A JOURNEY TO THE CENTER OF THE MIND

BOOK II:

The Police Officer Years
(1976 – 1987)

The journey continues…

A FORMER FBI PROFILER'S CANDID MEMOIR

By

James R. Fitzgerald
Supervisory Special Agent (Ret.)
Federal Bureau Of Investigation
Criminal Profiler/Forensic Linguist

Copyright © 2017 by James R. Fitzgerald

ISBN 978-1-4958-1315-3
ISBN 978-1-4958-1316-0 eBook

Published January 2017

INFINITY PUBLISHING
1094 New DeHaven Street, Suite 100
West Conshohocken, PA 19428-2713
Toll-free (877) BUY BOOK
Local Phone (610) 941-9999
Fax (610) 941-9959
Info@buybooksontheweb.com
www.buybooksontheweb.com

DEDICATED TO:

Wally and Alma (My parents)

Cass, Alma, and Marilyn (My sisters)

Sean, Dan, and Ryan (My sons)

...without whom, to a person, this book
would never have been written,
nor a fulfilling life led.

Acknowledgments

Although I've dedicated this book to my parents (now deceased), and my three sisters (Marilyn, now deceased), I would be remiss if I didn't again acknowledge my birth family here for raising me, supporting me, encouraging me, and loving me. None of this would be possible for me without the five of you at the start of it all.

As to the others to whom I dedicated this book…

I was later fortunate enough myself to raise (with their mother, Eileen) three great boys to great young men who are now, well, three great adults. I hopefully provided them with the same support, encouragement, and love as was earlier bestowed upon me. Thanks, sons, for being today who and what you are to me.

There are others too, of course, who I want to acknowledge and thank in terms of this writing project. They include a handful of former Bensalem Township Police officers (whom I consider friends to this day) who have each contributed here when my otherwise pretty sharp memory or archived documentation needed some level of factual reinforcement. These would include Tim Carroll, Bob Gorman, Fred Harran (still at the BPD), Jerry Judge, John Knowles, Terry Lachman, Steve Moran, and Rich Viola.

I'd like to publicly thank Jack Robinson here too. I did it in person many, many years ago, and more than once, but not any time recently. As my lieutenant and my captain (then demoted and re-promoted, you'll see what I mean) at the Bensalem PD, he was my first actual mentor and "Rabbi" in my nascent law enforcement career. So, thanks again, Capt. Jack, wherever you are, for taking me under your wing as you did back in the day.

I didn't do too bad, did I?

On a very sad note, I'd like to once again acknowledge and thank Kena Childers. She was the proofreader/light-editor of my first book in this series. She did a great job, too. Unfortunately, Kena died suddenly in April of 2015, not long after JCM I's publication. She was only 37 years old and a new mom. She never even got to see the book in its published form. At Kena's funeral service, I presented a signed copy of JCM I to her husband, her teenage son, and her baby son with some heartfelt written words about their wonderful wife and mom. It's the least I could do for her, and for them.

RIP Kena. You are missed.

On a clearly more uplifting note, for this book Lois Carter did an excellent job proofreading, light-editing, and formatting it for me. It took her a while as we both know it is not exactly a short book, but she definitely made it a better read by the time she was done doing her thing. Thanks again, Lois. I'll hopefully see you in JCM Book III.

Lastly, I wrote this book, in almost equal parts, in essentially three different if not disparate geographic locales. They are Chevy Chase, Maryland (thank you Natalie Schilling); Fiesole, Italy (thank you Natalie and Georgetown University); and Sea Isle City, New Jersey.

Each city, if not country, contributed in its own cultural and ethnographic way to the successful completion of my book. There's a little bit of each place and its respective peoples found within. Oh, and there's lots of both regarding a place called Bensalem, Pennsylvania, too. That will become very apparent in the forthcoming pages.

TITLE CONCEPT THANKS TO:

Jules Verne

From his 1864 novel,

Voyage au centre de la Terre

aka,

A Journey to the Center of the Earth

and

The Amboy Dukes

(Specifically Ted Nugent and Steve Farmer)

From their 1968 record album and single,

Journey to the Center of the Mind

COVER ART:

It is rumored that Ben Franklin, one of the U. S. Founding Fathers, conducted his kite and electricity experiments in the 1750s in what is now Bensalem Township, Pennsylvania. The metaphoric representation of clear skies turning to stormy skies, with lightning strikes tearing apart a badge and a police building, will become evident to the reader before long.

The cover artist is Stephen A. Jeter (www. stephenajeter.com) of Los Angeles and New York.

Table of Contents

Note: For additional background regarding me and my life during this timeframe, there are numerous stand-alone "Bonus Chapters" to JCM II on my website. Each one either relates to the chapter before it, the one after it, or it's set in the general timeframe of what you're reading.

You will see advisories (+ Bonus Chapter___) at the end of some of the chapters indicating the extra material. Go to www.jamesrfitzgerald.com to read them.

Prologue

In the early 21st Century, the men and women who are now Superintendents, Commissioners, Chiefs, Sheriffs, and/or in upper-management at many U.S. law enforcement agencies, spent their formative professional years during the same general timeframe as covered in this book. While rookie cops back then, many of these people are the "Top Cops" in charge at their respective police departments today.

To some degree, what I experienced and what influenced me back then is also what our current police leaders experienced and what influenced them during these same years. With little doubt, these myriad factors continue to have an effect on their current policy and decision-making processes - whether they care to admit it or not.

Only the jurisdictions, the names, and the ranks are different from my experiences related in this book to the experiences in these officials' own early professional lives. And while many things may have changed in my former profession over the years, much has stayed the same - certainly as it applies to that thing called human nature.

This is my story.

This is the story of Jim "Fitz" Fitzgerald and his (my) eleven years-plus as a police officer/detective/sergeant in a one particular department not all that long ago and not all that far away. However, in more ways than some of our current police leaders would care to acknowledge, this is their story too - at least many aspects of it. Of that, I can assure you.

Not surprisingly, the next generation of law enforcement management will also be influenced by today's current leaders, and so on, and so on, and so on. It's called human nature.

* * * * *

I never worked a midnight shift or "last-out" before, so I wasn't quite sure how to prepare for my first ever night of doing so, not to mention doing so for the first time ever as a uniformed police officer. After awaking every weekday for the last three months at 6:45AM at the Pennsylvania State Police (PSP) Academy with my fellow fifty or so municipal officers-in-training, I elected not to get out of bed too early over the past weekend or that Monday morning. Thus, I found my body's internal clock wouldn't permit me to take a nap that afternoon or early evening before reporting to work. That would have been the ideal preparation for the first night of a midnight shift, whether as a cop, a nurse, or in any other profession which requires overnight hours.

There's also no doubt that my adrenalin was pumping at full capacity that day of my first shift, which precluded me from any hope of resting, napping, or the like. The biological release of one or more of these natural chemicals within my body over this twenty-four hour period, in conjunction with the natural anticipation and excitement of it being my first ever cop-shift, each in its own way likely kept me wide-awake and alert for the entirety of that day and later my first ever overnight work assignment.

As directed by the Bensalem Police Department's (BPD) Lt. Jack Robinson on the previous Friday after my academy class's graduation ceremony in Hershey, Pennsylvania, I showed up at HQ on Monday night, November 22, 1976, at 10:15, about forty-five minutes early for my shift. Once inside, the first person I met that night was Sgt. Gene Ashton. He was there early too, before the rest of my other nine squad members.

Sgt. Ashton was in his mid-50s, about six feet tall, slightly overweight, and wore a dark black (and rather obvious) toupee, which didn't necessarily match his otherwise white sideburns very well. He was a former U. S. Marine, served in World War II, and had been on the BPD for as long as I had been alive at the time. He was apparently very content at being a patrol sergeant at this point in his career. He told me within ten minutes that evening he was eligible for full retirement from the PD, but he wanted to wait a few more years before doing so. As time went on I found Sarge to be an amiable guy who was serious when he had to be, but who could also joke around with his men when the situation permitted.

Sgt. Ashton treated me fairly and respectfully from our very first shift together. I would learn that his management style, at least as it pertained to me, would include public praise when I did something right, but also private admonishment when I did something, well, not-so-right. I should add each was deserved at times during my first year-plus on the BPD under his tutelage.

I found out later during my first night on the job from other officers an interesting story regarding Sgt. Ashton. It seems only a year or so before he had responded to what he thought was a routine mid-day robbery alarm. It was at a bank in a shopping center near Street Rd. and Hulmeville Rd., one of the busiest intersections in Bensalem Township. As it turned out, it was anything but a routine mid-day robbery alarm. Instead, the sergeant walked into an actual robbery-in-progress. Once inside the bank he was surprised, to say the least, by the bandits and disarmed and held hostage by them for a short while. When other officers arrived on the scene and learned of this now unfolding situation involving one of their own, they remained in the parking lot and effectively surrounded the stand-alone bank building. The robbers eventually exited the bank and engaged the officers in a moving shootout. Fortunately, no one, including Sgt. Ashton, was hurt and the two suspects were apprehended a short time later. The local K-Mart building didn't fare quite as well though. It took more than a few incoming rounds and shotgun blasts during the shootout. No customers were hurt either...again, fortunately.

I additionally learned after the fact it was unanimously agreed upon by a BPD shooting review board that Sgt. Ashton should never have entered the bank as he did without awaiting the pre-arranged coded response from a phone call to the bank manager by the BPD dispatcher. This was the protocol whenever there was a bank robbery alarm in Bensalem and in almost every other U. S. police department.

Sgt. Ashton never brought this incident up to me, nor I with him. However, I eventually discussed the matter with other officers who were on the scene that day who related the timeline of events and everything which occurred, right and wrong.

This bank robbery scenario and what happened to Sgt. Ashton, even though I wasn't present for it, nonetheless became a sort of retro-learning lesson for me. It was the beginning of an early habit I would develop over my law enforcement career. That is, I would attempt to gather as much information as I could regarding how other police officers, and later FBI agents, responded to certain calls, handled certain people, resolved certain situations, conducted certain investigations, etc., all in the hopes of not only doing my job to the best of my abilities, but also staying alive while in the process.

It's worked pretty well for me so far.

About thirty minutes into that initial shift, with Sgt. Ashton telling my whole squad to "be smart out there," before leaving the safe confines of the BPD parking lot, and just as I was about to drive onto Hulmeville Rd. and into the real world for the first time as a badge and gun carrying cop, I found myself looking out the car's open passenger-side window and up into the cold starry sky. Then and there, I couldn't help but wonder…

What excitement awaits me?

What professional challenges will confront me?

Where will this all take me?

For that matter, what will be my first official police function on this, my first official shift as a law enforcement officer?

The answer to the last question was right around the corner…really, as in a short drive away in my patrol car just a minute down the road.

The answer to the first question would come about ninety minutes later. It would result in front page headlines in the local newspaper for me the very next day.

However, the middle two questions would have to wait a bit longer to be answered - years in some cases – and I would be challenged in ways I never expected and taken places I never imagined.

And these challenges would not all be out on the streets of Bensalem while confronting bad guys. Hardly. Many would originate from right within the BPD HQ building I was just about to depart and the "guys" who work in it. The reader can decide along the way whether they're "bad" or not.

Just a few pages from now, it's on those Bensalem streets where we'll start.

* * * * *

My memoir series, *A Journey to the Center of the Mind* (JCM), is actually comprised of three separate volumes. They are Book I, Book II, and Book III.

In JCM Book I (2014), starting in the mid-1950s and going through the mid-1970s, my personal journey begins. It is focused chiefly on my youthful life experiences, accomplishments, and a few glaring mistakes, and how I survived them (mostly) in one piece, mentally and physically. In it I share many events of my personal life, from grade school through college, with various friends, my sometimes tenuous involvement with law enforcement before I was even engaged in that career, at my first real job (sort of) in the criminal justice system, and the effect of both the good and the bad experiences, and the good and the bad people I met during this time. On occasion, there are flash-forwards to events and investigations in my later life. Book I culminates with my admission to and graduation from the Pennsylvania State Police Academy in Hershey, Pennsylvania.

Sometimes in Book I, the interconnections between my personal and future professional life will be seen as being clear and direct. At other times, the impact of my life experiences, interests, feelings, and beliefs was less direct, but still influenced my subsequent career-related decisions, both on a moment-to-moment and long-term basis, and thus ultimately shaped some quite important career outcomes as well.

JCM Book III (scheduled publication in mid-2017), starting in 1987 at the FBI Academy in Quantico, Virginia, through my first assignment to New York City, to my promotion which brought me back to the FBI Academy in Quantico in 1995, completes my law enforcement journey as I become an FBI special agent, criminal profiler, and later forensic linguist, all the while investigating some of the biggest crimes of the 1990s and early 2000s. These cases include Unabom, the Jon Benet Ramsey homicide, the 9-11 attacks, Anthrax, the Washington, DC Sniper...just to name a few. It concludes with my retirement in 2007. In the Epilogue, I'll discuss some interesting and headline-grabbing cases I worked as a consultant with my Virginia-based company, The Academy Group, Inc.

In each of these books, to include this one, I provide accounts of some truly great people I've encountered in my life, some perhaps not-so-great, and some of truly questionable character, integrity, and motivation, all while attempting to capture the times and places in which I lived and worked. Some of these people, whether I realized it right away or discovered it gradually, through careful, initially amateur profiling at the time, turned out to be downright evil. Criminals, victims, witnesses, politicians, wannabe-cops, groupies, and yes, even a few fellow law enforcement officers, fall into the above categories, some where you would expect them to, and others into quite unexpected categorizations. And, while I'm at it, the reader will learn about my mistakes and lapses in judgment too. I hold nothing back here, whether to my own detriment or not.

For the record, life has definitely not "concluded" for me in any way, shape, or form - not as of late 2016, anyway. I'm a still very active criminal profiler and forensic linguist; adjunct faculty member at Hofstra University in Hempstead, New York, and The Richard Stockton University of New Jersey in Galloway, NJ; frequent guest lecturer at other institutions of higher learning (both in the U. S. and internationally); *Criminal Minds* co-technical advisor; *Sleepy Hollow* co-technical advisor; co-host and executive producer of A&E's *Killer Profile*; with frequent appearances on CNN as well as other major electronic and print media outlets. I was one of the seven forensic experts to appear on CBS television's much watched four hour docu-series, *The Case of: Jon Benet Ramsey,* in September, 2016.

As this book goes to publication, I am also anxiously awaiting the premier of the Discovery Channel mini-series, *Manifesto,* scheduled for the second half of 2017. In this multi-part scripted series produced by actor Kevin Spacey's Trigger Street Productions, the true-to-life story of the FBI's Unabom investigation will be told in great detail in an eight-part series for the very first time. As I played a critical role in the eventual identification and arrest of Theodore J. Kaczynski (the Unabomber), it will be told from the perspective of my character, James "Fitz" Fitzgerald. As a consulting producer on the series, I'm very much anticipating its premier.

Lastly here, and what is probably obvious by now, I'm a pretty busy writer too.

This book (along with Book I and Book III) invites you to join me as I chart the sometimes smooth, sometimes rocky journey of my life's course – the one I chose or somehow fell into, or both – and the one which ultimately led to me becoming very successful at what it is I decided I wanted to do, that is, a law enforcement professional, criminal profiler, and forensic linguist. Oh, and I think a decent human being along the way, too.

* * * * *

Author's Note: Everything written in this book (and/or in the bonus chapters found on my website) happened just as it's related by me, or at least as accurately as my still excellent memory allows. I back up a number of my anecdotes and experiences with the inclusion of newspaper articles, editorials, and where appropriate, journal entries as well as actual written "memos" I received or wrote in the workplace during my eleven years as a Bensalem Township police officer. If quoting someone and/or detailing a spoken conversation, the language therein is as close to what was actually said by me and the other person as memory permits. While it's possible a few words are off here and there, the overall gist of the dialogue is exactly as written.

For obvious reasons, some names in this book have been omitted altogether and other names have been changed. If it's not a person's real name, you'll know it. This was done to protect the "innocent," the "guilty" (in many cases), and/or those people who fall somewhere in between. If it's a person's full name, or an identified business, title, or position, it's the real thing and will be clear to the reader.

And, for the record, any opinions offered in this book are mine and not that of the FBI.

"Be always sure you are right –

then go ahead."

Col. David "Davy" Crockett

U.S. Frontiersman, Politician, Soldier

1786 – 1836

Part 1 -
The Rookie Year-plus

Chapter One

Back to my very first night as a police officer...by 10:45 the other squad members began strolling in to the dark brown wood paneled roll call area. In turn, I said "Hi" to each of them, introduced myself, and shook their hands. One of them was a fellow rookie with whom I spent time at the academy. Two others, also still rookies, were graduates of the suburban Philadelphia PSP Regional Training Academy from just a few months before me. The remaining five men were veteran officers to one degree or another. Some of them that evening addressed me by my name (after checking out the nameplate on my chest), be it either "James," or "Fitz." Others called me "Rook" or "Rookie," with at least one older cop simply referring to me as "Kid." I was fine with any of these references. They were accurate on all counts. This was certainly true of "Kid" as I was only 23 years of age at the time and the youngest person on my squad.

I was subsequently introduced by Sgt. Ashton to my training officer for this shift. He was a year or two older than me, had about three years on the job, and seemed like a decent guy... at the time.

At almost exactly 11:00, as the officers from the 3-11 shift were returning to HQ after their work nights, I lined up shoulder-to-shoulder with my new squad members for my first official roll call on my first official 11-7 shift. At that point, Sgt. Ashton formally addressed his troops. Reading off of his well-worn clipboard he relayed to us the relevant information we'd have to know before heading "out there" on this cold November night. Let's see...there was something about a local man who was wanted by the Philadelphia PD for some felony or another, there was a black Cadillac which had been stolen earlier from one of the train stations, there was the description of a purse snatcher at the Neshaminy Mall, and there was a building in one of the industrial parks where a faulty burglar alarm was ringing incessantly.

Okay...I got it!

Flipping the page on his clipboard, Sgt. Ashton next told us who was assigned to what car, to what sector, who was "backup," and other pertinent squad information. I wrote down everything Sarge said on the first page of my brand new pocket-sized notebook. Looking to my left and right I realized shortly afterwards that it was only the four rookies among us writing anything down that night. I guess the veteran guys have really good memories...or something like that. It didn't matter to me either way. I just wanted to make sure I didn't forget whatever it was Sarge had told us. It must have all been important or he wouldn't have spent the time at roll call imparting this information to us. That was my thinking anyway.

Upon being dismissed a minute or two later, the squad slowly began to disperse toward the door to the parking lot. One of the senior guys, before he exited the room, looked over and specifically said to me, "Hey Rook, did you get all that stuff down? You know, there might be a test later on!" He laughed afterwards as did a few of his/our fellow squad mates.

I turned around, caught the gaze of the older, still smiling officer and simply responded with my own smile, "Yeah, I got it all. Thanks for asking." I then turned away from him and left it at that. As it was the first hour of my first ever shift as a police officer, I'd reserve my more sardonic responses to similar such inane questions and comments for a future time when I would better know my squad mates, and they would better know me.

However, not now, not yet. I'm no fool.

Before leaving the roll call area, my training officer and I went through a checklist of the additional equipment I needed for the night. That included a rechargeable flashlight, a portable police radio, and oh yes, my ballistic vest. Upon the vest being issued to me by Sgt. Ashton, I went into the small adjacent locker room area and undid my holster and pants, took off my uniform shirt, and put on the white vest for the first time, one (of four) Velcro strap after another. It took a bit of getting used to as it fit snuggly over my rib cage and would later bulk up in strange ways after I would be sitting for a while. But, as the 1/8 inch of Kevlar material was proven to be very beneficial in many a shooting situation, having saved the lives of many police officers, I wore it religiously every shift of my future uniform-wearing law enforcement career.

I had been previously issued my gun, holster, baton, handcuffs, shirts, pants, and hat for training purposes at the academy and also for the graduation ceremony just three days ago. Now, I added the new vest to my take home collection of police paraphernalia. The flashlight and radio would be returned to the roll call area in their respective battery chargers after each shift, but everything else would come home with me.

My tactical wardrobe collection was rapidly growing in size. Lucky me.

Once my equipment was in order, I was taken to the dispatchers' office and picked up some other material. This included an incident report book, blank traffic violation citations, blank summary violation citations, a local parking violation book, several extra pens, and a map of Bensalem. I was also introduced to the two dispatchers who were working that night and assigned to my squad. Both of them were approximately my age and seemed like nice guys. I eventually came to learn that they also had taken the exam earlier this year to become Bensalem police officers, but they didn't quite make the grade. Now they were seeing us rookies (about twenty of us) for the first time as the ones who passed that same exam, passed the subsequent oral interviews, and got the jobs they wanted at a PD where they each had been employed for the last few years. Despite that issue, the radio dispatchers were good to work with and handled us new guys gently. As it turned out, most of the dispatchers I met during my first year with the BPD who wanted to be cops eventually did, in fact, make it onto the force. It just took them a few extra years and a few extra exams to do so.

After all this equipment gathering, admin stuff, introductions, etc., it was now about 11:30P.M. I was chomping at the bit to get into the police car and go out on patrol. After all, I had a newly assigned sector to patrol that night. Actually, two sectors as my training officer and I were designated as the "backup car" to sectors 3 and 4.

I learned that night there were four police sectors in Bensalem which were drawn up by BPD administrators years before my arrival. On each shift there would ideally be two officers assigned per sector, and two backups. That is, a backup for sectors 1 and 2, and a backup to sectors 3 and 4. Of course, the sergeant was always a "floater" and would roam the whole township. He would meet with and/or back up his officers as needed.

As I came to understand, Sector 1 was the northwest portion of Bensalem, also known as Trevose. Sector 2 was the northern portion of Bensalem, a mostly residential area known as Neshaminy Valley. Sector 3 was essentially the business center of Bensalem with several residential areas, Eddington and Cornwells being two of them, bordered on the east side by the Delaware River. Sector 4 was the southeast portion of Bensalem, also known as Andalusia, and also bordered to the east by the Delaware River. It was mostly residential with some business, commercial, and industrial areas. To its direct south just across the Poquessing Creek was the Northeast section of Philadelphia. Of course, Bensalem Township itself was/is trisected by Interstate 95, Route 1, and the Pennsylvania Turnpike. As I would come to learn, Bensalem was a very busy suburb of Philadelphia.

Out in the BPD HQ parking lot, as I was ready to put my carrying case with the newly acquired paperwork onto the back seat of the white and blue 1975 Ford Torino police car, my training officer told me to hold off as first we had to check under the seats. I wasn't sure at first why, but I soon learned that a patrol officer always wants to make sure there are no weapons, drugs, or evidence of any kind from the last shift left in the car which is now assigned to him or her.

As one can surmise, if there's no prisoner van, arrestees are generally put into the back of a patrol car for transportation to HQ for processing, interviewing, arraignment, etc. While the individuals should be completely searched before they're put into the back of the car, handcuffed, and all contraband removed from them, sometimes smaller items can be missed by the arresting officer, especially if it was a non-compliant arrest situation in an unfriendly or potentially dangerous environment. If not used against the officer at some point during the ride to HQ (which would be the worst case scenario if it is a weapon of some sort), the item or multiple items could then wind up secreted behind their seat, or kicked under the front seat, placed there purposefully in an attempt to avoid yet additional criminal charges being lodged against them. As the rear seats in all the patrol vehicles were by design not fastened to the car's floor, they were easy to pick up and search with the beam of a freshly charged flashlight to make sure nothing was there that shouldn't be there.

In fact, nothing was under the rear seat or the front seat of our car on that first night, so my training officer and I were off to a good start. This was another habit I would continue during my entire patrol career, and not just at shift-beginning, but also at shift-end if I happened to transport a prisoner that day or night. An officer could never be too cautious when it came to potentially dangerous items hidden inside a patrol car, whether from his/her own prisoner or a previous one transported by another officer driving the same car.

With a topped-off tank of gas, and after visually testing the two "bubble-gum machine" style red and blue lights on the car's roof, audibly testing the siren, and finding both to be in proper working condition, we were ready to go on patrol. My training officer verbally signed-in over the police radio using 10-code designators of which I was not yet familiar, with the dispatcher responding in similarly unfamiliar numeric-based language back at us. With that formality over with, we drove off towards the bowels of Sector 3 with me riding shotgun; literally, in this case, as there was also a 12-gauge in its dashboard holder directly adjacent to my right knee. It immediately reminded me from whence the term "riding shotgun" originated, going all the way back to the stagecoach days of the Wild West. I was confident my ride tonight would be a bit calmer than in those days. At least I was hoping so.

I was now equipped with both offensive and defensive gear. The police car was fueled and deemed to be fully operational inside and out. My partner and I were good-to-go.

So, this was it! This was that moment I had been anticipating for a few months, make that a few years now. After attaining my four-year BS degree in Law Enforcement and Corrections from Penn State University, after fourteen months as a store detective, and after twelve weeks of training at the PSP Academy, I was at this very minute about to start my first tour-of-duty ever as a sworn police officer. This was so cool!

(+ Bonus Chapter 1a)

Chapter Two

My first "official" police function that night entailed driving the patrol car approximately 300 yards onto a nearby 7-11 convenience store parking lot on Hulmeville Rd. Hmmm…let me guess, would we be asking the worker info about a recent robbery? Following up on a major theft case? Did he/she see a certain fugitive we're on the lookout for? Maybe the clerk is a snitch and has information about that guy wanted by the Philadelphia PD.

"Negative" as they say in police talk. It was none of the above.

Instead, while parking the car, my training officer asked me what I wanted in the coffee he was about to pick up for us. He just assumed I drank the stuff. I told him I didn't drink coffee. He asked me if I was sure as every other cop he knew drank coffee, especially on the midnight shift. I told him I was, in fact, very sure I didn't drink coffee. I even volunteered to him that I never had a cup of joe in my life. I could tell by his facial expression that he found this habit, or lack thereof, a bit odd. So as to not further disappoint him, or have him think I was truly a bohemian, I said I'd take a hot chocolate if they had it. He shrugged his shoulders and said "you got it" as he was opening his door.

I offered the training officer money for my beverage, but he told me that cops don't pay for coffees at this 7-11. I asked him if they charged for hot chocolates. As he was closing the driver's side door, he said he didn't know as he never asked for one there before.

After a few minutes, my partner came back to the car with the two hot drinks. No charge to me. I guess I started a precedent then and there, just before midnight, with 7-11 hot chocolates now being free to the cops too.

Whether or not LEOs should get free coffees, hot chocolates, cold drinks, or other similar items (yes, to include doughnuts for some) while on duty from willing vendors is an issue which has been long discussed, written of, and even legislated in various jurisdictions over the decades. I'm not going to delve into it here in any detail as to whether

9

it's right, wrong, moral, ethical, or the like. It is certainly a smart move on the part of the individual business owners, as they get repeated, random visits from armed, uniformed police officers on a twenty-four hour basis. In and of itself, that would tend to reduce the possibility of robberies at their stores, as well as thefts and other crimes.

However, is the attainment of these free items, in fact, ethical and moral on the part of the officers? Would the LEOs show favoritism as a result? Would they be doing anything in return for the business owners, besides simply stopping in the stores for several minutes at a time and providing "security," no matter how temporal and spatial, for the time they're actually getting their beverages or other similar items?

Well, maybe…but maybe not.

For the record, during my uniform police days, I did accept free hot chocolates (and ice-cold Slurpees in the warmer months) from the friendly and appreciative owners and workers at a local 7-11 store while I was on duty. However, I took nothing else from them or any other commercial enterprise in Bensalem or elsewhere. Also, in my first year as a police officer, I quickly learned that there were a few dining establishments whose owners insisted on providing those of us in uniform with free meals when we came there to eat. Caught off guard at first with a training officer, I did partake in a few free meals, but then left a tip for the food server which at least equaled the cost of the meal. That's how I handled this issue at first, but then I never went back afterwards in uniform. When I eventually bought my own house in Bensalem I would almost always eat my meals there, thusly avoiding this issue.

I also found that a uniform cop eating his meal in a public restaurant or diner was only looking for problematic results. Firstly, from the public who wanted to inquire, invariably in mid-swallow for the officer, about some matter with which they are presently dealing. Secondly, and potentially much worse, the cop doesn't always know who the cook is that night, or maybe doesn't even know the food server very well. If one or both were recently arrested or hassled by an officer somewhere for whatever real or perceived reason, and chose to add some special personally derived hard-to-see liquid or solid ingredient to the meal, it could make for a very unpleasant digestive period afterwards. While this never happened to me personally (as far as I know), I nevertheless learned early on to just avoid the public eateries in the first place, at least while in uniform.

There were no written restrictions to taking such free items in the operational manuals of the BPD, or many other police departments at the time of which I was aware. Perhaps there should have been.

Later, in my FBI years, I never took anything for free or even at discount from a store or business owner, unless it was a legitimate corporate-type benefit offered to other large institutions at the same time. There were, in fact, written regulations and restrictions regarding agents attaining free items from a store or business, no matter how trivial. So, needless to say, I obeyed the rules in this regard. It should be noted that since FBI agents don't wear uniforms, there weren't many offers of hot or cold drinks to be made by the local merchants. Those free 7-11 hot and cold drinks, during chilly and warm weather, respectively, were the extent of any "gratuity" I ever received during my uniform law enforcement career.

Returning to my first hour on the job, and now with covered 7-11 hot drinks in hand (yes, in our actual hands as cars in the '70s, to include police cars, did not have built-in cup holders), off we drove from the store. NOW we were finally officially on patrol. Or, so I thought. Instead of actually entering full patrol mode, shortly thereafter we stopped at a nearby empty shopping center parking lot to drink our newly acquired beverages. And, as if by pre-planning, another police car pulled up right next to us, facing in the opposite direction so the two drivers were within arm's length of one another and could talk out of their respective drivers' side windows. We then began a three-way chat which I learned was, in fact, pre-planned between the two of them before roll call. Actually, it was more of a four-way chat, as the other officer was K-9, and his sometimes whining German Shepherd also joined our conversation occasionally from his converted back seat perch.

I don't recall all the specifics of this police car-to-police car conversation, but both officers, while drinking their respective coffees, were asking me general questions regarding my background, education, sports interests, why I wanted to be a cop (specifically a Bensalem cop), if I wanted to climb the PD management ladder, if I knew anyone in township political circles, etc. They were vetting me, to put it bluntly. While sipping my hot chocolate, I answered their questions as honestly as I could. I then asked them some questions in return. However, my queries were less personally-related and more job-related. They answered them, even if a bit guardedly. We probably talked about twenty minutes in the parking lot that night and then upon being finished with the hot beverages, the Q&A, and after a quick "See ya later," the two cars containing three cops and one dog drove their separate ways.

Now I suppose finally in full patrol mode, I noticed the police radio to be an almost constant stream of chatter during the first hour-plus of that first night. I had to learn quickly what was important to comprehend and what was not. There were actually several other Bucks County police departments on our radio band, each smaller than the BPD, and I eventually acquired the skillset to mentally filter out their calls and conversations. Of course, if it was a car chase coming our way or an "officer needs assistance" distress call from one of the PDs was heard, everything was dropped and even cars from the neighboring jurisdictions responded posthaste to the appropriate area.

Otherwise that night, there was some cruising/patrolling back and forth on Street Rd., the main business artery in Bensalem. There were no calls to our unit, no car stops, and with seemingly no real plan at hand, or at least none that I could discern on the part of my training officer, we simply drove around. Nothing very exciting was happening so far on my first shift as a cop.

That was all to change, and in less than thirty minutes.

* * * * *

It was probably around 1:00A.M. that morning, only two hours or so into my first ever police shift, when my training officer and I received our (well, *my*) first official radio call. The dispatcher advised of a burglar alarm at the Two Guys Department Store, near the intersection of Street Rd. and Knights Rd. The radio call discourse went something like,

Dispatcher: "696 to 22-10?" (The BPD radio designator to our car call number.)

Me: "22-10!" (First time ever on a police radio.)

Dispatcher: "22-10, respond to a 10-90 at the Two Guys store." ("10-90," I learned, is an alarm.)

Me: "10-4, enroute." (Of course, I knew that "10-4" meant "okay" or "message received" and when and how to use it.)

We were less than a half-mile away at the time from the single-story department store. We responded without lights and sirens, for several reasons. Firstly, we were relatively close and vehicular traffic was at a minimum. Secondly, commercial burglar alarms are inadvertently tripped all the time for various non-crime related reasons, so they're really not something that an officer wants to drive to at a high rate of speed, running traffic signals, or utilizing other dangerous tactics, even with flashing red lights and sirens. Responding to such alarms quickly, but more importantly safely, was something I learned early on. Thirdly, when arriving on the scene of an alarm, if you did choose to activate the lights and sirens on the way there, you'd want to shut them off as you enter the area so as to not tip off the possible burglar(s). For all those reasons that night, my partner and I chose to drive the half-mile or so to the store without wasting any time, but with no true urgency. After all, as I was told, it was probably just a false alarm. It happens all the time.

We pulled our patrol car into the department store parking lot, which was dark and virtually empty at this time. We advised the dispatcher we were on location ("10-23"), and after turning off our headlights so we would approach the scene more stealthily (a good practice, just in case it was an actual break-in), we proceeded to drive along the front side of the building, from one corner of it to the other. As we approached the middle section of the building, where the main entrance was located, I noticed a broken pane of glass in one of the front doors. It was large enough for a person to squeeze through. After pointing it out to my partner, he picked up the microphone and immediately called for backup.

He said something to the effect, "This is 22-10. We have a broken-out window on the Street Rd. side of the building, front-center. Backup requested."

The nearest backup car, the same K-9 officer with whom we recently shared a hot beverage, radioed that he was about five minutes away. It was agreed we'd wait for him to arrive before exiting our vehicles and entering the store. Awaiting his arrival, my training officer and I drove back and forth in our marked car, headlights still out, in the front portion of the building so we could keep an eye on the broken window and anyone possibly exiting back through it. Simultaneously, we drove to each end of the building to check the two far sides of it, just to make sure no one was attempting to escape through exits there, loading a car up with stolen goods, or otherwise trying to get away with his or their illegal act. In effect, by initially driving back and forth as we were, our one patrol car could keep an eye on three sides of the building while we awaited the arrival of the backup officers. This type maneuver is also designed to potentially fool the burglars inside. If they are somehow looking out of a window or door at the arriving officers, they would be thinking that there were multiple police cars on location. That clearly wasn't the case here, at least not for the first five minutes or so when we were the only police responders at the scene.

Eventually, the backup cars arrived, including the K-9 officer. Very shortly after his arrival, he was out of his car with his very anxious

German Shepherd. We then positioned other arriving cars to various spots around all four sides of the building, and the three of us, well, four counting the dog, entered the building searching for the possible intruder or intruders.

The irony wasn't lost on me this night, my first actual police officer tour-of-duty, and on my first actual call, that I was back inside a department store once again. Although Two Guys was much smaller than my former employer's store, that being the Strawbridge and Clothier Department Store in downtown Philadelphia, knowing the latter establishment as I did helped me in having a pretty good idea as to what areas of this store would have fitting rooms, storage rooms, offices, and other potential hiding areas. In view of this ostensible working knowledge from my short-term past, I did my best to navigate the four of us, including the police pooch, in areas which I felt may be likely hiding places for one or more possible burglars.

Of course, the canine was pulling its master in a certain direction, as it was yelping and barking the whole time. This was not by happenstance either. The dog was trained to do just that in order to potentially scare whoever it is who may be hiding or on the run into voluntarily surrendering.

In a relatively short time inside the store, maybe in less than ten minutes, the culprits were found one at a time. They were three young men, aged 17, 18, and 19, all from Northeast Philadelphia. They were found cowering in or near the women's clothes department, in an adjacent fitting room, and under a dress rack. The K-9 dog was going crazy barking and pulling on his leash as the individual burglars were being located, one after the other. He seemingly wanted in the worst way to get a piece of each of these guys. But his police officer handler, as per their months-long K-9 training regimen, eventually uttered some magic code word to him and the dog immediately calmed down. The officer and his dog then stood behind the three men as we directed them to a nearby central store location and ordered them to lie on the floor. My partner and I completely searched them and handcuffed them, under the watchful eyes of the K-9 officer and his four-legged colleague. The three wannabe crooks now under arrest fixed their eyes on the dog the whole time. They were definitely more scared of the furry "cop" than the three uniformed ones.

At our direction, the BPD dispatcher contacted Two Guys' security personnel to tell them what occurred at their store and to meet the police there. We kept a patrol car at the scene by the broken window and the three felony burglars were separately driven back to BPD headquarters. The one we drove back in the rear of our police car said he was very happy to be away from the dog. Actually, so was I. That creature scared me too at times during the search and subsequent arrest of these three guys at the Two Guys store.

Maybe I should learn that code word.

Interestingly, in all my years of thinking about what and where may be my first official arrest as a law enforcement officer, I never envisioned a dog being part of it. But, he was, and I'm glad for it too. This wouldn't be the first or only arrest of mine in which a K-9 dog played a significant role. They and their officer handlers can be a true asset to any law enforcement agency and any potential crime scene.

As the Two Guys' store alarm was our initial radio call, this arrest belonged to my training officer and me. For me, this was pretty darn good considering I was barely two hours into my first ever tour-of-duty and here I am with a felony arrest; actually, make that three of them. I spent most of the rest of the shift learning how to process arrestees, fingerprint them, photograph them, read them their Miranda warnings, and take individual statements from them. I also learned how the juvenile arrestee had to be handled differently than the two adults, and so forth. Eventually, we would drive the two adults to the on-call district magistrate for them to have their preliminary arraignment. After his parents were notified, the lone juvenile would be taken separately to a youth detention center.

My training officer and I finished the arraignment of the two adult arrestees around 6:00 on what was now Tuesday morning. Several Bucks County constables took the prisoners to their respective detention facilities. We drove back to the BPD to finish up our paperwork and end our shift. Sgt. Ashton told us "good job," on the arrest. I thanked him in response for the nice words.

I got out of the PD right at 7:00 and drove home to my apartment in Northeast Philadelphia, about four miles from the police station, just as the sun was coming up. My wife, Eileen, was already awake getting ready for her job. She asked me how my first night was. I told her about the burglary arrests at the Two Guys store. She was happy for me, but had to leave right away for work.

In my now-empty apartment, I all of a sudden realized how tired I was. It was an exciting, but also exhausting night as my body was reminding me now after about twenty-two hours without sleep. So, I crawled into my warm bed and slept like a baby for the next eight hours.

Little did I know what was transpiring in the meantime between a BPD representative and a Bucks County journalist.

Upon awakening later that afternoon I called my parents, Wally and Alma. They were still living in the 3rd St. rowhome in Philadelphia where I grew up. I told them about my first night. My mom was generally interested in it, but when my dad eventually got on the phone he wanted to hear specific details of everything that happened. So I told him all I could recall about the arrest of the three burglars. He also said, "Good job," afterwards, coincidently the same words as Sgt. Ashton earlier this morning. For some reason, hearing those words from my dad meant just as much, if not more, to me than from my police sergeant. Funny how that works....

I relaxed after dinner with my wife that evening and around 9:00 started getting ready for my next night of work. I was wide awake for this, my second-ever shift as a police officer, thanks to my earlier full day of sleep.

However, bright eyed and bushy tailed as I may have been, I wasn't prepared for what happened to me upon barely stepping inside my brand new place of work that night. My greetings, if you will, were a lot different than my first night there.

Was it something I said? Something I did?

No, it was something that someone wrote.

I arrived at the BPD around 10:30 that Tuesday night, the last night of this abbreviated 11P-7A tour for me. Sgt. Ashton was there once again and right away asked me, "How does it feel to be a celebrity?"

I responded with some level of incredulity, "Excuse me, Sarge?"

Before my sergeant could answer, another of my new squad-mates walked through the door and said, "Hey, it's the hero rookie cop!"

I spouted out loud, even more incredulously now, "Uh...what are you talking about?"

He and Sgt. Ashton started laughing. It was clear they knew what was funny, but the topic of their laughter still eluded me up to this point.

Finally, another squad member walked in and said, "Here he is, the Headline Kid!"

With me apparently looking very perplexed, someone, I think it was one of the squad dispatchers, came into the roll call area and had a copy of that afternoon's (November 23, 1976) *Bucks County Courier*

Times newspaper. He handed it to me to read. On the front page, about halfway down, was the headline: "Rookie Busy on First Night."

Holy Shit! That's me!

In the six relatively short paragraphs that followed, with my name as the very first two words of the article, the story of the arrest the night before was related to the reading public. And, not without a bit of hyperbole added therein, I must say.

The way the article was written made it appear as if my training officer and I just came upon the Two Guys store broken window by chance while on "routine" patrol. Of course, we did find the broken window right away, but only after first being dispatched there as a result of an alarm call.

Next, the article described the physically implausible, if not impossible, in that it stated, "The two officers surrounded the building...."

Now, how could just two police officers surround a building the size of a large department store? It's clearly not possible, but nonetheless that's how the journalist chose to convey this part of the story.

Needless to say, hyperbolic reportage or not, it took a while to live down this headline and story. I wished not long afterwards that the article had never been written. Over the next week, some BPD cops on other squads I hadn't even met yet, during the various changes of shifts, would come up to me, look at my name badge to make sure I was the right guy, and act as if they were mad at me because my name was in the newspaper.

One then unknown-to-me officer even said, "Hey Kid, you know it takes years for some cops around here to get their names in the paper like that. How'd you do it on your first night? Who do you know?"

I assured him I had nothing to do with the article as I'm not the one who called the newspaper earlier that day. I was asleep all day, I told him. It didn't seem to satisfy him.

Another cop said, very sarcastically, "Hey Fitzgerald...don't let this front page newspaper crap go to your head. You're still just a rookie, don't forget!"

Geez! Where was this coming from?

At the beginning of, during the course of, and at the end of this shift, I assured anyone who broached this subject with me on my second night ever as a cop, 1) I had nothing to do with the publication of this story, 2) I don't even live in Bucks County yet and never even read this newspaper before, and 3) it is NOT going to my head in any way, shape, or form.

Slowly, the disconcertment related to my little front page newspaper story ran its course. I would learn even years later that some fellow cops never forgot the positive coverage, on the front page no less, I received in the media on my very first night. It bothered them when it happened and they let me know it. It bothered them even years later, and they let me know it then, too.

This article did not represent the only positive coverage I would receive in the local media over the next eleven years as a Bensalem police officer. It was simply the first one. I made some good arrests on my own during my BPD career, and not just in responding to burglar alarms either. These later arrests and the subsequent convictions in court were reported in very favorable fashion on many occasions. Not just in the Bucks County newspaper either, but in the greater Philadelphia area media sometimes too.

One other bit of media coverage which directly concerned me, but clearly not in the form of a traditional news story, was instead the lead editorial in the same *Bucks County Courier Times*. It would also be during the month of November, but nine whole years later. That editorial, and its obvious influence on the public just a few days later, arguably changed the course of my police department, Bensalem Township, and me, forever. This same editorial and other news stories which accompanied it also greatly disturbed some of my fellow officers; specifically, those in the highest ranks.

Too bad!

But we're not there yet. There's still actual police work, you know, cops and robbers stuff, to discuss here first. The politics of it all will have to wait.

Chapter Three

By Friday afternoon, December 10, 1976, I had successfully completed two nights of midnight shift, and two subsequent weeks consisting of a 3P-11P shift and a 7A-3P shift. Those first fifteen work nights and days were definitely a whirlwind learning experience. My training officer and I responded to car accidents, domestic disturbance calls, residential and commercial burglaries, armed robberies, retail theft arrests (I couldn't get away from the department store "beats," aka, shoplifters), miscellaneous thieves, drunks, fighters, sick and dead people (so far, only of apparent natural causes), and all assorted issues related to the human condition, at least as it involves crime or nuisances of some sort that only the police could handle. It was at times exhilarating, challenging, overwhelming, edifying, and even fun. It was never dull though, and that was the best part.

I felt very good about my first complete tour-of-duty rotation, and almost didn't want the scheduled long-weekend to arrive when it did. But, I suppose I did need some time off to catch up on my personal life. So, that Friday at 3PM, at the end of my shift, I was in a pretty good mood. Off for five full days after a great first two weeks-plus. No need to shave every day or put my uniform on again until 11PM Wednesday night.

Geez, I loved my new job. Who wouldn't?

But my joy was short-lived. In fact, in less than twenty hours, the real world would come for a visit to me. It wouldn't go away any time soon.

It was late the following Saturday morning, my first Saturday off since I graduated the Academy, when I heard the news that would shatter the thrill and excitement I was feeling about my first few weeks as a cop. It brought the undeniable reality of my new career, and my new life, into very clear focus for me.

Sometime during the night of December 11, 1976, in Montgomery Township, another Philadelphia suburb about eight miles from Bensalem, Officer David Hancock, age 41, a police veteran of twenty-one years, was killed in the line-of-duty while arresting a burglar. The felon was apparently caught breaking into a department store at a newly constructed shopping mall, and was subsequently arrested by the lone officer. At some point shortly after the arrest, in or near the patrol car, the burglar managed to get his hands on the officer's weapon and fire it point-blank at him. Officer Hancock was killed instantly. The small-time burglar had now elevated himself to big-time cop killer. He managed to get away from the scene for a short while, but was apprehended in the general area a few hours later by a torrent of law enforcement officers from multiple neighboring agencies who had descended upon the scene.

I heard this info on the TV news and read of it in the local newspaper over the next few days. It was very sobering. While I didn't know Dave Hancock, he was nonetheless the first police officer anywhere near Bensalem to be killed since I had been sworn in almost four months before. As good as I felt about the first fifteen days on the job just hours earlier, it seemed very different on this day, the first of my supposedly relaxing long weekend.

For me, this was a genuine case of the "for-reals." This is what we learned about at the police academy, but with unnamed and/or fictitious officers as the victims of the practice shooting scenarios. What happened to Officer Hancock was not a practice drill. He was real and it was as real a police scenario as it could get. He was also dead, and not miraculously coming back to life in the next classroom training exercise or 16mm movie vignette.

I found it hard to express my feelings to those close to me for several days after this incident. This included my wife Eileen, my parents Wally and Alma, my three sisters, Cass, Alma, and Marilyn, and assorted friends. I wasn't exactly sure how to cope with it. Most of my family and friends reached out for me via telephone and wanted to talk, and eventually asked me if I knew the officer from the nearby town, how I was doing, etc. I told them I was okay, but didn't really have any more information than what I had read and heard in the media, and no, I didn't personally know Dave. It was a challenging time too because I was just beginning five full days off from work. As such, I had no police "brethren" immediately surrounding me with whom I could discuss this sad and all-too-close-to-home event in my life.

I must add though, over that weekend, at no time did I suddenly regret my choosing of this profession, nor was I hesitant in the least to go back to work on the upcoming Wednesday night because of this tragic incident. In fact, for some strange reason, I found myself anxiously looking forward to getting back to work in a few nights.

Nevertheless, this feeling of hurt, frustration, and to some degree, anxiety, as a result of someone getting killed just doing his job (the exact same job as I now do), was a new experience to me. Especially as my first arrest ever, within two hours of my first shift as a police officer, just over two weeks ago, was apparently not all that dissimilar from Officer Hancock's call that night. Both scenarios involved a shopping center/mall, a department store, a burglar... but clearly with a much different outcome.

Why was the result of my burglary arrest different from Officer Hancock's? Could I be in a situation in the future, just like the one he faced, with an offender who tries the same thing with me?

Of course I could, and accepting that fact as my new reality did not come very easy at first to me. But I did eventually learn to accept it and to live with it. I'd have to, or find another line of work.

My first ever scheduled long weekend away from the police department was soon going to be cut short. I was called at home on Sunday afternoon by a senior BPD officer who asked me if I was available on one of my upcoming off-days to go Officer Hancock's funeral service.

I said "Yes," right away. The officer on the phone advised me there was no overtime or comp time (hours to be "banked" away for future use) involved, as it would be voluntary on my part. That certainly didn't change my mind. "Count me in," I told him again.

So, eight uniformed officers, comprising most of my squad which happened to be off on that December 14th, would drive to Montgomery Township in two BPD patrol cars and be part of the procession, service, and memorial for the slain officer. Yes, it cut short my long weekend, but it was something I wanted to do. It was something I had to do.

On that cold, dreary, late autumnal morning, while being an actual working police officer for less than a calendar month, I found myself for the first time in the middle of a police officer's memorial service. I experienced it simultaneously as sad, distressing, and depressing, while also strangely regal, impressive, and awe-inspiring. I can't really explain my mixed feelings from that day in any other way. It was an odd juxtaposition of deep emotional disconcertment and unbridled professional pride.

I felt horrible for this man and his family that I never knew, yet with whom I felt a kinship because we were now in the same profession, or I suppose *were* in the same profession, as he was no longer among the living. Concurrently though, I couldn't help but be impressed by the grand display of people and personnel to honor Officer Hancock, of whom the great majority here this day didn't even know. They were here to celebrate his service and his sacrifice, even if not necessarily him personally. I slowly began to understand this notion, and how it came about in my new profession, on that cold and overcast December day.

As the memorial service continued that morning and into early afternoon, there were the requisite speeches, prayers, and the eventual long motor vehicle procession to the cemetery with hundreds of lighted, spinning red-lights and blue-lights on an equal number of patrol cars from all over the tri-state area (Pennsylvania, New Jersey, Delaware) and beyond, representing many different local, state, and federal law enforcement agencies.

The formal service itself concluded with a bugler playing a very emotional rendition of Taps, and immediately afterwards a twenty-one gun salute. And then, as quickly as it had started, it was over. It was an emotional roller-coaster ride that day, to be sure.

The mass of uniformed personnel and the others in attendance were then invited to a luncheon. As with any luncheon or the equivalent after a funeral service, it was at times awkward and uncomfortable, but at times cathartic too. In this case, it was also a learning experience for me, one which I never forgot.

The officers at the luncheon who knew Officer Hancock were clearly complimentary of him, and none, of course, had a bad thing to say about him personally or professionally. However, among some of the officers in attendance it slowly permeated throughout the large banquet hall that afternoon what had happened that fateful night and what actually contributed to his murder.

It appears Officer Hancock made a critical mistake during the arrest of the burglar. That is, once he confronted the guy in the mall area, clearly coming out of a department store in which he did not belong, carrying items which were not his, Officer Hancock reportedly ordered him to drop what he was carrying and "freeze." The burglar apparently did as he was told. Then, and in what was later determined to be the primary causal factor in the officer's subsequent murder, he violated the first rule of arrest protocol. Officer Hancock handcuffed the arrestee in the front of his body, not behind the back as we were all repeatedly trained at the police academy.

Somehow in failing to follow this proper handcuffing procedure, the burglar had enough wiggle room in or near the back of the Montgomery Township patrol car to which he could somehow overpower Officer Hancock and grab the gun from either his hands or his holster. It's not entirely clear where the gun was at this point, but it was obvious that the burglar attained it while he was handcuffed in front. Then, within seconds, he shot the officer dead. While it's probably not impossible to wrestle a police officer's gun away from him or her with a suspect's hands cuffed behind him, it is very, very difficult and has rarely ever led to a lethal shooting. It turned lethal that night, however, because the arrestee's hands were cuffed in front, and they and the arrestee himself were still relatively mobile as a result.

Nobody wanted to criticize Officer Hancock the day he was ceremoniously laid to rest. And truly, nobody did. The burglar, now cop-killer, was the one ultimately at fault here. He was the lone causal factor for the officer's murder, not a simple (yet, seemingly lethal) miscue in arrest protocol. But, if for no other reason than to remind the officers in attendance who were still out there making arrests, and especially the rookies among that group (to include me), his murder, as tragic and unnecessary as it was, could still serve as a learning experience and possibly help save others' lives in the future.

This incident, this event, never left me. It was embedded in my rookie police officer's consciousness during that day-long memorial, with hundreds of other uniformed police officers around me, a fraternity of which I was now a welcome, albeit brand new, member. I was reminded that the protocols and training we received at the police academy were done over and over again for a very specific reason; to get it right, to create that virtual muscle-memory, for when such a situation presents itself. This, for the sole purpose of protecting the lives of all involved.

In future years, whenever I would come upon a young police officer, a newly minted FBI agent, or anyone involved in the business of law enforcement, whether they asked me for advice or not, I always made sure I told them one thing. That one thing was and is: never, EVER, trust a potential arrestee, an arrested person, a prisoner, or anyone in any custodial capacity. Whether the criminal offense and arrest is a minor white-collar crime, a nuisance-type crime, whether it's an old woman, a teenager, or a person the officer/agent may have arrested routinely over a dozen times before, NEVER fully trust that person when he/she is in custody, from the very beginning of the process to the very end. Their freedom has just been taken away, maybe for a really long time. They know more about what they may have just done and/or what they have done in the past than the officer may know at that time. They know more about themselves, their own history, their true motivations, their physical capabilities, their risk-taking propensities, their present state of mind (perhaps), than the arrester will know then or possibly ever.

So, when the in-custody person asks to be handcuffed in front because it's otherwise uncomfortable, or because he/she has a "sore arm" or an alleged condition of some sort, or asks to loosen the cuffs because it's cutting off the circulation in one or more wrists, I would just tell them clearly and professionally that they'll have to wait until the transportation to the precinct, district, police headquarters, magistrate, prison, or wherever, is completed. I'd suggest to them that they should sit still, not squirm, and it'll be addressed upon arrival to the destination, with other officers around. Of course, they should be fully searched too, certainly while cuffed and before being placed in the back of a police car.

I have no doubt that I may have violated some administrative protocols in some situations in my 31-year law enforcement career. However, based on what I learned of Officer Hancock's burglary arrest and subsequent murder in December of 1976, I always treated the newly arrested and/or prisoners I was transporting in the same very strict manner, handcuffs behind them and fully searched. While driving them, I would do my best to observe them the whole time too, even if only through my rearview mirror. There was never an exception.

In closing, there was no reason Officer Hancock should have been murdered that night. He did everything right during the initial approach and arrest of the subject; well, almost everything. However, that one error in judgment on his part ultimately contributed to his death. That cannot be denied.

Officer Hancock's legacy lives on in the warnings and admonitions I impart to these younger officers/agents regarding arrestees, whether asked for or not. Dave Hancock's murder, while tragic and unnecessary by any definition, may have nonetheless helped future officers/agents escape the same fate in their own careers. I certainly hope so....

(+ Bonus Chapters 3a, 3b)

Chapter Four

Ray Geary, my former Olney (Philadelphia neighborhood) buddy, classmate going back seventeen years at three different schools, co-valedictorian with me at our police academy graduation ceremonies, and now fellow-rookie officer on the BPD, and I did not have the occasion to actually work side-by-side yet. I would see him at shift-change at times, before or after roll call, but otherwise we were never on the same squad at the same time. We would socialize off-duty occasionally when our work schedules permitted, but that was pretty much the limit of our time together. We thought this may change early in 1977 when the patrol squads were to be re-aligned, but we wound up assigned to different squads once again. As it turned out, except for maybe one shift in which one of us switched and worked for someone else on another squad, we two long-time friends would never patrol Bensalem together at the same time.

As Ray had taken the Philadelphia Police Department entrance exam the same time as me, in May of 1975, when he was eventually offered a position by them, he decided after about a year on the BPD that he was going to return to his geographic roots and make that agency his law enforcement home for the foreseeable future. He had several good friends now on the PPD, including Gary Farrell (who, as related in JCM Book I, was one of the people with us for our barroom celebratory get-together a few nights before Ray and I started the Pennsylvania State Police Academy), and he felt that this move would be best for him for various personal and professional levels. Ray eventually graduated from the Philadelphia Police Academy and was hoping one day to work with Gary on the same squad in the same police district.

That reality, unfortunately, never came to pass for the two good friends. It was to be cut short by a bullet. (More on this tragedy forthcoming.)

In the early '80s, Ray Geary was promoted to the rank of detective in the Philadelphia PD. In 1989, he decided to enroll in Temple University School of Law. It took Ray the better part of four years going part-time, but he eventually became a lawyer and passed the Pennsylvania bar exam, all while still working as a Philadelphia PD detective. Not an easy task, to say the least.

After working in the PPD legal department and in their research and development unit, Ray left the police department in 1996. He is now doing very well as a defense attorney with his own private practice in Philadelphia.

* * * * *

Back again to my new job...I was scheduled to work the 7A-3P shift on New Year's Day, 1977. It was the first of seven days of day-work for me. On that Saturday through Friday shift we actually got one of those days off, working six of the seven days until the last Friday and the beginning of our long weekend. Somehow it meant that we were only working forty hours per week on average over the whole month. As a rookie, I was given Tuesdays off during my day-work shift. Not necessarily an exciting day to be off, but I took it nonetheless. I really had no choice.

The night before, New Year's Eve, was the first one of those festive holidays in which I was asleep in bed before 10:00PM since I was probably eight years old. As part of my newly derived mission and ambition to be the best I could be in my new profession, I made up my mind to get a solid eight hours of sleep on every work night. So, under the covers and skipping the usual midnight celebrations was the plan for me for the very last day of 1976 and into the first day of 1977. I adhered to the plan and I awoke fresh and ready-to-go at 5:45AM on that morning and was the first one from my squad in the roll call room that day.

Sgt. Ashton took off that day too, but this time he actually switched with another BPD sergeant, Bill Schultz, to work his shift. I didn't really know Sgt. Schultz at all, but I had seen him at shift change on multiple occasions during my month-plus on the job. He was in his late 30s, divorced with a kid or two, in relatively decent physical shape, and seemingly a nice guy. I didn't think Sgt. Schultz knew of me either, but on that morning at about 6:55, during roll call, he surprised me with an announcement which would allow us to get to know each other pretty well. He told the squad, and me, that I was going to be his driver that day. All day.

OK…what was this about?

I still hadn't patrolled the streets on my own yet (nor did any of my recently graduated fellow rookies), and had always been assigned to another patrolman as my training partner; two of them so far. Now, I just found out that I would have one of the BPD sergeants as my training officer for the day. That seemed somewhat odd, but that was his decision, so I really didn't have much say in the matter.

Once roll call was over, we didn't waste any time. Sgt. Schultz wanted to get on the road right away he told me. So, we gathered our stuff and walked outside into the cold air. We found his car, the one the sergeants drove, and put our stuff in the back seat. Geez, it even had the word "Sergeant" on both sides, and since I was the one driving it today it was almost like I was the actual sergeant. This was kind of cool, I thought.

When we finally got inside the car and settled in, me behind the driver's wheel, he in the passenger seat, I couldn't help but notice an unusual smell. I didn't want to sniff too obviously, but I just wasn't sure at first from where it was emanating. However, it took just one turn of my head to the right to determine that it was my sergeant/training officer-for-the-day who was the source of what I could best describe as an overwhelming aroma of mouthwash and aftershave, with a touch of alcoholic beverage in the mix. It wasn't too pungent of an odor, but one which nonetheless permeated the whole interior of the car, especially on this day when outside sub-freezing temperatures dictated that the windows would be all but closed tight the entire shift.

Okay, I figured I could breathe through my mouth that day if I had to and maybe crack the driver's side window a little bit later that day. I'd get used to it, I'm sure. I hoped.

Right after I filled the police car with gas and it was good to go, Sgt. Schultz "ordered" me to drive to the nearest 7-11 where he said he was going to get the biggest, strongest, black coffee he could pour, or maybe even two separate cups of coffee, whichever he deemed would best suit his present needs. Ah…that explains his haste to get out to the patrol car and onto the street. He needed a cup of joe, at least one of them, and right away. He readily admitted to me on the short drive there that he was out late last night (as in, the wee hours of this morning), wholeheartedly embracing the advent of the brand new year. Having done so, with acknowledged little sleep and a still-lingering hangover, he wanted me to be his driver that day. I guess I was to feel honored for this task. I still wasn't so sure though....

Bill slowly morphed into a friendly mood that morning, although he clearly wasn't in the best of form on that day due to his admitted excessive alcohol intake the night before. This explained his over-abundance of odor-masking liquids on his face and in his mouth, and his overindulgence of multiple hot, black coffees throughout the morning hours. I was hoping we didn't have to respond to a robbery or any other violent crime-in-progress, as I'm not sure the sergeant's physical reaction time would have been all that good. Luckily, those reaction times were not to be tested on this day.

Driving with Sgt. Schultz for the better part of that eight-hour shift was the longest time I had spent with any management member on the BPD. While we discussed police procedures, patrol tactics, BPD history, and the like, he would also switch topics and would enjoy telling the occasional joke and humorous anecdote about his own life, his career, and that of other officers. I would notice when attempting to make a point in one of his stories, or when delivering a punch line to a joke, he would take the back of his left hand and tap it gently against my arm or my thigh as I was driving. When he took the conversation into the sexual realm, which he did repeatedly that day in his telling of a few ribald jokes and/or relating stories of his alleged sexual experiences with various women (as he was just recently divorced), the number of "taps" on my appendages, especially my thigh it would seem, would escalate exponentially. No big deal, I thought at the time, even if I was a bit uncomfortable on each occasion that he touched me. I had simply surmised that Sgt. Schultz was simply a demonstrative, hands-on type of guy. I was a young, fresh-faced, and impressionable rookie, and he wanted to make sure I understood his stories and got his humor. He did so by being a bit touchy-feely with me. That's normal for a sergeant and his rookie driver, I guess. Right?

Or is it...?

I didn't know, as it was the first time I'd ever driven around with a patrol sergeant at all, much less for an entire shift.

The first day of 1977 was a quiet one in Bensalem and uneventful, at least as the 7-3 shift ended for us. As with each of my shifts so far at this cool new job, these eight hours seemingly went by fast too, even with Sgt. Schultz tapping away at my right-side arm and leg numerous times while traversing the streets of Bensalem Township.

Later that January, the BPD patrol squads were re-aligned and as it turned out Gene Ashton would continue to be my sergeant. During the selection process, I believe he "drafted" me from the rookies on the force. I guess I had impressed him in the two months or so we worked together so far and apparently he wanted me as a part of his new squad. That was a good feeling.

Most of the rest of '77 on the squad with Sgt. Ashton was pretty routine. I was still learning the job, the geography of the township, and the personalities of my fellow officers. On the whole, I thought Gene to be a very good sergeant, a very good leader. We interacted well while on duty with our squad. He seemingly knew the admin part of the job as well as the street part of the job (just watch out for those bank alarms), and would freely impart to us newer officers what we needed to know in both of these areas.

As that year would unfold, interestingly, when Sgt. Ashton wanted to take extra time to extend his visits to his Virginia farm before or after our once-a-month scheduled long weekends, he would trade a day here and there, and have Sgt. Schultz work the shift for him. So, on perhaps an every-other-month basis, Bill Schultz would, in effect, be a substitute sergeant for Gene Ashton and he would be my boss on those days. There may have been one or two extra day-work shifts that I drove him around after one of his late nights out. They were pretty much very similar to the previous New Year's Day's experience, with the odors, the story telling, and the ever-so-subtle backhand taps to make his points. Still weird I thought, but not necessarily all that bothersome to me.

Eventually, however, Sgt. Schultz's interactions of the personal variety with at least one other individual caused him some problems; make that some very large problems. Apparently, he really was a touchy-feely type of guy, except on several occasions it went too far. Make that way too far, and with a person who was way too young.

One afternoon during the fall of 1977, while still at my house, I noticed a very disturbing story on the front page of the just-delivered *Bucks County Courier Times*. Upon reading it, I learned that a Bensalem police sergeant was being investigated for child molestation of some sort. The sergeant wasn't named, and specific details were not otherwise provided in the story. With so few details, and no one to really call about this news who would have known anything, I didn't know what to expect when I got into work that Monday afternoon.

Was it my sergeant?

No, no way! Not Gene Ashton!

It couldn't be him.

Upon arriving at the station that Monday for the 3P-11P shift, I overheard two patrol sergeants (Gene Ashton being one of them) and two detective sergeants complaining out loud that their reputations were being maligned because the newspaper didn't specifically name the offending officer in the front page article, only that he was a BPD "sergeant," and it did not even distinguish between patrol or detective sergeant. Any one of them, and there were about eight sergeants at the time, could have been the child molester as far as the public was concerned. Some even said their neighbors and friends looked at them "funny" that day. As one of the patrol cars had the word "Sergeant" on each side, the uniformed sergeant who was just ending his shift that day said people were seemingly staring at him and pointing him out to others towards the end of his shift. He said he felt compelled to tell some with whom he came into contact that day that it was NOT him who was the referenced sergeant in the newspaper article, and he did.

So, who was it?

Everyone was attempting to learn just what happened and who, in fact, was the mystery BPD sergeant who was now in trouble for this most disturbing of crimes. But, mum was the word on that evening. We were to find out soon enough though.

Interestingly, as my shift ended, Sgt. Schultz was not there for his oncoming squad's roll call for the midnight shift. An acting sergeant was in charge that night. Schultz's absence should have been an early clue to me and my colleagues I suppose, however, nothing was officially said to my squad at roll call or for some time afterwards. Nonetheless, I knew it wasn't my sergeant. Gene Ashton was one of my early professional role models, at least from a young police officer's perspective, AND he actually worked that night. So...nah...it couldn't be him!

It finally came out after 11PM that night from within the police station that it was, in fact, my sometimes sergeant for whom I would sometimes drive, Bill Schultz, who was the child molester referenced in the paper.

Damn! The touchy-feely guy.

Apparently, over the last few months, Bill got a bit too friendly with a 16-year old member of the Bensalem High School sponsored BPD police cadet corps. He started fraternizing with the young man after work hours. Purportedly, some very personal touching took place (apparently much more personal than just light backhanded taps as with me during our car rides), and the youth eventually reported it to an authority figure. The world as Bill knew it then came tumbling down on him and his career a very short time later.

The following Tuesday afternoon, the day after the story was first publicized, the front page of the newspaper reported the remaining facts of the case, specifically naming Bill Schultz (to the relief of the other sergeants), and the fact that he was formally arrested for various criminal violations related to the sexual abuse of the teenager.

Coincidently, the Friday night before this story broke in the media, the 25th anniversary dinner of the Bensalem Police Department was underway. As the PD had been officially formed in 1952, a long-planned celebratory event took place on that Friday at a local restaurant. Many present and past members of the department, their significant others, as well as former and in-office politicians, and other township and Bucks County luminaries, attended the dinner that evening.

As I was still a rookie, not originally from Bensalem, and not involved at all in the long-term history of the department, I respectfully declined to attend the event. I knew that the department still needed officers to patrol the streets that night, so I thought I would do my part and agree to switch my shift with other officers who wanted to attend the dinner.

Sergeant Schultz was among the many attendees at the anniversary dinner that night. After all, he was from Bensalem and on the police force for a decade-plus at the time, so of course he would be there. But, neither he nor the vast majority of the other attendees knew about the ongoing investigation concerning him and the teenage boy. The very few in police upper-management who knew of it, as well as the two investigating detectives, decided that they didn't want to ruin the dinner by making it public then and there. So, instead, the story went public after the weekend, with Bill being formally charged and arrested at that time.

Interestingly, I was told Bill Schultz attended the semi-formal anniversary event with a young woman who was described by several as a "stunning redhead." There may have been some natural gray added to that red hair within the next few days, however, upon her being made aware of the "stunning" multiple media accounts of Bill's now much publicized criminal matter involving the teenage boy.

Bill Schultz's career as a Bensalem police officer, and sergeant, was now over. He would eventually plead guilty to his crimes. As part of the plea agreement, he was not sentenced to any jail time. He would move on in life, but not in any law enforcement capacity.

I never saw Bill Schultz again. The last I heard of him he was bartending at a neighborhood Bensalem drinking establishment. The young man he assaulted eventually became a BPD dispatcher and years later a police officer and a detective at another agency.

It was a great disappointment to me that this police sergeant, one with whom I'd had only a part-time association, but I nevertheless looked up to and respected and had learned from, had this secret side to his life. I wondered numerous times after his arrest if he chose me to drive him on that New Year's Day, 1977, and on a few other subsequent days, for reasons other than what he said at the time, that is, that he was simply hung over and needed a driver, any driver. He didn't try anything with me on those days (besides the incessant leg and arm touching), or anytime during the rest of that year. But I've always wondered….

At the time, I was only seven years older than the teenager Bill eventually abused, and I was told back then that I could pass for a good bit younger than my actual chronological age. Did Bill have other intentions on his mind for me? Was he testing me? Grooming me, of sorts?

This became a troublesome thought not long afterwards for me.

It doesn't matter. Bill did what he did (and not in any way to me) and ultimately paid a heavy price for it. To his credit, I don't believe he reoffended with any other youth any time after his arrest. Both affected parties seemed to have moved on, as did the Bensalem Police Department. Oh, and me too. Nonetheless, living through this episode taught me early on in life that many people have their weaknesses, their personal issues, even their demons, to include those of us who are supposed to not just follow the law, but take an oath to enforce it as well.

Bill Schultz died in 2013.

The next time I would have direct knowledge of a pedophile law enforcement officer, it was when I was in the FBI. And so was he. I was part of the team that arrested him.

(More on that case in JCM Book III.)

Chapter Five

After my innocent (I think) New Year's Day of being chauffer to Sgt. Schultz, my actual squad sergeant, Gene Ashton, came back to work on Sunday, January 2nd, 1977, for our 7A-3P shift. He surprised me first thing that morning by telling me at roll call that I was patrolling on my own that day. Yes, it was to be my first shift ever on patrol in a car by myself. He told me based on his evaluation of me over the last month-plus, what my two training officers had to say, and even having read a praise-worthy memo from Sgt. Schultz from the day before, he reckoned that I could now handle the streets of Bensalem in a patrol car on my own, at least on what is generally the quietest shift of the week, Sunday day-work. So, after being assigned Sector 3, which is the smallest sector land-wise, but perhaps the densest population-wise, off I went, solo in a police car for the first time.

Man! What an exhilarating feeling! I was free at last; in my own patrol car, as my own person, as my own police officer. I could drive where I wanted to drive (in my assigned sector), do what I wanted to do (while still in a police car and in uniform), check out who I wanted to check out (with the appropriate constitutional constraints), and I was essentially my own boss (well, sort of), for the first time ever. Naturally, I still had to be responsive to the dispatcher, to the sergeant, back up other officers when necessary who may have a call in or near my sector, and generally NOT do anything to cause trouble or get into trouble, but I could now do what it was that I signed up to do. That is, be a cop, doing my own thing, and hopefully doing it very well.

My training officer days riding in the passenger seat were behind me, and that was a very good feeling. Besides successfully passing all my course work at the twelve-week police academy, now, after just about five weeks of being assigned to training officers, I had passed that benchmark too. I was now primed, pumped, and ready to go.

And go I did, eventually working through all three shifts, on my own. Some of the coldest continuous temperatures on record were with us in the U. S. Mid-Atlantic region that January of '77. I remember even driving down to the Delaware River, which bordered Sector 3 to the east, and seeing it was frozen over - a very rare event. The single digit or even below-zero temperatures didn't bother me at all. For the next month, over each of the three shifts, I was as enthusiastic as a guy could be with a new job, very cold weather or not. I just wanted to be out there, on patrol, handling crimes and the concerns of the citizenry in any way I could. Catching bad guys would be an added bonus too, if possible.

Looking back, these early days of me being an officially sanctioned, solo patrol officer, were without a doubt the most interesting, invigorating, and fun times of my 31-year professional career. I was brand new at it, the majority of my co-workers at the time seemed positive and committed to each other and to our respective chosen profession, and internal politics (and infernal politicians) had not reared their ugly heads yet. Well, not that I had noticed, anyway. I was innocent and a blank slate, at least as it would apply to a rookie police officer. And, no one within the BPD had pissed me off nor had I pissed them off yet. It was a great place to be, at least from my personal and professional vantage point at that time.

If only I could have somehow stayed in that mental place, with that same naïve attitude throughout my entire career.

Could I somehow bottle up this feeling? Take it with me? Hold onto it forever?

Maybe?

No, I couldn't, and I wouldn't. This feeling, as it turned out, wasn't destined to last very long. It rarely does in life to those in similar new careers and professions, and it certainly didn't as it related to the temporal euphoric stage I was in at the time. It couldn't last with me, as the human dynamics of my police department and the unabashed quest for power among some within it resulted in the lighting of a long invisible fuse, one I and some others didn't even notice burning at first. But it would smolder and move ever so slowly for a while before it reached its political powder keg. When it did, most would feel the explosive repercussions right away, and all would live with the results for years, if not a decade-plus, to come.

* * * * *

In early February of '77, after the patrol squads were re-aligned, I was actually assigned to be the fill-in training officer of an even newer rookie on my squad. His name was Steve Moran. Now it was my opportunity, at least on a few different shifts, to show a new officer around Bensalem Township and also how to be a police officer. While I had a two month or so head start on him, Steve caught up quickly and we eventually learned a lot of our new profession and new township together, even after he was assigned solo duties in his own patrol car.

Steve was one of the few officers on the Bensalem PD who did not grow up in either Bensalem (as did the majority of the existing officers), or in Philadelphia or its suburbs (as most of us newer officers). He was from Erie, Pennsylvania, and travelled diagonally across Pennsylvania to take the written exam with the rest of us back in the spring of '76. He was appointed to the force a few months after me, went to the local Pennsylvania State Police Academy training class in the Philadelphia suburbs, and started on the streets upon graduation in early '77.

Steve and I became good friends over the years there. He followed me onto a few squads and even into management, each after I "blazed the trail" for him, as I would jokingly (and semi-truthfully) remind him at the time. Years later, Steve eventually rose up the ladder all the way to the rank of Director of Public Safety. He stayed there for about a decade through the early 2000s. I was glad for him and his professional ascendency within the department.

I reminded Steve years later that it was my on-and-off expert training of him during those few weeks back in early 1977 that taught him all he knew about the job and got him to the top of his professional law enforcement mountain, aka, the Bensalem PD. He laughingly responded it's what he later taught me that helped me land my next job. Touché....

* * * * *

There was another rookie officer with whom I became friendly on Sgt. Ashton's new squad. His name was Jerry Judge. He was a big and imposing guy, with a slightly crooked nose and hands the size of uncooked Easter hams. The crookedness of the nose and the size of the hands were not unrelated, as I would soon learn. He was good looking guy (despite the curvature of his nose), bright, with a great personality and sense of humor to boot.

After getting to know Jerry over the course of a few shifts, it turns out I had known of him, from afar, since my earliest years at my alma mater, Cardinal Dougherty High School. He was a great football player for one of our Philadelphia Catholic League divisional rivals, Father Judge High School (no relation to him whatsoever.) He had a great gridiron career while there, being named to the prestigious All-Catholic team more than once. He was three years older than me, and his reputation preceded him on a few fronts, one of which I was not fully aware of yet.

Jerry told me over a few hot beverages shared across the drivers' doors of opposite-facing police cars during our rookie year that his knees gave out on him not long after his high school playing days, so his college football career never really took off. When that fizzled, he decided to follow through on what else he was very good at doing. That was, fighting. After developing the basics on the streets of Northeast Philadelphia, he attained a seasoned trainer, learned the art of pugilism, and eventually decided he had what it took to become a professional boxer. His ring name became "Irish Jerry Judge."

During the late '60s and through the mid-'70s Jerry slowly rose through the ranks in the boxing world, earning a 17-8 (and 1 draw) heavyweight record, with fourteen knockouts to his credit. Among the highlights of his career was a 1971 TKO of Chuck Wepner, who was one of the few boxers to ever knock Muhammed Ali off his feet in the ring. In 1973, Jerry met future heavyweight champion Larry Holmes and only lost to him but by a close decision in their bout.

However, possibly Irish Jerry Judge's most notable and well publicized professional fight was not really an officially sanctioned one. It was more of an exhibition. It took place in April of 1975.

Upon being recruited by the event's promoter, Jerry travelled to Toronto, Canada, to be one of five heavyweight boxers who would meet former and future heavyweight champion George Foreman in the ring for three rounds each with him, all in one over-the-top (by anyone's standards) boxing extravaganza. The highly marketed event was covered live on ABC's *Wide World of Sports* by Howard Cosell with guest commentator Muhammed Ali, who had beaten Foreman and earned the heavyweight crown from him just six months before in the famous "Rumble in the Jungle" in Africa.

Foreman would "win" each of his five bouts that day, including his three rounds with Jerry, but not before Jerry had some fun with him, and landed some punches on him too. In an attempt to intimidate Big George, Jerry surprisingly kissed George on the cheek as he was trying to stare him down during the pre-fight advisories by the referee. Needless to say, Foreman didn't take kindly to this gesture on his opponent's part. Jerry was also reported to have told George during the actual bout that he (George) couldn't hit, something that no boxer likes to hear about himself, especially in the middle of an actual contest, be it an exhibition or not. Despite the bit of clowning around that day on his part, Jerry nonetheless stood his own with Foreman, was never knocked down, but ultimately lost the bout on overall points.

It was a wild and unusual boxing event, that goes almost without saying. But Jerry got some positive notoriety from it, having stood toe-to-toe with boxing great George Foreman for three rounds, and earning a decent paycheck for it too. Jerry went on to fight some more, (just one opponent at a time thereafter), but hung up his gloves for the most part upon joining the Bensalem Police Department.

To say the least, Jerry led a very interesting life before ever joining the BPD, certainly more so than this kid (me) from my Philadelphia neighborhood of Olney so far. He even lived in Hawaii for a year prior to becoming a police officer, with some great anecdotes to tell about that stage of his life too. At the time, I didn't know anyone personally who had ever even visited Hawaii, much less lived there for a year or so. But, Jerry's public legacy ultimately would live on in a small and very unusual way in another genre for the rest of his life, and not coincidently related to the boxing world. It would initially present itself in one of the most popular movies of all time, and be a constant reminder of his legacy to all those who saw it when it first came out, and anyone who has seen it since.

Sylvester Stallone, the lead actor and writer of the screenplay for the movie *Rocky*, had roots in the Philadelphia area. In researching the storylines for the movie, among other things, he had to come up with some names to be presented to the Apollo Creed character in the staging of his big upcoming fight at the Spectrum arena in Philadelphia.

In his third scene in the movie, Carl Weathers, playing Apollo Creed, rattles off several names of potential boxers he could face for his big January 1st Bicentennial Year bout. This after the "legitimate" opponent he was supposed to fight backed out at the last minute due to an injury of some sort. Creed's goal now became to choose a relatively unknown pugilist and to give that guy a shot at his title in this overly-hyped event although, of course, planning all along to retain the championship belt himself by beating this "chump."

In this particular scene, it's not the name "Jerry Judge" that's referenced, but darn close.

In going through a list of potential opponents, Creed's trainer says to him, "Bobby Judge is a good boy."

Creed passively responds, "...I don't feel heat from the name."

Eventually in that scene, the name of down-on-his-luck Philadelphia heavyweight Rocky Balboa surfaces, he's chosen as Creed's opponent, and the plotline continues through the climactic slugfest at the end. In 1977, among other accolades, *Rocky* won the Academy Award for Best Picture of the year.

It was well known in Philadelphia boxing circles that this quick name reference in the movie was a tip-of-the-hat to Jerry Judge as the type of local boxer that Stallone wanted his Rocky character to resemble. Of course, Rocky was an Italian-American in the movie, with a nickname of the "Italian Stallion," instead of "Irish Jerry Judge." It was probably for legal purposes that Stallone couldn't actually use the name Jerry Judge as the never-seen-but-referenced almost-contender in the movie.

In the end, Jerry Judge was perhaps just an average prize fighter in the annals of professional boxing history. Nonetheless, in his relatively short time in the ring he managed to out-box or at least hold his own with some pretty famous tough guys who eventually went on to make names for themselves, whether in officially sanctioned bouts or even the crazy five-opponent bout in Canada against George Foreman. With a very similar name reference in the very successful movie *Rocky,* even this "average" heavyweight contender's legacy will be in place for a long time to come thanks to that classic movie, and Sly Stallone's subtle tip-of-the-hat to Jerry.

Later in Jerry's police career, specifically during his two-year stint as the Police Benevolent Association's (PBA) President, as that earlier lit fuse of internecine departmental politics was nearing its explosive nadir and causing the whole department to publicly spiral downward, by his own acknowledgment, some of Jerry's toughest fights ever were to take place then. In that role, he wasn't necessarily threatened by a broken nose or fat lip from his foes, but instead the kind of knockout punch that's represented by the loss of his job or even being criminally prosecuted. And, by the way, that possibility existed for me too at the time, as I was Jerry's "corner man" during this several year political battle.

Ultimately, Jerry and I, along with dozen or so other BPD officers, fought to the finish our powerful and well-connected departmental opponents, utilizing every means legally accessible to us, both overtly and covertly. The ethically and morally challenged police management team who managed to take charge just a year-plus before, to include their sycophantic lower-level henchmen scattered among the troops, were terrorizing the other, hard-working PD members in their (the management's and henchmen's) ongoing pursuit of unabated and unquestioned authority over all they surveyed.

It would be a nasty, hard fought, knock-down, drag-out fight. And a TKO wouldn't suffice. It had to be by knockout, once and for all, that this scourge on the Bensalem PD and the majority of its officers, and for that matter, the public that it served, would have to be excised from power.

It would be great to have a former heavyweight boxer on our side during this time. Jerry could take a punch and deliver one too. I was glad to stand there with him, fighting the good fight alongside of him. Looking back, I was proud to be in the "ring" side-by-side with Officer/PBA President Jerry Judge during those divisive and politically challenging times. I couldn't think of a better guy to have my back.

But, we're not there yet....

* * * * *

I received a phone call at home on a quiet mid-week evening in February of '77. It was from John Tierno, my friend and former co-worker at the Strawbridge & Clothier department store, who just happened to catch me at home on a night off. He asked me how I was doing, how was the new job, my marriage, etc. I told him things were great in all categories, as I honestly felt they were. I asked him some similar questions and he told me he had since finished his master's degree courses at Villanova University, quit S&C, and was working for a suburban Philadelphia school district as a guidance counselor. It was nice to catch up on each other's personal and professional lives.

John eventually told me, however, that the main purpose of his contacting me was to ask if it would be okay if his long-time friend, Bob Yezzi, could call me. Bob purportedly had some questions to ask me about the Bensalem PD. I told him to have Bob call me the following afternoon when I was again off-duty and at home.

I remembered Bob well and immediately liked him the first time John Tierno introduced us well over a year ago when we walked the floor at S&C together looking for shoplifters. As mentioned earlier, Bob visited S&C a number of times to visit John and I thought him to be a genuinely nice guy.

Upon Bob calling me that next afternoon, we joked about some of our S&C experiences (even though he never actually worked there), and where his own future intentions and interests lay. Like John, he too was a Villanova grad, and decided over the last year that he wanted to become a law enforcement officer at the local level. Or at least start there. He had applied to two suburban Philadelphia police departments, Lower Merion Township and Bensalem Township (having taken the latter's entrance exam with me just about ten months before), and felt that both PDs were about to make him an offer of employment. Bob, at the time, was still residing in Southwest Philadelphia. He grew up in a rowhome and neighborhood somewhat similar to mine, but in an entirely different section of the city.

After exchanging other pleasantries and catching up on our respective lives, Bob got to asking me all sorts of questions about the BPD during our thirty minute or so phone conversation. They were good questions too. He asked about living conditions in the township, what were the veteran officers like and what was the caliber of the more recent hires at the BPD. He wanted to know about the PSP academy training, what was the proposed pay scale over the first few years for a rookie police officer, what were opportunities for advancement, and what was the quality of the equipment we're issued. He also wanted to know the condition of the police cars we drove and other related queries about the overall experience that was being a sworn officer on the BPD.

I responded in the positive to most of Bob's very astute questioning regarding my new department. I certainly didn't denigrate the Lower Merion PD, as I knew that agency to have a fine reputation. I did in some ways sell the Bensalem PD to Bob as I felt it was a progressive and professional law enforcement agency and that I was very happy with my career choice so far.

I knew Bob to be a good guy, a smart guy, in physically good shape, in mentally good shape from what I could tell, and that he would only enhance the existing attributes of the BPD and its personnel that were there already. So, in effect, I played the role of recruiter to him, at least to some degree. It wasn't my job to do so, but I found myself doing it anyway, since he called and was asking me all about it.

As Bob and I wound down our conversation, we both agreed that the ultimate decision was his to make. Both PDs were seemingly good places to land, and he couldn't go wrong with either. I told him I would welcome him, introduce him to people, and generally show him around once he got to Bensalem if he chose my agency to begin his career as a police officer. He thanked me for that as well as the time I took to talk to him that afternoon. He said he'd be making his decision within the next week. I asked him to let me know and wished him luck in the big decision-making task ahead of him.

Within ten days or so, Bob got back to me via telephone. He thanked me again for the advice and information I provided to him during our initial phone call. After much consideration, further research, a long car ride around Bensalem over the preceding weekend, talking to family and friends (he included me in that latter category), he informed me that he was, in fact, joining the Bensalem Police Department. He had already accepted their offer. His PSP academy class was starting in early March, he would graduate in late May, and be on patrol shortly thereafter.

Bob told me that my talk with him was a major reason why he joined the BPD. He added that it would be nice to have a friend already on the force to steer him through the early days on the job. I reminded him that we may not even work on the same squad anytime in the near future, but despite that, I could still get him acclimated to the place once he got there. We agreed that could easily be done.

I was happy for Bob, for the Bensalem PD for recruiting yet another quality police officer, and for me, for helping a friend, even if a newly made friend-of-a-friend, decide to join me on my department. That positive feeling remained constant throughout the next three-and-a-half years for Bob and I as our professional and personal relationship grew.

Then it all ended...overnight...literally...in the worst possible way imaginable.

More on this will be forthcoming.

(+ Bonus Chapter, 5a)

Chapter Six

Throughout the rest of '77 as a uniformed patrol officer, I worked all three shifts on a weekly rotating basis and experienced just about everything a law enforcement professional could imagine over the course of a year in a mid-sized suburban police department. (To include the extra "experience" of having one of the BPD sergeants arrested for child molestation by year's end.) I responded to homicides, attempted homicides, deaths by natural causes, fatal vehicle accidents, stabbings, shootings, drunken bar room brawls, shoplifters (yes, them again), robberies, burglaries, thefts, and the like, and made or assisted in arrests of individuals involved in most of these types of crimes.

While it certainly wasn't New York, Los Angeles, Chicago, or even nearby Philadelphia, Bensalem was busy enough considering its size, its proximity to the City of Brotherly Love, and with three major East coast highways running through it, i.e., Rt. 1, Interstate 95, and the Pennsylvania Turnpike. Throw in a large horse racing track (then known as Keystone Park, later known as Philadelphia Park) along with two large malls and just about every sort of crime that could be committed was, in fact, committed there. It was not to the volume or frequency of the much larger cities, but for a suburban town, the crime per capita was not insignificant.

While Bensalem had (or has) no truly rundown residential sections to it, or "Badlands" as they are known in some cities, suffice to say, for whatever reason, several then-newly constructed apartment complexes attracted some less-than-desirable individuals to them, and they brought criminal lifestyles with them, mostly from Philadelphia and from across the Delaware River from New Jersey. While I certainly arrested my share of Bensalem natives during my time as a young patrolman, it was pretty evenly matched with a newer influx of those criminal types from the other outlying areas, whether just travelling through town or actually living in my town.

Many of the families newly residing in Bensalem were looking to escape their crime-ridden cities and neighborhoods, but inevitably brought some of the criminal activity with them through their children and kin. Not all of them, of course, but some. In many cases, the newer residents themselves could be the victims of various crimes too. It resulted in a rise in crime in Bensalem starting in the early 1970s. No doubt, that was part of the reason federal grants were awarded to the Bensalem PD and resulted in my new colleagues and me eventually being hired there.

During the course of my first year-plus on the BPD, I found myself feeling relatively well-prepared to handle most of the types of incidents and crimes to which I was dispatched or otherwise came upon during the course of my duties. This preparedness was no doubt the direct result of my PSP academy training, my on-the-job experiences with several different officers, and generally the knowledge gained from my overall life experience so far, with a decent dosage of common sense thrown in for good measure. I'll readily acknowledge there was probably some luck in there too. Nonetheless, with all of these factors put together I'm proud to say that I didn't make any bad arrests, screw up any crime scenes, let a bad guy go when I shouldn't, crack up any police cars, injure myself or others, etc., during this first year of my law enforcement career.

I'm not suggesting everything I did during this time frame was flawless, it clearly wasn't. I made my share of administrative/paper-work mistakes, and even in some of the ways I may have handled the public in certain situations. But, on the whole, I think I was doing a pretty good job throughout 1977. Sergeant Ashton seemed to think so too.

There was one area, however, that I felt I didn't know my "stuff" as well, and where I probably made my share of early mistakes and misjudgments. It was in the handling of what every cop knows as the domestic disturbance.

There were a few hours, certainly less than four, allotted in our 12-week police academy training to the handling of the domestic disturbance call. In the one or two separate training blocks, various scenarios would be discussed in which couples and/or their older children could create such a toxic environment in their home that one of them would deem it rising above and beyond the "normal" familial arguing and abuse. That is when they would need the police to come to remedy the situation and protect the innocent. As we learned through an instructional training film or two, and several staged interactive role-playing vignettes, these situations could get out of hand very quickly. As they are almost always fueled by high emotions, anger, and frustration, with usually an unhealthy dose of alcohol or drug use involved, this was to be expected.

We also learned at the academy that many police officers were killed and/or seriously injured every year responding to these types of family feud-related calls. The offender would typically be the enraged, emotionally imbalanced, and/or intoxicated husband or boyfriend who felt particularly emboldened by the police who are now in HIS home and who were clearly NOT invited there by him. This would be exacerbated even more so as it was his female partner/wife who most likely called the police in the first place, ostensibly for her own protection or that of their/her kids.

When in my younger years I would imagine what it would be like to embark on a career as a law enforcement officer, the last type of activity that would come to mind would be as a household marriage counselor to warring couples in their own homes. These types of calls are rarely illustrated in television series or movies about police work. But as I learned early on in my rookie year, it was much more commonplace than I ever expected, with calls coming in several times a shift (more so on weekends and at night) to respond to and handle these various people's personal problems. Many were repeat customers and we knew who the players were and what they were capable of doing before we got there. Others were the occasional one-night wonders. Either could be equally dangerous to the responding police officers if he or she wasn't prepared for the worst-case scenario upon arriving there. In retrospect, some of my most memorable fights and altercations as a police officer took place amidst the three-piece leather sectionals, glass top coffee tables, 25" console TVs, and most unfortunately, small children, in these living rooms suddenly turned into couple-combat zones.

I initially found it very difficult as a police officer responding to these type calls; that is, coming into a family's home for fifteen to forty-five minutes at a time and trying to solve sometimes a decade or more of emotional despair, frustration, anger, abuse, and at times, unabated hatred. Especially for me, as a 23-year old guy, newly married, who did not live in or grow up in an argumentative or dysfunctional household, and really had little, if any, experience in how to handle these highly-charged domestic situations once inserted into the middle of them. The minimal police academy training at the time only went so far for me in learning the skills necessary in coping and succeeding, if possible, with these type scenarios.

As mentioned before, it would usually be the wife or other woman in the household who would call the police on their now out-of-control man. In most cases, it would be the man who had physically assaulted or threatened to assault one or more family members, and it usually involved alcohol and/or controlled substance usage on his part. The nationwide statistics are very clear and consistent on who physically abuses whom. That would be the men threatening, harming, seriously injuring, or even killing their female partners. Or, sometimes their own mothers.

On the topic of domestic abuse/assault cases, this one resulted in me coming the closest I ever have to actually shooting someone. It would have been fully justified, too.

In my second stint in uniform patrol, sometime in 1981, I received a call one Sunday night of a domestic disturbance at a house in the Nottingham neighborhood of Bensalem Township. A mother was having trouble with her reportedly out-of-control 18-year-old son. (Obviously, it's not always a husband/boyfriend causing the problems for a woman. It can be her offspring, too.) The son had physically mistreated his mom a few times earlier in the evening and she decided enough was enough and eventually called the police. I arrived there shortly afterwards with another officer, Dale Richardson, and we were greeted by the mom at the front door. She was a woman in her late 40s, but she looked much older on this night.

There were no markings on mom indicative of her being physically assaulted by anyone, but she was nonetheless highly emotional and very distraught. She told us that after arguing with her son all day long and him then pushing her out of his way one last time, the young man had locked himself in his bedroom. Mom was sure he was "high" on something as he had been acting very strange lately, and even more so on this night. He pushed her around several times that day, and after thinking about it for a while, she felt that calling the police was what she now had to do. She was afraid of him, and with no husband/father in the house, Dale and I were to be the temporary remedy for their present familial issues, or at least try to be so. Thus, we two officers were in the living room of her one-story house learning the facts as she related them. Next, we knew we had to get the son out of his nearby lair and talk to him.

The mom walked us to the son's closed and locked bedroom door. Dale and I stood outside of the door, called him by name, and attempted to reason with him, sight unseen. He didn't answer us at first or even acknowledge we were there. Eventually, after suggesting we were going to get into his room one way or the other, he told us to leave his house as we had no business being there. We politely, but firmly reminded him that it was actually his mom's house, she called for us, and we were just here to talk this matter out and resolve it peacefully. We didn't want to break the door down we told him, although his mother said we could if we felt it was necessary to do so. That's how scared she was of her teen in his present state of mind.

After a few minutes engaging in the closed door negotiations, the son went silent again. The mom, who was about ten feet away from the bedroom door, whispered that sometimes he sneaks out of his window and leaves the room and the house through the back yard. If that was the case and he was gone for the night, perhaps that would resolve the problem, at least for now. After all, as the mom had told us she didn't necessarily want to press charges against her son, there wasn't much else we could do at that point in time except talk to him, read him the proverbial "riot act," and encourage him to go somewhere else until he calmed down.

It wouldn't work out quite that way on this Sunday night, going into Monday morning, all because of some potentially lethal decisions made by the son. Stupid decisions, too.

Since it was believed the son left the house via his bedroom window, Dale went outside the front door looking for him. I stayed in the house talking to the mom for a few extra minutes. Then, as my partner was still outside the house, I heard the sliding glass door from the kitchen area being opened. The mom said it was "probably" her son coming back inside. I got on my police radio and advised Dale that the son was now "probably" inside again.

I then walked from where I was standing with the mom and proceeded in a roundabout way in the direction of the sound of the sliding glass door. Upon walking around the corner from the living room into the dining room, lo and behold, there standing about fifteen feet away from me was the previously unseen son. I saw him very clearly now. He was at least six feet tall, trim and fit, longish curly brown hair, and he had a wild-eyed look about him. Oh, and I saw very clearly that he was also pointing a rifle directly at me.

In that nanosecond it took my brain to tell my body I was in his line of fire and potentially in serious and imminent bodily danger, I immediately stepped backwards and behind the wall which partially separated the two rooms. At virtually the same time I drew my .357 Magnum and yelled at the top of my voice to no one and everyone, "Gun! He's got a gun!"

As I heard Officer Richardson back inside the house, I knew he could hear me at this point. I wanted him to know what I was seeing. I wanted him to protect himself too. I then told Dale, "Go toward the kitchen, but stay covered! He's in the eating area, gun pointed right at me!"

From behind the wall separating me ever so slightly from the former teenage domestic-abuser to (from my perspective) now-adult gunman, I told the young man in a very commanding voice to drop the weapon and get down on the floor with his hands where I could see them. I heard nothing of him or from him after that particular verbal order. I knew he hadn't moved much as I could see his reflection at an angle through a china closet glass door in the room where he was standing. He was still holding the rifle with its butt on his shoulder, his finger on or near the trigger, with the barrel pointed in the direction of me. Fortunately, I was safely (I was hoping) behind the plaster-board wall.

Upon both of us maintaining our respective positions for what seemed like a minute-plus, with the son ignoring my orders to disarm and drop to the floor, I could see through the glass door that for some reason he had lowered the barrel of the gun. It was now pointing at an angle towards the floor, but he was still holding it in both of his hands and it could be raised to my level in a half-second if he chose to do so. This was my chance, I thought, as his guard was temporarily down, or at least the barrel of the weapon was temporarily down. In view of that, I stuck half my head and my entire weapon around the edge of the wall, just barely exposing myself to the gunman, much like I had trained at the police academy firearms range while standing or keeling behind various wooden barricades. With my .357 Magnum now pointing directly at the son/gunman, I ordered him once again to drop the rifle and get down on the floor. I even told him, "I don't want to shoot you, but you're giving me no choice here. Now drop the f**kin' gun!"

After that last command, the two of us stared at each other in silence, me peering from around the wall, him standing in freeze-frame fashion less than twenty feet from me. I had already given three or so orders to the teenager to drop the weapon. He ignored me each time, even the last one where I laid it on the line to him in very clear, if not profane, language. He never did raise the weapon back up to where it was aimed directly at me again, but he was still holding it in a very dangerous position, certainly for anyone standing in the area where the barrel happened to be pointing. That would be me at this time and place.

In the meantime, the mother started screaming for her son to put the gun down. She may have been screaming ever since he came back in the house, but this is the first time I registered it. Obviously, the gun pointed at me focused all of my senses on it and the person holding it. While I was no doubt aware of my other immediate surroundings, I was nonetheless myopically attentive to the danger zone playing out in front of me, just a few rifle barrel lengths away. I then heard the mom state very loudly in a half-crying, half-moaning voice that the son had the .22 which had been kept by her late-husband in the backyard shed and that must have been where he went to get it. I instructed Dale to call for additional backup and to get the mom out of the house. He did both.

At this time, it was still just me in the adjacent room facing the son, eye-to-eye and weapon-to-weapon. Except now I had the slight advantage. He was standing with no protection in front of him, with his weapon angled slightly downward toward the floor, almost at where my feet would be if I was standing in front of him. I had my weapon in my left hand (my strong hand) with half my face exposed, but the rest of me all but hidden behind the wall, and with my finger on the trigger while pointing the revolver at his center-mass.

Who would make the next move?

Him or me, what's it gonna be?

All it would take would be one furtive movement on his part, a movement I was hoping he was smart enough NOT to make. My trigger finger was in no way itchy, but it was definitely ready to scratch.

In these few seconds, I knew this was the closest I had ever come in my five-year or so career thus far to either being the shooter or the shootee. I was hoping to avoid either of these selections in the next few minutes, but if forced to choose, I would greatly prefer the former to the latter. Not even close, actually.

Upon giving him one more order to drop the weapon and get down on the floor, the son ultimately half-obeyed me. He dropped the weapon and ran from where he was standing to his left, back into the kitchen and out the sliding glass door. There were shallow woods directly behind his house and I barely managed to see him disappear into them. I immediately picked up the weapon off of the floor. I did not want it to become a factor in anything else which may unfold on this night. I examined it right then and there and determined that it was, in fact, loaded. I next advised over my police radio where I observed the subject run. Other responding officers began searching the woods and the adjacent roads and streets looking for the wayward son.

We all but ordered the mother out of her house. She agreed that it was too dangerous for her to stay there, especially as we couldn't guard her all night. She drove to a relative's house, I believe, somewhere out of the immediate area.

The son was eventually found and arrested later that night. His actual arrest was made by another officer and it was uneventful. He had somewhat calmed down from the person he was when I was in his company. I told him his mom wasn't pressing charges against him. I was. I charged him with various weapon and assault violations as they related to my interactions with him in his house that night. He later told me he was sorry for the pain he's lately been causing his mom. I reminded him of the pain he almost caused himself and/or me just a few hours before, the kind as a result of bullets tearing through flesh. He didn't seem to have a clear memory of what had transpired just those few hours before. I made sure he knew what happened both while in the police station and later in front of the district magistrate as he was being arraigned on those various charges.

A few months later, when the case came to court, the son had already been in detention much of the time as he couldn't make bail, nor would his mom post it for him. Once he eventually got out he entered into a drug program and he seemed to clean up his act. Through his defense attorney and the Bucks County District Attorney's Office, a plea-agreement was reached where he would do time-served (I believe several months), stay in the drug program, and have no weapons in his house. In fact, the .22 rifle was destroyed as per court order, with neither mom nor son objecting. I believe the son straightened up after that and there were no further problems between him, his mom, and law enforcement.

In looking back at this domestic-assault-gone-potentially-very-bad, there is no doubt that I was in fear of my life and in imminent bodily danger from the threat this eighteen-year old and his .22 rifle posed to me. I didn't know for sure if it was loaded, but I would have been a fool to assume otherwise. I could have shot him dead then and there in his own dining room and been legally justified in my decision to do so. But I didn't. Something told me that this young man was more likely temporarily stupid due to drug usage than being actually homicidal. I also knew I had the upper-hand when he unconsciously lowered the barrel of the rifle from it pointing at me to pointing it more-or-less at the floor. (Luckily the well-placed china closet door glass offered me that reflective view of what he was doing.) Maybe, I recall thinking at the time, I could get out of this situation without having to shoot him or kill him. I really didn't want to, after all, as he was only eighteen years old and not a "real" criminal from what I knew of him. Although, pointing a loaded weapon at anyone, much less a police officer, turned him into one at that precise moment in time.

Even after many years, I second-guess myself at times when recounting this specific experience. It could have gone a few different ways. It could have gotten very ugly, and very deadly. Fortunately, the incident turned out as it did for the son, the mom, and me. He pushed the limits that night, but ultimately lived to talk about it. And, so did I. That's what really matters here.

In closing here in the area of domestic abuse, a senior cop on the BPD once told me he respected no one less than a man who would hit a woman, no matter what the relationship. (With fully justifiable self-defense, of course, being the only exception to this rule.) I agreed and still agree with him wholeheartedly. As a police officer, I was forced to arrest and/or to sometimes "hit" these same men myself on more occasions than I'd like to remember while affecting their apprehension. I always hoped it would be the one time "teaching moment" they would need in this category of life to NOT do it again. Unfortunately, when days, weeks, or months later I was called back to the same households, involving the same parties, for essentially the same reasons, I usually found out they learned nothing. And some of the younger male children who witnessed these sessions of domestic non-bliss were learning this same behavior the whole time, to only be repeated again by them in their later adult relationships.

It is a sad ongoing cycle that unfortunately remains unbroken to this day.

(+ See Bonus Chapter 6a, 6b, 6c)

Chapter Seven

The everyday and every night routine of being a patrol officer was continuing to grow on me, and in a good way. I felt I was learning more and more with every tour-of-duty, about my job, about me personally, and about the overall human condition, as I was now seeing it in ways I never imagined before my days on the BPD. It was still very enjoyable going to work as each day was different than the day before and presented new challenges and opportunities for me in almost everything I did. This is what I wanted to do, this is what I wanted to be - certainly for now, anyway.

But alas, I was starting to hear from the older, veteran officers of a changing wind slowly picking up strength within the Bensalem Police Department. I gradually picked up on it too, even without necessarily being forewarned by the senior guys. It would gust on occasion around us officers, then seemingly subside for a while. Then, it would be back, sometimes when it was least expected. It wasn't too long before even this politically naïve rookie cop (me) knew it was, in fact, a troublesome wind blowing down the hallways of our police headquarters building. It would carry over onto the streets of Bensalem too, almost like it was following us in our patrol cars.

This zephyr was unseen, but clearly felt by us all. It carried with it the effluvia of office AND elected politics, making it the worst of its kind. It may have been small town politics in comparison to some neighboring jurisdictions, but with potentially big consequences to anyone for whom it blew as a headwind instead of a tailwind. Yes, backroom political intrigue was rearing its ugly head, now more so than ever, according to the officers who had been on the BPD for a few years. And it didn't take me long to get wind-burnt by it, despite my clear attempts to avoid doing so.

One Tuesday in late 1977, I learned from the front page of the *Bucks County Courier Times* that after the previous night's weekly Bensalem

Township Board of Supervisors meeting, it was determined that Chief Larry Michaels was to be demoted. Well, sort of. He would still retain the title of Chief, and keep his same pay and benefits, but a certain BPD Detective Lieutenant, Theodore Zajac, Jr., would now be taking over the day-to-day operations of the department. He would be promoted to Deputy Chief within a short time, and the BPD would be his to run. Chief Michaels would be nothing more than its titular head, with Zajac now in actual charge of the whole department.

How could this happen? Why would it happen? I naïvely asked more than one of the senior BPD officers.

I was told this upwardly-mobile move on Zajac's part had been orchestrated for several years as his father, Theodore Zajac, Sr., had been a long-time Bensalem Township politician. He only recently stepped down from his position as one of five elected township supervisors. But a majority of the remaining members on the Board of Supervisors were still aligned with him and would apparently still cater to him in their various deal-brokerings. Ted, Sr., even now removed from his previous post, evidently worked behind the scenes to reconfigure the management of the police department by putting his son, Ted, Jr., in charge of it; this while Larry Michaels was still officially its lawfully appointed chief. Since Chief Michael's political capital had been spent, with no real strong supporters of him left on the Board, he apparently accepted his new role, and was just biding his time until he could move on to greener pastures, outside of the Bensalem PD.

This was all confusing to me. How can we have one "real" chief, who holds that title, but then have someone else who's just a lieutenant (albeit soon to be a Deputy Chief) actually running the department? What did this all mean to the BPD? And, yes, what did it all mean to me?

Some officers, I was to learn, were truly distressed about their future careers now that Lt. Zajac was put in charge. Others seemed truly happy for their careers now that Lt. Zajac was in charge. Interestingly, but not surprising in retrospect, these two sets of officers and detectives within the BPD who saw themselves so aligned, or so misaligned, didn't seem to be all that friendly with each other. The cliques were forming, morphing into two distinct groups in my police department, as much for the professional survival of each member as anything.

Me? I was neutral. I had neither attempted to kiss-the-butt nor kick-the-butt of either the present or former person in charge of my PD. But, what I didn't realize is that I was expected to choose sides at some point in the future, the very near future. Staying neutral wasn't good enough, not if one didn't want to be screwed over along the way. Kissing a butt or kicking a butt of someone was apparently in my future. I would NOT do the former, but be ultimately forced into the latter, in a figurative sense anyway. I now knew with whom it would occur, it was just a matter of when and how.

This political nonsense was all strange and new to me. I just wanted to be a cop. I didn't want to be part of this internecine side-taking which was slowly fomenting throughout the department. Thus, I avoided it, like the plague. I just continued to do my job.

And I did it well, if I may add. Strangely enough, it was about to pay off for me too.

* * * * *

In January of 1978, as announced at one of our roll calls by Sgt. Ashton and also listed in the departmental administrative book (which we were required to review and initial everyday), I learned that there were now three posted openings on the Bensalem Police Department Tactical Squad. The Tac Squad, as it was also known, was a (supposedly) elite six officer plainclothes unit headed by a sergeant. It was formed around the same time I arrived on the department, funded also by a federal grant specifically acquired to create one more tool within the PD to help fight crime in Bensalem. This would be the first time it was done here with the formal implementation of a squad of plainclothes officers.

The Tac Squad officers could dress any way they wanted and wear their hair in any fashion while on-duty. Thusly, its members generally had longer hair, a few had beards, and each wore various versions of faded jeans, beat up denim jackets, sneakers, boots, etc., to best blend in with the various assignments to which they were deployed on any given day. Essentially, its members' prime goal was to NOT look like cops. Likewise, the cars assigned to each squad member were also innocuous and could not readily be recognized as undercover vehicles. They each had police radios in them, but they were hidden under the front seats or in the glove compartments.

The assignments for the squad may be a surveillance of a specific neighborhood or apartment complex getting hit by daytime burglaries. It could be a nighttime surveillance of one or more convenience stores which were prone to armed robberies. Or it may be working at the large Neshaminy Mall, so named because of the tribe of Neshaminy Indians who lived in the area two centuries before, in the northwestern area of Bensalem Township. It experienced at least three to four car thefts per week, if not more, as well as known drug sales, thefts, and other nuisance crimes associated with a large suburban mall complex. Other times the Tac Squad would be assigned to the smaller Woodhaven Mall in the southeastern area of Bensalem, or at one of the two commuter rail stations located in Bensalem, as cars were also known to be stolen from those locales quite regularly. The schedules and assignments for the Tac Squad were flexible and on any given day could change at a moment's notice depending on what information would come available from sources, snitches, crime trends, or otherwise.

Being assigned to the Tac Squad would be considered a lateral move, and not technically a promotion for a patrol officer. Its members were still considered officers, drawing the same salary as those in uniform. Nonetheless, it was considered an elite squad, a great opportunity to make quality arrests, and more than a few officers wanted to be assigned to it.

When I first heard of the opening on this squad by Sgt. Ashton at roll call, it merely went in one ear and out the other, wasting little time in between. I was still a rookie patrol officer, with barely thirteen months under my belt (or holster) on the streets, and I simply felt it was too early for me to request any such transfer to a squad such as this one. So, I initially disregarded it.

However, with the deadline to apply for the squad coming up soon, Sgt. Ashton met me on the street one night after backing me up on a car stop. After talking for a while about general PD matters, he asked me if I was going to put in for the Tac Squad. I told him I wasn't interested as I wanted to get more experience as a patrol officer. Maybe next time, I said.

That's when Sgt. Ashton advised me, in so many words, that the notion of experience wasn't something necessarily measured in formally determined time allotments or gauged by someone else's subjectively contrived checklist. It could also be measured by what a person has individually accomplished, been exposed to, and how he or she handles the everyday situations as presented, regardless of the actual time frame involved and how new he or she may have been to it all.

I didn't necessarily disagree with what my sergeant had just said and I told him so. Then I asked him why he was telling me all of this.

Sgt. Ashton came right out and said that he thought I was a "damn good cop" and I should consider putting in for the newly posted openings in the Tac Squad. He continued that he'd hate to lose me as one of his officers, but he felt that with my "already well-honed street sense and cop instincts," I would do very well on such a squad. He said he'd put in a good word for me too, if I decided to apply. I thanked him for his suggestion and his compliments, and told him I'd think about it.

Hmmm...what do I do now? It would be really cool to be on such a squad. No more midnight shifts, Sundays generally off, I could let my hair grow long again, I wouldn't even have to shave every day, and oh yeah, I could make some really good arrests on this squad.

How do I handle this? What do I do?

Based on Sgt. Ashton's advice and recommendation (and who was I to disagree with my wise old...er...make that just wise sergeant), and running it by my wife, Eileen, I decided to formally apply for the Tac Squad on the last day of eligibility. I typed up the brief memo and put it in the mailbox of the detective lieutenant (now erstwhile chief), as instructed in the admin book.

I told a few of my fellow officers of my decision and they thought I was crazy because I was still a rookie and I wasn't politically connected to the new powers-that-be, or even the old powers-that-were. I agreed with them on both counts. However, I also felt that if I put in for this squad at this time, and even if I didn't get it, it would show my interest in advancing within the department and maybe it would help me get some future appointment or promotion. The bottom line is, all the top boss could say is "No," and if so, I stay in patrol doing work which I really still enjoyed doing.

Well, as they say, be careful what it is in life you ask/wish for. I asked (I really didn't wish), and yes, I received.

I answered the phone at home on one of my days off about a week after I submitted my memo and lo and behold, I received the news. I was advised by my soon-to-be new sergeant that I was being transferred to the Tac Squad at the beginning of the next work week. I was very excited when I heard the news, and I'm sure I didn't hide it very well at all, and thanked this sergeant a few times during the course of the call. Interestingly, as the several minute phone conversation progressed, I couldn't help but notice that the sergeant on the other end was rather stoic and off-putting in his comments and replies. As he was passively advising me of my new assignment, he repeatedly said back to me, "Don't thank me, it was Lieutenant Zajac who chose you."

Oh, yeah, right...okay.

Well, maybe that was just this sergeant's style or maybe he's just having a bad day. He lastly advised me in his monotone delivery that I was to finish up the week on my present patrol squad, take the weekend off, and report to him and the Tactical Squad the following Monday morning at 10AM. I enthusiastically said back to him, "Yes, sir, I'll be there…and I want you to know that I really appreciate…," and the phone line went dead.

Ok, that was odd. My new sergeant hung up on me. Maybe just a fluke, though. Right?

I mean, it almost seemed like the sergeant didn't want me on his squad and he was being forced to take me, to call me, and to soon supervise me. He was the only sergeant to ever manage the barely year-and-a-half old Tac Squad, so he certainly had a stake in its early formation, its management, and its direction. But what was his problem with me? We never even talked before today, or had any personal interaction at all in the year-plus I've been on the PD. Unless, it was simply the fact that it HAS only been a "year-plus" I've been on the PD.

Could that be this sergeant's issue with me? Was he doing this to the other two guys who were also recently transferred to the Tac Squad?

I'd figure it all out after I show up on my new squad. It'll work itself out, I'm sure.

Maybe.

Maybe not.

Nonetheless, after that somewhat strange phone call advising me of my promotion (okay, lateral transfer), I had to tell my wife, my parents, and all my friends about it. I was truly a very happy guy upon learning of this news. Less than eighteen months (counting my Academy time) on my new police department and I'm already assigned to a position on an elite squad. And I got it the old fashioned way. I earned it. That's certainly how I saw this transfer.

I wasn't politically connected. I wasn't anyone's "Boy." Sgt. Ashton may have put in a good word for me, but he wasn't my "Rabbi." (That's a secular law enforcement term of unknown origin relating to a mentor/supportive person of higher rank and status to a younger, subordinate officer, who shepherds his or her career.) No, instead on merit alone I achieved this position. I was convinced of it. I suppose all those decent arrests I made, writing my share of quality traffic tickets, my positive work ethic, rarely if ever calling in sick, etc., finally paid off.

This was really the first time in my relatively young life that I was given such an opportunity after such a brief amount of time. Things were coming together for me. This whole new attitude, this whole new level of maturation, this whole new ME, was working, at least so far. I couldn't wait for my first day on the job in my new plainclothes position. Ten o'clock Monday morning couldn't get here soon enough.

Well, that day and time finally did arrive, and I was there early as usual. Our squad had a small meeting room off of the detective division main room in the BPD police headquarters, and that's where I proceeded to meet my new squad mates. As I had learned, two other officers were also transferred into the Tac Squad with me. They weren't rookies though. They had each been on the PD for several years longer than me. I knew them both and I certainly had no problem with them on the squad.

I also learned that day that there were three officers who had been transferred off of the Tac Squad several weeks ago because their "attitudes" didn't quite gel with the new management of the PD. Their transfers out resulted in my transfer in. That's how life worked, I supposed. But does that mean my attitude did, in fact, gel with the new management? I didn't know my attitude had changed one iota between the time Chief Michaels was running the department and now with soon-to-be Deputy Chief Zajac running the department. I just figured my attitude was measured in production, that is, positively in terms of arrests, tickets written, etc. Maybe there was something I was missing. Either way, I wasn't looking for it right now. I just wanted to get working on my new squad and keep that positive production going, and from now on as a plainclothes police officer.

As I was about to confirm, my perception of my new sergeant's demeanor on the phone call the week before was an accurate one. When I met with him on my first day on the squad, his negative attitude toward me would become even more pronounced. And it wouldn't end at that first meeting either. I would learn very soon that he was the antithesis of Sgt. Ashton, in almost every personal and professional way. He seemingly did everything within his limited power and abilities to take me in the opposite direction of that which Sgt. Ashton (and even the occasional Sgt. Schultz) had attempted to guide me over the last year.

Instead of building me up and telling me what I did right, and constructively criticizing me when I may have done wrong, this guy did everything to deconstruct those positive feelings of professional self-worth in me. That was his sole management style. That was his personality, even in his late-30s. How he ever got promoted to sergeant was beyond me. What did this say about the promotional testing process within the BPD if a guy like him can be made a supervisor of officers? Not much back then, I would learn.

On that first morning's roll call, after assigning the six of us to work the Neshaminy Mall for the 10A-6P shift, and partnering me with one of the experienced Tac officers, the sergeant dismissed the squad. However, immediately afterwards he asked me to meet with him in an adjacent interview room as he wanted to talk to me, alone. So, I stayed behind.

We closed the door of the small room and sat down. The sergeant was behind the desk with me in the one unmovable chair directly in front of him. I figured this was arranged as if I was a newly arrested suspect here and he was the detective. He would have liked to maintain these roles while we were in here, but it wouldn't quite work out that way for him.

While the sergeant was initially busy writing or doodling in a thick black notebook he had with him, I couldn't help but further observe his wardrobe and overall look on this morning of my first plain-clothes tour-of-duty. Maybe he was on a special undercover assignment where later today he had to blend in with a certain sub-section of our community. Yes, that had to be it. I could only think this was the case and that he was now dressed like the criminals in the group he was going to infiltrate. If so, based on his eclectic apparel choices, these criminals must have been a hybrid mix of Amish farmers, jazz musicians, snake-oil salesmen, cowboys, and beatniks, because from top to bottom, these were the clothing styles seemingly randomly worn by my sergeant that day.

Starting at the very top, Sarge's longish, graying hair was barely combed and seemed to stick out from the side of his head in various uneven directions. Propped not very stylishly on the top of this unruly hair was a pair of cheap Elvis Presley-esque sunglasses. Not the cool ones from the King's early days, but the thick-framed metallic kind with holes on the side frame which the singer wore near the end of his career. Working downward, the sergeant was wearing some sort of a cherry-stained ascot or faux-turtleneck under a flannel shirt, the latter with several missing buttons. His heavy plaid outer coat was also missing a button. His pants were brown corduroy and had clearly seen better days and his wardrobe bottomed-out, literally and figuratively, with white sweat socks and unpolished black dress shoes. Adorning this otherwise unremarkable and severely unmatched clothing selection were various pieces of turquoise Indian jewelry, to include a necklace, a bracelet, and a pinky finger ring. At least the jewelry matched.

It turns out the sergeant was not on an undercover mission of any kind later that day. What he wore this morning, I would later learn all too well, was representative of his normal, everyday apparel choices. Needless to say, Beau Brummel he was not. *GQ* would not be calling him anytime soon for their cover story on "Well Dressed Men in Law Enforcement." However, I would come to learn, my new sergeant's mangy look was the least of my problems as this initial meeting and the next several years unfolded.

Back to our little meeting...once Sarge pushed his still opened notebook aside on the desk, he looked up at me and cut right to the chase. In so many words, he said to me:

"You know Fitzgerald, I didn't want you on my squad. In fact, I fought hard to keep you off the squad once your name first came up. But you're here, and I guess I'm stuck with you."

I couldn't help myself so I responded, "Well, Sarge, nice to finally meet you too."

He seemed a bit taken aback by my attempt at congeniality with him, although it was clearly dripping with intended sarcasm.

Most likely not even recognizing my attempted congenial OR sarcastic tones, he then said, "Look, Kid, I have nothing against you personally. I'm sure you're a nice guy and all of that."

I interrupted him again by sneaking in, "Well, thank you, I certainly appreciate it. And I'm sure you are too," with additional sarcasm continuing its steady drip.

Again, caught off guard, he refocused and said, "Well, ahem, yes, but I just want you to know that there are other more senior officers in this department who I think, quite frankly, would have been better qualified to work on my squad than you. You just don't have the time in yet, the experience, and things like that necessary to do this job right. I don't want you to be a danger to me or the other squad members."

Before this, I was sort of disappointed with him. But with this last statement, I was actually now getting frustrated...and mad at him.

I retorted somewhat forcefully, but still respectfully, "I assure you, Sarge, no one is in 'danger' because of me now being on this squad. Can we get that off the table here? I am not a liability to you or anyone else. I'm a hard working cop who already has a share of felony arrests to my credit and I plan on adding more to it. And...I know there may be a learning curve of some sort for me for a while, adapting from a uniform mentality to a plainclothes mentality, but I can do it. Trust me."

He was my new sergeant after all, for the indefinite future, and I didn't want to push him too hard here. So I sort of mellowed toward the end of my last response to him, replacing the sarcastic intonations with genuine attempts at humility and solidarity.

It didn't work.

Seemingly not being able to differentiate between the sarcasm and sincerity, nor possessing much more than the slightest modicum of managerial sensitivities, he replied, "Well, we'll see. And, just so you know, I'll be keeping my eye on you, each and every shift, documenting everything you do wrong. If it gets too bad, I'll work to get you off the squad and back to patrol. Understand?"

In saying that, and apparently in the form of a non-verbal exclamation mark, he slammed closed the black notebook he had in front of him. Before he did so, I had seen that it contained numerous pages of sloppily handwritten notes, indecipherable symbols, roughly drawn maps, stick people figures, etc. It also included a tabbed page with today's date and my name listed on the top with a black star alongside of it.

"Fair enough," I responded.

As I pointed to the book he just demonstrably closed I added, "But would you also document in your diary or journal or whatever it is you call your little book everything I do...correctly? And, if it's actually positive, will you acknowledge that I'm in fact doing a good job?"

As he stood up to open the door, he said impassively, "Yeah...sure. Now get with your partner for the day and go to the Neshaminy Mall - and don't get into any trouble!"

"Yes, sir," I retorted, with as much sarcastic emphasis as I could articulate in just two, one-syllable words. Killing him with politeness, I thought to myself.

Geez, where was Sgt. Ashton when I needed him? Or Sgt. Schultz? I'd even take TV's Sgt. Bilko right about now.

After that very inspirational pep talk (yes, sarcasm intended), off to the mall I then went with my new partner for my first day as a plainclothes police officer. During that otherwise uneventful initial day on the squad, I found myself to have never been so motivated by a supervisor to undertake a new role, a new position, or a new tasking - and then bust my ass to show him wrong.

I actually wasn't sure whether to laugh out loud at this poor excuse of a supervisor or quit the squad right then and go back to patrol and

Sgt. Ashton where I knew I was appreciated. This guy was without a doubt the poster child/man for personnel management malfeasance. Make that a 3-D, full color, mega-sized billboard from his head down to his toes.

I swore to myself that day, IF I should ever climb the management ladder and become a sergeant, or beyond, I would use this particular supervisor as a role model on what and who NOT to be. Sometimes reverse role models in life could be a good thing. I suppose everyone needs at least one of these people in their lives at some point to create a balance between the normal and abnormal, the right and wrong, the bright and the not-so-bright. I added this sergeant to my still relatively short list of these reverse role models early on in my new profession. As related in JCM Book I, the first of these men was an off-duty Philadelphia police officer who had me "arrested" at sixteen-years of age for lobbing pennies at a cat (to see if it was even alive and needed to be rescued from its elevated perch). Now, my new sergeant would become a permanent member of this not-so-very-esteemed group.

I learned from both of these guys. That is, what NOT to do as a patrol officer, on or off-duty officer, then what NOT to do as a supervisor, if I should ever happen to become one.

My imaginary (but unfortunately all-too-real) squad of law enforcement reverse role models was slowly growing. It would be comprised of a full complement of LEOs before I would retire.

From now on, I'll refer to my new supervisor as Sgt. Whacky.

Rookie busy on first night

James Fitzgerald probably won't forget his first night on patrol as a Bensalem Township policeman.

The rookie from Northeast Philadelphia, and his partner, Patrolman ████, were cruising in the area of ████ Street and Knights Road shortly after midnight today when they saw a window smashed at the Two Guys store.

The two officers surrounded the building and proceeded inside where they nabbed three persons, allegedly in the act of burglarizing the store.

The suspects, all from Philadelphia, have been identified as ████, 17, of ████; ████, 18, of ████ St., and ████, 19, of ████.

████ and ████ have been committed to Bucks County Prison in default of $5,000 bail each, while ████ has been remanded to the custody of his parents.

The suspects were arraigned before District Justice Dominick Spadaccino on charges of burglary, larceny and receiving stolen property.

23 November 1976, *Bucks County Courier Times,* Front Page

August 1977, left to right...
Officers Jerry Judge, Jim Fitzgerald, Steve Moran, Sgt. Gene Ashton

Part 2 -
The Plainclothes Years

Chapter Eight

If the first year or so in patrol was over-the-top cool, fun, and edifying, being a plainclothes cop starting the second full year of my career was even more so, despite the aforementioned leadership skillset, or lack thereof, manifested by Sgt. Whacky. Nonetheless, it required a new way of thinking, a new way of acting, a new way of looking, and definitely some new equipment. The new thinking and acting parts would come gradually to me once I got out on the streets. But, the new way of looking and attaining some additional equipment, or at least finding a different way to carry my old equipment, had to begin right away.

Regarding how I looked, there would be no visits to the barber for a while now that I'm on my new squad. I had to grow my hair long again, as that was still the style for men in the late 1970s. The last thing I wanted was to look like a cop. I may have been one, but I certainly didn't want anyone else to physically see me that way, at least not while on duty. I began shaving only about every third day my first few weeks on the squad. So even though my hair remained "cop-short" for a while, I still had a bit of a grubby look to me.

I also had to get some new gear; specifically, a new holster. My patrol leather belt holster obviously would not work for me while wearing jeans and t-shirts or sweatshirts on the job every day.

I mentioned my equipment needs to long-time former Olney neighborhood friend Rob McCarthy, now with three-plus years of service as a Philadelphia PD patrol officer, and he gave me a shoulder holster that he no longer used. I could wear this new apparatus under my coat, jacket, or whatever I was wearing while working. Fortunately, both of us were left-handers, so it was a perfect fit. I simply stuck my PD issued .357 Magnum into the holster, which was essentially under my right arm, and I was good to go. It was secured to my shoulder and my belt, staying in place even if I had to run after someone.

With an empty cylinder, I practiced quick drawing my weapon from its new holster a number of times, from different positions too, just so I could get used to this new motion if I would need to pull my gun quickly in a tactical arrest situation. I certainly had muscle-memory from my repeated training at the police academy in drawing my gun from my uniform side holster, but this was different. So, I practiced this new method of drawing by myself on a frequent basis (and always with a bullet-less cylinder) in an attempt to create that all-important new muscle-memory.

However, it wasn't just a gun I needed to hide under my clothing or have near me at all times. I needed at least three other items with me while working. They were handcuffs, extra ammo, and binoculars. The former two were relatively easy to hide on my person, the latter I simply kept in my glove compartment and used as needed. My handcuffs were simply stuck through my belt at the back of my pants, covered by my coat or jacket or shirt. My two plastic speed-loaders, holding six additional rounds of ammo each, were just as simply kept in one of my available jacket pockets. In addition, I put a whole box of ammo in my car glove compartment, with yet another in the trunk, just in case things got really bad. If in any potential shootout I expended 118 rounds of ammo, I would be in a whole heap of trouble at that point. I'd certainly hope by that time the reinforcements would be on the scene.

My new everyday "uniform" was pretty much just some basic mid-to-late 1970s style clothing. Some clothing was newer and nicer, other was kind of grubby. Depending on my mood while getting dressed each day for work, and/or the type of assignment I knew was coming up on my shift, I would alternatively pick out my nicer, every-day clothes, or go a bit retro and dig out some clothes I wore while still in college. At twenty-five years of age, I could wear either and get away with it. I made good arrests in each of the "looks" I presented, so I obviously made the right wardrobe choices when I had to, at least most of the time.

Bottom line here, these were the same clothes I wore off-duty almost every day for the last few years, but now with some hidden tactical implements concealed within. Picking and choosing clothing, where to hide secreted equipment, etc., all took a bit of getting used to in my first month or two on the Tac Squad, but I eventually did.

Unfortunately, with the aforementioned needed equipment, on even the hottest summer days, while working plainclothes, I had to wear a jacket, or at least an open button-down shirt over a t-shirt, to cover my holster and other equipment. But, that was one of the few downsides to working plainclothes. As a uniformed officer, no coat or jacket was needed in the summertime, but when wearing the ballistic vest underneath the shirt, it made for raised body temperatures and lots of uncomfortable sweating then too. There really is no way for a working cop to keep cool in the warmer weather. Not while carrying either a hidden or out-in-the-open handgun, anyway, not to mention the addition of a ballistic vest underneath it all.

By the way, I didn't wear my vest under my casual street clothes as a member of the Tac Squad. None of the other plainclothes officers did either. But I did keep it in the trunk of the car just in case I knew I was about to make a felony arrest, and I had the time to put it on. Depending where a plainclothes officer is working and what he/she is doing, it may be a good idea to wear it all the time. I would never question an officer who so chooses to wear it, even under otherwise stylish shirts and jackets. It could just save a life someday.

Now appropriately equipped and dressed, hair getting longer, that grubby appearance (when appropriate) slowly kickin' in, I was looking and doing my best to be a good plainclothes cop. The large Neshaminy Mall parking lot was actually a good training ground for making arrests in all sorts of crimes, and I slowly started to do so. The mall was immediately adjacent to two of those three major highways which traversed through Bensalem, that being U. S. Rt. 1 and the Pennsylvania Turnpike, with easy access from both to it. It made for an inviting target to those willing to ply their criminal trades there, of the small and large variety.

While it was the running joke in the BPD that our squad served as "Mall Security" there, it didn't bother us. There were enough felony and misdemeanor crimes taking place there that we were glad to oblige and lock up the people committing them, usually coming upon them ourselves, as opposed to calls from dispatch. These criminals, whether of the career type, amateurs, or opportunists, came in all sizes, shapes, and colors. They committed all sorts of crimes there, some that until becoming a plainclothes cop, I didn't even know existed. One "crime" in particular, of a very sexual nature, will be discussed shortly.

I recall being asked during my plainclothes tenure and even years later…how did I know who was about to commit a crime? What and/or who did I look for? And at the same time did I "profile" the potential criminals? (In this context, it didn't mean the behavioral assessments of unknown subjects that I later undertook as an FBI criminal profiler. Here, it was meant in the demographic sense.)

My answer would be that I never "profiled" any one person in particular from a demographic or racial perspective. Quite frankly, most of my arrests, certainly while in plainclothes, happened to be of white males. While driving around the malls and other areas of Bensalem looking for potential criminals, besides looking for males of any race aged fifteen to thirty (in those very active crime-committing years), I found that if I "profiled" at all, it would be of their automobiles, and not necessarily the persons inside of them.

Ratty cars back then were usually driven by, well, ratty people, out looking to commit crimes. Not always, but many times. And by "ratty," I don't just mean older cars. I mean messy cars with one or more lights broken, mismatched tires and doors, splintered windshields, expired inspection stickers and/or registration, etc., in other words, rolling multiple motor vehicle violations, inside and out. I would tend to follow those cars around the mall, just guessing that the driver and his occupants were probably up to no good. If they drove past a few open parking spaces, and/or more than once around the mall parking lot for no apparent reason, that would be a clue that they're looking for something to steal, sell or buy (illegally), or someone or something to violate.

While people have constitutional rights not to be picked on or harassed by police because of how they look, and I certainly respect and defend that principle to the utmost, cars don't have the same rights. There's nothing in the U.S. Constitution protecting the rights of motor vehicles, in and of themselves. So if that ratty car was first noticed at a mall, train station, or even just cruising the streets of Bensalem aimlessly, I would tend to follow it, many times not even knowing the demographic/racial makeup of its occupant(s). And many times, with the requisite probable cause fully established, arrests followed, for one type of crime or another.

I must add here that of course not every criminal, or potential criminal, drove a beat-up car back then. Some drove nice cars. Some took public transportation to their crime committing zones. Unfortunately, even times when the whole Tac Squad was at the Neshaminy Mall, or one or two of us at a train station, invariably a stolen car report would come in sometime during the day. Obviously, it was very frustrating as we were assigned there to prevent just that, and here it happened under our noses.

Or did it in every case?

When these thefts occurred while the Tac Squad was on duty at the mall, did these successful criminals drive nicer cars, thus throwing off our vehicular "profile?" Did someone drop them off and they went right to work on foot stealing their car without leading us around the mall first? Did they take a bus there?

Or, was it actually a false report of a stolen car?

If so, perhaps the car was never even at the mall that day and only reported stolen by the owner for insurance purposes. (He would have arrived there by other means after having ditched the car beforehand.) This exact scenario happened more than once in my time on the Tac Squad, with arrests that followed.

Bottom-line here, smart criminals do exist. They get away with their crimes more so than their less-smart counterparts. They knew back then (as well as nowadays) not to drive a car which would attract attention to them by the police. That's just one way in which they succeeded. Well, sometimes. I arrested my share of guys in nicer cars, and while they were on foot, too. And, yes, even while nicely dressed.

A plainclothes cop has several advantages over uniformed cops, certainly when making arrests. If done right, he or she is able to observe the criminal dynamic, at work, close up and in its natural form from beginning to end. I immensely enjoyed taking in this pre-offense behavior of these guys, doing so in many cases from a distance with binoculars in one hand and microphone in the other, ready to send my plainclothes colleagues or marked patrol cars into action.

Once a criminal was about to commit his crime, whether he was in a car, on foot, whether it was to steal another car, a bike, do a purse snatch, an armed robbery, sell or buy some drugs, or whatever his criminal intent that day may be, there was one very telling part and predictive element of this unfolding dynamic. It would potentially give him away almost every time, IF discernible by the officer up close or through binoculars.

As I would learn before very long, it was the eyes of an about-to-strike criminal that could potentially give him away. It is a "tell," as the better poker players know, which serves to measure and possibly predict the forthcoming movements of one or more of their opponents. With criminals, these similar types of "tells" allow a police officer to know that a crime event is imminent and so he or she has to be ready to pounce, right before or right after the robbery/theft/assault or whatever takes place.

I saw this non-sleep related "rapid eye movement" sometimes close up and personal when the potential perp had no idea I was slouched behind the driver's wheel of my police car right next to him, or even if I was some distance away and watching him through my binoculars. The eyes of a person about to commit a crime become very active, darting back and forth and up and down as he is about to ambush his prey, be it a person, or a car. That's when I knew it was almost time to ambush him, the criminal. It worked virtually every time. The eyes give these guys away virtually every time.

When those criminal eyes would perhaps look over in my direction, checking me out, wondering if I was the one last thing which stood between them and their potential crime, there's a little trick I learned to employ after a while as a plainclothes cop. It also involved equipment, and it helped to maintain my cloak of invisibility to the crook, or at least added to my non-relevance to them within their field of vision. It was small, simple, and cheap to get into its functional form, and actually quite enjoyable too.

It was a can of beer. Well, make that an empty can of beer.

I got the idea from arresting many a young male for various crimes big and small who happened to have beer cans in their car. Some were empty, some were full, some were being drunk at the time they were arrested. It's never a good idea, of course, to be driving a car and/or committing a crime while under the influence of alcohol. Unfortunately, it happens all the time. Obviously, it could be a crime in and of itself if the person was driving intoxicated. If that was noticed by me, the marked cars would be called in right away and an arrest effected for that crime. I'd worry about catching the guy stealing something another time.

But as my goal was to blend most unobtrusively into the dark night (or sunny day) to the criminal mindset, I found the beer-can-as-prop could be invaluable. If I was following someone, conducting a surveillance of them for one reason or another, and they possessed an above-average level of criminal sophistication, in some instances they would eventually spot me and then suspect me of being a cop. After all, there's only so many times a bad guy on the prowl for a crime of some sort could see the same car in his rear view mirror. If so, he would many times spin around, make a U-turn, let a passenger out on foot, or whatever, to further check me out. In doing so, when the time was right, and his line-of-vision unobstructed, I would simply put the empty beer can to my mouth, making sure the label could be seen on it (so he knows it's not merely a soda can), and pretend I'm gulping it down. For me personally, as there was nothing but air in the can, it was worse than drinking non-alcoholic beer. But hey, it worked in these scenarios.

If I really felt I had to act the part as the guy was really checking me out, I would sip it convincingly as if it was my last gulp, then toss the can out the car window. That usually confirmed my non-cop status, if I did it convincingly enough. I could always find a way to attain another empty beer can. That part was easy.

After numerous arrests of offenders for one crime or another, I'd interview them afterwards and ask them, among other things, if they had noticed me following them. I always wanted to hear from their own lips what they had to say about that topic so I could potentially improve my surveillance techniques in the future. Several times, if the now-arrested thief, robber, or assaulter admitted he did see me before the crime, and even if he did initially suspect me of being a cop, he'd tell me that notion went away when he saw me sip my "beer." He just figured I was another guy like him, looking to score something, and getting drunk while doing so.

Interestingly, at least one arrestee who saw me take a sip of "beer" was so convinced that I was drinking on duty that he attempted a subtle blackmail of me during his subsequent interview back at the station. He said he wouldn't tell my supervisors what I was doing (drinking on duty) if I dropped the charges against him. I dared him to. Needless to say, it didn't work.

I suppose in today's world, if I was a plainclothes cop, I'd want to have a fake joint or pipe on me at all times, or at least in my undercover car. Lighting up and toking away could easily convince a potential criminal that the guy he observed "getting high" was no one to fear. I'd just want to make sure that the perp didn't get too close to me. The smell of the burning non-marijuana leaves would be readily noticed and the person would know in seconds that something wasn't right and that the non-weed toker may be someone of whom he should be suspicious. Or perhaps that he was someone who got badly ripped off buying his last dime bag. Maybe that would work too.

Lastly in this category, whether a cop is carrying a fake joint, pipe, or an empty beer can in his or her plainclothes equipment stash, it is strongly suggested that a document of some sort be composed and placed in a paper or electronic file within the agency IN ADVANCE to doing so. It should be memorialized that this prop is, in fact, being utilized, and that it's fake or empty, and its use is strictly for "show" and ruse purposes. In other words, make it clear in writing that it's only in your possession to help maintain the undercover/plainclothes persona and fool the bad guys.

I submitted my document (we referred to them as "memos" back then) to Sgt. Whacky regarding the empty beer can several months after starting on the Tac Squad. I was the first on my squad to come up with this gimmick/ploy. Even my loopy sergeant approved of it, although it took him some convincing. I wanted to make sure some other police supervisor didn't see the empty can in my undercover police car and think I had actually been drinking that day. If my personal philosophy was to not even drink on the nights before my day-work shifts, I certainly wouldn't be drinking while on duty. However, I wanted the paper to prove it. The BPD had it, and I had my supervisor signed-off copy too in my personal file I kept at home, just in case the original was somehow "lost" by one of the bosses. And that could certainly happen, by accident or on purpose, I would later come to learn.

(+ Bonus Chapter 8a)

Chapter Nine

The criminals at the Neshaminy Mall who took me most by surprise, at least initially in my young plainclothes career, were the many "perverts," as we used to call them, found in that large shopping complex on a weekly basis, if not more often. They could be found inside, occasionally doing their thing in the men's bathrooms, but mostly we found a particular sub-species outside, doing their thing, their very strange thing, in the privacy of their own cars.

Sometimes, the pending perverts would have even just dropped off their wife and/or kids to shop and it's then, while outside ostensibly listening to music or a ballgame on the radio, that they would then ply their trade, their hobby, their "handiwork," of either the left- or right-hand variety. It's like they had an instructional book, a manual, on how to do what they did, each and every one of them. And again, this is long before the Internet, where there's now a website for virtually every perversion out there.

The scenarios always started the same way. One of my fellow Tac Squad members or I would pick up on a car slowly, but deliberately cruising around the mall. It would be after several spins around the parking lot, skipping over available parking spaces, slowing down sometimes, speeding up quickly sometimes, and even completely stopping sometimes, the driver's head turning left and right the whole time as if looking for some very specific person, place, or thing, but with no readily discernible pattern to any of it. Why they were doing all of this was not always immediately clear to us.

Was this person looking for a car to steal? Not likely, driving by himself.

Did he want to steal a stereo system or something else out of a car? Maybe.

Was he trying to hook up with his drug dealer or his drug customers? Perhaps.

But the modus operandi (MO) being utilized here, as well as each guy by himself in his car, didn't really seem to lend itself to these sorts of crimes.

What was it then?

I would learn before long that the always solo male, usually in his 30s or 40s, usually in a decent looking, newer car, and in many cases being a decent looking, well-dressed guy, was on the hunt for one thing and one thing only. That being, a female pedestrian walking through the expansive parking lot who met his fantasy-driven criteria. That's right, these guys were stalkers of opportunity, on the prowl during a time which was convenient to them, and at a mall with a target population of hundreds of potential female prey on any given day or night.

These guys' prime "hunting season" was the late spring, summer, and early fall, because, of course, women tended to wear less outer clothing then. I suppose that makes sense from these guys' perspectives. The perverts themselves though, at least while on these sex-driven hunts in the mall parking lot, rarely ever exited their four-wheeled, moving, self-pleasuring emporiums. They would simply attempt to locate the right girl or woman and position their car near her accordingly, depending if they wanted the target walking toward him or away from him. That is (and being politely euphemistic here), depending on whether he was a "front-side" man or a "back-side" man.

Once the positioning was ideal, the guy would then masturbate as the targeted woman would walk right by him, sitting in his car's driver's seat, pants undone, always with nearby lubricating gel of one variety or another and the requisite "liquid depository cloth" (again, being politely euphemistic). After all, these guys may have been perverts, but they weren't slobs. They didn't want the front seats, steering wheels, or dashboards of their cars stained, especially if the wife or kids were due to be picked up at the Sears store in half an hour.

Sometimes these guys found what, or who, they were looking for right away, other times we would follow these guys for an hour or more. Naturally, we weren't always initially sure they were potential perverts. I mean, they could have been looking to commit some other sort of felony crime. But regardless, we would follow them accordingly. If they slowed down when a good-looking, younger woman was in their general area, even if it wasn't their perfect or safest stopping point, that would be a strong indicator as to what they were up to. When we were pretty well convinced that it was, in fact, a pervert on the prowl, we'd break off all but two cars and let the other guys look for the real crimes at the mall. But as we never knew what these guys would ultimately do to their potential female prey, we felt it best for at least a few of us to stay with them and wait for them to strike. (Or stroke, if I may be non-euphemistic for once here.)

If the mall pervert du jour was really pushing the limit of our time and patience, the end of our shift was approaching, or we just wanted to focus on other potential criminals instead, we'd then mutually agree to proceed to Plan B. Well, let's make that Plan D. As such, we'll call the person primarily involved in this plan of action "Dee Dee," for reasons which will soon become obvious.

Dee Dee was a security detective at the large Strawbridge & Clothier store at the mall. I had met her there during my first few months on the job. We had shared anecdotes and experiences of my former gig in the downtown Philadelphia S&C store and hers at her Bensalem store. She was a nice person and an excellent store detective. She was late-twenties, tall, blonde, very attractive, and well-built. She would dress on most days to accentuate those latter features. When I or one of the other Tac Squad guys would have our dispatcher call the store for Dee Dee to come outside and meet us, she immediately knew the drill.

Upon learning that the Tac officers were requesting her in the parking lot, before coming outside, part of Dee Dee's prep would be for her to take off whatever outer coat or jacket she may be wearing, even on colder days. She'd then meet with one of us, out of the sight of the mobile pervert, and we would quickly tell her that we're following, for example, a white male in a dark blue, '76 Chevrolet Impala, and that we're pretty sure of his intentions. We'd then leave her to her own devices, so to speak. When Dee Dee would then see the so-described car approaching her she'd, well, start strutting those "devices" slowly off the curb and into the parking lot. She did her particular strut very well. And it worked with these guys too, virtually every time.

Dee Dee would wait on the wide department store sidewalk until she recognized the described car and she knew the driver got a good, long view of her. Once he slowed down and did his glaring drive-by, she would step off the curb, cross the drive, and then walk slowly and provocatively up the nearest parking lot aisle. Once the driver quickly spun around and was now approaching Dee Dee in the same aisle from either the front or rear (again, depending on the guy's particular angle-of-preference), she would many times coquettishly brush her hair with both hands at the same time. She would then gingerly walk toward the far end of the parking aisle with the pervert awaiting her to come to him or slowly trailing her from the rear.

Depending on where the car was, in front of Dee Dee or behind her at this point, she knew to attempt to walk directly alongside his driver's side window, even if it required a U-turn on her part and for her to then walk back towards the store area. She would then slowly stroll right by the guy's now stopped car and depending on what she saw him doing out of the corner of her eyes she'd nod her head to us. If a "yes" nod (it was never a "no" nod that I recall), that's when we'd quickly box the pervert car in with our cars, front and rear. We'd then come up to the car on foot on both sides, in the guy's blind spot, which was easy as at this time he was not looking in front of him, into his mirrors, or anywhere or at anything but at Dee Dee. With our badges out in one hand and with the other hand on our still-holstered weapons, just in case he was a potentially violent pervert, we told him that he was under arrest.

Upon seeing us somewhat long-haired, dressed-down if not grubby-looking plainclothes officers, with our badges clearly in hand and loudly yelling, "Police – You're under arrest!", the pervert would almost always throw his car into drive or reverse and do his best to get out of the mall parking lot as fast as he could, even through the narrowest of spaces. But he was never successful as we always had the car tightly boxed in. When he finally realized he had nowhere to go, he could then be seen zipping up and/or buckling his pants and throwing one or more shards of tissue paper onto the floor of his car.

These arrest scenes were never a pretty sight once they began to unfold, as these guys were always very surprised and completely disjointed and in disarray at the sudden arrival of police officers into his carefully orchestrated little mobile fantasy world. This especially after having just reached the climactic stage of physical ecstasy as the result of observing an attractive female pedestrian of his choosing (well, sometimes, but not always if we had implemented Plan D/Dee Dee), to now the complete opposite stage. That being, two or more cops on each side of his car telling him he was under arrest, which was clearly not of his choosing.

In quick fashion, we'd then order the guy to shut off his car engine, put his windows down, throw out his keys, get out of the car by opening the car from the exterior handle, with his arms and hands up in the air the whole time afterwards, in just the way that we learned about conducting felony car stops at the police academy. Even though this technically was not a felony car stop, it was nonetheless good practice for a real one. (As all cops know, it could develop into a felony at any moment if the driver should choose to do something violent.) We'd then turn him around, have him assume the prone position against his car, fully search him, and put him in handcuffs, while attempting to NOT touch his actual hands...as we knew what at least one of them was just doing, and where.

Rarely did these guys have any weapons or other contraband in their possession, but of course, they were searched just the same each time, as were their cars. We would then call for the duty-tow truck to remove the man's car from the mall and would have a marked patrol unit transport the now in-custody pervert/arrestee to police HQ.

After completing her extracurricular "job," admittedly above and beyond her everyday store detective duties, Dee Dee would simply walk back to S&C, usually very innocently with her arms modestly folded across her chest. On several occasions before leaving the scene, I saw her casually wink at the guy under arrest if their eyes happened to meet. I'm not sure if he appreciated it or not at the time, but I never saw a guy wink back at her. Oh, and we never gave Dee Dee up to them as our decoy. He would just think she was a regular, everyday shopper who happened to be walking through his hunting ground, coincidently dressed, preening, posturing, and looking just how the guy liked 'em to.

Back at police HQ, post-arrest, is where it got even more interesting, once we started to interview these guys. After reading them their Miranda warnings, they would almost always deny for upwards of an hour what they had been doing at the mall. When we told them what we actually saw, or what the female witness/victim told us they saw, many of them still stuck by their same story. That is, they had to "really pee" at that time and that's why they had their penises out and in their hands. We'd then ask the guys if they'd like us to send the tissues or cloths on the floor of their car to the lab for analysis. They would be asked, "Will the lab find urine or something else on the tissues?"

Inevitably, the guys would start crying and tell us about their wives, kids, and jobs, although not necessarily in that order. As mentioned earlier, sometimes these guys would tell us their wife and/or kids were still at the mall, no doubt looking for him about now. In these pre-cell phone days, it could be awhile before they actually hooked up again. Then once he was forced to tell his wife what happened, whether she was at the mall or at home, who knows how long before they would "hook up" again. Not our problem though.

When all was said and done in these cases, if nothing else happened at the scene of the arrest, no violence, no foot or car chase, and the guy didn't actually do or say anything to any of these women, (be it unsuspecting victims or our Dee Dee-coy), or attempt to touch them, we usually made a deal with these guys, right in the police station.

We would tell him that we would only charge them with a summary Disorderly Conduct violation IF they agreed to undergo psychological counseling. We would actually write that condition on the bottom of the summons. We would have him ask for a hearing in front of the district magistrate who would order the counseling as part of his sentencing. The defendant would have to bring some sort of proof to the court of his counseling record at a later date to keep it at a summary violation. We made it clear he could be potentially charged with Indecent Exposure, Indecent Assault, or other related crimes, which would automatically go into the newspaper and on his permanent record if he failed to follow through on the counseling. We also told him we would not call his home, his job, or anything like that to further inconvenience or embarrass him. All of this, of course, was conditional upon the guy having no other criminal record, especially one involving any sort of sex crimes. The "deal" seemingly worked as there was never a recidivist arrested in this category at the Neshaminy Mall, at least during my time there.

Some questions I pondered then and since then...

At the time and in my later years on the job, to include in the FBI, after attending various training seminars and in-service courses dealing with the then generically called "Sex Crimes," I often wondered about these so-called perverts and how far they would go in their activities if left unchecked. Were these guys potential flashers? Rapists? Kidnappers? Worse?

Was this a "gateway" crime, a precursor of some sort to more sexually violent crimes against women?

I was never aware of any of these men we arrested committing more serious sexually related crimes, but of course I couldn't keep track of all of them, especially if the newer crimes occurred outside of Bensalem and/or were after my time as a police officer there. And no doubt, there were plenty of men who were successful at doing this sort of thing and never arrested by the police, in Bensalem or elsewhere.

So did these men stop at this activity level, or move on to more direct interaction with their victims; that being, attempts of more violent interactions?

Or would adult women begin to bore them, not sexually challenge them anymore, and could it then be on to young girls, children?

All of the above, and worse, is possible, of course. In many cases it is safe to assume, if left unchecked and un-arrested, these men could possibly advance or "escalate" to more serious related crimes.

As far as I know, there has never been any documented empirical research investigating this particular hypothesis, specifically, regarding these guys who drive around in their own cars in public areas, and masturbate to females (or perhaps males) of their liking, or at least to whoever may have been visually available to them on those occasions.

And what about women? Could they be involved in some of the same type of masturbatory activities while driving around in their cars in a public place? If so in the '70s, none was ever observed or arrested in Bensalem Township.

Even from a legalistic perspective, if just inside a guy's (or woman's) own car, is it even a crime?

Well, if it could be seen through a car's windows in a public parking lot, it certainly was in Bensalem in the late 1970s, even if we only charged them most of the time with a summary offense. At least we got them into the criminal justice system, just in case they should re-offend in the future. Then the future arresting officers and the courts would know there is some sort of ongoing sex crime-related problem here and the men could be further adjudicated accordingly.

In the long-run, let's hope the mandatory counseling worked for the guys that we arrested, both for their sakes and their families' sakes. It seemed to….

* * * * *

As bizarre as it was arresting the occasional pervert that I did NOT know at the Neshaminy Mall and elsewhere in Bensalem, it was even more bizarre to happen to know one of them personally. That happened too, although I wasn't the arresting officer. But upon being caught "red-handed" doing his thing by the uniformed officer in Bensalem, guess whose name he embarrassingly gave up right away?

If you guessed my name, you are correct.

One of my neighbors on the street where Eileen and I eventually bought a house in Bensalem was a nice enough guy, but a bit on the odd side in some ways. He was married to an also nice, but occasionally demanding and sometimes loud wife. They had several kids, a dog, and members of their very large extended families and their own various dogs would stop by their house often, mostly on Saturdays and Sundays. Some days it would be when I was trying to sleep during the daytime as I had worked a midnight shift. Once or twice on those occasions Eileen would very politely ask our neighbors and the dozen or so kids running around their property if they possibly could keep the volume down to a reasonable level. They rarely did quiet down, and it caused some neighborly consternation between us.

After only a few years there, the woman-of-the-house insisted to her husband that their family move to the further suburbs. She was heard to state out loud that she and her kids had "outgrown" Bensalem and "these people here." She was also heard on more than one occasion bemoaning the fact that Bensalem was being overrun by "Philadelphia people," and not in a good way. Upon hearing her say that on one occasion in her presence, almost in unison, my wife and I said, "Excuse me?"

Realizing Eileen and I were both originally and recently from Philly, and realizing we were offended without us actually saying so, she would then add, "Well...uh...present company excluded, of course."

Thank you. She apparently forgot that her parents were born in Philadelphia, but that didn't matter. Since she wasn't born there, she could be the elitist, at least towards us and our fellow Philadelphians.

Our neighbor family eventually did, in fact, move away, but the husband couldn't quite keep out of Bensalem, at least at nighttime. You see, even though this guy had a decent fulltime job in sales selling something or other, he also liked to deliver pizza at night for one of the local pizza parlors. I really don't think he did this nighttime gig for the money. I think it was just to get out of the house and away from the kids and his wife every once in a while. So even when they moved a few suburban towns away, he kept his part-time, nighttime, job in Bensalem.

On a day shift sometime in '78 or '79, I recall a uniformed officer buddy of mine walking up to me inside police HQ. He had worked the late shift last night, but was in that afternoon for a court hearing. He saw me and came up to me and asked if I knew a certain pizza-delivery guy and gave me his name. I replied in the affirmative and said that he used to be my neighbor. The officer then smiled and warned me that I may not like hearing what he's about to tell me, but proceeded to relate the story to me anyway.

The patrol officer told me that delivery-man was observed the night before, around midnight, sitting in his car apparently watching a bunch of teenage girls congregating in a public parking lot. There was apparently a high school dance or basketball game in Bensalem that night and the girls were just talking and having fun after the event. When the officer got closer to check him out he further observed his car sort of bouncing up and down in an unusual way. Parking the police car about forty feet away from the car, with lights out, and walking towards the bouncing car while safely in the driver's blind spot, the officer got right up to the driver's side window and shined his flashlight into the interior of the car. In doing so, he noticed the solo driver with his pants around his knees. Yes, he was doing what the mall perverts do, but not at the mall. And he reportedly differed a bit from the well-known mall pervert's M.O. in that instead of a tissue or napkin of some sort, he had a white sweat sock in his "weak" hand as his makeshift liquid depository receptacle.

At first startled, when the officer asked pizza-man what he was doing, he responded, "Uh, nothing, Officer, just sitting here between my deliveries. I have an extra hoagie; would you like it?" This while quickly pulling up his pants and dropping the sock to the floor of the car.

The officer ignored his "bribe" and asked the driver for his ID, while smartly insisting that he pull it out of his wallet with his unsoiled hand. He did as instructed and handed it to him. Before the patrol officer could ask him another question, delivery-man blurted out, as if to garner grace of some sort from him, "Do you know Jim Fitzgerald? He's my good friend."

The officer responded that he did know me, but that it wasn't relevant at this particular time and place. (He was certainly right about that!) As the officer was aware of these guys' M.O. from Neshaminy Mall, he eventually handled this non-mall pervert pretty much the same way that night. As it was getting busy on the streets around that time and his patrol squad was short-handed, I don't believe the officer even took him into the police station. Instead, he merely wrote him a Disorderly Conduct non-traffic citation (summons) and issued it to him there on the spot. He then made sure his pants were fully up and buckled, so he could drive safely, warned him not to do this again, and then sent him on his way.

So I learn of this the next day and I was livid. I hadn't seen or heard of my former neighbor for a year or so after he and his family moved away from us "Philadelphia people." Then, to a fellow BPD officer he brings up MY name while caught doing THIS?

I was still on the Tac Squad at the time and was scheduled to work a 3P-11P shift in a few days. I knew what I had to do. I was going to find him at his pizza shop, confront him, and read my personal "riot act" to him. I must. He could have been doing a lot of things "wrong" that night and dropped my name. Ran a red light, too loud a muffler, stiffed a customer...I probably would have been okay with him mentioning me. But masturbating? To teenage girls? Into a friggin' sweat sock?

I don't think so....

It took me a few nights to finally track down my former neighbor between deliveries, but there right in front of the restaurant, as he was walking out with a few pizzas to be delivered somewhere, I trotted over to his car just as he was about to get into it.

He initially exclaimed, "Hey Jimmy-boy, long-time-no-see!"

I simply said, "Yeah, right. Hey, tell me, what happened with Officer _____ last week in the high school parking lot?"

Former neighbor/delivery-man replied in a much more subdued manner, "Uh...what do you mean? What, uh...what exact night last week?"

I retorted loudly for anyone to hear, "Do you really want me to repeat out loud here what I heard from the officer? Or shall I just check to see if you're wearing both your socks right now?"

He immediately lowered his head as well as the steaming pizza boxes he was still holding. He then turned and slowly put them onto the hood of his car.

"Oh, that," he said. "Yeah, that was kinda weird...I was just sorta playing around, you know, I was bored, had some time to kill, so I just pulled over...," and his voice trailed off.

I then stated to him, "Bored? Sorta playing around?"

With head lower than even before, he mumbled, "Yeah...I guess I wasn't thinking...," and again trailed off into an indecipherable whisper.

As firmly as I could to a guy standing in a dark parking lot next to a stack of pizza boxes on his car hood, I told ex-neighbor boy in no uncertain terms, "Listen, I don't care what you do in your private life, in your car, with or on your pizzas, hoagies, or cheesesteaks, but when you get caught next time doing what you're doing, you do NOT, I repeat DO NOT, drop my name to the investigating or arresting officer in this town or any other town! Do you understand me?"

After clearing his voice, and slowly raising his head just a bit so as to barely make eye contact with me, he humbly replied, "Uh, yeah...I hear ya. That was pretty dumb, I guess."

He couldn't help but add, "You know, Jimmy, or I guess it's Officer Fitzgerald now, it was the first time I ever did anything like that, really, and it was so weird that...."

I interrupted his stream of consciousness. "Yeah, weird is right! That's what they all say too...it's their first time. And, yes, I'm Officer Fitzgerald now to you. Let's keep it that way. Now go about your business and do not reference me again to another cop even if it's a jaywalking ticket. Got it?"

Pizza man's last words to me were, "Sure, Ji...I mean Officer Fitzgerald. I got it. No problem." As I walked away, he said, and I think very seriously, "Hey, uh, would you like a pizza? I can get you one from inside."

I didn't answer him. I got in my car and drove off.

That was the last time I ever saw my former neighbor and part-time pizza delivery man. I believe he quit the food delivery business not too long after that incident and our follow-up conversation. I know he pleaded guilty to the summons he received. I don't think he'd want to fight that one.

I knew one thing though, despite them having pretty good food there, I never wanted food from this guy's pizza shop again. I know my former neighbor never delivered any food to my house, nor do I THINK to the BPD, so that much was reassuring.

If he ever did though, I'd want to first determine whether he was wearing his socks or not. That would be a must....

(+ Bonus Chapters 9a, 9b, 9c, 9d)

85

Chapter Ten

As referenced in JCM Book I, one of my dad Wally's heroes, General Billy Mitchell, maintained a strong and persistent argument in the 1930s to enhance and improve air superiority in the U. S. military. After much resistance to him and his notions (including a military court martial), history finally proved General Mitchell correct.

I realized after designing and utilizing a hand-drawn pin "map" of the Neshaminy Mall, and plotting the ongoing car thefts at the mall from the "air" with the help of my multi-colored version of the location, how valuable it could be in car theft patterning and car thief apprehension. Now, could I put this idea to work in some other form, perhaps at some other Bensalem high crime area? It wouldn't be a map per se, but perhaps an element of "air superiority" in a way not done before, at least by the BPD.

I did put this idea to work again. This time, it wouldn't be a mall, but a large train station parking lot from which cars were also being stolen quite frequently. And this time, it wouldn't be me looking at a map on a wall of a high crime area merely after the fact in order to predict when and where the next theft would take place. Instead, it would put me actually up in the air, looking at the potential crime area from above, and making the arrests in real time. And, no, it wasn't in a BPD helicopter or aircraft of any sort.

How could I do this? Actually, quite easily, thanks in part to the "Mad Men" of the late 1970s advertising industry. Oh, and some rope, a car roof, binoculars, and a portable police radio, too.

The Cornwells Train Station, located on Cornwells Ave. alongside I-95, is one of dozens of similar stations of the Southeastern Pennsylvania Transportation Authority's (SEPTA) Suburban Rail lines that crisscross the Philadelphia area and its suburbs. The station is one of many which service the above ground line, the route of which originates in Trenton, New Jersey, and ends in downtown Philly. It is thusly called "The Trenton Line."

There were actually three separate parking lots adjacent to the Cornwells Train Station which back in the late 1970s held upwards of approximately two hundred cars. It was a commuter lot, in which people dropped off their cars early in the morning and picked them up later in the day, having ridden the train line in between to their destinations. Back then, the station office was not staffed, so no one was around to keep an eye on things, so to speak. (And, needless to say, this was years before outdoor security cameras were in place in such areas.) Hopefully, when the commuters disembarked the train to walk back to their cars after a long day at the office, most likely in Center City Philadelphia, it was still there. On some days, it was not. That's where the BPD Tac Squad came in.

My colleagues and I would be assigned to watch the train station lots on a sporadic basis, with no real regularity, depending on what else was happening in Bensalem that particular week. Simply parking somewhere in the lot in our unmarked cars and observing the various comings and goings of people, whether walking or driving, was the only way to really do it. And it wasn't always easy to find a spot there in which more than a few dozen cars could be observed at any given time. If a suspicious-looking car, with its equally suspicious-looking driver and passenger(s), drove into the lot, they would in many cases see our cars, see us sitting in the cars, get spooked (even if they saw me "drinking" from my empty beer can), and drive off. Mission NOT accomplished in our estimation. After all, our job wasn't to scare off potential car thieves. The officers in the marked patrol cars could do that. Our job was to catch them stealing the vehicles, in the act.

Sometimes, in nicer weather, during the middle of the day, I would park my car and simply stand at the station as if I was waiting for a train. With newspaper in hand and my portable police radio hidden under my jacket (along with my gun and cuffs, of course), I'd look out at the lot and watch for anyone acting suspiciously there. It worked to some degree, but was difficult to maintain for too long. Bad guys and potential thieves knew if they waited until a train stopped, and I didn't get on it, I was probably a cop, or at least someone they didn't want to chance watching them break into a car. I saw this play out too many times, when I was sure it was a thief or a car of thieves, ready to ply their dishonest trade, but then they saw me and changed their plans. They didn't necessarily know the long-haired guy in tattered jeans was a cop, but being overly cautious they would nevertheless drive off anyway.

Something wasn't right here. There must be a better way of working this detail and catching these guys in the act. We could do it at the malls as we could blend in, drive around, and not stick out among the other cars and people.

But at the Cornwells Train Station? What could we do differently? Better?

Just what would a forward projecting, hustling, starting-to-think-more-and-more-outside-the-box, plainclothes cop do in this type of ongoing crime scenario?

What would General Mitchell do here?

I know! He'd find his answer up in the air. And that's eventually what I did.

While assigned to the train station a few days in a row, I found myself straining my neck more and more each hour I spent there. Looking upward, higher than usual, was the cause of the strain, doing so either from my vehicle or while standing in the middle of one of the lots themselves. I was checking out more closely than ever a giant advertising billboard overlooking the three parking lots. Of course, I always knew it was there, as it can be clearly seen from I-95 and much of that area of Bensalem. But I never actually looked at it in this manner before, that is, as an implement of aerial surveillance, and not just as a place to shill beer, soda, and snacks. Besides advertising those and similar products, maybe it could also possibly help me catch the car thieves who have been hitting us hard lately. But first, I'd have to get up there to find out just what I could see and if it would, in fact, really function as the appropriate lookout. I'd need some equipment first for my initial reconnoiter. Let's see, 100 feet of rope, a milk crate….

On the next day I was assigned to the Cornwells Train Station, at the beginning of my shift, I brought along with me one of my Tac Squad colleagues for support (and just in case…gulp…I fell). I commenced my first journey up the ladder on one of the sign's two solid steel vertical support stanchions. The first rung was about twelve feet off the ground, so I had to stand on the roof of my car to attain the proper elevation to begin my ascent. Even on the car roof I still couldn't reach the bottom rung comfortably. That's one of the reasons I brought the 100' or so of rope with me. I managed to toss one end of the rope, to which I had previously fastened a small weight, through the fifth or so rung up the ladder. Then, lowering the weighted end down the back of the ladder, and pulling the two pieces of rope together and holding onto both strands now draped over this rung, I hoisted myself up to where I could get footing on the bottom rung. With both feet now steadily on the bottom rung, I then climbed the approximate sixty feet up into the interior of the billboard. I never was afraid of heights, and was in pretty good overall physical condition back then, so this ascent was not a problem for me.

At the top of the ladder, with my head just above the top rung, I could see that there was about a three-foot wide walkway in between the two separate signs that each faced I-95, one to the south (for the northbound drivers to see) and the other to the north (for the southbound drivers to see). As I hoisted myself up onto the interior walkway and began exploring the length of the sign, about fifty feet from end to end, I noticed that there were two square cutouts in the lower portions of each side of the billboard, measuring about three feet by three feet. They were designed so the authorized maintenance crews could access the walkways on the outside of each side of the signs.

Hmmm...I could sit behind this opening in this sign, the one facing southbound, with most of my body hidden from the ground, and have a perfect view of the train station parking lots down below and in front of me. Once I walked back and forth a few more times, I yelled down to my colleague, about six stories directly below me, that this was an ideal lookout and I told him this is where I would be working from now on when assigned here.

My fellow squad member, ever the pessimist, screamed back up at me, "Even in the rain? Would you want an umbrella up there then?"

So as to not further strain my voice from yelling down that far, I half-bent over the side above the ladder and just shrugged my shoulders towards him. I'm not sure he could understand my non-verbals from this altitude, but he was right. I would have to think about being up here in inclement weather. This may just be strictly a fair weather assignment, at least up in the billboard, that is. Unfortunately, I don't think the rain ever stopped car thieves before. It would be back to ground patrol on those days for me.

My fellow Tac Squad members would usually not be too fond of the assignment at the Cornwells Train Station. It was boring, difficult to work, and with little in the way of arrests to show for it. Unlike the Neshaminy Mall, where there was always something happening to keep us busy and our arrest records up. But there were cars being stolen from this train station too. And as it was now into the early fall of '78, with a long stretch of decent weather predicted by popular Philadelphia TV weatherman Jim O'Brien (the former "boss jock" radio DJ whom I had met in my very early lifeguard days...more on him later), I volunteered to do a two-week stint here, in the air, in the billboard, between the elevated twenty feet x fifty feet ads for chips on one side and a cold beverage on the other side, all the while looking for car thieves and/or other assorted ne'er-do-wells on the ground below.

Sgt. Whacky didn't understand why I was volunteering for this generally unpopular assignment, but he said if I wanted it, it was all mine. He didn't ask me any specifics regarding it so as usual I didn't volunteer any. Such was our relationship. I actually got to preferring it that way.

I was at my new billboard assignment that first day by 10:30AM. I parked my car directly beneath the sign. I had previously asked my Tac Squad colleague to follow me there. Once we were there together, I again got up on the roof of my car and maneuvered my feet onto that first rung like last time. This climb, however, I brought the rope up with me to the top. Upon reaching the top, I lowered it down to my colleague who then hooked it to a plastic milk crate that I had previously jury-rigged to hold the various implements which I would need up there with me. I then hoisted up the crate which contained or had hanging from it, in no particular order of importance, a light-weight folding lawn chair, binoculars, an AM-FM radio, a police radio, my lunch with a drink, my crossword book, and that day's newspaper. To me, that's all a billboard-sitting plainclothes cop would need to spend his day looking for car thieves sixty feet up in the air.

While I was the only plainclothes Tac Squad member to ever climb the billboard, it wouldn't be just me, of course, as a part of this newly devised plan of mine. As another Tac officer would normally be assigned on a daily basis to car theft duty at the nearby Woodhaven Mall, he would be my backup should something "go down." When in my now lofty but out-of-sight position I would observe someone suspicious at the train station, clearly on the prowl either in a car or out on foot, I would contact my colleague via police radio and he would come to my location to be positioned accordingly. Maybe I'd have him go on foot, or maybe stay in his car. Either way, from my sky-high perch, I would control the tactical elements in effecting the arrest of the car thief once the crime was committed and the person was about to leave the station area.

No one had a better overall view than I did of the situation, so it would be up to me to call the shots during the course of whatever illegal activity I was observing. Of course, the marked patrol cars would also be summoned to the outer perimeter of the station area in an attempt to block egress of the bad guy with his newly purloined vehicle, stereo system, tires, or whatever was on his shopping list for that day.

I must say, this plan of mine worked, virtually every time. I must have made a dozen or more felony car theft or other arrests (car stereo system thefts, drug deals, etc.) from my billboard perch over the timeframe I was up there. I would watch cars come up the ramp, circle the lot, sometimes stay awhile, sometimes leave almost right away, strangely not picking anyone up or dropping anyone off. Of course, before the cars left the lot, I would use my binoculars to copy down the tags of the drop-off cars or any other suspicious cars in the train station lot for future investigative purposes.

Invariably, many of those same cars would return later that day, or even a day or more after I first saw them. On their subsequent visits, the car would re-enter the lot, a passenger would be dropped off, and the car would exit the area. The dropped-off guy, instead of walking to the platform to await the next train, would choose a zig-zag route through the hundreds of cars parked in the lots, looking in windows and over his shoulder at the same time.

Once these potential car thieves got out on foot, and no matter how they arrived at the station, their M.O. each time was very similar. On one occasion, I happened to observe a twenty-something male get off an early afternoon train coming from Philadelphia. He walked at first in unison with the few other disembarking passengers as if he had somewhere specific he was going. He clearly wanted to blend in with them, at least at first. In this particular instance the guy walked down the long car ramp with his fellow passengers toward Cornwells Ave. But as they turned one way or another along the street, or were picked up by someone in a car, he instead made a quick turn and took the concrete and steel reinforced stairs back up toward the train station platform. That was strange, I thought. Did he just realize he got off at the wrong station?

No, he wasn't mistaken at all.

When this particular guy got back onto the platform, he looked around and saw what he thought to be a train station and parking lot devoid of any other human beings. He was right, except he didn't think to look UP in the air at that time. Of course, even if he had, it would have been difficult for him to see my head just barely visible in one corner of the three feet by three feet opening under the beer sign, about one hundred and fifty feet to his north, and sixty feet in the air.

As the soon-to-be-thief was now undertaking the well-known zig-zag walk between aisles, and looking through the glass windows of multiple cars, I got on my police radio and called for both my nearby Tac Squad colleague and at least two marked patrol cars to head over to my area. I made it clear to them not to come into the actual lot yet, but to just park along Cornwells Ave. a few hundred feet on both sides of the parking lot ramp. In those places, all angles of egress would be covered, but they would still be out of this guy's present line of sight.

This potential thief, like the others I observed from above both before and after him, started casually walking around the main lot with seemingly no discernible destination in mind. He eventually slowed his pace near a particular newer model car and began walking that little section of the lot in ever smaller concentric circles. While doing this, he was constantly looking around his immediate physical environment for anything which could potentially alter his preplanned course of action, with his head moving back and forth and his eyes darting right and left the whole time. I noticed he would also be glancing at his watch every few minutes. He was probably aware of the time the next train would be stopping at the station and wanted to be out of there, hopefully with a freshly stolen car, before then.

With my telescopically enhanced close-up view of this pending thief's about-to-commit-a-crime rapid eye movement, I knew he was ready to go, especially as he saw no one else anywhere near him in the parking lot. He was sure at this point he was the only one in the lot and in the train station area. He was technically correct in this observation, as there was no one else anywhere near him *in* the lot at this moment. But as he never thought to look up, he missed the cop looking intently down at him who was multi-tasking with binoculars to his eyes and a police radio to his lips.

Yes, that would be me.

Based on his perceived sense of isolation and safety, the thief-to-be slinked over to the vehicle he had chosen, pulled out his "Slim-Jim" car entry tool from down his pants leg (that explains why he seemed to be limping slightly), and in less than ten seconds of jimmying it down between the glass window and the outside door panel, he was inside the car. This guy was good. He had apparently done this before, I quickly surmised. He then closed the door right away, and immediately ducked down onto the front seat, out of my range of vision for a short time. But I didn't have to see exactly what he was doing at this point to know I had a car theft in progress.

It was definitely Go Time!

Knowing that he was probably less than a minute away from beginning his drive to either a "chop shop" or some stolen car "fence" destination, I instructed the two patrol cars to move along Cornwells Ave. to specific points where they could block off both eastbound and westbound egress from the station area. I wanted my fellow Tac member on foot, acting casually, near the bottom of the ramp, just in case the thief decided to exit the car and run upon seeing the police cars.

So, it was all set. Everyone was in place. It would be any time now....

Sure enough, within about ninety seconds from the moment the thief popped the lock on the car door and him crouching down to cross the ignition wires under the steering column, he and the now-officially stolen car were moving around the lot and toward the exit ramp. He took his time driving though the lot and down the ramp. After all, at this point, he was sure he was in the clear and didn't want to unnecessarily attract undo attention to himself. I, of course, now had him as the sole focus of my attention, advising my uniformed and non-uniformed police colleagues of the car's precise movements and the very soon estimated time of arrival (ETA) of it and him to their street locations.

Upon finally reaching the bottom of the ramp, the thief went to turn left, but saw a police car about twenty feet away blocking the whole street. He then made a quick right to go eastbound under the train track bridge, but saw it was blocked by yet another BPD patrol car.

What is a car thief, in his just-stolen car, to do? And no doubt he was thinking, where the hell did these cops come from? "I was so cautious," he must have been saying to himself, "I know I was."

Fortunately, for the cops and criminal alike that day, the thief in the car he just recently stole came to a complete stop on Cornwells Ave, almost directly under the train track bridge. Due to everyone's precise positioning, he really had nowhere to go. That's when my plainclothes partner, with gun and badge in his respective hands, ran up to the driver's side window and ordered him out of the car. He hesitated, looked into the mirrors and to his left and right (but still not up), and followed the authoritative orders of my partner and the two uniformed cops and slowly and safely exited the car with his hands up in the air. He was on the ground, with hands cuffed behind his back very soon and enroute to the BPD station before I could even get down from my perch, high above the just unfolded arrest. I did not want him to see me coming down the ladder. I wanted my newly utilized observation tower to be kept a secret, for as long as I could, from him and his car-stealing comrades.

After a number of these arrests took place, the only down side to my little plan was that it was never me who got to place the cuffs on these perps. Hey, I was still a relatively new cop, and I still enjoyed the actual arrest action. Nonetheless, watching the entire operation go down each time, and from high above it all, was quite a thrill. These were my arrests, of course, and I would be the one taking them to court, but I must admit I did feel somewhat tangential to the actual takedowns themselves from my tower position. But, as I was learning, all of life is comprised of sacrifices of sorts, and that was one of mine in the billboard-sitting stage of my plainclothes police career.

Most of these car thieves later pleaded guilty because they had actually been caught red-handed inside the stolen cars, barely off the train station parking lot, and with various "Slim Jims," screwdrivers, and other tools of the vehicle theft trade on their possession. But at least one fought the law, or at least his attorneys decided to do so for him, and it led to an interesting courtroom experience.

I recall going to trial in Doylestown, Pennsylvania, regarding one particular Cornwells Train Station stolen car case, and being on the stand testifying in front of the defendant, the judge, and the jury, and explaining my role in it. By design on my part, in none of my case related paperwork, on any court documents, nor in my testimony at the earlier preliminary hearing, did I reference the fact that I was up in a billboard when I observed the car theft unfold. I never wrote of it nor specifically testified to it at any time up to that point. I would clearly relate in writing or later in testimony the necessary probable cause in terms of what I observed the defendant do, how he did it, that he was found with various car theft tools, etc., but I omitted at least one bit of information because I truly didn't want to give away my location up in the billboard. I wanted to keep it as my little secret for as long as I could. Heck, my own sergeant didn't even know about it for the first few weeks I was doing it.

During the eventual cross-examination from a young defense attorney in this particular case, I had some fun with it, and him. I didn't initially plan it that way, but it just sort of developed as the lawyer's questioning of me continued.

During the cross, I answered truthfully and concisely each time. However, as his line of questioning was so focused in one narrow direction, he was increasingly missing what was becoming very obvious to the rest of the courtroom in my answers. He actually became rather flummoxed while doing his best to interrogate me on the witness stand. It was no doubt clear to the judge and I believe even the jury too what he was clearly missing.

The defense attorney had persisted in asking me questions concerning the distance from me to the defendant at the time I observed him stealing the car, what obstructions were in my way, how many other vehicles were in between me and the car "allegedly" being stolen, how was the sun reflecting off my windshield, other cars' windshields, was I wearing glasses, sunglasses, was I sitting, was I standing, etc. I answered all in complete honesty, citing approximate distances, the fact that there were no obstructions of any kind between my line of vision and the theft-in-progress, there were no windshield obstructions, I was sitting at the time, etc. I simply did not volunteer that I was in a billboard, looking down at the thief with binoculars, all while sitting in a folding lawn chair.

The defense attorney even brought in as a visual aid to the jury a blown-up, hand-drawn schematic of the train station parking lot (not too dissimilar in design from my Neshaminy Mall map/schematic), and attempted to have me pinpoint where I was located at the time of the theft. I told him my location wasn't on his blown-up schematic as my specific location, in fact, at the time was not visible on it.

My answers seemingly didn't make sense to the defense attorney. He thought he had truly compromised my testimony, all without ever asking me specifically where I was while observing the car theft take place. He knew I was about one hundred and fifty feet away from the scene of the crime, but he never asked nor did I volunteer that I was also sixty feet up in the air. Upon ending his cross-examination of me, in responding to my last answer, the lawyer turned to the jury and stressed to them that I could not have possibly been in a position to clearly observe the defendant steal the car, my testimony was meaningless, and he strongly intimated that I was lying. Those statements were objected to by the prosecutor, and they were sustained by the judge. Nonetheless, the defense attorney sat down, seemingly confident in his own mind that he had "won" this part of his case.

I knew at this point in my testimonial career not to get out of my seat yet. The Assistant District Attorney was chomping at the bit to ask me a few further questions. So, on redirect, the prosecutor, who knew of my billboard-sitting angle of observation, asked me one specific question.

The prosecutor commented and then inquired, "Officer Fitzgerald, despite the intentionally confusing, unclear, and even accusatory questions asked of you by defense counsel, since it was never explicitly asked, please tell the court exactly just where and how you observed the defendant steal the car in question."

"Yes, sir," I said. "Actually, it's quite simple. I was about sixty feet up in a commercial billboard, about one hundred and fifty feet from where the car was broken into and eventually stolen. I saw everything through my binoculars, clear as day, with no obstructions between my line of sight and the thief from the moment he entered the train station parking lot until my colleagues arrested him, following my instructions, in the stolen car as he was driving it onto Cornwells Ave."

The prosecutor ended the redirect by stating, "Thank you, Officer Fitzgerald, no further questions."

The defense attorney fumbled through his well-worn yellow legal pad for thirty seconds or so but then reluctantly advised the judge that he had no more questions of me at this time.

Within three hours, after a minimal defense was presented (I believe just a character witness or two for the defendant) and both the attorneys' closing statements, the jury came back with a verdict of guilty to felony car theft, receiving stolen property, and possession of instruments of crime. I believe it took them even that long because they had a county-provided lunch they wanted to eat before they left the courthouse.

Like most of the other car thieves I arrested, this one was eventually sentenced to 12-24 months in Bucks County Prison. I never heard from him again. Hopefully, he had stolen his last car, at least in Bensalem.

I sat in the billboard on and off, in nicer weather, numerous times in late '78 and throughout the nicer weather in '79. The fearless Sgt. Whacky finally figured out what I was doing there and while never complimenting me directly on my individual investigative initiative, I once heard him brag to his bosses about the upswing in car theft arrests among his plainclothes officers (not me specifically) at the train station. No surprise there. Hey, as long as our squad got some positive recognition, I was happy.

After probably thirty to forty total days up on the billboard during that year plus, I "retired" from that lofty assignment. The numerous arrests I made there all resulted in either guilty pleas or convictions.

The thefts from the Cornwells Train Station dropped off markedly toward the summer of '79, as I believe the word was out among the area's thieves that the lot was now being watched from above, specifically from a cop sitting inside the beer and chips billboard.

I'd like to believe that my initiative helped to stem the tide of car thefts from that area for years to come. Just these guys THINKING a cop was up there may have been all it took to keep them away from the station, at least for criminal purposes. Of course, that just means they went to some other train stations, or malls, to steal their cars, but we were there too, at least if they were in Bensalem. Just not necessarily up in the air.

I'm glad I did the billboard thing as there was never a negative side to it for me or the BPD. It reinforced to me what my dad and some others had strongly suggested to me throughout my youth. That is, to not be afraid to try something new, something different, to even BE different, if it helps to accomplish a particular goal or objective. It may not be successful each and every time, but it's worth attempting if more traditional methods don't seem to work. More times than not, these type initiatives worked for me throughout my life.

(+ Bonus Chapters 10a, 10b)

Chapter Eleven

The aforementioned billboard-related car theft and mall pervert arrests were nice, but I wanted to further expand my professional horizons. I had proven I could do this job from a faraway perspective, watching someone from ground-level, up in the air, etc., but how about up-close and personal? And I mean REAL up-close and personal. I was about to find out. It would ultimately leave me with a bad taste in my mouth, and more towards the management of my police department than the guy I would later arrest.

Drug investigations are, by their very nature, inherently dirty business. There are no good guys to be found in virtually any aspect of them. Everyone involved is either strung out, was very recently strung out, or sells to people for the express purpose of getting them strung out. Oh, and many of the former participants die as a result.

Of course, the exception to the above descriptions of the combatants in the so-called "War on Drugs" would be the investigators and the prosecutors. They are, on the whole, hard- working and very dedicated to this chosen field of endeavor within the criminal justice system. Their singular goal: to try to put the money-makers and corpse-creators out of business and behind bars. Unfortunately, as most of us know, when a person in either of these categories goes down for the count, another one rises almost immediately to take his place. They're like cockroaches. It's a non-stop, vicious, cycle with virtually no winners and many, many losers.

Over the years I've made some decent arrests of men and women with relatively small amounts of marijuana, cocaine, meth, PCP, etc. However, my career at both the local and later at the federal level never involved working narcotics investigations fulltime. My vocational path for various reasons just never took me in that singular direction. The occasional arrests I did make were generally in conjunction with other ongoing investigations, or car stops, or pedestrian stops, when controlled substances happened to be found on the person or in his or her nearby possession.

There was only one time in my thirty-one years as a police officer/FBI agent in which I undertook a specific proactive approach to the drug war. I did so by temporarily joining the ranks of this smarmy sub-group of criminal dregs, even if just attempting to look like and act like one of them for a very brief period of time. That was when in an undercover role, albeit a brief one, I bought PCP from a known drug dealer.

(PCP, aka angel dust, is known chemically as Phencyclidine. It comes in both powder and liquid form. It can be highly addictive and produces physiological results similar to someone having depressants, stimulants, and hallucinogens in their system. Its illegal usage in the U. S. seems to have peaked, coincidently, in 1979.)

Yes, as a member of the BPD Tactical Squad, it wasn't only car thieves and "perverts" at the malls and train stations that I was arresting. There were other arrests too. At least one of them involved me, dressed really funky, acting semi-stoned, and giving cash to an unsuspecting dope-selling cretin for his little bag of goodies.

Oh, and during the course of this drug buy and the planning for it, I also had to decide whether to directly disobey a BPD sergeant. He told me I shouldn't be carrying my .38 Smith & Wesson backup revolver on my person while I interacted, by myself, with the dealer behind the closed doors of a large apartment building complex.

What's an undercover narc to do in this situation, even if it's the first and only time he's in that role?

Obey his sergeant? Or protect his life?

The story of this drug buy itself is rather straightforward and commonplace to many other undercover drug buys. In February of 1979, one of the BPD detectives had a snitch who knew a certain PCP dealer was coming from Warminster, Pennsylvania, a suburb not far from Bensalem, to ply his trade. The snitch was in legal trouble for some other drug dealings of his own and, like many of his criminal compatriots facing potential jail time, he agreed to cooperate with the police. He was asked if he could introduce a plainclothes cop to any other drug merchants and he stated he knew just the guy. Most likely it was one of his drug competitors. That made no difference to us.

This entire operation unfolded in less than one hundred hours from the time this informant was initially pinched to when he agreed to cooperate with the BPD detectives. Once he agreed to do so, I was recruited to be the undercover cop to be introduced by this snitch to the dealer coming to Bensalem. Should be easy, I thought.

I agreed to make this controlled buy and started the lengthy and detailed preparation process. That consisted of not shaving my face or shampooing my longish hair for the next three days. Actually, that was pretty much the extent of my preparation. Oh, and I would need a good place to hide my backup weapon. Bringing my healthy-sized .357 Magnum on a drug buy just wouldn't work, so I dug out an old pair of brown cowboy boots that I wore only occasionally. My plan was to place my smaller-sized .38 on the inside of my right boot, just in case things went bad during the transaction. No big deal, right?

I came into work the morning of February 12th and I looked the part, well, more or less, in terms of what I was wearing, my facial growth, and my unkempt hair. I was ready to go, to make this drug buy. The snitch was coming in to the police station at noon, and the intro and buy was scheduled for around 1:00 that day. We debriefed this now-cooperating recent arrestee about where exactly we were going, with whom exactly we'd be meeting, what shared past did he have with this guy, and similar type questions. We agreed that I'd buy two to three grams of PCP, and I'd have $60 with me for this particular product, as I believe that was the going price at the time considering its alleged level of purity.

We had this drug dealer's full name, and some basic intel on him, but otherwise not a whole lot. He didn't seem to have a violent past to him that we could glean, so that was good news. We also knew he wasn't a top-echelon dealer, but more of the lower-level variety. That's fine with us too. We can start at the bottom and work our way up. That's how this game is played, after all.

After debriefing our allegedly former drug dealer at the police station, I wanted to talk to the detective who was handling him, as well as his sergeant who was actually running this pending drug buy on this particular day. The detective had to leave before long for a scheduled court appearance, so we talked briefly and then I met with his sergeant. This was not Sgt. Whacky, but a Criminal Investigative Division (CID) sergeant, who was much different than my immediate supervisor. He had his own issues though, much of which came out later over the next few years when the BPD internal politics really started hitting the fan. But there was one other issue too.

This particular CID sergeant's reputation was that he made very few arrests himself, going all the way back to his patrol days and even later as a working detective. That, in and of itself, could be tolerated by the troops within a squad, a division, or within a police department. But he also carried the very undesired professional baggage of being a cop who was known for NOT having your back should a physical altercation of some kind develop. That's never a good reputation for a cop to have among his peers.

This sergeant's perceived persona was the result of there being multiple examples from his days in uniform of him being at a domestic situation, a bar, or the scene of an arrest somewhere, in which a fight would break out between a guy being arrested and the uniformed officer making the arrest. The officer and the usually drunken and/or very emotionally unhinged male would wind up rolling around on the floor, exchanging punches, kicks, and the like, with this now-CID sergeant, then-patrolman, just standing on top of them and at best yelling, "Stop it! Right now! Both of you, just stop fighting!"

The then-patrol officer would yell loudly, be very demonstrative, and get on the police radio and request further assistance, but he wouldn't jump into the immediate fray to help his colleague. He was simply not the kind of cop you'd want backing you up on any call or arrest with the potential of it getting in any way physical. And that sort of reputation stuck with these types of cops throughout their careers, when they were patrol supervisors, and even CID supervisors. It certainly did with him.

Some years ago, as a patrolman, the now-CID sergeant studied hard for his promotional exam, passed it, and the subsequent interview process, and he was promoted directly to the detective division. It was surmised by the BPD higher-ups that he wouldn't function well as a patrol supervisor. So now, he's my supervisor, sort of, for this one-time undercover drug buy. Lucky me. It was two in a row for me of less-than-stellar sergeants since I left the patrol division.

We'll call him Sgt. Pansy. Not his real name, of course.

Preparing for this undercover drug buy included determining how I would get to the location, which other officers would be watching me, from where they would be watching, how long it should take, my potential words and actions with the drug dealer, etc. We also discussed what I should do if he wants me to smoke a joint or snort a line of white powder of some variety with him. It was decided, immediately by me, I wouldn't do it. I'd tell the drug dealer I had to report to my probation officer later that afternoon and I couldn't go stoned. If it didn't work, so be it and the deal would be off. Either way, I wasn't smoking or snorting anything this guy was giving me that day, or any other day for that matter.

In this pre-buy meeting, we also decided this wasn't going to be a "buy-bust." In other words, we weren't going to arrest this guy right away. We were going to have two other Tac Squad officers follow him in his car and see where he goes, with whom he meets, etc. We'd then have more information, and prepare the arrest warrant afterwards. This tactic was not unusual, and had been done before in the BPD if a guy was at least from our same county. And this guy was from Bucks County.

The prep was going relatively well, with the snitch in the room for part of this conversation and actually offering useful illegal drug-buying related tips. But as we were getting closer to departing for the site, Sgt. Pansy then asked him to leave the room.

Once the snitch was gone, the sergeant started to then tell me what I should and should not do during the drug buy, to make sure the deal goes through. I initially just nodded my head in benign agreement with him. I knew for a fact that he never made an undercover drug buy in his career, so what he was saying at this point didn't really hold that much value to me. But I listened politely and said "Okay," repeatedly. I just wanted to get out with the snitch, jump in the car, and get this buy over with. However, as my meeting with the CID sergeant was just about to end, he said something which totally surprised me.

Pansy told me I should not be carrying any weaponry with me that day. I should leave it behind in my locker.

I responded to the sergeant that I would not, in fact, be carrying my duty weapon with me. As per his suggestion, I would leave my .357 behind, in my locker. But, I told him, I would be carrying my smaller six-shot, .38 caliber revolver in my boot. I even showed it to him, well secreted inside my right boot. I reminded him I was going into this apartment on my own, with no other cops, not wired-up or with a two-way radio, and with at least two known drug dealers present with one of them HOPEFULLY now working for us. After that, I reminded him, there were a whole lot of unknown elements to this operation. In view of all of this, I told the sergeant I was going to have at least one implement of protection on me, that being my boot-hidden .38.

Sgt. Pansy vehemently disagreed with me. He brought up the notion that the guy may want to search me before any "deal" goes down and he'd automatically think I'm a cop if he finds the gun on me. I told him that was unlikely based on our intel to date, but even if he did, it would most likely be my torso area, and not down in my boot, with my stylishly-ripped and stained jeans over top of them. Plus, if that was the case, I told the sergeant I'd simply act upset and ask him (the drug dealer) in turn to then allow me to search him too. I knew, at least to some degree, how this game was played with these guys. But Pansy told me again that he didn't want me carrying my weapon, as it could negate the whole deal and our chance to get the next-level-up drug dealer.

This CID sergeant was now getting me almost as pissed off at him as that which I usually reserved for my own Tac Squad sergeant. That was saying a lot.

Just what is the promotional process in this police department? Geez....

I adamantly responded back to the supervisor (but not MY supervisor) that my own personal safety and going home that night meant more to me than this half-assed drug buy and whatever arrests we may get from it. However, the sergeant held firm in his decision. Out of frustration, I then suggested that I'd leave the gun behind if he (Pansy) went home, got changed out of his three-pieced suit and tie and into his own ripped jeans and old t-shirt, and went along with me on this under-cover drug buy as my backup. (As he was an overweight, middle-aged, pasty looking guy who probably didn't own ripped jeans or t-shirts of any kind, I knew he wouldn't, make that *couldn't*, take me up on this suggestion.)

Upon hearing my offer, the CID supervisor got up out of his chair, walked towards the closed inner-office door, told me again not to carry a gun as he knows what's best, opened the door and left the room. I muttered two very distinct words under my breath to him, made sure my .38 was still tucked securely inside my right boot, got up, found the snitch, and left the building. Once outside, I rebriefed the two other Tac officers who were my backup for this operation and we were ready to go.

On the approximately one-mile ride to the garden apartment complex where this drug dealer would supposedly be visiting today, I did find myself becoming a bit anxious. I had never before bought drugs in real life, much less surreptitiously as a cop. I never dressed like this, or looked quite like this, which was even funkier than I usually appeared for my daily plainclothes work. This would be different. It wouldn't be me just sitting in my car, or up in an elevated perch somewhere, waiting for the crime to be committed to then pounce on the guy and arrest him. No, today, this would be me, just me, one-on-one, mano a mano, going up against this experienced, street-level drug dealer. What we really didn't know was whether he was one of these paranoid types, thinking everyone he's dealing with is a cop, or a snitch, or someone about to rip him off. And here we had two of three of these types (a snitch AND a cop) in this apartment with him today. How observant, how worried, how paranoid would this guy be with me? I'd soon find out.

I decided on the way there that it was through subtle and indirect means that I'd have to convince the pusher-man that I was the real deal, so we could hopefully engage in a real deal. Of drugs, that is. I couldn't appear overanxious or nervous to him, but as if I knew what I was doing and that I had done it all before. Just act cool, laid back, and be myself, right? Well, not exactly like my everyday self, but like me if I was buying drugs from a dealer.

But wait, I've never done this before.

Hmmm...maybe this wasn't such a great idea. Well, at least I have my .38 with me, if he gets that suspicious and becomes violent. Hopefully, by that time, my backup in the parking lot would know something is wrong and come in to assist me. Hopefully....

The snitch and I reached the parking lot of the complex. Driving my non-police looking Tac vehicle, I found a spot to park and got out of the car right away and to the apartment. I really didn't want to spend any more time than I had to with this snitch, or his dirty friends inside the place. We also agreed on the way there that we couldn't rule out that we were being watched either from the apartment or from another car in the parking lot, so everything we did from the moment we were near the place, we did with that in mind.

Don't act suspicious, and certainly don't act like a cop, I kept repeating to myself.

Okay, I can do that. I think....

The snitch and I knocked on the apartment door. The occupant apparently looked through the peephole and saw the snitch, whom he recognized. The door was opened, and we were invited into the apartment by a simple sideways movement of the guy's head and a barely audible grunt. There was just one person in the place from my initial observation, this thirty-something year old long-haired guy. That was good to know. I took that it was this guy's apartment and he was awaiting his friend, the drug dealer, to stop by as per the appointment set up via the snitch. I was half-heartedly introduced as "Jim" (keeping it real,

105

right?), to this guy whose name, I believe, was "Beast" or "Animal" or "Dog" or some such anthropomorphic reference. I stood for a minute, then without being instructed to do so, I sat down on a sofa, awaiting the PCP supplier.

The place was a dump, with trash and uneaten food all over. It was seemingly decorated in early pizza box and Chinese food container style. The stereo was playing loud rock music, I think it was Jethro Tull's *Aqualung*, if memory serves. The music didn't bother me, as I was always a Tull fan. I was most concerned at this point with the prospect of having insects or other small creatures crawl up onto me and under my clothes from the dirty sofa upon which I was sitting. I found myself scratching myself almost the whole time I was there. Maybe that was a good move on my part, to look strung out, high, or something like that with the incessant scratching. But in actuality, I was really doing it because I was envisioning little bugs all over me, from their sofa nests onto me. I swear I saw some, but maybe it was my nerves too.

Anyway, after an intolerable ten minutes or so of loud music, inane conversation, and scratching, surprisingly almost on time our boy showed up. And by himself, so that was welcomed. The fewer the merrier in this potentially toxic situation I was thinking, and the safer, too.

I had viewed a mug shot of this guy in our preparations at the police station over the last few days. He looked pretty much the same, except his hair was now longer and he had a few days' growth of beard. He and Beast, Dog, or whatever his name was, walked directly into the kitchen before he engaged me or the snitch. I was trying to hear what they were saying, but it was impossible because of ol' Jethro and his melodious flute solo reverberating just a bit too loudly off the four walls. I was also trying to observe them over my shoulder, but I really couldn't and I didn't want to act too suspicious around them. I would just have to hope they brought no sharp utensils or other weaponry with them out of the dining and cooking area. I've certainly seen the results of that before while in other residences on various domestic disturbance calls.

The dealer then walked back into the living room area, sat down in a bean bag chair across from us and stared at me. He didn't say a word, he just stared.

Ok, this was weird. What do I now do?

Well, I decided to simply stare back at him. The snitch, after a minute or so apparently feeling some obligation to break up the staring contest then said, "Hey, Joe, we hear you got some good shit."

The dealer, never looking at the snitch, but still at me, says, "Oh yeah? Who'd you hear that from?"

I chimed right in, indicating the snitch next to me on the couch, and said, "From my man here, that's who."

My sudden answer to the dealer's question didn't really make sense, but it went unchallenged. We were fine so far.

The dealer, still staring at me through what I could now see were seemingly glassy eyes asked, "Ok, whaddya want and how much?"

"A couple of PCP," I replied without hesitation, quantifiers, or qualifiers. Right to the point, I figured. And, by the way, that was street parlance, or at least the best I could do-parlance back then, for two to three grams of PCP.

He looked at me, looked at Beast, then back at me again, and said, "That's $80 for you."

I knew if I didn't haggle a bit, there would be a loss of credibility on my part, maybe even a suspicion that I was someone other than what I was representing myself to be. Which, of course, was the case here, but I didn't want him knowing that.

So, I retorted, "I was told $60. Shit, man, that's all I got on me."

And I wasn't lying. I had no wallet and no extra money at all on me. That was on purpose. I only had the $60 from the BPD drug stash account, a set of car keys, and, oh yeah, a six-shot revolver in my boot.

The drug dealer, the snitch, and the apartment resident known only by a generic mammalian nickname, went back and forth with each other discussing the alleged quality of this stuff, how hard it was to attain, that $80 was the usual price for this amount, etc. I just sat quiet while they further debated several relevant, at least to them, economic issues, each framed within the context of supply-and-demand, manufacturer's overhead, distributor risk, travel time and expenses, ancillary costs, and the like. They could have been referencing tires, baby diapers, or bowling balls, but instead it was illicit controlled substances which were the focus of this fiscal-jabber.

Having enough, I finally looked at the clock on the wall and, taking a chance, extorted, "Uh…can we get to business here? I got other stuff to do today."

The Economics 101 discourse finally stopped, and the dealer said, while reaching into his jacket pocket, "Yeah, give me your $60. Here's the shit."

I gave him the three $20 bills, took the little black plastic film canister from him, opened it up and shook it around a bit to make sure it approximated the negotiated amount, which I really didn't know but just assumed it did, and then stuck it in my pocket.

My last words to the drug dealer were, "Hey, thanks, man."

"Yeah, right. I'm outta here. I got other stuff to do today too," the guy said while getting ready to leave.

I believed him. He probably did have other "stuff" to take care of today, equally unlawful as what just transpired. And I'd know about his other stuff soon as my Tac Squad colleagues were going to follow him everywhere he goes today after he leaves.

The drug dealer and the Beast undertook a five-part handshake of some sort with each other, said goodbye, and he finally left. I looked at the snitch, while the other guy was still at the door, and nodded my head just enough to him as if to say "good job." He nodded back in the same mode.

We passively thanked our "host" for the use of his dump for our drug buy, then the two of us walked out the door. I was poorer $60, but richer in another way with a pocket full of eventual court evidence. While still scratching and brushing away the real or imagined creepy crawlies from the sofa, we got into my car. We were careful in how we acted as we knew it was possible that we were still being observed. In any event, we left the area and took a roundabout way back to the BPD HQ, just to make sure no one was following us (they weren't), and we returned to the safety and security of the BPD CID room.

Once there, I took out the film canister of greenish material, logged it into evidence, and filled out a lab submission form. Of course, the material would have to be tested to determine its constitution, and then we would file the charges against this guy.

The results came back within a week that it was, in fact, decent quality PCP, and pretty close to three grams. At least the guy didn't rip me off. That would have really upset me.

When my Tac Squad colleagues followed the drug dealer in his car that day after our PCP-for-cash transaction, he made a few stops, but eventually went back to his residence in Warminster, an apartment unit in his name. His car was also registered to him. So, we now confirmed who he was, although we were all but sure beforehand that we knew his identity.

I swore a warrant out in the next week, and with Warminster PD detectives, we went to his apartment to arrest him. But we missed him. He wasn't home. His strung-out girlfriend was there and now she knew her man was wanted for something. We knew in no short time she would tell him, so now it would be somewhat more of a difficulty to find him and arrest him.

However, the neighboring Horsham PD finally saw him driving his car late one night about a week later and took him into custody. They even found drug paraphernalia in his vehicle; no surprise there. So, he had other issues to worry about other than just my drug distribution charges at the Beast's lair in Bensalem.

The drug dealer was transported that night over to BPD. I was called in off-duty to interview and process him. He didn't recognize me at first from our deal, as I was clean-shaven with freshly shampooed hair and better dressed, but eventually he said he thought he knew me from somewhere. I did my best to protect the snitch as I told the dealer that he (the snitch) was under arrest too, and Beast was next. A detective and I interviewed him for several hours, after reading him his Miranda warnings and him still agreeing to talk. But besides him saying that "maybe" it was him in the apartment that day who sold me "the shit," he didn't give any more info in terms of who was his supplier, who was the "Big Man," etc. He actually swore our little deal together was a one-time sale. I was his first and only sale of the stuff. Ever. We told him based on that untruth we wouldn't believe him anymore tonight even if he TOLD us he was lying. He wasn't sure exactly how to respond to that, but maintained his story nevertheless.

The dealer was arraigned that night, and down the line eventually pleaded guilty to various drug sale related charges from our little afternoon transaction. He was sentenced to a combined 3-5 years by the judge for the distribution charge, the paraphernalia found in his car, and the fact that he had now violated his probation. However, I believe he may have started helping the Drug Enforcement Administration (DEA) on one or more of their cases and got out of jail a bit early. That happens a lot in this seamy world. I didn't mind. If he could give the DEA a bigger fish to fry, that was fine with me.

Oh, and I guess Sgt. Pansy was right. I didn't need my hidden firearm that day during the undercover drug buy. I'm still glad I had it there with me. Just in case.

As I wrote earlier, this was my one and only deliberate incursion and involvement into the world of narcotics investigations. Other career aspirations and opportunities directed me elsewhere. However,

I'm confident that if I had chosen to do so during my time at the BPD, I could have flipped other arrested druggies, run with their information, made other controlled buys, and climbed that drug sale ladder to arrest higher-ups. But in a medium-sized agency such as the BPD, there were only so many rungs on that ladder to climb, mostly due to the limited personnel, smaller geographic area, and monetary aspects of this type work.

This type work would become even more difficult, as I would learn in a few years, when one of the five elected Bensalem Township Supervisors was allegedly involved in the local drug trafficking business, along with his brother. And this particular politician was a strong advocate of the newly minted Deputy Chief of Police, Ted Zajac.

It was going to get very challenging in Bensalem Township, and on the Bensalem Township Police Department, over the next few years. I'd be right in the middle of it too, with a big red target on my back.

I'd better keep that .38 in my boot...just in case. Like it or not, Sgt. Pansy.

(+ Bonus Chapters 11a, 11b, 11c)

Chapter Twelve

While we didn't directly work together, Bob Yezzi and I were getting closer as colleagues and friends. He was still in patrol in '78 and '79, and seemingly enjoying his time there on his squad. Our shifts and days on and off were obviously different, but every once in a while when our hours would coincide we would meet at one of the Bensalem malls, train stations, or elsewhere and catch up on our lives.

While chatting somewhere in the direct view of the public, Bob and I wouldn't park our respective police cars next to each other in the usual cop-like facing opposite ways, driver-side window to driver-side window. I wanted to keep my unmarked car as non-recognizable as possible to the criminal-types who frequented the mall. Bob knew this and we found other, less conspicuous places to meet and talk. Or, we'd just park about fifty feet apart somewhere and I'd walk over and sit in the front seat of his patrol car, as if a civilian with a problem of some sort.

Bob for a time was one of the several Sector 4 patrol officers who assisted me in the arrests of the billboard-observed car thieves at the Cornwells Train station. In fact, as Bob was driving one of the thieves in the back of his patrol car to BPD HQ, the arrestee provided him with a *res gestae* statement regarding his crime. That is, in this particular case, without any prompting at all from Bob, the thief just started blabbing away about his car theft abilities, what he did that day, how he did it, etc., and Bob just listened. This type of statement, without even the Miranda warnings being provided, is fully admissible in court. Because of this interaction during the perp ride to HQ, Bob actually became an important witness for me at this guy's preliminary hearing. With Bob testifying to this guy's voluntary back seat confession, it kept me once again from having to give up my location in the billboard. It was a win-win for all involved, well, except maybe for the defendant.

On a personal level, my wife, Eileen, and I thought so much of Bob that at one point at our house we introduced him to her younger sister.

It was pre-planned by us, but neither Bob nor my sister-in-law knew it. Lo and behold, before long, the two of them became an item. It was nice to see Bob at several family events, to "double-date" with him and her on occasion, and to have the two of them over for burgers on the grill some evenings. They made for a nice couple for the time they were together.

As it turns out, for various personal reasons, this particular relationship didn't last all that long for Bob and my sister-in-law. However, even after they went their separate ways they remained friendly. It certainly caused no issues between Bob and me, as I knew he treated her very well for the few months they officially dated.

Speaking of my wife's younger sisters, another one of them had met my wheelchair-bound friend Joe Widmeier through me. Before long, they started dating. This relationship did survive beyond a few months and in late 1978 they were married. Now Joe was not just my friend, but he was my brother-in-law too. He was a welcome addition to my extended family. I just had to keep the two of us out of the Penn State University bars and frat houses.

(See JCM Book I for more about Joe and our college-age antics together.)

* * * * *

Back to our respective police careers, during this time frame Bob Yezzi played a role in one particular arrest of which I'm very proud. Interestingly, the crime in and of itself wasn't really that big of a deal. I didn't bust up a major drug ring, catch a serial killer, a serial rapist, or save any lives at all in doing so. To me, it's more of how within the matter of just a couple of minutes of the crime being witnessed, I used my barely three years of experience to come up with an unusual arrest plan, almost literally on the fly at the time, and coordinated it with several other BPD colleagues, to include Bob. And, believe it or not, it involved a stolen car and me once again observing the crime from yet another elevated position. No, it wasn't from the train station billboard. Instead, it was from the roof of a dairy.

At the intersection of State Rd. and Street Rd., not far from the Delaware River, was located the Hillcrest Dairy Company. It was a small milk distribution facility, with a medium-sized one story building and an adjacent parking lot in which various size delivery trucks would be found during the off-hours. During the day, the place was bustling with activity as trucks were either bringing in their milk supplies from the various regional dairy farms, or leaving with the packaged versions of their milk products to deliver to various stores and homes.

At night, before the first workers showed up at around 3:00AM, the place was empty with no one around it. For some reason during this particular timeframe someone was targeting the place for vandalism and even break-ins. There had been numerous incidents over the prior month or so, each occurring sometime between 10:00PM and 3:00AM. Office items and petty cash had been stolen, some equipment vandalized or damaged, and it became an obviously problematic situation to the owner and his staff. In view of this, the owner asked the BPD if something could be done.

After the third or fourth burglary, theft, or criminal mischief report was taken, a Sunday through Friday nighttime pattern determined, and with no suspects at all, it was decided to assign two Tac Squad members to sit on the place and conduct a surveillance of it during those critical hours. Our mission was to attempt to identify and apprehend whoever it was that was engaging in this sort of criminal activity. Along with another officer, I was asked on a Friday afternoon to work this detail starting the upcoming Sunday night, and we both said we would. On that Sunday night, I arrived at the dairy with my plainclothes colleague in order to set up and figure out the best way to be out of sight but still in a position to observe anyone with ill intent who might show up.

As we soon discovered that warm summer evening, there was no place we could find to position ourselves where we wouldn't be readily observable to anyone driving by, or more importantly, to anyone who was casing the place for their nefarious late-night criminal activities. My partner and I continued to survey the parking lot and the dairy business building itself. We quickly determined that there was no readily logical place for us to either sit in our cars or sit or stand outside of our cars and not be seen by someone who drives or walks into the area. Maybe a windowless surveillance van with a periscope of some sort would have worked for us, but unfortunately, the BPD didn't have one at its disposal. This was frustrating. Once again, our job wasn't to scare away these criminals by just sitting out in the open, but to catch them in the act. So, we needed a plan.

After about ten minutes of walking around the closed-for-the night business and its property, my colleague and I stopped at one point next to each other. He saw me looking up at the roofline of the building,

113

slowly scratching my chin while doing so. He then said, "Are you going to do what I THINK you're going to do?"

As he was the plainclothes officer who occasionally helped me get onto the first rung of the billboard ladder, I replied to him without missing a beat, "Yep. Now help me get up there."

As my colleague had vertigo to one degree or another, he didn't do heights. It was up to me to get the best seat in the house for whatever crime or crimes were about to take place over the next few nights at the Hillcrest Dairy. And, interestingly, I would be above the fray once again, looking downward at the criminals when they did their dirty deeds. This time, however, I would be a bit closer to terra firma. The roof was only about twelve feet off of the ground, a much lower altitude compared to the sixty-foot height of the billboard at the train station. This time, instead of having a beer sign over me, I'd have a milk sign under me. Obviously, there were some very notable differences here.

Also, once the crime was about to be committed and/or underway, I could simply broadcast (quietly) on my radio what I was observing, bring in the troops, then hang from the side of the building and jump down and participate directly in the arrest or arrests. Geez, like in the movies, maybe I could even jump on one of the bad guys' backs while they're trying to escape. In any event, it would not be like I'd be sitting back and watching it all unfold from high up in the air as with the arrests at the Cornwells Train Station. I'd be right there as it happened at the dairy, really, just a few feet away from it all, and then fully participate in the subsequent arrest too. This could actually be fun.

Well, something did, in fact, happen on the second night of this detail, except it was not exactly what or how I thought it would happen, with the subsequent arrest going down much differently than any of us would have ever planned. And it didn't even involve the place we were watching. I never did jump on anyone's back from above that night, but the later arrest scenario itself turned out pretty cool nonetheless.

Once it was decided I was going roof-bound, like at the train station billboard, I drove my unmarked car to right alongside the building so I could use it to climb on top of it. I didn't need any rope for this particular perch, as I could just grab the top of the wall and pull myself up and onto the roof. The wall extended upwards approximately two and a half feet above the building's roofline, so I had a place to sit and observe all that happened beneath me by peering over the top, while my body was effectively hidden from anyone on the ground. I chose to position myself at the southeast corner of the roof, the one directly facing the intersection in front of me. That way, I could cover the two most likely entrance points to the parking lot and to the building itself. Once I confirmed this was the way to go, my partner moved my car to a faraway portion of the lot, he threw me my keys, my police radio, my trusty AM/FM battery powered radio, my binoculars, a small blanket (to sit on), a thermos bottle of water, and then he left and positioned himself about a block away on a side street.

The surveillance (stakeout?) was on.

As anyone who has worked a physical surveillance or stakeout of any kind, it is well known that they can be very boring and test the mettle of even the best and brightest. One functions best on these details if she or he has the kind of mindset that can think about disparate notions, ideas, concepts, and the like ("mind-occupiers" as I referred to them), while still not missing a beat as to what's happening in the surrounding environment that's under surveillance. I evolved into that type of person on earlier surveillances, especially of the stationary variety.

In daylight hours, besides listening to one or more fun radio channels for music, news, and sports, I would also rely on books and magazines of crossword puzzles and cryptograms to keep me busy. I learned I could multi-task and both challenge my brain, usually within a language perspective of some sort, while at the same time still carefully and dutifully observing what it was that I was supposed to be observing. I could also read a newspaper or magazine with no problem, and glance up after every paragraph or so at that which I'm supposed to be watching. Reading a book though, especially a good one, proved difficult for me while on these details. I would get too entrenched in the storyline and find myself not paying attention as much as I should to the surveillance itself. So, after a few times reading some fiction and non-fiction books while on a stationary surveillance, and initially missing a thing or two that I should have seen, I kept that type of engrossing literature out of my car. Give me something I can glance at, think about, then write down (as in a word puzzle book), while on a surveillance, and it works much better, at least for me. It keeps my mind occupied just enough on these otherwise boring missions, but not too much that I'm missing what I should be watching for.

These first two nights, however, my mind-occupier capabilities were at a minimum, as it was somewhat dark on the roof, with only enough ambient light to make sure I wouldn't miss a step and tumble off the roof. There was not enough light to read a book or magazine of any kind. I had a flashlight with me, but I knew I wasn't going to use it, lest someone down below possibly noticing it and me. So, the usually present reading material of mine was left in my car on this night. Any puzzles to be untangled and figured out while roof-bound would have to be mentally self-derived, all while staring over an empty parking lot out at the intersection of Street and State Rds.

As there were less and less cars driving by as the first two nights wore on, I made a mind-game out of counting them and then trying to guess in how many seconds the next one would drive by. Afterwards, I'd try to guess which way they were going to turn onto State Rd. It was boring up there, to say the least, especially as I could determine no patterning at all to the cars and when they would come by and where they would turn. I was doing everything in my power just to stay awake and on my toes while rooftop, but it wasn't easy.

So, those first two nights, it was me sitting alone on the roof, leaning back against the ledge at the roof's SE corner, with my head just slightly above it, which allowed me to overlook the premises below me and even beyond, as far as my eyes would allow on this relatively dark night. On one or both of those nights I had a Phillies baseball game on my play-radio, turned to very low volume. I whispered a radio check about every half hour to my Tac colleague, just to make sure the radios were still working and that he was still awake. I waited.

And waited, and waited, and waited....

Nothing happened at all on the first night. We knocked off at 3:00AM when the employees started arriving. But the second night, June 4th, at around 11:00PM, things got very interesting.

Similar to the night before, I was bored again on this night. It still was hot and humid, even as the clock approached 11:00PM. I was sweaty. I listened to the Phillies game on the radio and even that was boring as they lost to the Houston Astros, 3-0.

Now what do I do?

There's at least four more hours until the company's first employees show up and we're done our shift. But, here I am, with no crime, no anything of interest occurring, no one to be seen, and hardly even any car movement on the streets, anywhere. This was proving to be one of the tougher surveillances I'd ever worked, from a motivational perspective. Would anything come of this long week ahead of me? Geez, I hope so.

Out of this period of sheer and utter boredom, I came to notice an unusual series of seemingly innocuous events. They unfolded quickly, and as luck would have it for me (but not two others), directly across

116

the street from my rooftop location. While no one part of what I saw was in any way egregious or even necessarily that out of the ordinary, each individual aspect of it taken in totality began to slowly pique my curiosity. I initially considered ignoring what I was observing and not doing anything about it, but for some reason, perhaps the tediousness of this second night on this detail, I decided otherwise. And I'm glad I did.

It started innocently enough. From my quiet, non-eventful, and dull rooftop perch, at least so far that night, I first heard a car driving on the relatively deserted roads adjacent to me. It was moving toward me, in an easterly direction. There was something clearly wrong with the car as there was a loud clunking sound emanating from it. Shortly after I initially heard it, I then saw this dark-colored, mid-70s Oldsmobile Cutlass driving ever-so-slowly eastbound on Street Rd., toward State Rd. It was moving at a crawl by the time I had it in my sight, with the noise, whatever it was, noticeably quieting down too, as if in rhythm with the speed of the car. The vehicle eventually came to a complete stop on the shoulder of Street Rd., approximately fifty feet west of State Rd., and directly across from me at about the same distance. Only the Hillcrest Dairy parking lot and the westbound lane of Street Rd. was in between me and this apparently now-disabled car.

I didn't really think very much of this incident as it slowly developed in front of me. I was here to catch burglars, in the building right below me, and was still on the lookout for them. What do I care about this car? So a guy's car broke down, maybe a flat tire, maybe something else. It happens all the time, right? He'll fix it or find a nearby public payphone to call to get it towed.

Except, what happened next, and then what did NOT happen next, caused me to question what I was seeing and caused something inside me to react the way it did. Perhaps it was my intuition, my common sense, maybe it was my ever-developing street sense, aka "cop-smarts," or it was just something I couldn't quite define at the time. Hey, it could have just been my sheer and utter boredom added onto those things. Whatever it was, something inside told me to further explore what just unfolded here in front of me. So, I did.

With the seemingly disabled car now at a complete stop directly across from me, I noticed that within seconds both the driver's side door and the front passenger's side door popped open. Out came two males in their 20s. This movement in and of itself did not surprise me or appear unusual in any way. Of course they were going to exit their broken-down car. What surprised me was what they did next. That is, they pushed the car a few feet onto the shoulder so it was completely off of Street Rd., then the driver reached back into the driver's side door, grabbed something from on or near the dashboard, and took that item and threw whatever it was into the field directly adjacent to their location. It almost seemed like what he threw were the keys to the car, but I couldn't be sure of that from my vantage point.

Hmmm...this is turning strange.

The two males immediately started walking towards State Rd. They didn't seem to be talking to one another, they didn't once stop to examine the front or rear of the car, much less go to the trunk and remove any tools, or shine a flashlight, in an attempt to ascertain what the problem with their car may be. Instead, they merely got out of the car from their respective sides, quickly pushed it a few feet, threw something into the woods, and without even so much as a backwards glance at the car, they simply walked away from it. I curiously watched them cross State Rd. and I could see by the headlights of an approaching car that they were now attempting to hitchhike northbound, towards Bristol Township.

So, what do I have here?

A driver, and his passenger, in a newer, decent-looking car that breaks down at 11:00 at night, and neither of them tries to do anything to remedy the problem, or even attempt to figure out just what it may be. They don't look at the outside of the car even once as they exit it. I don't think they even locked the doors of the car before they left. You'd think the driver, if no one else, the one who is ostensibly the owner of the car, would want to know what to tell someone later who may ask him what the problem was with his disabled vehicle. Instead, both these guys just walked away, never looking back even once, as if they didn't care about it at all. As if it wasn't even their car it almost seemed. And, on top of all of this, the driver throws something from the dashboard area of the car into the wooded area next to him.

Something definitely wasn't right here.

Having observed this probably less than one-minute long scenario unfold in front of me, I felt I needed more information here. My curiosity was clearly getting to me. I had to know more of what was going on at this scene just fifty feet away from me. So, I took the first step. I got on my portable police radio and called my Tac partner at his location less than a block away. I asked him to drive over to the possibly disabled and oddly abandoned car on the shoulder and check it out. Specifically, I asked him to run its registration plate through DMV. I couldn't quite

118

read the tag from my rooftop location, even with my binoculars. The angle wasn't right for me, plus it was dark and the car now had its lights off.

I summarized to him on the radio what I had seen (which really wasn't much), and that the two former occupants had now walked beyond my immediate line of vision, presumably still hitchhiking on State Rd. I further advised my colleague not to pull up right behind the car to check it out, even though it was unoccupied and the occupants now gone. I still didn't know if these two guys had done anything wrong or not, but I figured either way, let's not telegraph to them what we were doing with their car.

My colleague pulled about one hundred feet behind the car and read off the tag number to the BPD dispatcher over his police radio. I further requested the dispatcher to run it every which way, including ownership and whether it was possibly missing, stolen, and/or wanted for a crime somewhere. All routine stuff so far. Probably nothing, my colleague and I were agreeing over the radio. But, hey, we were bored. We might as well do something here to break the monotony. Then we could get back to our regularly scheduled monotonous surveillance.

Within about thirty seconds, thanks to our dispatcher, that monotony was about to be broken, and in a pretty major way. The car, as it was learned, was reported stolen out of Philadelphia earlier that night.

HOLY SHIT!

The heck with the dairy for now, we gotta find these two car thieves. And quickly, before someone picks them up while they're thumbing their way to their next destination, which could possibly be their next car theft.

I immediately got on my police radio and requested my Tac colleague to come over and help me get down off the roof. He drove the very short distance, got out, and I threw down to him my various work and play equipment. I then hung over the side, jumped the rest of the way onto the parking lot, got my stuff from him, and went to my own unmarked police car. Before getting into my car, I yelled to my plainclothes colleague to drive north on State Rd. and let me know if he sees the two hitchhikers. I also told him as he was taking off that I didn't want him confronting them in any way…yet. We'll get them, but just give me a few seconds to figure out the best way to do so.

In the meantime, I knew Bob Yezzi was working Sector 4 that night, and since this area was on the border of his sector, I called him to our location. He responded that he had been listening to the radio broadcasts and he was less than a mile away and presently enroute.

So, while waiting to hear the status and location of the two hitchhikers, and the arrival of the marked unit, I started asking myself... how do I safely, effectively, and efficiently undertake the arrest of these two car thieves? If they hadn't already been picked up by an unsuspecting driver, they would just about now be approaching Neshaminy State Park, a wide expanse of wooded recreational area which runs along the Delaware River in Bensalem. On the other side of State Rd. from their now probable location was a large industrial park.

If I sent marked police cars to simply pull up alongside the two of them, with us plainclothes cops to assist of course, the perps would be able to run in either direction and hide among the trees in the recreational park, behind sheds and dumpsters in the commercial park, in playgrounds, under or inside trucks, or at dozens of other dark places on either side of State Rd., making the lives of the pursuing officers very difficult, if not dangerous. That was not what I wanted for me or the other officers I would be coordinating in this arrest. No, another plan would have to be conceived, and quickly too. I don't want them picked up by another car, even if done so innocently. We would lose so much control then and that driver could be in danger too.

Bob pulled into the dairy lot in his patrol car. He drove up next to me while I was standing outside my car. At just about that exact moment, my Tac Squad colleague radioed me that the two guys were, in fact, right near the entrance of the State Park, still hitchhiking. He drove straight by them and was continuing northbound so as to not draw attention to himself.

I responded to him, "Good. Now, go further up State Rd. and turn around when you can, out of their sight. Then, standby."

In the meantime, the Sector 3 car pulled into the lot, so we had some additional personnel for when the time came for the arrest. With both of the patrol cars parked in my direct vicinity, Bob Yezzi being in one of them, I came up with a plan. I didn't even run it by them, I just advised them to listen to what I was about to tell my partner on the radio.

On the police radio, I broadcast, "22-36 (me) to 22-39 (my Tac Squad partner), what's your 10-20 (location)?"

My fellow plainclothes officer responded, "I just turned around in a side street, a few hundred yards past the two perps. They can't see me but I can see them. No one has picked them up yet."

"10-4," I responded.

I laid out my plan, for him to hear on the radio and Bob and the other officer to hear in person, standing next to me.

"Ok, here's what we're doing. I'm going to pull out from the dairy first, with the two marked cars a short distance behind me. 22-39 (my Tac Colleague), you wait until you see three sets of headlights coming in your direction, then slowly start coming our way. I'm going to stop and offer the perps a ride. As soon as they're in my car, I'll drive a short distance and I want the marked units to do a car stop on me. I'll pull over, and all the cars can converge at that time and we arrest them. Everyone got it?"

"Gotchya" was the response from the two officers in the lot with me and "10-4" from my Tac partner on his radio. We were ready to roll, to make these arrests, in the most coordinated manner I could think of in the three minutes or so I had to put it all together. It should work.

I hoped it would work.

I left the dairy parking lot first, turning north onto State Rd. The two marked units, with Bob in the first one, took off about thirty seconds later, following behind me at an inconspicuous distance. About a half-mile ahead, I could see a set of headlights slowly pull out of a side street or driveway, and head towards me. I knew that was the other Tac car. Ok, all good so far. Now, if I can just spot these two walking car thieves. Let's hope they didn't cut through the State Park, or over into the industrial park. That wouldn't make sense, but you never know.

Then I started thinking…what, if for whatever reason, they decided to stop hitchhiking by the time I'm on top of them? What then? I guess it would be back to simply converging on them with lights and sirens and hoping to catch them by surprise and them not running. But it's Plan A for now, the one I hastily thought of under the dim lights of the Hillcrest Dairy sign.

Geez, where are they? I don't see them yet.

Sure enough, in one of the darkest areas of State Rd. on that evening, I could eventually see the two guys walking ahead of me, still on the shoulder. They were not facing the car coming at them, which would be me, so they weren't actually hitchhiking when I first had them in my sight. I slowed down to give them time to hopefully detect my headlights approaching them, spin around and stick out at least one of their thumbs, looking for that so far elusive ride.

Before long, with one of them apparently noticing over his shoulder the lights of a car coming at him, he turned around and out came his thumb.

Yes! As the car thief was now in official hitchhiking mode, I was in official hitchhiker pick-up mode.

With just the right distance between us so I didn't have to awkwardly jam on my brakes to stop for them and perhaps spook them, I gradually slowed down and pulled up on the shoulder, slightly ahead of the two suspects. I was looking ahead of me and behind me through my mirror at the same time to make sure I could see at least three pairs of headlights slowly coming my way. After all, I was beginning to think, I was taking a risk of some sort letting these two guys get into my car. I didn't know what kind of weaponry they may have on them. Even basic car theft tools, such as a long screwdriver, could be very dangerous at close range. I'd have to play it smart and safe here tonight. Surprise would be an important factor too, I thought to myself; us surprising them, of course, and not vice-versa. So far, we seem to have that in our favor.

Before turning off my police radio, I notified my backups that I was about to pick them up and feel free to stop me any time after I take off. Bob and the other officer each gave me a "10-4." I then turned off my car radio (which was out of sight under the driver's seat), and my portable radio, which I hid under the passenger seat. I didn't want any inadvertent, even unrelated, police broadcasts scaring them off from getting into my car. Also, at the last second, I decided I didn't want either of them sitting next to me in the passenger seat. If they were going to attack me somehow, I wanted both of them in one specific location, not spread out with one behind me and one right alongside of me. So, I had to think of a way to get them both into the back seat.

As my car came to a stop, I rolled down my passenger side front window. (While I had a nice, newer model, four-door, unmarked police car, it still didn't have power windows or locks in it. Remember, it was still the '70s.)

I casually said to them, "Where're you going?"

They responded, "Hey man, thanks for stopping. Yeah, we're headin' up to Bristol. You goin' that way?"

"I am," I lied, while motioning for them to get into my car.

"Cool," one of them uttered.

"Oh, yeah, my front door has a busted lock." I lied again. "Just get in the back seat. Okay?"

"Sure, no problem," they enthusiastically responded while getting into my unmarked police car, not knowing yet they were less than sixty seconds from being in handcuffs.

I was glancing in the mirrors at the ever-slowing headlights still several hundred feet behind me as I was talking to these two soon-to-be-arrested car thieves on the side of the road. Both patrol cars were back there, where they were supposed to be, just waiting for me to drive off.

As soon as the rear door closed, I did drive off. And immediately after slowly hitting the accelerator pedal, I could see through my mirror two sets of lights speeding toward me from behind. Looking out ahead of me, I could see another set speeding in my direction from in front of me. I was barely back onto the northbound driving lane of State Rd. and next thing I knew, as if on cue, two sets of red lights, with a few siren blasts, filled the interior of my car. The cops were pulling me over. This is almost always a bad thing for a driver, but I was pleased as punch to be felony car-stopped at this particular moment. After all, I planned it.

With the red and blue lights flooding the interior of my car, and the siren shrieks temporarily deafening me, I said loudly over this sensory stimulation, while still maintaining my role as merely a hitch-hiker picker-upper, "What the hell is this? Are you guys wanted for something?"

While shifting back and forth and taking all of this in, one of them responded very adamantly while looking out the rear window of the car, "No! Are you?"

Before I could answer, the other car thief/hitchhiker/soon-to-be-arrestee said, "Hey, man, just keep driving! Cross the bridge into Bristol Township. The cops can't follow us there! It's the law."

He was wrong on several counts. I wasn't going to "keep driving," despite his bold attempt to have me do so. And, for the record, the police officers behind me would be authorized to go into another juris-diction during a hot pursuit, which this would have turned into if for some reason I wasn't a cop and I did "keep driving." This almost-arrested thief must have been watching too many old movies or TV shows. But none of that was important right now as I was obeying the law here. I was going to stop for the policeman.

Oh, that's right, I AM a policeman too, and this was my friggin' arrest plan!

I pulled over and put the car's automatic transmission lever in park, shut off the engine, and pocketed my keys. No matter what happened here, I didn't want one or both of these guys somehow stealing my unmarked police car. That would be truly embarrassing and problem-atic to us on many levels.

At this point, I didn't waste any additional time nor take any additional chances as I did not know what weapons they may have on them, and/or how they would choose to react in this immediate crisis. So, I dropped my nice guy "where are you going" persona. In doing so I turned around in my seat and loudly and authoritatively voiced to them, "I'm a police officer! Hands all the way up, touching the roof! You're under arrest for car theft!"

At the same time, I drew my weapon from under my loosely-fitted unbuttoned shirt and pointed it in their direction. I wasn't worried about them seeing my badge at this exact moment as the uniformed guys were just seconds away from ripping the back doors open.

Interestingly, in the few moments it was just the three of us in the car, I found myself in an oddly contorted physical position as I was holding them at bay with my gun. That is, I was sitting behind my car's steering column, with my body twisted halfway to the right, while holding my gun on the two suspected felons in the back seat. That was a first for me and something that I realized then I hadn't been trained to do at the police academy. I also realized immediately that I had to hold my weapon in such a fashion as to make sure it was away from them, beyond their arms' lengths, so they couldn't easily grab onto it and use it against me. Luckily, I'm left-handed, so I could hold it in my strong hand, but it was nonetheless at an awkward angle for me, extended away from my body, with my wrist unusually bent so I could point it in their direction. But, most importantly, it was far enough away from them, with the back of my hand almost touching the dashboard, so that they couldn't readily get to it. If they came after it, or me, all bets would be off and the trigger would have been pulled. Luckily for all parties, that did not happen, as in just a very short time, both rear doors were ripped open (I previously made sure they were unlocked), and these guys now had guns pointed at them from at least two other directions.

One of the car thieves then yelled, "Okay, okay, put the f**kin' guns away! You got us!"

They were clearly simultaneously surprised, shocked, and scared by what just happened. That was our quickly put-together plan which developed into a successful arrest scenario.

With that, the two of them were taken out of the backseat of my unmarked car, separated, searched, handcuffed behind their backs (of course), and each placed into the rear of the marked police cars.

I thanked the two patrol officers, Bob Yezzi included, for having my back for this arrest. Oh, and my Tac Squad partner too. I told them I appreciated each of them reacting so quickly to what had unfolded so suddenly. Heck, it hit me that it had been less than five minutes from me first seeing the car break down, these two guys exiting their car as oddly as they did, and now exiting my car as surprisingly (to them) as they did. Good work done by all, I must say.

Back at the police station, a detective and I interviewed the two arrestees separately. Both of them denied any involvement in the car theft in Philadelphia or even being at the scene of the broken down car in Bensalem. Eventually, the passenger admitted to being in the stolen car, and knowing it was a stolen car, but said he was just hitch-hiking earlier in Philadelphia, and this driver that he never met before picked him up, and so on. Next thing he knew, the car had a mechanical problem (its crankshaft collapsed), they both exited the car, and they started hitchhiking again, this time on State Rd. where I kindly invited them into my car. Likely story....

Since no witnesses or police officers, including me, saw them actually steal the car in Philadelphia, by Pennsylvania criminal statute, I couldn't charge them with the actual car theft. (Nor even could the Philadelphia Police.) However, I could charge them with the crime of Receiving Stolen Property, since they were observed by me in possession of the stolen car. They were also charged with Criminal Conspiracy, since there were two of them, and they must have somehow planned it together, or at least talked about it. They were arraigned later that morning by the on-call district magistrate and remanded to Bucks County Prison on relatively high bails.

(Apparently, hours before, the car's legit owner had left his keys in the car where it was parked in Philadelphia. One or both of these guys came upon the car, saw the keys in it, and stole it. When the car developed its problem, for whatever reason, the driver tossed the keys into the adjacent wooded area. The next evening, after a brief ground search in the fading sunlight, my partner and I found the keys.)

Months later, these two guys went to separate jury trials. As it turned out, in the first trial in late '79, the passenger was acquitted of all charges. The jury believed he was merely an innocent hitchhiker, picked up by this unknown (to him) driver. So, he got off scot-free. In the second trial, in January '80, the driver was convicted of both charges. This, after he claimed he was in the process of repossessing cars that evening, and perhaps took this one inadvertently. The jury did not believe him as he had no proof of any kind that he was so employed as a repo man that night. He eventually received a sentence of 18-24 months in county prison.

This crime, arrest, prosecution, and its results are interesting for several reasons to me. Firstly, regarding the crime, I'm glad I reacted the way I did on the rooftop that night when I saw the car abandoned as it was by the two men. Secondly, regarding the arrest itself, I'm proud of how my quickly assembled team of uniformed and plainclothes officers came together that night and successfully and safely effected the two men's arrests. No one was hurt on either side, and with only a minimum of time and energy expended by us. Thirdly, regarding the prosecutions and their results, they remain memorable to me in that the acquittal of the passenger on both charges at his trial represents one of only very few arrests of mine, at any jurisdictional level of my career, in which a full acquittal was the result. This passenger is in rarified air in being one of only several defendants to have ever "beaten the rap" of an Officer/Special Agent James Fitzgerald arrest and prosecution. (Thanks also to some great prosecutors I worked with over the years.)

I tip my police hat to the aforementioned hitchhiking passenger in the Street and State Rds. stolen car case, and later to his defense attorney too. In my thirty-one year career of arresting people, or later consulting as a profiler and a forensic linguist on other legal matters, this guy was just the first of very, very few to ever walk from one of my arrests or analyses which had resulted in a prosecution.

Something tells me before long this guy would be arrested and found guilty of some other crime, somewhere, somehow, and the charges would stick on that occasion. Or, maybe he learned a lesson that night, and he went on the straight and narrow path afterwards, to include not getting into stolen cars anymore, whether hitchhiking or not. For his sake, I hope so.

Oh, and speaking of that Hillcrest Dairy assignment, my Tac Squad colleague and I did spend the rest of our nights there that week. A very boring and unfulfilling assignment it continued to be, certainly after that second night. We never caught anyone breaking in or otherwise committing any crimes on the property. Some on-and-off surveillance of the facility took place over the next few weeks, but no further crimes were committed and no one ever caught. Frustratingly, this remains unsolved.

But at least we caught the car thieves that night, with one of them ultimately held responsible for his crime.

Chapter Thirteen

"...beware of the Dark Side. Anger, fear, aggression; the Dark Side of the Force are they. Easily they flow, quick to join you in a fight. If once you start down the dark path, forever it will dominate your destiny, consume you it will..."

(Yoda, *The Empire Strikes Back*)

Despite some interesting and innovative arrest scenarios, making new friends, and my still-sort-of-a-rookie exuberance in doing my job every day, it wasn't all kicks and giggles being a Bensalem plainclothes police officer during this time frame. Internal departmental developments continued to play out which would ultimately detract from the enjoyment of doing my everyday job, and even more importantly, the future effectiveness and success of the BPD and its mission.

By the fall of '79, Larry Michaels was still the official BPD Chief of Police, but it was a title only and nothing more. I believe his main role at this time was administering to the fleet of police vehicles, to include an early "green" initiative involving changing them over from gasoline to propane powered engines. As previously decreed from the majority faction of the five elected township supervisors, the now-Deputy Chief Zajac was put in charge of all other aspects of the department, with no one or nothing seemingly in his way from eventually being named its actual chief. He only had to jettison Chief Michaels somehow from the office and position that he so desperately coveted. Then, all his puzzle pieces will have fallen into place.

From even my limited knowledge of BPD history and its political structure at the time, it nonetheless seemed on multiple personal and professional (not to mention political) levels that something wasn't right or fair here as it related to Chief Michaels and his recent involuntarily derived downward mobility. It was all unfolding less as a result of what was ostensibly good for the department and more for what was ostensibly good for one particular person and his handful of minions.

How could a situation like this take roots and ever evolve to begin with, and in a police department, of all professional environments? A place where law and order, equity and integrity, brotherhood and camaraderie, should rule the day.

Yeah, right! Not in this place in the late 1970s.

Interestingly, there were no significant negative departmental issues, at least none known to the rank and file, which could be construed as a rationale for Michaels to be stripped of his powers and all but his actual title. He had no disciplinary problems of his own or job-related issues of any consequence involving his officers, the Police Benevolent Association (PBA), etc., the overall PD stats were very good, he apparently knew how to manage the PD's allotted yearly budgets, he oversaw the hiring of us newer officers which effectively doubled the size of his department, and he was still very well-liked by the community and the local media. But it seemed that none of this mattered anymore. Chief Michaels' role was effectively marginalized within the police department to that of car jockey and the occasional ombudsman on matters of minimal importance.

I was told about some senior officers and mid-managers in the department who had worked well with Chief Michaels in the past and who were even supposedly his good friends, but who now gave him the cold shoulder as they had to instead shift their allegiances to Deputy Chief Zajac...or else. This movement had started at the top and would soon be filtering downward to the rest of us. Anyone of us in the department could be similarly marginalized, or worse, it would soon be learned.

The new boss was definitely not the same as the old boss.

However, this whole process wasn't going to be that simple for Zajac, as he and his numerous departmental sycophants would come to realize over the next several years. Not when unbridled political maneuvering, gamesmanship, personnel suppression AND oppression, as opposed to individual talent, intelligence, demonstrated leadership skills, and fostering an open and desirable workplace environment, are the means by which one person is attempting to ascend to the top of an organization.

If the formula a person is using to achieve that ultimate promotion, to attain that ultimate position, to climb that highest professional mountain, is based solely upon his daddy's political influence among his recently elected buddies, that person better make sure that those buddies stay in office, stay in power, and even stay alive, for the foreseeable future. More critically, he better hope he doesn't underestimate the personnel he's now attempting to lead by using this particular nepotistic formula. Some may see through him and his self-promotional, career-enhancing machinations and loudly question in various forums what is otherwise becoming the "new normal."

These questions were, in fact, starting to be asked by some within the BPD. The answers, however, at least for the short-term, were not what many of us wanted to hear.

Cliques were beginning to develop in the BPD, two to be specific. Officers, dispatchers, and even the civilian clerical staff, were all but forced to start taking sides. Either you were a "Zajac boy (or girl)," or you were not. If the latter, you were seen as a pariah, somehow against the "prince" and the rise to his self-appointed "king" throne, with the "kingmaker's" (daddy's) help, of course.

Not surprisingly at this time, no one was a "Michaels boy/girl," as there was no apparent future to it. The actual Chief wasn't even attempting to hold on to his powerbase anymore, as it was already severely diminished by the voting edicts of those politicos above him and with whom he fell out of favor. Larry certainly wasn't actively recruiting anyone to side with him so few, if any, openly aligned with him. He was a lame duck chief, he knew it, and so did the rest of the department and much of the citizenry of Bensalem Township. It was rumored he was going to retire soon anyway. It was just a matter of time for him to say goodbye to his PD of over twenty-five years and allow for the politically connected police officer son of a former elected township official to take over the reins of his little kingdom.

It was around this time that I learned the hard way that if one was not a card-carrying and outspoken advocate of Deputy Chief Ted Zajac, especially if in an appointed position of some sort (e.g., me on the Tactical Squad), that person was seen as a problem who had to be dealt with by one means or another. Through initial persuasive coaxing by the officer's peers to have him join the Zajac band wagon, to next, if needed, the officer's sergeant making very strong suggestions to join up "or consider the consequences," to, as a last resort, being at the receiving end of an unexpected transfer to an unwanted squad, detail, or shift, were all methods employed to solicit others to dutifully worship at the altar of Ted Zajac. This was the approximate order of progression in the attempted recruitment of me into what we non-team members would soon refer to as "The Dark Side." (Thank you, Yoda.)

I found out I was perceived as one of those problem officers. I was caught a bit off-guard because of my basic naïveté as to what was expected of me in terms of who I was supposed to support within the BPD and how I was supposed to go about it. My actions, or mostly lack thereof, as non-threatening to Zajac as I thought they may be, were not enough. I soon learned that it was also what I was doing off duty, and even with whom it was that I was doing these things, which placed me even deeper into that alleged trouble-maker category.

I must add here...I wasn't a complete political rube at the time. I knew, of course, that it was then-Detective Lieutenant Zajac who was ultimately the one who chose me over a year and a half ago to my position on the Tac Squad. I let him know of my appreciation through my early repeated "thank yous" to him and even more so, I believed, through the quality arrest record that I had amassed while on the squad. After all, those stats made him and the department he was now running look good too. However, I soon gleaned that more was required of me.

The eventual deputy chief and his next-in-commands expected me to not just blindly go along with his political maneuvering and manipulating. That's what I pretty much had been doing as I was more or less apathetic about it all at first. I really just wanted to focus on arresting bad guys. Really! However, he/they later also clearly expected me to outwardly and explicitly support him and his BPD coup-de-tat at the same time. In so many words, he would want me to actively campaign for him and be one of those aforementioned peer counselors who would bring other officers over to his side.

I couldn't just be a purchaser of Amway (aka, Zajac) products. I had to sell them (aka, Zajac) too.

I knew that being a shill and pitchman for this guy, or any person for that matter who is cutting corners, playing politics at this level, and engaging in duplicitous games with people's very livelihoods in an effort to achieve his/her upwardly mobile professional goals, is not what I do. I never have been that type of person and never would be, certainly not in an obvious power-grab situation such as that which was unfolding in my department at the time. That I knew for sure. My parents raised me differently than to overtly endorse this type of person for any role, from dog catcher to police chief.

So, rightly or wrongly, I initially kept my distance and maintained my silence. Just let me do my job and make my arrests. Don't bother me, and I won't bother you.

I learned, however, this stance couldn't be maintained. The reality of it all kicked in before long, as well as my realization that things were really not going well in my police department. I had to start looking behind the curtain at what and who was controlling the inner-workings of the BPD. It may have taken me a bit longer than some others to actually peek behind that curtain, but once I did, I could see the great and powerful Zajac was nothing of the kind.

DC Zajac had learned through one or more others (my Tac Squad sergeant no doubt being one of them) that at best I was basically neutral about what was happening within the BPD during his ascension to power. Apparently, my sources later told me, he and his departmental cronies couldn't get an accurate fix on me, my politics, or my loyalties, especially as it was Zajac who initially appointed me to the Tac Squad, and as a result my allegiance to him should have been omnipresent and unequivocal. When he later was told that I was actually seen to be quasi-friendly with some department members who did NOT necessarily support him and his climb to the top, I knew my days on the Tac Squad were numbered.

The big question to me was…do I pull the plug first or does the DC?

I suppose the beginning of the end of my association with the ever more Darkening Side occurred within the last few months of Eileen's pregnancy. (Yes, I was going to become a first time dad.) During that May and June, we had decided to attend Lamaze birthing classes together at St. Mary's Hospital, in nearby Langhorne, Pennsylvania. As it turned out, two other BPD officers' wives who were also pregnant were coincidently taking the same classes with their husbands. The three Bensalem police officers, with our respective wives on the floor mats next to us, showed up at these classes together for a few weeks in a row. We collectively joked that there was never a Lamaze class and its participants so well protected from bad guys as was this one.

By the second class, the six of us agreed to go to dinner at a small Bensalem restaurant, the Maven Haven, not far from our HQ on Hulmeville Rd. We probably had dinner together after the classes two different times at that same restaurant in the course of a month or so. While PD matters were no doubt discussed at these meals to some degree by the three men/officers at the table, they were not the main topic of discussion by any means. The pending births of our children, the first ones for each of us, tended to be the primary topic of the three couples while munching away at our various entrees. We cops could always meet while on duty and discuss departmental matters if we so desired. With our very pregnant wives at our sides, we kept it more about them and our soon-to-be-born kids. The direction and tone of our dinner conversations actually came rather easily on our collective parts. The pending birth, child, and parenthood discussions clearly won out over any otherwise mundane PD matters.

I should add here, the two other soon-to-be dads/BPD officers at these classes and meals were assigned to the patrol division. Each of us started at about the same time on the force. Like me they were college grads, hired from outside of Bensalem, and intelligent guys who I learned were not afraid to share an opinion or two about our employer, the BPD, and the guy who was now running the show, DC Zajac. They wouldn't necessarily engage in the overt bashing of any supervisor specifically, but would nonetheless ask probing questions regarding our new management and raise concerns about various evolving departmental issues as the transition from Michaels to Zajac became more pronounced. They would engage in these discussions with other officers in somewhat open forums while in HQ at roll call, at our occasional Police Benevolent Association (PBA) meetings, and with various members of the police department. Others would occasionally overhear them and the word would eventually filter back to Zajac, et al., about discontent fomenting within the ranks. The list being kept on these malcontents was growing. You can probably guess whose name was about to be added to it.

Even though I was plainclothes and these two co-workers from the Lamaze class were uniformed patrolmen, we were still at the same pay grade, still under three years on the PD, and would occasionally cross paths and talk while on duty. They/we were among the ranks of mostly newer hires who were finding themselves increasingly more uncomfortable in how the department was currently being run, the whole DC quick climb to the top, and what the future may hold for all of us and our colleagues, especially if not a part of the slowly expanding Team Zajac.

While at the time somewhat isolated from the everyday matters of the uniformed officers, I nevertheless knew that many of them, especially the newer ones, were asking these questions and sharing these concerns about what was happening in our PD management ever more frequently now. Some officers, I learned, were being harassed (squads changed suddenly, vacation time cancelled, no overtime details), just because they were perceived to be "enemies," or in some cases simply because they were not seen as outright supporters of the new regime. And, to make it worse, other officers in turn wouldn't support those being harassed because they were worried about their own names being placed on the departmental hit list and being duly harassed themselves. Many of these officers were brave and rough-and-tumble guys who wouldn't hesitate to take down the front door of a known felon or wrestle a 300-pound drunk to the ground to make an arrest. They'd cower and become shrinking violets, however, when they or their peers were faced with departmental sanctions and edicts which were blatantly unfair on the very surface.

All because of this slow abuse of power on the part of one man. It started at the top directly impacting Chief Michaels, went unchecked for a year or more, and was now slowly working its way downwards. A select handful of Zajac "boys" were benefitting from this, but many others, including the rest of the department and certainly the citizenry of Bensalem, were not.

Lord Acton's axiom from 1887, "Power tends to corrupt, and absolute power corrupts absolutely…," was bearing all too true in the BPD by the late 1970s and early 1980s. It was getting absolutely more corrupt-like as each day went by.

In June of '79, just a few weeks before my son was born, right after roll call one morning, Sgt. Whacky was told by Deputy Chief Zajac that he wanted to address our squad and a few members of the detective division. After grabbing a few loose chairs, about ten of us then crowded into the deputy chief's office. The meeting was a brief one, but certainly an enlightening one for me. While some benign issues regarding equipment, cars, overtime, or similar such topics were initially discussed, after a few minutes it turned into a pep rally by the head of Team Zajac himself. Then, it quickly, and strangely, turned into a rally to beat a recently diagnosed form of cancer. Well, sort of….

The deputy chief began his initial soliloquy by telling us how hard he was working, to include late nights, weekends, etc., to bring this department together, to create better conditions for all of us, and to assist each of us to do our jobs even better. He seemed very serious and adamant in his tone and his delivery during this brief speech.

Okay, this all sounds good to me. Bringing people together, improving working conditions, helping us make our arrests, I can live with that. Maybe he really is trying here.

So far, so good.

But then Deputy Chief Zajac shifted demonstrably in his chair. Clearly, his mood shifted demonstrably with him. Things seemed to be getting darker in the room. Much darker....

With the veins in his neck and on his forehead becoming more engorged as each minute passed, DC Zajac proceeded to tell us that there are members of the Bensalem Police Department, mostly "out there" (tilting his head in the general direction of the patrol officers' roll call area), who are spreading rumors and vicious lies and working to undermine the valiant efforts he's expending to fix this place. In doing so, he even more angrily added, these misguided ones only wish the worst for their fellow officers, the future of the PD, and the citizens of Bensalem.

"These men are a cancer growing within our ranks and must be dealt with accordingly," I then heard him exclaim to all in the room with elevated purpose and volume.

A cancer...? Within our ranks...? Must be dealt with...? Geez, these are pretty strong words. Machiavellian-like, some would say.

Okay...and this is interesting too. He seems to be looking in my direction more so than at the others while pontificating here.

Am I imagining this...?

The DC ended his little cancer-infused motivational speech by now staring directly at me. It wasn't my imagination. He then emphatically stated, with his two eyes most definitely affixed upon mine, "If these guys are your friends, if you want to meet with them for dinner at a restaurant up the road, that's on you. But you won't be spreading this f**kin' cancer while working for ME in THIS division."

Geez, the cancer analogy again. What's up with this guy and his terminal disease references today?

While consciously adjusting my body position a bit to avoid the direct, and quite admittedly, uncomfortable stare of the very resolute deputy chief, I happened to notice at least four other guys in the room staring at me at the same time and nodding their heads up and down in obvious agreement with what was being said. It's almost as if they knew in advance what the sermon topic would be today. My own lamebrain Sgt. Whacky and the doughy CID detective Sgt. Pansy, the one who forbade me from carrying my hidden revolver on my undercover drug buy, owned at least two of these vertically bobbing heads.

Being sometimes a bit slow on the uptake, it nonetheless finally hit me.

This whole meeting, this whole speech, was about me, Jim Fitzgerald.

It must be about me because 1) almost half the people in the room were staring at me during Zajac's strongly worded admonition; 2) it struck me that the DC must be talking about my recent dinners with the two patrol officers who could loosely fit his description of the "cancer" spreading throughout; 3) it must be the Maven Haven as it is coincidently the only restaurant "up the road;" and 4) it must be "THIS" division, as it's now in the Detective Division where I happen to be assigned and where I'm presently sitting.

So, it's not my imagination.

Now what do I do?

I realized leaving the meeting that morning that, in effect, it was being strongly suggested to me that I shouldn't eat dinner with, perhaps go to birthing classes with, and I suppose even otherwise socialize with, BPD members who do not fit the mold or have the membership qualifications of the numerous Team Zajac political adherents. Don't even think of having them as my friends. Not in this cancer-free zone.

I realized for the first time that morning that I was now an outcast, an outlier, on the Tac Squad and in the CID, having been recently diagnosed as being cancerous, or at least suspected of being a carrier of some sort. Since it could be contagious as far as the boss was concerned, I had to be dealt with, somehow.

What could be the cure? Who should prescribe it?

The medicine, or at least the temporary Band-Aid, wasn't too far off.

Prior to any movement on anyone's part in this regard, there was some relatively good news for me in terms of my every day job, and with whom I'd be doing it. Two senior members of my plainclothes unit left to become acting detectives in CID. Yes, they were both out-spoken advocates of the new regime and thusly "earned" their way into the then faux-competitive tested detective ranks. Because of this, there were two new patrolmen added to my squad in their stead. One was Steve Moran, who started on the job just a few months after me and I helped train when he first came to my patrol squad. Now I'd be training him again, but this time in the art of undercover police operations. The other new Tac Squad officer was Terry Lachman, who actually came onto the BPD in the academy class right before mine in '76. Essentially, all three of us started on the job within about six months of each other, so we were all still pretty much new officers. For that reason, as well as the fact that they were good cops and good guys (and from what I could tell, more or less neutral regarding the current management situation), I welcomed them wholeheartedly onto the squad.

Interestingly, I suppose because I was so new upon first coming onto the Tac Squad when I did, by the time these two men came to join me it was seemingly not a big deal for them or anyone else. We newer guys now represented half the squad. Sgt. Whacky didn't seem to direct his animus towards them as he did me when I first started. Good for Steve and Terry. I certainly didn't want them to feel as unwelcome on the squad as I did when I first arrived. With that in mind, I did everything I could to make them feel at home. They appreciated it, they told me at the time and later too.

While the squad and the work itself were a bit more tolerable now with these two new members on board, I still knew that things weren't as they should be and I wasn't very happy in my position anymore. The bloom had definitely come off of the departmental rose for me. I'm not sure if it was just being on this particular squad and under the all-too watchful eyes of this maniacal sergeant who reports directly to the deputy chief. Maybe it was the BPD itself or perhaps I was just losing verve of being a police officer all together. It was definitely a time of deep reflection as to who I was, where I was, and what it was I was doing for a living.

Something, someone, had to give here. No doubt soon, too.

After the lecture by DC Zajac, I recalled three other incidents that obviously were designed to let me know that I'd better shape up and get on their team or changes were a-coming.

The first involved me losing an earned (or so I wholeheartedly believed) day off with pay because of a departmental policy which rewarded officers who did not have a vehicular accident the calendar year before. I would have had that day off in '79, except during an ice storm the previous winter I slid while turning, hit a curb, and bent the front wheel of my unmarked car. It was not an accident per se, but Sgt. Whacky wrote it up like it was one and that I should not get the bonus day off. So, I didn't that year, unlike every other year so far.

I also recalled that in April of '79, there was a call of a suspicious vehicle somewhere in the township and for some legitimate work-related reason I did not immediately respond to it. Whatever the initial call and the car was supposed to be, it turned out to be nothing. Because of my non-response to roll on it right away (as per my ever diligent sergeant), I was ordered to write a memo to both the sergeant and the deputy chief. Nothing officially ever came of it, but just the fact that I had to write the memo and it was now a permanent entry in my personnel file was a clear attempt at the time to maintain control over me and remind me again of just who was in charge here.

Lastly, there were the basketball court confrontations with the Deputy Chief. Fouls could be called on him (we self-refereed, of course), defense could be played, and his shots could be blocked, but one better be prepared to pay the price then and off-court for the next few days or longer back at the PD. That's when the "technical" would be called on the offending, or defending, player/officer.

Someone on the PD had a contact at one of the private Catholic schools in the township. Every Thursday night we had the full size indoor basketball court to ourselves. Just cops versus cops. It could be a good workout, a morale booster, and a healthy competition on most of those nights for the eight or ten of us who showed up. That is, unless Deputy Chief Zajac donned his jersey, laced up his sneakers, and decided to join "his men." If you wound up on the team opposing him, you better choose not to play defense on him. The little guy didn't like it. If he hacked you while taking a shot or dribbling toward the basket for a layup, it wasn't wise to call a foul on him. He didn't like that either.

If in any way an opposing team member did something to make Zajac look bad on the court (and he really didn't need much help in that area), the wise-ass and confrontational comments from him would begin. Initially they would be somewhat subtle to the defender or foul victim himself. Then, as the aggrieved DC was walking away from the scene of the foul, he'd be heard to make other less-than-positive remarks about the same player to a fellow Team Zajac (basketball-wise AND departmental-wise) member. Not to the guy's face at that point, but as backs were turned. Yet he always made sure the insulting comments were loud enough for most to hear. And, of course, his sycophants would laugh with him, even if they were on my team.

Yes, I stole the ball from Zajac. Yes, I blocked his shots. Yes, I called HIM for a foul on me. Each time, it would be met with long looks of disgust, obvious anger, and then the walking away from me, just barely audible snarky comments, all from this so-called leader of men. It was even more interesting to watch as other players, those who were either scared of the Deputy Chief or one of his departmental flying monkeys (as in *The Wizard of Oz*), or both, would not play defense against him at all, ever call a foul on him, and the like. It was actually quite funny and quite sad at the same time.

After a few of these basketball court-related or next day confrontations, including one in which my nicer, newer unmarked car was taken away from me for a few days for no real reason, I had enough of the orange ball, at least on Thursday nights with my fellow PD members. It just wasn't worth it. I'd find other ways to exercise and blow off steam. The Deputy Chief's everyday antics in the workplace were enough to bother me. I didn't need to see him while playing a game I spent a lifetime enjoying. He found something else to ruin for me there, too. What a leader!

Regarding the other issues, I realized later that year that other Tac Squad officers had sustained dents and dings on their cars of their own doing, and/or caused damage costlier to fix than my one bent wheel, yet still got their "earned" days off with pay. On other occasions, for whatever reasons, fellow Tac officers had also not responded or tardily responded to one call or another, and/or missed a felony crime committed right in front of them on one of their details, yet did not have to sit down at a departmental IBM Selecta-type like me and pound out a written mea culpa as to why they didn't do or see what they were allegedly supposed to do or see. It was just me on the Tac Squad, as it turned out, who was selectively chosen to be reinforced with more negatives than positives, to include on the basketball court too. These minuses can mentally add up after a while, especially with an otherwise lack of pluses on the other side of the ledger.

It was dawning on me, and more so with each passing day, that I was clearly not a favorite son of the BPD powers-that-be, and it was only a matter of time before things would change somehow for me. But at the same time, I realized I had my own favorite son. His name was Sean. (He was my only son at the time.) His birth in July of '79 was forcing me to think in a more abstract and future-oriented fashion, about him, about me, about my slowly growing family, my job, my profession, and what would be best for all of us at this time.

Yes, it was time for a change. It would no doubt lead to better things for all of us. It had to. It was only a question of how, when, and to where to best effect that change.

Sometimes, I learned around this stage in my life, different and even unrelated matters suddenly come together and line up concordantly to assist in the making of one or more decisions at a given time. It may just result in being hit with a figurative "thunderbolt," to borrow a mind-altering, decision-enhancing metaphorical reference from Mario Puzo's *The Godfather*. That was about to happen with me. It would involve my job, my wife's job, a new police contract, and Villanova University.

It was all starting to fall into place now. And being struck by that forthcoming bolt of figurative lightning wouldn't hurt me a bit.

Chapter Fourteen

I want to make it clear here again that even during this ongoing frustrating time in my early Bensalem Police career, I still had that "Eye of the Tiger," as it applied to my everyday duties. I loved being on the hunt for bad guys and arresting them whenever the probable cause permitted. Whether it was roaming the shopping centers and strip malls, the streets and highways, on surveillances in billboards, or stakeouts at other locations, it didn't matter. At the beginning of each shift, once I cleared the parking lot of the BPD headquarters and its growing toxic effluvia of political moroseness, I felt like a new and inspired man and a duly rejuvenated officer of the law.

Bring it on, criminals! Give me the best you got! I'll find you and arrest you, or at least I'll give it my best in trying - internal politics be damned!

That being said....

At the same time, as a Tac Squad member, I was enjoying less and less my close proximity to the political machinations which were taking place at the top of the organizational pyramid, and the increasing machinations taking place by some (but not all) of my fellow officers closer to the bottom of the pyramid where I was dwelling. These included several of the senior guys with whom I was assigned to work alongside of every day. Ones who were supposed to "have my back" in potentially dangerous situations, or at least ones I hoped would have my back, and front, in such situations.

What I was hearing and observing every time in the "backroom," aka CID, aka the detective division, to include the number of closed door meetings (with sometimes the deputy chief's office door being purposefully and forcefully closed once I was spotted in the area), I could clearly see that the rift developing between the Zajac boys and those who weren't in the same camp was clearly widening. I was growing exceedingly tired of the personality clashes between members of the two sides, even if sometimes subtle, but which could nonetheless effect the personal safety of the officers (including me) while on the street. I wanted to once again just focus on my job. I also did not want to feel I was supposed to be eternally beholden to a certain deputy chief just because a year and a half ago he appointed me to this then seemingly desirable plainclothes position. It was becoming less desirable every day for me to show up for my job as a marked man, at least from an internal political perspective.

I just needed one extra factor in my everyday life to make that move, to somehow effect that change in my professional life.

Well, how about four of them?

Through the summer and fall of '79, my wife was off from work on official maternity leave. It was a very enjoyable time for her and us. We were debating how to handle the upcoming demise of that generous program from her company near the end of the year. We were leaning towards her quitting all together and becoming a full-time stay-at-home mom. Just when that seemed the logical thing to do, her company offered her a compelling option. Knowing she was a brand new mom, the management folks there asked her if she wanted to work part-time, from 8A-1P every day.

Hmmm…was that possible? Could we do that?

Eileen and I talked it over. We didn't want to go the babysitter route. Not when Sean was still an infant, anyway. And I knew my Tac Squad sergeant would not allow me to work steady 4P-12A shifts, which would then have afforded me the opportunity to be home with our son in the morning hours while my wife was at work. Although there were generally at least two of us plainclothes officers working that later shift on a weekly basis, I knew Sgt. Whacky wouldn't give it to me fulltime if I asked. It was not his style to give me something that he KNEW would make my life easier, especially not in these ever widening contentious times between the two growing factions within the PD.

So, what would be another option here…?

I know. How about if I left the Tac Squad and went back to the patrol division?

That's a definite possibility…more so than I've recently thought. If I did that, with the present patrol officers' schedule, there'd only be four days of day-work each month in which I could not be at home with Sean. Either my wife wouldn't work those days, or we would somehow find a trusted, part-time babysitter to help out on those days.

Plus, although I'd be returning to the same rotating shift schedule as when I had originally started on patrol, i.e., a week of midnights, a week of evenings, and then six (out of seven) day-works, with a five-day long weekend afterwards, there was a strong rumor floating around that the BPD was looking into permanent ten-hour shifts for the patrol officers; in other words, no more rotating around the clock. The rumored new shifts for the uniformed officers would be steady midnights, evenings, or day-work, respectively, with some overlapping evening hours, and ten-hour tours per shift. That would result in fifty-two less work days per year, it was calculated. The officers would work the same number of hours per year, of course, but doing so only four days per week on average.

I had always enjoyed the second shift the best, as it was the busiest, so IF I transferred back to patrol, and IF they eventually changed the schedule, I would ask for the proposed 3P-1A shift. That should work for me and my wife's new part-time opportunity.

Interesting option here. Should I put in for that transfer, back to patrol?

Hmmm...maybe not yet. Let me think some more about it. This would be a major decision on my part. It would affect substantive parts of my life and could alter the direction of my present career path, whatever that may be right now. Being a plainclothes cop is a nice assignment, there were some very real bennies to it. Perhaps it's not THAT bad...at least for now.

With all this going on, that is, me contemplating changes in my professional life which would certainly affect my personal life, and for reasons still not completely clear to me after all these years, I began thinking more and more about my formal education during this time frame. I was wondering if there were any options out there to enhance my existing academic achievements, to possibly open up some future doors for me; if not in the BPD, then perhaps elsewhere. Having my four-year degree from Penn State provided a great start to my young career. It no doubt already opened a few doors for me. However, I came to realize that in any profession the more formal education a person may have, to include actual degrees in one or more related fields, the more potential long-term benefits there are for the degree holder. That was no different in the law enforcement profession in the late '70s and early '80s in the U.S.

I was aware of officers being promoted in other nearby departments and agencies to upper-management or even the position of chief of police. While some of them had four-year degrees, none of whom I was aware had a master's degree, or was even working on one. Quite frankly, at least one of the reasons they didn't was because there were very few criminal justice- related graduate program choices during this time frame, at least in the general Philadelphia area. If so, they were generic majors such as sociology or public administration. While there is nothing wrong with either of those degree programs or areas of concentration, I felt if this was something I wanted to pursue, something in which I was going to invest my time and my money, I would want it more germane, more specific, as it related to my every-day duties and responsibilities, or the duties and responsibilities I was someday hoping to attain, such as in mid- to upper management in a law enforcement agency.

While having a four-year B.S. or B.A. degree was rare enough in the police ranks during this time period, having a master's degree was all but unheard of in law enforcement. Maybe in places like the NYPD or the LAPD officers could be found with an M.S or M.A., but most likely not anywhere near my town of Bensalem. Maybe I could be a groundbreaker in that regard. I was still pretty young, barely 27 years old. If I could have this advanced degree by my early 30s, that would possibly mean I could move to the head of the pack of those competing for management positions either in the BPD or outside. Maybe....

In my late teens and well into my twenties, I certainly never pictured myself progressing that far in one or more academic environ-ments. I figured by the time I had graduated from Penn State in '75, a full sixteen years of formal education under my belt was enough for me and should be all I needed for any upward mobility in my chosen career. But now, for some reason, additional keys to unlocking additional doors in front of me seemed necessary to pursue and attain. It's as if I slowly realized that something was missing from my life, professionally anyway, and I needed to fill that void in a way that it wasn't being filled at my everyday job.

What did this all mean to me? I really didn't know yet. But I was gradually coming to the conclusion that the CID, and possibly even the BPD itself, may NOT be my home forever. IF I was to go back to patrol I realized the logical course from the Tac Squad to the detec-tive division was now derailed, perhaps so forever, certainly under this present regime. If I was to advance in my career, either here or possibly elsewhere, it would most likely have to be in a management position where there was competitive testing to attain those positions. While I think I had it in me to be a good manager/boss someday, I knew that having yet another diploma to help get me there, within or without the

BPD, would certainly make sense. So, at some point down the line, I'll have to check on this. Yes, one of these days....

One of those days happened to be actually at nighttime, in the late fall of '79, while on a Tac Squad stakeout at some quiet location with nothing of relevance happening at whatever it was I was watching. While reading sections of the *Philadelphia Inquirer* Sunday newspaper that I had brought with me to pass the time, I gradually found myself perusing the multi-page employment section. In that section every Sunday was also an "Education" sub-section, which highlighted, through short articles and paid advertising, various schools in the Philadelphia area and the numerous classes, programs, and degrees they were now offering.

I happened upon a four-inch by four-inch square ad in the upper corner of page two or three of that newspaper section. It was for the Villanova University Graduate School. Under the emboldened all upper-case school name were the words, "Master of Science in Human Organizational Science." Beneath that, it listed in bullet form the three tracks in that program in which a student could enroll. They were Nursing, Correctional, and Law Enforcement. The first two didn't necessarily interest me but the last category clearly caught my attention. As I read to the bottom of the ad, I learned that the program was being offered part-time, with one-night per week of evening classes, and with no Graduate Record Exam (GRE) required for entry. Only that this test had to be taken sometime before graduation.

Hmmm...I had been thinking about graduate school for some time now and here, when I wasn't even seriously searching for it, this program sort of falls onto my lap, interestingly under the dull whiteness of my unmarked car's interior dome light. With Villanova being less than an hour away from Bensalem via (mostly) the Pennsylvania Turnpike, I figured this may be worth further exploring.

After an uneventful work shift the previous night, the next day I called the phone number at the bottom of the Villanova ad and spoke to a program representative. She enthusiastically described the degree program as a combination of Organizational Psychology and a Master's of Business Administration (MBA). It was designed for public sector institutions and agencies, with academic tracks for present or future nurse managers, prison administrators, and police department supervisors. This program was brand new, certainly in the greater Philadelphia area, officially starting in the next year, and the more we talked that day the more it seemed right up my newly planned professional alley.

If not during the first phone call, it was during a subsequent one that I even talked to the professor who was heading up this new degree program. He was very informative and equally enthusiastic as his staff member. He said there were a number of Philadelphia police officers and other suburban and state police officers who had contacted him and he was looking forward to the vibrant mix of professionals gradually enrolling in the program for these courses. I thanked him for his time and told him he may just have one more name before long to add to that growing vibrancy.

That would be, of course, IF I was in the mood to go back to school after almost five whole years away from text books, classrooms, studying, term papers, mid-terms, finals, instructors, etc. The professor to whom I most recently spoke seemed like a nice enough guy, committed to this new program, and not an egghead or someone who acted like he was permanently locked away in the protective shell of his ivied walls. He seemed to know his stuff, could talk the talk, and seemingly understood the world of law enforcement. He also recognized that there was a need for further education and learning opportunities within my field and certainly within the metropolitan Philadelphia area. I decided in one phone call that I liked this Villanova professor and his attitude, without even having met him yet. That was a good sign.

So, what was my mood at the time? Was I ready for this possible new adventure? Was I ready to renter a college classroom, of all places?

Upon not all that much internal reflection, my present mood did tell me that I needed something outside of my own daily employment at the BPD to further professionally motivate and reward me. Being appreciated for who I was and what I was doing, especially when being done rather successfully, would be nice again. The way things were going at the BPD, these types of little rewards weren't going to happen there anytime soon. So even if for the next few years it was in a graduate school classroom, and the appreciation was simply in the form of a positive response to me raising my hand to offer an intelligent (hopefully) point of view, or receiving an "A" (again, hopefully) on an exam or paper I had previously submitted to my professor, that could work for me. Plus, even more importantly, it would potentially open wide those future doors for me, in my own PD or somewhere else.

Per my request, the Villanova University rep mailed me a brochure and a grad school application. I talked it over with Eileen and I decided within a few weeks that I would apply to this brand new program.

Of course, as with any college or university application, there is no guarantee that one will be accepted into it. Villanova University was and is a highly rated academic institution and it doesn't admit just anyone. I made sure to write a very strong and positive "mission statement" regarding my professional goals and aspirations, which was required as part of the admission application along with my Penn State transcript and other material.

But before actually mailing off the application, I had one more issue to research. I wanted to confirm in our recently negotiated three-year police contract, in which the BPD had agreed to pay eighty percent of the tuition of any officer's college or university courses which were "law enforcement related," that it also covered grad school classes and not just undergraduate ones. Upon discussing this matter with our on-retainer PBA lawyer, it was officially determined that the legal language therein didn't differentiate between the two. That was good enough for me.

The Human Organizational Science (HOS) degree program at Villanova, as well as the individually listed courses on the law enforcement track syllabus, were certainly related to my job and my profession, so my goal was to have the BPD pay for it, or at least four-fifths of it. The only condition was that the officer/student attains at least a "B" in each course. I could do that. I would do that. As I wasn't necessarily flush with extra cash flow at the time, I would need these not-inexpensive graduate courses to be mostly paid for by my department if I didn't want to go into debt. That alone was incentive for me to work for at a minimum a B-grade in each course, with an A-grade naturally as the actual goal in each.

So, it all made sense as far as I was concerned. It had all just come together. I only needed that acceptance letter from Villanova. And I received it within a month. I would soon be not just a Bensalem cop, but a Villanova University graduate student too; a part-time one, anyway.

By the end of December of 1979, only my wife and Bob Yezzi were aware of this plan of mine. I told him because, firstly, he was a trusted friend and colleague, and secondly, he was a Villanova University graduate. When telling Bob of this for the first time, I peppered him with various logistical questions regarding the campus, parking, the professors, student body, etc. These queries were similar in some ways to his phone call to me just a few years earlier when he was first contemplating coming to the BPD. Just as I advised him back then, Bob was now advising me of what I needed to know about a future venture on my part. As I was to him a few years ago, Bob too was very supportive of this initiative on my part.

Before long, finding some alone time one evening in the detective division, I sat down once again at a departmental IBM typewriter and watched as the spinning metallic ball, following electronic orders from my fingertips, placed individual letters which turned into individual words onto the blank piece of white paper behind the machine's cylindrical carriage.

When complete, under the "To," "From," and "Date" headings, the memo read as follows:

> "For various personal and professional reasons, I respectfully request a permanent transfer from the Tactical Squad to the Patrol Division.
> Thank you."
> (End of memo.)

I initialed next to my name and put it in Deputy Chief Zajac's mailbox outside of his office door. I know for chain of command purposes I should have cut a copy to Sgt. Whacky, but I didn't. He'd find out soon enough and he'd be so happy he wouldn't care I skipped him in this step. So what, he'd give me a hard time because I didn't give him a copy? What would be the difference then as opposed to practically everything else I did on his squad? We'd both be ultimately glad with what was requested in this memo, and even gladder when the request was granted. No doubt about it.

It was done. And in just those few words I utilized in that memo, I felt it spoke volumes. It was clearly "personal" and it was clearly "professional" factors that led me to take this step, and I wanted to make that clear to DC Zajac in my own minimalist way in that one sentence. I was tempted to add a third adjective to modify my reasons, that being "political," to make it even more accurate, but I decided against it at the last minute.

As for the timing of my request, I wanted to work "normal" hours for my new baby's first Christmas, so I dated and handed in my memo a day or two after the holiday. Within days, by means of a similarly formatted and minimally worded memo in my time card slot, I had my response from the boss. I was to be reassigned to the patrol division the very first week of 1980.

It was a somewhat unexpected ending to the decade, and a somewhat ominous beginning to the next one. However, at least to some degree, I was now in control of my destiny. I'm the one who made the decision to move on, move back, move sideways, whatever way one chooses to look at my request to rejoin the patrol division. I'd have to relearn the tactics and techniques and even some new paperwork as a patrol officer again, but that shouldn't be a problem. I succeeded as a brand new patrolman right out of the academy just a few years before. I can do it now again, this second time around, with ease.

My uniform pants, holster, etc., still fit. That was good news. All I needed was to get a haircut. It had been awhile. Hopefully my barely six-month old son Sean would recognize me with shorter hair. It would actually stay short after this for the rest of my law enforcement career and well into my official retirement years. Men's hair styles were changing too around this time; just like me in many ways.

In closing here and looking back at this self-initiated transition in my career, it is interesting to reflect on where I was in life at that time. At the beginning of this just ended decade, I was a junior at Cardinal Dougherty High School in Philadelphia. At the end of the new one, I would be an FBI special agent assigned to the New York City office. This night, marking the virtual center point between the beginning and end of these two decades, I realized that I had just voluntarily transferred out of an allegedly elite plainclothes squad and was about to be a patrol officer again. Yet, approaching midnight on December 31, 1979, and as it turned into January 1, 1980, I wasn't thinking of ten years backwards or ten years forward. It was mostly about my family and where I was in life with them right then and there. I hoped that I had done the right thing, for both my and their sakes.

It was a major career decision for me. One I wasn't technically forced to make, although it probably would have been made for me eventually by those on The Dark Side. It would undoubtedly play well for me from a political perspective, i.e., not being around or directly associated with Team Zajac anymore and being forced to witness up close what they were doing, or for that matter, they witnessing up close what I was doing. From a personal perspective, my wife could work part-time while I was home with Sean in the morning hours and it would also facilitate me later attending graduate school.

I was concerned with how the next year or two would play out as it related to my future and the future of the Bensalem Police Department and its leadership. I didn't like the way the latter was going. Maybe something or someone would change things. I could only hope. I had to make these changes right now though for me. I had no regrets so far.

I didn't really make an official resolution that New Year's Eve approaching midnight. It was just me and Eileen, with Bob Yezzi and a lady friend of his, celebrating it quietly at my house with my baby son asleep in his bedroom. At the magic hour, the four adults in the house that night each raised a glass of relatively inexpensive champagne and wished each other a healthy, happy, and successful 1980.

If 1980 was a healthy, happy, and successful year for the four of us at its beginning, things clearly changed on August 12 of that year. It would be anything but after that date - especially for one of us in the room that night.

March 1979, Bensalem PD vs. Philadelphia Eagles

July 1980, Jim Fitzgerald and Bob Yezzi

Part 3 -
Back in Patrol Division

Chapter Fifteen

The transition back to patrolman status for me was not all that difficult beginning in January of 1980. As mentioned earlier, it was time for a change. I initiated that change, and this is where I would now be assigned for the foreseeable future. I would make it work for me. I was back on the same rotating eight-hour per shift schedule as when I started, although with a different squad. All of the patrol division was waiting to hear from management as to if or when the new ten-hour day schedule would be implemented. Some officers were really psyched over the possibility of it. Me, I didn't waste time worrying about things over which I had no control. If it happened, it happened. I just had to get re-acclimated to my old schedule and wearing a uniform again.

My new patrol sergeant had been previously assigned to the detective division. His name was Robert Eckert. He was assigned as a brand new sergeant to the patrol division two years ago. It was about the same time I went to the Tac Squad, so our paths had not officially crossed up until this time. Now, he was my new boss.

Sgt. Eckert was in his early 30s, about six feet tall, in relatively good physical shape, with a mustache which was just a bit longer than but otherwise very similar to Adolph Hitler's famous lip hair. I guess it worked for him. Eckert was also in the military reserves. One weekend per month, and two weeks every summer he would go off on his reserve duties. During that time, if our squad was working, there would be an acting sergeant in charge. I was still pretty low on the seniority totem pole, so there was never an occasion during this second stint in patrol that I was asked to assume that mantle. I was fine with that.

Eckert was not a very personable guy, at least with his squad subordinates. At the same time, he was a by-the-book sort of manager. Every "i" had to be dotted, and every "t" had to be crossed with him, both literally in our report writing, and also in our appearance, how we comported ourselves on the street, in HQ, and the like. I had no problem with this form of personnel management. Thanks to my parents, sisters, some good teachers, and others, those work habits were formed in me early in my life and carried over to my first three full years on the BPD.

Sgt. Eckert never displayed much of a sense of humor, emotionality, or even personality, but that didn't bother me either. Others on our squad didn't always handle these attributes, or lack thereof, so well, but they would eventually learn how to get by. As for me, Eckert's more-or-less robotic persona was not a problem.

Sgt. Eckert was no Gene Ashton on multiple levels, but thankfully he also wasn't my most recent managerially-challenged Tac Squad sergeant either. I knew what I had in this guy and I'd like to think he knew what he had in me. In that regard, and in that regard only, we complemented each other well. For these very basic and surface reasons, I respected him and got along with him at the time in our supervisor/subordinate time together in patrol.

This relationship would change drastically within about four years when each of our roles within the department would be different. What I didn't realize upon initially working for Eckert were his secretive affiliations with the Dark Side and his long-term political ambitions within the department. These ambitions even included his wife becoming a player in Bensalem politics before too long. She probably was already so-engaged in same but the two of them kept it on the hush-hush to the rest of those without a "need-to-know."

This family-member-as-politician promotional technique seemed to be a discernible and pervasive pattern within the BPD during my years there, whether initially explicit or implicit to those of us in the rank-and-file. That is, an officer's father and/or wife would be elected to or appointed to public office in Bensalem, who thus would work, if not legislate, to further facilitate their loved one's career and potential upward mobility. (Ted Zajac has the lone distinction of actually having one of each in office at separate times during his tenure; first a father then later a wife.)

I certainly learned very soon that this sort of daddy/bride-on top management pyramid is NOT an effective or efficient way to run a police department, or no doubt any organization for that matter. It is known as nepotism. It may be great for the few related family members, but not so great for those among the unrelated others.

Sgt. Eckert was covertly on Team Zajac, a sleeper, hiding in plain sight if you will, as would become all too evident within just a few years. He was probably sent to the patrol division in '78, maybe even volunteering for it after he first made sergeant, to be the eyes and ears in that division for the burgeoning Team, checking for signs of a further metastasizing cancer among its members, and dutifully reporting name after name to the deputy chief once so diagnosed. It probably wasn't a coincidence that I wound up on his squad. What better way to monitor my associations and demeanor as those near the top continued to build their political dynasty.

Despite Sgt. Eckert's leanings in one departmental political direction, and my leanings in the other, we managed to survive each other during the time of this professional relationship. The first eight months or so in patrol were relatively routine for me. Some decent arrests (one in particular to be discussed shortly), some interesting calls, but with a new son at home, weekday morning times with him while my wife worked, and grad school on the horizon, my priorities had been shifted. Show up for work on time, put in your eight hours, do your job well, keep your mouth shut (well, mostly), and go home. I was professionally much more than that for most of my career so far at the BPD, but it's where I had to be for now, just for survival sake.

Chapter Sixteen

Without a doubt, excelling in some upcoming grad courses would be great, but I still considered my accomplishments on the street as what truly defined me as a law enforcement professional during this stage of my career. One of the more significant of these accomplishments occurred when I was a uniformed police officer. It is one of the arrests of which I am most proud during this stage of my career. At the same time, I fully understood and was sympathetic to the fact that it was the result of a very unfortunate incident which greatly traumatized a person.

The arrest was for a sexual assault and rape.

In the early spring of 1980, a Canadian company sent a dozen or so of its employees to a two week-long management training program at a commercial facility in Bensalem. They were all staying at a large two-story hotel, part of a nationwide chain, near the intersection of Street Rd. and Route 1. The program, however, was never completed by one of the women who was part of this group of eager young mid-level corporate managers. During the second week of her otherwise enjoyable workplace management training course with her co-workers, she was brutally raped by a complete stranger in her hotel room sometime after 2:00 in the morning.

That night, while working an 11P-7A shift, I was notified by dispatch to respond to this particular hotel for a report of a break-in and a sexual assault in one of the rooms there. I wasn't far from the location and within a minute or so I arrived and parked in front of the lobby. Once out of the car and inside the lobby I was directed by hotel staff to turn to my left down a long hallway to a room with its door open and a few people milling around. As I was directed inside the room by an older male (later identified as one of the supervisors of this Canadian group), I noticed two other women there. They both appeared to be in their mid-twenties. One of them was lying in the fetal position on the floor in a corner. She was crying uncontrollably. She was wearing a white bathrobe with its belt tied tightly around her waist. The other woman was dressed in jeans and a t-shirt and kneeling alongside her while attempting to hold her and stroke her hair and comfort her in any way she could. It was clearly not working despite her gallant efforts.

As I approached the two of them and knelt down beside them, the woman who was in the somewhat vertical position whispered to me what little she knew so far. Between the sobs of the woman on the floor she told me that Susan (fictitious name), her friend and co-worker now lying next to us, had called her room across the hall about a half hour ago. She was hysterical on the phone and at first what she was saying didn't make much sense. Finally, it came out that she (Susan) had been sound asleep in her bed but had been suddenly and very rudely awakened by a man who had climbed in through the first floor hotel room window. He then grabbed her very tightly around the neck, tore off her bed clothes, and "forced himself" on her. This all occurred sometime in the last hour. Once he completed his violent mission, the friend continued, he exited the room by the same means which he entered, that is, through the window. It took a few minutes over the phone and later in the victim's hotel room to learn of this information, but that's all she could tell me right now.

I thanked the friend and turned away from her to next try to talk to the still crying woman maintaining a horizontal position on the floor. She finally opened her eyes, saw that I was a police officer, and unconsciously grabbed onto my hand. I took her hand in mine with the most reassuring and comforting grip I could offer back to her. I then bent over a bit and told her I needed some very basic information from her and, if she was up to it, I'd like to ask her a few questions as soon as she's ready. Upon hearing my request, she slowly came out of her sideways fetal position and while still holding my hand the whole time she managed to sit herself up in the corner. As she wiped away the tears with the terrycloth robe sleeve on her free hand, she simply said with what appeared to be a newly found purpose, "What do you want to know, Officer?"

Although I was already told it by her friend, I nonetheless asked the woman her name. "Susan," she responded. I asked her to please call me Jim.

I then stated, "Susan, I'm a Bensalem police officer and I'm here to help you. I'm here to find out what happened to you and find the man who did it. Could you answer a few questions for me?"

Susan nodded her head up and down and whispered a barely audible, "Yes."

I then asked her, "To the best you can remember, I need to know what happened and the description of the man who did this to you. Can you tell me?"

While what the friend told me was potentially important, I still had to get the information from the rape victim herself, at least at this very preliminary stage of the investigation. There was something I had to do in the next few minutes but I needed her first to answer just a few basic questions from me. I had to do it gently though. Her well-being and mental condition was the priority right now in her very understandably fragile and vulnerable state.

While still sobbing a bit, and pushing aside her long brown hair which had sort of matted onto the right side of her face, Susan responded by stating, "I think it was right at 2:15 when I heard the window slide open. Geez...why was it ever unlocked? Anyway, it was kinda dark but I recall looking at the bedside clock as soon as the noise woke me up. Then, right away he, this man, jumped on top of me, grabbed my neck, told me to be quiet or else, ripped off what I was wearing. Then...then...he...it was awful. I feel so dirty...and..." She couldn't finish her sentence.

I said, "That's okay. We can talk about some of this later. I know it was dark in here but can you give me any description of this man...his age, race, clothing, anything at all about him that you can recall?"

Susan hesitated some, but then now sitting up a bit straighter against the wall stated with some confidence, "All I can say is that he was white, probably in his 20s, medium-length dark colored hair, a mustache, I guess an average build...and that's about it."

As I was writing this information down in my little notebook, I asked if there was anything else, maybe even something seemingly minor, something different about him, which she could possibly add to his description.

After momentarily thinking about it, Susan replied, "Well, now that you asked...I remember him having some sort of a necklace or chain around his neck. I could see the little bit of outside lighting coming in through the open window reflecting off a piece of it, either a medal or locket of some sort in the front of it, dangling and moving back and forth as he...well, you know. That's really all I remember. I don't even know what he was wearing, when he was wearing his clothes. It was really dark you know, I closed my eyes for most of it, he was hurting me...oh, this is so awful and disgusting. Why me? WHY ME!?"

While squeezing her hand to express my best attempt at non-verbal understanding and empathy towards her, yet never answering her last question, I told Susan what she told me was valuable information and I thanked her for it. She squeezed my hand back in silence, perhaps as her own non-verbal sign of appreciation toward me. I next advised Susan we were going to take her to a local hospital for a check-up. I asked her if she would be okay with that. She nodded her head up and down to signify "Yes," then broke down and started crying again. Her friend, I learned her name to be Jocelyn, still kneeling beside her, took her back into her arms and pulled her closer towards her. They both began rocking back and forth at this time in a slow but constant motion on the floor. I excused myself after gingerly extricating my hand from Susan's, but telling her at the same time that I'd be right back. She again nodded her head and very reluctantly allowed my hand to slip from hers.

Upon attaining this very preliminary information from the victim, I stood up and quickly exited the room. In the hallway, with a few more of the victim's fellow employees now milling around, I used my portable police radio and contacted the BPD dispatcher. I advised him to send the rescue squad right away and to also notify our detective division because this was a confirmed sexual assault and rape. In a separate message just seconds after speaking to the dispatcher, I also broadcast what cops call the "Flash Information" regarding a crime. Since this crime of rape had occurred less than an hour ago, I wanted to put out the rapist's description to my fellow officers and the other neighboring PDs on our radio band. In doing so, I related on my portable the exact description that Susan had told me with the hopes that this guy was perhaps hitchhiking or walking somewhere, or that maybe one of my fellow officers had a run-in with a guy fitting this description earlier in the evening, or maybe even in the last sixty minutes. I knew it wasn't much of a "Flash," but I had to get it out there.

Within fifteen minutes, the rescue squad arrived at the hotel room. Before going with them, Susan told me she wanted to take a quick shower. I told her politely but matter-of-factly that she couldn't do that. I advised her that part of the reason she was going to the hospital, besides checking her for any physical injuries (besides the obvious injuries a rape victim has already sustained), was for the doctor to look for evidence of the crime which just occurred. A shower could possibly destroy or eliminate that evidence. She nodded her head once again in apparent understanding and we prepared to leave the room.

Despite Susan being able to walk, the rescue squad personnel nonetheless carefully put her onto a litter and rolled her out to the waiting ambulance. She and Jocelyn (who had collected some clothes for her to wear later) went to the hospital together. I told them I'd meet them there in a few minutes. Susan asked me to reassure her that I would meet her at the hospital. I advised her for the second time I would be there for her. She nodded again and even almost smiled at hearing me say that. It was an almost smile, but not quite a full one.

I decided then and there that this was my case and I was sticking with it and sticking with Susan. I so wanted to nail the bastard who did this to her.

Before I left, I had another officer respond to the hotel room scene. His job was to guard the inside and the outside of the room to make sure it was not disturbed by anyone. There was a strong possibility that there was evidence of some sort from the rapist in or around the room and I wanted to preserve it in an attempt to later identify him. The room would, in fact, be searched in a few hours. But first, I had to drive to the hospital. While enroute, I heard Det. Ken Hopkins sign on via the police radio. I advised him to meet me at the Frankford-Torresdale Hospital, which is less than a mile across the city line from Bensalem in Philadelphia. I was glad to be working with Ken. He was a good detective and a good man.

By about 3:30AM, I was in the ER with Susan, her friend/co-worker Jocelyn, and shortly thereafter, Det. Hopkins. In an adjacent private room, the doctor and two nurses did a complete examination of the victim. About an hour later, they came out of the room. One of the nurses handed Det. Hopkins a large and bulky envelope and had him sign a piece of paper for chain-of-custody purposes. In it was a completed medico-investigative "Rape Kit." Contained therein, among other items, were cotton-ended Q-Tips and other similar material of various swabbings of the victim's genital and other body areas. Also, there were combings from her pubic hair. This kit would be sent to the Bucks County Crime Lab and any evidence detected would be duly analyzed, assessed, and put into a written report.

The contusions on Susan's neck were also noted by the doctor in his verbal comments to us officers, as well as some abrasions and evidence of very recent forced sexual activity. He would include these findings in his own written report.

After this examination was completed at the hospital, Susan was allowed to get dressed in her regular clothes and was free to go. Det.

Hopkins politely then asked her if she would accompany us to the BPD HQ for a more formal interview as to what happened earlier this morning. She agreed at this point without hesitation. However, she made one request of us first. She wanted a coffee. This was a good sign I thought. She's regaining some semblance of who she is and what she wants. We both immediately agreed to her request. Det. Hopkins drove Susan and Jocelyn back to our station and I volunteered to pick up several coffees from the closest 7-11. (It was a hot chocolate for me, of course.) We must have realized collectively that none among the four of us had any decent sleep over the last twenty hours or so (to include me trying to sleep during the daytime) and the caffeine in these hot drinks would buy us a few more hours of functionality. At least we all hoped.

The CID area was still empty when I got there as the dayshift detectives weren't in yet. Heck, the sun wasn't even up yet. I met with Det. Hopkins and the two women in one of the larger interview rooms and distributed the various hot drinks. I even picked up a few bagels with cream cheese for us to munch on. They were appreciative of the food and drink items, especially Susan as she had the toughest night of any of us, without question.

As I would find out, when Det. Hopkins first arrived at HQ a few hours earlier to get his CID car, he had called the phone number for Women Organized Against Rape (WOAR). This was a relatively new organization at the time with well-trained people, mostly volunteer women, who would assist rape victims at any and all stages of an investigation. Ken knew of a few of these volunteers from prior sexual assault investigations and he called and requested one in particular. She showed up about the same time the rest of us arrived at the BPD. It was my first experience working with a WOAR volunteer, and I was impressed from the start. The introductions were made and the WOAR representative had a few calming and encouraging words to the victim right away. Susan was very appreciative of her being there with us now.

We were doing our best to make this most horrible of nights at least a little bit more manageable for Susan. It seemed to be working, ever so slowly.

Det. Hopkins asked Jocelyn to sit outside the interview room while the three of us interviewed Susan. At first our victim didn't want her friend to leave her side, but Ken assured both of them that it would be for the best. He wanted to make sure that Susan would answer our questions without the influence of her colleague, even if none was intended. This was a common law enforcement interview practice and neither party seemed to mind once the overall rationale was explained to them. I gave the friend a copy of the Philadelphia newspaper and with her coffee she kept herself busy at one of the nearby desks while we talked to Susan.

During about an hour of very delicate and sometimes very personal questioning, Susan provided me, Det. Hopkins, and the WOAR representative, the most detailed information she could. It wasn't easy ascertaining from her what we needed to hear. It took some time and repeated asking of the same questions to make sure she understood us. She eventually did and provided some great information and never once contradicted herself in what she was telling us. Needless to say it was very difficult for her to force herself to recount the degrading and traumatizing experience of what had happened only several hours earlier. But we could see that she was a strong person and now more in control of her emotions, senses, and even the situation at hand. She almost now seemed empowered to some degree. Again, this was another good sign.

The WOAR person did a great job in reminding Susan that SHE did nothing wrong in her hotel room this night. We all agreed with that notion, of course. Our victim was now more angry than hurt, more determined than sad, and more than anything she wanted to help us to find and arrest this man, this monster…her rapist. We told her we genuinely appreciated her attitude and we wanted nothing more than to arrest him too. She thanked us for what we were doing for her. We in turn thanked her for being such a brave woman, despite the ordeal she had just suffered through.

With the interview complete, the WOAR representative gave Susan one of her cards, an informational booklet, and said goodbye. She promised that she would stay in touch throughout this whole process, even by phone to Canada if necessary, whenever Susan needed to talk. Susan expressed thanks to the WOAR woman for her being here this night and of her pledge of further assistance down the line. I next gave the two co-workers a ride back to the hotel room.

Back at the hotel, Susan went into her room and under my watchful eye (I didn't want her taking any evidence with her), carefully packed her remaining belongings to go home. It was decided that Susan was going to fly back to Canada that afternoon with another of her co-workers accompanying her. Oh, and we did permit her to take a shower at this time.

Susan eventually left her room but not before giving me a farewell hug. She thanked me for making the most terrible night of her life just a bit easier for her before it was over. In return, I thanked her for working with us and reassured her that I would stay in touch. I followed her as she left the room, got into her colleague's rental cars, and drove off to Philadelphia International Airport for her flight home.

I also thanked Susan's co-worker and friend Jocelyn. She was very helpful that night and on subsequent times with Susan and the continuing investigation.

Det. Hopkins returned just a few minutes later as we had one last function to perform in terms of the early stage of this investigation. That is, we had to thoroughly search the hotel room for evidence.

With the help of two day-work shift detectives now on site, we searched the room. Since it was my case from a patrol perspective, I was authorized to stay over a few hours and assist. I'm glad I did, despite now being on the very tired side. During the course of the several hour long search, I decided to walk outside of the room and check the area where the rapist would have climbed through the sliding glass window to gain his entry. Once arriving there, on the ground, almost directly below the window but under a bush or two, I observed a shiny object. It was now just visible in the bright sunlight of this brand new day. Upon making my way closer to the object I saw it to be a man's style gold necklace. I noticed that it had a locket of some sort on it too. This must have been what Susan had described to me and later to Ken as what the rapist had been wearing around his neck. Apparently it somehow detached from his neck and stayed behind here at the scene, directly outside the window where he entered and then exited the room.

When I told Ken Hopkins what I found, he made sure to come outside and take a photograph of it, right where it was located and before anyone moved it. I then attained a plastic evidence bag so I could pick up and securely store the necklace. I did so with my pen, because I didn't want my fingerprints on it. I added this small plastic bag to the other bags of evidence slowly growing in the room, to include the sheets off of the bed, Susan's bed clothing, and latent fingerprints off the windows and sill.

As it would turn out, this necklace would be the item which would break the case wide open. But that would have to wait, at least for a few hours. Ken and I were now running on fumes, sleep-wise. We knew we had to go home and get some shuteye. We both had shifts starting later in the day and we agreed to drop off and properly store all of the evidence and when we're both fresh later tonight, we'd start over again. Before he left, Ken requested that after the room search the other two detectives interview the remaining guests at the hotel as well as the victim's co-workers for any information they may possess. Ken and I then said goodbye, goodnight, and went to our respective homes for some much needed sleep.

In the early evening of that same day, upon receiving telephonic permission from the shift lieutenant to return to work early after about five hours in bed, I began assisting Det. Hopkins in the ongoing rape investigation. In doing so, we went over all the evidence and the additional interviews from earlier today. Some of the evidence, like the bed sheets and Susan's torn bed clothes, would have to be sent to the lab for microscopic examination for hairs, liquids, etc.

(Being 1981, this was a decade-plus before the advent of DNA technology to solve these sorts of crimes. Nonetheless, hairs, fibers, and blood-typing were still valuable pieces of evidence to potentially identify someone if law enforcement also had hairs, fibers, and blood or other liquids from them too. It would not be individual evidence such as DNA would later offer, but it could be class evidence, which at least could place a person into a potentially very narrow pool of suspects based on the specific findings of this type of evidence.)

As the necklace and locket I found outside the window had piqued my curiosity, even as I was falling off to sleep at home just a few short hours ago, I wanted to examine it before anything else. It was too coincidental that Susan, the victim, described the rapist as wearing a necklace with a shiny metal piece hanging from it. She couldn't offer too much more in the way of descriptive features of her rapist, but she did know he was wearing some piece of jewelry around his neck. Then, a necklace is found right outside the same window the offender used to sneak into and then out of the room. It clearly hadn't been on the ground that long either as it had not been covered by dirt or debris of any sort. More likely than not, this WAS the necklace Susan described to me and Ken. But what, if anything, could we learn from it?

Upon putting on surgical-type gloves, Ken and I proceeded to open the plastic bag with the necklace. We examined it, measured it, took another photograph of it, and eventually popped open the square locket. Once it was fully open, we saw that on the left side of the three-quarter inch by one-half inch locket was a picture of a heart.

On the right side of the open locket was a black and white picture of a 20-something blonde woman.

Without hesitating, and at the same time surprising Ken, I looked at him and said aloud, "I know that woman!"

Recognizing the woman in the little picture was the easy part. I knew her from somewhere, somehow, in my professional travels on the BPD. But...had I arrested her? Given her a traffic ticket? Was she a witness to a crime? Was she a victim of a crime? I just couldn't figure out where I had seen this face before or in what context. At least not now with only the bare minimum of sleep under my belt, not to mention having less than one square inch of a face to work with here. Work with it I did though, even using a magnifying glass in some hope of detecting something on her which would strike a chord in me.

Despite this, her facial features, while familiar, still couldn't be connected to a name, or even a place by me. I may have to find an alternate means to ID her.

Later that evening, I went to the BPD photo room and started going through the mug shots of white females who had been arrested over the last few years. It took me at least an hour, but as I flipped through the several hundred photo files one-by-one, eventually I found a face that looked very similar. Her hair was not quite the same shade of blonde in the mug shot, and she wasn't smiling as in the locket, but I was pretty sure it was her. A little mole on one of her cheeks then confirmed it for me. It was only observable by me using the trusty magnifying glass to examine both pictures. What a great investigative tool. No wonder Sherlock Holmes always had one nearby.

My next stop was to the records room to check her name for past arrests. The woman-in-the-locket, I discovered, had been previously arrested just one time. It was at the end of a bar fight to which I responded several years ago. She was one of about fifteen people arrested that night after the donnybrook broke out among a bunch of drunken guys at a problematic bar in Bensalem. She was under 21 and was thusly arrested for being at the wrong place at the wrong time and, oh, with the wrong guy too. That's how I recognized her, although I didn't remember her specifically from that arrest as there were a number of other men and women arrested and/or issued summonses at the same time.

I found Ken back at his desk and told him that I identified the photo in the locket. Right afterwards, we both looked her name up in our intel card file (different from the criminal record files), and it turns out she was, as of a few years ago, the girlfriend of a well-known local criminal. His description matched what Susan had provided us. When we accessed it, so did his mug shot picture to me as he was arrested at the bar that same night too.

When we additionally checked out this guy's criminal record, we could see it was quite a long one besides just the bar fight arrest. It included being a peeping tom two separate times in his late teens, as well as a later sex offense. Plus, as an extra bonus, upon running him through the National Crime Information Center (NCIC) database, lo and behold, there was a bench warrant for him for failure to appear at a hearing a few months ago for yet another criminal case. If nothing else, we agreed, we'll lock him up on that warrant later tonight.

Ken and I now knew we were onto something, and we were barely twenty hours into this investigation so far. This was too much for it to be a coincidence. Here was a guy with known sex offenses in his past and a necklace/locket with HIS girlfriend's picture in it which just happened to be found at the scene of a rape.

What are the odds it's NOT him? We were willing to test those odds later that evening.

There was no good address found for our rape suspect, but Ken and I found the locket lady's present residential address. She was living in a nearby apartment complex. We assumed they were still a couple, otherwise, why would he still be wearing this necklace and locket?

We decided we didn't want to go to the girlfriend's place without our suspect/her boyfriend being there. The girlfriend may want to protect him and later warn him to skip town if we don't catch him there the first time. If we do get there and it's just her, we'll still talk to her as she may know something about what her guy was doing in the wee hours of this morning.

We'd also need some "props" for our interview, Ken reminded me. So, we took several colored Polaroid photos of the necklace/locket, including one close-up with the locket open and clearly showing the girlfriend's face. Our strategy for confronting the girlfriend and arresting her boyfriend was slowly coming together.

Ken and I agreed as I was leaving to go out on patrol with my regular squad that I should check on the apartment every once in a while and see what kind of activity is there. If it was determined she's there, and if our suspect is there (as we also now knew his vehicle information), we'd go pay them a visit.

Back on patrol, now with my squad which just came on, I made sure between routine calls from the dispatcher to drive by the girlfriend's apartment every hour on the hour of my remaining shift. Finally, after not seeing the car there for the first several hours, at around 1:30AM, I saw it in the parking lot around the corner from her apartment. I even jumped out of my vehicle and felt the hood. It was warm. Good, that means he just got there. I put over the police radio for our dispatcher to contact Det. Hopkins in CID and tell him our guy was now where we wanted him and to meet me at the apartment.

About ten minutes later, I met Det. Hopkins a short distance from the apartment. Then, after quickly finalizing our strategy, I pulled up and purposely double-parked my patrol car behind our suspect's car. Just in case he jumped out of the back window of the residence (since he seemed to have a talent for window ingress and egress), I didn't want him driving off in his car. That would not be good.

Strategy in hand, Ken and I knocked on the apartment door. It took her a while, but a woman finally answered the door. It was, in fact, locket lady. The now 22-year-old woman's hair was still blonde, but of an even lighter shade now than in the mug shot or the locket. We identified ourselves and told her we had a few questions for her. She didn't want to let us in the door at first, but we sort of convinced her it would be better if she did. She acquiesced and we entered her foyer area. She was fully dressed and we apparently did not awaken her. We didn't say too much more other than we were working an investigation and we wanted to show her something. She then more or less agreed to look at what we were about to show her. Of course, we were keeping our eyes and ears open the whole time for any movement around the apartment. The boyfriend was probably in here, but we didn't want her (or him if he could hear us) to know yet that he was the reason we were there.

Ken didn't hesitate at all at this point. He opened his file and showed her the Polaroid picture of the necklace, but with the locket closed. We asked her if she recognized this piece of jewelry. She hesitated at first but then said she didn't think she ever saw it before. Then, we showed her another Polaroid of the necklace with the locket open, but from enough of a distance that one couldn't really make out whose picture was in it. She hesitated even longer this time and then finally said, "Hey, what's this all about anyway?"

The girlfriend knew something was up, she became visibly more nervous, and she knew whatever this was now involved her boyfriend. We asked her again if she was familiar with this piece of jewelry.

This time she said she wasn't sure. Then, we showed her the close-up Polaroid. We asked her directly, "Is that your picture in the locket?"

The girlfriend responded in the affirmative. She then asked, "Where did you find this necklace? I gave it to...," but she caught herself and stopped.

We then lied. A little bit. Okay, maybe a lot.

Ken and I had pre-planned our response to that last question and, just as we predicted, she asked it.

Ken told her the necklace was found last night next to one of the dancer's cars at a local go-go girl bar and we just wanted to confirm that it's her boyfriend's.

The girlfriend then lost her cool, much as her boyfriend had very recently "lost" the necklace. She responded in now increased volume and pitch, "Yeah it's his alright. I gave it to him as a gift over a year ago. But he told me this morning when he got home that he lost it at work. And he told me he wasn't going to that f**kin' titty bar anymore! That lyin' son of a bitch!"

While the girlfriend was this emotional, Ken and I knew we should do nothing to extinguish her intense internal fire. In whisper tone, I then asked her where the guy was right now. With her arms now folded across her chest and her lips firmly pursed in obvious anger, she motioned with little reluctance via a slight sideways head twist that he was in the back bedroom. Ken quietly ordered her to stay in the living room area as we walked through the hallway toward the bedroom.

Once in the bedroom, I flipped on the light switch, but nothing happened. There was no light. Fortunately, I had my flashlight with me. I pointed its beam all around the room. The boyfriend/rape suspect wasn't behind the door or in the closet. I made sure to determine that right away. I then shined the beam of light onto the queen-sized bed itself. I noticed that the bed was unmade. The sheets and covers were in an elongated pile in the center of the bed, strangely running from the pillow area down to the bottom. As I bent down to assure there was no one under the bed, I couldn't help but notice when looking straight across the covers with my flashlight from mattress level that in the middle section of that elongated pile, the bedding material was moving up and down ever so slightly. It was almost as if someone was breathing beneath them, perhaps someone even heavily breathing beneath them.

Acting on a not too wild hunch here, I called the guy by name and had him come out from under the covers with his hands up. Both Ken and I had our guns out at this point from different vantage points in the room and we advised him as such as we had no idea what he had under those covers with him, weapon-wise. Ever so slowly, the guy put his hands out first, then head, then the rest of his body, stood up, and after re-holstering my gun, I put handcuffs on him. He said he had been sound asleep, but when I pointed out that he was in his jeans and a sweatshirt with sneakers on his feet he quickly gave up on that ruse.

The guy then told us that he knew why he was being arrested. Ken asked, "Why would that be?"

The guy responded, "For missing that court date last month, right?"

I learned early on in my police career that whenever a potential bad guy gives up a relatively minor crime or questionable activity right away, especially when not even asked about it, you know he's hiding something much bigger. There was no doubt to me that this guy was hiding something much bigger as I tightened the cuffs around his wrists. Oh, and I noticed too that he had longish brown hair and a mustache. And he was in his late twenties. Just like Susan said he would be.

I was sure we had our rapist.

We did have our rapist.

While the suspect didn't give anything up that night back at HQ regarding the rape, despite our attempt to ascertain it from him after reading him his Miranda warnings, he was still held without bail for the bench warrant for "Failure to Appear." Within a few days, a partial print from the hotel room windowsill was found which we confirmed belonged to our boy. Det. Hopkins and I swore out an arrest warrant for the rape and related charges and it was served on him in the detention center by week's end.

After one continuance, a preliminary hearing was held about a month after the incident and arrest. The Bucks County DA's office flew Susan and Jocelyn back to the area. The DA's office put her up in a Bucks County hotel, but not the same one as where the incident occurred, of course.

At the preliminary hearing, with the now-defendant (who was being held without bail) in the courtroom with her, Susan provided excellent testimony as to what happened that night. While she couldn't point out the rapist specifically, as it was simply too dark in the room that night to positively identify him, her basic physical description of him and my later testimony regarding the locket, the girlfriend, the fingerprint, etc., served to connect the dots. There was a prima facie case found by the magistrate and the matter was held over for trial.

I went out to dinner that evening with Susan, Jocelyn, and a Bucks County detective who was now also assigned to the case. (Ken Hopkins was not available this evening for some reason.) It was a nice dinner and Susan seemed to be a whole different person at this time. She was still hurting, of course, from what she had to endure in that hotel room just about one month ago, but she was in a much better mood and made it clear that this incident, this man, was not about to get in the way of the rest of her life. We actually toasted her and the rest of her life and it made for a pleasant evening. The rape or the earlier court proceedings were not discussed at all after that toast. We hugged again in the parking lot after the dinner as they were going back to their hotel. It would be the last time I would see Susan.

A few weeks before the trial was set to begin later that year, the rapist pleaded guilty to his crime. (As part of his plea agreement, he admitted he was doing his "peeping-tom thing" around the hotel grounds that night, looking into the first floor windows, noticed a lone female in her bed, found the window unlocked, and then decided to do his "rape thing.") He was sentenced to 10-15 years in state prison. I never heard from him again. I believe his girlfriend broke up with him. Either way, neither of them asked for the return of the necklace or locket. I wouldn't want it back either if I was one of them.

I stayed in touch with Susan and Jocelyn by phone and occasional letter for a year or so after the incident, but lost track of them after a while. She was doing well during that time frame and was even promoted at her workplace despite never officially finishing the Bensalem training program. (She was awarded the certificate of accomplishment anyway.)

I can only hope today Susan is still doing well and that this particular long ago winter night in Bensalem, Pennsylvania, is now a distant memory for her. She was an unfortunate victim of a violent crime. However, once finding herself in that never asked-for position she found a way to become an excellent witness against the perpetrator who violated her.

If only every criminal case had such an excellent witness.

Chapter Seventeen

Bob Yezzi now had about two and a half years on the BPD, and he was looking to affect some professional changes in his life. Specifically, he wanted to try something other than be a patrol officer at this early juncture in his career. In exploring these options, we had talked about the possibility of him returning to his Villanova University roots and joining me in the new graduate program there. However, he made it clear that for him right now he wasn't interested in going back to school, be it at his alma mater or not, for these classes. He wanted to first see how I enjoyed it, the course content, its relevance to what we do, how I worked it out with my schedule, the reimbursement policy, and perhaps after a year or so he'd consider joining me there. That made sense and we agreed that once I started I'd give him updates as to the program's merits, weaknesses, overall viability, etc.

In the meantime, the BPD was still attaining various Law Enforcement Assistance Agency (LEAA) grants for different projects and initiatives. Bob heard of one which had just been secured by management and for which he felt he would be ideally suited. It was a grant to set up a Crime Prevention Unit, aka, CPU. It would be a one-officer operation, at least initially, with the set-aside budget paying the salary of the full-time officer and that of a staff person assigned to the unit on a part-time basis. The basic premise of the unit would be, of course, coming up with ways for community members to prevent crimes and/or to avoid becoming victims of crimes. This mostly entailed theft of some sort, and in Bensalem, the predominant reason for one's personal property being stolen was as the result of either commercial or residential burglaries.

Bob had been smart enough to mostly keep his mouth shut regarding the ongoing political shenanigans within the department, or at least he was never overheard saying anything of dubious intent by one of the growing handful of known Dark Side operatives. Also, as he wasn't necessarily known for being all that friendly with me (since we never actually worked on the same squad nor attended Lamaze classes together) or other known dissidents, he was seen as eligible to be appointed to a position such as the new CPU. Somewhat as important as an officer's political and social leanings at this time in the BPD, it was also clearly evident that Bob was a bright guy, well-spoken, presented an excellent professional image, and a very competent police officer in his few short years on the job. In view of all of this, he applied for the lateral transfer to the position as the BPD CPU Officer.

Lo and behold, in short time Bob was appointed to the new post by the Deputy Chief. So, like two ships crossing in the night, just as I was coming back to patrol division, Bob was being newly assigned to the Detective Division, under which the new CPU would be administratively managed.

I was happy for Bob. He fit well into this new program and put lots of energy and initiative into it from the very beginning. Along with the guidelines and recommendations attached to the LEAA awarding of the grant monies, Bob also came up with some excellent ideas on his own. Initially, he would become very busy with the marketing of the new unit throughout Bensalem. He utilized various media outlets to do so. There was also the engraver-loan program, in which residents could borrow one of dozens of the newly acquired electronic engravers from the BPD CPU to permanently engrave their driver's license numbers onto everything of value that they owned. IF the item was stolen and (hopefully) recovered, the police would have a quick way of determining the item's ownership.

Bob would later tell me that upon request he would travel to numerous Bensalem residences, mostly senior citizens in these cases, and help the folks engrave everything from cameras to their dentures. He would also address various community and neighborhood gatherings as to how to better protect their properties from break-ins and thefts; he would talk to local business owners regarding installing upgraded alarm systems at their facilities, providing better lighting to the exteriors of their buildings, making sure the BPD had current contact info just in case a break-in was detected late at night; and he would go to the schools to advise the students how to avoid being victims of crimes involving stranger assaults and the like.

All in all, the whole Bensalem community benefited from this program now being run by Officer Yezzi. From homeowners to apartment renters, from large corporations to mid-sized warehouse facilities to small retail stores, from younger children to senior citizens, each was on Bob's weekly list of people to meet. He'd talk to them at HQ, meet them at their homes or businesses or schools, loan them engravers (which, as some of them started to go missing, he made sure they too had the requisite identifying engravings on them), gave out "Operation ID" window and door stickers, not to mention authoring and distributing professionally prepared four-color brochures on how NOT to become a victim of a crime.

Bob took his new unit and new assignment very seriously. The residents and business owners of Bensalem Township appreciated his hard work and dedication and the fact that he was very responsive to their needs. He was making a good name for himself throughout the township and representing the police department well. The new BPD CPU clearly had Bob Yezzi's name engraved on it, literally and figuratively, and it was off to a great start under Bob's stewardship.

As the summer of 1980 moved well into the warmer weather, there were a few weekends that Bob came over to my house for cookouts. He was now the lucky one, schedule-wise, working mostly Mondays through Fridays with weekends off. I was the one back with the rotating schedule and only having that one long weekend off per month. Nonetheless, when our schedules would permit, I'd invite him over. Sometimes it was just him, sometimes he would bring his new girlfriend, who happened to be the daughter of one of the BPD dispatchers, and we would hangout, drink a beer or two, eat some burgers, hot dogs, or barbecued chicken, and talk about whatever interested us. Sometimes it would be the job, and the never-seeming-to-end political issues now ongoing there, which Bob was getting to see and hear first-hand as he was now in the proverbial belly of the beast in the Detective Division. But most of the time when we were together we would simply discuss other personal matters. We did have lives, after all.

Whenever he'd visit my house, Bob also enjoyed playing with Sean, now a one-year old toddler. If weather permitted, in the backyard they'd play hide-and-seek, roll a ball back and forth, and he'd push Sean on his little swing set. I remember Bob clearly telling me on several occasions, "I want one of them someday," referring to my son. It was very obvious to me and my wife then that Bob would make a great dad when his time came to be one.

Bob advised me during one of these summertime visits, it was in mid-July of that year, that he had a recent clash with Deputy Chief Zajac. It involved the relatively new CPU, how he (Bob) was running it, what he was doing or not doing therein, or the like. Bob further offered that the disagreements were less of a specific or substantive nature, but instead seemed more personality-driven between him and Zajac. I nodded my head affirmatively in support of him, saying to him in so many words, "Been there, done that!" Bob ended this particular conversation by telling me he wasn't sure he'd be heading up the CPU much longer and that he may be joining me back in patrol before too long.

Hmmm…this sounded all too familiar.

I asked Bob if he heard anything yet about a spreading cancer within the department from the DC. He said he had not, but he'd keep his ears open. I told him when Zajac started talking or lecturing him about a terminal disease of any variety, the die was more or less cast for him and it would be time to "exit, stage right." He seemed to appreciate my diagnostic and exit strategy.

Bob and I commiserated about our recent run-ins with BPD management. I was sort of used to it by now, but he wasn't. I felt bad for Bob, as he had only been in this new position for about seven months and he seemed to enjoy it. More importantly, the CPU and he were getting great reviews from various community organizations. I knew this as I would meet with residents at various times while on patrol when responding to calls and they'd tell me so.

However, Bob and I agreed that things must be getting desperate among the powers-that-wannabe. I assured him that IF he was "demoted" back to patrol division, it probably meant he was, in fact, doing his job very well. It was the people who excelled in this administration that seemed to be punished. Those who did less or performed in sub-standard ways were promoted or at a minimum left alone to do what they liked. That is, of course, if they were in the right political camp, and unequivocally paid homage to the new camp leader.

In early August, on a Saturday afternoon, one of our other police department colleagues had a cookout at his townhome in the Neshaminy Valley neighborhood of Bensalem. It was attended by mostly newer members of the BPD, that is, those of us hired in the last four years or so. Bob was also invited and shortly after arriving he pulled me aside to tell me something. We walked to a corner of the smallish, fenced-in yard and he advised that just the day before he had received a memo which, as we suspected, instructed him he was being transferred back to the patrol division, effective immediately. DC Zajac became incensed at him for something unrelated to the prior issue, a life-threatening disease was indeed referenced, and the transfer order subsequently issued. I was somewhat surprised at how fast it all occurred, but then not really.

So, here's yet another BPD officer, Bob Yezzi this time, appointed to a specialized squad or unit, by all accounts doing very well while there, but then apparently doesn't play ball, or doesn't want to be on a certain team, and away he goes, back from whence he came to the Patrol Division. I had beat the management cronies to the punch with my proactive transfer request about eight months before, but Bob obviously waited just a bit too long in his case for his exit strategy.

Bob was ultimately fine with the transfer. He pretty much laughed it off. Being in the CPU was a positive overall experience for him as he made some good contacts, some good friends outside of the PD, and he and they know he did a stellar job while head of the department's first ever such unit. Bob eventually told the whole crowd there at the cookout that day that he was "coming home" to join them, and as virtually all of us in attendance were in the Patrol Division, we collectively welcomed him back with a raised toast of various cold beverages. It's not that bad, I and others reminded Bob. I further reminded him that he'd appreciate being further removed from the everyday political nonsense too. He concurred.

Once again, as it turned out, Bob and I would be on alternate shifts as he landed on a different patrol squad than mine. Maybe by design, we agreed. Nevertheless, a few days later we assured each other during a phone call that we'd get together before too long, either at my place for a cookout, or to a movie or local restaurant. As Bob had only recently moved into his newly purchased first home, he suggested that perhaps I could come to his place for a cookout one of these days. I replied I'd be glad to as he was always bragging about his skills in cooking Italian food. He told me to make sure I bring that cute little boy of mine as he would cook him some real spaghetti in genuine homemade gravy for the first time. (I learned through Bob that "real Italians," as he would say, call spaghetti sauce "gravy.")

Bob and I ended our phone conversation with the fact that I was going "down the shore" with my family for a few days in about a week and a half. When I returned we'd get together, we agreed. We then said goodbye.

And goodbye it was to my dear friend.

Chapter Eighteen

Like Bob Yezzi from just a week ago or so, I had my own recent run-in with management. With me it involved Lt. Bob Hughes, the guy who worked the grants to get us new officers hired at the BPD just a few years prior. Hughes had since prostrated himself to the ever rising-in-power Deputy Chief and whenever he (Hughes) could further ingratiate himself by taking a shot at one of the real or perceived enemies within the department, he would. It was my turn on August 5 of that year.

One day before, August 4, I was among several officers on my squad assigned to a "speed-trap" detail on Byberry Rd. This type detail involves officers at a specific, measured, street location with a certified electronic device operated within a stationary police car by a certified operator, all of which is designed to measure the speed of passing cars. While on that assignment, one of the speeders caught in the trap that day happened to be a niece of Lt. Hughes. So, I ticketed her, as I had done approximately seven other people so far that morning. She was doing 39 mph in a marked 25 mph zone. So, she was issued a traffic citation with a total fine and costs of $63.00. The speed-trap electronic device was operated that day by an older, soon-to-retire sergeant.

The very next day, while inside HQ for some reason, I happened upon Lt. Hughes sitting at his desk. As I would notice him doing many times in his office over the years, he was reading a newspaper. While barely looking up from what I believe was the comics section, Hughes said to me very officiously, "You're going to fix the ticket from yesterday, right?"

I responded with my own question. "What ticket?"

Hughes said, "Don't play with me, Fitzgerald. You know what I'm talking about. The speeding ticket you gave my niece. You knew it was her too, didn't you?"

I replied, "No, I really didn't, but either way, I don't fix tickets. Sorry. Tell her to ask for a hearing."

The bad lieutenant then said, ominously, "You WILL take care of this for me, Fitzgerald, or I will make life very difficult for you around here."

"Yes, sir, I'm sure you will," I ever so politely retorted as I left his office area, with my mind now more made up than ever NOT to fix or adjust the ticket for him. Sgt. Ashton would have been proud of me - well, at least for the politeness part.

I never did "fix" Lt. Hughes's niece's ticket. She asked for a hearing and it was scheduled for October 22. I was there that day, the niece was there that day, but amazingly, the sergeant didn't show up that day. He called in sick. Without the availability of his testimony about his electronic speed device, how it functions, its calibration, certification, etc., the ticket was dismissed by the district magistrate.

I didn't personally care one way or the other regarding the outcome of the ticket hearing. But clearly the "fix" was in from the start. It just manifested itself from a different direction.

Whenever he later had a chance, Lt. Hughes, eventually becoming Captain Hughes, would take a shot across the bow at me with every possible opportunity. Despite that, his vindictiveness was the last thing I would be thinking of starting in just about a week. What was to happen in the next few days paled in comparison times a billion to that man's contemptible and threatening rhetoric towards me.

* * * * *

On Sunday afternoon, August 10, 1980, my small family, but increased somewhat by Eileen's ten-year-old brother, and even our part-Labrador Retriever, Mickey, drove to Sea Isle City, New Jersey. Months before, we had agreed to sub-rent a small house from a friend for that Sunday through Friday for five days of relaxation and fun in the sun "down the shore." The weather forecast called for temperatures to be in the high 80s, low humidity, with no rain. The house was only a block from the beach, so it was looking like a great mini-vacation ahead for all of us. I knew I needed a break from the PD, so the timing was excellent. Or, so I thought.

I should add, at this time, very few rental houses at the seashore had telephones in them. Some didn't even have cable TV yet. This house did have the latter, but not the former. And, of course, it was long before anyone had cell phones or the internet was even imagined. So, when one made a decision to go away for a day or a week or more to the South Jersey shore, usually that person was out of contact with his or her "real" life for the entire time. Of course, one could go to a nearby payphone and call home, the workplace, or wherever, to check on things, but that was about the only option back then if every day real life connections were to be maintained on the personal or employment front.

While a few people may have known where I was during this particular week, including my mother (my father had died in 1979), it wasn't many more than her. I wasn't required to, nor did I choose to, notify the BPD of where I was during these scheduled days off. Why bother, I thought. They'd be fine without me, and vice-versa.

I believe the first full day there, Monday, was a bright and beautiful day of which we spent mostly on the beach. It was Sean's first time ever at the ocean in his young life, and he seemed to love it. My young brother-in-law hadn't travelled to the seashore very often in his life, or at least not this particular beach in Sea Isle City, and he was enjoying himself as well. While sunning and taking the occasional dips in the ocean, we happened to notice some charter fishing boats cruise by us not far off shore, as well as the banner-pulling planes above advertising for the same local fishing boats. I learned then that my young in-law had never been fishing before nor had he ever even been out in the water on anything but a rowboat. So, we decided while still on the beach that later we'd walk to the local boat dock and make a reservation to go "deep-sea fishing" the next day. He was really excited about it and couldn't wait to do so.

That next morning, August 12, we awoke early to meet the boat at the nearby dock for the 8:00AM departure. Before breakfast, as usual, I had to decide what I was going to wear that day. A pair of shorts and sneakers would be an easy choice from the waist down, but what shirt should I wear. Let's see...what did I quickly pack for myself before we left on Sunday? Oh, interesting, my old Bensalem Police Department softball team tee-shirt. I'm one hundred miles from home, who will care today if I wear it? Who will bother me on a boat? What could be the downside?

So, without even thinking anymore about it, I put it on.

For perspective here...In the late '70s, the BPD rookies would occasionally play the veterans, and even sometimes other PDs, in softball at a local Bensalem field. In view of that, the shirts were ordered en masse back then for around twenty-five of us officers. Our yellow embossed badge numbers were on the back, with "Bensalem

Police" in script written also in yellow on the front of the otherwise blue color mesh-style shirt. However, the potentially unifying trend of playing a friendly game of softball sort of faded away as of late when the political maneuvering became overwhelming by 1979. If we did play amongst ourselves by this time, it would pretty much have to be Team Zajac vs. the rest of us. (And no strikes better be called on the DC while he's at bat.)

Besides softball games and the two charity basketball games we played against the Philadelphia Eagles and Philadelphia Phillies, I should add that my personal habit at this time would be to never wear this shirt outside my house or backyard in Bensalem. It's not that I was particularly ashamed of the BPD or what I did for a living, but I just wouldn't want people possibly recognizing me from my everyday job when I'm otherwise off duty. It could lead to problematic situations, on multiple levels, especially as I lived in the town where I worked, and would sometimes arrest people not all that far from where I resided, shopped, etc.

In view of all this, on that warm, crisp, salt-air laden August morning, after randomly donning my rarely worn Bensalem Police tee-shirt, my young charge and I both sat down to eat a hearty breakfast. Right after that, with my wife happily staying behind with our son and the dog, off we went on our excellent fishing adventure.

Without the TV or radio on that morning, none of us had any way of knowing what had happened back home just a few hours earlier, and to one of my best friends.

In many ways, these were to be my last few hours of relative innocence in my life.

When making the fishing boat reservations the day before, I only made them for a four-hour cruise. I figured if this was the first time on a boat for my kid brother-in-law, we better keep it from just 8:00AM to noon. If he was to get seasick, at least he was less than four hours from returning to land.

Our fishing excursion went fine that morning. We both got a little bit of motion sickness, but nothing a heave or two over the rail didn't temporarily cure. The first-time fisherman beside me caught at least one fish during our trip, I believe a flounder, and that was excitement enough for him. Since neither of us ate fish, nor were we about to gut the thing, we chose to throw it back into the sea.

The only strange part of this whole fishing experience, and it started on the dock before we even sailed off that morning, was that I noticed a few people staring at me sort of oddly, and more than once that morning. No one said a word to me, other than the boat hands helping us out with our rods, lines, getting bait, etc. But the whole time, and especially when looking back later that day, I couldn't help but notice some of the other fishermen and fisherwomen sort of glancing down at my tee-shirt, then glancing up at my face, then just slowly turning away, perhaps while whispering something to the person next to them.

Okay, so I was wearing my Bensalem Police shirt. I suppose some people react differently, or oddly, to someone they surmise is in law enforcement, especially when in this case we're sort of stuck together for a full four hours on an eighty-foot charter fishing boat. Whatever... No one was rude or impolite, so I just did my thing that morning, more for my first-time fisherman/brother-in-law than for me or anyone else.

Once we unceremoniously returned to the marina and we docked, we simply gathered our stuff, got off the boat, and went back to the house. Not before a few more lingering stares I couldn't help but notice, but I again ignored them and left the area. The kid thanked me profusely on our short walk home and once there he couldn't stop telling his older sister about how much fun he had on the boat that day, catching his first fish, getting seasick, etc.

After lunch, all of us changed into our swimsuits and we spent another great afternoon on the beach. So far, I couldn't have asked for a nicer day.

If only I had known.

We probably left the beach by 4:30 or so that day and came back to the house. We showered and settled down to get ready for an early dinner. When I was done in the bathroom and dressed, I happened to turn on the TV in the living room to see what was happening in the real world. I may have bought a newspaper the morning before, but other than that so far this week I had been far removed from what was happening anywhere near or far from me. That's what vacations are for, right?

My regular TV news habit at the time was watching the local ABC affiliate, Channel 6, *Action News*. One reason was because of the presence of my old buddy, Jim O'Brien, from my lifeguarding days. Well, he wasn't really my buddy, but we did have those few brief interactions back in '72 as he would be walking one way and I would be walking the other at his former apartment complex which had the swimming pool where I lifeguarded. (See JCM Book I for details of these interactions.) The least I could do now is watch his newscast every day. Plus, I may add, he was very good at it too. Besides also being the everyday weatherman, the former Boss Jock was now the everyday anchor for the 5:30 – 6:00 news broadcast.

As I plopped myself down on the orange vinyl couch in the brown wood paneled room, with Sean and my wife in there with me playing and getting dinner ready, respectively, the all-too-familiar percussion-based theme music introducing the nightly news began. Then, as on each weeknight now at half-past five, there was the seemingly ubiquitous one, Jim O'Brien, voicing his usual teaser regarding the two lesser important stories in the news, and like I had seen and heard him do hundreds of times before, next was coming "...but the big story on Action News is...."

Okay, these other two stories are the usual routine matters of the day. No big deal. Let's see what's REALLY important today in the news. Tell me about it, Jim.

Once those last eight words left Jim's lips, his next words were "...A tragedy in Bensalem early this morning...."

Hey! That's where I live! That's where I work! What's this all about?

Before the news anchor could respond to my mental self-query, I observed a black-and-white picture of Bob Yezzi on the TV screen, upper-right from Jim's image. It's then that I heard the familiar voice say, in words which didn't immediately register, that a Bensalem police officer was killed early this morning when a car hit him on Richlieu Road during an arrest.

Huh....? What did Jim O'Brien just say?

Jim continued that the officer and his partner were attempting to arrest a robbery suspect when a car came along and struck both officers as well as the suspect. The other Bensalem police officer was Tony Rihl, a K-9 officer, who was seriously wounded and in the hospital in critical condition at this time. The guy they were attempting to arrest was also injured, but not too seriously.

What the...?! I could only repeat to myself, now out loud for all to hear.

Upon hearing and seeing this, my wife walked from the adjacent kitchen area and joined me on the couch and before long began crying. Sean and my young brother-in-law, who was still in his bedroom getting dressed, didn't initially know what any of this concerned. However, our dog, Mickey, knew something was drastically wrong with the two adults in the room. Domestic animals seem to have that sense about them. He was most definitely on-the-mark this time with his primal instincts.

How did this happen? What went wrong? Do they have their facts right? Maybe it's a mistake…. Yeah, that's possible, right?

Jim O'Brien, please tell me you got this one story wrong!

Oh, who am I kidding? Of course the facts are right, the basic ones here, anyway. The media don't always get things one hundred percent correct the first time around, but they wouldn't release Bob's name and these specific details of what happened if it wasn't true and accurate.

Before long, with Jim still relating the story, along with several of his reporter colleagues on the ground in Bensalem, there were the requisite aerial shots, or at least a map view, of the road where Bob was killed and Tony was injured. I knew the area well as I had traversed it many times on patrol, responding to calls, following suspicious cars and myriad other reasons.

Then, there was Chief Larry Michaels on the screen. He was holding a press conference of some sort at BPD HQ. I forget after all these years exactly what he said, but something to the effect that this was a sad day in Bensalem, we lost one of our own, Officer Yezzi was a great man and great police officer, he will be missed, we're all pulling for Officer Rihl, and justice will prevail in regard to the arrest scenario and the car and driver which hit them and killed Officer Yezzi.

Hmmm…interesting it was Michaels speaking to the media, who was nothing but the titular head of the BPD now, relegated to car-jockey duties, and not Zajac, who was actually running the department. Some varied thoughts flashed across my brain at that instant, politics-oriented, "cancer" related, Bob's recent surprise transfer…but I suppressed them. Now was not the time for these issues to obfuscate this dire situation. No, not right now. They'd have to wait a bit.

Instead, focus on Bob. Bob Yezzi, my good friend, my colleague. He's the guy who I had recruited to some degree to my PD, as early as during a walk-around at my old department store, to later through a phone call. He was now dead, killed in the line of duty.

Jesus! How do I handle this? What do I do? I had never felt so low, so helpless. And here I am, on vacation, literally one hundred miles away from the scene of the crime, just finding out about it, fifteen or so hours after it happened. I'm on a fishing boat this morning, and later relaxing on the beach, when one of my best friends, certainly on the BPD, was in a body bag and later on a slab in the morgue undergoing the requisite autopsy. This is so terrible….

Wait! The fishing trip earlier today! That explains it! Now it makes sense! The odd stares, the double-takes, the comments seemingly made, and me wearing that tee-shirt this morning while at the dock and on the boat. Dear God in Heaven, THAT's why! Some of those people obviously heard or saw the news this morning on the radio or on TV and knew of the Bensalem officer being killed. And here I am, an actual Bensalem officer who for some strange and bizarrely coincidental reason was wearing my one and only BPD shirt this morning but NOT knowing of the tragedy. And, with a stupid shirt I hardly EVER wear anymore.

I can't believe this...!

If only someone had told me this morning what they knew, what they heard. But, if it was when we were already on the boat, out in the water, what would I have done?

Damn! This is all so surreal, so bizarre, so sad....

Jim O'Brien that night eventually moved onto the next story. We turned off the TV. Still on the summer beach house-style faux-leather couch, with my head buried in my wife's shoulder as we each attempted to reassure one another and get through this horrible situation playing out in real time before us, one-year-old Sean got up from playing with his toy cars and trucks and waddled over to us. He too knew at this point that something was wrong. We jointly hugged him and the three of us bonded very profoundly at that exact moment. We were each hurting in our own ways, even if Sean didn't quite grasp the significance of it all yet.

Afterwards, my mind started wandering. I began thinking of other parts of my life, my past, sad ones for some reason. It struck me that my dad had died just about a year and a half ago, and that still hurt so bad. But this hurt too, in a different way, and for right now, it seemed to be even more painful. Older men, like my dad at age 75, die. It's the normal course of life. We all know that. But men in their late 20s don't die. Not like this. Not doing the same job that I do every day. Not my good friend, Bob Yezzi, who may not have ever even been a Bensalem police officer if not for me and my "recruiting" of him.

Oh my God, I hadn't even thought of it this way before, but it's a possibility....

Was I responsible, even if just indirectly, for Bob's very untimely death?

Okay, I must calm down here. Bob's death is NOT my fault. At least...I don't think so.

I have to go out and call the police department from a pay phone and find out more about what happened. I need details. I need something or someone else to get me through this, maybe someone who has unfortunately been through this before.

For some reason, I wanted to be on my own when I made the phone call to the BPD. I did, however, put the leash on Mickey and brought him with me for the walk. I found a nearby payphone on the promenade, aka boardwalk, near the center of town in Sea Isle City. I threw in a few quarters, and reluctantly called my PD, not really wanting to hear what I knew I was about to hear.

It must have been about 6:00 on that Tuesday evening. While overlooking the beautiful Atlantic Ocean, with hundreds of joyous people and kids walking and biking by me the whole time, and with others still down on the beach having fun, I had to proceed with this phone call from hell, or maybe to hell, my own private hell, for the time being at least. If only these people around me knew at the time how different, make that how difficult, my life was from theirs, maybe they'd be quiet, more respectful. But they couldn't, they wouldn't, and no, they shouldn't. This was for me to handle, for me to deal with, on my own for now.

I initially talked to the BPD dispatcher and learned from her that I was the only one of the eighty or so sworn on the PD that they could not contact earlier today to tell me the news. Either the other guys were working, or they could be reached at their residences. What are the odds of being away from home when something this bad happened and with no way to contact me? As per my request, the dispatcher eventually patched me through to Lt. Jack Robinson.

There wasn't too much more information Lt. Robinson could provide at this point, as both Tony Rihl and the robbery suspect that he and Bob were attempting to arrest this morning were not physically able to give a statement yet. From what could be pieced together though, it seems that at about 3:00AM, a man had taken some money or other valuables at knifepoint off of a person at an apartment complex on Richlieu Rd. The victim called the police shortly afterwards, gave the suspect's description and the direction in which he was walking. Officers Yezzi and Rihl then received the call from dispatch.

As Yezzi and Rihl drove along Richlieu Rd. in their separate marked cars, about a mile from the location of the incident, they eventually came upon someone matching the robbery suspect's description. Upon calling in on the radio what they were about to do and where, they exited their respective cars and confronted the alleged robber. However, as was eventually learned, instead of cooperating with the officers, the suspect immediately and demonstratively denied his complicity in the robbery and began wrestling with the officers as they attempted to handcuff him. At some point in the thirty second or so-long scuffle, a knife was brandished and the suspect broke free from them and ran onto the two-lane highway. At that precise moment, a lone woman on her way home from work was proceeding on Richlieu Rd. in their direction. She rounded a bend in the road and suddenly came upon the scene of relative mayhem playing out in front of her. But even though (or because of) the rotating blue and red police lights temporarily blinded her as to what was happening and who was doing what in front of her, she for whatever reason didn't take her foot off the gas and thus maintained the same speed in her car the whole time. She then drove into the middle of the skirmish. In doing so, she struck all three people, each wearing dark clothing or dark uniforms on this otherwise dark night on this all too dark stretch of highway. All three were hit by her car with one, Bob, apparently dying almost instantly due to severe head trauma.

So, now I knew the story, or what was known up to this point in time. It didn't help at all or make me feel any better I realized. Whether Bob had been shot, knifed, or hit by a car in a scenario such as what actually happened, he was still killed performing his sworn duty. I was still without my very good friend, one whom I saw and/or talked to only about a week before and with whom I was going to meet sometime in the next week.

But that wouldn't be happening now, would it?

I asked Lt. Robinson about when Bob's parents and his sister were contacted. Fortunately, if that's the right word, they were notified not too long after it happened and before the media released the information to the public. I had never met Bob's mom, dad, or sister, up to that point, but would be doing so in just a few days in the most uncomfortable and unbelievable of settings.

I was told by the lieutenant the funeral plans weren't confirmed yet, but they would probably be on Friday night and Saturday morning, in Philadelphia, near his extended family and his geographic roots. I thanked Robinson for the info and his compassion and hung up the phone.

After the phone call, Mickey and I went for a long walk on the beach. I don't think dogs are even allowed on the beaches during the summer months in Sea Isle City, but I walked on it with him anyway. I really didn't care. He was on his leash and not bothering anyone and he was good company for me. I think we walked the whole length of the beach, all the way to Townsends Inlet, a narrow body of water which separates Sea Isle City from the small resort town of Avalon. That's about a six mile walk, roundtrip. When the dog and I finally made it home after ninety minutes or so of being away, Eileen wanted to know what I learned. I told her. It didn't help her cope any better either.

We stayed over that night at the beach as I just wasn't in a mood to drive anywhere, much less back to Bensalem, my real world. However, the next morning we packed up and left the seashore to go home, two days earlier than was planned, and for a reason that I could have never imagined.

After dinner that first night back in Bensalem, I wanted to go to the police station and talk to the likes of Sgt. Gene Ashton or Lt. Jack Robinson again, the two senior officers I knew, respected, and trusted the most at the time. Maybe they could possibly offer some comfort to me and help me with what I was experiencing here. Perhaps they could tell me how long this pain would last. Any words of guidance, almost anything they could offer, would be appreciated, I assured myself and later them.

As I drove to the station, I noticed the U.S. flag in front of our building at half-mast, as I had noticed some other similarly positioned flags in front of other commercial buildings I had driven by on the way. When I walked toward the main glass doors of the station, I observed the black bunting over the entranceway. It reminded me that it had only been in 1975 that Bensalem buried its first officer ever killed in the line of duty. His name was James Armstrong. I had never met him, as I was hired a year-plus after his death. And now, just a bit over five years later, my mid-sized department was about to bury yet another officer.

I don't recall to whom I spoke at police HQ that night. Perhaps it was Sgt. Ashton, perhaps Lt. Robinson again. I recall observing for the first time that night they and the other officers and dispatchers were wearing little black mourning bands over their badges. I was issued one too that night for the next time I put on my uniform. Clearly not a piece of equipment that I ever wanted issued to me. But now I had one and I'd be wearing it for the next month.

After a few short conversations with different BPD staff and officers, I walked back to our locker room area. There, I noticed Bob's locker with various notes and black ribbons on it. There were flowers at its base. Nothing elaborate, just pieces of paper and other items with short handwritten messages to Bob, with a few rose stems propped up on the floor. The notes included, "We'll miss you, partner," and "Thanks for being a friend," and "One of Bensalem's Finest," and the like.

I found a piece of paper and hastily scribbled three words on it and taped it on the locker. I'm not even sure what I meant in this message which I very well knew that Bob would never actually read. But they were the first words which came to mind when I saw this makeshift memorial and I impulsively wrote them down and placed it among the other messages. I then immediately walked out the back door and drove home, speaking to no one else for the rest of the night.

My message read, "I'm sorry Bob."

Chapter Nineteen

Bob's viewing was a few nights later at a funeral parlor chosen by the Yezzi family. It was deep in the heart of Philadelphia, around the unofficial border of Center City and South Philadelphia. There was traffic congestion the whole evening around the place. The Philadelphia Police did their best to direct traffic and make sure attendees and regular local drivers alike could park and also drive through the busy intersection and surrounding streets. It was surreal seeing a dozen-plus Bensalem Police Department patrol cars in the heart of Philadelphia. It was a strange visual nexus juxtaposing my former life and my present life, brought together by this most unwelcome and tragic of events. I realized that this Philadelphia-Bensalem juxtaposition applied to Bob, too.

Inside the parlor that evening, for the first and only time in my life, I was assigned to be part of an official honor guard detail at a funeral service. Those of us in our police uniforms took turns for fifteen-minute intervals standing at attention on each side of Bob's casket for the duration of the three-hour viewing. Yes, we each wore the small black bands on our badges, as well as the larger black bands across our right upper-arms. It was by far one of the most difficult official or even unofficial functions I've ever had to perform, before or after that night. I should add that it was also my first and only time at a funeral service involving a very traditional Italian family. To say the least, it was an emotionally traumatizing and draining experience for me and everyone else there.

At first that night the family paid their private respects to Bob in the large, lavish room of the funeral parlor set aside for him. The ongoing sounds of human distress and complete and utter non-acceptance from within were very evident to the rest of us outside the initially closed doors to the room. Calling it very unsettling to us in waiting would be a gross understatement. When those doors finally opened, with Bob's family still in there and still visibly upset and shaken, the BPD officers were permitted in next to pay homage to their fallen comrade. Afterwards, when friends and others wishing to pay their respects to Bob were allowed in the room, the officers assumed the honor guard duties, in no particular order among us.

At some point during the several hour viewing, it was my turn to stand alongside Bob's coffin. His mom, dad, and sister, other close family members, and friends were sitting in the rows of chairs almost directly in front of it. This included John Tierno, our mutual friend and the person who introduced me to Bob during my store detective days. It had been at least four years since I had last seen him at the downtown Strawbridge & Clothier location. Never did I think our next time would be at a viewing, much less Bob Yezzi's viewing.

While performing my one quarter-hour honor guard detail, which seemed to me to last much longer, I was there to witness a very traumatic and moving scene, especially as my time coincided with the Catholic priest presenting his words of comfort and prayers to the large gathered crowd. They were nice words I must say, but they did nothing to stem the tide of despair and sadness in the room that night.

Bob's poor mother, who I believe was born in Italy, was crying uncontrollably the whole time. She was screaming aloud about how this should never have happened to her family, to her Bobby, her baby, inquiring vociferously as to where is her God when she needs Him, how could He allow this to occur, and similar heartfelt, sincere, and sometimes faith challenging admonitions and questions. They were recited in a sometimes barely understandable hybrid of English and Italian. I so wanted to leave my guard post position and kneel down next to Mrs. Yezzi, take her hand, and somehow try to say something, anything, which would possibly make her feel better. But I knew there was nothing I could tell her or do for her at this moment in time. She lost her only son, and she was grieving as any mother would do in a similar situation. Of course, I also knew that I had to maintain my post, looking simultaneously stoic and statuesque, until my "shift" was over and I was formally relieved by the next officer in line.

When that time finally came, I saluted, turned to my left and then to my right in the most official militaristic form I could muster, and continued to walk in-step with the other just-relieved officer to a back room where my various BPD fellow officers were congregating.

I didn't plan on what happened next, and I surprised even myself as it unfolded.

Upon entering the room with the three dozen-plus other uniformed and suit-wearing BPD officers, bosses, etc., and now out of the sight and hearing range of any family members or friends, something involuntary took over me. As hard as it had been for me an hour or so ago when I paid my own private respects to Bob, I found it immeasurably even more difficult to watch his mom, dad, sister, various aunts, uncles, cousins, and friends grieve as they did from my almost-on-top-of-them honor guard perch. I felt so helpless standing out there in my attempt to assist Bob, or at least his family members in this most distressing of times.

So, after these last fifteen minutes of watching Bob's spiritually and mentally devastated parents and family members, and as the doors closed behind me, I strode deep within the group of my colleagues. As a reaction to those pent up emotions and feelings of not just the last hour, but of the last seventy-two hours and perhaps even the last few years, I instinctively ripped off my police officer hat and flung it about twenty feet across the room into one of the corners. I then yelled loud enough for anyone to hear, "F**k Zajac and his f**king political games! Bob is dead because of them!"

I consciously recall afterwards I didn't say "him" at the end, meaning Zajac himself, but instead "them," referring to the political games which I knew resulted in Bob being just recently transferred, against his will, back to patrol. Of course, the interpretation was relatively clear and concise to all who may have heard me.

The room went silent for the next fifteen seconds or so. I'm not sure after all of these years if Deputy Chief Zajac was even in the room or not at the time, but I know many of his sycophants were there. And I didn't give a f**k either, then or afterwards.

A few of the guys slowly came over to me after my brief outburst, put their arms over my shoulders and walked me to the opposite corner of the room. They could see I was very upset. Quite frankly, this particular moment in time probably still stands as the most emotionally charged and physically out-of-control I have ever been in my adult life. But after a minute or two, I gathered my emotions and put them somewhat back into check. People slowly started talking in whisper tones again. Someone brought me over my hat and a cup of water. I thanked those who came over to me, but told anyone within range that I meant what I just said. That's because I did.

The viewing ended and we eventually drove home that night. However, we all knew there was more of the same to come in just a few hours.

The next morning, the whole BPD was up early. (Except for one officer and one officer only. He told me "I don't do funerals. They're too difficult for me." Okay...) We formed a procession of marked police cars from our Bensalem HQ and drove south on I-95 back to the funeral parlor. From there, the longest line of police cars I had ever seen, including from the Philadelphia Police Department, the Pennsylvania State Police, and dozens of other municipalities from the area and even surrounding states, each with its red lights flashing, proceeded to a Catholic church for the funeral Mass, then to a cemetery in Delaware County, in one of the western suburbs of Philadelphia. There, Officer/son/brother/friend Robert Yezzi was permanently laid to rest after a beautiful, traditional ceremony, including the playing of Taps, a twenty-one gun salute, calming words by important people, including Chief Michaels, and ending with a nice (I guess) luncheon afterwards.

I hated every minute of it.

When all the pomp and circumstance was done, all the timeworn speeches delivered, and after each and every police car was driven back to its home department, I was still without my closest friend on the Bensalem PD. I hated that feeling too.

None of it made any sense to me. I had a good friend one minute, and he's gone the next, in the prime of his life.

And for what? For who?

For some half-assed armed robbery suspect, confronted in the middle of nowhere, hit by a car being driven faster than it should have been driven at the time? There was no reasoning or sense to be made of this at all. I needed some rational explanation for it, but none was to be found, then or even decades later.

When he was physically and medically cleared, the perp who was the cause of the whole incident that fateful night was eventually arrested and charged with robbery, theft, aggravated assault, resisting arrest, and other related crimes. If he was charged with Bob's homicide, I believe it was dropped at some point in the subsequent legal proceedings. He ultimately served a few years in prison for his deadly misdeeds that night, but was released before the 1980s even reached their halfway point. I don't know what happened to him after that. I didn't care.

The driver of the car was not drunk or under the influence of any controlled substance that night. She was cited for reckless driving and perhaps a few other motor vehicle violations for her highway carelessness, but that was it for her. I don't know what happened to this woman either, and no, I didn't really care about her either.

Most importantly in regards to the eventual outcome of this whole sorry event, Officer Tony Rihl eventually recovered from his injuries. That was at least some good news. He was out of work for a year-plus on full disability, and could have easily and deservedly claimed such for the rest of his life. If he had done so, his annual salary would have remained at least what it was at the time of his injury, with even more "take-home pay" as it would have been taxed at a lower rate. However, to his great credit, Tony worked very hard to get his broken bones and other damaged internal body parts back into working order. By the end of 1981, he returned to the BPD fulltime as a patrolman with his faithful K-9 dog at his side.

Upon the official BPD investigation being completed, with the only living witnesses, Officer Rihl, the robbery perp, and the car's driver all being interviewed, it was agreed that Bob Yezzi's death was the result of a bad situation which then got worse, much worse, as the approximately one-minute long confrontation and arrest attempt unfolded that night. How the police cars were positioned on Richlieu Rd., how the felony suspect could have perhaps been approached differently, the two officers maybe waiting for additional backup to assist them in the arrest or even closing down the highway first, and many other scenarios were floated as to how Bob's death could have been avoided.

As cops, we all realized that it could have been any of us out there that night, or some other night, doing what we were trained to do. But then, with the unexpected, the intangible, the worst case scenario manifesting itself out of nowhere, it led to this very tragic and uncalled for loss of life and serious bodily injury.

Officer Robert Yezzi did nothing wrong that night, except perhaps not looking both ways when crossing a street. I'm not being flippant in that seemingly simplistic statement. I'm being realistic and matter-of-fact to make a point here.

How often have I, or other police officers and first responders, confronted people on the streets and highways in Bensalem, in Pennsylvania, in the United States, or in any country in the world for that matter, and let the actions of an errant suspect, a hot-headed and/or drunk driver, a mentally unbalanced pedestrian, or whomever, dictate an arrest scenario which then puts that public servant in harm's way?

I can assure you, from my own experience and the known experiences of other law enforcement officers I've met through the years, exactly what happened to Bob that night also happened to me and still happens every night to others as well. It may not necessarily be at 3:00AM; at a curve in a road; on a streetlight-less stretch; on a virtually moonless night; with an oncoming driver suddenly blinded by bright, flashing police car lights; who maintains her speed instead of reducing it; and with people in the roadway wearing mostly dark clothing.

It was the perfect storm that early morning of August 12, 1980, of things that could go wrong for Bob and Tony. One of them paid the ultimate price during that storm, with another coming close to suffering the same fate.

I should add here that despite my emotional outburst the evening of the viewing, I don't directly blame Deputy Chief Zajac for Bob Yezzi's death. Bob was a well-trained, intelligent, and capable police officer when he met his fate that night in the most improbable totality of dire circumstances. DC Zajac clearly didn't push him in front of the car on Richlieu Rd. However, it was no doubt a politically-motivated decision of the Deputy Chief which removed Bob from his good work in the Crime Prevention Unit and back into the Patrol Division just a week or so before his untimely death.

So, did Deputy Chief Zajac kill Bob Yezzi?

No!

Did the political culture within the BPD, the game playing, the manipulation and maneuvering of personnel at a whim for purposes clearly designed to promote and advocate DC Zajac's rise to the top at least contribute to Bob's death?

I'll let the reader decide on that one. I know I'm firm in my opinion, even these many years later.

In closing to this sad episode of the BPD and my life, and this tragic end of Officer Yezzi's life and the grievous injuries to Tony Rihl, there was something good to come out of it. I suppose....

I was proud to be a part of the initial developmental committee and at the eventual grand dedication of Yezzi Memorial Park. It is to this day a beautiful series of seven ball fields and several play areas located on a multi-acre tree lined expanse on Hulmeville Rd. in the Cornwells section of Bensalem Township. After a year plus of working with the Bensalem Parks Committee, and with others who devoted their time, efforts, and money to the design of this park, I was very gratified to be part of the opening day ceremonies on April 24, 1982.

On that bright spring day, we officially unveiled a portrait of Bob that the BPD had commissioned a well-known local artist to paint. It would later hang in the BPD HQ, alongside a previously painted portrait of James Armstrong. Their badge numbers, 32 for Officer Armstrong and 51 for Officer Yezzi, were forever retired in the BPD.

Members of the Yezzi family were there too at the park's dedication, and his parents and sister were also presented with smaller lithographs of the portrait of their son/brother. While it was a festive day for most in attendance, there were a few of us there that day who knew what unfortunate event led to Bob's name being forever attached to this now bucolic and play-oriented environment.

I was only one of numerous speakers on the dais that dedication day, to include politicians and other Bensalem and Bucks County luminaries. I kept my words short and to the point, mostly focusing on Bob Yezzi the person and how if he was somehow here today he would have thoroughly enjoyed this park and its future potential for the community.

However, to put the festivities of the day in perspective, I ended my talk with the following: "Let's hope there are many more parks in Bensalem Township like this. But let's hope it's the last one to be named after a Bensalem police officer."

While James Armstrong Memorial Park was opened up a year later in another part of the township, at the time of this writing, these are the only two parks in Bensalem to be named after slain police officers or other first responders. Two remains way too many by my count, but fortunately for those who served before me, with me, and those after me, Bensalem is holding steady at that number.

I hope and pray it stays that way.

* * * * *

In the very final note here, I have referenced Jim O'Brien, the former radio Boss Jock and *Action News* weatherman and anchor, at least two separate times so far in my writings. First it was when I was a young lifeguard (see JCM Book I), then again in the previous chapter when I was a still relatively young member of the Bensalem Police Department. The initial time, in 1972, it was interesting and cool to just have said "Hi" to a very popular celebrity from the Philadelphia area, and him respond with a seemingly genuine "Hi," along with a few other words, back at me. Then, of course, the next time I had any meaningful interaction with him, in 1980, it would not be in person, but via the television screen and with him as the deliverer of terrible news to me and the whole Philadelphia region. These two interactions were quite different scenarios, to state the obvious.

In any event, I followed Jim's career in the Philadelphia media market, along with a million-plus other listeners and viewers, through the 1970s and early 1980s. When watching the local television news, it would be his station I would watch, mostly because I liked his style, his look, and his overall demeanor and persona on the screen, while remembering some of that in person from my lifeguard days at my first poolside assignment.

Unfortunately, like Bob Yezzi's life being taken way too soon, so ultimately was the popular news anchor's life. In September of 1983, just about three years after Bob's death, Jim O'Brien was killed in a skydiving accident near an airfield in suburban Philadelphia. He was an accomplished and experienced skydiver, and it was on a Sunday afternoon that all of Greater Philadelphia learned of this tragic news. Ironically, it was reported on *Action News* by his own co-workers, a most difficult assignment for them, no doubt.

Jim's legacy continued, however, and it was also on the small screen. That's because a few years later one of his two daughters, Peri Gilpin, gained an acting role which made her quite famous in her own right. She played the character "Roz," on the very popular NBC television series *Frasier*, which ran from 1993 through 2004.

* * * * *

Bob's legacy continued in its own way in the form of Yezzi Memorial Park. Obviously, he, as well as the rest of us, would have preferred it not to have been as the result of his untimely death.

Knowing Bob as I did, he would have instead wanted his legacy to be carried on with "one of them," as he pointed to my young son in the backyard that time. Life didn't permit Bob that opportunity, or that legacy, for reasons I still can't fathom.

I miss you, Bob.

I'm sorry, Bob....

(+ Bonus Chapter 19a)

Top: Brochure, page 2, Yezzi Memorial Park Dedication
Bottom: April 24, 1982, Jim Fitzgerald, Supervisor Don
Bell, Chief Richard Viola, Sheriff Larry Michaels

Chapter Twenty

There wasn't much rest for the cop-funeral weary during that late summer and early fall of 1980, certainly as it applied to friends and colleagues of mine in the Philadelphia area. As mentioned in an earlier chapter, Gary Farrell, a Philadelphia Police officer and a guy I knew pretty well from my old Olney neighborhood, was killed in the line of duty as he attempted to arrest a robbery suspect.

Gary's murder was barely forty-four days after Bob Yezzi's tragic demise. Just when I was starting to recover somewhat from Bob's death, this happened again to someone I knew well. Most definitely, this wasn't an easy time to be a police officer in Philadelphia or its extended suburbs, especially as I was already contemplating just what it was I wanted to do with myself at this juncture in my life, professionally-speaking, that is.

But for now, I had a job to do. Despite the political nonsense still unfolding within the BPD, and much more importantly the violent deaths of two police officers with whom I worked or socialized, or both, I was nonetheless dedicated to my sworn duty once my uniform was put on and I was out on the streets in patrol mode. I owed it to the taxpayers who paid my salary, but even more so I owed it to myself. I couldn't and wouldn't do this job half-way or half-assed. That wasn't in me. So, despite the nonsense taking place within the four walls of my police HQ, and the very tragic loss of two police officer friends of mine, I was just as focused as ever to undertake my sworn duties and perform at the high level which I had previously set for myself. And, I should add, based on recent events, to assure more than ever that I would learn from what happened to Bob, Gary, and other slain police officers of whom I was aware, I would do as my dad had strongly recommended several years before to me to do at the end of every shift. That is, to simply make sure I come home. I was more focused than ever now to follow my late dad's advice.

* * * * *

Chief Larry Michaels finally retired. Within a year or so he would run for Sheriff of Bucks County. He would win that election and a few more after that and it was a post he would successfully maintain for the next fifteen years or so.

Despite the former Chief Michaels now officially out of the way, things were not necessarily going all that well for the guy who essentially forced him out, or at least orchestrated (through his father) all of Michaels' power and responsibility being taken away from him. That would, of course, be Ted Zajac, Jr. As Deputy Chief, he was still running the department and plotting and planning its official takeover with him as its formally named chief. However, much to his chagrin, the political structure of the township had changed as a result of the most recent election. There was now a Republican majority, at 3-2, controlling the elected board of supervisors, and this majority wasn't as gung ho and blindly supportive of the present Deputy Chief as their elected predecessors had been.

This new majority of three elected supervisors had the unmitigated gall to actually ask the Deputy Chief questions about what he was doing with the BPD as its interim CEO and how he was doing it. These questions concerned his form of leadership, his management decisions, budgetary issues, crime clearance rates, and related matters. This had been previously unheard of during the first two years of the unofficial Zajac regime. Upon receiving incomplete and otherwise unsatisfactory replies to their legitimate queries, these Johnny-come-lately elected interlopers even told the Deputy Chief that he may not be, after all, the heir apparent to the top job in the Bensalem PD. They had even boldly gone where no Zajac boss or supervisor had gone before and proffered that perhaps competitive testing for the position of chief of police in Bensalem was the more effective way to go in this regard.

Deputy Chief Zajac was advised at one of the regularly scheduled Monday evening public Board meetings that, in so many words, no one was saying he could not be the next chief of the Bensalem Police Department. Perhaps, in fact, he would merit that promotion. However, at this particular time, the majority faction of the board of supervisors felt it best for all involved that the chief position itself be advertised and opened to other potential candidates, both from within the BPD and without. After a battery of tests, including a written examination, a polygraph, formal interviews, background checks, etc., all taken into account, the best person would then be selected for the job.

Who could possibly argue with the fairness of this hiring/promotional protocol?

Ted Zajac, Jr., that's who, and adamantly so through most of 1981.

Ted Zajac, Jr., the self-appointed (actually, indirectly dad-appointed) Deputy Chief, lowering himself to take a competitive test to attain this position, make that any position, within the BPD? That's not how it's supposed to work. Not for him, anyway. There's no precedent for this. Well, not for Ted. Didn't they know who his father used to be and who he now wanted to be?

They did, but apparently they really didn't give a shit. Well, three of five of them (elected township supervisors) didn't anyway.

All of this information was great for a slowly growing number of police officers on the BPD. And, yes, it was amazing to watch as the tide was gradually turning just a bit against Team Zajac in early 1981. Numerous officers who beforehand were outwardly on his team were now slowly hedging their bets and migrating over to the other side. Just in case, I suppose.

Regardless of whose side one was on, most of us anxiously anticipated Tuesday afternoons to read the accounts in the *Bucks County Courier Times* as to what happened at the weekly Board meeting the night before. Sometimes, we'd have leaks of the Board's discussions and decisions during the course of the night if we happened to be working a midnight shift. One officer would get the info from some source of his and slowly pass it around to his like-minded colleagues. Other times, we'd have to wait for the next day's newspaper account of the potential future of our department. Either way, this year was definitely different for Team Zajac as things were not going his or their way.

I guess that damn cancer had now also spread to the Bensalem Township Board of Supervisors, or at least three-fifths of it, and the Deputy Chief was starting to feel its effects more than ever. That's a shame.

But wait, is there a doctor in the house? Is there anyone who could possibly assist this ailing patient?

Yes, there was. The Deputy Chief did have at least one very avid supporter, an unrepentant advocate, a stand-by-your-man kind of guy among the now-minority political faction on the Board of Supervisors.

His name was Stephen Kelly. He was in his late 30s with a flowing mop of brown hair, and an engineer of some sort at his official day job. This particular elected official, in office for several years at this time and whose political mentor was former supervisor Ted Zajac, Sr. (the daddy), would seemingly stop at nothing to see that his man, Ted Zajac, Jr. (the son), would be the next chief of police in his town. He worked tirelessly and did whatever it took to see that no person other than Zajac could or would assume the admiralty position of his police department ship. Apparently, he wholeheartedly believed in the merits of Deputy Chief Zajac and everything he stood for and represented.

Interestingly, just about one year later, with large, screaming newspaper headlines and the accompanying television and radio news coverage, with both Stephen Kelly and his brother as their focus, the Bensalem community and beyond would shockingly learn that he and his sibling and others had allegedly been "engineering" some other products within our town over the last few years.

Hmmm…a coincidence?

Chapter Twenty-One

By midway through 1981, Zajac and his minions were now on the defensive more than the offensive. That meant, among other things, they weren't screwing with officers as much as before. In fact, they were even trying to woo some of us onto their side. Hard to believe, but that even included me.

Most of us knew that the whole idea of the Patrol Division moving away from rotating eight-hour tours of duty to steady shifts of ten-hour tours of duty was devised by the new regime as an attempt to buy officers and curry favor, especially among the uniformed personnel. So, when the new steady-shift schedule was finally put together, it was surprising that one afternoon in the roll call room DC Zajac himself called me over and said he wanted to show me something. This had literally been the first time I had any real face-time with him since I sat in his office maybe a year and a half ago and was read the riot act by him about my patrol friends, post-Lamaze class restaurant meetings, a spreading cancer, etc.

Zajac on this day walked me into the empty sergeant's office and showed me a copy of the new ten-hour shift schedule. He wanted me to personally look at it and let him know if it seemed workable. I thought at first he wanted me to take it with me and study it later when I had time. But after he handed it to me, he stood right next to me and asked me what I thought of it.

I told the Deputy Chief that since there are eight legal pad-length pages here, which list each shift over the course of a calendar month, I would need some more time to review it and I couldn't say anything either positive or negative right now about it. After he kept insisting that it was great, everyone benefitted from it, etc., he expected me to agree with him right then and there and tell him that it was, in fact, great, beneficial, and so on. If it was those things, however, I needed time to realize so. I even asked him if I could borrow this document for a while and review it when I'm back out in my patrol car. He then

207

abruptly took it off of me and walked away with it and simply said frustratingly, "It's my only copy. Forget about it!"

Okay, perhaps it was a good, even great new schedule, but I couldn't and wouldn't validate it right there. I needed more time to study it. But that didn't seem to matter to DC Zajac. He wanted a quick favorable response from me, maybe to then tell others that "Hey, even Fitzgerald approves of it."

I couldn't do that for him. Not then. Not there.

As it turned out, by the early spring of '81, the BPD ten-hour steady shift was made official. It wasn't the schedule that Zajac had tried to force-feed me to advocate, but an altered version. Each patrol officer was given a first, second, and third choice as their preferred shift. I chose the 3P-1A shift. Fortunately, a week or two later, I got it.

I wasn't then (and am still not now) a fan of awaking before the sun is up, so I didn't want the 7A-5P shift. And, as I hated the midnight shift for the obvious sleep altering purposes, I didn't choose the 9P-7A shift either. To me, the late afternoon to just after midnight shift was the best one. Plus, it was generally the busiest shift. I liked to keep busy when I worked.

The Patrol Division implemented the new schedule and the officers immediately liked it. Before long, for various reasons, the second shift's hours were switched to 5P-3A to overlap more with the midnight shift and the busy 1A-3A hours (when the bars would be emptying), but that was no big deal. Those of us on it were still done by 3:00A, and even if we slept until 11:00 that morning, we still had a bit of the morning and a good part of the afternoon left ahead of us before we had to be at work again. Plus, we never worked more than four days in a row. During one part of every month, the tour was only three days in a row. With a total of fifty-two additional more days off a year (while still working the same number of hours per year) it was a win-win for all of us in the Patrol Division.

IF there was one thing that Deputy Chief Zajac proposed during his time that was a positive, this was it. In fact, it may have been the only positive thing he did during his tenure, at least for the betterment of the department as a whole.

Over many years, the BPD still worked this ten-hour shift. As empirical research has shown that a lifetime of weekly rotating shifts can take ten-plus years off of a person's life, I'm glad for the sake of my fellow officers at my former agency that this innovative work schedule finally took hold and a version of it is still in effect there.

* * * * *

There were several phone conversations with my former Olney friend Rob McCarthy over the course of a few weeks in which we tried to align our respective work schedules (me on the new steady 5P-3A shift, with varying nights off, Rob still working the standard rotating eight hour shifts with varying nights off). Finally, on a Friday night in April or May of '81 that we both had scheduled off, he invited me to join him at the Philadelphia Police Department Fraternal Order of Police (FOP) Hall. This facility was located in a building near the intersection of Broad St. and Spring Garden Ave., in downtown/Center City Philadelphia.

The FOP administrative offices and conference rooms were on the above-ground floors, but in the basement, down a long flight of stairs, was their hall, aka barroom. It wasn't a small basement by any means, as it contained a large and well-stocked bar, numerous tables and chairs along the sides, and even a dance floor in the middle. There was always music playing there, and on at least the several Friday nights I was there during the 1980s, there was usually dancing taking place too. It was a friendly environment for officers of the PPD, as well as guests from other law enforcement agencies, and even invited civilians; yes, to include female law enforcement officers and those females who were not employed in our field. There, the cops and guests could let down their hair and enjoy each other's company in a bar where almost everyone knew your name, if not rank and assignment.

On this particular April or May evening, while walking around the floor of the FOP barroom with Rob, he introduced me to some of his PPD buddies. I was a novelty, of sorts, as I wasn't in their department, but instead an outside cop, a suburban cop. There were a few jokes about me patrolling farm fields, moving cows off of the highway, etc., but after a while we'd talk about salaries, benefits, pension plans, schedules, and they'd individually tell me that I had it pretty good at the Bensalem PD.

"If only I had applied to Bensalem or one of the other suburban PDs when I was younger…," was a refrain I heard from a few of them once they were alone with me. Also, "Are they hiring there?"

I told them the BPD had its problems too and further added that sometimes I regretted turning down my chance to have joined the PPD when I was offered the position about four years ago. But I assured them that I would not be changing jobs any time soon. Most concurred with me regarding their present situations, too.

One of the officers I spoke to that night introduced himself as Dan something-or-other. Because of the loud music being played at the time, I didn't quite catch his last name as we were shaking hands. We talked for the better part of twenty minutes about his five years on the PPD, his assignment to the 6th District in Center City with Rob (but on different squads), growing up in Southwest Philly, me in Olney, his department, my department, and just general cop talk while sipping our respective beers. He seemed like a genuinely nice guy, from as much as I could hear of him while we all but yelled in each other's ears over the loud music in the background. After chatting for a while with Dan and this group of guys individually and collectively, Rob and I then gradually walked over to the other side of the bar and mingled with some people he knew there from his former patrol district. All in all, I remember thinking it was a pretty good night as we left the place around 1:00AM. Rob knew some cool guys on the PPD and I was glad I got to meet them and talk to them during our few hours at the FOP bar.

As we drove back to Rob's house (my car was parked there), I asked him a bit more about some of the various people we met that night, including Dan who was assigned to the 6th District. I asked Rob his last name. He told me it was Faulkner, Danny Faulkner.

I'm not sure if I made it back to the FOP later that year or not. As Friday nights were the best night to visit the FOP basement bar, I just don't believe Rob and I had that many of the same Friday nights off, or if he did have it off, he had to be on duty early Saturday morning and he didn't feel like going out the night before. Either way, as it turned out, it was a one-time meeting I had with Officer Danny Faulkner in the spring of '81 at the FOP. As with many people one meets briefly during their lifetime, even the very friendly and the clearly-got-their-acts-together type people (which was Danny), the memory of him or her may stay for a brief time, but then it may fade after a while. Regardless of where he was in my consciousness on December 9th of that year, Danny Faulkner's name and person came back to me. It has stayed with me and millions of others ever since, from Philadelphia and around the world, for various personal, professional, and/or ideological reasons.

My personal memories of that night at the FOP came back to me on December 9, 1981. Around 3:00AM that morning, Officer Daniel Faulkner was shot to death while lawfully arresting a cab driver in the Center City area of Philadelphia. Also found shot and injured at the scene, and subsequently arrested, was an individual with the birth name of Wesley Cook. He was the cab driver's brother and came to assist his now-in-custody sibling as Officer Faulkner was placing him into handcuffs.

At the subsequent 1982 trial, the jury was told by numerous witnesses and experts that the injured Wesley Cook was found at the scene with a handgun on or very near him. Receipts later proved he had previously bought and possessed the handgun. Rounds fired from that weapon were ballistic matches to those found in the body of Danny Faulkner. A well-aimed round from Officer Faulkner's gun had also been found in Cook as the uniformed patrolman managed to get off one trigger pull of his service revolver after he was initially shot from behind and before the officer collapsed and died from multiple additional shots, fired at him execution-style.

Based on the evidence presented at the trial, the jury convicted Cook. He was sentenced to death by the same jury one day later. He's been in a Pennsylvania prison ever since.

Oh, and Wesley Cook goes by another name, one by which he's much better known today. That is, Mumia Abu-Jamal.

I'm not going to recount any more of the story as it relates to Officer Faulkner's murder and the subsequent trial of Cook/Abu-Jamal, or the legal appeals, media articles, television specials, documentaries, movies, books, protests, sit-ins, petitions, and the national and international notoriety that this case has garnered. It's all been done, if not overdone, already.

Incomprehensibly, based on some of the false information out there about this crime and this convicted killer, there are even two cities in France where the mayors and city councils agreed to name streets after Abu-Jamal. One was in St. Denis and the other in Bobigny.

Yes, you read this correctly. The streets are NOT named after Officer Faulkner, a dedicated law enforcement officer, but instead his convicted murderer.

For reasons which escape me to this day, this is the cause that many entertainment figures and celebrities, at least two French mayors and their city councils, as well as others looking for their yearly something-new-to-protest issue, latched onto in terms of further vilifying the alleged injustice of the U. S., its penal system, the courts, the death penalty, "the Man," and/or any other aspect of society of which they were not in favor. Only, they forgot or somehow never knew in the first place that Mumia Abu-Jamal was, in fact, convicted with overwhelming evidence of killing the police officer who was merely carrying out his sworn duty. No legal appeals, even after thirty years, have convinced any number of judges that Abu-Jamal did NOT shoot and kill Officer Faulkner or that his rights were violated in any way at the scene of the arrest or during the later investigation.

It was becoming very tiring to hear this rhetoric over and over again from some well-known Hollywood actors and other entertainers who knew so little about the facts of the case, only that Abu-Jamal was on death row and he should be thusly acquitted of all charges against him. They seemingly were not satisfied just doing away with his death sentence and having it reduced to life in prison, but completely freed from prison too and/or pardoned for his crime.

(I should add here that I respect the differing opinions regarding the death penalty in the U. S., or anywhere for that matter. I've vacillated myself in the past as to its legitimacy and efficacy. However, these arguments over the years regarding Mumia Abu-Jamal went well beyond the focus of simply this particular issue.)

In 1995, around the world, the U. S., and certainly in the Philadelphia area, this matter was at a fever pitch as various legal appeals of Abu-Jamal's death sentence were coming to the forefront, and there was the expected over-the-top media coverage and related partisan activism regarding all of these new developments. It was a difficult time to be living in Philadelphia if one was a law enforcement officer of any sort, not to mention having actually met Danny Faulkner, even if it had been just briefly fourteen years earlier.

In July of 1995, as a newly minted FBI profiler having just completed my three months of behavioral training at the FBI Academy, I was sent on a long-term assignment to the Unabom Task Force in San Francisco, California. Part of me was glad to be away from Philadelphia, seemingly the "Free Mumia" epicenter of the world, and the constant bombardment of information, much erroneous and biased as it related to this case, this man, and his violent crime. The coverage many times conveniently failed to mention that a police officer had even been killed, or if so, just in passing. Nonetheless, being in San Francisco, some 3,000 miles away, would be a welcome respite for me from the non-stop media coverage of these almost circus-like events regarding the "rights" of Mumia Abu-Jamal. Or, so I thought.

On that first jet-lagged night in the City by the Bay, after unpacking my suitcases and various case materials, I walked out onto the fourth floor balcony of the Opera Plaza condo at which the FBI had arranged for my lodging. I wanted to stretch, take in some fresh air, and wrap my head around this new and challenging assignment awaiting me. Upon casually looking across Van Ness Street and then upwards at the top of a nearby five-story building was a clearly displayed and well-lit billboard. On it, in big black lettering, were the words "Free Mumia Abu-Jamal Now," with a picture of the convicted cop-killer next to it.

Damn! Is there anywhere I can go to escape this stuff?

The Van Ness Street billboard "ad" came down a week or two later and the story eventually went away for a while, at least from the everyday headlines. The rest of my time in San Francisco, I'm glad to say, was relatively Mumia-free.

In 2011, after years of appeals by an onslaught of defense attorneys, the Philadelphia District Attorney's Office finally announced that they would not fight a judge's recent order which effectively took Abu-Jamal off of death row. His sentence was now life in prison, with no possibility of parole. I guess his side won, although his advocates continue to fight even this sentence, wanting him completely exonerated, if not pardoned, for his crime.

Of course I would have been personally and professionally affected by the murder of Officer Faulkner in 1981 whether I had ever actually met him or not. He was a brother law enforcement officer killed in the line of duty. But it was even more difficult as two police officer friends of mine had also been killed/murdered in the fifteen months prior to his death. Adding to all of this was the fact that I spent a brief moment in time with Danny, a genuinely nice guy, in a friendly conversation that previous spring night in the FOP bar. It somehow brought it all even closer to home. To include even years later when I was far from home in San Francisco hunting yet another violent killer, the Unabomber.

RIP, Danny Faulkner, one of PPD's finest, and a great guy to all who knew him.

Chapter Twenty-Two

Back to Bensalem in the early 1980s...

The political soap opera continued to play out within the four walls of the BPD. It was seemingly growing more intense every day as the spring of 1981 moved toward summer. The *Bucks County Courier Times* (BCCT) rarely had a week's worth of its newspapers go by in which the contest for the BPD police chief job, and the ancillary stories associated with it, were not front page, above the fold articles. Even the big city *Philadelphia Inquirer* picked up on the various plotlines along the way and would run the occasional story about it.

Every once in a while, along with the articles, some local resident and alleged concerned taxpayer would write a letter to the editor to the BCCT supportive of Zajac and the supposed professional way he was running the department. Within a few days, there would be another letter posted, this one attacking Zajac and the supposed way he was running the department. He seemingly had an equal share of advocates and enemies, at least if you only read the local newspaper.

The 3-2 Republican majority Board of Supervisors continued their stated agenda that the next chief be selected as a result of fair and open testing. Also continuing was the loud and vociferous stated agenda of Zajac's strongest ally on the board, albeit now a minority member, Supervisor Stephen Kelly. But despite his pointed remarks and unabashed support for the present Deputy Chief to become the future Chief, the competitive hiring process had begun.

We rank-and-file officers knew little about the machinations behind what was actually going on at the time. We heard through the grapevine that anywhere from a dozen to a hundred candidates applied for the position which had been listed in the local Philadelphia area newspapers, and also in *Police Chief*, the monthly professional journal. Some applicants, it was subsequently learned, were quickly cut after the written test. Some were dismissed after the interview stage. Some were out of the running after the background investigation. Some were gone after failing the polygraph examination. Just who was in and who was out and even how many were still in contention was a mystery to the rest of us as the summer wore on.

It was rumored that both Deputy Chief Zajac and another supervisory officer, Lieutenant Ron Traenkle, applied for the chief position. However, it was unclear where they stood in the rankings, or if they were still in the running at all towards the end.

Despite this ongoing mystery as to who our next boss would be and when it would all come to fruition, I wasn't just sitting around on my hands. I was there to do a job, and that I did. My patrol duties from 5P-3A, four days a week, were my primary focus each day when I put on the uniform. Regarding the quest for that top BPD position, all I really wanted was to be assured that it was a thorough, comprehensive, and objective testing regimen being undertaken in the process. From what I was hearing and reading, it seemed it was so. If after everyone had been vetted it was determined that DC Zajac was to be the one, then that's what was meant to be. I'd have to live with it. However, along with everyone else in the department, I would have to wait a while to hear who would be the ultimate winner of this promotional contest.

Interestingly, I would meet one of the candidates for the BPD chief position months before any hiring decision was ultimately made. In fact, it was well before most of us knew this person existed or that he had already applied for the job.

No, I wasn't asked all of a sudden to join the chief position search committee. Instead, the unplanned meeting occurred on the streets of Bensalem. How I met this candidate was in the most unusual and potentially tragic of ways. He could have lost his opportunity to possibly serve as our future chief right then and there. He could have also lost much more than that; me too, for that matter.

Was it a coincidence how I met this person on that fateful afternoon? Was it orchestrated by the BPD Dark Side to go down as it did? I'm not sure after all this time, but nothing would surprise me during this turbulent lead-up in the hunt for our next chief of police.

The story unfolded this way....

Late one afternoon while on patrol in the late spring of '81, I received a message over the police radio from the dispatcher to call the Detective Sergeant in CID. I promptly found a street-side payphone and called him. This happened to be Sgt. Pansy, the same CID supervisor that I was forced to deal with when making the undercover PCP buy a few years earlier as a plainclothes officer. Our relationship since then had been strained, to say the least. His loss, not mine, I reckoned.

During this particular phone call, Sgt. Pansy advised me one of his "reliable sources" told him that there was a suspicious red Cadillac cruising around the Doral Apartment complex and it wasn't the first time he (the source) saw it there. This several hundred unit rental community, with its known share of crime and drug related problems, was located at the intersection of Knights Rd. and Dunks Ferry Rd., right above the Philadelphia city line in Bensalem. In the car, I was told, was "a lone, smarmy looking white male, approximately 40 years of age, maybe dealing drugs."

Pansy also gave me the car's plate number, which he further advised that when he ran it through DMV it came back "No Record Found." He added that he didn't want to put the call over the police radio as his source said to him that the suspicious person may have a police scanner in the car. So, he had me call in by telephone to relay this information to me. It was strongly suggested that I locate and observe this guy and his activities for as long as I could, see if he was committing any crimes, then stop and identify him if possible.

Okay, I can do this, I told the sergeant. But, why me?

I reminded the CID sergeant that I'm in full uniform in a patrol car now and not in the plainclothes Tactical Squad anymore. Where are those guys? I suggested he send them or one of his detectives if he really wanted to find out what the alleged smarmy guy in the red Cadillac, whose tag has no record, is doing in the Doral Apartment complex.

Sgt. Pansy advised me that all the Tac Squad guys were tied up on another matter as were the detectives. But, he offered in an obvious condescending tone, he knew with my prior surveillance experience I'd be the go-to guy here, even in uniform and in a marked car. I told him this was sort of a strange request, the attempted surveillance of this person with me in a marked car, but as things were quiet on the streets right now and with the help of my trusty binoculars (which I still carried, even as a uniformed officer), I'd do my best to stay at a distance and observe what the guy was doing. The detective sergeant thanked me and he quickly ended the call.

I didn't trust Sgt. Pansy before this telephonic conversation, going back to quasi-working with him when I was on the Tac Squad, and I still didn't trust him at the time of this request. There seemed something fishy about this whole scenario. Knowing his professional history and also that he was one of Zajac's Boys didn't engender with me all that much confidence in him either.

Again, why me here?

But I said I'd do it and I figured I'd carry through. The back of my neck hairs were up though the whole time and my senses were on full alert. For exactly what reasons I wasn't sure, but my life experience to date told me to be so.

After a partial drive-thru of the complex, I saw the red Cadillac off in the distance without, I believe, the driver initially seeing me. The engine was idling and the driver was sitting behind the steering wheel hardly moving at all. He was just staring off into the distance as if waiting for something to happen. For the next ten minutes, I watched this guy from afar through my binoculars, also waiting for something to happen. He was stationary this whole time and I maintained my position on the west side shoulder of Knights Rd., above the complex, where I could look down and watch him through my binoculars. Eventually, somebody came out of one of the apartment buildings and walked over to him. They exchanged a few words and an envelope or piece of paper or something of the sort. The Cadillac then pulled away and out of my sight.

Okay, what was that all about? I didn't necessarily see a crime being committed, but something strange did seem to be going on here.

I decided to leave my somewhat elevated observation post on the street and drive into the complex again to look for the car. I didn't see the Cadillac at first but upon turning a corner there it was, parked in another spot, still with the engine running. As I had no choice but to drive my marked car directly alongside the Caddy, the unshaven, cap-wearing, suspicious-looking guy stared at me as I slowly drove by. Then, once I passed his car, he took off from his parking spot and drove straight ahead toward one of the complex exits.

Well, I was asked to check out this guy and I figured now was the time to do it. As I was now "made" by him after inadvertently driving right next to his car, I decided to pull a car stop on him and find out what the heck he was doing here in the complex. Did he just conduct a drug deal? Receive a payoff for something? Was he now holding contraband of one form or another? I suppose I should find out.

I did a U-turn and started back in the direction of his car. We were both still in the large complex parking lot when I pulled up behind the slowly moving car and turned on my red lights. I could see the driver look in his rearview mirror. He knew I was behind him, but strangely he didn't stop. He just kept driving at a slow rate of speed. He went right up to one of the exits onto the street, but instead then turned and continued to drive back through the complex. I stayed behind him, my red lights still on, and decided to give him a blast of the siren. Now, even with both visual and auditory commands to stop, he still for some reason refused to do so. It was a car chase, sort of, but at a very slow rate of speed. This was getting even weirder, I thought.

I broadcast over the police radio that I was attempting a car stop in the Doral Apartments parking lot and that this guy was not pulling over for me. At least one other nearby police unit responded that he was enroute. Finally, the driver drove to an exit and turned left onto Dunks Ferry Rd., which runs on the north side of the complex. After travelling westbound a few hundred yards, in the fading sunlight under a flickering street lamp just coming to life, in a place with few other people or cars around, the driver decided to finally pull over his red Cadillac.

At the same time I was calling out my exact location to the dispatcher, I observed the driver sort of angle his body to his left, use his right arm to reach down and possibly grab onto something on the seat next to him, then bend over to his right as if to put that something on the floor of the front passenger seat.

Not a good sign, I said to myself.

Small hairs on neck, stand up, please. Make that stand up even farther, please.

I purposefully exited my patrol car and slowly walked up to the driver's side window, which I noticed was now in the down position. I had my flashlight in my right hand with my left hand hovering alongside my holstered weapon. The driver just stared ahead with his hands on his lap, with no initial acknowledgment I was even there. As was my custom on all car stops, while standing on the street somewhat behind the driver in the front seat, I did my best to visually assess the backseat and the front passenger seat of the car to make sure there was nothing or no one that could possibly harm me. The car, so far as I could see, appeared clean. It was then, while assured that he was alone in the car and his hands were empty and I was about to say the usual, "License and registration, please," that I shined my flashlight into the front seat area of the car and saw what every cop fears when he confronts a suspect on foot or in a car.

That is, a gun.

I could clearly see the brown grips sticking out from under the passenger seat. Damn, I thought in a nanosecond - that must have been what he contorted his body to remove and try to hide under the seat just as I was pulling him over.

Needless to say, in the very next nanosecond I had my .357 Magnum out of its holster in my left hand, backing up just a step so he couldn't reach out and grab it from me, and I was pointing it directly at the driver's head. At the same time, I yelled authoritatively, "Hands on the wheel! Now! THEN DO NOT MOVE!"

The driver slowly looked up at me, smirked a bit, and put his hands in the 10:00 and 2:00 position on the steering wheel, strangely in a manner suggestive of the fact that he's done this before. Then, in almost too calmly a manner, he said back to me, "Kid, relax. My .38's on the floor, out of the way. It's all good."

I replied to his statement in a very adamant fashion, showing that I was in charge of my level of relaxation, the scene, my .357 Magnum, and him, "Yeah, and it'll stay 'all good' as long as your hands don't move off of that f**kin' steering wheel! You move anything but your lips, I start shooting! UNDERSTAND?!"

"Yeah, yeah...Kid, I told ya, it's okay. I'm 3-6-9," again, in a voice much too calm for the situation unfolding in front of us here, at least from my perspective.

"3-6-9?!" I repeated out loud, in a voice no doubt giving away equal amount of surprise, incredulity, and anger, as to how this scene was rapidly playing out.

I knew right away what he meant. "3-6-9," at least in the latter part of the 20th century and in the general Southeastern Pennsylvania area, was a "code" word, or more accurately I suppose, a "code" number. It was utilized when one police officer wanted to identify himself to another police officer, whether off-duty or in a plainclothes capacity. Its origin is unknown, although probably has something to do with the police 10-code.

"Tell me more, but keep those hands on the wheel where I can see them," I all but shouted to the driver, with my gun still pointed at his head. I remained standing slightly behind him, just as we were taught at the Academy, so he had to look back and up at me from his driver's seat position. He did, in fact, manage to keep his hands on the steering wheel of his car this whole time, a smart move on his part.

"Okay, it's like this...hey, what's your name, by the way?"

Geez, now he's asking ME questions. It's like we had just met in a bar or something.

"It's Fitzgerald. Now I want your name and badge and ID and with just one hand, and do it all in slow motion," I instructed him firmly.

While very deliberately using one hand to pull out, flip open, and show me his weathered leather wallet with badge and photo ID card inside, which upon quick examination looked authentic to me, he finally offered more in the way of explanation.

"All right, Officer Fitzgerald, here's the deal. I'm a sergeant with Philly Major Investigations Unit. Rich Viola is my name. I'm investigating a team selling drugs and guns all around this area, and one of the mopes I'm dealing with lives in your apartment complex back there. I knew you were watching me but if I had pulled over when you first put on your lights and I had to identify myself it would have blown months of work in this operation. And I figured if you saw my gun right away, you'd draw down on me, so I put it under the seat, but I guess not all the way, and...."

I interrupted him with a combination of anger and impatience, "So you're a Philly cop on a stakeout in Bensalem! Is that what you're saying? Did you tell anyone in my PD what you were doing here?"

"Ah...well, no, I didn't. This meeting sorta all came together quickly today. Plus, this place is right over the city line. But I guess I should have, right? I will next time, I swear," he offered in a not-so-earnest fashion.

By this time, a backup BPD patrol car pulled up behind us and the officer got out and went to the other side of the Cadillac, just as he was trained to do. I finally put my gun back in my holster, told my partner this guy was a Philly cop, and proceeded to walk back to my patrol car.

I was fuming at this point. Once I reached the front of my car I slammed my fist onto the hood and yelled out loud for no one in particular to hear, "Jesus Christ Almighty!"

I meant it reverently, of course.

As a cop and later as an FBI agent, I didn't necessarily like having to pull my gun on anyone, much less than holding it point blank at that person's head. But I ESPECIALLY disliked doing so when it was a fellow law enforcement officer's head, and an on-duty one at that.

Damn!!

How the hell could this scenario have reached this point? One working cop pulling a gun on another working cop? As I was trained at the police academy five years earlier, my finger was not actually on the trigger during this minute-plus confrontation, but it was real damn close and ready to go there in one of those aforementioned nanoseconds. I wondered afterwards if a nearby car had coincidently backfired at the same time, or some neighborhood kid lit off a firecracker, would I have moved my finger onto the trigger, pulled it, then...well, who knows what then? It would be a classic case of "friendly fire" in which a law enforcement officer shoots and/or kills one of his own in the course of a misidentification of some sort.

Damn again...!!

Coincidently, the other BPD officer who showed up happened to have a brother in the Philadelphia Police Department. Once things calmed down at the scene he started talking to Sgt. Viola and it was soon determined that he (Viola) knew his brother, and lieutenant so-and-so, and captain what's-his-name, and he (the other BPD officer) nodded to me that Viola was apparently the real deal. Well, the real deal in Philadelphia, anyway. He's now in Bensalem though. What does that make him here? I was still pissed off that he was in MY town doing HIS police work. He should have told someone within our higher-ups in the BPD.

Right?

Or, should he have...?

Sgt. Viola eventually got out of his Cadillac and talked to the two of us on the side of Dunks Ferry Rd. He wasn't a particularly tall guy, maybe 5'9" or so, but solidly built. And he wasn't as ratty or "smarmy" as he was described to me over the phone by the Pansy one. He was wearing some nice clothes and what looked to be very expensive leather boots. And he's driving a Cadillac. What is up with this guy?

Viola explained, without even being asked, that he used his personal car (with his portable police radio) for these type assignments so as to better conceal his identity when working these cases. He knew if these guys saw him driving a plain Ford or Chevy of some sort, they'd make him for a cop right away.

Well, he certainly fooled me the whole time, that's for sure. In my law enforcement career, up to that point anyway, I never knew a plain-clothes cop to be driving that nice of a car for his work assignment. In fact, I never knew a cop who even owned a Cadillac.

Anyway, before Sgt. Viola left the area, after a seemingly genuine "Sorry about the mix up, Kid" and handshakes to both of the BPD officers on the scene, the Philly cop promised that he'd contact my agency the next time he was working in Bensalem. I didn't really believe him, but then upon reflection a part of me didn't really blame him. My fellow BPD officer later agreed with me in that regard.

As the two white and blue Ford patrol cars and the red Cadillac sedan individually pulled away from the car stop scene, I knew what I had to do. I didn't bother to find a payphone to call Sgt. Pansy. Instead, I drove to HQ to tell him to his face what had just happened. But surprise, surprise...he wasn't there. He took off the rest of his shift for some reason. No one else in CID (yes, there were detectives milling around the office area when I got there) seemed to know anything about his "request" of me from just an hour or so earlier.

How about that?

I didn't see this supervisor until the next evening shift when I finally tracked him down in his CID office and told him what the suspicious car/person scenario developed into, with my gun to the head of another cop and all. He acted surprised and even mad that this Philly cop would encroach on our territory.

"How dare he?" Sgt. Pansy was heard to say several times over.

After twenty-four hours of thinking this thing through, I didn't believe this Zajac Boy/CID Sergeant for a second when he told me he was surprised OR mad. I felt he somehow knew more than what he was relating to me, and he knew all of this yesterday, before he sent me to check out the alleged suspicious person.

Damn, these hairs on the back of my neck were standing up again. I realized later I wasn't sure if they were up because of having to deal with this sergeant, the mission he sent me on, or because I was back in the Belly of the Beast, aka CID, aka the Backroom, still run with an iron fist by the now chief position-challenged Zajac, staffed by his appointed uber-loyal zealots, with this detective sergeant near the top of the zealotry totem pole.

Needless to say, I didn't stay in CID long that evening. Before leaving the room, however, I told the detective sergeant to use one of his own boys the next time he wanted a surveillance of someone "smarmy," especially if they may actually be another cop. I walked away before he could respond.

Was being sent on this "mission" all just a coincidence? Was it by happenstance? Did Sgt. Pansy really have source information about a "smarmy guy in a red Cadillac dealing drugs" in the Doral Apartment complex? Or, did this info come from somewhere else, somewhere higher up within the BPD or the Township?

Was it something more sinister, more devious, on the part of the CID and BPD and those within its upper management? Did they know Philly PD was doing part of their investigation in the Doral

Apartments? Was this investigation infringing on one of the BPD's investigations or possibly someone else's operation? Or was this particular Philadelphia PD Major Investigations Unit sergeant on their "list" for some other reason?

And was I chosen because the bosses knew I would do it right, but at the same time if something went wrong (as it almost did that evening), they'd then have the benefit of plausible deniability, as I was not one of DC Zajac's favorite sons?

I simply wasn't sure what it all meant back then immediately after it went down, but a few months later, the puzzle pieces finally came together.

I would meet Rich Viola again. It would be in Bensalem Township again. The next time, however, it would be a completely different scenario. No one could describe him as looking smarmy that night.

Geez...and I held a gun to this guy's head? Now what am I in for?

(+ Bonus Chapter 22a, 22b)

Chapter Twenty-Three

After an invigorating and overall pleasurable nine-day international vacation throughout New England and Nova Scotia, my family and I were back home in Bensalem. One car, two bikes, and three people all made the return trip in one piece. After a restful weekend plus a few extra days off, once all the unpacking, laundry, and minor car and bike maintenance were completed, Wednesday, September 2nd, was upon me. I was scheduled to go in for my regular 5P-3A shift later that day.

At 4:40 or so on that Wednesday afternoon I jumped on my now even more well-travelled Fuji 10-speed, and off to work I pedaled for the very short trip to work. (Yes, I was really into biking during this stage of my life. Even biking to work.) No rolling hills or picturesque seaside vistas on this ride; just the banality of Hulmeville Rd. during rush hour.

This first post-vacation shift back at work wouldn't be just any normal day though. It would be the day that the BPD's new chief of police would be announced. At least that's what I had reconfirmed telephonically from my PD buddies over the last week. I was glad to be working this night. I may be among the first to hear the news.

Would I be rejoicing at the announcement? Dismayed by it? Or, perhaps be only neutral about it? Time will tell, I told myself.

As it turned out, within several hours of the start of this shift, I would be rejoicing; well, more or less. By the next morning I would be dismayed; and definitely MORE so, not less. How could that be?

This could only happen to me, I thought, and only involving the Bensalem PD.

After a predictable first few hours on patrol that September Wednesday evening, to include my usual (and always welcome) thirty-minute dinner at home with Eileen and Sean, I began the last two-thirds of my shift at around 7:00. I was not one of those officers that liked to hang around HQ unless I absolutely had to for an arrest processing, equipment change, a formal talk with a boss, or something like that. Tonight would be no exception. So, instead of just coincidently showing up at 8:30 or so to use the bathroom, pick up equipment, run a tag through DMV, or the like, which would be the estimated time the new chief was to be introduced, I came up with an alternate idea.

Earlier in the shift I asked our dispatcher to make the announcement on Channel Three of our radio band (an administrative channel) when she heard the news from upstairs. She agreed to do so, and I told a few of my squad mates of the pending message. It took her until almost 9:00 for her to find out and then instruct the several of us interested officers to make the channel switch.

It went something like…

"696 to 22 (Bensalem) cars, switch to channel three," the dispatcher spoke into her mike with a hint of newly gained knowledge resonating in her pitch and timbre.

Several, if not all, of us on duty that night switched over, with some electronically stepping on each other in the process. We individually replied, "22-7 on Channel 3;" "22-10, here;" "22-12 here, tell us what you know."

That last one was me.

"22 cars, be advised the Board of Supervisors, with a 3-2 vote, just appointed a former Philadelphia Police Department commander to be Bensalem's new chief. His name is Richard (and what sounded through some ill-timed static like) Bolla. That's all that's available so far, back to channel one now."

There were a number of "10-4s" among the troops. Some officers were dead silent afterwards. Some were clicking their mike buttons non-stop, sort of a cop's way of giving a round of applause or non-verbal affirmation over the radio. At least one officer, who was clearly holding his mike an arm's length away from his mouth so as to not be readily identified, was heard to state "Bye-bye Teddy Z, don't let the door hit you in the ass!"

That last one was NOT me, whether I was thinking it or not.

Okay, so it's official. It's a done deal. We now have a new chief of police. It's not Zajac. Thank God! But what was his name…?

"Bolla, Richard Bolla?"

Hmmm, that name sounds familiar, I was thinking, possibly even saying it aloud in the solitude of my patrol car. A former Philly police commander…I wonder what his rank is, or was. Did he quit the PPD job just for the Bensalem position, or was he already retired and maybe working somewhere else for a few years? If he was a commander, he was high up there, no doubt. Of course, he's high up there once again as he's now Chief Richard Bolla in Bensalem.

Dang, I know I recognize that name; maybe from the Philly media. I'm sure he was one of those guys on TV speaking to the reporters at the scene of a big homicide or major drug arrest. But I'm not so sure. I also wonder if he came up through the ranks of patrol or investigations. That could make a difference in this guy's priorities once he assumes command.

So many questions....

A few of us talked that evening from car to car, but none of us had any more information to share with the others. We all kept saying this guy Bolla must have been a major player in the Philadelphia PD, an Inspector, Deputy Chief, or something like that. But as we knocked off our shift at 3:00A (me a bit later as I got tied up on a last minute call), we/I didn't know much more about our new chief than when the dispatcher informed us at 9:00P.

Yes, it is confirmed that we have a new boss. No, it's not Zajac. All good so far, but just who is this new guy?

Richard Bolla...geez, that name sounds familiar. I guess I'll learn more about him tomorrow from the newspaper and certainly when I get back into the police station at 5:00. It'll be interesting.

To say the very least, it would prove to be "interesting," and to no one more than me.

I was up by 10:00 the next morning, getting no more than six hours of sleep that night, almost two hours less than usual. Eileen was already at work and Sean was at the morning babysitter's house about three blocks away. I would always walk or bike over to pick up Sean shortly after I awoke on work days and we'd come back to eat my breakfast and his lunch together. Today though, I went outside first to fetch the newspaper.

Coincidently, like many other newspapers at the time, the *Bucks County Courier Times* (BCCT) had only several months before become a morning newspaper, ending its decades-long run as an afternoon paper. It proved very timely for me, certainly on this day. I wanted to quickly check the front page of the September 3rd BCCT as I knew its dedicated journalists would have additional information to provide to their readers regarding who was our new chief of police. So, before I even reentered my front door, I removed the rubber band and unfolded the newspaper and there it was.

The headline read something like, "Bensalem Appoints New Chief by 3-2 Vote." Okay, I knew that. But in the split second it took me to read the headline, I momentarily failed to take in the black and white photograph directly beneath it and off to one side. Then my eyes focused slightly downwards and to the right and there was a handsome man, in his mid-40s, semi-smiling, in an expensive looking suit, glancing directly at the camera, directly at ME it seems, while walking out the township building's front doors.

So, this was the new Chief. His name is Richard J. Viola. It must be as that's the name below the photo.

Wait! I thought his name was "Bolla!" But it's not "Bolla," as we heard (or thought we heard) over the radio last night, and which I had never bothered to later confirm.

No, it's "Viola!" Richard J. Viola!

NOW I recall from where I know that name, or the version of it I heard, or thought I heard, last night. And it's from not that long ago and not that far away.

If I drank coffee and had been holding a cup of it at the precise moment this all synthesized in my brain, I assure you I would have dropped the hot liquid on my feet while still outside my front door. Instead, I let out a much too loud "Holy Shit!"

As my neighbors still had their windows open on this relatively warm September morning, there's no doubt some of them heard what I just said. It left my lips at this somewhat elevated volume for a very good reason. I just now realized who this guy WAS. I just now realized who my new boss IS. He's not a former high-ranking Philadelphia PD commander. That "rumor" threw us off last night in connecting his name (which was also mispronounced/misstated/static-y) to what he used to do and who he used to be. According to the paper, he had been a sergeant in Philly, assigned to the Major Investigations Unit.

Again, Holy Shit! I met this guy on a previous occasion, an unlikely previous occasion. Yes, it's all coming back to me very clearly now; way too clearly, as a matter of fact.

This is the guy at whose head I pointed my .357 Magnum just a few months ago near the Doral Apartment complex. He was in the suspicious red Cadillac who took something from a guy, he wouldn't pull over for me, he had a gun on the floor, he was kinda smarmy looking at first, and yes, he was a cop, a Philly sergeant in the MCU, Richard Viola.

What the heck does this all mean to me?

Geez...Zajac never really liked me and treated me as such, but at least I had never pointed a loaded gun at his head. How would now-Chief Viola react to me, an officer who drew down on him, two feet from his head no less? If I ever even talk to this guy, do I bring up the incident? Do I wait for him to discuss it? Do I apologize? Do I deny it was even me there that day?

Okay, I was starting to think some silly things here. But, hey, could anyone blame me?

A self-imposed question came to me that morning before long, while still reading and re-reading the article in the paper. I asked it of myself in all seriousness, and more than once. All I needed each time was a way to find an answer. That question was...How many people in the history of the U. S., let's even make that the whole planet Earth, somehow ever found themselves with a new boss, manager, supervisor, superior, tribal leader, church head, chief of police, or whatever, and it so happened that their one previous interaction with that person involved holding a deadly weapon of some variety within twenty-four inches of that same person's head while threatening to shoot/hit/smash that same person in said head?

I answered myself in all seriousness that I was pretty sure very few people in the history of humankind fell into this very specific, if not unique, category. Nonetheless, I was now in this no doubt minute unnamed group (if not all by myself) of weapon-holders-at-head-of-future-bosses. And I wasn't very happy about it; no, not at all.

Okay, I gotta get my act together, get my thoughts collected. Plus, I have to go over and pick up my son. Let me go and do that now. Then I'll figure out just what to do and how to handle this ever-so-murky situation.

As I was walking the few short blocks to get Sean, I couldn't help but still think - of all the candidates who applied for this BPD position, how many was it, a hundred, at least a few dozen, whatever the number - of all those people, why is it that the one guy whose head just a few months before was at the pointy end of my gun barrel is now the new Chief?

Why my gun? Why his head? Why my Chief?

What are the friggin' odds of this all happening to me?

The odds don't really matter at this point, do they? This is my fate, my destiny, divine providence, kismet, whatever it is. My new boss, a position I couldn't wait to see filled by anyone other than Ted Zajac, Jr., is now a man who I almost shot to death. Well, not really, but damn, it could have happened....

I finally picked up Sean that morning. The babysitter, of course, knew I was a police officer, and in an attempt to make small talk during my short visit, told me she had read today's newspaper and asked me what I knew about the just-appointed chief. I politely told her I really didn't know too much about him yet but that I was very sure I would be meeting him soon. When I finally did meet him, I added, I'd tell her more. I didn't dare mention I had already "met" him once before and how that little meeting went down on that occasion. As I hadn't worked out this whole unfolding scenario in my own brain, I wasn't about to share it with my kid's babysitter. Not yet, anyway.

Sean and I slowly walked home. Once inside we ate our respective meals together and spent a nice afternoon having fun on the swing set in our backyard. Playing with Sean and my two later boys, whether on swings, having a catch with a ball, or just generic dad/son stuff, always made me feel better about myself and help me see the world just a little bit more clearly. It did on this day too.

I decided I would go to work later on and act like it was just any other day. The new Chief will have to make the first move. When he does, and IF the Doral incident comes up, we'll discuss it then. There, it's that simple. I think....

Sean finally went in for his nap by 2:30 and I started getting ready for my shift. Eileen came home from work at her usual time, right around 4:30, and as usual on days when we both worked we had only a brief time to chat. I had called her during her lunch break earlier that day for a few minutes and explained the bizarre situation now in play at my work. She remembered me telling her the story back in the springtime about when I stopped the Cadillac, pulled my gun, eventually ID-ing the driver as a Philly cop, etc. This afternoon, as my wife and I crossed paths, after her workday and before mine, she simply wished me a heartfelt "good luck" as we parted company. I said "Thanks, I'll need it" back and told her I'd see her in a few hours for dinner.

My ride to work that afternoon was the quickest bike ride I had ever undertaken. Or, at least it felt that way. I wanted it to last longer, but alas, I was already dismounting my bike and rolling it into the squad room within just about four minutes of leaving my house.

I was wondering…would Chief Viola address our squad today? If so, what would he say? What is he even like? I only knew him at the end of my gun, not in any other situation, much less at a police roll call. Geez, this is going to be so awkward. I didn't tell any of my squad mates or other police personnel of this uncanny connection I have with the new chief. I think for now I'll leave it that way.

Sure enough, after an otherwise routine squad roll call with the sergeant, into the room strode the smartly attired Chief Viola. He was in another expensive looking suit, different from the one in the photograph in the newspaper from last night. He was accompanied by Lt. Traenkle. Hmmm, this was a strange pairing, I thought. I guess the lieutenant was brought in to show him around, introduce him to various people, and the like. I would find out within a few weeks that Traenkle had his own politicians in his pocket, that he was a "player," and that he was about to be rewarded for it.

Back to our roll call, without much time wasted, Lt. Traenkle introduced Chief Viola to us. We learned that he already addressed the day-work squad at 7:00 this morning, and now he was meeting with us. He'd be back at 9:00P, he told us, to address the squad coming on then.

The Chief's talk to us that afternoon was relatively short and to the point. I noted that he wasn't a man who seemed to waste many words. He spoke well, had a rich vocabulary, but didn't mince or overuse his words. He started off his address to us stating that he knew the Bensalem Police Department was a political quagmire, with morale run into the ground, to include people getting promoted for doing no work and people getting punished for doing good work. That was all going to change, he said. EVERYONE will work, and if they do a good job while at it, they'll be justly rewarded for it. If they don't want to work, they'll be out of a job, he assured us.

Okay, pretty ballsy statement, but I can live with that.

The Chief at some point looked over his right shoulder and saw the time clock on the wall where each of us would punch our timecards as we began and ended our shifts every day. He told us that the machine was going to be taken off the wall and trashed. Cops were professionals, not "factory workers," and they don't punch clocks, he matter-of-factly related to us.

The time clock issue never really bothered me, but if the new boss wants to end its use, that's fine with me. I guess using one does potentially make us less "professional," come to think of it.

After further promising us that he would do his best to get us new cars, better equipment, "uniforms that don't make you look like bus drivers" (referring to our light gray shirts over dark gray pants), and do all that he could to make it easier for us to do our everyday job, that is, arresting bad guys, Chief Viola ended his talk by telling us to simply be safe tonight. He then turned to his left toward the hallway. Before leaving the roll call room though he came to a sudden stop right in front of where I was standing. He looked at me in the face and then down at my name plate.

The Chief then said, "Fitzgerald...Fitzgerald...Yeah, I remember you. Hey, how's it going?"

"Uh, ahem, uh...fine sir, thanks...thanks for asking," is all I could muster back at the time, having to clear my throat before I could say much of anything.

"Yeah, we'll talk one of these days," were Viola's final words before disappearing down the hallway with Lt. Traenkle trailing him, presumably enroute to his new office.

"Yes...yes, sir!"

Okay, what the hell does that mean, "We'll talk one of these days?"

Was he referencing JUST me when he said that? Or, did he mean the other eight officers in the room too? I think it was just me, as he was looking at just me and even said my name, but I'm not so sure.

And what would we talk about, "The Almost Gunfight at the Not-OK Doral?"

Hmmm....

As it turns out, the Chief would attempt to talk to everyone in the department in the next few weeks. That included, of course, a first day showdown with Deputy Chief Zajac in his former office, now the new departmental home of Chief Viola.

That sort of put things in perspective for me, once I started thinking about Zajac's situation, and not just mine. I mean, here's a guy who through his father's decade-plus of agenda-driven politicking and then his (the son's) own brand of office politicking, thought he had the brass ring to the BPD. Zajac's hostile takeover of Chief Michaels' department three years ago, then all the carefully laid out plans, promotions, demotions (of one sort or another), harassment, and the like, and now it was he who was the one having to answer to another chief, one whose powers he couldn't as readily usurp as Michaels' powers.

Not that I felt sorry at all for Zajac, of course. As in the Gospel of Matthew, "Live by the sword, die by the sword." That was certainly the case here and now.

Interestingly, the two swords in the BPD of the two "Chiefs" would be out of their respective scabbards a number of times over the next few years. One swordsman would finally prevail, but not before a whole lot of slicing and stabbing, slashing and jabbing, took place. Much of it on the arms, legs, and in the backs of other BPD officers. That would include me.

Teddy, Jr., would eventually need another family member to take the reins of elected officialdom to yield his sword effectively once again. But, as I do sometimes, I'm getting ahead of things here.

First, Chief Viola had to deal with Zajac's most stalwart supporter on the Board of Supervisors. That would be Supervisor Stephen Kelly. That headline-grabbing day was coming in just a few months.

Chapter Twenty-Four

Whether Zajac was in charge or Viola was in charge, as I've stated numerous times so far in this book, when I was working the streets of Bensalem Township, I didn't let one or either of those two guys affect how I undertook my sworn duties. I'd like to think I was on top of my game every day and every night I was on the job, whether it was on a surveillance/stakeout as a plainclothes cop or on patrol as a uniformed cop.

Interestingly, however, when asked after all these years what was my "best" arrest ever, another one I put at the very top of that list (along with the rapist of the Canadian woman earlier the same year), occurred just about two weeks after Chief Viola was named our new leader. This arrest certainly didn't hurt me in the eyes of the new chief, as he was looking to bring up the departmental arrest numbers, especially in the area of violent felonies. And it's the arrest I am also very proud of because it was not the result of a call from dispatch, a long-term investigation, or even confidential source information, but instead the result of me being consistently aggressive in the everyday performance of my job. It was a major arrest too, with prosecutions spanning a few years, and with some serious jail time involved for several of the bad guys.

Oh, and this felony take down may have been the closest I ever came to being killed in the line of duty. But he never got the chance because of my employment of excellent tactical police procedures and, believe it or not, forensic linguistics. Well, sort of, as it relates to the latter topic area.

Allow me to tell the story from its beginning.

On Monday, September 21, 1981, around 9:00PM, I had just finished a later-than-usual dinner at home. It was delayed due to, if I remember correctly, an earlier routine but time-consuming shoplifting arrest and prisoner processing. I had just signed back in on the police radio after a reheated but nonetheless filling meal and proceeded in the direction of my sector to resume my patrol duties. I had brought one of my Villanova University text books with me so later, when things slowed down a bit, I could read the assigned chapters for my graduate class the next night. (Yes, I had finally started my first course just two weeks ago.)

I made some basic rounds of my sector when I eventually found myself stopped for the red light on Kingston Way at Street Rd., right across from the then-Holiday Inn. It was a warmish night, with dry conditions, with nothing to block my vision or my (by now) pretty well-honed intuitions and street sense.

The police radio was relatively quiet and I was hoping for a not-too-busy next six hours until my shift was over. However, at one particular residence in my sector, it was anything but quiet for its occupant and his guests. I didn't know that yet, but I was about to pull a car stop on the major player in that incident, without even knowing at first it was him or that a crime had even been committed. It would be written language which would give him up to me, and in the most unusual of ways. It wasn't a formal, full forensic linguistic analysis I conducted in a matter of seconds that night, but it was as close to one as could be considering the circumstances, and it put this guy and others in jail for a decade-plus.

At approximately 9:40 that Monday evening, while stopped in my marked patrol car at the aforementioned red light on Kingston Way, I noticed two vehicles, a light blue Ford van followed closely by a white AMC Hornet, both run the just-turned-red traffic signal while travelling at a pretty good rate of speed in an eastbound direction on Street Rd. It was kind of unusual seeing two vehicles both clearly blow a solid red light at their somewhat elevated speed while driving that closely together. Usually it's just one car doing so. Since they were unlucky enough to do this right in front of a cop in a marked patrol car, there was at a minimum a car stop coming up, and maybe a ticket too, for at least one of the vehicles. No doubt the drivers of both saw my police car and knew this was about to happen too.

The traffic light turned green for me and after making sure no other cars were following these two through the red light, I immediately turned right onto Street Rd. to proceed eastbound after one, if not both, of them. As I floored my car's accelerator to catch up with the two vehicles, I noticed that when the leading Ford van came up to the next cross-street, Richlieu Rd., it made a quick U-turn and in a flash was now heading back westbound on Street Rd. But, for whatever reason, as I pulled up almost directly behind the trailing Hornet, the driver decided to continue driving straight on Street Rd., and not make a U-turn to follow the van.

I turned on my overhead lights at that exact moment in an attempt to pull over the one vehicle still ahead of me. As I was only one police officer, in one patrol car, I really couldn't do anything about the van which also clearly ran the red light behind me. But if I could get one of these vehicles, and ticket the driver accordingly for what was a dangerous violation created by one if not both of them, I'd still be doing my job.

As the Hornet was slowly pulling alongside an out-of-business gas station at Street Rd. and Richlieu Rd., I picked up my microphone and broadcast my car stop location as well as the make and model of the car. As I was about to read the registration number to the dispatcher, I noticed that the car actually had no tag on it. Instead, it had a piece of paper taped to the inside of the rear window with some numbers and letters scribbled on it. I couldn't decipher them from my vantage point so I just re-broadcast the make and model and added that it was of an early '70s vintage with what appeared to be a lone male driver.

The dispatcher responded with a "10-4." Hopefully she wrote down the minimalist description and the location that I provided.

As was a habit of mine from the police academy training and my earliest days on the force during night time car stops, once completely stopped I next aimed my car door spotlight directly into the inside rearview mirror of the Hornet. This is done to temporarily blind the driver from what's happening behind him or her. It may not seem fair to the regular, everyday law-abiding driver, who may have simply ran a stop sign or red light, or who perhaps was going a few miles over the speed limit, or had an expired inspection sticker on the car and nothing else, but it adds greatly to the tactical advantage to a police officer about to expose himself or herself to what is the most dangerous part of the job - that being, the never "routine" car stop. In doing so that night, I would later learn, my spotlight usage may have contributed to me still being alive to write this book.

I next stepped out of the car with my regular flashlight in my right hand to approach the driver. Nothing else was ever in my left hand during a car stop as I always wanted it available to reach for my gun, if so needed. (Of course, it's just the opposite for a right-handed police officer in this situation.) Once again, this was a skill I learned early on that would prove beneficial to me on this very night.

I slowly walked up towards the car on the driver's side, shining my light in the rear side window to see what or who may be inside the car. I could right away see it was full of different items, mostly looking like junk and various sized boxes, but no other humans were observed.

As I approached the driver, he already had his window down. I could see he was a white male, in his late 20s, with long hair and a scruffy beard. He wasn't a small guy either, as I could see by the length and breadth of his arms, or at least initially his left arm. As I stood to the rear of him at an angle, to make him strain his neck to look back at me over his left shoulder, again giving me a tactical advantage, I made to him my usual request in these situations, and with almost the identical language and level of firmness.

That is, "License and registration, please!"

After a few verbalized "ums" and "ahs," the driver's response to my request was very matter of fact. He didn't have his wallet or his various ID cards as he left it and them at home. I was immediately unconvinced by his too convenient of an excuse. Nonetheless, we continued our conversation.

I asked the driver about the missing tag on the car. He said it was stolen the night before. I then asked him if he reported it to the police. He responded he did not as he was simply too busy throughout the day to do so. I inquired as to where the theft may have happened, and he replied he didn't know. I requested the car's tag number from him. He didn't have it memorized, he said, but was sure it began with an "8." I next asked him, sort of sarcastically, if he had his name and date of birth memorized. He replied in the affirmative and gave me an alleged name and an alleged birthday, but something told me they didn't actually belong to him. I wrote them down on my little pad anyway while never taking my eyes off of him.

During this police officer-to-traffic violator bit of discourse, I continued to shine my flashlight into the interior of the car. Something just didn't seem right here. The driver's demeanor as well as the missing identification about the car and him, the odd piles of junk stacked up in the car, not to mention the speeding red light violation (of two vehicles) which was why I pulled him over in the first place, all told me this guy was playing games with me for one reason or another. Even the front passenger seat next to him was full of cardboard boxes, some open, some sealed shut, newspapers, empty fast food bags, I believe part of an old stereo system, and the like. I wasn't sure what exactly was beneath these items but I wanted to make sure his hands couldn't quickly get to it...just in case it was something which could prove unfriendly towards me.

Our next bit of verbalized back-and-forth went something like....

Me: "Put your hands on the steering wheel where I can see them."

Driver: "Okay, sure." (Somewhat contemptibly, but with his two hands now on the steering wheel.)

Me: "Do you know why I stopped you?"

Driver: "Uh, I guess because I ran the red light back there."

Me: "That's right. Anything else?"

Driver: "Uh, no tag on my car?"

Me: "Yep, that too, plus speeding. Oh, and by the way, who were you following?"

Driver: "What do you mean? I wasn't following anyone."

Me: "You were tight on the bumper of a blue van when you both ran the light going much faster than you should around here. Then it made a U-turn right in front of you. You can't tell me you weren't with that van. Who was in it?"

Driver: "No, I wasn't, I swear! I don't know who was in it...really! Uh, can we get moving here, I have some other deliveries to make."

Me: "Deliveries? What kind of deliveries? Who do you work for?"

Around this time, while maintaining this lively conversation with this squirrely driver, yet learning nothing about him or his car, I also continued to move my flashlight around the interior of the vehicle. In doing so, along with the other junk, I happened to notice a yellow legal pad lying flat on the dashboard, directly in front of the steering wheel. I never reached inside the car for it, but instead moved a step or two forward and pointed my light downwards through the windshield and onto the pad. While making sure I could see the driver's hands at the top of the steering wheel the whole time, I visually scanned the top page of the pad.

The pad's entirety consisted of what appeared to be handwritten addresses, one per line, with numbers and then streets listed one after another down the page. I noted to myself, somewhat curiously, that none had the city or town names next to any of them. That was a bit strange I thought as besides nearby Philadelphia, there were a number of different municipalities immediately outside of Philly and Bensalem as well as further west on Street Rd. I momentarily wondered how this guy would know where each address was located for his supposed deliveries without the town/city being also listed.

While very briefly perusing this document, and in utilizing a skill-set which I somehow developed before then and still have to this day,

I quickly "read" the sheet of paper, probably more sub-consciously than consciously, for any possible pertinent information which may be contained therein. I won't say I've ever had a photographic memory of any sort, but I can rather readily perceive nuanced language usage, to include punctuation features, misspelled words, unusual words, etc., on printed and handwritten communications, with just a single quick glance. I don't really know its physiological or psychological origins within me, how or when I "learned" this skillset, but it's just something that seemingly always came natural to me. And on this night, during this car stop, on the top page of this legal pad of paper, I took in as much information as my brain could absorb in the less than ten seconds or so that I had it in my sight line, through the car's windshield illuminated by my handheld flashlight, no less. I definitely got the gist of it, I unconsciously surmised.

As I glanced at this list on this yellow piece of lined paper, however, I remembered thinking that only one of the addresses was recognizable or made sense to me as being from anywhere in the immediate area. Yes, right in the middle of this long list of maybe twenty different addresses, about halfway down the page was the address "1234 Oakford Road." (I changed the street number for the purposes of this book. It was, in fact, Oakford Road, though.)

Okay, so there's one Bensalem address on the list. None of the remaining addresses registered with me at all. I'm not sure what all this means, but it's in the brain for future retrieval, if necessary. Let me focus back to the driver for now.

Our little talk continued....

Me: "So what sort of stuff were you delivering, and to whom?"

Driver: "I'm working for a...a...guy who has me dropping of...uh... spare parts and stuff...for, you know, music equipment and stuff...."

Me: "Right! Okay, stay here with your hands on the steering wheel. I'm going to check things out."

Driver: "Yeah, but can you hurry. I have these other deliveries to make tonight." In saying that, he seemed to be getting more agitated, frustrated, and more worried. About something, but I wasn't sure just what.

I walked back to my patrol car. I got on the police radio and called in his info. I didn't copy down the car's vehicle identification number (VIN) yet, as I wanted to wait for my backup to arrive before I started spending the time and effort in doing so. That would be next though,

I thought, once I had another officer with me. Assuming the VIN was intact, it would tell me lots about this car, and maybe even the driver.

Without any great surprise, the dispatcher got back to me in no more than a minute and advised that there was "No record found" on this guy or the handwritten tag number in the rear window. The car, at least via the paper tag number, wasn't reported stolen or wanted for anything, but there was no info at all on it, or this guy with the date of birth he provided. I now KNEW something was up, but just what it was I still couldn't figure out.

As I heard one of the other marked patrol cars broadcast that he was just a half-mile or so away from me, I decided to walk back toward the pseudonymous driver and tell him that neither he nor his car exists according to the DMV. Hopefully, he could help me further clarify his and his car's very existence. I had just shut my door and while back on foot was near the front bumper of my own car. That's when I heard the ominous sound on the police radio that causes every officer to react with a visceral response. No matter what the officer is doing at the time, upon hearing these particular electronically produced signals, he/she better sit up straight, take a deep breath, and get ready to move fast.

It was three loud beeps; yes, THOSE three loud beeps. When the dispatcher pushes those buttons that means a serious and most likely violent crime of some sort has just taken place, and the officers on patrol were about to receive the flash information regarding it. If you're sitting still and parked with the engine off, as soon as you hear those three loud beeps you know to start your engine, put the gear shifter into Drive, and be prepared to go somewhere, anywhere, quickly, ready for the worst. Except for me, I was out on foot, with my portable radio on, and walking toward this so far unregistered car and undocumented man.

However, once I heard the beeps, I stopped my forward momentum and waited for the next burst of noise, that being the verbal stimuli. Within seconds over my portable radio I heard it from the dispatcher, and within several additional seconds I reacted accordingly.

"BEEP-BEEP-BEEP...696 to all 22 cars, be on the lookout for a blue Ford van, no tag! It's wanted in conjunction with an 03 (crime code for armed robbery) which just occurred at 1234 Oakford Road. It was a home invasion involving four to five armed men. They pistol whipped one occupant and duct-taped the others before taking their money and valuables. They fled the scene in the blue Ford van. More information to follow!"

In those two seconds, the radio broadcast information went in my ears and then from one side of my brain to the other. The synapses connected quickly.

A blue Ford van? That's what THIS car was closely following when I watched them run the light back at Kingston Way!

1234 Oakford Rd? That's the one, and only one, Bensalem address on the pad of paper!

Damn! If this guy isn't one of the home invaders himself, he certainly knows who they are in that van which got away.

I have to act quickly now. I'm not sure this guy heard the three loud beeps on my portable radio, or the transmission that followed immediately afterwards, but I better assume that he did and also assume he's already a step ahead of me here.

Actually, and for obvious reasons, this guy has been that step ahead of me here the whole time. That explains nothing matching up so far. He KNEW he was involved in this home invasion, but I didn't find out until just now. But I do know now, so I better get busy here, and do it safely and smartly.

As I looked up, I could see the other patrol car coming towards me on Street Rd. Via my portable radio I immediately advised him and all the others who were listening that I presently had one of the armed robbery suspects on this car stop. (I may not have had "proof" yet that he was actually in the house committing the armed robbery with the others, but I certainly knew I had probable cause here to detain, if not eventually arrest, this guy for this crime.)

I instructed the patrol car which was approaching me to pull directly in front of the Hornet and box him in as I was about to order him out onto the ground. The just arriving car gave me a hearty "10-4," crossed the oncoming lanes of traffic and pulled up right in front of the suspect car, almost bumper to bumper with it. The officer then jumped out with his gun drawn, but staying behind his open car door for protection.

I was trying to do the same thing from my position, but on the driver's side of the Hornet. While staying well behind the driver, who now saw his car boxed in, I commanded him to put both his hands outside of the driver's door. It took a bit of time, but he ever so slowly complied. My uniformed and gun-pointing colleague came up a bit closer now on the other side of his car, and I ordered the suspect to open the door using the outside handle, with both hands exposed the whole time, and slowly step out of the car and kneel down on the ground.

"What's the problem? All this because of a missing tag? Officer, there's been a mistake here." He was heard to say in various forms a few times, straining his neck back and to his left to talk to the police officer (me) standing behind him.

"Shut the f**k up and do exactly what I tell you to do!" was my emphatic response to him as our little conversation continued.

(Yes, it was one of those moments in police work when one particular expletive was used a few times by me in an attempt to maintain command and control and assure that we were all safe here. He seemed to understand it very well by the second or third mention of same. My harsh use of that particular word was, no doubt, the last thing on this guy's mind at this moment in time.)

Other patrol cars arrived, one blocking off the right side lane of Street Rd., and at that point I approached the kneeling suspect and placed him in handcuffs, behind his back, of course. I searched him and didn't find anything of value on him. I did notice, for the first time that evening, that the suspect had some sort of white dye, or maybe even spray paint, covering certain parts of his hair. I hadn't noticed it previously when he was sitting in his car, but it was clear to me now in the brighter lights. Regardless of this oddity, which was meaningless to me at the time, I instructed one of my colleagues to place him in the back of his patrol car as I had a radio transmission I had to quickly put out there.

As the arrested person was being placed into the rear of a police car, I contacted dispatch and advised them that I last observed the blue Ford van heading westbound on Street Rd. I instructed her to notify Bucks County Radio, Montgomery County Radio, and the Pennsylvania State Police radio (each of which covers other police jurisdictions west of Bensalem yet not directly reachable via my police radio) that the "03" suspect vehicle was possibly heading in their direction and police should be on the lookout for it. The message was dutifully sent by the Bensalem dispatcher.

Less than forty-five minutes later, thanks to that alert being received by at least one astute police officer, the Ford van was stopped in Whitemarsh Township, Montgomery County, around ten miles away from the Bensalem location where I first saw the two cars run the red light together. Upon the van being stopped, four men ran from it as soon as it came to a rest on the side of the road. Two were captured after a brief foot chase, but the other two got away.

My suspect was brought into BPD HQ and turned over to Det. Ken Hopkins. I was glad it was him. This would be the second major case I worked directly with Ken this year alone. The rape case involving the locket-girl was the other. Ken ran with this home invasion case from this point on, with my able assistance, of course. After eventually determining the driver's actual identity and reading the 27-year old his Miranda warnings, we both interviewed the suspect in a small room in CID. We found out (although he never admitted it) he was an affiliate of a Philadelphia area outlaw motorcycle gang. Possibly because of that, he didn't give anything up at all to us that night. He admitted nothing to us and before long said he wanted his lawyer. Okay, we told him, we'll just have to go with the evidence found on him, in his car, and in the van over in Whitemarsh Township, which we learned had significant Oakford Road robbery-related evidence in it.

Before we left the interview room, however, the guy was asked about his grayish/whitish hair, which was clearly the result of a hasty and haphazard application of something presumably alien to his normal grooming style. But he still had nothing to say. We took pictures of his ill-colored mop top and later that night attained a search warrant for random clips of his unprofessionally highlighted hair. We then cut away some of his gray locks. He did not appreciate two police officers cutting his hair. Too bad.

When the Hornet was subsequently towed in from where I stopped it, a full inventory search was undertaken of it. Of course, the yellow legal pad with the incriminating address on it was confiscated for evidentiary purposes. Also, and somewhat disturbingly, found under the debris on the front passenger seat and within very easy reach of the driver (if he had chosen to do so), was an item which could have changed my life, or for that matter, ended my life. It was a loaded, double-barrel, sawed-off shotgun. The victims of the home invasion later provided information that one of the perpetrators who happened to match my guy's description was, in fact, brandishing a sawed-off shotgun throughout the hour-long ordeal.

I'd learn more about this guy and the shotgun placement in about two years. It wasn't right next to him on the passenger seat initially that night. He moved it there from the back seat as I pulled him over.

He had been prepared to use it. On me!

As far as the home invasion itself, an intrepid newspaper reporter, Anita DiBartolomeo, who covered the Bensalem beat, contacted the main victim the next day (after BPD detectives further interviewed him and his family and friends) and wrote the following article in the September 24, 1981 edition of *The Bucks County Courier Times*. Portions of it read as follows:

> "Just as the TV show 'That's Incredible' was ending around 8:30 p.m. (the victim) said four men with stockings stretched over their faces pushed into his Oakford Road home.... One of the robbers, he noticed, had white spray paint on his hair.
>
> "(The victim) said the robbers forced him to lie on his living room floor, along with two women and a man who were visiting him. A short time later, his parents dropped by and they too were forced to the floor.
>
> "(The victim) said the robbers bound their hands and feet with tape and began ransacking the house. He said the thieves placed pillows near their faces and at one point flipped couches over them to prevent them from watching.
>
> "During the hour-long ordeal, (the victim) said the robbers struck him with a tire iron and slashed him with knives, cutting open his shirt. He said he received 12 stitches in the head later at Holy Redeemer Hospital....
>
> "Police said the robbers escaped with more than $800 in cash, which included money taken from the victims' wallets, as well as four rifles, a five-gallon jar of change and a bottle of dimes."
>
> (End of article.)

The guy I arrested was arraigned later the next morning on charges relating to robbery and eleven other offenses. He was remanded to Bucks County Prison in lieu of making bail.

After the main victim was interviewed again by BPD detectives over the next few days, it was learned that he had been "holding some marijuana for a friend" that night, over twenty pounds worth. In other words, this home invasion was, essentially, a drug-ripoff. What no one counted on was the innocent friends being there, as well as this guy's very innocent parents who just randomly happened to stop by that night. If he had been at home by himself, who knows if he would have even called the police? The others being there clearly changed that whole dynamic.

Within a few months, the man in the AMC Hornet that I arrested, and the two men caught in or near the Ford van in Whitemarsh Township a short time later, each pleaded guilty to the various offenses stemming from the home invasion. Bucks County Assistant District Attorney (ADA) Peter Hileman was the prosecutor assigned to this case and worked with the various defense attorneys and public defenders as well as the multiple victims of the crime until all agreed to a viable plea agreement. There were two men still on the loose, of course, and we didn't forget that fact, but for now, putting three-fifths of the crime team from that night behind bars for 7-10 years wasn't too bad.

Case all but over, right? No, not quite.

In January of 1983, I received a collect phone call at the BPD from an upstate Pennsylvania prison. It was the guy I stopped in the Hornet who was now serving his time there. He wanted to talk to me and to ADA Hileman. In our brief phone chat, he told me that he wanted to get out of prison. To possibly facilitate this, he was willing to give up the two other guys. One of them, he claimed, was the alleged mastermind of the whole home invasion scheme. He wouldn't tell me either of their names now, but if we came to see him....

The convict on the line wanted to know if I was interested. I told him I may be and I'd get back to him.

I contacted ADA Pete Hileman, told him of the call, and we agreed to travel to the vicinity of the Pennsylvania Poconos to meet with the guy at his new maximum security home. After all, the case was not technically closed as the last two suspects were not in custody. So why not see what this guy has to offer us. Our respective bosses approved of it and off we went.

After prior coordination with the prison authorities and a two-hour drive upstate, we met with the convict in an interview room far away from the general population where he was otherwise housed. As he was escorted into the room by the correctional officers he was seen to be wearing the facility's ubiquitous orange jumpsuit. His hair seemed of a more natural color though, that being dark brown. There was no need to spray paint his hair for our visit today. Hiding his true hair color for disguise purposes was only for pulling robberies, I suppose.

The prison officials left and it was just the three of us in the room. The inmate was initially hesitant to tell us anything. He first wanted us to know that he was NOT a snitch but, well, maybe just this one time he'd consider being one. After some unrelated small talk, Pete and I finally got him to open up to us.

To prove his intent right away, the inmate gave us the names of the other two offenders in on the robbery that night. Yes, there were five total. And at least one of them was the mastermind/ringleader of the whole operation. Yes, it was a drug ripoff and it was one of these two co-conspirators that first heard of the Oakford Rd. location and put the plan together. He didn't like these two guys and resented the fact that he took the fall for the home invasion, not to mention getting the most prison time of the three people arrested so far for it. He reinforced that while he didn't like being a "snitch," for him it all came down to the fact that he didn't like prison even more so. Thus, he decided it was time to do this, for his sake and his sake alone, not because he liked cops, or DAs, the system, or anything like that. He continued without prompting that if he could get a significantly reduced sentence, maybe even time served up to this point, he'd be willing to provide more information and even testify if necessary.

Pete and I remained all ears and told the man in the orange jumpsuit to keep talking. He told us with his girlfriend the two of them sloppily attempted to color his hair that night with some sort of theatrical spray dye, for one purpose and one purpose only. That was, to alter his appearance for any future potential identification of him by victims/witnesses. The convicted robber also provided for the first time the reasoning behind the yellow legal pad address list I found on his dashboard, which directly led to his arrest. He said its purpose was simply that of a prop. All the other addresses were made up, he continued, with the only real address being the one in the middle of the page of their intended target that night. He figured when he knocked on the locked front door to gain entry into the house, if the homeowner questioned him, he could just show him the makeshift handwritten list of addresses, tell him he has a delivery of some sort, point to the address in the middle to "prove" it, and the guy would simply let him in. That was the plan, and it actually worked.

Although we felt we had plenty of good information so far, before too much more was told to us, the convict wanted to get a guarantee of some sort, in writing that day from ADA Hileman, that his sentence would be greatly reduced, if not vacated, before he would provide any additional information and/or evidence. Pete very clearly told him that the system doesn't work that way, that we'd need lots more from him, a written statement, etc., to even begin this process. There would be no guarantees and he'd have to provide testimony at any future trial or trials to even be considered. THEN, at that time, a sentence reduction application could be filed by the DA's office to the courts on his behalf.

The now-somewhat cooperating inmate (but don't call him a "snitch") thought this over. He knew the DA's office held most of the proverbial marbles, with him holding only a few. After a period of silence with him staring down at the floor in what appeared to be deep contemplation, no doubt slowly realizing he only possessed two of those marbles (representing the remaining two robbers), he raised his head, met our eyes, and reluctantly advised us that he would follow the process as it was just laid out to him. Anything, he said, to get out of this "hellhole," as he described his present involuntary custodial environment.

So, Pete and I got to work, both taking several pages of handwritten notes regarding what the inmate had to tell us. While I stayed silent about it, the irony wasn't lost on me that Pete and I were writing this guy's statement on the pages of yellow legal pads. The three of us in that room each knew, and I'm sure even more so the prisoner across the table from us, that it was a yellow legal pad with the Oakford Road address written on it which sealed this guy's fate that night; this especially as the AMC Hornet he was driving was never observed by the victims at the scene of the crime. We kept quiet about this bit of ironic coincidence. He was cooperating with us now and we didn't want to unduly upset him.

Interestingly, as the convicted man proceeded to tell us more of the "real" story behind the home invasion robbery, he advised that one of the two other named men, in fact the alleged leader of the crime team that night, just happened to be one-half of a set of identical twin brothers. And as far as the inmate knew, they still wore their hair in the same style and donned almost identical eyeglasses to make it even more confusing for people to tell them apart. He felt that the twins maintained their very similar appearances for purpose of making it difficult for police and witnesses to potentially identify which one of them may have committed a crime, was at a certain place, or with a certain person at a certain time, etc. Not a bad strategy, IF you happen to have an identical twin sibling and IF you are interested in fooling people, whether through harmless practical jokes or in the commission of violent felonies.

I didn't really think too much about this twin issue as a possible legal defense strategy while the information was being related to us by the inmate. I suppose it could make our job of arresting and convicting one if not both of these two newly identified guys a bit trickier down the line. We'd have to wait and see if it even gets that far, of course.

After about ninety minutes the meeting with our own convicted home invader had pretty much run its course. Pete and I silently nodded our heads at each other to signify that we got, for now, what we came for. In view of that, the ADA asked to be excused for a few minutes to call his office and run some of these various issues by his supervisor. He wanted to make sure he wasn't tentatively promising something to the cooperator ("snitch") that the DA's office couldn't deliver. Upon being buzzed out of the room by the officer just behind the glass, it left just me and the inmate in there together.

As the two of us were making our own small talk (as much as one can with a guy dressed in orange and in a prison setting), he confided in me some additional information from that night of the arrest. He had no real reason to offer to me what he did, but in his doing so, I believed him. What I heard from him made my heart skip a beat, although I never let him know it.

While not exactly word-for-word, this relatively brief part of the conversation between the two of us went pretty much as follows:

Inmate (known previously as "Driver"): "You know, Fitzgerald, you only got me that night because we missed the turn off from Street Rd. onto the Pennsylvania Turnpike. I was following the van and the dick who was driving it missed the f**kin' exit. We were trying to make the U-turn back toward the turnpike exit but then you stopped me. That's the only reason you ever caught me…I just wanted you to know that."

Me: "Okay, I appreciate it. I guess sometimes in life we just get lucky…or unlucky, depending on your point of view."

Inmate: "Oh, and another thing, you know how close you came to dying that night?"

Me: "No, tell me."

Okay…now he was getting to the point.

Inmate: "You know I had the loaded sawed-off in the car, right?"

Me: "Yeah, that's one of the several reasons you're here doing hard time."

Inmate: "Well…it had been in the back seat hidden under some stuff when you first pulled up behind me. As your cop car was getting closer to my car and I was pretty sure you were going to pull me over, you probably couldn't see it but I quickly reached behind me and pulled the shotgun up onto the front seat next to me and put it under some other stuff I had there. That's where you found it, right?"

Me: "Yeah, I saw the photos my colleagues took when they first found it in your car. The butt was facing you and it was within easy arm reach from the driver's seat. I guess you put it there to be picked up and used if need be. Right?"

Inmate: "Yeah, you got it exactly right! And I seriously thought of using it on you that night too, just before you got out of your car to walk up to me. I'm tellin' you, I was this close, man!" (He showed me his index finger and his thumb about one-half of an inch apart.)

Me: "So, why didn't you use it on me then?"

Inmate: "Well…I gotta tell ya, and I've been thinking of it ever since I've been in this f**kin' place, it's because you did everything right that night after you stopped me, you know, from a cop perspective. I'm not just blowin' smoke up your ass either. That f**kin' car spotlight you shined in my rearview mirror all but blinded me. I couldn't tell from that point on if you were a solo cop or had a partner with you on the other side of the car. I was pretty sure you were all by your lonesome, but I couldn't be sure."

Me: "So, the spotlight technique works just like they taught us at the academy, eh?"

Inmate: "It wasn't just that. The way you made me turn my head to look back and up at you by standing behind me…it just threw off my sense of, I don't know, balance and judgment. From what I COULD see after that, I did notice that your left hand was held close over your gun the whole time you were standing outside the car. I even noticed your fingers sorta twitching right next to it, as if you were ready to pull it at any time. I knew you'd pull it out and get your rounds off before I could get off mine."

Me: Staring back at him in silence…on purpose.

Inmate: "Yeah, so all things considered that night, I gotta hand it to ya, you know what you're doin' at a car stop. Well trained, I guess. You just never gave me the chance…."

Me: "That's the plan actually, each and every time."

Inmate: "Anyway, I just wanted you to know that. Good job, I guess."

Me: "Yeah, thanks…I guess."

Inmate: Staring back in silence…probably on purpose.

Me: "Do me, and you, a favor…when you get out of this place, and you WILL get out sooner or later, do not THINK about shooting any other police officer, no matter what the situation may be. Because, as you figured out already, you know if you did try to shoot me that night you may have hit me, but I assure you that you would have been shot dead too. IF you somehow survived it, then you'd be a cop killer now in prison and you wouldn't be talking to another cop right now about getting an early release, no matter what info you had to offer. You'd be in a 'hellhole' of your own making for life. Know what I mean?"

Inmate: "I hear ya.... I'm gonna go straight when I get out, I swear...."

Me: "Uh-huh...." (Incredulity implied.)

At about that moment Pete Hileman came back into the room with the correctional officer. He told the inmate that he'd be hearing from us. We said our goodbyes, and the two of us left.

During the first half of our drive back to Bucks County, Pete and I discussed our options regarding this new information, how to approach it, how to investigate it, etc. We still had some work to do to verify what our guy told us, and we'd certainly do that. During the second and final hour of our drive, we were both relatively quiet. I'm not sure what was on Pete's mind, but I know my mind was aflutter with the information that I was provided about my car stop "technique" on that two years ago-plus September evening.

This was a first for me. That is, the first time I was ever critiqued one-on-one by a person with whom I engaged in a tactical-style arrest takedown, from one side of the badge and gun to the other. It was revelatory and thought-provoking at the same time, while also, I gotta admit it here, a bit mind-blowing. It was somewhat scary learning from a guy, who really had nothing to gain by sharing his little anecdote with me, that he had seriously considering killing me at that time and that place.

Okay, besides that today, how was your afternoon, Jim?

The more I later thought about what the convicted armed robber told me, the more I became somewhat proud of myself and ever so thankful for adhering to the PSP academy training principles I had received years before and continued to put into practice since then. But, at the same time, I also couldn't help but think that if I had performed my duties just a slight bit differently that night, on one of several fronts, I may not be alive to talk (or write) about it now.

I didn't tell Pete about the private conversation I had with our now cooperating prison witness. He wasn't a gun-toting first responder like me, he wasn't confronting these types of guys on the street on a regular basis, and I'm not sure he would have appreciated what I was told by

251

the robber/inmate. In fact, I rarely told anyone of this story until just recently. I didn't want to upset my wife or family or friends, so I just buried it deep within my professional, and to some degree, personal psyche. But, I must say emphatically here, I'm very glad the guy I put in prison told me what he did those few years later. It reinforced in me the utilization of proper police tactics when confronting virtually anyone on the street, to even include the undertaking of one of those "routine" car stops.

After two months of further investigation, to include reinterviewing all the home invasion robbery victims again, and also continuing to talk to the convicted robber/now-cooperating witness from prison, I attained arrest warrants for the two other men involved in the September, 1981 crime. In early March of 1983, the twin was arrested at his home. Later that same night, the other suspect turned himself in to police upon learning there was a warrant for his arrest. Before the end of 1983, the trial was set to start. Unlike the previous three defendants, neither of these two guys was looking for a plea agreement. They were going to trial.

Just a few days before the jury trial was to begin, the guy who came real close to shooting me with his double-barrel, sawed-off shotgun, surprised both Pete Hileman and me once again. He got cold feet (even in the "hellhole") and suddenly told us that he would not testify at the trial. Since he couldn't get in writing that he would be released from prison the next day after his testimony (which NO ONE ever promised him), he then refused to take the stand and tell the jury what he told us numerous times over the prior year.

The trial was held nonetheless, even without our "star witness." ADA Pete Hileman did an excellent job. I testified as to everything I knew regarding the crime and subsequent investigation. So did several of the victims from the robbery itself. They consistently and separately identified the two defendants in the courtroom as being part of the robbery team. It looked pretty good for the Commonwealth of Pennsylvania's case to attain two convictions in this matter.

However, when it was his turn, the defense attorney for the identical twin defendant played the best card, maybe the only card, he had in his deck. That's right, it was the *you-can't-possibly-tell-them-apart* defense.

The lawyer had the twin NOT charged in the crime and NOT on trial come into the courtroom on a certain day and he pointed out to several of the crime victims (and the jury) how closely alike the brothers looked. He even had the siblings dress very similar to each other that day, no doubt just like their mother did for them when they were kids. Fortunately for them (and I suppose their mom), and unfortunately for the Commonwealth of Pennsylvania and the rest of society, it worked.

The twin on trial was subsequently acquitted of all charges by the jury. The remaining defendant was convicted of the main charges against him. Unfortunately, it seems, he didn't have a doppelganger to bring into the courtroom.

Whether we, the BPD and the Bucks County DA's office liked it or not, it was Case Closed, for sure now.

So the arrest/conviction fraction rate was now at four-fifths; that is, four out of five of the home invaders were convicted or pleaded guilty to the crime and were in or off to prison. We tried our best to convict the fifth one, but it's never easy convicting an identical twin if he, his twin, and one or more defense attorneys are willing to play the same-face-but-different-guy game in the courtroom. (Although, I'm sure that strategy could have been defeated IF our prison witness would have agreed to follow through on his testimony promise. But, alas, it was not to be.)

I learned a lot from this whole series of events which began on that Monday evening at 9:40 in September of '81. Very fortunately, what I had learned through my training, experience, and life itself prior to that evening's car stop, allowed me to survive it and tell of it in the future.

I'm glad the Hornet driving, yellow legal pad-address writing, home invading armed robber, contacted me from prison and told me what he told me. It ultimately led to the conviction of at least one more of the two other bad guys involved in the violent felony. And what he also told me on the side about my car stop techniques that night was much appreciated too. People don't get professional validation like that too often in their careers, especially when their very life was on the line by the guy providing the validating.

I hope the convicted robber's remaining years in prison were uneventful, that he eventually got out, went home, and, in fact, did "go straight," as he told me he would. One can only hope, for his sake and that of other police officers who may confront him in the future.

Chapter Twenty-Five

Wikipedia defines the term "Renaissance Man" as "...gifted people...who (seek) to develop their abilities in all areas of accomplishment: intellectual, artistic, social and physical."

I was finally invited, along with a steady stream of other officers at varying times, to sit down with Chief Richard Viola in his office about three weeks after he was sworn in to his new job. Coincidently, or not, it was the day after my car stop arrest of the home invader robbery suspect. Starting with that conversation, as well as spending additional time with him over the next few years, mostly professional but some personal, brought me to the realization that at least up to this stage of my relatively young life, Rich Viola was the closest that I'd ever come to a guy fitting the aforementioned description of a Renaissance Man.

Needless to say, I wouldn't put Viola in the category of Da Vinci, Michelangelo, Copernicus, et al., although each was, interestingly like him, of Italian heritage. But within the professional world(s) I occupied in my then-less than thirty years so far on this planet, he seemed to cover all the requisite bases of that esoteric typology, certainly more than anyone I had personally met so far in my life. I mean, without even knowing anything about him, I knew his last name was identical to that of the bowed instrument developed in Italy around 1500 and since then a staple in classical music. Was there a connection somehow in his ancestry? (Alas, none of which he knew, he later told me.)

The Chief didn't even have to open his mouth yet during that initial meeting in his office for me to notice that he was, well, somehow different from other men I knew. I observed this shortly after sitting down across from his desk. (Yes, it was the same chair I was sitting in when I was told of that spreading departmental cancer, etc., by DC Zajac just a few years before. It was a much, much different atmosphere now, to say the least. A true cancer-free zone...).

While Viola was shuffling some papers, to include what I could see was clearly my personnel file, I noticed that something was a bit unusual about his hands. He had a seemingly high-quality gold pinky ring, with a diamond in the middle of it, on his right hand little finger, but that wasn't it. He wore monogrammed and expensive looking cuff-links on each shirt-sleeve, but that wasn't it either. I noticed a Rolex watch on his left wrist, but that still wasn't what made his hand-area look somewhat unusual to me. He signed something quickly with a Mont Blanc pen, but it was still something else that was drawing my attention.

Hmmm…what was it that was different about him, or at least his hands, which distracted me from our upcoming conversation while he was multi-tasking with paperwork and a just-received phone call?

Wait, I know! It's…it's Viola's fingernails; all eight fingers and two thumbs, as far as I could determine. They're…they're…polished. They're nicely cut and trimmed and have a clear veneer to them.

Geez, I was thinking, what kind of man gets his fingernails polished? (The term "metro-sexual" was still almost fifteen years away at the time from being added to our lexicon.) And…what cop, or especially chief of police, sits down for a manicure every week or two just to have his fingernails look like they could belong to a hand model, which I postu-lated his could have successfully passed for even with my then (and still) limited knowledge of the world of hand modeling. Regardless, this was the guy whose office I was now sitting in and as my new boss was about to discuss the first five years of my career in the BPD, and perhaps the next five years, or more.

Don't get me wrong here. I wasn't judging Viola negatively in any way, shape, or form simply because he wore nail polish, albeit of the clear variety. I was merely attempting to do what all humans do upon first meeting another human, in one manner or another. That is, to size them up and to attempt to determine the best possible way to interact with them. I'd still be myself, of course, but it wouldn't hurt to put together a conscious strategy, even if just on-the-fly within a minute or two here, in trying to present myself in the best light to Viola, the new Chief of Police, and my new boss. But in trying to do so in his office that day, for some reason the reflection off his cuticles threw off my thought process in terms of building that strategy. I eventually got there though.

I would learn over the next two years, as I had the opportunity to work closer with the new chief, that he had a very interesting background and past personal and professional life. He was born and raised in the Kensington section of Philadelphia, then as well to this day a rough-and-tumble lower economic area of the city. His father, Rich Viola later told me, had an "association" with Angelo Bruno, the head of the organized crime family of Southeastern Pennsylvania and southern New Jersey throughout the 1960s and 1970s. (Many say the fictional Vito Corleone of *The Godfather* book and movie fame was loosely based on Bruno.) Young Richie would spend time in Bruno's South Philadelphia home while his dad would visit there for "business" of one sort or another. My new chief didn't hide this association between his dad and the Philadelphia mob boss. However, young Richie clearly did not follow in the footsteps of his father.

After finishing high school, Rich Viola enlisted in the U. S. Marine Corps. Upon his honorable discharge, he joined the Philadelphia Police Department in the mid-1960s. He eventually took the sergeant's promotional exam, passed it, got to know then-PPD Commissioner and future Philly mayor, Frank Rizzo, and after a few very productive years in the patrol division was assigned to the Intelligence Unit. After a stint there, he was the first and only commander of the newly created Major Investigations Unit (MIU). This squad was for four years unofficially run by Rizzo, both as the top cop and later, even more unofficially, as mayor. It was a plum and much sought-after position for any PPD officer, with its officers assigned to work only the biggest cases in Philadelphia. Viola later told me that if he had taken additional promotional tests and passed, he may have lost his position managing this elite squad. So, he happily stayed as sergeant in the MIU, doing what he did best, investigating major crimes.

While working on this squad, then Sergeant Viola had the occasion to meet with some art dealers in the Philadelphia area. These businessmen got to know him and asked him at some point if on his days off he could transport various expensive works of art to New York, Miami, and even internationally. Up to that point, these art dealers told him, they would occasionally get robbed of their very valuable merchandise while in transit and they liked the fact that this young, ambitious, and honest cop, who was also street smart, happened to carry a gun, and knew how to use it, could better protect their merchandise on its way to a customer, a gallery, or a museum. So, they hired Viola on an occasional and informal basis.

On several of his trips to Paris, with various pieces of artwork either coming or going with him, Viola even brought his .38 revolver along for the ride. He would store it in his checked bag on the flight.

But once on the ground there, he would wear it in concealed fashion the whole time. He was being paid to protect these very costly pieces of art, and he wasn't taking any chances, he said, even if it meant being an off-duty City of Brotherly Love police officer carrying a loaded gun in and about the City of Lights. Rich never had to pull his weapon internationally, he claims, nor did he ever lose any merchandise. Maybe there was a connection….

Before, during, and after undertaking these off-duty trips, because of the kind of guy he was, Rich Viola took it upon himself to begin learning about the art world, its paintings, its artists, and the business itself. Prior to him departing on one of these details, Viola negotiated with the local dealer that instead of being paid for his services in U. S. currency, for his compensation this time he would instead like to keep one of the small prints he was transporting of a certain well-known artist. The deal was agreed upon. It was the same agreement that he worked under during the course of the next several years which allowed Viola to acquire additional pieces of art, each in trade for him protecting the ones he was transporting for the various dealers. Then, one of the artists whose works he now owned unexpectedly died. In doing so, the value of all that artist's paintings skyrocketed. Owning a few of this artist's works, Rich Viola now became a relatively wealthy man, at least in terms of the small but valuable artwork collection he now had in his home. He sold some, bought others, and his collection continued to grow.

Over the years, starting in Bensalem, and later in other residences around the U. S., I was invited into Rich's homes where he and his lovely wife Sandy would give me a grand tour of their small but impressive art collection. I was amazed, to put it mildly, of not only the paintings and also sculptures themselves, but also of my then former chief's knowledge of individual past and present painters and the art world itself. It definitely got me interested in this world which was previously unknown to me other than through a few art history classes back in grade school.

Years later, after I left the BPD, Rich Viola, knowing of my newly found interest in art, was nice enough to give me a belated going-away present. It was an illustrated coffee-table style book of the late 19th-century French artist Henri de Toulouse-Lautrec. In it, among other paintings and illustrations by the famous artist, was one from 1899 titled "At the Circus, Horse and Monkey Dressage." (Also known as "At the Circus: Performing Horse and Monkey.")

Years later, coincidently, I linked this particular painting to Ted Kaczynski, also known as the Unabomber. Due to my rudimentary knowledge of the art world and the Toulouse-Lautrec book, both thanks to Rich Viola, I was able to put together the one last missing piece of the Unabomber puzzle.

(More on this fascinating case and the intertwining of the lives of Henri de Toulouse-Lautrec, Ted Kaczynski, Rich Viola, and Jim Fitzgerald, in JCM Book III.)

In attempting to furnish the full mosaic of Chief Viola as a Renaissance Man, at least in my limited world at the time, I should add that he was in very good physical shape from his daily workout regimen. He's a guy I wouldn't want to tangle with in an alley fight, and I happened to know back then that there were still a few guys in prison who tried, but failed. Also, he was an excellent marksman on the pistol range. I know that from shooting next to him on more than one occasion and observing the small saucer-size groupings in the center of his paper targets.

Rich was also well read, able to quote Shakespeare, Twain, Churchill, and the like, sometimes with purposefully added invectives of his own for emphasis. Lastly, speaking of language, even though he was not formally educated beyond high school, Viola had an excellent command of English and could do so eloquently in front of a large audience or one-on-one, with a journalist, or with a grieving wife whose BPD officer husband became an on-duty stabbing victim. On occasion, he could readily lace his language with words of the four-letter variety, usually for purposes of emphasis, but sometimes as modifiers too. He was by no means a "dese," "dose," and "yous guys" kind of speaker. He may have pronounced "water" as "wooder," but that's understood. Practically all of us Philadelphia natives do that.

One could debate the interpretation and application of the term "Renaissance Man" all the way to Florence, Italy, and back. All I'm saying here is that I hadn't met anyone quite like Rich Viola in my life up to that point, and if asked back then to identify a living version of such a man, well, it would have without hesitation been my new Chief.

Returning to my initial "interview" in the Chief's office that day, after a short, one-sided phone discussion with an FBI agent and after the two of them apparently agreed upon a place and time to later meet, the Chief told me it was now my turn. I sat up even straighter in my chair and said, "Yes, sir."

Viola initially congratulated me on my arrest from the night before, which he knew actually led to two other arrests the next county over. He knew the guy's name, where and how it happened, and more. Obviously, he did his homework before talking to me. That was impressive, I recalled thinking to myself. He then told me that this is the kind of aggressive police work he was looking for in his department, from uniformed to plainclothes to detectives and from his management people. Keep up the good work, he said a few times to me that day, and "You'll go far here."

Okay, sure...I'll try, I more or less acknowledged back to him. I thanked him too for his nice words regarding the arrest. Interestingly, I never actually heard any nice words at all while in this office on previous occasions under the last regime, so this was definitely a different experience for me.

Viola further related to me he was attempting to personally meet with every officer in the department in the first month in his new position. He had talked to about thirty of us so far. It wasn't necessarily that easy to do as the officers were working steady shifts, he reminded me, and that's why it took so long for him to get together with me. But he was coming in early some days and stopping by after dinner on other days to work through this process. That's why he was meeting with me now, shortly after my just completed 5:00P roll call. He asked for me specifically today, he told me.

Hmmm...because of last night's arrest, or something else? Yes, I was still waiting for the other shoe to drop regarding the first time I met Chief Viola, well, Sergeant Viola, back in the spring. There was nothing yet though mentioned regarding that encounter.

The Chief's stated goal here was to sit down with each officer for about ten minutes and go over their respective backgrounds, personnel records, what they've done in their BPD career so far, where they've been assigned, and where they may want to go within the department. Today, it was my turn to discuss these matters with him. Since I was sure I was the only one in the department to have pointed a loaded gun at him, this may last much longer or much shorter than the allotted ten minutes. Time, literally in this case, will tell.

Next, saying little more than, "Let's see...what do we have here?", Viola opened my personnel file, leaned back in his new leather chair, put his feet up on the corner of his desk, and started going through the paperwork. He saw that there were several less-than-positive one-page memos in it relating to me. They were all written by my former Tactical

Squad sergeant, the Whacky one. Two I knew about, a minor-car accident and me supposedly not responding to a suspicious vehicle call at some point, both while I was on the Tac Squad. The other three or four memos were about matters which were never discussed with me, much less shown to me. They mostly concerned my "attitude" on the Tac Squad and how it wasn't conducive (my word, not a word Sgt. Whacky could pronounce, spell, or comprehend) to him running a cohesive (my word again, for the same reasons) squad. Also in there was Lt. Traenkle's memo relating to my disciplinary action over the called-in-but-not-responded-to burglar alarm incident the night the Phillies won the Series just about a year ago.

Upon reading the topics of these various documents aloud to me, the Chief simply crumpled them up with his (manicured) fingers and said each time, "This is trash," as he deposited them one-by-one in the round can on the floor next to his desk. He then told me that he already heard I was a good cop, an innovative cop, saw I had a degree from Penn State, was taking grad courses at Villanova, and couldn't believe I didn't have any commendations in my file for the various past arrests I had made of which he had recently become aware. I shrugged my shoulders in tacit agreement. I honestly did not have an answer for him as to why those type "atta-boys" were not in there except for the fact that I was on the bright side of the Dark Side. Viola knew that too.

The Chief advised me that he was putting me in for a commendation for my robbery arrest from the night before. I thanked him. He further added that he believes in positive reinforcement as a management style, not negative. I was thinking to myself that this was just the opposite of the last regime, or almost-regime, under Deputy Chief Zajac, certainly to those perceived to not be on his side anyway.

As my ten minutes were all but up, the Chief asked me if there was anything else I wanted to discuss. He had to leave in a few minutes to meet with the FBI agent who had called earlier, he told me. I was about to get out of my chair and tell him, "No, that's it," but I couldn't resist the temptation. I HAD to mention our little incident from back in the spring at Doral Apartments and get it off my chest. So, while standing up and approaching the closed office door, I said it.

Our little post-meeting conversation went more or less like this:

Me: (Unapologetic, yet deferential.) "Uh, sir, I just want to say… uh…the incident a few months ago at Doral…you know, you, in your Cadillac, I…uh…was just doing my job, you know and, uh…."

Chief Viola: "Jimmy, Jimmy, stop right there! Don't worry about it! You think you're the first cop to draw down on me? Hah! You're not! It happened to me in Philly a few times. No, you did an excellent job that day 'cause you didn't know who the hell I was and you saw a gun. You did it all by the book. I would have done the same thing. All's good. Keep up the good work, that's all I ask of you."

Me: "Uh…okay, fair enough. I will. Thanks for your time today. Take care."

I left the Chief's office and that was it. The elephant in the room was freed and on its way. To where, I didn't know, nor did I care. I did know that neither the big animal nor the Chief held any grudge or animosity towards me then or anytime in the future for what happened a few months ago in the past. It was done, over, and off the table. In fact, I had it reinforced on that day in a strange sort of way in this law enforcement profession of mine that it may have actually been a good thing that happened between the two of us with this incident. It served somewhat as sort of a cop-to-cop bonding moment for us; ESPECIALLY as I didn't actually pull the trigger that evening.

Obviously, the level of bonding would have been somewhat different if I HAD pulled my gun's trigger. But, we won't dare go there.

Chapter Twenty-Six

The next few months were actually a joy to work at the BPD under our newly appointed chief. I felt almost like a rookie again. It was much like I felt my first year at the BPD before the nadir of ugly politics and equally ugly people (in a figurative sense, well...mostly) manifested within the department, or at least before I noticed it and them.

Various training opportunities were suddenly made available to the rank-and-file in the department for the first time in a long time. There may have been some of it offered over the last few years, but not to those of us who were allegedly on the team playing opposite Team Zajac.

One opportunity that Chief Viola made available to us through his former professional colleagues was for interested officers to spend a week on a 4:00P-12:00A shift with a squad of plainclothes officers in Philadelphia. I signed up for it right away and in mid-November of '81 I spent a Monday through Friday working with these officers in their very busy North Philadelphia police districts (as so-called in Philadelphia; not "precincts" as in many other PDs) chasing drug dealers, armed robbers, and other miscreants in and around an area which came to be known as the Badlands. I didn't actually work that week in my old Olney neighborhood as, fortunately, the crime there wasn't that bad...yet. But being not too far away from there, and finally working as a cop in my city of birth was quite a thrill, even if it was only an "Away Game" for me for those five nights.

And speaking of the Deputy Chief, it turns out he wasn't very happy with his new everyday assignment under Chief Viola. Zajac was put in charge of the motor pool and issues related to the gasoline pump, car speedometer checks, vehicle inspections, and the like. He played no role whatsoever in the management of the department. He was put in the office right next to Viola's, who was now actually in Zajac's old office, and worked a steady 8:00A-4:00P shift. Oh, and he was now in full uniform too. I had never seen him wearing a police uniform prior to this assignment. However, he was ordered to wear it and he did. He didn't have much choice I suppose, did he?

Interesting that Zajac, indirectly through his dad, only three years ago orchestrated exactly what was happening to him now, but with Chief Larry Michaels as his then-foil. Michaels was effectively allowed to keep his title and his pay, but stripped of all official duties within the department. Now, ironically, the same thing was happening again, but only with Zajac in Michaels' place.

In some cultures and/or philosophies there is a word for this. That being, Karma.

My favorite expression in regard to Zajac and his situation back then was simply, "What goes around, comes around." The question was... had what gone and come "around" fully completed its cycle, or could it go and come "around" again? No one at the time knew the answer to this question, but the wheels of this cycle certainly continued to turn. They would be spinning completely out of control before too long.

* * * * *

Amazingly and unbelievably, three of these proverbial wheels fell completely off whatever was left of the Zajac "cycle" before the year 1982 was even four days old. It was less than four months into Rich Viola's tenure as Chief at the BPD that the unthinkable happened. Well, at least unthinkable to my still somewhat naïve and unsuspecting mind at the time, and no doubt with many other people in possession of a similar mindset. It would alter the shape of Bensalem politics, its police department, and the reputation of both, for years to come. It was all just beginning in that first week of January.

That would be the arrest of Bensalem Township Supervisor Stephen Kelly and his brother Michael for what were initially state charges involving drug manufacture, car theft, gun possession, and related crimes. The arrest was under the direction and supervision of Chief Viola and a few BPD detectives.

What the hell was going on in my suburban Philly town? In my suburban police department? Supervisor Kelly, an elected official, arrested? With his brother, too? For drug related charges, along with gun violations and car theft? This couldn't have just happened. I mean, he was Deputy Chief Zajac's biggest supporter. He had previously publicly vowed to fire Viola once he had the votes.

Okay, wait a minute! Were there dots to be connected here? Were they just, in fact, connected in a very straight line by this arrest?

264

I may be politically naïve to some degree, but something is rotten in...Bensalem.

Where is this whole thing going to lead?

For one thing, it eventually led to the matter being prosecuted in the federal system as both the Bucks County District Attorney and U. S. Attorney agreed that the charges and subsequent trial belonged there. Yes, the charges were that serious.

Damn, this is going to be interesting to follow over the next year or two.

I'll once again use the cogent words of *Bucks County Courier Times* reporter Anita DiBartolomeo to summarize what occurred on that cold winter night, and a few days and nights before then. This particular snippet is from an article she wrote in late 1983 just before the federal trial was to begin in Philadelphia.

"(Federal) court documents indicate (Stephen) Kelly is to be tried as a result of two basic allegations:

* That last New Year's Day (1982), Kelly burst into the Levittown (PA) home of (E. B.), an automobile mechanic whom he had never met before, and brandished a small, chrome-plated revolver.

  Kelly was paying the call because E. B. had taken $2,000 from the supervisor's brother Michael as part payment for a half pound of methamphetamine, commonly known as speed, and then never delivered the drug.

  The supervisor demanded the money, but said he would take instead a gallon of phenyl-2-propanone, known as P2P, an illegal chemical used to manufacture speed.

  As collateral, they stole a 1969 Plymouth E. B. was buying from a friend. The scheme started to unravel when the real owner of the car called Bensalem police and an investigation was launched with E. B.'s cooperation.

  E. B. secretly recorded two telephone conversations, one with the supervisor and two with his brother, before both Kellys were arrested Jan. 4.

  Federal officials provided E. B. with a gallon of P2P and Michael was apprehended under the Indian-style totem pole at the Neshaminy Mall after he accepted it. Stephen was arrested several hours later as he arrived at the municipal building for a supervisor's meeting.

- That on Dec. 26, 1980, and Jan. 16, 1981, (Stephen) Kelly bought a total of $517.50 worth of phenylpropanolamine hydrochloride from an Illinois company. Kelly allegedly paid by check for five kilograms of the chemical to be delivered to his brother Michael at the supervisor's apartment."
(End of article.)

The Kelly brothers proceeded through the criminal justice system the same as any other arrested and charged persons. Later the night of their arrests they were arraigned at a local district magistrate's office, eventually made bail, and were subsequently released from the detention center. Within a few weeks, a preliminary hearing was held and both brothers were held over for trial. Within months, the state charges were dropped and the federal charges were lodged.

Supervisor Stephen Kelly became scarce over the next year and a half, rumored to be living anywhere from Virginia to Georgia to Colorado to California. His supervisor seat was not officially vacated, but obviously he wasn't there to vote on any township or police department matters.

Geez! Does it get much more serious than these charges? No one was killed, fortunately, but still…drug manufacturing, guns, car theft, threats, etc., all allegedly undertaken by a duly elected official of a mid-sized U.S. town? With surreptitiously recorded phone calls by seemingly viable witnesses linking the Kelly brothers to the crimes?

Yes, this is serious, very damn serious.

I had thought the soap opera elements of Bensalem Township and my police department over the last few years were bad enough already. But this really puts matters into the stratosphere. Could it possibly get any more bizarre?

Yes, it would.

The cast of characters would grow exponentially and it would become a Bensalem-based passion play in its own right on full display in the media and subsequently in the courtroom. The ending of this multi-act stage show was unforeseen in these early days. By curtain call, it would surprise all involved, protagonists and antagonists alike, not to mention those of us in the audience watching it unfold before our eyes.

Chapter Twenty-Seven

Life and everyday police work continued in the BPD in early 1982, despite one of the sworn elected supervisors no longer performing his sworn elected duties. It's amazing how municipalities and governmental agencies can still survive, if not thrive, without one or more of these officials' daily or weekly involvement…or interference.

Maybe we simply need fewer politicians in the world. Things MAY run much more effectively and efficiently that way. We don't necessarily have to arrest the surplus ones, just not elect as many of 'em.

But again, I digress here.

My career was going along just fine in patrol working the steady shifts. I got very used to working ten hours in a row, knowing that it gave me an extra day off per week. It provided for more family and personal time and was a very welcome addition to my life, as well as the others in the patrol division of the BPD. I was also into my second semester at Villanova grad school (just one evening course per semester) and with the extra day off and using a bit of comp time, I never missed a class.

In terms of the administration of my patrol division, it turns out that Lieutenant Ron Traenkle was promoted to Captain by Chief Viola before the end of 1981. He was now in charge of us uniformed officers. I guess he was at the right place at the right time, especially as he was just a patrolman barely four years before. We called these guys/gals "Blue Flamers" later in my FBI career. That's because their careers were moving so rapidly upwards it was like a jet engine's blue flame was coming out their butts. Sometimes, after a while though, they sputtered and crashed to earth. Especially those who moved up too quickly and never mastered the requisite management and supervisory skills along the way. It could certainly happen in a place like the BPD too. And it would.

One of the now-head of patrol's first decrees was that uniformed officers were allowed to roll up the sleeves on their winter shirts while on duty, but only a few inches and folded no more than two times. I believe they were called "French Sleeves" in this particular context. Capt. Traenkle actually put an addendum in the patrol officer's handbook which allowed for this daring uniform fashion modification. It occurred within a few days of his assuming the position as it was a pet-peeve of his from the past.

I was never crazy about the winter long-sleeved shirts anyway because it meant we also had to wear our clip-on ties too. (No ties were required when wearing our short-sleeved summer shirts; we wore them open-collared during these warmer months.) I didn't care one way or the other whether I could roll up my sleeves or not. I guess Traenkle did though, and since he was now in charge of the uniformed officers his first official policy change was that he and the rest of us could wear the sleeves a la the French.

Merci beaucoup, I guess....

Chief Viola also needed someone in charge of his detective division, aka CID. Before too long into 1982 he surprisingly appointed Lt. Jack Robinson, who before this was always either in patrol or in an administrative function within the department. I heard that Jack at first hesitated to take this new position, quite frankly, because he had not been a detective and/or investigator previously. However, he was eventually convinced by Viola to take the position. His job, after all, was to be the detectives' supervisor, not to actually investigate crimes. He came to understand this and after his initial reluctance he welcomed the new professional opportunity.

Viola was not a dummy when it came to appointing people to certain high-ranking positions within the BPD. In considering someone, he had to first know they were dedicated, committed, intelligent, and the like. (Well, mostly anyway.) And, almost as importantly, he had to know they were not a Zajac zealot, at least not for these upper-level positions in management. He didn't need someone who drank the exiled Deputy Chief's Kool-Aid now attempting to undermine him (Viola) in these important administrative functions.

It was known to all in the department that Jack Robinson and Ted Zajac were NOT friends. It seemed to go back a long time too, so Viola's appointment of Jack seemed to make perfect sense. Plus, he was dedicated, committed, and intelligent too. Even better!

Interestingly, and maybe not coincidently around this time, many of us got to see an old black and white photograph of a very young Bob Hughes, Ted Zajac, and Jack Robinson, each in their crisp, new uniforms, at or about the time they graduated from the police academy in the late 1960s. In the photo, the three of them were lined up with the shorter Zajac in the middle, each with their hands straight down at their sides. This was done, Jack Robinson later told us, because Ted had failed yet again to qualify at the pistol range at or near the time of their graduation and thusly couldn't be lawfully issued his gun. So, at someone's suggestion it was agreed as the photo op was being staged that the other two, with guns clearly in their holsters, were to stand alongside of and slightly in front of the future Deputy Chief and, in effect, block for perpetuity the view of Ted's empty holster with their hands.

Apparently, Jack occasionally kidded Ted over the years about this picture and his poor shooting skills, and the latter didn't appreciate it. So, for that and other personal and professional reasons they never, shall we say, bonded all that well.

When Viola put all of this together, he knew that Jack Robinson was the man for him. He would eventually be promoted to captain in January of 1983 and become the Chief's closest advisor, serving as a bridge between Viola's sometimes intense Philly PD style of management and the more laid back Bensalem PD way of doing things. Jack had a few local political and business movers and shakers in his back pocket too, so it didn't hurt Viola to gain these connections as he was brand new to our township and its way of conducting business.

The blossoming Viola/Robinson was a match made in heaven, or at the very least somewhere along the Philadelphia/Bensalem border. They were nevertheless two very different men with very different backgrounds and personalities. However, they complemented each other well in the management of the BPD. I'd get to know this even better before long, sometimes straddling the line between the two of them and their varying temperaments and managerial styles.

Before long in his new position, Jack Robinson needed some new blood in his CID; new detective blood, that is. Chief Viola agreed with this line of thinking and told him to start the promotional process. It's then that Viola hit the roof when he learned how the existing detective promotional process worked.

Under Zajac's command of both CID and later the whole department during the prior six or so years, when there was a position open for a new detective, he would simply personally appoint an officer who had expressed an interest in same. This man would then work under Zajac's tutelage for six months. After that, the acting detective would take an alleged two-hour written detective promotional exam in a room by himself. Once he completed the test he handed it in to Zajac. Guess who then graded it? Yes, Zajac had the alleged answer key and would determine if the acting detective had passed his exam or not.

In other words, it was the good old boys' network at play here in a directly upward mobility promotional opportunity. (Remember, my Tac Squad appointment was NOT a promotion. It was a lateral move. I was still a patrol officer.) Under this old system, Zajac would appoint one of his long-proven patrolman supporters to an acting detective role, and if he did well in that position over a half year, not just solving crimes but continuing to worship at the altar of the BPD high priest himself, he was in the club. All he had to do was pass this little exam. Remarkably, every acting detective appointed by Zajac did, in fact, pass the test.

What are the odds?

The official detective position was an actual upgrade in rank and pay too, with a five percent pay raise and lots of overtime to earn in working after hours, going to court on days off, etc.

When Viola heard of this competing-against-yourself promotional process for the detective position, with Zajac as the school marm who graded the tests, he scrapped it then and there. He had no problem with appointing acting detectives for a few months at a time, but at some point they and any other interested officer would take an actual competitive written exam, followed up by an oral exam, all administered by an outside professionally-sanctioned testing entity. When this was announced in early 1982, it was very positively received by the rank and file and the Police Benevolent Association (PBA).

Finally, this department was approaching professional standards. It was about time! Thank you, Chief Viola.

The good old boys on the BPD would have to find other ways to get promoted. (Unfortunately, they did again only a few years later and in the most bizarre of manners. More on that will be forthcoming.)

Regarding departmental promotions, it seemed that the testing process for the sergeant and lieutenant positions had been relatively legitimate starting about the time that I got to the BPD. (My managerially and otherwise challenged Tac Squad sergeant had been promoted just before I got there.) Written and oral exams for those positions, undertaken by outside entities, were the norm for the few years I was there. This may have been the result of the federal Law Enforcement Assistance Administration (LEAA) funding being made available to the department, and the prescribed departmental rules and regulations which were supposed to be followed accordingly.

But good things couldn't and wouldn't last forever. Not under the former regime.

In early 1981, with Zajac still running the show as Deputy Chief, there was one or more openings for the position of sergeant in the BPD and it was announced that a promotional exam was to be administered to any and all who coveted that slot. I'm not sure I truly coveted that slot, but I signed up to take the test anyway. It would be the first attempt in my career at an official promotion. There were some recommended books and study guides which were suggested, I purchased them, I read them, and on a cold winter day, once again at the Bensalem High School where it all began for me five years before, about twenty patrol officers and detectives took the written exam. In about two weeks, the results were released within the department.

I came in about fourth or fifth. I honestly don't remember exactly how high (or low) I finished, but it was around there. What everyone back then did remember and focus upon was who came in first. In doing so, he was well above everyone else as he attained an almost perfect score. This guy was a senior patrol officer on the department, with perhaps twenty years or more under his belt, who Zajac had recently appointed as the acting sergeant of a squad. He was a nice guy, I liked him, but as he was a die-hard Zajac boy, certainly at this stage in his career, I was hesitant to get close to him in any professional or personal manner.

Supposedly, before I was hired on the department and since then, this now-acting sergeant had taken several other promotional exams for sergeant, and he scored very low in each one. However, this time, in early '81, somehow, someway, he scored well above his closest competitor. His score was in the very high 90s, with perfect being 100.

What was going on here? Did this guy all of a sudden become super smart? Did he finally buy the study books this time? Did he hire a tutor? Did he really, really, cram for this exam, unlike the others he took before this one? Or, was there something else going on here? Just who graded this exam? Was that same school marm involved?

I along with others in the BPD started asking questions and bemoaning the fact that this officer, who again, was a decent guy, a good cop, and an okay acting patrol sergeant, just couldn't have scored on the test what the results said he did. And, like with a detective promotion, this too would be an official rank enhancement as a sergeant enjoyed a ten percent bump in salary once so commissioned.

With this testing anomaly so evident, the department's PBA put in an official request to review ALL of our written tests, the scores, and related materials before the next phase of this exam process, that being the oral component, would take effect. Some in the BPD were supporting this acting sergeant with the almost perfect score, and even Zajac made personal appeals for him at one or more roll calls over the next few weeks. However, it was in our contract to somehow have access to the test results if a certain number of officers wanted to see them. Apparently the higher-ups did NOT want anyone to see them (as we never did), and the test and the results were eventually deemed to be null and void.

No one ever admitted to providing the test answers to this officer, or him somehow cheating by any other means, but all parties backed down once the test results were officially challenged.

Within a year, with Viola now in charge, another round of promotional exams would be given. The former acting sergeant wouldn't even take the tests, but many others did, me included. The results were quite different this next time.

Chapter Twenty-Eight

Changes were coming for me, and soon too, the BPD, even though no one knew it yet.

Through the early winter of 1982, however, I was still responding to domestic calls, robberies, thefts, car accidents, and other similar type "jobs" consistent with that of a uniformed patrol officer in a busy suburban police agency. One call, actually it was a few separate calls over a several month time span, would open an interesting window to my future in law enforcement as an investigator and later as an FBI profiler. That would be when I would occasionally respond to, among other places, a residence on Fleetwood Ave. in the Trevose section of Bensalem Township. It happened to be the house where one of the most horrendous mass murders in U. S. history occurred.

On March 12, 1976, close to the date I took the written exam which would lead me to eventually become a Bensalem police officer, a 24-year-old man named George Geschwendt broke into a two-story single home a block or so away from where he lived and methodically murdered, one by one, five members of the Abt family, and the boyfriend of the oldest daughter. He laid in wait for each of them as they came home that afternoon and early evening, shot each one as they entered the front door, dragged their bodies down the basement stairs, and then went back upstairs quietly anticipating the arrival of the next family member.

Geschwendt's primary goal was to kill Michael and Clifford, the two Abt boys closest to his age who used to tease and torment him when they were all younger. The two older Abt brothers and George went their separate ways by the time they reached their late teens, but apparently the overwhelming negative memories lingered for George, and he chose to carry out his plan to "get even" with them on this particular Friday night after months of pre-planning.

Before the carnage was over that evening, shot to death were parents John, 49, and Peggy, 46, along with children Margie, 19, Johnnie, 14, and Kathy, 13. Also killed, in a classic wrong-place-at-wrong-time scenario, was Gary Engle, 20, the boyfriend of Margie, who just happened to accompany her to the house that evening.

George didn't stop at killing only human beings, however. While on his mission he even put a bullet to the head of Heidi, the family's ten-year-old St. Bernard.

Geschwendt would clean up the blood in the hallway area near the front door after each shooting. That way, as each forthcoming unsuspecting victim walked through the doorway they wouldn't initially notice anything unusual. They'd be caught off guard as George would come up to them from behind and shoot them in the head. He then laid each body alongside the last one on the basement floor.

George apparently covered the faces of each victim with pillows and/or blankets once they were placed on the concrete slab of a floor at the bottom of the stairs. Later in my career as a profiler I would learn that this type of post-offense behavior was known as "Undoing." Wikipedia defines this term as "…a defense mechanism in which a person tries to 'undo' an unhealthy, destructive or otherwise threatening thought or action by engaging in contrary behavior." Sigmund Freud first wrote of this concept in his development of the various theories relating to psychoanalysis. In the case of the Abt family victims, it was the covering of their upper bodies so Geschwendt wouldn't have to look into his prior victims' eyes and their faces each time he reentered the basement to add to his impromptu ever-expanding mass grave.

As reinforced in my FBI profiler training, when someone undertook this sort of action at a crime scene, specifically at the disposal site of one or more bodies he personally killed, these usually served as indications that the offender was either feeling remorse or guilt for what he did, and/or that he possibly had a personal connection, in some manner or form, to the victim(s).

George Geschwendt did know each of the Abt family members as he had been one of their neighbors for virtually all his life. But ironically, the two family members he most wanted to kill, because of their alleged harassment and teasing of him when they were all teenagers, never came home during the several hours he was on his lethal mission at their house. Unbeknownst to George, one brother, Clifford, 23, was in Bucks County Prison, serving a year-long sentence as the result of a forgery arrest and conviction. The other brother, Michael, 21, was out and about in his car that day, not getting home until about 7:30PM.

When Michael arrived at the unusually darkened house, certainly for that time of night, with no family members or even a dog greeting him at the door, he instantly knew something was amiss. Before long, after calling out various family members' names, he casually walked down the basement stairs. There, Michael found the lifeless bodies of five of his family members, a friend, and his pet, each representative of the indescribable slaughter which had taken place in his own house and ending only a short time before he walked through the front door.

Michael's first reaction in attempting to mentally decipher the tragedy he had just observed was to run down the street to the house of a Bensalem police officer. The officer was off that night, and upon answering his door and being told in barely understandable yet highly emotional language by Michael what he had just seen in his basement, the officer called on the phone for police backup, got his service revolver, and walked with Michael back over to the Abt house. With Michael waiting outside, the off-duty officer entered the front door, gun drawn, and walked down the basement stairs. There, once he secured the scene to the best of his ability, in other words, making sure no one else was in the house, he confirmed that, in fact, each of the victims was dead. It was then that the uniformed officers showed up, further secured what was now a major crime scene, and called for detectives.

As the preliminary stage of the investigation began that evening Michael was questioned at length as to what could have possibly caused this horror to befall his family. He was no angel, and had his share of run-ins with the police, but he assured the detectives that this had nothing to do with his current life or anyone who was "out to get him," and that he clearly would not have done this himself. He was checked out fully and his story and alibi ultimately was confirmed, at least in regard to his own direct complicity in the murders.

The obvious next person to question was Clifford Abt. Not necessarily as a suspect in the actual crimes themselves, of course, but as to why this may have ever happened in the first place.

As such, Clifford was brought out of his cell around 1:00AM the next morning to meet with BPD detectives who had travelled to the Doylestown, Pennsylvania, Bucks County Prison for just this reason. First, naturally, they had to convey to him as delicately as possible that all but one of his family members had just been wiped out, each shot to death in their/his home. Not an easy task to undertake, as one can surmise, by even hardened detectives. Clifford at first didn't believe the two detectives, then got very angry at them and temporarily lost control of himself. He yelled, screamed, pounded his fists on the table, then eventually broke down and cried.

Upon Clifford slowly pulling himself together during those early morning hours in the prison interview room, the detectives began to inquire of Clifford as to whether he believed any of his former illicit dealings with people in matters even remotely related to his life of essentially petty crime could have possibly resulted in this violent episode against his family. Could he have pissed off anyone while out on the streets or now in prison badly enough that someone would massacre his parents, three siblings, a friend, and even the family dog?

Clifford couldn't think of anyone who would do such a thing. The detectives accepted this as true at the time. Like his brother, Clifford wasn't an angel either (after all, he was in jail at the time), but he maintained emphatically that he was never involved with any activity, in the streets or now in the joint, which could have possibly led to this massacre of his family. There may be a few guys both inside and outside of prison upset with him for one reason or another, but nothing, he posited, would result in anything even close to what happened to his mom, dad, and three siblings.

At the conclusion of the interview that night, Clifford asked to be let out of prison to assist in the investigation of these multiple murders. If these murders WERE about him, he maintained, he would find the culprits. Unfortunately for Clifford, any early release or furlough, other than to attend the upcoming funeral service for a few hours, was not going to happen.

Eventually, it would be good, old fashioned, detective work which solved this horrific case. A victimology assessment of each murdered person was undertaken. In other words, their personal backgrounds were checked over and over for indicators that someone, anyone, may have wanted them dead for one purpose or another. Nothing of any consequence was uncovered and all of the family members and friend were eventually deemed to be low-risk victims.

Repairmen and delivery men who may have made recent visits to the Abt household were identified and interviewed. They each had solid alibis and no discernible reason to slay the family.

A neighborhood canvass was undertaken at the same time in which every neighbor within a three-block circumference of the Abt household was interviewed. In some cases, for various reasons, people were reinterviewed. Every person's individual criminal record was reviewed, alibis checked, and information about each resident was figured into the ongoing investigative strategy.

Slowly but surely, George Geschwendt was interviewed once, then again, and then again, at his home less than a quarter-mile away from the Abt residence. He readily admitted to knowing the various Abt family members, and that he used to run around with Michael and Clifford in his teens. He added, however, that he hadn't really seen them or been in contact with them for years now. George's juvenile criminal record was later reviewed which showed he was arrested a few times back then, mostly for nuisance type crimes.

It was also subsequently learned that George had purchased a specific make and model .22 caliber firearm just a month or two prior to the murders. Interestingly, a few days after the murders, he filed an official report with the BPD that the weapon had been stolen from him. The forensic laboratory examiner told the detectives shortly after the murders that the .22 caliber rounds found in the bodies of the victims had each come from the same make and model of firearm. It was the same type that George had recently attained and had even more recently reported stolen from his home. In view of this, George was requested to come to the BPD HQ for one last interview. When confronted with this information, and later failing a polygraph exam, he ultimately confessed to the murders.

Geschwendt killed the family, he told the detectives, out of a delayed revenge for what Clifford and Michael did to him, or he thought they did to them, from five to ten years ago. He let these misguided perceptions foment internally over the preceding decade or so, eventually acting upon them on that March late afternoon-into-evening in 1976. His only regret, he told the detectives, was that he didn't wait around longer that night for one or both of the older brothers.

At the conclusion of his trial a year or so later, George Geschwendt was found guilty of six counts of first-degree murder and sentenced to the death penalty. It took the jury thirty minutes to reach their verdict. His sentence was later reduced to multiple life sentences when the courts ruled the Pennsylvania death penalty was unconstitutional. He remains in prison in Pennsylvania at the time of this writing.

As mentioned earlier, I was not yet on the BPD at the time of the Abt family mass murders and the subsequent investigation of the crime. However, later in my patrol career, specifically in '81 and early '82 when I was assigned for the first time to work Sector 1, which covered the Trevose section of Bensalem Township, I had a few of my own interactions with the two surviving Abt brothers.

Neither was exactly walking the straight and narrow path in life before the murder of their family, and neither chose to necessarily walk that path after the fact either. They were never what I would consider hardcore or career criminals, but instead more involved in nuisance-type crimes, usually at this time related to drugs and other intoxicant abuse.

Clifford was eventually released from prison, his eighteen-month or so sentence served, and he and younger brother Michael lived back at their Fleetwood Ave. family residence on and off for years afterwards. On more than one occasion I would respond to calls there from dispatch for loud parties, fights, and otherwise bothersome and rambunctious activity originating either inside the house or from the exterior of the house. The complainants were usually nearby neighbors.

On one such occasion, I responded there with another BPD officer who over the years working Sector 1 had developed a professional relationship, of sorts, with Michael. A neighbor had called the police at approximately 1:00AM because of a fight on the street outside of the house. Upon arriving, we were met by Michael. He was alone in the house as his "guests" had either voluntarily left or were forcibly and loudly evicted by him. The younger surviving brother was drunk and/or high and at first was very contentious because he thought we were immediately going to arrest him. But recognizing the other officer with me on the scene, with whom he had prior encounters, Michael eventually calmed down. Since he intuitively seemed to know it was my first time inside the Abt house, he offered in barely comprehensible verbiage to give me a "tour."

It wasn't really much of a tour, but Michael did point out to me the kitchen window which Geschwendt broke and used to climb into the house on that fateful day. He showed me the piano where George admitted to the detectives that he hid behind while awaiting dad, mom, Margie, Johnnie, Kathy, and Gary, his sister's boyfriend, to come into view. Michael later learned that George hid there because it gave him a view of both the front door and the rear door of the house at the same time.

Michael then pointed to the doorway leading to the basement. He asked me if I wanted to go down the steps. Before I could answer, he took a deep breath and led the way. I followed him, taking my own deep breath as I descended the first few steps. It was dark and musty in the basement, but Michael made a point of showing me exactly where the bodies had been laying when he came home that night. Neither the other officer nor I said a word. We knew what happened here and we both later agreed it was almost like sacred ground of some sort.

Within a minute or two, we followed Michael back up the staircase to the first floor. Halfway up he stopped, turned around, and with slurred words to both of us from slightly ahead and above he said, "You know, that motherf**ker killed our dog too! He killed Heidi! Who the f**k would kill an innocent dog? Jesus, who the f**k would kill an entire family? F**kin' George…!" Michael's voice then trailed off, he slowly turned around, and he and we reassumed our ascension of the stairs.

Upon reentering the living room area, Michael collapsed onto his sofa and advised us that he's done for the night, the "tour" is over, and he's going to sleep. He'll cause no more problems, he assured us. We two officers looked at each other, shrugged our shoulders, and agreed to leave. No arrest tonight of Michael Abt. As long as things quieted down, and his guests and/or combatants were all gone, the neighbors would no doubt be fine. I then drove off to my next call.

Two to three times again while still in patrolman status I had my moments with Michael Abt, perhaps even Clifford too. I believe it was on a car stop one time and another time at a local bar. I never arrested either of them, but other officers did when they simply could not control them or essentially had no choice in the matter. Everyone in the BPD felt somewhat sorry for Michael and Clifford, the latter of whom had his own additional demons to face for the rest of his relatively short life. But when one or both of them were acting up or involved in criminal activity, even of the minor variety, the laws of the land had to be enforced. Well, sometimes, anyway.

If Michael hadn't been one of only two survivors of a family mass murder in which he and his brother were the actual targets of the killer, perhaps the police would have handled him and them somewhat differently on those occasions. But as long as no one was actually hurt, or the quantity of some controlled substance was not all that large, sometimes we officers would look the other way for the sole remaining members of the Abt family. (We'd still dump the drugs into the street or toilet, however.) We'd let them sleep it off somewhere or even drive them back to their house and make sure they would pass out harmlessly on their living room couch…the one next to the piano.

Years later, as an FBI profiler, I would be assigned many a serial killer, serial rapist, or mass murder case to assess from a behavioral perspective and even a forensic linguistic perspective. These included Unabom, DC Sniper, the Philadelphia Center City Rapist, as well as others. During these assessments and analyses, I would occasionally find myself drifting back in time to my interactions with Michael Abt, to include the quick walk-through of his house some five-plus years after the murder of his family. It reminded me that the victims of murderers and rapists are NOT only the dead and/or assaulted themselves, but others associated with them or related to them; especially if that person had actually been the intended target of the offender from the onset of their insidious mission.

Talk about survivor guilt....

According to a *Philadelphia Inquirer* article dated March 3, 1991, written by Larry King (not the TV host), Clifford Abt died in 1989 of complications related to narcotic ingestion. He was 37. Michael Abt, 36, and his girlfriend were expecting their first child in '91. They were living in a rundown motel in lower Bucks County.

The oldest two Abt brothers were certainly not the most upstanding of Bensalem citizenry, but they didn't deserve what happened to them; nor did their family, the friend, or even Heidi the dog. Six people may have died on March 12, 1976, but the heart and soul were torn out of Michael and Clifford at the same time. In a way, they died too that night, as do other survivors and loved ones of murdered victims, each and every time it happens.

Chapter Twenty-Nine

I came into work one afternoon in early February at around 4:45, ready for a regular 5P-3A work shift, and found an envelope in my former timecard slot. (Yes, as promised, Chief Viola got rid of the time clock for his police officers. Where we used to keep our timecards were now our mailboxes.) I waited until after my roll call was complete and opened it. Inside was a memo, signed by Lt. Jack Robinson, advising me to report to CID as an Acting Detective in one week's time.

This transfer was not a complete surprise to me as a few days earlier Jack sought me out after a roll call and invited me back to his new office in CID. He told me that afternoon behind closed doors that he and Chief Viola wanted to get some "new blood" into CID right away and they both felt that based on my arrest and conviction record, as well as my overall experience and positive working attitude so far on the BPD, I was one of the top candidates for the job.

Lt. Robinson told me the rules had changed, however, and it wasn't going to be like the old days where an acting detective appointed by DC Zajac would do his six months, take an alleged test, have it scored by an alleged grader, and then be officially anointed and promoted as detective. I told him I was very glad to hear this news as I was a strong advocate of competitive testing, certainly within the BPD. He continued that I could be acting detective for the next few months but as there was going to be a legitimate detective exam and a legitimate sergeant exam in the next four weeks or so, everyone would have to abide by the final results. If I placed high enough in one or the other exam, I could stay in CID and/or become sergeant. If not, I'd be back out in patrol, acting status over. I told Jack it doesn't get much fairer than this, and I had no problem playing by these new sets of rules. We stood up, Jack shook my hand, congratulated me, and said "See you Monday morning. Suit and tie, please."

"You got it," I happily replied.

Wow! This all came about so quickly. I guess I had been impressing Lt. Robinson all along over my six years so far, and more recently Chief Viola too. Some recent high-profile arrests of mine didn't hurt either.

This was going to be different for me though. I had been in CID before, but as a patrolman/Tactical Squad member under the old regime. Now it would be as a detective, albeit in an acting capacity. However, getting this experience under my belt early on, even before the detective exam, would certainly not hurt my promotional chances for that position or even sergeant.

Geez, if I do well in both of these tests and I'm given the offer, which one do I take?

Okay, I'm getting way ahead of myself here; one step and one test at a time.

Ironically, my friend and fellow rookie and fellow Tac Squad member for a while, Terry Lachman, had been asked in the waning months of the Zajac regime to do the whole acting detective thing, take the test, then be officially promoted if he "passed." He played by those rules and he was made a detective sometime in mid-'81, a year and a half after I left Tac. I didn't begrudge his promotion. Terry was a good guy, a good officer, was developing into a good investigator, and he merely did what was asked of him at the time. Except, interestingly enough, he was advised under the new Viola regime that since he wasn't out of his detective "probation" period yet, he'd have to take the upcoming competitive exam if he wanted his position to become official.

Terry may have had a very winnable legal argument to make that he was duly promoted under the old rules of the old regime, and that he was, in fact, an official detective. But he chose not to go the litigation route. He took the forthcoming exam with the rest of us and he ultimately passed with flying colors. He's the only officer in the history of the BPD to become a detective via the old compete-only-against-yourself method and then the new compete-against-everyone-else method, all within about a year.

Along with Terry and a mix of twenty or so patrolmen, I took the separate detective exam and sergeant exam at Bensalem High School about one week apart in early March of '82. In less than seven days the grades were posted at HQ.

I forget my exact placement after all these years, but I was definitely within the top two to three in both the detective and the sergeant exam. I was happy, but not elated, as I wasn't number one in either. But this was only fifty percent of the overall score for the positions. There was to be an oral exam at the end of March. The top seven candidates in each written test would come in and sit before a board of non-BPD police managers who would interview them regarding various topics and areas related to investigations and management, depending on which area, if not both, the candidate was testing. That would make up the other half of the score total. Then, the rankings would be combined, finalized, and the promotional lists officially posted.

Where would I come in on the final detective list? Where on the final sergeant list?

I sure didn't know these answers at this time. I know I've always been a better interviewer than written test taker. Maybe I'd still have a solid chance yet to finish number one after my board interviews. And, strangely, no one was clear about how many slots were open for both detective and for sergeant. So, even if I didn't get promoted right away, and if I'm not TOO far down on the list after the oral interviews, maybe I'd get one of those slots within the two-year lifespan of the test. I could live with that.

I learned right away, along with every other interested party, when the written test results were posted that there was one officer, a guy with whom I attended the police academy in Hershey five and a half years ago, who scored off the charts. He was in the very high 90s. I congratulated him accordingly. I meant it too. It so happens he was one of the officers with whom I had attended the Lamaze birthing classes about two years before, had dinner afterwards with him and another officer and our respective three wives, and was then effectively reprimanded for it by Deputy Chief Zajac in his cancer-spreading office speech.

Unlike the Zajac-sponsored sergeant "test" a year earlier, when that other senior officer scored so high, no one suspected any hanky-panky on this Viola-sponsored one. The officer on top in this 1982 written exam had a good head on his shoulders, was a college grad, and obviously an excellent test-taker. Some among us just conceded that he would naturally come out on top after the orals, and the rest of us would simply be vying for what's left in either CID or possibly as a sergeant in patrol.

This patrolman did, in fact, score really high in the recent written test and his lead seemed insurmountable. I agreed. It was seriously doubtful that he could go much lower on the final lists after his oral exam results were tabulated into his score. Geez, all he had to do was show up that day, be decently dressed, have his hair nicely combed, not belch or scratch his butt in front of these guys, answer their questions even so-so, and he'd still likely maintain his overall number one position.

Furthermore, it was known through several PD friends of mine that this officer had gotten together with some former officers who had been fellow rookies with us but who had quit the BPD (during the former Zajac regime) for law school, to get their MBAs, or to move on elsewhere in their careers. With them, I learned, the high scorer was undertaking multiple practice oral exams at their various homes over the few weeks prior to the big day. These ex-officers role-played the interviewers and he role played, well, himself, the interviewee. Not a bad idea, I suppose.

I wasn't invited to any of these practice sessions, however. I guess I wasn't as friendly with some of these ex-officers as I thought I had been when we were still working together. Oh well, no big deal. My various friends and colleagues still on the PD who were taking the oral exam with me discussed some basic strategies amongst ourselves. Yet, no one thought to help each other in the way this other guy was going about it.

Maybe it would have been a good idea. That is, practicing these type interviews with my fellow oral exam competitors. I don't know. Some personalities with whom I was familiar within the BPD wouldn't go for this sort of collegial approach with so much on the line. I was sure of that and I wasn't going to press them into a situation in which they may feel uncomfortable. So, no practice interviews for the rest of us, at least as far as I was aware at the time, only for the high scorer. As if he even needed it.

So, when the time came for my board interview, I went in raw. No role playing or practice sessions for me; only in my head, with myself. My only experience in this area was my six or so similar board-style interviews in 1976 when I was attempting to get hired by various police departments in the general Philadelphia area. I knew back then I was presenting myself as more confident and more competent as I underwent each of those successive interviews, with my last one being in front of the Bensalem PD board who, of course, eventually hired me. Obviously, my written score AND oral score were together high enough to get me hired at the BPD. So, I guess I learned something in that regard in 1976 by the last of these board interviews.

But would all of that carry over here? Was it too long ago? Was I rusty in this area?

I'd have to wait to learn those answers, wouldn't I?

I admired my one colleague for how he was prepping, but I ultimately chose to do any prepping on my own. I decided to bring to the table just the person I was at that time, with no recent outside role players/former officers to possibly confuse or confound issues. I recall thinking at the time…how would they know they were asking the right questions of their friend? How would they know if the interviewee was giving the right answers?

Clearly, they wouldn't and he wouldn't know for sure.

I was confident I knew my stuff and could present it as well to these three men who were about to determine the next few years of my professional life. I'd be dressed decently, coiffed nicely, and wouldn't scratch anything of mine while talking to them. And I already knew my responses to their questions would be well above the "so-so" level.

That was my plan and I was sticking with it, for better or worse.

One morning in late March of '82, after six weeks or so being assigned some routine burglary and theft cases in my new role as an acting detective (which I figured was my form of REAL role playing), I walked upstairs for my scheduled oral exam. They were being held in the township auditorium, the same place where I had my hiring interview back in '76. Sitting officiously in a row behind the long and elevated table were the three unknown (to me, anyway) police managers from other Pennsylvania departments, wearing their starched white shirts, and looking very serious and matter-of-fact. I returned that look immediately upon entering the room. I don't remember their individual names, their PDs, or their exact questions after all these years, but I do recall they asked me about mostly investigative and management oriented matters (I was a candidate for both positions), as opposed to the more generic patrolman-oriented questions when I did my previous oral exams six years earlier.

Bottom line, when finally done, I felt I answered each of their multiple-leveled questions honestly and accurately. No one question or scenario caught me off-guard or threw me for a loss. As with any of these type multi-person exam boards, no matter what is answered by the candidate initially, it is almost always challenged to some degree by one of the other interviewers, just to try to trip-up the interviewee, or make him/her retreat from his/her initial answer. There was some of that, but I fended off the counter-questions/counter-scenarios very well, I thought. After forty-five minutes or so, with a now somewhat sweat-soaked new shirt under a now somewhat moist brand new suit, they thanked me and excused me. They gave me no indication one way or the other as to how I did… not that I expected it. Nonetheless,

I thanked each of them by name and/or title, shook their hands, and left the room.

Whew! Deep breath time!

I was so glad that was over. No matter what the outcome, I was relieved that the month- long testing process was now behind me. I could relax a bit as it was totally out of my hands at this point. I realized my immediate professional future lay instead in the hands of these three all but anonymous oral exam board members.

It would be another three weeks before us candidates for detective and sergeant would learn the final results. There would be surprises for a few of us.

I always wondered if the various role-playing scenarios in which my high scoring colleague participated included how to react to the results once they were posted, no matter what they may be. It probably would have been a good idea for him to have done so.

First though, I'd have to deal with an attempted homicide of one of my fellow police officers and friends. This took immediate priority over any testing matters.

* * * * *

On Saturday night, March 27, 1982, while responding to a report of a disturbance at a bar, several BPD officers went into the Mercury Beef and Beer on Rt. 13 in the Andalusia section of Bensalem Township. Jerry Judge, the former heavyweight boxer, was one of them. As was quickly learned, about six members of the same family, mostly men but with a woman or two among them, started fighting with each other and any additional patron in the bar who chose to or was forced to join in the escalating physical altercation. After the manager finally called the police, the two initial responding officers (Jerry being one of them) reluctantly became invited guests into the drunken family brouhaha which was now in full action mode. As the two officers entered the darkened bar, they could see right away bottles flying, pool sticks swinging, and punches being thrown. This is never a good combination in a bar already full of drunken people, especially if a sizable component of these drunks belongs to one extended dysfunctional family.

As most of the patrons in the joint seemed to be involved in the throwing and swinging of inanimate and/or animate items that evening, even with two uniformed cops now well inside, the officers got on their portable radios right away and requested back-up. They knew this wild-west saloon free-for-all was not going to end anytime soon. Jerry was ready and willing to go and begin to break it up, but even he knew he may need the cavalry here in the form of his fellow squad mates before long. He fought George Foreman in the ring just a few years before, but at least there was only one of George and he carried no weapons other than his two fists. Times this barroom scenario by twenty, with multiple weapons of varying sorts, and it's more of a wrestling cage match than a boxing match. Jerry knew this and he knew to call in the troops.

One thing I learned working with Jerry Judge on the streets on and off during the prior six years is that he rarely, if ever, needed to resort to his nightstick, blackjack, or even .357 Magnum, when things got physically challenging to him. He was so big, so strong, and his fists were so quick and targeted, that they were really all he ever needed when these type scenarios presented themselves. And let me be clear here, Jerry never hit anyone who didn't throw a punch or push him or another officer first. It took Irish Jerry Judge a great deal of physically aggravating circumstances and/or seriously threatening actions for his "Irish" to manifest itself. Once it did, however, it was a lightning strike out of nowhere that always ended the immediate problem in a very effective and efficient knee-buckling manner. I don't doubt that Jerry would even pull his punches on occasion just so he wouldn't actually break some drunken loudmouth's jaw or nose who wanted to fight him. He didn't punch for fun, I observed in these instances, he did so to maintain the peace.

Yes, Jerry Judge punched for peace. I said it and I stand by it.

However, is there is a potential downside to using one's fists as weapons all the time? Sometimes, even a former professional boxer can get overwhelmed in the wrong situation at the wrong time if there are enough people involved and at least one of them has a potential lethal weapon of his own and he's about to use it. This is exactly what happened to Jerry at the Mercury Beef and Beer on that Saturday night.

As Jerry and the other arriving officers were slowly clearing the deck (bar) of the rowdy relations and anyone else who may have sided with them or fought them during the ongoing drunken brawl, one of the 22-year-old male family members managed to get close enough to stick a four-inch knife blade into Jerry's gut. It went in right below Jerry's ballistic vest and above his leather holster. There would "only" be one stab wound of this police officer that night because before the guy could pull it out and try for a second thrust of his blade, Jerry instinctively came around with a left-handed jab to the front of his head that knocked him out cold. He wasn't pulling any punches on this night, especially with the point of a knife now several inches into his mid-section.

If not before then, an official "Assist Officer" call was put out on the radio and the rest of the BPD working that night responded to the scene of the now even more out-of-control Family Feud and bar fight. It was messy inside the Mercury, but things finally calmed down as Jerry, with the knife still protruding from just above his waist, managed to also knock out the stabber's older brother and their father, one after the other in a rapid left-right combination when they came to assist their now down-for-the-count brother/son. The additional arriving officers, some using their fists but others mostly swinging nightsticks, blackjacks, and heavy-duty flashlights, managed to quell the one-half of the dysfunctional family members who were still standing as well as the few remaining unrelated booze-emboldened fighters. As for the other half of the family now in various stages of unconsciousness on the suds and sawdust covered floor of the Beef and Beer, they'd soon be awakening to a very bad headache, some broken face bones, missing teeth, and handcuffs on their wrists.

The rescue squad was called and Jerry was taken to the nearest hospital, Frankford-Torresdale, not far into Philadelphia from the location of the bar. He was examined, sedated, rushed into surgery, and the ER docs fixed him up. The knife wound was deep and potentially serious, but the blade had missed Jerry's vital organs and he was going to be okay. He'd be in the hospital for a few days, but he'd be home before long.

The knife was recovered at the scene and about ten people ultimately arrested that evening. Once back on his feet, the 22-year-old stabber was arrested for attempted homicide, among other charges, and arraigned accordingly.

My role in the fight itself was non-existent (I was off that night), but I was later involved in the follow-up investigation. Over the next few days I was part of several detective teams who interviewed the bartender, manager, and other customers in the establishment that evening, at least the ones who had been sober enough to remember what they saw that night, in order to build our case against the 22-year-old. I was going to visit Jerry in the hospital after one of these interviews, but he was released a bit earlier than anyone thought he would be. It pays to be in tip-top shape like this former heavyweight. I eventually saw him at his home where he was resting comfortably with his small kids and his great wife Ethel at his side.

The barroom family members, believe it or not, later actually accused the BPD officers of police brutality at the bar that night. The charges didn't stand and were quickly dismissed. It was (and is) a common ploy by defense attorneys to claim these abuses. Yes, it is justified sometimes. But not this time. One of the family members actually stabbing a police officer somewhat diminished their legal argument.

The 22-year-old stabber eventually pleaded guilty and did a few years in prison. I heard he got his front teeth replaced in prison that Jerry removed for him that night. Good for him. Hopefully eating food for a while with only his gums in the front of his mouth would remind him to never stab a police officer again, or anyone else for that matter.

Jerry eventually returned to his squad in a month or so. He was no less of a bad-ass when he went back onto the streets in patrol. I know he mostly still relied on his left and right fists to manage most physical confrontations when warranted. It almost always worked for him.

* * * * *

By the second week of April, once we knew Jerry Judge was going to be okay and back to work soon, many of us re-focused on the promotional exams of last month. (For whatever reason, Jerry wasn't interested in the promotions. He liked being a street cop. There's nothing wrong with that either.) We were told that at 10:00AM on April 20th the results were to be made available to everyone. I was working an 8A-4P shift that day in CID.

Okay, so today's the day. What will the results be? Where will I place? How high? How (gulp) low? Where will I be spending the next few years within the BPD, and doing what?

I know it won't be as an acting detective, that's for sure.

C'mon, it's almost 10:00. Get this over with already. Post the friggin' results!

As the two separate lists were posted, by of all people Lt. Bob Hughes, with the combined written and oral grades, it was now official. I saw my name on the top of the individual lists. Yes, the very top. I came out number one in both the detective and sergeant exams.

Bob Hughes, again of all people, as administrative lieutenant, was the first person to congratulate me that morning. He knew I was on the "A-Team" now, and he was no fool. I guess he forgot that I didn't "fix" his niece's ticket a few years ago. Actually, he didn't, and he'd indirectly remind me of same a few years later.

But, for now, Hughes wanted to be my friend, or at least pretend to be. How convenient. He also handed me and the other candidates in the room that day individual envelopes. Inside these envelopes were brief summaries written by the three-officer promotional board relating to the individual candidates.

Mine read as follows:

> "(Candidate Fitzgerald) was one of the best candidates interviewed by the board for both of the jobs. His responses were well thought out, well-articulated, and showed a fine grasp of police work and the need to direct and control police officers. He also showed a sensitivity to differences in different types of situations and an ability to look at a factual situation from a number of differing points of view. While this candidate could perform both jobs well, there is a feeling among the board that he may be 'wasted' in the investigative division."

Wow! I can't believe this! What nice words from the three board members. I never expected this result. That is, being number one on BOTH lists. Especially with the other officer who scored so high in the written exam. I was hoping for maybe the number two position on one of the lists. But I was instead on the very top of each list. I considered myself on the top of the world at this exact moment in time too, as I fondly recall.

As it turned out, the high-scoring candidate did poorly on the oral exam. Very poorly, he even told a few people. Apparently, when one of the three board members asked him what his top qualification may be in attempting to earn a promotion to either sergeant or detective, he responded by saying, "Well, I scored highest in the written test of anyone else in the PD. That should mean something, I hope." Uh... apparently it didn't. His answer didn't sit very well with the board members. Their immediate body-English told him so, he later advised his colleagues. At the end, his combined scores turned out to be so low that he didn't place on either the detective or sergeant lists. Talk about a turnaround....

To his credit, this officer, with whom I was somewhat friendly back in the day, came up to me later and shook my hand and congratulated me. I believe he meant it too, despite his own obvious disappointment. Within a year he would leave the BPD. It just didn't work for him there anymore. I never saw him again and I'm not sure whatever became of him.

Maybe NOT attaining the sergeant or detective rank was a blessing in disguise for the former number one candidate, especially as things would develop politically over the next few years at the BPD; lucky me in that regard.

For now, though, let's stick with my just attained promotion.

So...what do I do? After a hearty handshake, a slap on the back, and a loud "Attaboy, Jimmy," I was told by Chief Viola the choice was mine as to what position I wanted. I had forty-eight hours to think it over.

I suppose take the sergeant position, right? After all, that's an official step up the management ladder. And a ten percent pay raise too. Geez, I hadn't even thought about that before. A promotion was NOT just a different position and responsibility, but it meant more money too. I could certainly use that right now. But I may have to leave the CID then and go back to patrol, just as I was growing into the whole detective thing. I had some decent, even if relatively minor, cases I was working, and had actually cleared some burglaries and theft cases and made arrests in them in my short time as an acting detective. I was getting into the whole detective thing....

However, after a day or two, a decision, more or less, was made for me. Lt. Robinson and Chief Viola called me into the latter's office that morning. The door was closed. The Chief asked me if I would consider taking the sergeant promotion but then staying in CID. In other words, I'd be a detective sergeant. Stupidly, in retrospect, I said back to them collectively, "Are you sure? I mean, I've only been an acting detective for two months or so...."

Jack responded, "I've seen you in action, I've seen you around the other officers in patrol and now in CID. They respect you. I know you got the street-smarts and I'm confident you can do the job."

Viola was nodding his head the whole time in agreement. I was flabbergasted as once again this was happening so fast. Without too much more thought (and being afraid I'd say something stupid again), I simply blurted out, "Well, okay then, I'll take the sergeant stripes and work back here. It's a deal! Thanks for this offer. I'll do my best, I swear."

Viola said, "We know you will, Jimmy. Otherwise we wouldn't have offered it to you."

They both shook my hand and out of the office I went. Later that afternoon there was a meeting of CID personnel. Lt. Robinson told all the detectives in attendance that I was going to be the new detective sergeant, effective April 29. Most of the detectives gave me a positive head nod or an actual verbal "glad to hear it," or some such comment. Some sat quiet in the back of the room. No coincidence, as they were the leftovers from the previous regime. They weren't thrilled about this brand new sergeant and virtually brand new detective now as their new boss. But, of course, it went much deeper than that. They were Zajac's people, and I wasn't. The new Detective Sergeant James Fitzgerald wasn't thinking that way right then, but I found out before long that's how they saw it.

Det. Ken Hopkins walked up to me after the meeting. With a cigarette dangling from his mouth (which was not an infrequent sight), he told me he knew I was a bit anxious about going from acting detective to detective sergeant within just a few days. In conjunction with that, and in front of Det. Terry Lachman, Lt. Robinson, and Chief Viola, he said to me and anyone who was listening, "Hey, Sarge, don't worry about the new job. You'll be fine. Let's just hope there's not a homicide on your watch the first week. Other than that, it'll be a piece of cake."

We all laughed as Ken stubbed out his cigarette in a nearby ashtray and walked back to his desk.

No one in the room that afternoon could guess how truly prophetic Ken's words would become. Like I said, he always was a good detective.

* * * * *

On Thursday morning, April 29, 1982, I was presented my gold sergeant's badge by Chief Viola and Bensalem Township Manager Marge Strange in the upstairs township conference room. It was my first gold badge. The color signified the fact that I was a detective. The word "sergeant" across the top signified, of course, that I was a detective sergeant. I never imagined that color and that word would be on a single badge of mine, certainly not this early in my career, anyway.

After the badge ceremony, while saying a few complimentary words about me, the Chief commented to the small crowd in the room that he was not aware of a younger detective sergeant anywhere in the tri-county area, to include in his former Philadelphia PD. He assured the people in the room that day that despite me being *just* 28 years of age, he knew that I would do a fine job as Bensalem's newest sergeant, now officially assigned to the Criminal Investigative Division.

I wasn't too thrilled at the time with Viola letting everyone know my exact age and the lighthearted reference to my youthfulness. But he said what he said and there wasn't much I could do about it. After all, he was the chief and he was telling the truth in this matter.

As we all know, later in life, people are hesitant to have their age made public because… well, they're older and don't necessarily want others to know they're older, or at least not have the actual number put out there. On this particular day, I didn't want my actual number put out there because…well, I was younger, and apparently younger than all the detective sergeants in the area at the time and in the recent past. Maybe some people, including my peers and soon-to-be subordinates in the CID, would possibly think I'm less capable, less experienced, less…I don't know…supervisory because of my young age. It didn't help that I did not even look my age, not to mention that I was younger than everyone of whom I was about to be in charge.

Damn! That curse of youth!

Well, the cat was out of the bag regarding my chronological time on earth thanks to the well-meaning words of my Chief. So, I guess I'd just have to prove anyone wrong who looked at my youthfulness as a weakness or a handicap.

I would, in fact, do so. It would just take some time.

Oh, and that last Thursday of April of '82 was a very extraordinary day for yet another reason. In the morning I was promoted to sergeant. In the afternoon I found out I was going to be a dad again. Yes, Eileen confirmed that she was pregnant with our second child. The doctor told her that the baby was due the end of November.

Wow! And I didn't think this day could get any better. It just did, and immeasurably so.

I started a day-work shift on that Thursday which would go through the beginning of the following week. The detective sergeants, of which there were now four, three of them senior guys, rotated back and forth on 8A-4P shifts and 4P-12A shifts. No midnight shifts, luckily, for us. The detectives themselves had a slightly different schedule, and there were no set squads where certain sergeants were assigned with certain detectives. Their schedule at the time was similar, but one detective every night shift worked a 7P-3A shift, just to be available for any late-night crimes which may need immediate CID involvement.

Thursday and Friday, the last two days of April, were relatively quiet for me. I was learning some of the paperwork, how to do the end-of-month CID report (cases opened, cases closed, arrests, convictions, property recovered, etc.), familiarizing myself with the evidence closet (of which the detective sergeants were in charge), taking calls from the local media folks regarding any "press releases" over the last twenty-four hours, and the like. I also had a few old cases of mine from my acting detective time I was still working and did so during those first two days in my new position.

While busy, this Thursday and Friday for me as a brand new detective sergeant was quite literally the quiet before the storm. Things were about to break wide-open for me in one more day.

Ken Hopkins's earlier admonition did, in fact, prove very insightful. Again, he's a helluva detective.

Top: April 1982, Acting Det. Jim Fitzgerald escorting Theft suspect
(Photo courtesy *Bucks County Courier Times*, Jay Crawford)
Bottom: April 1982, Township Manager Marge Strange and Chief Richard
Viola presenting Jim Fitzgerald with Detective Sergeant badge

Part 4 -
The Detective Sergeant Years

Chapter Thirty

For me, and mostly just by happenstance, the first seven weeks in my new role as BPD detective sergeant was less about being a supervisor and more about working cases. Several of them were headline producing cases, as a matter of fact.

I determined from the very beginning in my new position that the detectives didn't need an everyday boss looking over their shoulders and micro-managing them while they worked their respective caseloads. For the most part, I allowed them the autonomy they needed to do their jobs. I was there to assign them their cases and facilitate them in any way I could. I told myself, and them, that I wasn't there to be their babysitter. The detectives seemed to appreciate this particular management philosophy on my part.

Of course, some people work well within that supervisory (or lack thereof) framework, but others sometimes take advantage of it. I'd have some of both before too long.

I did my best in my new role as CID sergeant to not come across as officious to the detectives who were working for me on any given shift. I mentally juxtaposed my two most memorable sergeants in the BPD so far, that being Gene Ashton and my Tac Squad bizarro-boss. In doing so, I leaned heavily towards Sgt. Ashton's managerial skillset and as far away as I could from Sgt. Whacky's. It seemed to work for me at this particular point in time.

I learned early-on as a supervisor that I could get more by "asking" a detective working for me to undertake a specific task or tasks rather than by "telling" him to do so. Of course, by me *asking* him as his sergeant he knew at the same time that I was more or less *telling* him to do whatever it was I needed done. But, in this way, it came across as much less of a command and more of a request of him. I found that most people, at least most of the time, respond well to this type of manager/subordinate relationship. It always worked well for me with my supervisors.

Things would drastically change for me in the not-too-distant future and I would have to adapt my management style to an entirely different paradigm. Then, at times, officiousness on my part was necessary, even if it was not always very effective. I knew what I was doing then and it was done for a very specific reason. In the long run, the very long run (and an exhaustive one at that), it all worked out for me.

This referenced timeframe is a year and a half away though. There are more interesting issues to discuss before those dark days.

In my first seven weeks as a detective sergeant, encompassing the late spring and early summer of 1982, there were at least five cases and arrests which broke wide-open in the BPD. All five received extensive local media coverage, some national, with at least one case attaining headlines internationally.

The first of these cases starts below. The remaining ones are highlighted in the next four chapters.

* * * * *

On May 1, on what started like a very routine Saturday morning in the BPD Detective Division, even for this new detective sergeant who really didn't have an actual routine yet, things were about to get busy. Really busy! At 8:00AM on that bright and sunny morning it was only the relatively new Detective Terry Lachman and the brand new Detective Sergeant James Fitzgerald working in the CID backroom. It was mostly typing reports and reviewing evidence and information from some older cases we were both working. Then, with one phone call to dispatch, it all changed.

Terry and I both heard the call broadcast at the same time from the portable radio we always had on full volume in its battery charger on a shelf in the CID. The dispatcher was heard to be sending two patrol cars for the report of a possible shooting and/or a homicide at a warehouse on State Rd., in the Andalusia section of Bensalem. Terry and I looked at each other and with bated breath we waited to hear the responding officers' findings. It could have simply been an industrial accident of some sort, initially misconstrued as a shooting. Maybe it was even a false report filed for one reason or another. If it was an actual founded call, there was a good possibility Terry and I would be proceeding to the State Rd. location. The question we pondered aloud to each other was...Would it be for an accident investigation or a homicide investigation? Both, of course, are taken very seriously but the latter would involve a different set of rules and protocols to be followed than the former. An industrial accident is normally just that...an accident. A homicide is not an accident, and there are always one or more people responsible for its purposeful commission. Therein lies the critical difference between the two.

It took about ten minutes, but once the officers got inside the warehouse location they immediately confirmed the initial report. I heard one of them transmit on his portable radio, "...One adult white male, dead..." on the floor of this business. He was bleeding from the head. There were spent shell casings around his body.

This was no industrial accident or false report. It was a bona fide homicide.

Even though Terry Lachman and I worked together for a time on the Tac Squad, we got to know each other a bit more over the prior few months when we were both essentially acting detectives in the CID. We had arrived there by different promotional means, but we were now there officially, sans the "acting" before our title thanks to the recent test results. And I was his supervisor too.

That was weird, by the way, to virtually overnight go from becoming someone's peer to someone's boss. But that's how it was in a mid-sized police department and that's the dynamic we shared starting just a few days ago. It was actually easy with Terry. Like me, he was also born and raised in Philadelphia, a Penn State grad, and a stand-up guy who played by the rules and didn't succumb to the political nonsense practiced by many in the BPD at the time.

Terry had married his attractive, long-term girlfriend Janice just a year or so prior, and they were a fun couple. I reveled at his stories whilst in Tac or sitting around the CID backroom of his/their various scuba diving experiences while vacationing in the Caribbean. They had no kids, Janice worked, they managed their money well, and at least twice a year they spent a week or so at some island resort, diving during the day, and dining under the starry seaside skies at night. They had a very nice life.

While I was very much content being married to Eileen with one child and one on the way, I must admit, sometimes hearing of Terry's "adventures in paradise" made me a bit envious of him; in a healthy way, of course. I was happy for Terry and Janice, and all I really did was make it my personal goal to someday get to some such places and do my own scuba diving, and yes, maybe even some romantic dinners at a beach somewhere on a starlit evening. It would take me a decade or so, with any romantic aspect somewhat limited as our kids would come with Eileen and me, but it was still worth the wait.

Back to that Saturday morning...Terry and I drove to the site together in a CID car. We had our crime scene evidence kit in hand, packed into a large, gray suitcase designed for just such a purpose. Once we reconfirmed what we had at the scene, that is, the lifeless body of a man sprawled on the floor with several obvious bullet holes in him, I instructed the dispatcher to call in several off-duty detectives. They responded there before too long. It was now a full-fledged crime scene investigation which would eventually morph into a full-fledged homicide investigation.

The deceased's name, we quickly learned, was Robert Suckle. He was 38 years of age and was a steel executive who owned the warehouse facility where he was found murdered. One of his employees coming to work that morning found him on the floor near his office door. It appears that he was shot several times only an hour or two before. At the later autopsy, it was learned that there were both .25 caliber and .32 caliber rounds in his body. That means two separate guns, two separate shooters.

Somebody really wanted Robert Suckle dead; but who, and why?

(The employee who found Suckle and called the police had a rock-solid alibi for that morning. It wasn't him who was one of the shooters. That much we knew early on.)

The motive didn't seem to be robbery as Suckle's wallet with some cash was still in his pocket. We also later determined that nothing was reported missing from the building itself, nor were there any signs of a forced entry. This was a strange one, right from the start, without robbery, burglary, or theft figuring in as a possible reason for Suckle's murder.

Determining the ultimate motive and the identity of the killer or killers would be the task of Det. Lachman, as it was to be his first officially assigned homicide case. And I would be his supervisor on it, at least for an initial period of time.

After I assigned two detectives to personally notify the family of the deceased, one of the remaining tasks for later that day was for an investigator to attend Mr. Suckle's autopsy. It was the policy in every homicide or suspected homicide investigation that a BPD detective would attend the procedure in an attempt to maintain chain of custody of any evidence found in or on the victim, take photographs, as well as to be there when manner and cause of death was preliminarily determined by the medical examiner (ME). As I had never attended an autopsy before, I volunteered (actually assigned myself, as I was the supervisor at the scene) to be the investigator to go to the morgue. After making sure the crime scene was secure, the family notified, multiple potential witnesses interviewed, that's where I headed...to the morgue.

The autopsy took place around 5:00 that afternoon at Lower Bucks Hospital, in Bristol, Pennsylvania. It was conducted by nationally, if not internationally, renowned forensic pathologist, and at the time Bucks County Medical Examiner, Dr. Halbert Fillinger. Outside of his office, adjacent to the hospital's morgue, I met Dr. Fillinger for the first time. The mid-50s, distinguished looking, gray-haired gentleman was putting on his green scrubs and after a brief conversation regarding the circumstances of the crime, he told me he had a question for me.
I simply said, "Yes, Doctor, of course, what is it?"
After moving over to the other side of the room and now beginning the meticulous process of washing his hands in the bowl of a shiny stainless steel sink, and while looking down in the direction of the water rapidly flowing out of the stainless steel spigot, Doc Fillinger turned his head halfway in my general direction and asked, "Sergeant Fitzgerald, are you hungry?"
Hungry? At a morgue? When we're about to participate in an autopsy?
Before I could answer, the ME told me he was ordering cheesesteaks from a local pizza shop and wanted to know if I wanted one too. It was his treat, he said, and they were really good ones with extra cheese and fried onions and grilled-just-right thinly sliced meat portions.
I wasn't sure what the protocol was regarding eating while formally examining the body of a homicide victim, but nonetheless I respectfully told the good doctor, "Thanks, but no thanks," to his generous culinary offer. While drying his hands, Doc shrugged his shoulders, said "No problem," and gave the diener (also spelled "deener," and "deaner;" basically a morgue attendant or autopsy technician) the food order to call in for the two of them. After that, with the three of us properly attired and scrubbed, it was into the examining room we went. Dinner for the diener and the ME would come a bit later.

There on the table of the sterile and well-lit autopsy room was the same person I saw removed from the floor of a warehouse just several hours before, that being Robert Suckle. He was brought to the hospital in a body bag by the ambulance squad after the scene was fully processed and photographs (or so we thought) taken of his body in place. Within minutes of us entering the autopsy room, without being told what to do, the up until now all but silent diener slowly began doing his job with various cutting instruments and power tools. He's apparently undertaken this procedure many, many times before, as he seemed very effective and efficient in what he was doing. Between the very distinctive sounds of sawing of bones and cutting of tissue, I couldn't help but hear the diener ever-so-quietly humming a song tune to himself. Yes, as in a popular song one would hear on the radio at the time. I don't recall the name of the song after all these years but I do remember his humming disconcerting me a bit while standing there next to him. No more, however, than watching him saw and cut away various human body parts.

When the sawing and slicing was complete, and once Dr. Fillinger could see what he needed to see both outside and inside of the cadaver in front of him, he began talking into his portable tape recorder and listing various measurements, weights, colors, conditions, etc., regarding what he was observing and assessing of the external and internal parts of the body. These verbal notes would eventually be transcribed into his formal written report.

In respect to Mr. Suckle and his family, I will not go into any further specific details of the autopsy at this time. However, to say the least, the attendance at my first-ever such procedure was an emotional if not a physically draining three-hour experience. All I did was stand there and take some notes and photographs of the procedure. And I wasn't even involved in any of the slicing, dicing, bagging, or use of power tools.

At some point during this process the cheesesteaks were delivered to the hospital. We knew this because another morgue assistant walked casually into the autopsy room with the food in hand and said matter-of-factly, "Hey Doc, you want it here or in your office?"

I was wondering if they'd actually eat their dinner IN the room, with the "patient" right there with us. Fortunately, they didn't. Instead, Dr. Fillinger announced we were taking a break. The tools and recorder were abruptly put down. We left the autopsy room and locked the door behind us.

I was SO glad at the time I didn't order anything from the pizzeria. I was so NOT hungry at this point. In fact, I couldn't even watch these two guys nonchalantly begin to eat their respective cheesesteaks. In lieu of that, I graciously departed Dr. Fillinger's office to make a phone call and leave those two to dine in privacy. Upon locating a payphone, I called the CID to find out if anything was new in the investigation and to make sure everything that could be done at the time was being done. In reality though, I just needed to talk to someone, anyone, who was not dead, not cutting into a body, not speaking of it into a tape recorder, or eating greasy sandwiches during an intermission to these processes. Luckily, Terry answered the phone and he brought me up to date regarding the investigation. I did the same from my end.

Before long, the doc, the diener, and I were back in the room finishing the job we came there to do. I stood directly across the autopsy table from the ME the whole time, never flinching once. I may have been semi-traumatized at times as I observed what was being done to the body before me, but I never showed it. At least I don't think so.

I'm aware of stories, some being perhaps apocryphal, of officers/ detectives passing out or running out of the room holding their mouths at their first autopsy experiences. I was NOT going to be one of those, I said to myself, as I walked through the morgue doors the first time. And I did not become one of those people. I'm still glad I didn't eat the cheesesteak that evening though.

As we parted company that evening, Dr. Fillinger provided me a marked, see-through plastic bag with the several spent rounds which he found and removed from Suckle's body. They would eventually be submitted to the Bucks County Laboratory and their ballistic evaluations undertaken there. As referenced earlier and later confirmed, they were of two different calibers, again meaning two different guns and more likely than not, two different killers.

But who were they, and why did they kill Robert Suckle?

As we learned over the next few days and next few weeks, Mr. Suckle had some issues. The primary one, and where we focused our time in the beginning, was the fact that he was previously a big-time gambler. This gambling, by the way, was NOT in Atlantic City where it was now legal to do so. Instead, it was on the streets and through various bookies in the greater Philadelphia area. He would bet on almost anything, we found out, including numerous professional and college athletic events, boxing matches, and racehorses.

In doing so, it seems Mr. Suckle had accrued some large losses which he apparently hadn't been paying up. After much in the way of purported threatening dialogue, the Philadelphia "Family" (in the non-blood related sense) with whom Suckle was placing these bets eventually gave him "an offer he couldn't refuse." The eventual agreed upon deal included Robert Suckle's father paying off the approximately one million dollars in gambling debts of his adult son to these not-so-nice and unrelated Family members. However, the older Suckle insisted on only paying the one million dollar debt itself, not the accrued interest or street "vig," which was significant. So, because of that, there was one extra stipulation put in place by the bookies. That was, Robert Suckle could never gamble again. He reluctantly agreed to this stipulation and his "account" was forever closed.

Or was it?

As it turned out, the apple didn't fall far from the tree in the Suckle family. The teenage son of Robert Suckle seemingly developed his own gambling habits shortly after his dad had involuntarily ended his. The kid had somehow managed to place his bets with some of the same bookies his dad used and, like his dad, he lost heavily. Also like his dad, the kid wouldn't or couldn't pay off his own now sizable gambling debts. You think between dad and granddad, the teenage kid would have learned his lesson. Apparently, he did not.

Sometime later, whether through a "Family" misidentification between the father and son (as in who was actually placing the bets), or simply them wanting to send a message once and for all to the Suckle family and nipping this new unpaid debt in the bud, Robert wound up being shot to death on that Saturday morning.

Lesson learned, I guess. Too late for Robert though.

I ran leads for the next several weeks with Det. Lachman. We travelled to the Suckle home in Cheltenham Township several times. This was an area in Montgomery County, Pennsylvania, to the immediate north of the Philadelphia city line, bordering very close to my old Olney neighborhood. I used to ride my bike throughout the area as a kid with friends to check out the "rich people" who lived in the big single homes there (as opposed to my little rowhome). Now, one of these people had been murdered in my new neighborhood of Bensalem, and it was my job, along with others, to find out why and by whom.

Det. Lachman worked this case very diligently for several months, then several years, then several decades. It didn't help him or the investigation that the numerous crime scene photographs, taken by another detective that Saturday morning, could somehow never be developed. In other words, due to a faulty camera, faulty film, faulty darkroom procedures, or simply a faulty on-scene detective, there were never any photographs of the body at the crime scene. This is never a good start in the investigation of a homicide.

Early on and through the years Terry had assistance from the entire BPD detective division, the Bucks County Detectives, the Cheltenham PD, the Montgomery County Detectives, the Philadelphia PD, the FBI, and various other law enforcement agencies. Despite all of this personnel and time spent, I'm sorry to report that after thirty-plus years this case, essentially MY first homicide case too, remains officially unsolved.

The "Family," which used to (and still does) run the illegal gambling trade in Philly, could never be completely ruled out as being complicit in the homicide. However, other suspects eventually surfaced too. Specifically, they were two men who had an ongoing business relationship with Robert Suckle back in the day. The case could never quite be made against them, at least not made well enough to arrest and convict them. One of these suspects is now deceased. The other, as of this writing, is still alive.

Robert Suckle's son, the then-teenager who ran up the gambling debts and whose actions may have been a contributing factor in his dad's murder, died of a drug overdose in the 1990s.

In the early '90s, after vesting his municipal police pension, Terry left the BPD and continued his very distinguished law enforcement career as a Bucks County detective, solving many cases, including other homicides, while there. Interestingly, in 2013, on the morning before his retirement luncheon, literally about one hour prior to the beginning of the function, he received a phone call at his office. It was from the youngest son of Robert Suckle, with whom he had not been in contact for a decade-plus, coincidently calling on Terry's last official day as a sworn law enforcement officer. He wanted to know from Terry if there was anything new in his father's case. Between farewell handshakes from colleagues and cleaning out his desk, Terry told him, unfortunately, there was nothing new he had to share with him.

Alas, the murder of Robert Suckle remains open to this day.

I've asked myself more than once since May 1, 1982…would a more experienced detective and/or detective sergeant have made a difference on that Saturday morning of the homicide? Would "he/she" or "they" have solved the case right away or at least at some point in the not-too-distant future?

I happen to doubt it.

These two men, whoever they were, managed to get away with murder, literally in this case. Terry Lachman has strong suspicions as to who he now thinks did it, but yet the case remains where it is, that is, unsolved. Like me, he wouldn't make an arrest without the evidence being there, in full, for a likely conviction. We both respect that concept within the criminal justice system and based our investigative and professional philosophies upon it.

The unresolved murder of Robert Suckle is an outlier in the respective careers of Terry and me. I'm confident enough to say that about both of us, certainly after all these years and the other successes we've attained throughout our working lives.

Sometimes people, to include even violent criminals, are just plain lucky. Terry and I were not necessarily "lucky" on that first big case as a detective and detective sergeant, despite doing everything possible to solve it then and for years later on Terry's part. Perhaps one of these days that misfortune will be reversed and Robert Suckle's murderers will be identified, dead or alive, and the case formally closed.

As it turned out, Terry Lachman and I weren't done working cases together yet, by any means. In less than two months from the date of the Suckle homicide, I would make an arrest (with Terry's assistance later that night) of a person for a crime the type of which had been fomenting behind closed doors within a certain well-established institution for decades, if not much, much longer. The ramifications of this arrest, these crimes, and how this particular institution chose to handle them, continue to this day.

Chapter Thirty-One

While Bensalem Township was not then or is now a white-only community, up until the early 1980s, the BPD itself had been one. In terms of minority hiring, the first female officer was brought on board with me in 1976. The first person-of-color was finally hired in '82. His name was Juan Diaz. He was Hispanic. He was thin, about 5' 9", at most 22 years of age, and looked even younger.

In what was kept at first very top secret, it was decided by Chief Viola early that year that upon Juan graduating from the police academy, he would NOT be going right into uniformed patrol as did every other officer ever hired at the BPD. No, the Chief was aware of a festering problem in the township, and he also knew of this very young new officer who looked even younger than his chronological years. So, he put together a plan of action.

As there was a perceived burgeoning drug issue in the Bensalem High School (BHS), it was mutually agreed upon by just a few people that Officer Diaz, once having completed his formal police training, would be immediately enrolled in the high school as a "transfer student" from New York City. His purpose was to infiltrate as best he could any drug trade within the school, take names, turn over evidence, record conversations and transactions occasionally, and when the time finally came, effect the arrests.

Only Chief Viola, one of the trusted elected township supervisors (NOT Stephen Kelly, of course, who was now indicted federally for his own alleged drug distribution), CID Lt. Jack Robinson, Det. Ken Hopkins, the Bensalem Township School Superintendent, and the BHS principal, were initially aware of this undercover operation. I was brought into it about halfway through. Everyone else in the BPD and in Bensalem Township was in the dark about it, to include, most importantly, the several thousand students enrolled at BHS.

On a cold March morning in 1982, off went "Juan Gonzalez" on his first day at his new school. He had a fake academic file meticulously prepared for him and he was set to start his classes as a just-transferred-in senior. The back-story which was created for him was that his parents were divorced and he had some problems in his old NYC school where he attended while living with his mom. Because of this, it was decided by his "parents" that he was to now live with his dad and transfer to BHS. On occasion, to further this cover, the BPD even "borrowed" an Hispanic police officer from the Philadelphia PD (thanks to Chief Viola's connections there) to playact as Juan's dad in a local apartment which had been rented for just such a purpose. After all, if Juan could bring other students to his house on certain afternoons or Friday nights and there was a cool dad there who sort of looked like him, and with whom he could even speak the occasional Spanish, it only enhanced his pretend story.

As it turned out, Juan Gonzalez began blending into the student population almost right away. He was quickly making friends and influencing people. He was popular, could talk-the-talk, walk-the-walk, was good looking, and most importantly...he acted "cool." There weren't all that many Hispanic students in the school at the time, some African-Americans, yet Juan managed to fit in with most every segment of the school; especially, as he was instructed, with the drug-selling segment.

Juan was carefully warned early on by his everyday handler, Det. Ken Hopkins, about the legal construct of "entrapment." He had to be careful to not be the one suggesting to the students that certain crimes be committed. Once he hears of a potential crime being carried out, he could say he's interested in participating, helping, driving people, etc., but essentially, the person committing the illegal acts would have to be pre-disposed to such activities already, even if Juan hadn't been around. But, if Juan happened to hear about it and could somehow participate in it, these people and what they were doing were then all fair game from a legal perspective. There would be no entrapment issues then.

While hanging out with one or more of these groups within the BHS, it was interesting to later learn that some of Juan's fellow female students actually became interested in him. Romantically inter-ested, that is. As he would report his activities telephonically to Det. Hopkins each afternoon or evening after school (kiddingly, this was referred to as his "homework" as he wasn't doing any actual school-related homework), these non-criminal associations had to be officially documented too. It later came out that he may have kissed one or two of these females at various social events, parties, in a car, or wherever, in an attempt to maintain his cover, but it never went farther than that. He swore it never did. Juan was warned repeatedly that any arrests could be thrown out and it could cause everyone great embarrassment IF he would go any farther than a plain "undercover" kiss with a female, as opposed to literally going undercover with them; especially if they were not yet 18. He never did, or at least neither he nor any female student ever reported it. That was a good thing, of course.

While Juan was never a disruption in class, he also never did any actual assigned homework and managed to fail most of his tests. This was on purpose. The teachers threatened him with summer school, no diploma, no graduation, no prom, to call his "dad," etc., but he didn't care. This classroom image worked well for him in bolstering his "bad-boy" persona and reputation. It seemingly made some students trust him more readily and feel freer to include him in their ongoing illicit activities.

Juan also had a car which was assigned to him. It was an older sports car of some make and model. Nothing real fancy, but still pretty cool for a high school senior in 1982, especially a student who didn't seem to care at all about his grades or anything to do with his everyday classes. Oh, and the car had a built in tape recording system and microphones in it for when there may have been a drug pickup or sale taking place. These recordings proved very valuable for later prosecutorial purposes.

When all was said and done in this operation, by late May of that school year, there were about a dozen students who were identified as having sold drugs of some sort to or in front of Juan. The warrants were attained and the arrests themselves were scheduled for a regular school day. I was on board with the arrest planning by this time and it was me in CID that morning who finally told the other detectives and Tac Squad officers about the several month-long undercover operation. It was "going-down" today, this morning, at the BHS. We were to all meet at a certain section of the high school parking lot at 9:30. We were then met there by Chief Viola, the school principal, and for the first time in public in his uniform, Officer Juan Diaz.

The plan was to have Officer Diaz, in full uniform, go into individual classrooms and arrest each of the twelve students with a warrant for the crimes for which they were charged. Of course, he had other officers with him as back up for each arrest. I happened to be the officer with him for his very first arrest.

On this initial arrest with now-Officer Diaz, the two of us simply walked unannounced into a history class, blocked both the front and the back doors, and asked for the charged student by name. Once he stood up, Juan walked over to him and slapped handcuffs on him right in the aisle. Then, we marched him out of the room to a holding area set aside in the school. Before he could talk to any of his fellow students, he was whisked away to the police station by other officers.

I still remember walking into that first classroom with Juan. He initially tipped his police hat to the teacher (who was reportedly not very appreciative of Juan's everyday student alter-ego), and upon seeing his former slacker student now in full police uniform, the man almost lost his footing and had to grab onto his chair to gently sit himself down right away. At about the same time I heard a female student say aloud, "Hey, look, it's Juan Gonzalez! He must have joined the cops!"

Yes, he did, young lady, but you have the timeline wrong. Oh, and the name, too.

Fortunately, or unfortunately, depending on one's point of view, it seems that Bensalem High School back then was not the den of drug iniquity that some thought it to be. While a few of the arrests were for sale and distribution of meth, most of the sales were for marijuana, and all were of lower quantities. None of the arrestees did any hard jail time, but they didn't graduate with their class either. For that matter, neither did Juan Gonzalez.

Juan Diaz went on to have a successful, albeit short, career with the BPD. When the Dark Side returned to power a while later, Diaz saw the writing on the wall for an Hispanic officer and left to join the U. S. Border Patrol. When the Dark Siders were finally vanquished for good (yes, I know it's confusing right now...we'll get there), Juan came back to the BPD for a few more years. Then he left again to rejoin the Border Patrol of his own accord. The last I heard, it was in that agency where he finished his stellar law enforcement career.

I still wonder after all these years, when the BHS Class of '82 has its reunions every five years or so, do some graduates still ask, "Whatever happened to Juan Gonzalez, that transfer student who came in near the end of senior year?" Then, of course, others would remind the inquisitive one, "No, he joined the cops, remember?"

Actually, I'm sure they all remember, even to this day.

Chapter Thirty-Two

The call came in to dispatch mid-morning June 15, 1982. It involved an abandoned newborn baby having been found in one of the vestibules at the very large Doral Apartments complex. The uniformed officer arrived there and requested CID and a rescue squad right away. From the portable radio blaring away in the CID, I could hear an infant wailing away in the background of the officer's transmission. I just happened to be the one representative in CID available at the time. Everyone else was tied up on their own investigations or in court. It seemed like an interesting case, I knew I wanted to continue to broaden my investigative experiences, so I thought, "why not?"

I "ordered" myself to the scene and arrived there within twenty minutes.

Upon entering the second floor apartment, now with two uniformed officers, a patrol sergeant, several ambulance personnel, as well as what appeared to me to be a newborn infant in the arms of one of the female rescue squad members, I managed to locate the leaseholder of the apartment. She was a single mom, in her mid-30s, with two small children herself. I'll call her Pamela. Once I identified myself to her, and without even having to ask her, she started telling me right away what had happened. I was all ears....

Pamela advised that about an hour or so ago she heard what sounded like a baby crying somewhere in the vicinity of her residence. Initially she thought the muffled sounds were coming through the walls or from the outside of her building. However, when the crying didn't stop, and even got louder and more persistent, she decided to open her door. Upon doing so, there just on the other side of her threshold, on the floor at her feet, was the infant, carefully wrapped in several blankets. Pam brought him in and called the police right away. The officers and the ambulance personnel each arrived within minutes, and me not long after.

The rescue squad personnel, from their initial observations of the baby boy, stated that he appeared to be in relatively decent condition, all things considered. His umbilical cord had been properly severed, with several inches of it still protruding from the baby's navel (which, of course, is normal). The newborn also seemed to have been cleaned up to some degree and perhaps even fed, as if whoever gave birth to him took good care of him for the first few hours of his life. Then, for whatever reason, he, she, or they decided to abandon him at this particular time and place.

This was a first for me. Not a lost child…but a found child, a newborn infant no less. And, at of all places, he was found in the doorway of a woman who already had two kids of her own.

Maybe the person or persons who left the baby knew Pamela was a good mom and felt she would be a good caregiver for her/their child. But, geez, there are ways of finding a good foster or adoptive parent for your just-born kid other than leaving him on the proverbial doorstep.

Something just didn't seem quite right here.

It wasn't.

The newborn was taken by the rescue squad to the hospital for a full checkup. I stayed behind after everyone else had left and reinterviewed Pamela. I made sure, to the best of my ability, that SHE was not the actual birth mother. I even directly asked her so. She denied it wholeheartedly. She further offered that I could search her apartment for any evidence of her having given recent birth. I took her up on it. Between no findings of anything suggesting that a natural childbirth had just taken place here (that is, bloody sheets, towels, carpeting, placenta, umbilical cord cuttings, etc.), and the fact that she seemed very physically capable to walk around, bend over, pick up her own two kids, and the like, I quickly ruled Pam out as the birth mom of the just-found newborn. Plus, her two children were now up and walking around and they didn't seem to suggest that mom had been pregnant or had just given birth or anything of the sort.

Okay, so Pamela was NOT the mom. I was convinced of that. But if she wasn't, then who was? And what role, if any, did Pam play in the big picture here?

I've got some investigating to do….

There were six separate apartment units in the building in question. Two of them were below the floor where the baby was found and two were above. I decided to start my investigative canvass in that very building and to each of those five other apartments. I wanted to know if anyone saw or heard anything earlier this morning that could help identify this child and his mom and/or dad. It took me until well into that evening to find someone at home in four of those units, but I eventually did. Nothing of value, investigation-wise, came from any of them. However, it seems I could not get a response from the apartment of the resident directly across the hallway from Pamela. And, interestingly, Pam claimed she didn't really know much at all about the person who lived there. She couldn't even tell me whether it was a man, woman, a family, or anything of the kind.

Hmmm…that's a bit strange. Pamela seemed to know of her other building neighbors, both upstairs and downstairs, and they seemed to be familiar with her, but she claimed to know nothing about the person directly across the hall from her. I didn't bother asking the other neighbors too much about the as-of-yet NOT interviewed person from across the hall on this first canvass. I just figured I'd talk to that person eventually and move on from there.

As can be imagined, it didn't take long for the media to pick up on this "abandoned baby" story. It was a front page headline and story in the *Bucks County Courier Times* the following morning. The three Philadelphia television stations were covering it on their news programs too. Somehow a picture of the newborn from the hospital was attained by the media, and that along with interviews of Pamela, were all over the airwaves and in print. The BPD offered no official comments other than to say that there was an ongoing investigation and, oh yes, Sgt. James Fitzgerald was heading it.

I went back first thing the very next morning to the one person's apartment in that building I hadn't interviewed. The one right across from where the baby was found. There was still no answer at the door. I found a phone number for the unit, had it called by one of the CID secretaries, heard it ringing through the door, but no response that way either as it just kept ringing away.

I next proceeded to the Doral Apartments management office. While there I learned that the mystery resident was a single woman, around 30 years of age, she had three kids, and had lived there about one year. I'll call her Maureen. As I told her the little bit I knew of that particular building's social dynamics, the rental office representative was surprised to hear that Pamela claimed to not know anything about Maureen, her across-the-foyer neighbor. She was all but positive they were good friends, and that the as of now uninterviewed and unreachable Maureen even sometimes babysat for Pam's two kids and Pam for her three kids.

As I was leaving the rental office that morning, I had a sudden hunch about something, make that about someone. I asked the rental rep one last question. I inquired as to the last time she may have seen the so-far unaccounted for female resident. She responded it was about one month ago when she came in to pay her rent. I asked her about her physical appearance, if it's changed lately, and/or if there was anything at all unusual about her. The woman thought for a minute, advised that she deals with hundreds of different people here in the complex and sometimes mixes them up, but then said, "You know, I hate to say this, but Maureen may have put on some weight over the last few months. Neither of us acknowledged it to the other, of course. I mean, I wasn't going to say anything to her about it. Uh...does that help?"

I simply responded to the management rep by saying "You never know." I thanked her and left.

Things were slowly coming together here, well possibly, anyway. The great abandoned baby caper of Doral Apartments may just be starting to unravel.

From the rental office I went directly back to the apartment building where it all started the day before. I parked around the back of the building and walked as silently as I could into the foyer. Up the first stairwell, upon putting my ear to the door, I heard nothing from Maureen's apartment. Next, as I rested the side of my head up against Pam's door, I could hear the TV, numerous kids, and at least two adult female voices. I then knocked. No one answered the door. I knocked again, harder this time, stating to Pamela through the door who it was and that I really had to talk to her. She eventually opened the door looking guilty as hell. It clearly wasn't the Pamela who I interviewed at least twice the day before, or saw on the 11:00 news last night. Something was different about her. She invited me in nonetheless.

Once in the apartment, I looked around and noticed five kids in the apartment. I asked Pam to whom the other kids belonged. She simply stated they were a friend's kids. I inquired if anyone else was here in the apartment. Pam took her time but responded in the negative. I then told her that I could have sworn that I had heard two adult voices from inside the apartment just a few minutes ago. Pam hesitated again and then told me unconvincingly that she may have been on the phone.

316

I retorted very officially, "You MAY have been on the phone or you WERE on the phone? Which was it?"

Pam just looked around the apartment vacantly, avoided meeting my eyes, bit her lower lip, and didn't reply. The silence was deafening. More for her than me, I could see...and hear.

I eventually told Pam that unless she was asking and answering her own questions in different voices whilst on or off the telephone, I KNEW that someone else was in here. I then asked very firmly, "Who is here and where is she?"

The oldest of the five children now in the apartment, belonging to whom I'm not sure but probably around six years of age, heard me ask that question to Pamela. After a big sip of something from her kid-lidded plastic cup, I watched as the little girl silently pointed down the hall towards the back bedrooms. Well, I thought, at least someone is being cooperative here. I stayed silent too and just tilted my head and focused my eyes toward the little girl. Pamela followed suit until her eyes met her little girl's and saw that she still had her arm up pointing down the hall. Pam, now seemingly exasperated, said out loud, "Maureen, come out here! Come out here now! This is too much! I can't do this anymore!"

Within thirty seconds, out of one of the rear bedrooms walked, make that waddled, a woman that I had not seen before. She told me her name and advised that I probably wanted to talk to her. I said, "Okay, let's talk."

The two of us sat down on a couch, me right away but I noticed the woman sitting down rather gingerly, as if she was in some discomfort. Pam took all five kids into one of the bedrooms, and with just the two of us in the parlor and without hesitation, the woman I now knew as Maureen told me what I had suspected since my very recent visit to the rental office.

Yes, she was the mother of the newborn baby.

Maureen continued to tell me that she gave birth by herself on her kitchen floor around 6:00AM the previous morning. There was no dad in the present picture, and no family of which to speak. She was scared, she wasn't ready to be a mom again after having three kids already, on welfare, no medical insurance, little money, and with babe-in-arms, weak, bleeding, hurting badly, and not knowing what to do, she called for Pamela across the hall. Pamela came to her apartment, helped her clean up the baby, helped clean up HER, the kitchen floor, etc., and they together hatched the "abandoned baby" idea. Their thinking was that some couple or family would eventually take the baby from the hospital and give him a good home.

Since Maureen was not in custody at the time, and I was not interrogating her (I was just listening at this point), I allowed her to talk away. For those reasons, I did not have to read her the Miranda warnings. So, I didn't and she kept elaborating. Eventually, she started repeating herself as she went on, crying, saying she knew what she and Pam did was wrong, but that their only concern was for the new baby, her other three kids…and that's all. She also defended Pam, saying that nothing should happen to her regarding this matter. She insisted that it was all her (Maureen's) fault.

I sort of felt sorry for Maureen, and also Pam. Yes, they both reacted to a situation with poor judgment, yet at the same time with good intentions. Although, come to think of it, Maureen did have around nine months to prepare for yesterday's big event; Pamela, by all indications, only fell into her role after the fact, after the birth. Yet, it was Pam who lied to the police, and the media too, for that matter. But it wouldn't be lying to journalists which would get one or both of them into trouble. That's not illegal. Lying to police officers, and/or filing a false police report…THAT'S illegal!

I told Maureen that she should go to the same hospital where her baby was and check herself in. She should be fully examined too as she just went through a difficult childbirth with no medical attention or anesthesia at all. She agreed. With Pam watching Maureen's existing brood, I drove her to the hospital ER, made sure she got checked in, then left to go back to BPD HQ.

I now knew what had happened regarding the little boy, but my head was spinning. I had to run this whole matter by some people in charge.

Once back in CID, we all agreed this was a different type of case; really different. Not only had neither I nor anyone else in the BPD ever handled an investigation quite like this, we had never even heard of a similar abandonment case such as this before. Sure (and unfortunately), newborns are abandoned all too frequently in the U. S. and elsewhere. Sometimes it's done in a relatively careful and controlled scenario like with this little boy, but most other times it's not undertaken with such care. In fact, in many cases there is a deadly outcome for the newborn child, whether so intended by the abandoner or not.

After speaking with Chief Viola and Lt. Robinson, it was agreed that I should call the Bucks County District Attorney's Office. I needed to speak to one of the Assistant District Attorneys there. I did, and after patching in the DA himself in a phone call a short time later (as he was familiar with the case from the TV news), it was agreed that both women should be charged. The charges would be Filing a False Police Report, Endangering the Welfare of a Child, and Conspiracy. As it was agreed that the baby was never technically "abandoned," no charges relating specifically to that issue were filed against the two women.

I swore out the warrants that afternoon, went to their respective apartments later that evening, and strongly suggested that each of them turn themselves into me at police HQ the next day. They did. I didn't go to their apartments and drag them out in handcuffs or anything as draconian as that. It wasn't necessary. I knew these weren't seasoned or "real" criminals at all, but nonetheless, they did use poor judgment in how they handled this matter, tied up various law enforcement and ambulatory resources for hours if not days, and as such they ultimately had to pay the legal price.

They were arraigned later that day and both set free with no or minimal bail.

Of course, now the local media was in a feeding frenzy. This was an even bigger story to the journalists now. They wanted to interview the women, the neighbors, the doctors, and of course, me. I turned them down because it was a pending prosecution. The DA's Office had a standard style press release, but it was agreed not too much in the way of details would be released in it. Various versions of the story ran anyway. Most of the facts were correct in this case.

There was a preliminary hearing within a few weeks. Both Pam and Maureen had been appointed attorneys from the Bucks County Public Defender's Office. After my testimony at the relatively brief hearing before District Magistrate Chris Ritter, he ruled that prima facie evidence existed and the matter should be held for trial.

The case never went to trial. A plea agreement was reached through the DA's office, I concurred with it, and no jail time was served or even fines set. Each woman was put on two years' probation and had to do some community work, but that was the extent of their sentences. After the two years, if there were no further arrests or criminal issues, they would be off probation.

I don't know whatever became of the two women or the little boy. I'm not sure if Maureen ever sought or attained custody of her fourth child, the never-really abandoned one. Perhaps she put him up for adoption, which of course would have been very easy to do in the first place and would have caused everyone much less grief and aggravation.

I simply lost track of these two people and their kids as many other cases, investigations, and arrests came my way before long at the BPD.

This included one with international implications the very next night after the discovery of the not-abandoned baby.

Chapter Thirty-Three

In the early evening hours of June 16, 1982, I was in BPD HQ finishing up some routine paperwork from the now never-really-abandoned-but-still-a-crime baby case. I was typing a report and undertaking other administrative duties while at the detective sergeant's desk in CID. At some point right before I had planned to go home for dinner, Chief Viola walked through the CID back door and into his office talking to another person. In their apparent haste, and with my back to the Chief's office door, I didn't actually observe the Chief or the other person as they closed the door behind them, but I knew it was him with at least one other person whose voice I didn't recognize. Oh well, it didn't concern me so I'll just keep doing what I'm doing here, then I'll be off to my dinner at home.

As the evening slowly started to unfold from that point, I knew dinner wouldn't be at its normal time tonight, if at all. That would become very clear, very soon.

Within about ten minutes of his quick closed-door office meeting, Rich Viola came back out and directly over to my desk. He told me initially he was glad to see I was working tonight. Without even a chance to respond, he then instructed me to call a few specific people to meet us in the CID room right away. He made it clear that something big was going down tonight, but mum was the word for now. I made a few phone calls and a police radio transmission or two and got the requested people to CID. Before long, there were about six of us awaiting the Chief's orders regarding this "something big."

Just what this "something" was, and exactly how "big" it was, would not be learned for another hour or two. It was all a mystery until then; understandably too, as we would find out.

Eventually, some other people came into the CID area, and I could now plainly see that they were wearing blue U. S. Marshal's (USM) raid jackets. The big letters on the back made the men and their agency name hard to miss. Before long, the Chief wanted me to assemble the group in the CID area for a briefing. There were six BPD officers of various ranks, Chief Viola, and four USMs. Those of us not yet in the know were anxiously waiting to hear what this was all about. We were just minutes away....

Viola had everyone quickly identify themselves and then he turned the floor over to the supervisor of the USMs. This tall and well-muscled special agent stood before us and told us that an international fugitive has been tentatively identified as residing in one of the Bensalem apartment complexes. We, as in the presently gathered BPD and USM personnel, were about to go and get him. He told us that additional USM personnel were already on the scene in various unmarked vehicles watching the fugitive's apartment.

As we later learned this supervisor was familiar with Chief Viola from his Philadelphia PD days, he knew he could trust him to assign the right people to assist his squad on this major arrest. I was glad to be considered one of these "right people" selected for this task.

While holding up an enlarged black and white mugshot photo, the USM supervisor continued on in his briefing that this fugitive was a known killer. He had escaped from a U. S. prison several years before and was known to have high-powered and fully automatic weapons. He was expected to run at a minimum, or turn his arrest into a firefight at the maximum, if the element of surprise was somehow lost. We were advised that in the several months he lived at his present location he may have been involved in some local bank robberies and possibly even two homicides in Bensalem. Yes, and that would include the murder of Robert Suckle from just six weeks prior.

Geez, this guy was the real deal. Luckily, so were those of us now assembled in the CID room.

The USMs have been hot on this man's trail for a few years, have a long-standing federal warrant for his arrest, and have come close to capturing him before. But they feel right now, if their information is correct and the plan goes accordingly, it would be their best opportunity to apprehend him. So, we were told for the time-being to "stand-down" and wait here in CID for the signal.

I later learned that it was Chief Viola himself who greatly assisted the USM agents in locating this fugitive. He did it by quietly reviewing records of the Bensalem Rescue Squad and determining that the fugitive's stepdaughter (whose name was known to the USM and previously supplied to Viola) had been taken by ambulance to an area hospital in April. That was all the information the feds needed in ascertaining where this guy was living, that being at a specific address in Bensalem Township.

It had now all come together on this specific date.

By around 8:00 that night, the rest of what was supposed to come together at the apartment complex apparently did so. Our group, now wearing our ballistic vests, some with shotguns and other high-powered shoulder weapons and extra rounds of ammo, travelled in separate unmarked cars caravan-style to the Brookwood Apartment complex on Street Rd., just east of Hulmeville Rd. There, we met at a certain interior parking lot. Radio silence was ordered, just in case the fugitive had a police scanner.

As the sun was about to settle beneath the horizon, the "go" signal was given. USM and BPD, working together and in tandem, quietly surrounded the front and the rear of the apartment unit. The man, for whatever reason (but seemingly on schedule according to the USM), stepped out of his residence that evening to light up his cigar. In doing so, the fugitive wanted in several countries for several years was surrounded by at least eight of us at varying distances with .357 Magnums, long rifles, and shotguns pointing at his head and body. I was no more than fifteen feet from him at the time of the arrest, pointing the barrel of my handgun at him the whole time. (We made sure to avoid any cross-fire positioning, a common cause of "friendly fire" deaths to law enforcement officers.) While that close, I could notice his eyes frantically scanning his immediate and extended environment as he was undoubtedly thinking about somehow effecting his escape. But, as I and others commanded him, he ultimately went down to his knees. He knew he was outnumbered and outgunned. With the slap of handcuffs on his wrists, and a fully loaded .25 caliber handgun removed from his waistband, he was now in the official custody of the USMs, with some help from their new friends at the BPD.

It was confirmed at the scene once he was in custody and once he was also put into ankle cuffs just who he was. There was no mistake. This was the very-much wanted man.

His full name was William Joseph Arico.

In the next day's *Bucks County Courier Times*, coincidently sharing headlines with my semi-abandoned baby case, was the article about the fugitive's arrest. It was written by Anita DiBartolomeo.

The headline read, "**Two Countries Elated after Area Arrest**." Portions of the story read as follows:

"No lawman had been able to snare William Joseph Arico since the slightly built alleged 'hitman' shimmied through a window in a cell in Rikers Island prison off the coast of New York City and leaped into the swift current of the East River.

On Wednesday night, nearly two years later, the search for Arico – nicknamed 'The Exterminator' – ended more than 100 miles away in the parking lot of the generally quiet Brookwood Apartments in Bensalem as a team of heavily armed police swarmed around the 46-year-old man."

"...When police searched his apartment...they found a cache of weapons, including four revolvers, an automatic rifle with a tripod, a sawed-off shotgun, a machine gun, ammunition, two bulletproof vests, and a hand grenade."

"...Arico was being held overnight at the Bensalem police station, where he had a round-the-clock guard plus a closed-circuit television camera installed in his cell. He was to be taken to federal court in Philadelphia today, after which he was to be transferred to New York, police said."

(End of article.)

Bottom line, Arico did NOT escape from the BPD holding cell that night. He was in our custody and out of it in about twelve hours. I spent an hour-plus sitting on a chair diagonal from his cell, within eyeshot and earshot of the prisoner. Nothing was being left to chance with this guy.

As my brief time that evening with Arico dragged on, he started asking me my name, my rank, what I do here, etc. I kept my responses to him polite but to a minimum, giving him nothing he could use to fully identify me. I was instructed, make that ordered, by Chief Viola to not engage this guy in any way. So, I didn't. Arico left the next morning with the USM under heavy guard to his next home behind bars.

Case closed, wanted international fugitive/felon behind bars once again.

I lost track of Arico over the next several years, but I was surprised to find his name in a book I was reading in 1985. It was titled *In God's*

Name, published in 1984, and written by David A. Yallop. The book's subtitle was "*An Investigation into the Murder of Pope John Paul I.*"

John Paul I became Pope in late August of 1978 but was found dead in the Vatican just a month later. Conspiracy theories regarding John Paul I's untimely death surfaced almost immediately. The theorists mostly suggested that the brand new Pope had uncovered corruption within the Catholic Church and/or the Vatican Bank, along with other irregularities, and he was poisoned by someone close to him. Yet, his death was purportedly the result of a heart attack.

As the book details, a U. S. and Italian joint investigation regarding the corruption within the Italian banking system was underway in Italy in 1979, a year after the Pope's death. Its tentacles reached the Vatican Bank. The Italian Mafia played a substantial role in this matter too. One of the government witnesses scheduled to testify in an upcoming trial regarding the alleged corruption was a lawyer and banking liquidator named Giorgio Ambrosoli. He had uncovered criminal wrongdoing at the highest level within several of the Italian financial institutions dealing with the Vatican Bank.

On page 316 of *In God's Name*, Yallop writes:

> "By (June 9, 1979) the man who was given a $100,000 contract to kill Giorgio Ambrosoli had been in the Hotel Splendido, Milan, for twenty-four hours. He had checked in as Robert McGovern. He was also known as 'Billy the Exterminator.' His real name is William Arico. At this first-class hotel near Milan Central Station, Arico dined with the five men who were to assist him with the murder. His two main accomplices were Charles Arico, his son, and Rocky Messina. Their weapons included an M-11 machine gun specially fitted with a silencer, and five P-38 revolvers. Arico hired a Fiat and began to stalk Ambrosoli...."

(End of book reference.)

A summary of the next few related events is captured succinctly in Wikipedia:

> "Ambrosoli was killed shortly after he had a talk with Palermo Police Chief Boris Giuliano, who discovered checks and other documents which indicated that Michele Sindona (a corrupt Sicilian banker) had

been recycling the proceeds from heroin sales by the Mafia through the Vatican Bank to his Amincor Bank in Switzerland. Ten days after the killing of Ambrosoli, Giuliano was shot and killed by the Mafia on July 21, 1979."

(End of Wikipedia reference.)

Back to *In God's Name*, in a footnote on page 353, Arico's ultimate fate was described once and for all:

"On February 19, 1984, William Arico fell to his death while trying to escape from the Metropolitan Correctional Center in New York City. Arico and Michele Sindona were due to face an extradition hearing two days later. The Italian authorities wanted to put both men on trial for the murder of Giorgio Ambrosoli."

(End of book reference.)

William Arico was believed to have played a direct role in both the murder of Guiliano and Ambrosoli in Italy. No doubt there were others too, both in Europe and in the U. S.

Although we tried through witness and forensic evidence, no other Bensalem area murders, including the Suckle homicide, could be positively linked to Arico. However, as a result of the search of Arico's apartment after his arrest, dye-stained money was found. It was subsequently linked to a bank robbery in nearby Middletown Township on March 11, 1982. He was eventually indicted for same although, for obvious reasons, it never came to trial.

In closing to this matter, I've arrested my share of bad-asses in my 31-year career, but this guy I would clearly put near, if not at, the very top of the list. I played no direct role in actually locating William Arico that night in Bensalem. The U. S. Marshals Service deserves the credit for that aspect of the case, as well as Chief Viola. I'm glad, however, I was there for his actual takedown.

There are no doubt numerous people around the world who managed to live out their full lives thanks to Arico being placed in custody on that June evening in 1982. I'm glad that I followed my orders and I didn't provide him my name that evening whilst keeping an eye on him through the jail cell door, especially when I learned later that he murdered the Palermo, Italy, police chief.

As it played out, the next time "The Exterminator" would leave the confines of a prison, he would be a "free" man for only those few more seconds of his life. Arico's momentary taste of freedom was spent rapidly falling down the outside of a prison building. As it turned out, he was his own last victim.

Top: May 1982, Sgt. Jim Fitzgerald with confiscated weapons cache
(Photo courtesy of *Bucks County Courier Times,* Sally Hunter)
Bottom: June 16, 1982, Sgt. Jim Fitzgerald at arrest of William Arico

Chapter Thirty-Four

I was working what started out as a very ordinary 4P-12A shift on Tuesday, June 22, 1982. Later that evening, in the last ninety minutes or so of my shift, I interviewed an overnight employee of the then-Hilton Hotel on Rt. 1 in the Trevose section of Bensalem. It involved an old theft case I was still investigating from my pre-sergeant days. I drove there on my own in an unmarked CID vehicle.

After the routine twenty-minute interview, just out of habit from my patrol and Tac Squad days, and with less than an hour to kill until my shift ended, I found myself driving around the parking lot of the hotel looking for anything or anyone of interest. My ride-around had nothing to do with the interview which brought me there, but I suppose old routines are hard to break. While the location was not exactly a crime hotspot, there were the occasional stolen cars, vehicular break-ins, and drug deals which occurred in the parking lot and the general environs. So, I figured I'd circle the perimeter a time or two and look for potential ne'er-do-wells. I'd give it one, maybe two drive-bys, then call it a night.

I should add here that the Hilton Hotel was immediately adjacent to the Lincoln Drive-In Theater. Yes, as in a classic watch-it-from-your-car-under-the-stars outdoor movie venue. In my late teen years, travelling from my Philly neighborhood of Olney and going to the drive-in movie was an enjoyable way to spend a Friday or Saturday night. This 1950s to 1980s (more or less) rite of passage for teenagers was usually with a car full of friends, male and female alike, with one or two extra movie-goers sometimes hiding in the trunk of whosever car was being driven. It wasn't even that expensive to go to the drive-in for a night, but as they charged per person then to gain admission, it seemed like a cost-effective (if only slightly illegal) thing to do at least once in a while for some teens, or those with teen mentalities.

In the Lincoln Drive-In's early days, regular "G," "PG," "PG-13," and "R" rated movies were the norm as to what was presented on the giant screen every night, usually as part of a double- or triple-feature event. It could actually be a wholesome family outing on some evenings, depending on what was playing. However, due to a reported decrease in the number of outdoor movie watching patrons, at some point in the early '80s the Lincoln Drive-In management made a corporate decision to change its fare. It went from mainstream cinematic productions to adult-themed cinematic productions...make that VERY adult-themed and "X" rated; what some then called pornography. In doing so, they had to then make sure more than ever that the screen could not be seen from any nearby highways and/or adjacent properties.

Easier said than done....

Back to that June night in '82, under a starry Bensalem sky, there was a double-feature of now-long forgotten (if ever known in the first place by me) sexually suggestive titled porn movies flickering away on the large white painted plywood "screen" at the northwest end of the Lincoln Drive-In property. Most vehicular patrons paid their way through the tollbooth-like entrances off of Rt. 1. It was a flat rate at this time, so the art of trunk-hiding had died a very natural death. However, in a more contemporary version of watching a movie for free, yet without the teenage antic element involved, others would routinely sit in their cars in the rear of the Hilton Inn parking lot and watch silently through a few broken-off vertical wooden fence slats along the property dividing line. After all, as more than one of these guys would tell me in my uniformed days when I chased them away from their side-row view while sitting in their cars' bucket or bench car seats, sound isn't really necessary for a porn movie.

The Hilton management would complain to the drive-in management to fix their broken fence sections and they usually did within a few days. However, as soon as the missing fence slats were dutifully replaced, they would mysteriously be broken off or removed again within one or two nights.

As I did my first circle around the hotel parking lot that June evening, I happened to notice a full-sized American made car parked nose-in at an area with clearly several missing fence slats in front of it. There was no other car on either side of it. I didn't initially notice anyone in the vehicle when my headlights illuminated the rear of the car from left-to-right as I made the turn behind it. I figured that the car is just parked there away from the main hotel parking lot for a legitimate reason. As there was no crime readily observable right then, I didn't put any extra thought into this particular automobile.

After what was going to be my last time around the lot, and as I was pulling up behind the same car with my headlights following the same illuminated path as just a minute or so ago, for the first time I saw what appeared to be a smaller, seemingly male head through the rear glass in the right side back seat. Now, focusing more intently on the car's interior as I was very slowly completing my turn, I also noticed a smaller, seemingly male head in the front passenger seat. And, just by coincidence at that very same moment, I saw another male head come into view as it arose from the vicinity of the lap of the front seat passenger. I couldn't help but notice that this third head, attached to a person now sitting behind the steering wheel, was slightly larger than that of the other two.

Okay…something was going on here. This wasn't just a guy getting his jollies peeping through the fence at the naked actors on the side-viewed screen. He was involved in something inside his own car and he had company with him, at least two others, while doing it. And by the looks of the three head movements and two of the head sizes, it may even be something illegal.

I radioed the dispatcher the make and model of the car, along with the tag number, but kept driving. I pulled into a parking space about six car-lengths away so the driver wouldn't think I was interested in any way in that in which he was involved. If this person was doing something untoward and/or illegal, I wanted to try and catch him in the act. To do that, I gave him as much time, about one minute, as it took to find out from the dispatcher that the car wasn't stolen or wanted for anything.

Learning the car was "clean," and after grabbing my ever-present flashlight and portable radio, I exited my vehicle. At first, I walked at an angle away from the suspicious car, but once passing its rear I cut back and walked toward the car. As I mastered in my former Tac Squad days, I mentally calculated the driver's rearview mirrors' blind spots so upon walking up to the door I would hopefully catch the occupants off guard.

I learned in life to never underestimate the value of the element of surprise. Whether in sports, relationships, or police work, the "surpriser" almost always has the advantage over the "surprisee." Each person just better be prepared for what happens next. In my case that night, I was prepared; the other guy, and his passengers…well, not so much.

As I approached the driver's side door, I noticed the windows were open only about two inches from the top. And, the windows themselves on that side were a bit fogged-up. Because of that, I couldn't immediately make out whether the driver was still sitting up or leaning over again. At this point, I expected to find a couple of lovers, maybe even two couples occupying the front and back seats, perhaps each in the prone position. I've seen that here before and I would usually just chase them away if there were no drugs or underage alcoholic beverage issues at hand. However, what I observed upon walking directly up to the partially opened window and shining my flashlight into the interior of the car was something that disconcerted even this relatively experienced cop.

With my trusty handheld portable light source now fully illuminating the front and rear seats, I noticed the back of a head of a gray-haired man now bent over with his face directly on the lap of a person in the passenger seat. Following the flashlight beam upwards, I managed to observe the passenger's surprised face before I could see the man's face. With a carefully aimed shining of the light beam I could further see the person sitting upright was a teenager, no more than 14 years of age. Upon my directed light beam sweeping the rest of the car, the older man immediately sat up and began wiping his mouth. The boy, and that's all he really was, quickly put his hands down around the zipper of his pants, moved a bit up and down, and eventually put his hands on his lap.

What the…?

I now KNEW what is going on here, but I never saw it up close and personal like this before, and not involving someone this young. And there was another boy, around the same age, in the back seat too.

My brain didn't take long at all to synthesize the fact that this was clearly statutory rape, corruption of a minor, indecent assault, sodomy, you name it…and no doubt there were two counts of each as I was sure the boy in the back seat had been also victimized by this man on this night. All of this was going through my brain at this preliminary point, and no one has even uttered a word yet.

I immediately ordered everyone in the car to put their hands on the steering wheel, dashboard, or the seat in front of them, respectively, depending on where they were sitting. I wasn't taking any chances here. However, upon surveying the totality of the situation over the

332

next fifteen seconds or so, my own personal safety and security wasn't my utmost concern at this time. Instead, it was to find out from one or both of the boys just what was going on in the car while they ostensibly peered through the broken fence toward the sex flicks. I had no doubt that there was as much sexual activity going on in this parked car as there was on the screen, except it didn't involve consenting adults here in the Hilton lot; well, not two out of three of them anyway. These were two young kids and an adult male who was clearly a pedophile, or at least engaging in pedophilic acts.

What kind of man would do such a thing?

I would find out before too long. It would shock me like few other situations have before in my life, both personally, professionally...and spiritually.

As I was wearing a sport coat and tie (and not a police uniform), I eventually identified myself, showed my badge, and asked the driver what was going on inside his car. He intimated that he was simply fooling around with the two young men in the car. (He actually referred to them as "young men" a few times that evening, no doubt attempting to somewhat upwardly age them for his own defensive-oriented purposes.) I asked him what he was doing when I first walked up to his window and saw him bending over onto the passenger seat. His response was a nonchalant, "Nothing really, Officer. I was simply looking for something I dropped on the car floor."

Hmmm...it was almost like the man had practiced this line before or had actually uttered it in the past to someone.

"Simply something on the car floor, eh?" I repeated/inquired with clear incredulity.

I then asked the boy in the passenger seat what he had just done with his hands on the front of his pants. He stated rather unconvincingly, "Uh, uh...I had to pee...that's all. Really...."

This car was now reeking of incredulity, inside and out. All the parties, including me, knew it. Now it was just determining how to get to the truth of what was really happening here. I knew to do so I had to separate these three people from each other. Otherwise, the truth would be much harder to ascertain.

I readily determined of anyone involved in criminal activity among them, it would be the older male passenger. In view of that, I prioritized him among the three. As such, I ordered him out of the car. He hesitated at first, but eventually upon me opening the door for him, he stepped outside and stood next to me. I noticed right away that he was an out-of-shape, smaller man in his 50s. He was dressed in every-day casual clothing; nothing unusual in that regard. It would be a few hours later that I'd discover another style of clothing he would wear. By then I'd know why he's not so attired at this particular time.

I next asked the two boys to step out of the car. I told one to stand at the front of the car, and one at the rear, and to not say a word. For the most part, they didn't. They seemed scared. That wasn't a bad thing at this moment in time as it would eventually play in my favor. But I couldn't get a read on the older man. He seemed a bit too calm. Again, like he's been through this before.

As I knew this wasn't the place to resolve this matter, I called on my portable radio for two patrol cars to meet me at the rear of the hotel lot. Before long, the sector car and the back-up car arrived. I had them each put one of the boys in their respective back seats. I instructed the officers to search them but not to handcuff them as they weren't under arrest. They were potential witnesses and/or victims of a crime I told them. After a search in which no weapons or evidence was found, they were put in the backseats of the separate police cars.

The older man, I decided, wasn't going to be treated quite the same way. I had him turn around, place his hands on the roof of his car and I thoroughly searched him. No weapons or evidence found either. I then handcuffed him and placed him in the back of my CID car. On the way onto the back seat, I told him he was under arrest for child molestation. He didn't say a word.

As I sat down in the car behind the steering wheel of my car, I next asked the man his name. He hesitated, but he eventually told me while looking up sheepishly from the backseat into the rearview mirror.

"My name is Robert Hermley."

I was initially just going to lock Hermley's car, take the keys, and leave it in the parking lot. But after all parties were safely in their respective cars, I took my flashlight and exited my vehicle and gave the car one more visual sweep from the outside of the interior of the car. What I saw through the now un-fogged windows, just slightly sticking out on the rear floor from under the front seat, really threw me for a loss. There, in plain sight, was a *Penthouse Magazine*, a tube of some kind of lubricant or jell, and what appeared to be a 6" to 8" penis-shaped vibrator.

Okay, this was now more of a sophisticated crime scene than I had envisioned before. This guy had a plan; a well-designed *modus operandi* in undertaking these parking lot trysts inside his car. No doubt, he's done this before. Tonight was definitely not the first night something like this happened in his life, and in this very car.

I got on the police radio and called for the duty-tow truck. This car was apparently chockfull of evidence, and I hadn't even looked under the seats yet, in the glove box, or in the trunk. That would all happen back at HQ. In the meantime, I called for another patrol car to sit on Hermley's car and eventually follow it in so the chain of custody could be maintained the whole time. A warrant may or may not eventually be needed for the full search, but I'd worry about that later. First, I wanted to interview all of these people, young and old alike, innocent and guilty alike, and determine just what the heck was going on inside the car. I knew it wasn't anything good, and most likely illegal, but to what extent? These and many other related questions would be answered by night's end.

The three police cars with each separate person eventually wound up at the BPD. Before long, and without talking to one another, each person was put into a separate interview room. Hermley's car was towed in and secured behind a locked fenced-in area in the rear of HQ. First, before officially searching the car, I wanted to find out what I could from these people, especially the boys. Luckily, Detective Terry Lachman was still on duty working the 7P – 3A shift. I requested his assistance in this matter and we got to work right away.

I told Terry what I observed and what I knew from the Hilton parking lot. He took it all in and agreed we most likely had a serious crime here, if not multiple crimes. With Hermley now securely handcuffed to the wall in his interview room, we decided to start talking to the boys who were sitting in two separate interview rooms. As they weren't under arrest or even suspected of a crime, we didn't officially need their parents or guardians to be with them at this time. We told them we were going to call their parents soon, but we wanted to hear their side of the story which would hopefully explain what had happened earlier tonight. They separately agreed to talk to us.

After they each gave us their biographical information (one was 13, one was 14), each told us individually in just a few short minutes that they knew Robert Hermley from their neighborhood and their former elementary school. They had just graduated eighth grade and were going to high school in a few months. They gave us details about how long they've known Hermley, how they met, and what they were doing parked next to the drive-in movie. Well, almost.

Neither boy, in their separate interviews, was initially willing to admit whether any sort of sexual activity was occurring while in the Hilton parking lot. But eventually, after carefully reminding them what I actually witnessed at the scene, and that they don't want to now be lying to police officers, they individually gave it up. They told us that the man liked to perform oral sex on them. He did on this night and on other occasions over the prior few months.

The boys, while still separated, admitted it wasn't the first time they'd been sexually abused by the man. Interestingly, they kept calling him "Bob," and never "Mr. Hermley," or anything more formal than that. I finally asked one of the boys to describe in detail exactly how they met. He was hesitant, as this was the last part of the story that he apparently did not want to give up, but eventually he just put it out there. He somewhat reluctantly acknowledged that he was a former altar boy at his Roman Catholic parish church, and he met "Bob" while performing those duties.

Oh, and "Bob" went by another name there, or more precisely, another title, the boy added. That was, *Father* Robert Hermley, as in Roman Catholic priest, Father Robert Hermley.

Terry and I looked at each other while sitting across from this boy and all but let out a collective gasp. However, we maintained our poker faces and stayed the course. We thanked the young teenager and allowed him to call his parents. We went in to the room holding the other boy, and after following almost the same back-and-forth discourse with him, he eventually told us the same information. Yes, it was Father Hermley; and no, this wasn't the first time that he had engaged in sexual activity with him, his friend in the next room, and supposedly other boys that he knew from his church and school.

I allowed this kid to call his parents too. Before long, both sets of parents were on their way to the Bensalem PD to retrieve their sons.

Terry and I decided that no one would be retrieving Bob Hermley anytime soon. Not if we could help it. But next, we had to hear from him what the kids just independently told us. That would require a formal interview of Father Hermley, to include his Miranda warnings being read to him right up front.

With another detective now sitting with the two boys, taking additional background information from them, Terry and I entered the interview room with the awaiting handcuffed-to-the-wall priest/suspect/pedophile. After reading Hermley his constitutionally mandated warnings, and him agreeing to waive same, sign the form, and talk to us, Terry and I began asking him all sorts of questions about earlier tonight, who he is, what he does, how he knows the boys, etc. At no time did he admit he was a priest, nor would he admit to any sexual misconduct with the boys. He really only confirmed his full name to us, his address, and that he was 55 years old. Terry and I continued to play along with him as if we didn't know any other details.

Finally, after directly asking him one more time by whom he was employed, and Hermley stating nothing more than he was a high school guidance counselor in a private school in Wilmington, Delaware, and continuing that the boys were simply young friends, their parents knew about him and their relationship, and that nothing "bad" had happened tonight, I had enough. I started pressing him a bit.

"Are you familiar with the Ten Commandments, Bob?" I emphatically asked him while not really being sure how he'd respond to the religious overtone of the question.

"Uh...sure, I guess so. Why?"

"How many do you think you broke in the last few hours? Up 'til and including right now in this room? Rough guess? How many do you think?"

For some reason, I thought playing the religious card would have some effect here. It didn't. Well, at least not right away.

"I don't know what you're talking about, Officer. I mean, I may have run a red light at some point tonight, is that what you mean? Is there a Commandment for that?" Hermley was smirking a bit when he made that remark and while posing the asinine follow-up questions to me.

Terry gave me the non-verbal that he now wanted a shot at him. I gave him the non-verbal back to go ahead. He asked Hermley, in so many words, "Bob, how does it look that you were caught parked by a broken fence next to an X-rated double feature with a 13- and a 14-year-old boy in your car? And that Sgt. Fitzgerald here saw you with your head, face down, on one of the boy's laps?"

Hermley responded without missing a beat, "You know, we just pulled up there in the lot right before you got there (pointing to me). I didn't even know that the fence was broken at first or it was a drive-in movie next to us. Then, we just sat there for a while and talked. I dropped some change on the floor, bent over to pick it up just as you got there (again, pointing at me). That was it, I swear."

Terry told him, "I see. Well, you know, besides the X-rated movies outside, we found some X-rated items inside your car. Would you care to comment on those items?"

Hermley asked, "What do you mean? What kind of items?"

I took over and said, "Bob, on just a cursory glance, without even having yet ripped your car apart with a search warrant, we already found one nudie magazine, a dildo, and some sex lube. Now, what the hell would you be doing with those items in your car, especially with two teenage boys as your passengers?"

"You found THAT stuff in my car? Really? Well, it's not mine. You know, I lend my car to other people sometimes and maybe...."

I had enough of this sham, of this bullshit, of this man. Slamming my fist on the table in front of Hermley, I stated in very clear hi-fidelity and hi-volume, "STOP F**KING LYING TO ME! TO US! YOU HAVEN'T SAID A TRUTHFUL GODDAMN WORD SINCE I FIRST CONFRONTED YOU IN THE PARKING LOT TONIGHT!"

Hermley lowered his head and gazed down at the top of the desk.

I continued, now staring at the top of his head, "STARTING RIGHT NOW, AND I MEAN RIGHT NOW, YOU'RE GOING TO BEGIN TELLING US THE TRUTH OF WHAT HAPPENED TONIGHT! DO YOU UNDERSTAND ME?! CAN I BE ANY F**KING CLEARER?!"

Then, I strategically lowered my voice. I wanted him to know I was upset, didn't believe him, but could be reasonable and listen to him now explain to us what we wanted to hear; that being the truth.

I added, in my normal speaking tone, "You know, Bob, the two boys told us everything. We know who you are and what you are. We know the specifics of what happened tonight, not to mention what I witnessed myself. Now, do you want to tell us what we already know or shall we tell you what we know and how much you've been lying to us? I'm sure you're aware, down the line, any judge you go before will be told of your lack of cooperation with us tonight. Do you want that known when it comes time to making bail later this morning? Do you want a jury to hear that you repeatedly lied to us here in this room?"

"Again, Detectives, I'm really not sure what you're talking about here. Those boys sometimes make jokes, make up stories, and...."

Slamming my fist again on the tabletop, but in a somewhat lower volume than when I last slammed my fist I stated, "Stop lying Father Hermley! Yes, we know you're a priest. However, that's the last time I'll put the word 'Father' in front of your name tonight. You've disgraced the priesthood, the Roman Catholic Church, you've violated your vows, and you've violated those two boys. And, there are others. Yeah, we know about them too."

Okay, I didn't have specifics yet about the last part, but I was sure that these two kids with him tonight were not Hermley's only sex abuse victims. He never denied it, so I was sure I hit on something here.

Hermley sat in silence, looking at no one in particular.

Terry, seeing that I had decidedly morphed into the "Bad Cop" in our interview scenario, decidedly morphed into the "Good Cop" in an attempt to break the silence. It was a smart move on his part.

Terry said, "Father, you gotta see that there's nowhere for you to go tonight except to be forthright and honest with us. We have two independent yet virtually identical statements from both of these boys. They told us all about you and specifically that you performed oral sex on them tonight, right in the Hilton parking lot. Are you going to tell us if we swab your car's seat covers, the boys' pants, your clothes, any tissues or napkins in the car, YOUR MOUTH, that we won't find traces of semen? Do you really want us to go there? Do you really want to deny this in front of the judge in a few hours, again in district magistrate court in a few weeks, and eventually in front of a jury of your peers? We have really good evidence against you, you know. Telling us truthfully what happened tonight can be the first step in making this very bad situation for you into a manageable one down the line."

I simply added to Terry's statement, "Bob, do I have to remind you of what I SAW just about two hours ago, in your car? I witnessed you giving oral sex to a 14-year-old. Do you really want to deny that? It's NOT just those two boys saying what happened. I SAW what happened. Do you understand that? You really gotta consider helping yourself out here."

I really didn't care whether Hermley would consider "helping" himself or not in this situation, but I wanted to get a statement from him of some kind. People in these police interview scenarios tend to selfishly think of themselves at times like this and perhaps we could convince him that the system would go easier on him if he told us the truth about tonight. In reality, the system DOES reward truth-telling in these situations, so we weren't lying to him in that regard.

Father Robert Hermley looked up at some point and met both of our eyes, but he maintained that just self-imposed vow of silence. He didn't say a word…yet.

Terry advised with great solemnity, "You know, Bob, I'm usually the one confessing my sins to a priest, but now the shoe is on the other foot, isn't it?"

Morphing back to a less-than Bad Cop, I simply added, "Bob, do this for the boys. Don't drag them through this anymore. Tell us what is going on here. It can help them and you in the long run."

Hermley took a deep breath. He actually took a second, and a third deep breath. Then, very slowly but very surely he began to tell us he has a "problem" with young teenage boys. He finds that he's, well, "sexually attracted to them." It's made him think in "bad ways" about them for years now.

Okay, that's a start....

Hermley eventually admitted he brought these two boys to the parking lot adjacent to the Lincoln Drive-In, a place he's been before, for the specific purpose of engaging in sexual activity with them. It's like he had to get that statement off his chest, out into the open. It seemed as if it was almost an epiphany for him. But then he sat back in his chair, folded his arms across his chest, and quieted down. When Terry and I gradually asked for more details regarding the extent of his sexual misconduct, how many other boys, their names, etc., he abruptly decided to stop talking to us. In so many words, Hermley suggested to us that he has probably said enough already tonight and now wished to end the interview.

Terry and I at that point had no choice. We ended the interview. At least we got out of him to some degree what had happened earlier this evening. In a sense, Hermley confessed. Not to the whole picture, of course, but it was something. It certainly would help our case when it comes to his later prosecution.

One of the last things Hermley said to Terry and me as we were getting up to leave the room was that he was "genuinely sorry." We believed him, but we later agreed that we weren't sure if it was for what he had done to the boys tonight or just for getting caught. With most criminals who utter similar type apologies, it's the latter reason.

The boys' parents individually showed up at BPD HQ an hour or so after we called them. It was about 1:30AM at this point. Terry and I briefed them about all that happened. They were in denial at first. One mother was adamant that Father Hermley, who she stated she has known for several years, could not have done this to her son. Something was amiss here, she insisted. We had our facts wrong, it was a different man, we misunderstood the boys, or something like that. I told her what I had visually witnessed and what Hermley had admitted, even if just partially, to us during the interview. She was still in denial.

Terry left the area and brought the two boys to their parents. After the more distraught of the moms talked to her son in private for a few minutes, she hugged him and started crying out loud. She now believed what had happened. It didn't make it any easier for her, or the other set of parents, but they now knew the full scope and implications of what had been happening, to some extent, right under their noses.

The parents hadn't done anything wrong, of course. I mean, who couldn't trust a priest with their kid? But, that's how I later learned these guys, be they priests, teachers, soccer coaches, even law enforcement officers, liked to operate. Gain the trust of the parents first, then work on the kids.

Before they left, we told the parents that they would be contacted by Det. Lachman and/or me in the next week or two regarding the preliminary hearing. We told the two boys that they may have to testify at the hearing if so requested. They agreed then and there to do so.

I also assured the parents that I would be calling the Archdiocese of Philadelphia the next day to advise them of the arrest of Father Hermley. The parents appreciated this and said they would also do the same as well as advise the pastor of their parish who seemed to know him rather well.

I finally thanked the parents, and their sons, and reminded the two boys before they left the police station that they had done nothing wrong with this man. He was the bad guy, not them. They were victims of Father Hermley, not co-conspirators. He used them and abused them for his own selfish, sexual, and illegal purposes. There was also no reason why they could not go on and have very "normal" teenage lives, I reminded them. I lastly told them that their names would never be released to the media or the public, as the law forbade it. Sons and parents alike were relieved to hear that bit of information as they left the building to go home. They thanked Terry and me as they departed. It was much appreciated.

But our job wasn't over yet that night.

I next requested of Terry that he transport Hermley to his preliminary arraignment with a uniformed officer. He agreed to do so. He started on the affidavit and other paperwork which was needed for Hermley's appearance later this morning before the district magistrate to be officially charged and his bail set. I, in turn, went out back of the police station to the mini-impound yard to further search the car. Since the car was legally impounded, we didn't need a search warrant to fully examine it for evidence, contraband, and the like. Before the search was over, found under the seats were eighteen other pornographic magazines of varying nature. Every item was photographed where it was originally located in the car, removed, packaged, and formally entered into evidence.

And yes, for various reasons, I wore gloves during the entire search. Protecting the evidence was only one reason for doing so.

Next, I wanted to search the trunk of Hermley's car. Upon opening the lid, I observed in the relatively large and uncluttered space what appeared to be a custom fitted red carpet remnant lying flat on the surface, butting up against the spare tire. There, on top of the piece of carpet, was a neatly laid out set of men's clothes. Not just any man's clothes, mind you, but a full set of priest's clothes; that being, from my left to right, from feet to neck, a pair of black shoes, black pants, and a black shirt with a bright white priest's collar affixed to it. Sticking partly out of the shirt pocket was a crucifix on a chain.

I recall thinking how convenient it was for Hermley to be able to go from the interior of his car, pop open his trunk lid, don these priestly accruements, and in doing so quickly switch from one persona to another. I suppose when he was wearing his black priestly clothing, the apparel of his other persona then took its turn riding in the trunk for when it may be later needed. It seemed almost too convenient....

In those few remaining moments in the confines of the darkened BPD impound yard, searching for additional evidence in Hermley's car, I wondered to myself when and where would be the next time he would wear the black priestly clothing, to include the crucifix around his neck, and assume his priestly duties. Then I realized that I found myself less concerned about when he would be wearing these particular items of clothing than when he would next be dressed casually, such as he was tonight. That, apparently, is when bad things occurred. (Although, the initial "grooming" of his intended victims most likely always started when he was wearing his priestly garb. No doubt, he had it down to a science.)

Closing the trunk lid on Hermley's alternate dress attire, search now completed, the juxtaposition came to mind of those teenage antics from the not-too-distant past of hiding friends in their cars' trunks to sneak them into the drive-in theater. The teenagers' rationale, of course, was always for kicks-and-giggles and ostensibly to save a few dollars on movie admission prices. Here tonight, I could see that Father Hermley also chose to hide something in his trunk while at or near the drive-in theater -- that being the visual representation of his priesthood, laid out from shoes to collar. But, unlike those semi-wayward teens of just a few years ago, Father Hermley's present rationale was much more sinister and devious.

The surface nexus between the two scenarios was obvious: teenagers, drive-in theaters, and each car having something hidden in its trunk. With the teens, it was innocently hiding their friends. With

Father Hermley, just what was he hiding? Was it the fact that he was a priest? Or, that he was a pedophile?

To me, at least in Hermley's case, they were inexorably linked.

After putting the relevant items from Hermley's car into the evidence locker (I didn't take his priest wardrobe, I just took photos of it), and before I left to go home that night, I somehow felt obligated to undertake one more activity regarding this matter. It came to me rather quickly and I didn't put all that much thought into it. Maybe I should have.

I decided to call my parish priest. His name was Monsignor Edward Musial. He was the pastor of St. Ephrem Church, where I was a member at the time. I knew him somewhat from Sunday Mass and various other church and police functions over the last few years. Rumor had it that he was a distant cousin of baseball great Stan Musial. But it wasn't baseball I was going to discuss with him this night, during this call. I thought he'd want to know a fellow priest had been arrested for sexual misconduct with two minors in the area of the parish of which he was the pastor for almost a decade now.

When I called the rectory Monsignor Musial answered the phone. It was clear that I had awakened him. I politely apologized for doing so and then identified myself as a BPD detective sergeant and a parishioner. He seemed to recognize me, or at least my voice. Without wasting any time, I told him about the arrest and even gave him Hermley's full name, his religious order, etc. However, Monsignor Musial didn't seem all that interested in what I had to say. He simply told me to call the Archdiocese offices in the morning and tell them the news. I told him I would do so and that I was again sorry for bothering him this late at night. We said our goodbyes and I hung up the phone.

I'm not sure what I expected as a result of the call to the pastor of my church. I think I saw it as sort of a professional courtesy to him, but maybe I was also looking for some words of comfort or reassurance as I was now caught up in a very uncomfortable situation personally, professionally, and spiritually. I must admit, arresting a priest for such charges was quite difficult for me at first. I had looked up to and respected these men, these servants of God, my whole life. Now, I happen to catch one in the act of giving oral sex to a pair of young teens. Damn! Talk about one's world being rocked, and on multiple levels at the same time.

But, for whatever reasons, my brief dialogue with Monsignor Musial didn't seem to obviate any of the intended reasons for the call as it ended very shortly after it started. Neither party seemed to have gained anything from it.

In any event, I'm not suggesting in any way that Monsignor Musial's apparent lack of interest during the phone call regarding Hermley's arrest was indicative of the fact that he was not concerned about what I had told him. In retrospect, I'm sure he was concerned. However, I suppose if I was called out of a sound sleep to be told news such as this about a man I may not have even known (although in my same profession), I may have adopted the same attitude.

To this day I'm not sure why I called my pastor during those very early morning hours. Was it for his benefit? Was it for my benefit? I simply don't know.

I saw Monsignor Musial again over the years on multiple occasions at various church functions, but this topic was never raised between us. He didn't mention it, so I chose not to mention it either.

In the large scale investigations over two decades later in Philadelphia regarding sexual abuse by Catholic priests, Monsignor Musial's name was never brought up in any such allegation of any sort. He led a long and respected career as a priest and pastor.

Musial's life ended tragically as the result of a fatal car accident in 2005 in Philadelphia.

The day after the arrest I did, in fact, call the main office of the Philadelphia Archdiocese. I asked for someone in the legal department in the Cardinal's office. I figured what I had to say was pretty important and I should tell someone relatively high-up, and why not go to their legal counsel. Once I got that person on the line I identified myself as a Bensalem Township detective sergeant and told him of the arrest of Father Hermley the night before. The person, whom I believed to be a church lawyer, took the information, thanked me, and quickly said goodbye. I never heard from him or the Archdiocese again.

It was one and done with that phone call to the Cardinal's office. No follow-up, no request for details, no stated interest in the young boys… nothing. Oh well, they'll handle it internally, I was sure. This particular priest will never see the light of day again, or at least never be assigned around kids again. No way! And he'll probably be defrocked too.

I was wrong, on all counts.

As it turned out, there never was a preliminary hearing for Hermley. Lawyers for the Archdiocese showed up at the district magistrate's office on the scheduled day and waived Hermley's right to his hearing.

The two boys never had to testify in open court, nor did I. Ultimately, through a deal worked out with the Bucks County District Attorney's Office and the Archdiocese of Philadelphia's lawyers, Father Robert Hermley pleaded guilty in November of that same year to the lone charge of Indecent Assault. For his plea, he received three years' probation. There was no jail except for the very short time, maybe only a few hours, he spent in detention immediately after his arrest. He was bailed out within a day by none other than the Archdiocese of Philadelphia.

I played no role in Hermley's plea agreement. I was not contacted by the Archdiocese or the Bucks County DA's office regarding this "deal." Detective Terry Lachman played no role in it either. If I had been asked, I would have expressed my strong unwillingness to essentially let this guy off with only the proverbial slap on the wrist. I would have insisted on some jail time and mandatory psychological counseling. But, alas, my opinion was not sought at this final stage of the judicial process and Hermley was a free man. He was still an active priest too, as I would find out much later.

I learned during the course of writing this chapter that Robert Hermley actually had a direct Bensalem Township connection several years prior to my arrest of him in 1982. It seems he was one of the priests-in-residence at the Our Lady of Fatima parish and school in Bensalem during the mid-1970s. He apparently did not teach at the school there, according to my information, but instead simply resided in the rectory on the parish grounds while he was assigned as an educator at a nearby high school in Philadelphia. Living at this parish would perhaps explain his familiarity with the area of the Lincoln Drive-In and even the convenient Hilton Inn parking lot next door.

I can only hope Father Hermley did not sexually abuse any boys during the time he actually lived in Bensalem. As I was a rookie police officer during at least some of those years, it would bother me greatly to find out that this may have been happening under my nose, on my watch, in a rectory about a mile from my police station, as well as about a mile from my home.

In 2005, I was a supervisory special agent working at the Behavioral Analysis Unit (BAU) as a profiler at the FBI Academy in Quantico, Virginia. One of my colleagues with an expertise in sexual victimization of children had been assisting the Philadelphia District Attorney's Office (PDAO) with their newly initiated investigation of the Catholic Archdiocese of Philadelphia and its handling of multiple sexual abuse cases involving priests and their child victims. The PDAO's reps were coming to our offices to attain some potential investigative, behavioral, and prosecutorial strategies as they were moving forward with their large-scale case. On that day, I sat in on the round-table consultation to offer my assistance.

It wasn't too long that morning before one of the visiting assistant district attorneys (ADA) started going through a litany of dozens and dozens of priests who had been accused of and/or arrested for sexually assaulting children over the last two to three decades in the Philadelphia area. In doing so, the name Robert Hermley was referenced early on. At the time, I hadn't thought about him or my arrest of him in many years. In fact, his name had even slipped my mind. But as the ADA was providing summaries of each priest's alleged misconduct, with Hermley's arrest being adjacent to a drive-in theater, etc., I immediately recognized that they were talking about the arrest I had personally made some twenty-three years earlier.

I couldn't help but interrupt and stop the ADA in his tracks and offer to him and the group that I happened to know a great deal about this particular priest and his arrest. The ADA who was the primary spokesman that day looked at me somewhat quizzically. I then told him that I was the arresting officer in 1982 of Hermley. Barely saying another word, he opened a nearby file-folder, searched some additional documents he had on Hermley, and sure enough he began to read aloud to the whole group part of the probable cause affidavit from the arrest warrant. There was the name "Sgt. James Fitzgerald" clearly referenced throughout. I half-kiddingly added, "See, I told you it was me."

The ADA told the group, of course, that he believed me right away, but he still wanted to make sure it was the same priest, same arrest, etc., before we continued. Once he confirmed it to be so, he informed the group in the room that Hermley's 1982 Bensalem PD arrest was later determined to have possibly been the very first arrest ever in the Philadelphia area of any priest for such a crime. The ADA further stated that before even coming to Quantico to visit with the BAU, his office concurred that the arrest of Hermley was an important case to them as there was an actual law enforcement eyewitness to the crime (me), as well as an eventual confession (partial), and guilty plea on the priest's part. It had opened the door years later for further investigation into how the Archdiocese handled these sordid matters, and these many sordid priest/pedophile criminal acts. The fact that Hermley's charges were ultimately reduced to Indecent Assault and that he was only sentenced to three years' probation was unfortunate, we all agreed, but it certainly didn't reflect on me or the BPD at the time. It was the Bucks County DA's Office, apparently under high-level pressure from the Archdiocese, which led to the reduction of the much more serious charges to that of a misdemeanor Indecent Assault.

Thanks to the PDAO, I learned more that day in '05 of the details of the '82 arrest and what happened after the fact than I had ever known before. I found out once Hermley was released on bail, and within just days of his arrest, he was sent to Johns Hopkins Medical Center in Baltimore, Maryland, for a psychological evaluation. There, reportedly his diagnosis came back as "routine" and/or "normal" and no further therapy, treatment, or counseling was mandated. And, apparently just a few weeks after his November 1982 guilty plea in front of a Bucks County judge, he was assigned by his religious order to a parish and school in Vienna, Virginia. Nine years later, in 1991, he was assigned to a parish in Fredericksburg, Virginia.

I was surprised at how much I ascertained about my decades-ago arrest of Robert Hermley, and what occurred subsequent to it, during the '05 visit of the PDAO lawyers and investigators. I know they were appreciative of the behavioral advice that I and my BAU colleagues provided them that day too.

It would take another six years or so for the PDAO to complete its investigation. As a result, a high-ranking Archdiocese of Philadelphia official (and priest), Monsignor William J. Lynn, was subsequently arrested for the charge of Child Endangerment. Although he was never accused of abusing any children himself, he was viewed as a facilitator of the abusive priests over the past several decades as he allegedly played a substantial role in secretly transferring the so-identified priests to other parishes and even other dioceses where, in some cases, they would continue to sexually abuse other children.

After a long trial, Lynn was convicted in July of 2012 in a Philadelphia court of one count of Child Endangerment. He was sentenced to a three-to-six year prison term. It was considered a landmark case at the time and unprecedented in the U. S. legal system. According to some, the Catholic Church, as represented by the Archdiocese of Philadelphia and its leadership, was finally being held accountable for its apparent systemic handling (or more accurately, mishandling) of the multiple pedophile priests over the decades and the subsequent cover-ups once they were identified as offenders and even re-offenders.

However, Lynn's lawyers appealed, and his conviction was overturned by a unanimous decision in late 2013 by a Pennsylvania appeals court. He was subsequently released from prison. As of this writing, the PDAO is now appealing that decision to the Pennsylvania Supreme Court.

It is unclear if Hermley ever reoffended, that is, abused any other young boys after his 1982 arrest. There were later allegations that he sexually offended some teens prior to my arrest of him, but the records from the PDAO's office do not indicate another arrest of him for any additional child victimization. However, there is no doubt that the church authorities, no matter in which geographical diocese he may have landed, placed Father Hermley in venues with access to young children. For that, there is no excuse.

Learning what I did about pedophilic behavior some years later in my law enforcement career as an FBI profiler, something tells me that the two boys I happened to catch Hermley sexually abusing that June night in 1982 would not and could not have been his only victims. His thinking in "bad ways" about 13- to 14-year-old boys most definitely did not begin or end on the night of his arrest at the Lincoln Drive-In.

Robert Hermley died in 2009. He remained a priest until the end. Whether he remained a pedophile until the end, or acted upon those sexual urges, is known only to him, his God, and perhaps some additional child victims. Let's hope those "bad ways," if they still existed within Hermley for the rest of his years, were limited to only his mind, and not his actions.

I must add here in closing...despite the likes of Robert Hermley and his pedophile priestly ilk, and the decades-long systemic machinations of the Archdiocese of Philadelphia, other Roman Catholic Church leadership throughout the U.S., as well as other parts of the world, to protect priests who sexually abused children and/or covered-up their actions, I am also aware of some truly fine and dedicated priests. These men take their vows very seriously and at the same time condemn to the fullest the behavior of these rogue ordained sexual predators and the system which protected them.

I am personally aware of many devoted priests who perform their religious duties as well as any man or woman of the cloth, Catholic or otherwise. They reflect the priesthood and its mission as it should be, with dedication to God and the many congregants they serve.

The exceptions to the rule, of course, are the Hermleys and other priests like him. However, their numbers are dwindling rapidly, through serving prison time, being defrocked, and/or dying. I'm told there are now multi-level safeguards in place in the Catholic Church to prevent these sorts of individual and/or institutional atrocities from occurring again in the future.

I certainly hope so…for I, and others, will be watching.

Chapter Thirty-Five

While there were some interesting criminal cases I was investigating, even as a detective sergeant, I still had to remind myself at the same time that I was now first and foremost a CID supervisor. And with that supervisory role came responsibility, to include making difficult decisions and occasionally being given undesirable supervisory-like assignments.

As referenced earlier, it was strange going from a peer relationship with my fellow detectives one day to being their boss the next day. But that's how it is in a smaller to mid-size agency, institution, or company when such promotions occur. Personal affiliations and associations are forced to alter somewhat, on both sides of the supervisor/subordinate paradigm. That certainly happened during this time in my personal and professional life at the BPD. I may have initially looked at my present co-workers the same as I had in the recent past, but it didn't take me long to realize that they were looking at *me* differently now.

In terms of the BPD as a whole, there had been at least one major change in the police department management over the last month or two. For reasons never entirely explained or clear to me, Captain Ron Traenkle was transferred from heading up the Patrol Division to heading up the Administrative Division. That means he was put in charge of the secretaries, auxiliary police, cars, uniforms, and the like. It wasn't a demotion or a promotion, but a transfer to a less-than-sexy position which I'm not sure Traenkle was all that thrilled about.

I was a bit dismayed to learn that Lt. Hughes was then put in charge of the Patrol Division, but Chief Viola needed someone to run it, and I suppose Hughes was the only one of that upper-rank level who was available despite (as I would learn later) the Chief's general dislike and mistrust of him. Viola wanted to keep Jack Robinson as head of the CID (their offices were very close to one another), as he was also an important everyday advisor to him.

Bottom line, the managerial pyramid had been shifted around a bit, but things still seemed to be running very well in the department. Arrests were up, convictions were up, recovered property was up, and overall officer morale, at least among most within the PD, seemed to be up. The new chief couldn't ask for better numbers or conditions than those.

On that same hypothetical managerial pyramid chart, the position of the former "Chief," Deputy Chief Zajac, would have been visually connected by a horizontal dotted-line to a separate, stand-alone box off on its own somewhere. I never did really figure out what his role was during the year or so after Viola was appointed as the new Chief. I don't think he was ever given a specific role by Viola. I know he spent some of that time working the dispatch desk talking on the phone to complainants, sending officers on calls, managing the car fleet, etc.

In essence, Zajac was still around at the BPD, but barely, and changes were coming for him too. His box would be off the aforementioned chart before too much longer, and not in a good way for him.

For various administrative reasons, including the fact that Zajac seemed to have for some reason secreted various investigative files within the department after Viola was placed in charge, the Deputy Chief was unceremoniously terminated in October of '82. There was a headline or two in the *Bucks County Courier Times* over the next few days and some later coverage about Ted's appeal of his firing, but in effect, after his firing the man was a *persona non grata* and off almost everyone's radar for the foreseeable future in Bensalem.

Perhaps someone should have been assigned to watch the radar screen and monitor Zajac's movements and activities during his time in exile. Or, at least those of one of his family members.

It may have already been too late though.

* * * * *

If there was any one consistent serious property-related crime that plagued Bensalem in the early 1980s, and its new chief and CID head, it was burglary. They were mostly residential burglaries, but with the not-so-infrequent commercial break-ins too. The former would take place during weekdays when residents were at work, the latter overnight and on weekends when the facilities were generally closed.

When I first came to CID, there was no rhyme or reason as to how the follow-up burglary investigations would be assigned to the detectives. Along with other cases, each detective would have a mix of residential and commercial burglaries he was investigating which happened to be spread around the four corners of Bensalem. It didn't take me long to come to the realization that there must be a better way to assign these cases, one in which individual detectives could perhaps specialize in these types of crimes in an attempt to put a dent in the number of them. So, after running a set of ideas by Viola and Robinson, and receiving their joint blessings, I was fully authorized to initiate the "Bensalem Police Department Burglary Unit." So, I did.

Once approval was granted, I simply asked if any two of the approximately ten detectives in CID would be interested in working burglaries on a fulltime basis. I explained that they wouldn't be responsible for any other type cases as residential and commercial break-ins would be their only everyday investigative responsibility. Within a few hours of the announcement of this new unit, two detectives contacted me and told me they wanted in. Lt. Robinson agreed with them coming onboard and it was a done deal. While I'd still be a regular CID detective sergeant, I would also separately supervise these two detectives in this brand new unit.

At its inception, and by design, I gave the two detectives autonomy to self-assign the burglaries to themselves as each new crime report came in to the CID. I would first review each one, put the basic facts (date, time, location, method of entry, what was stolen, etc.) of each burglary into a logbook on my desk, and then put the patrol officer's report in the Burglary Unit assignment box. This box was on a small table which sat alongside their now adjacent desks.

I had the two detectives working alternating day-work and evening shifts each week (with no late-night shifts or weekends, which no doubt also made the new squad more desirable to them), with an hour overlap each afternoon (3:00 – 4:00) so they could discuss their respective cases and compare notes. Each day, the two detectives would individually review the reports and take the cases most similar to what they've worked already, or which occurred in one of the four patrol sectors they were unofficially assigned. They'd then put their name next to that case in the logbook so I knew who was working it. If a burglary call came in to dispatch while they were on-duty, they could also respond to the location with the responding patrol officer and start the investigation right then and there, to include a thorough forensic examination of the crime scene.

I had learned during my earlier patrol officer days, when at the scene taking the initial report of a burglary, be it at someone's house or someone's place of business, that burglars had certain tendencies, patterns, and habits which were readily identifiable upon a close-up examination and comparison. Later, as an FBI profiler, I would learn that serial killers, serial rapists, and other serial offenders, each have what is called a "Signature" which would manifest itself at their individual successive crime scenes.

A criminal's signature, in a behavioral context, is defined as actions and/or deeds at the scene of a crime which are NOT necessary for the successful commission of the crime itself. They are instead the result of need-driven behavior for the personal satisfaction (to include sexually-oriented) of the criminal himself. Signature is separate from *modus operandi* (M.O.). M.O. includes actions and/or deeds which, in fact, are necessary to successfully commit the crime. The M.O. a criminal utilizes may change over time. Signature rarely changes, or at least not in any substantive form.

The actions of serial burglars also manifest these two features in various forms. Basic examples of M.O. at a burglary scene would be the consistent use of one or more specific tools to gain entry into a residence or business; the burglar bringing his own bag each time to carry out the valuables he steals; using a pillow case from one of the bedrooms for the same purpose; or, it could be consistently leaving the drawers of dressers or desks open in a certain fashion. (It is well known to burglary investigators that an experienced burglar, when searching for valuables in a set of drawers, will start at the bottom and open them one at a time moving upwards to the top. That way, he doesn't have to close each drawer to check the next one, thus saving valuable time and also making less noise.)

An example of a criminal's "Signature" at a burglary scene would be him eating food while there; defecating while there (yes, I've seen that a number of times in both residential and commercial burglaries, and not always in an unflushed toilet); looking through photo albums; playing videos/DVDs on the TV (perhaps before the TV itself was removed from the premises); switching on a radio to a certain music station and leaving it on even after departing; turning tabletop family pictures upside down or face down; masturbating; and the like. Clearly none of these are necessary for the successful undertaking of a burglary, yet cases I investigated or of which I am familiar over the years included one or more of these listed peculiar activities.

(In the 1990 movie *Home Alone*, in a rather silly yet by definition accurate example of the concept of "Signature," one of the two professional burglars collectively known as the "Wet Bandits" insists on leaving a kitchen water spigot running over a plugged-up sink drain upon exiting each residential break-in. The subsequent flooding of the house then becomes their prideful "mark," aka signature, in so doing. In this subplot of the movie, it is this signature act which serves to link all their prior burglaries and which leads to their eventual arrests.)

In view of all of this, and the fact that burglaries were still very prevalent in Bensalem when I was first promoted to detective sergeant, it made sense to me to conceptualize and then start such a unit devoted to just one crime. The two detectives would work only burglaries and investigate each one for various commonalities in M.O. and Signature (although I didn't use this specific term back then), along with forensic, geographical, and other similarities which could potentially link them and then hopefully identify the offenders.

I mandated that the Burglary Unit detectives also hang a township map on the wall near their desks and use multi-colored pins and small labels to create a visual representation to chart the various residential and commercial burglaries over time. They both knew of my successful car theft-related pin map of Neshaminy Mall (which was still hanging nearby), and readily agreed to get the new map on the wall and update it with each new offense.

It all worked. For the first time in Bensalem PD history, we had a unit of two detectives working fulltime on nothing but burglaries. I allowed them to remain more or less autonomous and work each case as it came along. I, along with the two of them, when noticing various burglary trends in terms of days of weeks, times of day, neighborhoods, items stolen, M.O., signature, etc., would work with the Tactical Squad (now under new leadership as Sgt. Whacky had been reassigned to patrol), and set up stake-outs and surveillances of certain areas when deemed appropriate.

All in all, the unit made numerous arrests, recovered property, and shut down a few different burglary rings over the next 18-plus months. Some offenders were local teenagers and twenty-somethings offending in their own neighborhoods. Those cases were usually easy to solve. Others, however, were professional burglars with long records. Some were from Bucks County, some were from Philadelphia, and others were from neighboring areas. No matter their level of expertise or from where they hailed, we were glad to put the burglars, be they professional or amateur, local or long-distance, behind bars.

The very successful Burglary Unit remained intact and very functional through early 1984 with its two detectives, under my tutelage, making multiple arrests and attaining multiple convictions along the way. But the unit was then disbanded by the "new" person in charge. The map itself was unceremoniously torn off the wall in early '84 by none other than one of the two detectives who I had initially assigned to the unit and with whom I worked well (or so I thought) lo those eighteen months. The rationale for his attitude and the disbanding of the unit, if there is one at all, is forthcoming. As I would learn starting in very early '84 in the BPD, rationality would rarely be present in any comprehensible or definable form.

(+ Bonus Chapter 35a)

Chapter Thirty-Six

The very best day of 1982 came for me near the end of the year. That's when my son Daniel was born. Eileen and I now had our second child, and Sean found himself suddenly with a little brother to play with. The house was getting a bit more crowded, and there was now another mouth to feed, but we managed it all just fine.

Chief Viola called me into his office just a few days after Dan was born and congratulated me for my recent good news. I thanked him and gave him the customary cigar. It wasn't a particularly expensive one like he may have normally smoked, but he was appreciative nonetheless as he put it inside his jacket pocket for later use. He then closed the door and said he wanted to run a few things by me.

I said, "Sure. What's up?"

"Jimmy," the Chief started, "Traenkle is burning out doing the Admin job, or at least he's telling me he is, and I was wondering... would you be interested in doing it for maybe six to nine months or so? I figure with the new baby you may appreciate working a steady Monday to Friday day-shift with your weekends off."

I couldn't help but immediately respond, "Uh...are you okay with my work as CID sergeant? That's not the reason why you're suggesting this transfer, is it?"

"No, no, not at all," Viola replied, half-laughing, "your work there is fine. The Burglary Unit is working great, you're an excellent supervisor, especially with some of the guys you've inherited back here, and the cases you've handled have all had excellent results. Even in this short time, you've proven yourself in CID, first as a detective, and now as a detective sergeant, so believe me, it has nothing to do with your job here."

Rich Viola was not one to mince, waste, or conflate words to make his various points. That much I knew, so I genuinely believed what he had just told me.

The Chief and I went back and forth a bit more discussing various details of this re-assignment. He told me, unfortunately, this move would not entail a promotion in and of itself, nor would it even have an attached "Acting" title in front of "Lieutenant" or "Captain," but that I'd do it as a sergeant, my present rank. I was okay with that notion. I saw it as providing more long-term career benefits to me than necessarily short-term, so keeping my current three stripes for the relatively short duration of this assignment was fine with me.

Viola also assured me that Jack Robinson was on board with this concept despite "losing a good man" in me, but he (the Chief) really needed some help in the Admin department and I was their logical choice. We agreed that me working for the first time in the budgetary, purchasing, and personnel side of the department would not be a bad thing. It could only enhance my resume as I would attempt to progress through the ranks of the department, or elsewhere, in the future. So, after our ten minute or so chat, I let him know I would do it. I would take over these duties during the first week of January, 1983. We also agreed that it would be for no more than nine months. That would be after a new round of officer hiring would be completed. Around September, I could decide then where I wanted to go. It could be either back to CID or into the Patrol Division, or even stay on as the Admin head if I so desired.

I shook hands with Viola, and it was a done deal. In about a month I'd be leaving CID and working in the office directly adjacent to his, the Admin Office. It was presently occupied by Capt. Traenkle, but he wanted out, or the Chief wanted him out. (That part was never made entirely clear to me). Maybe I would want out too in a few months, but I'd at least give it a try. Traenkle was already a captain but I was still two ranks away from that position. If this stepping-stone would help me eventually get there, then why not give it a try? Viola seemed to think it would help, and I trusted him implicitly.

When I went in shortly thereafter to see Lt. Robinson, he informed me he knew the Chief wanted to give me a try at this new position. He told me to take it as a compliment that the boss thought I had what it took to undertake this assignment change. It's not an easy one, Jack said, but it's an important one. He even warned me that dealing with salespeople, vendors, township accountants, insurance agents, and sometimes even crying secretaries, could be as stress-inducing as other jobs on the department. But he also knew of several disciplinary run-ins I've had over the last few months with at least three detectives, and said maybe it would be a nice break for me from those malcontents. I assured him that neither of them posed any concerns to me personally or professionally, but Jack said, "Well, take it as an added benefit. I'm still stuck with these malcontents, don't forget."

Robinson was also one not to parse his language or play games by saying one thing but meaning another. So, like with Viola, I believed him too. Then, he said, he had two more things to tell me.

Jack first told me that as of the next township supervisors' meeting he was to be promoted to the rank of captain. It wasn't known around the department yet, but as Viola put him in for it (it was an appointed position, not one attained by competitive testing), he wanted to tell a few people first, including me. I congratulated him. He shrugged his shoulders and responded with a simple "Yeah, thanks."

Jack next divulged to me he would soon be going away to Quantico, Virginia, for three whole months. He added that about a year ago Viola had put him in for, and he had just been accepted at, the prestigious FBI National Academy (FBI NA). I congratulated him once again for this known career-enriching opportunity. However, I next advised him that although I had heard of the NA over the years, I wasn't exactly sure what it was or how it worked.

The soon-to-be-captain proceeded to tell me that less than one percent of U. S. law enforcement officers ever had the opportunity to attend this most renowned of police management training academies. It is truly an honor, he told me, to be accepted and then to graduate from it. It is managed and taught by the FBI at their Academy in Quantico. It was started in the 1930s by J. Edgar Hoover, is designed for sergeants and above in rank, and is offered in four different sessions each year. Each session includes approximately 250 officers, and they are housed in several dormitory buildings on the grounds of the Academy. Most of them are from U. S. law enforcement agencies, but there are always approximately twenty officers from other countries there too. The course lasts eleven weeks and is management oriented, to include workplace supervisory issues, public speaking, dealing with the media, constitutional law, and other related courses, all designed to assist the management-level police supervisor in making that next career step, perhaps even becoming the chief at his or her own department.

Jack was on a roll. He continued by telling me that the courses taught at the FBI NA are all done so in conjunction with the University of Virginia (UVA). Each FBI agent instructor there is also an adjunct professor at that esteemed institution of higher learning. Jack finally ended the fact-filled part of our conversation by telling me that nowadays most police departments in the U. S. actually require that their candidates for the position of chief be a graduate of the FBI NA. (Rich Viola was not an FBI NA graduate, thus he was an exception to the rule as the relatively new BPD chief. He was, however, a graduate of multiple U. S. Marine Corps leadership courses over the years, thus he had his own prestigious level of formalized training in this regard.)

After taking all this in, I told Jack I was really happy for him and that this was a great opportunity for him, his career, the BPD, his family...but before I could go much farther in articulating my views, he stopped me. He reminded me that he was local guy, born and raised in Bensalem, he never lived anywhere else, he did not enjoy travelling away from home, and he was only doing this to keep Chief Viola happy. I was mildly taken aback from his almost-reluctance to attend this very exclusive training experience, this opportunity of a lifetime, but he maintained his opinion that he would be just as happy if he didn't have to leave home for "a whole three goddamn months." He did lighten up shortly after all this, telling me it would be nice to "get away from this goddamn place" for a while. I laughingly agreed with him.

Then, what Jack said next, really floored me.

Soon-to-be Capt. Robinson told me that he had already talked to Viola, and they've already officially requested the FBI to put my name on the list for a future NA slot. It may take a while, he cautioned me, as each FBI division across the country only gets so many NA openings per year for officers within their geographical jurisdictions. But with Viola's pull and recommendation, Jack maintained, it may not be too long before I could attend.

Me? At the FBI NA? I was flabbergasted. Up until about ten minutes ago, I wasn't even sure how the whole NA thing even worked. I mean, I had heard of it, but who went, for how long, what it exactly entailed, was all more or less a mystery to me. I knew lots more now, of course.

I was definitely caught off guard by this revelation by Jack and showed my enthusiasm accordingly. At that point he said, "Hey, do you want to go in my place? I'm sure they wouldn't mind."

I knew Robinson was kidding about that last part, but about the other part I knew he was dead serious. I thanked him profusely for this information and the forthcoming potential opportunity for me to go to Quantico for what would truly be a once-in-a-lifetime professional experience for me.

Jack ended our little chat with, "No problem. You've earned it. Just don't hold your breath. It may take some time."

The lieutenant was right about that. And actually, it worked to my advantage.

(+ See bonus Chapter 36a)

Chapter Thirty-Seven

In retrospect, 1983 could best be described as an up-and-down year for me, for a few other officers, and for the BPD itself. January and December would make for odd and disparate bookends to the months in-between for almost everyone employed at my police department. And those of us who were paying attention and trying to figure out where certain late-year events would lead us came to realize that even by December 31 the future of the BPD and the Township itself was a very large unknown.

We'll get there, but let's start with the known....

As planned, starting in very early January, I took over Capt. Traenkle's old job and began my duties as the head of BPD administrative matters. It was pretty cool those first few days settling into my very own desk in my very own office. It was the first office space or even desk that I ever occupied completely to myself in my career so far.

Within the first hour in my new digs I began taking Traenkle's stuff off the wall and desk and replacing it with some of my own personal mementos. For some reason, the now-former admin captain was reluctant to remove his personal items either on his last official day in the office or now, on my first official day in it. So, after a day and a half, I did it for him. I put them all in a large box, sealed it, and put it in the nearby patrol squad room with his name on it. When he saw it the next day he got mad at me and let me know, but he also finally took his mementos home with him. His stuff was gone, that's all I really cared about. His new office didn't have the room for displaying his various trinkets, etc., so apparently to his basement or attic they went.

In my new office on one wall I proudly hung a recently attained Penn State football championship clock (they were NCAA collegiate champs in '82), and on another wall I hung my framed PSU diploma. On my desk, I placed a picture of my two young sons, as well as other personal mementos designed to spruce the place up and add some color and personalization to the otherwise bland brown paneling which comprised the four interior walls. This approximately 15' x 15' room would be my workplace for the next ten months, five days a week for at least eight hours per day, so I wanted it looking and feeling right for me. I was attempting to make it as reflective of me as I could, and I think I did.

With the minor redecorating over, it was now time to get to work.

As Chief Viola had previously advised, my new position involved me dealing with all the people, companies, materials, supplies, and issues that contribute to a police department's overall functionality on a daily basis. Very few decisions regarding these varied entities and objects could be made without knowing from where in the annual line-item budget the funds would be available to pay the various people or companies for their products and services to remedy the various issues at hand or to order new equipment. I quickly learned I couldn't spend monies which had run out and/or the township hadn't previously allocated for certain items or services within that calendar year. So, I routinely checked with the upstairs offices before spending said monies. I handled these purchases somewhat like I handled my own in my personal life, that is, I didn't spend money I didn't have. This part of my new position came rather easy to me.

In my new position I had nothing to do with payroll, salaries, or benefits, thank goodness, as the township offices upstairs handled those matters. But if it was service related or equipment related within the PD itself, from uniforms to cars to copy machines to bullets to toilet paper to gasoline, I was the person who bought it, leased it, authorized it, and/or somehow got it replenished. I was "The Man" in charge of all these sundry items and issues.

Lucky me.

This new position was a true learning experience for me as I had never done anything like it before. I found I was slowly developing into more of a purchasing agent, office supply manager, and clerical supervisor than anything law enforcement-related at this juncture in my career. But I knew this going in and I figured for less than a year, I can do this. I even told Chief Viola after a while that this was really a job for a civilian, perhaps one with a business degree or some such related education or certification. He didn't disagree with me. For now though, he reiterated, it was me and me alone undertaking these duties, with a B.S. in Law Enforcement and Corrections, and a few grad courses in Human Organizational Science now under my belt. I continued to remind myself that I could do this, I could do this right, get the notch on said belt, move on, and maybe even move up.

Yeah, that's the plan. Well, with a slight alteration to a prior part of my plan.

* * * * *

When it came to those grad courses at Villanova University, I must acknowledge here that I made a difficult decision during the previous summertime, and it's one that I came to regret not too long afterwards. I found that my then-casework and new supervisory role and shift work were simply getting in the way of me taking these courses. I had done fine academically in the first three of them, but I felt that my work schedule and professional responsibilities were hindering me getting to class on those nights (it was about an hour drive each way) and completing all my course-related assignments.

Well, sort of....

Okay, that's only partly the story. While I did enjoy the courses themselves, the subject matter, the professors, and meeting other working students in my field, something intangible at some point went missing and/or was lost from my own self-perceived big picture, my roughly-drawn out life plan, etc. It would be about eighteen months later that I would realize what had happened here. I was hoping by then it wasn't too late to make up for the lost time and misperceptions.

I believe what I lost was what I referred to earlier in this book as the "Eye of the Tiger." The "Eye," this time, would be in relation to my graduate degree program and at least one of the multiple paths (the academic one) I had chosen to pave the way for my various long-term professional goals and aspirations. I lost it, I believe, because I was doing TOO good at my job and, quite frankly, succeeding very well so far in all associated professional undertakings. These "successes" would have included being recently promoted (with a ten-percent pay raise), supervising other detectives and their cases, working and solving my own cases and investigations, making good arrests, attaining solid convictions, receiving excellent media coverage for many of these accomplishments, and with essentially all aspects of my life progressing in a very positive direction for me.

The bosses who were actually running the PD (Viola and his number-two man Robinson) liked me and respected me and, if not directly, clearly intimated that I had a future in this department, to include even at its higher ranks. So hearing this, seeing this, experiencing this, and believing all of this, something happened to me.

While still working hard every day I nonetheless got comfortable, I settled, I became complacent to some degree, and worst of all, I became somewhat enamored with who I was, where I was, and my various professional accomplishments to date. Mix in a bit of youthful naïveté and this all lulled me into a false sense of professional security.

That's never a good thing.

In later years in the FBI, I would hear the not very desirable descriptor that a certain person had become "fat, dumb, and happy" in his/her life, career, etc. Well, I was neither "fat" nor "dumb" in a literal sense in my life or career, but I suppose I was "happy." Based on this perceived happiness, mixed in with my own perhaps over-exaggerated estimation of my level of success at this time and place, I decided the further pursuance of the M.S. degree at Villanova University was not in the cards for me anymore.

My logic, in part, hinged on the fact that I was not even 30 years old yet and here I was a detective sergeant in the fifteenth largest police department in Pennsylvania. So, why do I need more schooling? I've already made it. I can take another promotional exam, make lieutenant, then who knows what's in the professional wind for me after that.

In light of all this, I had simply lost the drive, the ambition, (the "Eye?"), to continue my education in the form of a graduate degree in a field related to my career. I felt that I would be wasting my time to proceed with it. I didn't need that M.S. degree to get where I was now, right? How could it be of help to me in the future?

So, I got to thinking…

Sitting through two ninety-minute classes per week? *I work 40 hours per week already!*

Reading assignments? *I have officers' and detectives' reports to read and review!*

Writing term papers? *I have "real" reports to write!*

Taking exams? *I've already "passed" my real-world promotional exams!*

Actually, I was clearly NOT thinking…at least not very forward-mindedly.

Late during the summer of '83, I called the Villanova department head and told him that I was taking some time off due to overwhelming work responsibilities and having recently undertaken a new position within my police department. I didn't officially quit the program, I just told the professor the timing was bad right now to continue classes and I needed a few semesters off. He stated that he understood and that I could come back within a year or so without having to officially reapply to the program. I thanked him and said goodbye. I actually recall believing that this may be the last time I would ever speak to this professor.

I knew deep down that if I had really wanted to do so I could have kept going to these classes. But that's just it, I didn't really want to do so because I believed my career was already on the rise and I didn't need further formal education for it to continue to do so. After all, as previously noted, in the early 1980s, most cops didn't even have undergraduate degrees (if any college credits at all), much less an M.S. or M.A. degree. So, with my B.S. alone I figured I should be fine for the rest of my career. I mean, look at my career already and I only have an undergrad diploma so far. In fact, I see it every workday hanging on the wall of my new office.

So, no classes, no courses for me at Villanova or anywhere else during calendar year 1983. I was too busy at work. I was too busy at life. I was already on my way.

Or so I thought.

As it would turn out for me, the eye of that mythical tiger hadn't closed completely. Rightly or wrongly, it was just in resting mode for now; well, more or less. When once again reopened and fully focused, by forces as of yet unimagined, it would be so with a greater determination and purpose than ever, with another academic degree just one of the several "prey" in its near and far sights.

* * * * *

During 1983, two separate investigations of which I played no role eventually resulted in the termination of two detectives from the BPD. They were senior officers, and it took many of us by surprise when each occurred.

The first incident involved a detective who was off-duty and in a local drinking establishment one evening. He apparently had been imbibing his share of alcoholic beverages while there. A confrontation with one or more other patrons at the bar took place, the detective pulled his handgun from his holster, and as the other people were leaving (or running from) the bar, he fired off a few shots out the door into the night sky. Fortunately, no one was struck by the bullets and there was no known property damage.

The Bensalem police were called to the bar. The shooter was identified by witnesses as the off-duty detective. Within a day, an internal investigation took place at the BPD. Based on the results of that investigation, Chief Viola decided the detective was to be terminated. The next day the detective turned in his ID, his badge, and his handgun and he was no longer an employee of the BPD. He had been fired for several violations of police department rules and regulations.

The second detective who was terminated was involved in something a bit more complex, even if not as potentially lethal, than shooting off his gun at a bar. The matter is best summarized in a 1983 article written by Anita DiBartolomeo, a staff writer at the *Bucks County Courier Times*.

The headline reads, "**$1,200 missing; Bensalem officer fired**."

The article reads, in part:

> "A Bensalem police detective has been fired on charges that he failed to properly handle $1,340 confiscated in two criminal cases. Most of the money is now missing, although the detective...is not charged with stealing it, officials said.
>
> "Police chief Richard Viola said he fired (the detective), on the force for nine years, after money taken from suspects as part of two separate investigations was not recorded on departmental records.
>
> "Viola said (the detective), who was handling the case for Bensalem in conjunction with Philadelphia police, did not record the confiscated money on a property receipt or an evidence log. The money was noted on records kept by the city police involved in the case, Viola said.
>
> "(Viola) said (the detective) contended he had placed a bag of confiscated items in a police station evidence locker, to which other officers have access, and never saw the money."
>
> (End of article.)

And so, this officer subsequently turned in his ID, badge, and handgun and he was no longer an employee of the BPD. His firing too was the result of various violations of the departmental rules and regulations.

While I had worked on-and-off with the two aforementioned officers in the past, I was not particularly friendly with either of them. It would have been readily obvious to anyone who would listen to them or observe their actions that they were very closely aligned with former Deputy Chief Zajac. In fact, both of them had been promoted to the rank of detective as a result of Zajac's previously self-designed, non-competitive testing protocol. They undoubtedly owed him much in return. They made no secret of it either, even after Viola took the BPD reins and Zajac was ousted.

The detectives' allegiances to Zajac aside, it was still disconcerting to learn that two of my fellow officers had been independently terminated from their jobs, only a few months apart. Even if both were guilty as charged of their respective offenses (of which I didn't know one way or the other), I was nonetheless sympathetic toward them. They had families to support and bills to pay too, just like me.

At the same time, a sworn police officer can't just go off and discharge a weapon multiple times out of a barroom door, and/or somehow misplace drug suspects' money that he's supposed to retain as evidence, and not ultimately be held responsible for it. I'm not sure if firing them was the only recourse at the time. Perhaps another lesser form of discipline would have been more fair back then. I simply don't know all that went into the decision making by Chief Viola, et al., at the time.

While these two guys clearly both engaged in careless activity to one degree or another which resulted in their ultimate firings, they certainly also made it relatively easy for Viola to "take out" two of Zajac's more vocal on-duty supporters. I'm not suggesting at all that this was the rationale for the two detectives being terminated. Nonetheless, it is something that I could never completely dismiss despite neither the chief nor anyone else at the BPD ever confiding anything such as this to me. However, as the two detectives basically handed their separate violations on a silver platter to the current chief...well, I suppose that current chief just took what he was given and ran with it as far as he legally and departmentally could.

For perspective here, allow me to assure the reader that if Deputy Chief Zajac had still been in charge, even with the exact same circumstances in each case, neither officer would have received disciplinary action at all. Or, it would have been a slap on the wrist at the very most. If Zajac had been in charge and it had been, let's say, an officer named Jim Fitzgerald involved in similar off- or on-duty circumstances, allow me to assure the reader once again that he (as in me) would have been terminated too, if not also criminally charged.

As the worm would turn, however, regardless of the level of sympathy I or others may have had for these two detectives post-termination, its duration would be short lived. Things would be very much back to "normal" for both of them before too long, as well as for the guy who had earlier promoted them.

* * * * *

By the spring of '83, as the BPD purchasing agent, office manager, and clerical administrator over all I surveyed (again, lucky me), my internal and external research brought me to the realization that there was a growing trend in the private sector, as well as in many government agencies, to "computerize" the clerical and record-keeping aspects of the workplace. As I was learning, police departments were no exception to this latest trend. However, as I and others were also learning, my police department was woefully behind in this area of electronic office enhancement.

I became determined to do something about it.

After speaking to Chief Viola and, with his permission, the township manager and her staff, it was agreed that it was time for our department and the township offices, "to join the 1980s," from a computerization standpoint. With the approval of the chief and the township manager, a small team of police and township employees was assembled. In due time, as part of our tasking, we collectively reached out to several neighboring departments and municipalities which in turn put us in touch with various computer hardware companies' vendors and consultants. As a result, the BPD was soon on its way to joining the digital world, even if a bit later than we would have preferred.

Through a salesperson at IBM with whom we eventually contracted, Bensalem Township began the snail-like journey of computerizing the PD and the upstairs administrative offices. Early on, as arranged by this IBM rep, a PD clerical employee and I travelled to a police department near Allentown, Pennsylvania, to assess their relatively new computer system, see how it worked, determine exactly what it did, how fast it operated, etc. After an informative half-day in this agency about sixty miles due north of Bensalem, I was convinced of the system's efficacy. I came back to Bensalem that day and told the chief and others what we learned and that this was the hardware and software that we needed to acquire, sooner rather than later, if we wanted to become the truly modern law enforcement agency to which we all strived.

After a few months, and some township budgetary realloca-tions to acquire the necessary funding, a brand new, state-of-the-art, "mainframe" IBM computer was purchased by Bensalem Township, along with approximately ten separate but networked desktop computers for the PD as well for upstairs in the administrative offices. As part of this purchase plan, of course, various employees, includ-ing me, were provided at least one day of training on how these new devices would function and ostensibly make running the PD more efficient, more effective, and serve to streamline our overall adminis-trative operations. After the wiring and set-up stages were completed, I was standing there with the IBM consultant team on the day when the computers were first plugged in and turned on.

Looking back, I remember with great pride and purpose the feeling that day of seeing the monitor lights flicker on and the little cursor first start blinking away. It was an equally great feeling to know that I, along with a few others, had played a somewhat significant role in this first acquisition ever of computers for the BPD.

"Finally, we're in the 1980s," someone snidely remarked from the back of one of the newly equipped offices. The person's welcoming wish, sarcastic as it may have been, was appreciated by all despite everyone knowing it came a few years later than we would have liked.

Welcome to the Computer Age, BPD. We were Luddites no longer.

* * * * *

As per my agreement with Chief Viola, I left the admin branch of the BPD in the fall of that year. Both the chief and now-Captain Robinson wanted me to come back to CID as a detective sergeant and essentially take over my old job. After a day or so transitioning (I believe it to be) Lt. Hughes to my admin position, I cleared out my office and desk and I was assigned back to where I was very comfortable and, quite frankly, to where I wanted to be all along.

I made this move with my head held high as I gave the PD ten good months, admin-wise. I accomplished lots while in that office. Along with the aforementioned computer project, I also facilitated the testing of and hiring another ten or so police officers, attaining their required uniforms, equipment, and academy training. I even coordinated the purchase of a dozen new police cars.

Much of the admin job was boring and definitely not related to why I chose this career in the first place, but like the chief and I agreed early on, someone had to do it. For those ten months, I was that "someone" and I think I did the job pretty well.

Now, it's back to CID. Let's see what the end of '83 has in store for me, and the PD.

* * * * *

There was no one big investigation I was assigned or personally worked my first month or so back in CID. I spent my time routinely supervising the detectives, assigning them their cases, monitoring the still-successful Burglary Unit, helping to rearrange the evidence room and update the process for the logging of evidence, and otherwise doing what a detective sergeant does during the course of his normal every day (or night) work shift.

I recall during the latter months of '83, and not necessarily very fondly, of my first ever one-on-one experience with a local television news program. It stemmed from a man who was "flashing," or exposing himself, to young children at school bus stops in the mornings and in the afternoons in Bensalem. There was a partial description of the offender, and a partial description of his car, but not too much else to go on. There were at least three incidents attributed to this offender over the prior several weeks, and it had become an important investigation in Bensalem. I had assigned a detective to the case, and I arranged for our plainclothes Tac Squad to cruise around various bus stops during the kids' drop-off and pick-up times. When that didn't produce the desired result, meaning an arrest, and when yet another exposure incident occurred involving a child, Chief Viola decided to get the media involved. The BPD had to make sure the public knew about this case, for all the obvious reasons.

As this serial flasher was becoming bolder, having struck at least four times so far, and who knows what he could try to do next to a boy or girl, the chief decided to go proactive and get some television news coverage of this story. He wanted to put the limited information we had about the offender out there with the hopes that maybe a viewer could assist in identifying this guy. From his Philadelphia PD days, Rich Viola had become friendly with a local CBS-TV news reporter named Bill Baldini. The chief called him one afternoon and the results were all but immediate.

The next morning, less than a day after the fourth and most recent offense, Bill Baldini and his cameraman, Frank Goldstein, came to the BPD. Frank was a Bensalem resident and I came to know him and his wife and kids pretty well over the next few years. Bill, the reporter, initially interviewed the chief. Frank did some B-roll (usually silent filming of people routinely talking, walking, etc.) around the interior and exterior of our HQ. I was aware of all of this but I was pretty much just minding my own business and doing some paperwork at my desk while it was going on. However, when the reporter requested of the chief that he be authorized to travel to some of these bus stops where the actual flashings had occurred, Viola told him that he had just the CID sergeant to assist him with the rest of his story. In fact, I actually heard the chief say out loud as he was standing outside his door, "Jimmy Fitzgerald will take care of that, Bill. He's one of our new sergeants and he knows all about the case. Jimmy, where are you?"

And with that command/request of Viola's, I was to have my first direct on-screen television exposure as a police officer, or for that matter, as a human being. It would be an odd one, at least in regard to my first few seconds on the big screen.

"Uh, over here at my desk, Chief," I responded.

The chief then called me into his office and there was the reporter sitting comfortably in one of the chairs. Viola introduced me to his "friend," Bill. The reporter stood up, grabbed my right hand with his, and we shared a firm handshake.

I said, "Hi, I'm Jim Fitzgerald."

He replied, "Nice to meet you Sarge, I'm Bill Baldini."

He didn't have to say who he was, certainly not by name, certainly not to me. But, I thought it was nice that he did. This reporter was a well-respected TV news fixture in the Philadelphia area for almost twenty years at the time. In fact, as I channel-surfed a bit back in August of 1980, in the days after the on-duty death of my good friend and colleague Bob Yezzi, I recall Bill Baldini's very moving television tribute to the slain officer. Bill even commented in Viola's office that he saw Bob's picture in our PD lobby and recalled being here within hours after his death to cover the story. I complimented him on the piece he did back then, and he thanked me in return.

Chief Viola allowed us these few minutes for us to more or less feel each other out, to discuss my friend's death and Bill's follow-up report-age regarding it, but then he semi-politely reminded us that we have a potential child molester to catch and we should probably get to it.

Always the pragmatist was our chief. He was right in this instance to get us moving here. Time was crucial.

So, after clearly having already discussed with Viola what he'd like to do with this story, and Viola apparently having already agreed to it, Bill asked me if I could drive one of our CID cars around to some of the same school bus stops where these offenses had occurred. Frank, the cameraman, would be riding shotgun in the passenger seat to film me, the bus stops, and maybe even some kids if they happened to be around during the time we're driving. Bill told me, if it was alright, he would be asking me some questions at the same time. Viola was nodding his head in the affirmative as this was being discussed, so I simply said, "Sure, let's go do it."

So we did. The three of us drove around the Cornwells and Andalusia areas of Bensalem where a few of these offenses had occurred. The cameraman got his additional B-roll out the car window and of me as well as some cogent (I think) sound bites from me about the case, these types of offenders, how kids can protect themselves, what parents should be looking for, etc., as I was driving and answering the questions from Bill in the back. This whole filming-and-interviewing-while-driving car ride probably took no longer than an hour from beginning to end. Of course, we weren't actually hoping to catch the criminal in the act, but to just drive around and film in the areas where he's been doing his thing for the last few weeks. The two-person news crew agreed before long that they had enough footage and material so back to HQ we drove.

At HQ, I did another quick film interview with Bill at the entrance to the building, Frank assembled his gear, and we said a collective goodbye. As they were leaving, Bill told me it should be on the 5:00 news that evening, probably the lead story, as well as on again at 6:00 and 11:00. I thanked him, he thanked me, and off in the WCAU-TV10 news van he and the cameraman departed.

Okay, that wasn't too bad. Bill made me feel very comfortable when he interviewed me, when he had the mike up to my face, and it all felt sort of natural. I recall thinking that I probably came across okay for my first time, but I suppose watching it on TV later that day and that night will determine just how well I really did. But that would be a few hours away yet. I still have some work to do.

Hopefully, and most importantly, this news story will help in catching this flasher, this potential child molester. That's why the chief set up the whole thing. Let's hope it works.

This would be a first for me, that is, being interviewed on television. Perhaps I should call some people and let them know about it. They'd be mad if I didn't tell them. So, I called my mom, my three sisters, a few friends, and I made sure I was home with Eileen, four-year-old Sean, and one-year-old Dan, to watch the news at 5:00. In fact, to make sure we didn't miss anything, we tuned in to Channel 10 at about 4:55.

From the confines of my rec room I learned later that day how editing, timing, screenshots, voiceovers, and captioning or lack thereof, can be very influential on how a story or a person is presented to and perceived by a television viewing audience. And how first impressions really do mean something. This can be especially true when a film editor perhaps doesn't have all the time he or she would have liked to fully complete the editing process, like say when airtime is at 5:00 and he/she perhaps receives certain raw footage at around 3:30. Throw in a news producer and what he or she deems as important, and things can get lost, misplaced, or at the very least, confusing at times.

As it turns out, if you were watching Channel 10, the local Philadelphia CBS affiliate back then, right around 4:58PM, and you happened to see the everyday-at-the-same-time ten second promo for the upcoming News at Five, one would have seen the video and heard the following voiceover from Larry Kane, the well-known and very popular news anchor:

"Coming up at five… (pregnant pause) …there's a pervert on the loose in Bensalem Township. Do you know him? More in two minutes."

Okay, so the audio alone sounds fine, right? I agree. It's clear, succinct, and to the point. It captures and encompasses the gist of the story in only a few words and in less than ten seconds. I perhaps wouldn't have used the word "pervert," as it's not a legalistic or behavioral descriptor for this sort of offender, but that's a relatively minor issue.

However, as I was sitting in my paneled rec room and absorbing this micro-burst of sensory information on my 25" color television, it was the accompanying video of that ten second promo which proved most bothersome to me, and when viewed simultaneously with Larry Kane's spoken words it could be potentially confusing to anyone watching it.

Geez, it confused me, and I was there earlier today when they filmed it.

You see, the video was clearly of me, looking straight ahead while driving the unmarked car, and in this particular clip not saying a word. It was sort of B-roll within B-roll, if you will. But, when one then heard the anchorman stating "…there's a pervert on the loose…do you know him?" and at the same exact time it's the right side of MY friggin' face up there with no text captioning on the bottom of the screen providing my name, my title, that I was cop, or anything, one could confusingly conclude that…gulp…I was, in fact, said "pervert."

It was a very troublesome next minute and forty-five seconds for me until the 5:00 news actually began. I was hoping, literally praying, that they somehow got the rest of the story right and it would be precisely explained who the cop was and who the pervert was, and they weren't one in the same.

Anchorman Larry Kane did eventually fully explain things, but for whatever reason it wasn't the lead story. It came on maybe three minutes into the newscast. I was thinking...if anyone happened to see the promo but didn't bother watching the upcoming news show itself, or past the first few minutes, they would think the guy driving the car, that being Jim Fitzgerald (even if unnamed) was, in fact, the Bensalem pervert.

Oh, and by the way, I was watching CBS/WCAU at 10:58 that evening, just two minutes before the 11:00 news was to start, and they showed the same promo. Geez, didn't the editor and/or producer have time to fix it by then?

Later that evening and the next day I talked to some of my BPD colleagues and even friends and family members. Most complimented me as to my on-air presence and I thanked them. But a few who saw the promo beforehand also thought the same as me. They knew me. They knew I certainly wasn't a pervert. They were hoping for the viewer's sake (and my sake too) that who the pervert REALLY was, and who he was not, would be clarified during the news story itself. It was, thankfully.

A few friends and work colleagues with wry senses of humor had some fun with the whole thing, and I wound up eventually laughing about it too. But at first, I gotta say, it was a bit upsetting to me.

I know in the long run this whole matter wasn't that big of a deal. Perhaps it bothered me more than it should have initially. It was my first time ever being interviewed for a television news show and I wanted to come across the best I could. I think I did during the actual piece itself. It was just those two promos, two minutes before the 5:00 and 11:00 newscasts which threw me off, and could lead some to think that the guy on the screen, driving the car, was the actual "pervert."

I eventually got over it.

Most importantly, in a week or two, the REAL pervert was identified and arrested. The newscast did result in some positive lead information from a viewer who first called the TV station, then the BPD. One of our detectives ran with the new info, and ultimately did a great job in investigating, arresting, and achieving the conviction of the Bensalem school bus stop serial flasher. The guy never physically touched any children, but what he was doing was bad enough and it certainly could have escalated to more serious crimes. He was off the streets for a while thanks to this arrest. That was a good thing.

In closing to my on-air TV news initiation, the above incident wouldn't be the only odd and bothersome interaction of mine in dealing with the media over the course of my later career. There would be many more to follow, of both the print and electronic variety, and even at the national level. These problematic interactions would encompass different issues, but nonetheless with occasional similarly disturbing results. (More on additional odd media incidents in JCM Book III.)

*****

As 1983 was coming to an end, one other news story concerning Bensalem Township was garnering its own headlines and TV news coverage. Not just in Bucks County either, but throughout the entire Philadelphia news-reading or news-watching region. Bill Baldini would be covering this soon-to-be-breaking "Big Story" too. His cameraman, Frank Goldstein, would actually play a critical role in it too…in the most bizarre of ways.

But first, let's go back to 1982, for just a bit.

The much anticipated trial of Bensalem Township Supervisor Stephen Kelly and his brother Michael, both arrested in early January of 1982 by Chief Viola on various state drug-related charges, which were then dropped and the two of them subsequently federally indicted, was originally slated to begin in late August of 1982. The jury had been picked and both sides were raring to go. The co-prosecutors for the government were William Carr and Frank Sherman.

On the eve of the trial, Stephen Kelly's Bensalem-based lawyer, Barry Denker, argued in a pre-trial suppression hearing against the admissibility of the three telephone calls which were recorded between the Kellys and the cooperating witness (the auto mechanic) in the case. Denker's argument before the court suggested that the witness was "coerced" to record the calls by the police and for that reason they were not "consensual" and should not be admissible. So, the judge had to make a decision.

Anita DiBartolomeo, of the *Bucks County Courier Times*, filed the following news story.

The headline read, "**Judge won't allow tapes in Kelly trial.**"
The story read, in part:

"Philadelphia - A federal judge ruled here yesterday that three potentially crucial secretly-recorded
telephone conversations in the drug conspiracy case
against... Supervisor Kelly cannot be used as evidence
at the trial.

"In doing so, U.S. District Judge Edward Cahn
reversed a ruling he made Monday night that the tapes
would be allowed as evidence in the trial of the 34-year-
old supervisor and his 31-year-old brother, Michael.

"At the time, however, Cahn indicated he had reservations about whether ..., a Levittown automobile
repairman and self-described drug user, voluntarily
consented to wiretap a Jan. 2 (1982) conversation with
Stephen Kelly and two others with Michael on Jan. 1.
The conversations were allegedly about a drug deal.

"...Cahn, however, left open the possibility that he
might change his mind about the tapes again today after
listening to oral arguments from attorneys...."
(End of article.)

Judge Cahn never did rechange his mind yet again, ruling ultimately
to suppress the use of the recorded calls as evidence. In view of this, the
trial was immediately halted at the behest of Assistant United States
Attorneys Carr and Sherman. The two co-prosecutors requested and
were granted a postponement for purposes of appealing the judge's
just rendered, or rerendered, legal decision. They knew without the
recorded phone calls containing talk by the Kellys of threats and drug-
deal transacting that their case was not as strong as it could be. So, the
just-chosen jury was summarily dismissed and the trial was put off
until the Pennsylvania Third Circuit Court of Appeals could rule on
the matter.

And...it would take a while, which brings us back to 1983.

The Kellys' federal trial didn't resume until December 12, 1983. It
would proceed, in fact, with the three tape recorded drug and threat
laden telephone conversations being heard by the jury. Barry Denker's
motion of suppression, on behalf of his client, Stephen Kelly, and Judge
Cahn's decision in his favor, was overturned on appeal by the Third

Circuit. The appellate court ruled that the calls were consensual and not at all coerced, so they were free to be played for the jury to hear during the trial.

Before we get back to the Bensalem Trial-of-the-Century (even though it actually took place in Philadelphia), in an attempt to more fully grasp the nuances regarding this case and this legal proceeding, not to mention Township politics in the early to mid-1980s, it would be beneficial for the reader to better understand one of the key characters in what I previously referred to as the Township's ongoing "passion play." That character is Bensalem resident Barry Denker, Stephen Kelly's attorney. Coincidently, or not, he would also be the defense attorney to generally the worst of the worst of the criminal world in the Philadelphia area during this period.

Barry Denker could best be described during these years as an early prototype of the Saul Goodman character from the AMC television series *Breaking Bad* (2008-2013) and *Better Call Saul* (premiering in 2015). Not necessarily in physical appearance, but certainly by way of Denker's legal and illegal dealings and undertakings at the peak (or some would say depths) of his lawyerly career.

Yes, if you were a Philly area mobster, outlaw biker, drug dealer, or for that matter a local politician charged with, let's say, P2P distribution and drug conspiracy, it was Bensalem attorney Barry Denker that you "better call." He didn't come cheap, but he did have a very good track record in terms of his clients "walking," and that's why these guys tended to hire him and pay him the big bucks; many times in brown paper bags containing carefully wrapped wads of $20 and $50 bills.

Allow me at this time to borrow the words of the *Philadelphia Inquirer* staff writer Alfred Lubrano in describing Mr. Denker from a 1996 "article" he wrote.

It reads, in part:

> "Barry H. Denker's life had two acts – first as a corrupt, fur-coated lawyer who wore a wire and helped convict three Philadelphia judges on the take, the last a pseudonymous patron of American crafts in the South.
>
> "...At 6'2" and more than 300 pounds, Mr. Denker cut an impressive figure in the criminal courts of Philadelphia during the 1970s and '80s handling about 500 cases a year. He sported a full-length fur coat, favored

cowboy boots, and disbursed enough cash to grease the wheels of justice, making sure they turned his way.

"Typically, Mr. Denker would offer judges money in exchange for favorable decisions, or bribe court officials to steer his cases away from the most pro-prosecution judges, investigators said.

"…Mr. Denker decided to become an undercover informant in August 1986 after investigators taped him bribing a state parole agent.

"One of his primary contributions to the city involved wearing a wire and collecting evidence against three judges whom Mr. Denker had identified as corrupt: Kenneth S. Harris, Thomas N. Shiomos and Herbert R. Cain Jr. In the fall of 1986, Mr. Denker secretly taped all three.

"One such recording captures Mr. Denker talking to Cain about a case: 'I want a not-guilty on this one,' Mr. Denker is overheard saying. Cain complied, investigators said, soon dismissing the case after accepting Mr. Denker's $1,500.

"Eventually Mr. Denker testified against all three, who were all convicted of extortion in 1988.

"Mr. Denker received a death threat, so authorities moved him to Albuquerque (New Mexico), where he ran an art gallery…."

(End of article.)

Ironically, after being sentenced to a year and a day in prison for his various crimes, attorney Barry Denker wound up in the same U.S. city in which the *Breaking Bad/Better Call Saul* television series were based.

What are the odds…?

Is this a classic case of art imitating life? Did the creator of these two TV shows ever actually meet Barry Denker at his Albuquerque gallery and then decide to base the "Saul" character on him?

I don't know for sure, but it certainly wouldn't surprise me.

(Of course, Barry Denker is far from the only corrupt lawyer to ever practice his craft in the U. S. But the similarities between the fictional Saul and the non-fictional Barry are certainly noteworthy.)

Back to the trial….

On December 30, 1983, by whatever varied machinations Barry Denker employed in the Philadelphia federal courthouse, he and his client attained the results for which they were hoping so desperately. In a jury trial presided over by Judge Cahn, Stephen Kelly, as well as his brother Michael, were acquitted of all charges.

Amazingly, Saul Goodman, I mean, Barry Denker, did it again!

As 1983 was drawing to its close, the stage of the seemingly never-ending Bensalem passion play was now re-set, if not soon to be re-cast. The newly acquitted Stephen Kelly would be triumphantly returning to his position as Bensalem Township Supervisor (he had never officially resigned) the first week of January. This, almost two years to the day after he was arrested by Chief Viola, the man he previously threatened to fire once he had enough votes to do so. Now, it was all but certain that Kelly was ready to resume his place on the Board of Supervisors and carry out his threat.

If it's possible to make this "play" of passion even more interesting, as township politics and recent election results would have it, ousted Deputy Chief Ted Zajac's wife, Patricia, was now herself a newly elected township supervisor. Amazingly, in his early police career, it was Ted's father on the Board of Supervisors. Now, it was his wife soon to be in the same elected position.

What a public-service oriented family are those Zajacs! And with her there was a new majority on the Board with Kelly slated to be at its helm, starting the first week of the New Year.

Not just was Stephen Kelly back, but he was soon to be back in charge, soon to be the head of a 4-1 voting majority juggernaut.

Talk about rising from the ashes....

So, what would all of this mean to the Bensalem Township Police Department?

To Chief Richard Viola?

To Capt. Jack Robinson?

To Sgt. James Fitzgerald?

To other hard-working, by-the-book, police officers?

To the present and future ne'er-do-wells plying their trade in Bensalem Township?

The answers to these questions would be coming shortly and they wouldn't be pretty. Not for Viola, not for Robinson, not for me, or for many BPD officers and employees.

I'm not sure about the various ne'er-do-wells in and around Bensalem Township. I could certainly guess though.

New Year's Day of 1984 and the weeks, months, and years beyond were ominously foreboding for many within Bensalem and its police department, me included. What would this New Year be bringing to me, to my law enforcement colleagues, to the township as a whole?

None of us knew. We hadn't a clue. It was right around the corner, but we'd all have to wait for the ball to drop on New Year's Eve. Shortly afterwards, the shoe would drop...and no doubt kick many of us in our collective butts.

Again, it wouldn't be pretty. No...not at all!

(+ Bonus Chapter 37a)

Part 5 -
The Dark Side Strikes Back

Chapter Thirty-Eight

Because New Year's Day fell on a Monday that year, the usual meeting of the Bensalem Township Board of Supervisors occurred twenty-four hours later, on Tuesday evening. Some of us would later half-kiddingly/half-seriously look back at January 3, 1984, as "a date which will live in...idiocy." No, I wouldn't dare compare it to another date from 1941 which truly lives in "infamy," as per President Franklin D. Roosevelt at the time. Instead, for what was about to be unleashed on this third night of the New Year, what I would witness in my office space that very evening, where it would all eventually lead, and what it would ultimately cost the taxpayers of Bensalem Township, "idiocy" was clearly the operative word here.

This idiocy, at least for me, initially reared its ugly head on my first night of a 3P-11P shift on New Year's Eve, still several days before the Big Meeting. While everyone on the BPD, including me, had been wondering since the Kelly acquittal the day before just what would be in store for our agency once the nascent political regime took over in the New Year, I had my first taste of how it would affect me on the last night of the Old Year.

On that evening, as many civilians were getting ready to celebrate the end of one year and the start of another, some of us dedicated public servants were at work. While doing so at my desk in CID, I noticed from afar one of the veteran patrol sergeants quietly approaching me. His name was Bob Dechant. Upon stopping alongside my work area, and after carefully looking over his left and right shoulders to make sure we were alone, he proceeded at low oratory volume to advise me that he had something important to share with me. Before I could even respond to his barely audible advisory Dechant went on to state that just a short while ago he had overheard two detectives (he identified them) in a private conversation. As they had mentioned me by name, he thought I should be made aware of what they were planning to do.

Without bothering to look over either of my own shoulders, I simply glanced up and him from my chair and replied in normal oratory volume, "So...?

With that single syllable response, expressed as an interrogative, the low-talking Sgt. Dechant was assured he could now continue. And he did.

I knew that both of the detectives Dechant identified were closely aligned with the former (yet possibly soon to be resurrected) Deputy Chief Zajac. I also knew this sergeant standing beside my desk to have also been previously aligned with Team Zajac. However, to his credit, he exhibited at least a modicum of workplace survival skills in that he was deferential and respectful to Viola during the past several years. Dechant knew how to play the game, in other words, and very well I might add.

Back to Sgt. Dechant's reason for being here, and with his verbal volume never increasing above that of a loud whisper, while still peering cautiously around the office area several times during our talk, he eventually got to the gist of what he allegedly overheard. He told me these two CID guys were talking in the patrol squad room about how they were going to hire a lawyer and file a grievance with the Police Benevolent Association (PBA), and maybe even before the courts in Doylestown, regarding the sergeant's test that I had taken and passed some twenty-plus months before. Dechant added he wasn't sure as to what the two of them were specifically referencing but that they seemed adamant and committed to the fact that something was wrong with the test because they and others didn't get promoted from it and, apparently, because I did. The sergeant quickly aborted his commentary when he thought he heard footsteps approaching us. "That's it, I'm outta here, good luck, Fitz," he muttered as he rapidly retreated from the CID area.

I responded for anyone to hear, "Yeah, right, Bob. Oh, and a Happy New Year to you, too!"

Okay...this alleged information makes for an interesting end to calendar year 1983. But there was more of the same yet to come.

Making the end of the year even more interesting, about an hour later, when the 9P-7A squad came in, I had yet another visitor from the patrol division. It was Sgt. Pansy, the former detective sergeant with whom I debated a few years back about whether I could keep a .38 in my boot during an undercover drug purchase. He had been transferred to the patrol division sometime after Viola took over. On this night, he walked over to my desk and related that he had something important to tell me.

I again said, "So…?

Yes, Sgt. Pansy that evening also heard the same thing about a potential legal maneuver by some officers to invalidate the promotional exam from which I made sergeant. He wasn't quite as secretive or paranoid as Dechant about telling me what he did just a short while ago, but remarkably the message was virtually the same.

Okay…so what do I have here now?

Two separate patrol sergeants, both previously (still?) aligned with the former Deputy Chief, telling me essentially three nights before the well-publicized Big Meeting that the results from an over a year and a half ago exam were about to be challenged by these two detectives, who also happen to be aligned with the former Deputy Chief. The sergeants conveniently didn't know any specific grounds for the purported challenge, but they just wanted to advise me, "sergeant to sergeant" about what they had innocently heard.

Upon receiving the second set of talking points that evening, I somewhat sarcastically thanked Sergeant Pansy for going out of his way from his otherwise busy schedule to tell me this very important information. I mentioned to him as he was leaving that I didn't concern myself with rumors around this place and that when and if they become a reality I would respond accordingly. Oh, and I wished him Happy New Year too, but I don't think he heard me.

After the shift ended and I was driving home that evening for a quiet midnight celebration with my wife, I found myself not all that concerned with the nebulous "facts" of what I had just heard from these two different sources. I knew my promotional results were legit and no one would or could change the outcome. They may try, but I assure you, they would not succeed in taking away my stripes, certainly not without a fierce battle from me.

On my short commute home during the last hour of 1983 I came to realize, especially after the second sergeant visited me this evening, that this was a calculated move on the Dark Side's part. It was directed, if not ordered, to these two sergeants from the almost-in-charge-again top of the former (maybe future) management pyramid. What it reinforced to me was what I had already been warned by others. That is, I was going to be in the crosshairs of the new regime once it returned to power in just a few nights.

The more I thought about it, the more sense it made.

I was promoted under Viola.

I worked well under Viola.

I was successful under Viola.

In effect, I made him and the BPD look very good (and actually be very good) during that timeframe.

The more I thought about it, I knew this could not stand...not with the new regime about to take over.

Jim Fitzgerald as a sergeant in CID, or in any managerial position within the BPD, not to mention also as the newly elected Vice-President of the Bensalem PBA, would not sit (or stand) well with the new, actually old, top brass when/if they eventually retake the place.

But wait! Is there a ray of hope on the horizon? Someone out there to run interference for me, with me, against whatever gauntlet the new/old Team may have me run?

Sure, there was still Chief Viola and Captain Robinson. They had to be the bigger targets than me, right? Plus, they wouldn't abandon me, right?

I was wondering, what were they hearing about all of this as the calendar pages from 1983 were being discarded for the new calendar pages of 1984? What were they doing? What were they saying?

Their silence at this particular time, for me, was deafening. But in retrospect, I understood their predicaments too.

My next few 3-11 shifts were routine through that holiday weekend. I was the only boss around CID on those days, with just one or two detectives working but who chose to not be around the office very much. I didn't care one way or the other as long as no new case was breaking or no one walked into HQ having made a prior appointment with one of them.

However, when I arrived to work on Tuesday, January 3, just before 3:00, I found the place to be abuzz with activity. There was something definitely different about this frenzied activity than on previous days.

Upon approaching my desk, I heard for the first time from one of the secretaries just what had happened. She told me that Chief Viola had just been taken out of police HQ in a wheelchair to an awaiting ambulance. It seems that shortly before I got there, the Chief called a meeting with his captains. During that meeting, when he went to sit down in his big black executive-style chair in his office, it somehow rolled away from him, and down he went flat on his back, his backside, or both. Regardless of whatever body part hit the floor, his spine was now apparently out of whack and he needed help from his captains to even stand up. He couldn't walk very well and he needed assistance being placed into the wheelchair by the responding paramedics. They even put a neck brace on him, I was told. So, by the time I came in to CID that fateful day, the Chief was already gone and at the hospital.

What the hell does THIS mean?

After settling in at my desk a bit, I walked into Jack Robinson's office and he was in a noticeably sour mood. He was there when the Chief injured himself as he was in Viola's office when it happened. He related this information but other than that he wasn't saying much to me or anyone else. Detective Ken Hopkins also stopped in Jack's office as his day-work shift was just ending. We commented among ourselves several times that we hoped Viola was going to be alright. The three of us slowly changed the subject, however, to commenting among ourselves regarding the fact that tonight's Supervisors' meeting would determine the immediate and long-term future of the three of us and others, as well as that of the PD itself. It probably wouldn't be good for the three of us, Jack stated more than once. Not for the PD either, Ken stated more than once. I agreed with each of them…more than once.

Captain Robinson specifically told me to "be scarce" tonight and to not sit around CID and wait for "all this shit to flush downhill." Either go home early, he advised, or go out in a CID car and cruise around or whatever, but I shouldn't stay in here as it may get ugly. I nodded my head that I heard him but I didn't verbally respond to Jack's suggestion one way or another.

Before long it was 4:00 and Jack's and Ken's shifts were over. We said our collective goodbyes, they wished me luck, I wished them the same, and they left the building to go home. As Captain Traenkle was nowhere to be found, and who knows where Lt. Hughes was, I was now there on my own, the only representative of BPD management in the place. That wouldn't last long though. Bosses and others would be crawling around this place like cockroaches shortly after tonight's Big Meeting. I was pretty sure of that earlier in my shift and it was very loudly confirmed later in my shift.

Quite frankly, I didn't know what I'd be doing that night when the edicts from above would filter down to the rest of us. However, there was a morbid curiosity about me as to what would happen, how it would happen, and who would be the players involved in it all. So, what do I do? I wasn't about to run away and hide from these people. That's never been my style, and it certainly wouldn't be that night.

But I was assured after the events of this afternoon that neither Chief Viola nor Captain Robinson would be in CID tonight. Captain Traenkle wouldn't show his face either. It would be just me, Sergeant Fitzgerald, the now highest ranking member of the so-called Team Viola left in the building.

And so it came to pass...

I didn't attend the meeting upstairs, but starting at 7:00 I could hear it from my desk chair down in CID. There was lots of cheering, applauding, yelling, and foot stomping, much like jubilant home team fans at an athletic event of some sort. But it wasn't an athletic stadium or a game or match of any kind taking place above me. It was a scheduled meeting of five local politicians and township officials with numerous members of the community in the audience. Also in that audience, I learned later, were approximately twenty of my fellow police officers. I read in the next day's newspaper or heard from somewhere that when Stephen Kelly, just recently acquitted of federal drug conspiracy charges, was introduced as the new Chairman of the Board of Supervisors, there was a standing ovation for him, including all of the cops in attendance.

What the...?!

So it was police officers I was hearing through the upstairs meeting room floor/downstairs CID ceiling, loudly cheering for a guy who had just beat federal charges of conspiring to distribute P2P? This because he was about to vote in their favor, or their ex-boss's favor, and this is where their collective loyalty now lies?

Has the world, or at least Bensalem Township, turned upside down?

Yes, through his later-proven corrupt defense attorney, Stephen Kelly beat the rap. I get it! And, yes, I'm a firm believer in the legal principle of "innocent until proven guilty." Kelly wasn't proven guilty so now he's back in town and undertaking his sworn duties as an elected official. Fine! But do my fellow police officers have to give the man a standing ovation and sing his praises now that he's Top Dog in Bensalem politics once again? Really? I guess because of what they surmise he's about to do, and with those cops about to directly benefit from what they surmise he's about to do, they'll continue cheering loudly and euphorically like rabid fans rooting for their hometown baseball team on opening day.

For me though, it was a cold winter evening, literally and figuratively. Before long the coldness and frigidness would be enveloping me as I'd be learning more about what occurred just about ten vertical feet above my head in the same building, but in what seemed to be another world; a true Bizarro World as I saw it at the time.

In a 4-1 vote, with Kelly and Mrs. Ted (aka Patricia) Zajac comprising two of those votes, the following was so decreed:

- Chief Viola was suspended immediately without pay, with intent to fire,
- Captain Robinson was demoted to lieutenant,
- Deputy Chief Zajac would be un-fired and brought back to run the department,
- An official investigation would be launched into non-specified administrative wrong-doings and alleged criminal activities of now-suspended Chief Viola during his two years in office, with lawyer Barry Denker to be retained as counsel for the investigators;
- Now-Lt. Robert Eckert (my former patrol sergeant) would head the Viola investigation team, and his wife Theresa Eckert appointed as Tax Collector at the same time;
- The detective who shot off his gun at the bar months ago and was fired, was officially reinstated,
- The detective who was accused of mishandling drug money months ago and was fired, was officially reinstated.

(I will add here that this detective had appealed his earlier firing, took it to civil court in Doylestown, and a judge found his termination to be unwarranted. It was subsequently ruled he should get his job back. The Bensalem solicitor initially appealed the judge's decision and that is where this legal matter stood as of late 1983. That appeal was dropped and he was back on the BPD, as a detective, effective on this very night.)

At about 8:45 that evening, from the two different entrances into CID, it was as if a crowd of twenty or so English football hooligans was descending into the room. A number of them were taking turns high-fiving each other and were very loudly repeating proclamations such as, "We're back and now it's our f**kin' turn," "Heads are gonna start rollin'," "It's payback time," "Happy f**kin' days are here again," and "F**k Viola," to list just a few of the rantings and ravings that I could readily decipher through the unbridled and unchecked enthusiasm running amuck throughout the Detective Division at this time. I remained at my desk, with paperwork spread in front of me and at least looking busy. For the most part, I was ignored by the revelers. I wasn't one of them in spirit or philosophy and was actually glad I was being overlooked. But at the same time I wanted to observe and take in all that was playing out before me. I was a witness to Bensalem history here tonight, whether I liked how it was unfolding or not.

Before too long, while many in the crowd were still congratulating and applauding each other and the events of the evening, one of their fellow celebrants, a detective, seemed to be looking around the office for something. He eventually found it. It was an audio cassette player. A few of these were maintained in CID for sometimes interviewing people, listening to tapes of interviews, statements, dictating reports, and the like. I observed him as he plugged it in, turned it on, and brought it over to the center of the room where he proceeded to insert a cassette tape into it that he took out of his jacket pocket. I was watching this guy the whole time out of the corner of my eye and wondering just what the hell he could be doing here and for what purpose. Well, I was soon to find out, and once the sound started I would know that it wasn't a recording having anything to do with a suspect's confession or admission to a crime.

Instead, it was a cassette with at least one song off a then-several month old record album. The officer did his best to quiet everyone down and announced the song's start as if he was a disc jockey introducing a brand new "hot hit" to his listening audience. When the crowd of officers heard the first few bars of the song that he had obviously cued up beforehand, the noise in the room was reduced to a low murmur. It took the better part of ninety seconds to get there but when the chorus finally reverberated out of the cassette player's tinny little speaker for the first time, everyone started cheering and chanting repeatedly in unison, "inn-o-cent, inn-o-cent, inn-o-cent," with some simultaneously throwing punches in the air and others karate-style kicking the walls.

The song was Billy Joel's *An Innocent Man*.

As an aside here regarding the aforementioned song, I don't think the sing-along crowd realized at the time that the lyrics refer to an unspecified man wrongly accused of something of a very personal nature by his lover. The accusation/allegation seemingly has nothing to do with legal, philosophical, or ideological issues. But that didn't really matter to the musically engaged cultists at that otherwise highly-charged moment in time in the CID office.

I guessed early on that the "innocent man" so referenced in the lyrics was supposed to represent certain specific innocent "men" in the course of this performance by Mr. Joel of his song. Those men, of course, would be Kelly, Zajac, and the two detectives who were brought back into the township and departmental fold on this bizarre January evening.

I actually liked the song then, and still do now after all these years. Interestingly, and perhaps not surprising, I can't listen to *An Innocent Man* anywhere or at any time without remembering where I was one of the first times I ever heard it. That being, at my former CID desk, essentially surrounded by a group of on-duty and off-duty law enforcement zealots, all celebrating the return of an accused, but recently acquitted, P2P distributor/co-conspirator, and the Deputy Chief who he now reappointed to run "his" department.

After all, as of that night, they were "innocent" men.

For the rest of my shift that evening, until 11:00, I remained at my desk, work in hand, observing all of this bluster and macho collective-aggrandizing. It was scary to some degree to me. Not in a personal sense, but in an unruly mob sense, make that even in an almost cult-like sense. It's as if their Fearless Leader, be it Kelly or Zajac or both, along with Lt. Bob Eckert, Lt. Bob Hughes, lawyer Barry Denker, and others all now present in CID, had just risen from the ashes, each like a phoenix, and was now poised to deliver them to the promised land, wherever that was and whatever that may represent to them as individuals or as a whole. It was strange and almost hypnotic in a sense watching these guys I knew, some better than others, prance, preen, and posture in such a manner, with even musical accompaniment for a portion of it. I don't even think they had been drinking. Maybe a few of them, but I wasn't about to pull out the Breathalyzer at any time on this night to test them. Not my job, not my problem, nor did I care.

Surrealistic doesn't begin to accurately describe this precise episode in my life. It's as if I was on LSD watching live scenes from the movie *A Clockwork Orange* which had been redirected by Federico Fellini and now starring the Marx Brothers AND the Three Stooges, with the barroom scene from the original *Star Wars* movie as the backdrop. That is how I felt taking in this mind-numbing display of approximately twenty adult men, some in full police uniform with guns at their sides, engaging in this almost tribal-like ritualistic behavior. The only things missing were a bonfire, speaking in tongues, and human sacrifices. However, the night wasn't over yet.

I recall after a while watching the reinstated detective who was fired for mishandling the drug monies pull himself away from the madding crowd and sit down at one of the IBM Selectric typewriters in CID. There he pounded out three or four relatively short memos. Two other detectives stood next to him to make sure no one (I guess me) could look over his shoulders and observe what was being typed. They must have been very important and for-your-eyes-only memos because when he was done his typing the detective opened the lid on the electric typewriter, removed the ribbon cartridge, and took it with him. He wanted to make sure no one, no how, knew what was just typed, even prohibiting a potentially curious person from later pulling the cartridge apart and reading word-by-word in linear fashion the message so imbedded on the black ribbon. One of those memos made it immediately to the departmental administrative book maintained in the patrol squad room. It announced Viola's suspension and Robinson's demotion. The other two or three never did surface, or at least I never saw them.

With the shift over, I was home in my kitchen by 11:15 that night. I did something unusual for me after a work night, especially when on my own with everyone else asleep. I cracked open a cold beer; only one I told myself at first, just to take the edge off and to maybe help me in some way better assimilate what I just experienced. As the beer cleared my palate and the alcohol disseminated into my blood stream, I realized it really didn't help me figure out or understand anything more about tonight. No surprise there. But I suppose it didn't hurt either. I knew the next few days and weeks would be trying for me, but I had to go in and do my job, whatever it may be now under the new, or is it old, regime.

Maybe I should consider pursuing some other options too. Let me think about this some more...okay, with one more beer.

With the first sip of that second beer, it hit me. Geez...how the hell did it ever come to this? What the hell went wrong? Is this the future of the BPD? If so, what is MY future?

Not a bright one, I convinced myself under the influence of now almost two whole beers.

After finishing that second beer, I went to bed. I slept well that night, and I awoke with a clear head and a clear plan. Well, sort of....

Oh yeah, and as a long-term result of that next day plan, there would be one more strategic playing of a certain song in the CID office at some point in the future. It would be another DJ that next time. The tune would be an oldie by then, but still very appropriate to the moment in which it was performed, and also for the person it would represent.

The very last stanza of the song sums it up well:

> "Some people hope for a miracle cure
> Some people just accept the world as it is
> But I'm not willing to lay down and die
> Because I am an innocent man."
> (Billy Joel, *An Innocent Man*)

I decided the morning of January 4, 1984, that Jim Fitzgerald wasn't going to "lay down and die." Not for these people, not for no one. I realized at the same time there would be no "miracle cure" nor would I "just accept the world as it is," at least as it related to the world of the BPD. Someone, some group, some entity, would have to step up and find that "cure."

And some would....

Maybe these lyrics aren't that unrelated to this situation after all. Well, at least the last stanza.

Thanks for the inspirational words, Billy.

Chapter Thirty-Nine

The next day, Wednesday, the 4th of January, I was scheduled to work the last of my 3P-11P tour of duty for that week. I was wondering the whole morning and early afternoon what I would find when I arrived at the police station that day. Of course, the *Bucks County Courier Times* had the whole "Viola Fired/Zajac Rehired" headline and article on the front page, above the fold. The article listed basic information of which I was already aware from the night before, along with a few quotes of various people and a photo or two, but I knew there was much still to find out about all that was happening at my place of work.

I talked to a few of my trusted police buddies that day on the phone, but no one knew a whole lot more than me about what was going on at the PD. Those in-the-know would be working today but I didn't want to call them at the police station because they wouldn't be able to talk, or at least not talk without a fear of being overheard by the numerous spies, or at this point, overt human listening posts dedicated to protecting their newly re-crowned king. So, I'd have to wait.

When I finally walked into CID at around 2:55, it was a very strange sight to see Viola's office now occupied by the former but now present and I suppose future Chief, Ted Zajac. I guess he was still technically a Deputy Chief, but as before, everyone was once again calling him "Chief." Strangely, as I strolled by his open office door, I heard him loudly bellow from his desk for all to hear.

"JIM FITZGERALD! HOW ARE YOU TODAY?" This was a tradition of Zajac's that began on this, his first day back on the job. He would do this to me it seemed several times per month whenever he'd see me in a hallway or walking by his office. Sometimes it would be my name with a generic rhetorical question after it. Other times, it was just my name he would yell out loud. It was an odd if not annoying habit of Zajac's that he developed now that he was in charge once again. I never heard him do it with people he seemingly liked or trusted. In response, at least initially, I would answer in normal tone and volume with a

397

simple "I'm fine" or "Hi," depending on the perceived level of fake discourse with me the DC desired.

When I finally had a chance that afternoon to talk in semi-privacy with Jack Robinson in his office I told him about the off-the-chart festivities I witnessed the preceding night. What bothered him most was that Stephen Kelly and Barry Denker somehow made their way into the PD, not to mention into CID. I agreed but told him there wasn't much I could have done about it since it seemed they were specifically invited and actually accompanied by the Deputy Chief himself. Jack simply commented that he'll "duly note" it. I'm not sure exactly what he meant by that and I let it go.

Hmmm...maybe I should start duly noting some things too around here. (Fortunately, I did - for reasons important to back then and for reasons important to the eventual writing of this book.)

Jack then brought me up to date on the latest news around the PD, or at least that of which he was aware so far. He told me that after some difficulty this morning the new regime finally found a key to the chief's office and gained entry to it. (Viola had a new lock installed when he first took over.) One or more detectives packed all of Viola's personal items from his desk and what was hanging on his walls and put them in several boxes. They were delivered to him, Jack believed, by Lt. Hughes at Viola's house just a few hours later. Viola's gun and badge were officially taken from him at the same time by Hughes after he "served" him with some sort of official township papers demanding same. I'm not sure down the line who wound up being issued those two items. The badge said "Chief" on it, but I don't think Zajac would be carrying it...yet. Even he wouldn't be that ballsy...yet. But, who knows? Nothing would have surprised me at this point at the BPD.

I actually WAS surprised just a few minutes later when now-Lieutenant Robinson began to tell me of now-civilian Rich Viola's current employment status. I was all ears. I had to be as Robinson was talking to me in very low volume. He told me, among other developments that day, he was specifically instructed by DC Zajac not to close the door on his office for any reason while he (Robinson) was in it. So, from this point on, if we wanted to talk about what was happening, it had to be done in very quiet tones.

Geez...I have a newly-recommissioned Deputy Chief who now yells to me, and a newly-decommissioned Lieutenant who now whispers to me. If I had been wearing a hearing-aid back then, I would have been readjusting its sensitivity level every few minutes.

Back to that surprising information...Robinson went on to advise me that although Viola was suspended without pay at the Big Meeting the night before, probably sometime around 7:30PM, what happened around 2:30PM earlier that same day would trump the later action and have a long-ranging effect for him as well as the township. That was because Viola had already called the Township Manager yesterday afternoon and begun the process of "going out IOD."

Virtually all first-responders in the U. S. know what the three letters "IOD" represent. It's something to be avoided at all costs in one's career. However, if it does happen, it's good to know the policy and protocols which would kick in. Then-Chief, now-civilian Viola apparently knew of them too.

The initials stand for "Injured On Duty." Yes, being placed in injured on duty status can be the result of an officer being shot, being stabbed, being struck by a car (Officer Tony Rihl was IOD for almost two years after he was hit by the same car which killed Bob Yezzi), or, as I would learn, it can be for falling off of or out of one's chair in an office. As long as the officer of any rank is officially "on the clock," whether on patrol or at his or her desk job or somewhere in between, and if he or she is in the "official performance of his/her duties," if that person gets hurt in any way, shape, or form, the same exact benefits are available for as long as it takes to be cured, healed, mended, or fixed. Oh, and one other very important benefit, at least in Pennsylvania, was that an officer on IOD status could not be fired.

What this all means was that despite Viola being suspended without pay pending termination the prior evening, once he filed his IOD paperwork regarding his verifiable injury which occurred BEFORE the official suspension, and with the appropriately submitted doctor reports supporting said injuries, a whole separate state-governed compensatory system would kick in. In Viola's case, he would now be receiving approximately eighty percent of his former full gross pay, at a significantly lesser tax rate (as by state law), and an additional stipend through worker's compensation. In summary, this means despite being suspended without pay only a few hours later, because he was injured on-duty PRIOR to that, he'd now be bringing home even more money per "paycheck" than before his injury. And, his health insurance benefits would remain in full effect for the duration of his IOD status. With injured vertebrae, damaged disks, a nagging sacroiliac, or some combination of these ailments, it could mean being in an injured status for a potentially long time. Viola knew it, the Township Manager knew it, and no doubt the Zajac/Kelly team now knew it.

So…was Viola smart like a fox and was this a clever counter-move on his part?

Or…was Viola legitimately injured?

Could it be both?

Did Viola have advance knowledge of his pending politically-oriented suspension set to occur on the evening of the 3rd with the chair accident coincidently happening as it did on the afternoon of the same day?

I didn't know the answers to these questions.

As a memo was placed in the administrative book on this first full day of Zajac's retaking of his long-sought crown, I would not have the opportunity to ask Viola about any of this. You see, the new memo hereby ordered everyone in the department, staff and sworn officers alike, under the threat of suspension and/or termination, to cease and desist any and all interaction with the former Chief. If an officer or employee was known to be talking to Rich Viola either in person or by phone, he/she could be summarily fired. At least that's what it said in the memo.

So much for the First Amendment in Bensalem, I suppose. I could perhaps see such a prohibition against talking to Viola while on-duty, but during off-duty time too? I mean, he hadn't been arrested or charged with any crimes. This was just administrative and political nonsense.

Regardless of the basic constitutional issues here, Jack and I agreed that Viola was too much of a hot potato right now and that it would be wise not to contact him at all, whether in person or by telephone. We didn't rule out that Viola's house may be under surveillance by Dark Side operatives or even his phone tapped. So, I refrained from contacting Viola…for now, that is.

Back to Jack…I asked him how HE was doing, now that he's been demoted. He shrugged his shoulders and told me he was not happy to have lost his rank and the extra salary that came with it but he was taking it in stride and biding his time for now. While I didn't directly ask him about it, I knew he had one or more local lawyer friends and I had no doubt he was already in contact with them to contest what was a clearly politically-oriented reduction in position and pay. He even joked with me, in a gallows humor sort of way, that recent graduates of the eleven-week FBI National Academy course usually come back to their respective agencies and in short time get promoted. Here, at the

BPD, he comes home with the impressive certificate in hand and within a few months he's demoted. Only in this "God-forsaken place," I heard the now-lieutenant repeatedly say that day.

Jack quietly ended our short time together in his office that afternoon by strongly suggesting that I should look to get out of this, as he again referred to it, God-forsaken place. Especially, he added, after Zajac told him earlier today that now it was HIS (Zajac's) turn to start firing people around here, just like Viola had done during his time in charge. We stated to each other at almost the same time that if an off-duty officer is recklessly shooting off his gun at a bar or had somehow misplaced legally confiscated drug money, perhaps he SHOULD be fired.

As he was putting on his coat to leave that day, Jack reminded me that I was still young and I can go elsewhere and start a whole new career. The BPD is going to get much worse before it gets better, he assured me, and I'd want to get out on my own terms, not the Dark Side's terms. I thanked him for his sage, if barely audible, advice. I told him I had a plan in mind already. He didn't ask me anymore about it, he only said, "Good."

Jack left right at 4:00 that day and afterwards it was just me in CID in terms of management. Fortunately, it turned out to be an uneventful evening. I handled some new evidence that had to be logged, assigned a case or two to the detectives, and was preparing the year-end CID report which was due in a few days. The other detectives acted relatively professional and nothing of any consequence, negative or positive, occurred to me on that shift.

It was the quiet before the storm.

* * * * *

At 9:30 one off-night during the first week of the new regime, after my kids were in bed, the phone rang at my house. It was my friend and fellow BPD officer, Pat White. He was a patrolman and, like me, a newly elected PBA officer. He held the title of Secretary. (As a reminder, the preceding year I had run for and was elected to the position of PBA Vice-President.) He told me during our short talk that the PBA President (another BPD officer) had called him and wanted me to provide him with a copy of "the final sergeant's test listing" from twenty months ago. Pat continued to tell me it was because a certain detective (it was only one of them now) wanted to file a grievance against the test list and all promotions resulting from it.

I chuckled a bit out loud and told Pat to tell our brave PBA President (who wouldn't call me directly on this night) that I'd really love to help him and grant his request but coincidently I had just given my one copy of the test results to my lawyer a few days ago.

"Oh, okay," Pat casually responded. "Uh, I guess they'll want to know who your lawyer is."

I sardonically replied, "Sure. It's C. Patterson from Philadelphia."

Pat repeated the name to himself as he was apparently writing it down.

I lied to Pat, but I had my reasons.

"C. Patterson" was actually a reference to Chippy Patterson, a very successful criminal and civil attorney who was a legend in Philadelphia during the earlier part of the 20th century. My father, even as a non-lawyer, had been a fan of his unorthodox legal style and talked of him often as I was growing up. Years ago my dad even suggested I read his biography, which I eventually did.

Chippy was now long dead but I gave Pat his name anyway to tell the PBA President who was now apparently in cahoots with the various Dark Side members. I knew neither he nor anyone on that side of the PD political ledger was well-read or otherwise knowledgeable enough to know of this long-ago (yet relatively famous) Philadelphia lawyer, so I thought I'd give his name as my present attorney just to mess with him/them.

Pat took the information, thanked me, and hung up. I didn't like lying to my friend, but in this instance it was for a very specific purpose. I knew the other side was trying to screw with me, so I thought I'd do the same back at them. It was reassuring to know that it was probably only a few minutes later when the detective and his minions would begin researching and looking up in various Philadelphia phone books and directories the name "C. Patterson, Esq." Of course, they wouldn't find it. It would only add to the mystery for them.

A few days later on Sunday, while working the 7A-3P shift in CID, a fellow officer whom I trusted implicitly, John Knowles, told me he got wind of a few things which I may find bothersome…but as a friend he still wanted to tell me. I told him, "Sure, John, but from what I've been hearing lately I doubt if it will truly be anything new."

John advised me nonetheless that he heard I was going to be demoted. He even gave me his source, another Zajac flunky. I jokingly told John that he and anyone else would have to start getting in line to be relaying this type of information to me. He smiled but then quickly added that I seemed to be the primary target of these guys from mid-management and down. We agreed that it's apparently the Big Wigs in the PD such as Zajac and Eckert who were going after Viola, Robinson, and Traenkle, but it was the lower-level guys, sergeants and detectives, who had been assigned to come after me. It was their division of labor, I suppose.

Almost on schedule to support this theory, John opened a manila folder he was carrying and showed me a copy of a pre-printed roster of all BPD personnel that he found in the patrol sergeant's office. I had seen versions of it before but I noticed that this one had check marks on it next to certain names. Those names so-indicated were clearly the perceived "Viola supporters." There were about fifteen names which had been checked. Each of these names, including John's, had a single check next to it. My name had two checks beside it.

Geez, two checks? I guess they were pretty serious about coming to get me...and my stripes.

So, recapping the last nine days...two sergeants separately told me of the grievance possibility on New Year's Eve; the call at home from Pat White on behalf of the PBA President; the demotion information from John Knowles; and the check list of names, with mine being double-checked. Finally, on the morning of January 9th, came the actual grievance filed by the allegedly-grieved detective.

The aforementioned grievance was poorly written, ill-conceived, with no apparent legal basis to it, yet was still presented to the pre-selected PBA Grievance Committee. At its next meeting and after some discussion, it was voted on and despite a close vote (Viola supporters vs. Zajac supporters) the detective's grievance to throw out the previous test, and my subsequent promotion, was ruled as unfounded.

This particular matter of my demotion and/or a somehow bogus testing protocol seemed to go away after this vote. However, the issue would be resurrected one more time in a few months for me.

(I should add here that even if the grievance had been "founded" by the Committee, there would still be other legal steps which would have had to take place to invalidate that test, my promotion, etc. But, with the PD's own Grievance Committee seeing it as meritless, it severely curtailed the detective's chances.)

I, of course, never gave the detective, the PBA President, or anyone else the twenty-month old promotional list, nor did my "attorney," Mr. C. Patterson. If they wanted it so bad, they could find their own copy somewhere in the township building. After all, it wasn't my responsibility to help them with their nonsense case. They played their pseudo-psychological games to try to get to me, and I played my own same games back.

So far, I was winning, I still had my stripes. Not by very much though, I was realizing.

While the Dark Side and its various hardcore as well as revolving door sycophants would like to have taken my hard-earned promotion from me during the first few weeks of the neo-Zajac regime, it wasn't meant to be. They'd try again though, just by other means the next times.

Geez...the price I was to pay for taking one of the first legitimate, fully competitive, promotional exams in BPD history, and then also coming out on top. It was a very expensive price in Zajac-land, I came to learn.

* * * * *

I took four hours of vacation time on Monday, January 9th. (I had planned this time off before I first read the official grievance that same morning.) At about noon that day I drove to downtown Philadelphia and parked my car in a public garage near the intersection of 5th and Arch Streets. At that location in Philly happens to be the U. S. federal building, and that federal building happens to house the offices of the FBI. I went there for the specific purpose of picking up an application for the position of special agent. This had been something I had been contemplating for several years, but when things started going relatively well under Chief Viola, I put it on hold, much like my Villanova M.S. program. But I knew it was time to start reevaluating options such as this in my life, and so here I was. Maybe returning to Villanova would be next; one step at a time though, one step at a time....

Coincidently, while walking through the main lobby of the FBI offices, I ran into a former Bucks County Assistant District Attorney. He was now in private practice, doing most of his work in the Doylestown courthouse, but for some reason was in the Department of Justice building and FBI office space today. He was a good attorney and a nice guy who was on speaking terms with members of both factions at the BPD. He knew Viola and he knew Zajac, and worked with them in the past on various criminal-related matters. We both seemed sort of surprised to see each other in this building at this time. Neither of us offered a reason why we were here but we exchanged pleasantries nonetheless.

I was wondering after I parted company with this attorney how long it would take for it to get back to at least one faction in the BPD that I was spotted at the FBI offices. When this information made its way to the top, would Zajac and company think I was there looking for employment (which I was)? Or, would he/they think I was there looking to provide information to one or more agencies regarding possible federal violations?

The more I thought about it, either one of these alternatives was fine with me. Let 'em think what they want back at the BPD. In reality though, I just wanted out of that place. Submitting an application to the FBI and taking the entrance exam would be my next step in attempting to accomplish this goal.

It struck me…here I am back to taking standardized written tests, and once again at the federal government level. But it had to be done. I just hope I have better luck this time than with the fed PACE test I took in '76. I just missed the cutoff score by a half point to become a special agent with the Bureau of Alcohol, Tobacco, and Firearms back then. I'd need to score higher this time I convinced myself, much higher, to eventually get out of this, as Lt. Robinson would say, "God-forsaken place."

(+ Bonus Chapter 39a)

Chapter Forty

I want to briefly clarify something here once and for all if I haven't made it crystal clear already in the preceding chapters. That would be a comparison between the leadership styles of Rich Viola and Ted Zajac, Jr. I believe it's important to do this because it is exactly what I found myself doing during this timeframe when days of future past were back again as the Deputy Chief rode his steed (alongside his newly elected wife and a newly acquitted politician) back into Dodge for his second stint in charge in early 1984. It was during this period that the two chiefs' respective styles of running the BPD became even crystal clear-er and solidified for me my opinion of each.

I've already provided numerous examples and anecdotes of how Zajac and Viola individually chose to lead the BPD during the two years-plus so far each of them had the reins to the place. In doing so, it should be somewhat obvious at this point that they were pretty much as different as night and day. The how and the why of their differences are naturally found somewhere in the then-approximately four decade personal and professional life history of these two individual men. Therein lie the roots of their respective management and leadership styles, not to mention their overall personalities and life skills... or lack thereof.

I believe at its essence and its fundamental roots, Ted Zajac's organizational approach to the BPD was based on his own insecurities. Some people at the time claimed his lust for power and how he went about attaining and maintaining it was the result of, at least to some degree, a Napoleonic Complex. He wasn't a tall guy, maybe 5'9" with shoes. Perhaps this issue alone affected him and allowed his personality to evolve in such a way over the years in an attempt to over-compensate for his, well, perceived shortcomings.

My personal belief, however, is that Zajac's general character and its resultant manifestations were based more on a deeply ingrained subconscious issue. That would be the internalized self-acknowledgement that he only attained the lofty heights of BPD upper-management through initially his politician father and then secondarily his politician wife. Ironically, when one looks at him through this prism, it becomes obvious that HOW Zajac achieved his very success at the same time may have actually contributed to the development of his myriad insecurities. In view of this, and perhaps because of this, his management style became closely aligned with various Bensalem and other elected/appointed officials with whom he was familiar (if not related) who achieved their positions and cut their political "deals" in similar nepotistic or underhanded back-room manners.

Like some of those from whom he learned, Zajac eventually adopted a "scorched earth" policy of running his police department. He would demand nothing less than one hundred percent blind loyalty and unconditional support for him and all he decreed upon his officers and his agency. Disagreement, or even perceived neutrality in many cases, would be seen as a form of insubordination worthy of punishment. Conversely, continued mindless head-nodding and, more critically, ongoing and adamant support for Zajac and his departmental dictates were repaid with special assignments, overtime details, promotions, and related ancillary benefits, regardless in most cases of the officers' overall work ethic or their on-the-job results. These men would be recognized and recompensed as card carrying members of the Dark Side, with all the expected (and ultimately provided) advantages of said membership.

Viola, on the other hand, was essentially the polar opposite of his nemesis. There was no silver spoon in his mouth when he was born, or anytime thereafter. Coincidently, he wasn't a tall guy either, maybe about the same height as Zajac. However, that issue (or anything to do with Monsieur Bonaparte and his rumored Complex), played no apparent role in Viola's general disposition, behavior, and certainly not in his leadership style. From what I came to learn about Viola, at no stage in his life and career did either election politics or nepotism have anything to do with his ascension to positions which he desired and ultimately achieved. This climb up the management ladder started professionally with Rich's stint as a patrol sergeant in the Philadelphia Police Department (PPD), later as the head of a specialized crime fighting unit in the PPD, at the same time reaching the rank of Lt. Colonel in the U. S. Marine Corps Reserves, Commanding Officer of the Marine

Air Base, Squad 49, at the Willow Grove (PA) Naval Air Station, with eventually becoming Chief of Police at Bensalem PD.

As with any supervisor, Viola would naturally want loyalty from those around him in their varied positions of authority. There's nothing wrong with that. However, he specifically told anyone upon promoting them to such positions that he didn't want any "Yes-Men" on his staff. They were free to disagree with him at any time to his face, even vehemently so if they felt that strongly about a certain issue. Most in the BPD management, including me at its lower level, had no problem with this style of leadership. Essentially, if you had ideas on how to make the BPD a better place, you were invited by Viola to tell him about it, at whatever rank or position you may have held. If you chose not to, for whatever reason, perhaps because of your allegiance to the then-former Deputy Chief or that you just wanted to work your eight or ten hours a day and do your job and nothing else, that was fine too. Viola nor any of his subordinates would bother you or expect otherwise of you in that regard.

Bottom-line under Viola's regime, there was no punishment for NOT bowing down and kissing his feet or any other body part. One didn't have to perform such actions at the BPD while he was in charge. If you were a hard worker, made good arrests, got along with your fellow officers and supervisors, didn't abuse your sick time, weren't late for work, and followed everyday fundamental workplace policies, Viola left you alone. If, with this type of positive work history and/or arrest history, you desired a special assignment and made the Chief or upper-management aware of it, you'd be provided that opportunity or something similar to it when the time was right.

Yes, Viola was a strict disciplinarian at times, and yes, two officers were fired during his reign as Chief (albeit, now back at work), but that's what managers have to do sometimes. I didn't necessarily agree with everything Viola did as Chief, but I knew I wouldn't be punished for such disagreements, even if/when I let him know about it...which I did on occasion.

In sum, these were the differences between the two Chiefs. You may not have agreed with or openly supported one of them (Viola), but as long as you were doing your job you would be left alone to do it. If you disagreed with or did not support the other one of them (Zajac), no matter how you did your job, you would NOT be left alone to do it; not for very long, anyway.

So, now that Zajac was back in charge, and Viola was not, I came to realize once again that how I did my job at the BPD really didn't matter to him or his team. Like Viola's career track, my police career track was antithetical to Zajac's. Like Viola's, mine was based on merit and hard work. That was an unfamiliar concept to Zajac, certainly in terms of those with whom it was he chose to surround himself. His police career and his current position were based almost solely on two relationships, of the blood (father) and legal (wife) variety. Otherwise everyday standard workplace dynamics as they related to Zajac or his minions were largely unimportant to him. This was clearly reflected by those now again in management and specialty positions within the BPD.

In light of all of this, I would now have to reconcile who I was, what I was, and come to grips with the "leader" now in charge again and deal with who and what HE was. With two years of Viola now part of my management perspective, not to mention a third or so of a master's degree in organizational science completed, I came to realize what a true leader was and how that leadership style facilitated the successful running of an organization, one with the singular goal of achieving its maximum potential in a fair and equitable manner to all involved.

I also now knew more than ever that I couldn't and I wouldn't lower myself to Zajac's management and personality style of gamesmanship, politics of personal and professional destruction, and the reward and punishment paradigm which had now been reestablished for what was said and done for or against him. I was fully cognizant of the fact that there would be no forthcoming rewards for me at the BPD. I could honestly live with that. But I also knew there would be punishment of some sort, at some level, heading my way. It would be a bit tougher to live with that issue. Zajac's possible behind-the-scenes orchestration of my attempted demotion (or at a minimum, his tacit approval), not to mention his strange new Tourette Syndrome-like habit of yelling my name out loud on random occasions, were indications of his overall negative attitude towards me, what I stood for, and what I earned in legitimate fashion in his absence.

Despite knowing that I would never descend to the Dark Side's manner of running the BPD, I also slowly came to realize something else. I still had to survive. I had a family to support. Because of this, I couldn't nor wouldn't be stupid and thoughtless enough and go out of my way to cause any overt problems and/or face-to-face personality clashes. I'd certainly TRY to avoid these conflicts anyway. I'd do my best to bite my tongue, pretend I didn't see or hear certain things, and otherwise just bide my time. I'd do my job every day and, as I believed

Jack Robinson was now doing too, I'd start keeping a record of what was happening to and around me. These copious notes, newspaper clippings, and workplace memos to me (eventually lots of them) that I retained over the next few years would assist me in working through this very difficult time and ultimately becoming an agent of change in the BPD.

However, in that darkest and coldest of winters of 1984 at the BPD, I couldn't dare look too far ahead to the department's future or certainly my own. It would be one day at a time, one slight at a time, one harassing memo at a time, and slowly working to build a case to make the BPD a better place for those who simply wanted to perform their lawful duties and be good cops in a non-hostile work environment.

It wouldn't be easy though, not on any one of those days during the next few years.

* * * * *

There was at least one minor victory for the good guys before the month of January was over. That is, Jack Robinson's legal action in which he contested his demotion was heard before a judge in Bucks County Court. As such, his demotion was overturned. Kelly's stated reasoning at the January 3rd meeting was, "The Board is highly concerned that there has been an over-inflation in rank in the Bensalem Township Police Department and this is costing the township a lot more money than we should be paying for police services."

As the judge ruled, there was no listed cause for Capt. Robinson's demotion; none, except the alleged "over-inflation" excuse. The "Pennsylvania Police Tenure Act" requires misfeasance, malfeasance, or the like to be the reason behind an officer's demotion or termination. Kelly, et al., were wrong. It wasn't the first time nor would it be the last time either. Interestingly, Kelly's "over-inflation" rationale as it pertained to the recent BPD promotions would prove to be very ironic near the end of 1985. That would be when he presided over a spate of his own unwieldy elevations of rank for a number of officers. We'll come back to this....

Alas, despite Jack's courtroom "victory," as it turned out, the new regime wouldn't have Ken Hopkins to kick around anymore. "Victory" for the Dark Side, I suppose.

With an investigative position offered to Ken in the security department of one of the new Atlantic City casinos, he gave his two weeks' notice and quit the BPD.

Ken would be missed by many of us, including me, although the current regime was no doubt glad to see him leave.

One down! Now how many more to go?

John Knowles, show me that departmental hit list again....

Interestingly, but not surprisingly, Ken wouldn't be the only one leaving the BPD. Officer Juan Diaz, of rookie undercover Bensalem High School "student" fame, also saw writings on the walls of the BPD starting in '84. (He also saw a check next to his name on that aforementioned list.) As a result, he had applied to the U.S. Border Patrol and in 1985 they hired him and he quit Bensalem PD.

The current regime wouldn't miss Juan either. They never could convert him to their way of thinking. Juan told me before he left that he thought it was a language barrier of some sort. I knew what he meant by that and I also knew he was probably correct.

Geez...who else would be leaving the BPD now that the new regime is in place?

Well, at least one other would be leaving soon, but he wouldn't be quitting his job. He wouldn't be fired or suspended either. And it wouldn't bode well for me.

* * * * *

In mid-February of '84, the once-again Captain Jack Robinson called me into his office and advised me that he had some good news for me for a change. I didn't initially believe him, but he wasn't kidding. He had received a letter from Penn State University's Justice and Safety Institute earlier this day advising him and the BPD that the officer they had recommended last year to attend their POSIT-POLEX course had been officially approved. The two-week training course would start on April 30 at the main campus of Penn State in State College, Pennsylvania, and they would expect that specifically named officer to attend as a slot was now open for him.

That officer was, in fact, me.

POSIT is an acronym for "Police Supervisory In-Service Training." POLEX stands for "Police Executive Development Training Program." The related courses almost always run during back-to-back weeks, ten days total. The instructors are mostly Penn State faculty members with retired supervisory troopers from the Pennsylvania State Police also on staff. As the course titles suggest, they're designed for police supervisors from sergeant and above. These courses were very well-respected, much sought out, and considered by some as the Pennsylvania version of the FBI National Academy, albeit much shorter in duration. They were and remain an important stepping-stone for any Pennsylvania police officer in attaining a promotion from one supervisory rank to the next. These courses and certificates earned from them would open doors for such upward mobility if he/she so desired.

I was aware that Captain Robinson had put me in for this course about a year ago but I had honestly forgotten about it with all that had been going on lately. Jack advised me, however, that this just-received letter of acceptance could develop into a very interesting scenario at the BPD for me. He knew that Zajac would never put me in for this highly-regarded training nor would he have any interest in "rewarding" me by sending me to it. But as literally every other sergeant and above in the BPD had already attended prior training sessions, it would be difficult for him to turn me down for it. This was especially true as it was my actual name on the acceptance letter and the BPD would lose the slot and maybe even future slots if I didn't attend. Costs wouldn't be a factor either as the "tuition" was state-subsidized with the only expenditures being the attending officer's lodging, meals, and travel.

So, Jack told me to sit tight and when the time was right he'd run it by Zajac and hopefully get his okay, if even reluctantly, to send me to the training.

I was seriously hoping to go. Two weeks out of this place would be a God-send right about now. It certainly wouldn't hurt my career aspirations either, wherever such aspiring may take me.

It took a few days but Jack eventually told me that it had been approved by Zajac for me to attend the upcoming Penn State course. I expressed my gratitude to Jack and later that afternoon while walking by the Deputy Chief's office I actually stopped and thanked him for allowing me to attend the upcoming training. He barely looked up from his paperwork but still said, "You're welcome." No, he didn't yell it or my name out loud this time.

(By the way, neither Jack nor I ever told Zajac about my nomination last year to the eleven-week FBI National Academy. We knew an actual invite was at least a year away and, more importantly, we also knew there wasn't a snowball's chance in hell that the Deputy Chief would ever allow me to go to that prestigious training. One step at a time we figured. Let's just get me to the POSIT-POLEX course first.)

* * * * *

On February 20th, I was working a 4P-12A shift. I was at my desk in CID. After the usual Monday night township meeting ended upstairs I happened to hear a loud, bellowing voice coming down the back stairs toward the area of CID. Upon turning around from my desk I could see it was none other than Ted Zajac, Sr. (Apparently bellowing runs in the family.) The former elected official was now just a regular civilian but with his son running the show downstairs in the PD I suppose he could waltz through our work space anytime he wanted. So, he did.

On this night, after some backslapping and handshakes with his accompanying hangers-on, Senior slowly made his way to Junior's office. Once he was observed leaning up against the doorframe and chatting with his son, a few Team Zajac detectives got up from their desks and crowded around the old man. An awe-struck patrolman or two sauntered back this way too. I could overhear some portions of the several minutes-long conversation but I wasn't paying much attention to it as I really didn't have any strong desire to listen to these guys remind each other how great they are and laugh out loud at one or both of the Zajacs' attempts at humor.

However, at some point during this multi-generational, non-partisan discourse, maybe specifically for me to hear or perhaps merely as the result of the uncontained ebullience of the various participants, Ted, Sr., was heard to say something very revealing about their Team's collective mindset. It was said louder than anything else I heard from him that night. Yes, one could say it was even bellowed.

What Ted Zajac, Sr., very demonstrably exclaimed was, "Wait 'til we get rid of Caesar! Then bombs will really start dropping around here!"

As expected, raucous laughter followed his proclamation.

As the mirthfulness slowly died down on their end, I mentally replayed the mixed metaphor ("Caesar" and "bombs…dropping"?) statement on my end a few times. It became clear that this somewhat confused student of Roman history, Zajac the Elder, whilst bloviating as a modern day Brutus to Zajac the Younger, as well as to the assembled centurions outside the latter's office, was referring to one man and one man only. "Caesar" was, of course, a very obvious reference to Rich Viola. After all, he was of Italian heritage and they were trying their best to "get rid" of him. Right?

Right.

After a few more laughs and a few hearty "take it easys" and "see ya laters" to his friends and countrymen, the elder statesman made his grand exit out of the building, bellowing as well as bellicose all the way out the door. Ted, Jr., walked his dad outside to his car. It was a Hallmark-like father and son moment.

The other Brutus, the one from the 1st century B.C., would have been proud. Actually…probably not.

* * * * *

At some point, I couldn't resist. I needed some reaffirmation, a shot in the arm, something, anything to remind me I was still normal and it's the inmates around me in this asylum that are the abnormal ones. In attempting such, I had to break the law. Even though I was a sworn law enforcement officer, I just had to do it.

Okay, it wasn't exactly "the law" I would be in violation of, but instead the early January edict prohibiting any BPD member talking to or having any interaction with the former Chief. So, bucking tradition, on a Saturday afternoon in early March, I called the suspended/IOD/under investigation/soon-to-be-fired Rich Viola. It was from my home phone to his home phone. I was hoping the wiretap authorized by Barry Denker was down by now. (That last part was a joke. I don't THINK the lawyer could authorize a wiretap back then. Not a legal one, anyway.)

It was strange when Viola finally answered the phone. I didn't think about it beforehand, but what do I now call him? He never insisted on me calling him "Chief" for the two years I worked for him, but I did anyway. I believe even Viola's number two guy, Jack Robinson, routinely called him by his official title whenever I saw them interact. I never heard anyone associated with the PD call him anything but "Chief." I didn't feel "Rich" was in order, so I continued to refer to him how I always did. After all, he wasn't officially fired yet. Everyone knew it was coming, but technically, he was still the BPD chief…I guess. Whatever, once I heard "Hello" from the voice on the other end that I recognized as his, I simply responded, "Hi Chief, it's Jim Fitzgerald."

"Jimmy, great to hear from you! How are they treating you there?" Inquiring minds, especially when suspended and/or injured and/or incommunicado, wanted to know.

We talked about fifteen minutes. I filled him in on everything of relevance from the last two months. I even told him about the "Caesar" remark. He laughed out loud and said he'll be sure to tell his lawyer of it.

Of course, the actual purpose of my call was to hear from Viola regarding what he and his legal team were doing about the coup d'état and his "overthrow" which occurred at the BPD those short nine weeks ago. Right away and very confidently Rich told me that he was fighting his suspension/intended firing tooth and nail, he had some excellent Philadelphia lawyers on the case, and he would ultimately prevail. That was a relief to hear, even if just general speculation at this time. What Viola couldn't provide me was any sort of a timeline in terms of when this would be accomplished. He knew he had done nothing wrong while in office, he knew it was all political, and that whatever they were trying to accuse him of would be unfounded. But, he regretfully added, this all may take a while.

"Jimmy," Viola went on changing the subject, "get out of that place, and the sooner the better. I'm sure you're trying. You've got a lot going for you but that place and those people will tear you apart if they can. Take your skills somewhere else. You should consider the Feds. In the meantime, just stand tall and stick it out. Don't take any shit from anyone there, but do what you gotta do to survive. And keep good notes. You'll be glad you did someday."

The Chief-in-exile borrowed from his years in the Marine Corps as he ended the call. He told me he learned from his days as a young Marine. He said, "Remember, if you're doing something and it hurts, keep doing it until it doesn't hurt anymore."

Good advice, I told him, and we both said goodbye.

I wasn't at first sure what Viola meant by that USMC expression. Did it refer to push-ups, sit-ups, running, and those types of physical activities? Or was it a bit more esoteric, and could it apply to what I'm going through right now with the Dark Side?

I took it to be most applicable to the latter. In other words, I should get over the initial shock of Zajac and his cronies being back in charge, keep doing what it is that I do to get by, and it won't "hurt" anymore, or at least not as much.

Okay, I think I can do that. Emphasis on I *think*....

* * * * *

Over the next month or two, as a CID sergeant, I found that my role was relegated to basically that of a pencil-pusher, phone answerer, and for a while yet, evidence custodian. My supervisory duties were all but stripped away from me, and even if I did give a detective a case or a specific assignment to handle, it was many times ignored or delayed. This was not every detective, of course, but some. Those perceived to be in lockstep with Team Zajac, naturally, were the ones giving me the most kickback and grief. Ironically, for the most part, I got along very well with the majority of these detectives over the prior year and a half, or at least I thought I did. Presently, however, it was a different story as they were feeling their oats and thumping their chests as now being among the chosen ones.

Capt. Robinson wasn't faring much better in his role either, and things were heating up even more so for him. He was ordered to frequently appear at the so-named "White House," located directly behind BPD HQ, now commandeered by Lt. Eckert and his Viola Mini-Task Force. Jack would be interviewed multiple times by Eckert who was conducting his fulltime witch-hunt in an attempt to get the goods, any goods, on the former chief. After Jack's most recent interview session with Eckert he was advised that he would next be administered a polygraph exam. This was because, according to the investigating lieutenant, some of Jack's responses to his questions weren't sufficient, or at least they didn't help advance their case far enough yet against Viola.

One afternoon in late March, when I was just starting my shift and Jack was about to go home, I could see he was in a bad mood. I believe it was only a few days before his scheduled polygraph exam. I suppose he wanted some misery to join his company so he proceeded to advise me that he had been called into Zajac's office earlier today and among other topics discussed was me. Zajac told Jack during that meeting that he didn't want me in CID anymore as I was "green and inexperienced" and "couldn't handle a homicide." Zajac continued that he knew that I had trouble handling the detectives in CID. He ended his assessment of me and my situation to Jack by stating that he'd like either Sgt. Pansy or Sgt. Whacky as the new CID supervisor.

As Capt. Robinson was very aware of the multiple and varied personal and professional shortcomings of the two men proposed as new CID sergeants, and the fact that they'd be working directly for him (yet reporting HIS every move directly to Zajac), he wasn't thrilled to hear their names as possible replacements for me. There was no timeframe set here by the Deputy Chief and I was later told by Jack to just sit back and see how this all plays out. That's what HE was trying to do he told me, well, once he got this damn polygraph exam out of the way.

Hmmm…I guess I thanked Zajac a bit prematurely a few weeks ago.

Of course, everyone in the BPD knew that my first big investigation as a brand new CID supervisor was the Robert Suckle homicide from almost two years ago. But I wasn't the only investigator who hadn't yet solved that case. I certainly wasn't the veteran detective (and Team Zajac member) who came to the scene that day and left the lens cap on the camera, or whatever he did, so no photos would ever exist of it. Plus, I've supervised other homicide and attempted homicide cases since then, investigated other high-profile cases, and did just fine with all of them, right up to their successful convictions.

But, again, I had to slow down here and re-remind myself of something. I knew it, but I still had to bang the side of my head every once in a while in order for it to sink back in. That is, none of this was about my actual experience, skillset, or the lack thereof which was allegedly important to DC Zajac. It was about my perceived loyalty and deference towards him, or the lack thereof. Once that bit of knowledge found the appropriate synapse connection from one side of my brain to the other, I was fine. I could relax and not beat myself up.

Hey, I said to myself, put me back in patrol! I could be a patrol sergeant, no problem. In fact, I wouldn't mind at all. I've got plenty of friends in the Patrol Division. But I'm not going to make it easy for the powers that be. Not like last time when I wanted out of the Tac Squad. No, this time, YOU Deputy Chief Zajac, will have to order me out of this position.

* * * * *

Forging ahead…from April 30 until May 11, despite being green and inexperienced, or perhaps because of it, I was sent to the Penn State sponsored POSIT-POLEX course. The Deputy Chief kept his word.

The combined courses made for an exceptional two weeks. It was even more exhilarating for me as I was returning for the first time to my alma mater since I graduated nine years earlier in 1975.

The course itself was very challenging, but at the same time informative, edifying, and inspiring. If only I worked in a law enforcement agency at which I could practice some of the management and leadership techniques which were discussed during the ten class days. Of course I used to, but not anymore. But, that's okay. Maybe someday, somewhere….

I was taken aback, in a good way, on the very first day when my fellow students and I were advised by one of the professors in the program that this eighty-hour course could also be worth either three undergrad or three graduate credits once completed. The professor told us that this course is recognized by virtually all other U.S. universities and the credits would be readily transferable. If we were so interested in attaining these credits, there was a certain form to be filled out and submitted by the end of the last day of the course. I filled out that form and submitted it by the end of the first day of the course.

418

This information was just what I wanted to hear. It was what I needed to jump-start my fledgling academic career, or at least part two of it. This could now be one more course under my belt towards my eventual M.S. at Villanova University. I decided right then that when I get back home after these two weeks of training I'll call Villanova, confirm that they will accept these credits, and then restart their program. It won't be too late from what they told me a year or so ago. I knew it was time to get back to school. My batteries were recharged on several levels now and I was rarin' to go and complete that degree program.

I eventually attained the transcript from Penn State which reflected my grade of "A" for the POSIT-POLEX course. I submitted it to Villanova. They accepted it and I was back in grad school by the fall semester of '84. I was on my way, at least academically, one more time and I felt great about it. The BPD job certainly wasn't doing anything for me presently, but at least my family and my new academic pursuits would keep me going in the meantime.

Now, to just find another job....

* * * * *

Sometime that late winter, the FBI got back to me via a letter to my home. It was in response to the application I sent to them shortly after picking up the special agent position paperwork at their office back in January. There was a test scheduled on a certain upcoming date and if I was still interested, I should recontact the Philadelphia Division and let them know right away. So, I did.

Early one April morning, after either taking the day off or being on a scheduled day off, I drove to the downtown Philadelphia FBI office and took the written test with about one hundred other applicants. The male applicants were all wearing dark suits, white shirts, generic ties, and brown or black shoes. The female applicants were all wearing dark business suits, white or beige shirts, with brown or black mid-height heels. There were virtually no exceptions in either gender category. Me included.

We were told at the beginning of the day by the FBI proctor that the same test was being given today in each of the 56 FBI field offices. Geez, that means today alone over 5,000 people were taking it? And they administer this test five to six times per year? What are my chances here?

Regardless of whatever the calculated odds were of me getting hired by the FBI as a result of my performance on this test on this day, I took it anyway. It wasn't an easy test, but then I didn't expect it to be.

The proctor told us it would be several months before we would hear from them regarding our results. The letter would explain in full our options at that time, whether we passed it or...well, if we didn't pass it.

After the four-hour test, I left the building exhausted and drove back to my home in Bensalem. I had no idea how I fared on it. Along with everyone else who took it, I'd have to wait the requisite months to learn the results. So, I forgot about it for now.

Back at the BPD during the next week, however, I'd be reminded once again of the last test I took BEFORE the FBI one. Yes, the now almost two-year-old sergeant's test matter reared its ugly head yet again, but this time from an unexpected source. After my reaction to this unexpected source, I'd be called on the carpet for it. It was to be my turn to go to the White House, and not the one occupied by President Reagan at the time. Hardly....

Chapter Forty-One

On April 17th, 1984, the *Bucks County Courier Times* had an article in which allegations of "promotional tampering" at the BPD, under the prior chief's watch of course, were now being investigated by the Viola Mini-Task Force. Yes, it referred to the same test by which I was promoted, just about two whole years ago now. And a specific BPD patrolman was quoted in it, or at least referenced in it, as being one of the officers ostensibly concerned about and affected by this matter. I couldn't believe that this issue had resurfaced yet again and now, for the first time, in a public forum for all to read. It truly lit my fuse.

Despite that fuse being lit, I never did lose my cool. I never exploded but I did simmer over the next few hours. Whilst still in simmering mode, and when I happened to see the so-referenced officer at HQ around 12:30 that afternoon, I made the conscious decision to confront him. It was probably a mistake, but I had been biting my tongue for too long around this place so far.

The officer was a patrol officer who came on the job around the same time as me. However, I never really worked with him or got to know him. Up until this point, I had nothing to say good or bad about this guy as I simply hadn't spent any time with him, either personally or professionally, to develop an opinion of him one way or the other. I wasn't even sure in what "camp" he would have positioned himself during these days of overt partisanship in the BPD, nor was I even aware that he took the sergeant's test lo those several years ago. I had seen this officer as being a more or less neutral guy regarding anything to do with Zajac and Viola, which was fine with me.

But now, with Zajac back in charge just a few months, and with a supposed "objective" investigation into alleged official violations by Chief Viola while in office, this officer all of a sudden gets the gumption to somehow take his complaint to the task force because apparently he did not finish higher in the last promotional test. This accusation was then added to the list of the many other trumped-up charges being investigated against the former chief. Then, somehow, it made its way into the newspaper article this morning.

So early that afternoon, without actually looking for this officer I nonetheless happened upon him in the patrol locker room area. I walked up to him. It was just the two of us. My words to him were measured and tempered, and they were not threatening, loud, or officious in any way. I simply told him that I had read today's newspaper account and that I truly hoped he knew what he was talking about and he had some level of proof in his making of such serious allegations regarding the now-two year ago testing process. He stalled and stuttered but never really did provide any salient comments of his own except to say that he didn't know how his complaint made its way into the *Courier Times* article. I told him I found that hard to believe. He reiterated that it was the truth then turned his back on me. I left him as he was fiddling with one item or another inside his open locker. As I walked away I simply suggested to him that if he did NOT have proof of "promotional tampering" with that test other than him not scoring as high as he would have liked, then he really should make that clear to Lt. Eckert and company and leave this thing to die once and for all.

That was it. My mostly one-way conversation with this most recent test-related accusatory police officer lasted less than a minute. I went back to my CID desk, moving on from this topic and my little chat with the officer. He obviously had earlier made his complaint to Lt. Eckert and/or to the media, and/or Eckert talked to the media, and/or maybe Eckert's "counsel" Barry Denker called the *Courier Times*, or some combination of these possibilities. However, as it somehow found its way into the newspaper I felt I had to at least talk to the officer who was specifically mentioned in the article. So, rightly or wrongly, when I came upon him by happenstance that day, I did.

But it wasn't meant to end there.

Apparently immediately afterwards, the officer went to the White House and advised Lt. Eckert of our just completed interaction. He told him he felt "threatened" by me, a BPD sergeant, because of what I had said to him and my "overall tone."

At 3:30 that same day I was hand delivered a memo at my CID desk. It was initialed by Lt. Eckert. It instructed me to come to the White House, but it didn't state for what reason. It was my first invitation to the central hub of the Get-Viola investigation. I did not consider it an honor nor was I looking forward to it.

When I arrived at the White House I was immediately brought into what I suppose was the former dining room but now office of this two-story single home. (Yes, the exterior of the building was white, ergo, its name.) The retro-fitted dining room door was closed on the two of us and I was then "interviewed" by the lieutenant. He wanted to know what happened with the patrol officer earlier that day in the locker room.

I was surprised to learn this is why I was here at the White House, but I nonetheless told Eckert without hesitation exactly what happened, what I earlier read, what I later said, how the officer responded, and that was it. Eckert then wanted me to put in writing what I just told him. So, I went back to CID, typed up a very short memo recounting same, and walked it back over to him. I was ordered to stay at the White House.

Five minutes later, after reading my written version of events in private, Lt. Eckert called me back into the interview room. He then told me candidly that even he thought the promotional test tampering allegation was untrue. But despite what he believed and despite the issue being made public in the newspaper today, I still shouldn't have confronted the officer about it as I did. I shrugged my shoulders, not necessarily showing agreement or disagreement to him. He added that he understood why I and some others in the BPD got upset over the news piece today but he denied that he or his office released this information to any journalists. The lieutenant then ended our "interview" with what I found to be rather strange advice. He told me I should do my best to find out who did, in fact, release it to the media and confront them with my anger.

Okay, I recall thinking, let me get this right. You're now sanctioning me to confront "them" with my anger? But you just told me I shouldn't have said anything to the patrolman who came to you? With other people it's approved by you though? What do you know that I don't know?

So be the mindset of Team Zajac, even from its second in charge.

As no other officers were referenced in the article that day, just that one by name, I really didn't have too much more to go on, no one else to "confront." So, I let it drop. I said what I said to the patrolman and later that day to Lt. Eckert and for once and for all this bullshit test tampering allegation was put to rest at the BPD.

I never said anything else to the patrolman after that day, nor did some others in the BPD for that matter. I and others lost respect for him because of how he chose to run to the lieutenant and complain about me and my addressing of the situation with him as I did. It's simply not the way things were usually handled within police departments, or at least not at the BPD back then. There was no accusation of a crime here at any level, there were no threatening behaviors or insinuations, yet this officer felt he had to report me and my actions to a supervisor. He couldn't have handled it with just me, then and there, on his own? Apparently not.

If I had been in this officer's situation, I would have acted differently. I would have handled it one-on-one with the other officer, talked through it man to man, and worked it out as adults. There would be no "parent" or "teacher" involved, or in this case lieutenant, being advised of any such discussion between two police officers. But I suppose that's how this officer and I differed in our personalities and demeanors, certainly on a professional level.

The allegation regarding the test issue was dropped from the Viola Mini-Task Force and there were no further challenges to it. However, with the issue now having gone public, there would unfortunately always be a taint to my and others' promotions of two years ago because of these unsupported and baseless accusations. I knew it was a legit test, with legit results, and I was a legit sergeant; whether this new regime liked it or not.

* * * * *

In the summer of '84, I came into work one day to find things very much changed in CID. Most importantly, Jack Robinson was gone. He was now out IOD with a bad back. Yes, like Viola, he had also hurt his back while at work. In Jack's case, he was trying to open a heavy filing cabinet drawer in the evidence room and somehow twisted his back in the process. He went to the doctor, his back injury was confirmed, and he was in official Injured-on-Duty status for the foreseeable future.

With Capt. Traenkle also out for various reasons for one or more extended periods during this timeframe, and another non-Zajac Team detective sergeant eventually going IOD with his bad back (geez, was it contagious?), it left me at the BPD as the highest ranking member of management associated with the Viola administration - yes me, a lowly sergeant. Now, there was an even bigger red target on my back. And I thought it was bad before.

With Robinson gone, Lt. Eckert was directed by Deputy Chief Zajac to relocate from the White House to CID as he was now the new Detective Lieutenant, replacing Jack. While he would still be running the Viola Mini-Task Force in Zajac's/Kelly's attempt to find ANYTHING they could pin on the former chief as it related to alleged misfeasance, malfeasance, criminality, fixed parking tickets, impoliteness, unshined shoes, ANYTHING, Eckert's other position now would be as head of CID. A genuine hack-of-all-trades was he.

What would this mean for me? Well, that answer would be forthcoming, and very soon.

On June 25, my first day back after a week off, working the 4P-12A shift, before I even sat down at my desk I was ordered by Lt. Eckert to turn over all my keys to CID. This meant the key to his new office (Capt. Robinson had issued me a key to his old office) and the keys to the evidence room as well. I was told I was no longer to be the evidence custodian.

Okay, that's fine with me. What will be my duties in CID if not working with evidence? I didn't know, yet. He did though.

On the very next day, there was a CID meeting with all the detectives and sergeants in attendance. (There were four sergeants now; me, two old timers, and the newly ubiquitous Sgt. Pansy.) The meeting was chaired, of course, by Lt. Eckert. It seems everyone had their jobs and positions laid out for them. There was to be a newly formed Varsity Team of senior detectives who would handle the major crimes. Then, there was a back-up Junior Varsity Team who would handle the minor crimes. Eckert didn't actually use those two athletic-oriented terms, but after the meeting that's how the mostly JV Team members referred to the newly constructed divide in CID. Oh, and the successful Burglary Unit which I had originated eighteen months ago was disbanded. After all, who needs burglary arrests?

What was created in place of the Burglary Unit was a Narcotics Unit. It was composed of two of Zajac's top boys. Over the next year-plus, one or two other officers (all Zajac boys) switched in and out of it, and amazingly they had one thing in common. It was a well-noted level of consistency that they maintained throughout the entire time Zajac's (and Eckert's) drug squad was in place. That is, they made virtually no arrests; literally, none. The exception, if it really even was, happened when patrol would apprehend some guys in possession of small or even mid-sized quantities of various drugs. They would then take over the arrest but coincidently, it would never go farther than that. No one up the pot/coke/meth/PCP/heroin chain of distribution was ever arrested during these two years. Or, if they were, it was by patrol and the Zajac appointed narcs just processed the paperwork.

More on this unit and at least one of its members forthcoming.

Back to me and my place in CID as a result of this meeting, I wasn't assigned to any team or squad. The detective sergeants essentially had no listed functions. There was nothing articulated from the lips of our new commander himself or written on the various documents which were handed out during the meeting explaining our place in this new set-up. The sergeants now didn't assign cases (Eckert did), we didn't read and approve detectives' reports (Eckert did), we couldn't approve overtime for the detectives (Eckert did), there was no evidence to handle (someone else was now delegated these duties), and as far as we could determine there was absolutely nothing for us sergeants to do. Yet, we were still there, in CID, but with no discernible purpose. Strange….

To add insult to injury, in the next day or two one of the other older sergeants overheard Lt. Eckert tell Sgt. Pansy that when he (Eckert) was on vacation over the next week, "Don't let Fitzgerald do anything but answer phones."

When the same Sgt. Pansy was put in charge as acting lieutenant during Eckert's vacation week, he actually had the gall to ask me, "Jim, are you upset that I'm in charge of CID for the week?"

I responded to this sergeant, "Of course not. You're clearly the MAN for the job."

The wimpy sergeant seemed to detect my sarcasm.

I would, in fact, undertake my assigned duties from him or whoever was in charge. Give me a legal order and I'll follow it. The only problem was…I didn't know what the hell my duties were, well, besides serving as the CID receptionist.

I would have a very specific investigatory responsibility before long though. It would be an important one too, according to the lieutenant.

On July 10, via a memo, I was advised by Lt. Eckert that I (and I alone) was now in charge of all vandalisms which occurred in Bensalem Township. Vandalisms! Yes, as in criminal mischief, graffiti, soaping of car windows, toilet paper rolls tossed over houses and trees, bad language written on bathroom stalls, you name it. I clearly wasn't on the new Varsity Team, not even the JV Team. Maybe the intramural team? Actually, I think it would be more akin to the guys who clean up the arena after the sporting event is over. I mean, I wasn't even in the game here. I wasn't even an undrafted walk-on to the team!

I didn't let it get to me. When the various reports of vandalism came in, I investigated them. I even solved some of them. On July 13, just two days after being awarded this lofty assignment, I even made an arrest of a kid I spotted vandalizing a house or business somewhere in the township. I believe I was on my way to or from lunch (as I wasn't allowed out of the building for any other reason at this point) when I saw the kid and I made the collar. Lt. Eckert wasn't very happy with me actually making an arrest, but hey, he put me in charge of the vandalism non-epidemic. If not me, who?

Rumors abounded at this time that I was going back to patrol. I may have even helped spread some of them. Again, I would have welcomed the change at this time. But, as I decided a while ago, this time it would be their decision to transfer me. I wanted it to be on them. Secretly though, I was hoping for it. Maybe one of these days if I REALLY screw up, or if I keep arresting those local vandals, I'll get my wish.

* * * * *

On September 4th, I was back at Villanova University. It was great to return to the classroom and this time I knew I was in it for the long haul. A few of the students I got to know from my first stint were in my class and it was great to see them again. With the three credits I transferred in from the Penn State POSIT-POLEX course, I was really only one or two courses behind some of these folks. I figured sometime in '87 or so I could have my M.S. degree if everything played out just right. Hopefully, anyway.

Geez, where will I be then? I could only wonder. I could only hope.

Since I was scheduled on a 4P-12A shift for that first night back at school, I had to use 3.5 hours of compensatory (comp) time to take off. Before classes even restarted for me, I calculated just how much comp time I would need over the next few semesters to make sure I could attend all of my evening classes. When I would very rarely work over my eight hours per day, I had been purposely taking comp time instead of overtime for this very reason. But those calculations (and that comp time) proved unnecessary as the result of a pleasant surprise I was to receive the day after my very first class.

Via memo (which is really the only way my lieutenant communicated with me now, as we virtually never spoke to one another, and even though my desk was right outside of his door), I was informed that starting next week I was to work a permanent 8A-4P shift, Monday through Friday. That means no more evening shifts and no more weekends.

Okay, what did I do to deserve this? I assure you, if the bosses knew I had just restarted my classes at 'Nova, they would have put me on straight 4-12 shifts in a heartbeat and forced me to use all my comp or vacation time to go to my classes. Something was up, but I didn't know nor did I care. All I knew was that I wouldn't have to take any time off for the foreseeable future to attend classes. Thank you Lt. Eckert/DC Zajac, although you have no idea what you just did for me.

* * * * *

Chairman of the Board of Supervisors, Stephen Kelly, couldn't keep his mouth shut (or his typing fingers still) for too long regarding the police department he now once again oversaw through his Deputy Chief. He knew there were "malcontent" officers who complained about how the BPD was being managed under the new regime, essentially HIS new regime, about the witch-hunt (my word, not his) against former Chief Viola, transfers, schedule changes, overtime details to the selected few, rumors of firings and demotions, and the like. So, what does an elected official choose to do in such a situation? Of his many options, he chooses to write an op-ed to the *Bucks County Courier Times*. Did he do it to appease his officers? No, he did it apparently for just the opposite reasons.

Addressed in Kelly's op-ed, among various deficiencies and problems which HIS Chief, Ted Zajac, was attempting to address and fix, was that department members were engaged in various illicit activities. He even went as far as to compare the BPD to the Philadelphia PD which in the very recent past had been rocked with highly publicized corruption charges which resulted in the arrests of numerous officers. According to Kelly, maybe THAT sort of investigation of similar types of corruption is what was needed in the BPD now. Fortunately, he wrote, that's what Deputy Chief Zajac was working hard to remedy.

Kelly's piece was published on August 21st.

One would believe the entirety of the BPD would be up in arms and seething in anger over printed comments such as this by one of Bensalem's elected officials. Every officer, one would think, would be highly agitated and offended by these remarks by Kelly.

Think again.

The Team Zajac members reacted to Kelly's op-ed...well, actually, they didn't react at all. Even after a follow-up newspaper article appeared the day after the op-ed was published, most everyone in the BPD acted as if nothing just happened, instead of their entire agency being torn apart by the Supervisor's reckless and derisive comments.

Not surprisingly, our PBA President, who was so in lock-step with Zajac at this point, stated that he wasn't about to touch this issue. He simply put his head back in his hole in the ground (or perhaps somewhere else) and pretended nothing was wrong. However, as the PBA Vice-President, I knew the BPD had to respond to Kelly, somehow, someway.

After a few days I finally convinced the president to talk to Zajac and see if he'd respond to the op-ed with words of his own, adamantly asserting that his BPD was NOT a corrupt agency. Zajac declined to do so.

Okay, no surprise there. So, what's our next step?

On August 30th an "emergency" meeting of the PBA was called. I requested it. Approximately thirty officers showed up. After much discussion a vote was taken and by a count of 21-9 it was decided that a formal letter would be sent to Kelly by the PBA in which we would demand that he recants his earlier words. I helped compose the letter, it was signed by the five PBA officers (reluctantly so by the President), and it was sent to Kelly AND the *Courier Times*. It was printed in the newspaper and it seemed to work, well, sort of.

On or about September 7th, Kelly wrote another letter and walked-back some of his earlier language. Not all of it, but parts of it. Essentially, the BPD was not THAT corrupt, he wrote, and after that it was mostly just praise for Zajac and the job he was doing to make sure these types of corruption issues would never occur in his BPD.

It was at minimum a partial victory for the good guys on the BPD. It wasn't that much of a recanting but at least Stephen Kelly, as well as Ted Zajac, now knew that there was a faction of officers in the BPD which would have to be reckoned with in the future, especially if pushed too far. Despite this, however, the regime found its own little way of getting back at the rank and file. No surprise, once again.

On the same day as Kelly's letter of clarification was made public, the word spread around the PD like wildfire that on September 17 four to six unnamed officers would be fired. When I came into work on the 7th, I saw where the date September 17 was circled in red on my desk calendar. Hmmm...and about two weeks prior to this there was a Miranda warnings card placed in the center of my desk. Now it was all coming together for me.

Was this another warning from above? Punishment for me stoking the fires as PBA Vice-President? Yes, I was convinced, on both counts.

Well, the good news out of all of this was that no one was fired on or around September 17. Nor was I arrested and read my rights that day either. It was just another one of those strategic rumors (and game-playing) that would pop up every once in a while at the BPD. We all knew the regime would very much have liked to fire at least that many opposition party members, but easier said than done they were finding out.

* * * * *

There was some other bad news I received around this time. It was not related to any of the ongoing nonsense at the BPD, well, at least not directly anyway. It came in the form of a letter to my home. It was from the FBI. Upon opening it, I learned I did not meet the required passing score in my FBI special agent test from several months ago.

Damn!

Double-damn!!

As I continued reading the one-page form letter, I saw that I would have to wait at least six months to take the test again. Then, that would be it for me. A candidate for the position of special agent is only allowed to take the written test two times in total. That means, if I didn't pass it the next time, I could say goodbye to any potential career in the FBI.

Perhaps the next time, make that the final time, I should buy one of those test-preparation books and actually study for the entrance exam. Maybe I'm simply getting the same types of questions wrong each time.

Yes, IF I do it again, I'll definitely prepare for it next time. Yes, definitely....

But that next time would have to wait. Because of various economic conditions in the U. S. in the mid-1980s, President Ronald Reagan suspended most, if not all, federal hiring for the better part of two years. Just my luck! It seems if I wanted to escape the BPD anytime in the next year or two, it would have to be at a job other than the FBI.

* * * * *

Then, there were the headaches.

Not the normal little ones I occasionally had growing up or the ones that I woke up with back in my college years after a night of perhaps too many libations. No, these were different. These were sudden, long-lasting, persistent, painful, and very disruptive to my well-being, my psyche, and my life. They were occurring now at least two to three times per month, usually in the middle of the day, and more frequently as time went by. The first of them seemed to begin earlier this year.

What the hell is causing them? No aspirin or other medicine seemed to work. I would have to go to bed, with the room completely darkened, the house completely quiet, and try to fall asleep. That usually helped me get rid of the headache in a few hours. Usually, but not always.

I would live with these headaches, always popping up at very inopportune times, for the next year-plus. I would eventually get checked out by a neurologist. The diagnosis would be scary, but then very understandable at the same time. Until then, the great discomfort and debilitation would continue, and I never knew when or where it would materialize.

Chapter Forty-Two

"JIM FITZGERALD! HOW THE HELL YA DOIN'?!"

Yes, it was the shrill, disembodied voice of the Deputy Chief. I had just turned down the main hallway at HQ one afternoon, didn't see him behind me at first, and there it was at full or close-to full volume for all to hear.

Why does he do this to me? What does he get out of this oratorical exercise involving me, and apparently only me?

Regardless of the "why" or the "what," I responded to Zajac a bit differently on this day. Instead of the usual "Fine," or "Okay," I half turned my head around and responded, "Actually, not very well today. I have a bad headache. But thanks for asking."

I wasn't really serious about thanking him, but I was serious that my head was hurting.

"Yeah, well take the rest of the day off. We'll be just fine around here," the Deputy Chief unsympathetically offered in response at a somewhat reduced decibel level as he turned into his office.

"Nah, I'll stick it out. You never know when the big one will break and I want to be here for it."

I know he heard me, but he never acknowledged what I said as he slammed his office door behind him.

Of course my retort to Zajac was meant to be glib, just as his prior words to me were likewise meant to be glib. But that's the game we played with each other now. He knew that my role in CID was now as phone answerer and vandalism investigator. If these newly assigned duties of mine (or lack thereof) were not the result of his direct orders, I knew he was fully supportive of Lt. Eckert giving them to me. However, I couldn't help but let him/them think that I was still here and for all the right reasons. I also wanted him to know that I wasn't leaving this place, meaning CID, either for the afternoon or for the rest of my time here without him ordering me to do so. Especially as I was now working a darn good shift, at least for a police officer, that being, straight day work with weekends off.

I relegated myself now to just showing up, doing what was asked of me, and going home. My real life was with my wife and kids, extended family, friends, and going to school again one evening per week. No one inexplicably and very weirdly yelled my name out loud in those places. I was, in reality, doing just fine in the areas of life which really mattered to me.

Except for these damn headaches! They seemed to be following me outside of work now too. What's up with that…?

* * * * *

Headaches notwithstanding, things would change for me in the month of November in the BPD, finally, and in some very dynamic ways. I'd be leaving CID, but not without a bang. There would also be headlines, as well as other newspaper coverage, two separate stories actually, all in the first week of my new assignment. The Deputy Chief and the Detective Lieutenant wouldn't like any of it. But I deemed it, and even partially planned it, as my way of saying "thanks" to them on or around Thanksgiving Day. As a result, it seemed to give both of them their own headaches.

Welcome to the club!

Despite being the newly-anointed chief vandalism investigator, I worked one other case during the month of November, 1984. For that matter, it was just about the ONLY non-vandalistic matter I was assigned the entire first year of the new regime. It strangely stood alone in that regard. It was personally assigned to me by Lt. Eckert himself. This particular assignment to me, of all people, and from him, of all people, made little sense, especially considering how it turned out.

Or, did it make sense to Eckert? Or maybe his wife? I'm still not sure.

As it so happened…

One day in mid-November, Eckert stepped out of his office towards my desk, handed me an incident report from patrol the day before and said, "Here, Fitzgerald, check this out."

It was one of the few times the lieutenant actually spoke to me in CID.

"Okay."

My brief response was one of the few times I actually spoke to Eckert while in CID.

Usually, as mentioned earlier, it was by written memos that we communicated, which I later very much appreciated. It made eventual evidence gathering for me so much easier.

But back to this new case…I immediately assumed what the lieutenant had just handed me was yet another report of vandalism for me to investigate. As such, I began gathering up my usual evidence kit of gloves, magnifying glass, latent print powder, camera, etc., but upon a quick review of the report I realized it wasn't the sort of assignment I had been used to lately.

The standard one-page BPD incident report, written in longhand by a patrol officer, related the concerns of a parent in the Cornwells area of Bensalem Township. Apparently, a mother had learned from her teenage son that a certain local man in his early 30s was acting strange, perhaps even in a sexual manner, when associating himself with her child and some of his friends. The patrolman's report didn't relate too much more in the way of details, so once assigned the case, I decided to contact the mother and set up an interview to learn what I could from her and her son.

It's what the good lieutenant expected of me. So, of course, I did it. It was seemingly an important matter to him and he wanted his best vandalism investigator on it. That would be me.

I told Eckert what I was about to do and he actually gave me permission to leave HQ to follow-up on this investigation. In retrospect, I'm not sure what he was thinking, but that's what he did.

I eventually found my way to the house of the complainant and met with her, her husband, and their fourteen-year-old son. After the basic introductions, and the son seeming a bit sheepish and verbally gun-shy at first, he finally began to open up to me. He said he knew of this man who lived somewhere in the Cornwells area of town. He gave me his full name and advised me he was also a "big shot" in the Boy Scouts and in the local Catholic Church parish.

I continued listening and taking notes….

The teen continued that this guy would drive up to certain local street corners looking for the boys, or even go to their houses, and with the respective parents' approvals, they would get in his car and drive around Bensalem and the neighboring areas. The usual plan was that they were going out for ice cream, to a McDonald's, a Burger King, a pizza parlor, or some such place and this man would be their means of getting them there and back. He'd even treat the kids sometimes, although supposedly not all of the time. They would inevitably park somewhere afterwards, maybe in a mall parking lot, or near one of the restaurants, and the sometimes as many as five boys, along with their older driver, would then start talking about various "stuff" while finishing up their cold or hot treats. These multi-young teen/one adult discussions would go on for an hour or more at times. The conversations, practically every time according to my young interviewee, would eventually turn in some strange directions. Specifically, to that of a sexual nature; actually, he emphasized, of a very personal and detailed sexual nature.

At this point in the interview, I could see the boy was getting a bit nervous. After all, he was sitting in his living room with his parents both alongside of him and presently talking to a police officer about what was clearly a rather uncomfortable subject matter for him. When he was becoming even less specific and less detailed about what he was telling me, I politely asked his parents if they would mind leaving us alone for a few minutes. They agreed and left the room.

With now just the two of us, the boy started telling me, hesitatingly at first, about what this man would be discussing with him and his friends. Once he became somewhat more comfortable with me he told me just how far these car talks would go. He related to me that the guy wanted to know if the boys ever looked at "dirty" pictures of women like those found in *Playboy* or *Penthouse* magazines. If so, did they like what they saw? Could they describe the women? He'd also want to know if they had kissed any girls, touched any girls, and/or had sex with any girls. If "yes" to one or more of those questions, he'd want to know of the young teens what it was like, how it felt, if they used condoms, did they reach orgasm (using other words), etc. On more than one occasion, the man even gave the teenagers condoms and told them to feel free to use them when needed, but that there was "a catch." The "catch" was…he wanted to hear all the details afterwards. My young interviewee on this day in his house found it necessary for some reason to swear to me that he never took any condoms from the guy. I reassured him it was okay, whether he did or not.

The teenager ended this part of our conversation by telling me that all of his friends felt this guy was a bit weird, and they sometimes felt a bit weird talking to this adult male about these particular subject matters. However, they nonetheless continued to see him and "hang out" with him several times per month because, well, it gave them something to do, it got them out of their immediate neighborhoods, and he was "fun" in his own sort of odd manner. Anyway, their parents knew about these ride-arounds with the guy, at least most of the time, so it wasn't like they were doing something wrong or sneaking behind their backs. I nodded in agreement and told him he and his friends were NOT doing anything wrong here. He seemed to appreciate me saying those words. I lastly asked the boy for contact information for his friends and he gave me names and phone numbers for three of them.

I invited the teen's parents back into the living room and we discussed in general what the boy had just told me. I advised them I was going to contact the other boys he mentioned in an attempt to get further information from them about this guy. Of course, for my own purposes, I also wanted to corroborate the information this kid had just given me too. I eventually would.

I left it with the family that I would get back to them when I knew more of what was going on here. They thanked me and walked me out the front door.

These parents seemed like very nice people who had a genuine concern for their son and his friends. They suspected something wasn't right about the man in question and they wanted the police to determine just what he was up to and what his agenda may be with these young boys. I wanted to know that too.

As I would soon learn, however, not all of the parents in this investigation would act like these two. Not even close.

Naturally, before I would do anything else on this case, I would check out this man by his full name and learn as much as I could about him. So, back at HQ later that same day I ran his criminal history. I saw that he had no previous arrests or any criminal record within the BPD. Okay, that's good to know. Let's see, what else can I find out about him? I'll check these records, these reports, this card file. Oh, here's his name....

Okay, here's his local address. He's 32. He's single. Whoa! Are you kidding me? Can this be accurate?

Yes, it apparently is!

What I didn't initially know, what this first boy and his parents didn't know, nor what Lt. Eckert didn't SEEM to know (or tell me), was that this man wasn't just your everyday, run-of-the-mill weirdo. No, he was a politically-connected weirdo.

This was Republican Committeeman Joseph R. Scheck, Jr.

Oh, and make that Bensalem Township Auditor Joseph R. Scheck, Jr. Say what?!

This guy obviously had some political clout in Bensalem. He knows important people, relatively speaking, and they know him. Otherwise, he wouldn't be holding these relatively important positions within the township political machine and within the government itself.

(As it so happens, I did NOT know Joseph Scheck or had ever even heard his name prior to this investigation. He had been missing from my local political radar up until this point in time.)

So, let me get this right. Scheck is moving in these political circles and holding these two positions and at the same time he's hanging out with teenage boys? Not eighteen-year-olds when they're "legal" (which even then would still be a bit odd), but with kids all around fourteen years of age? And talking sex stuff as well as distributing condoms to them?

Okay, I'm not a subject matter expert regarding the sexual exploitation of children (not yet, anyway), but something isn't right here. What he's doing with these kids may not technically be illegal, but it's only a step or two away from illegality at this point in time. Or, maybe it's already happened.

Either way, I have to get more intel on this guy. I gotta talk to these other kids.

The next day, I went to the homes of the three other boys. Interestingly, and right away, at least two of the separate parents involved became very defensive regarding Mr. Politico.

The first mom told me, "How dare you come to our house and ask questions such as these? Do you know Joe Scheck is our committeeman? Do you know he's the township auditor? He's a sweet man. He's a kind man. He would NEVER do anything to harm these boys."

"You're treading on thin ice," another mom at another house told me regarding this sort of inquiry. "Joe Scheck is in the Boy Scouts and very active in our church, too! He's done nothing wrong! Go search out some real criminals!"

Geez, was she talking about graffiti artists and nighttime window-breakers? What did she know about ME and my present assignment?

I was also wondering if Mom #1 had called Mom #2 when I was on my way to the latter's house after the first interview. #2 seemed very much prepared for my brief encounter with her son and husband regarding Joe Scheck.

I should add here that neither of these parents nor their two sons denied that they knew Scheck, or that he drove the boys around on occasion and even talked sometimes about "sex stuff." Whatever of this information may have been meaningful to them or not, it seems they simply did not appreciate me investigating the ride-arounds, this man, these boys, or their budding in-car relationships.

Hmmm… this is getting even stranger. Didn't they read in the newspaper about the priest I busted not even eighteen months ago? He started with his fourteen-year-old boys in many of the same ways. I guess they don't get the local paper or follow the news or they have short memories. I hope that's all it is.

Fortunately, at least the one remaining teenager did confirm in some detail what the first boy told me. He didn't think it was that big of a deal, nor did his mom and dad, that Joe would sometimes talk about sex, even very specific sexual situations.

"Hey," these particular parents told me, "they're all males here, what could go wrong?"

Hmmm…I knew LOTS that could go wrong here. It just hasn't happened yet, or at least not of which anyone was willing to admit.

Bottom line here, after four different teenage boy interviews I knew I didn't have the probable cause to arrest Committeeman/Auditor Joe Scheck. He's weird and has some strange sexual preoccupations involving young boys, granted, but I would need more than what I've heard so far to get an arrest warrant for him. I will go and talk to him though. Let's see then what he tells me about his various interactions with these kids. He probably already knows he's in my sights as some of the kids OR their parents may have already contacted him. It wouldn't surprise me at all, especially how some of these parents seemed to defend this guy to me.

I guess he's one heck of an auditor and committeeman, or for that matter Boy Scout leader and/or Knight of Columbus grand pupa.

Interestingly, this whole episode brought me back to my own days as a teenager and having a somewhat similar coming-of-age experience as these boys. Growing up in the Olney neighborhood of Philadelphia, my buddies and I, all around the age of fourteen, made friends with an unmarried guy who was literally twice our age at the time. His popular nickname was Big Ed. He was called that because he was, in fact, tall and heavyset, and his name was Ed. He was actively involved in the Catholic Church too, specifically our St. Helena parish. He would drive us around in his very nice car, we'd go places to eat, and yes, we would sometimes talk about sex. But that would be pretty much the extent of it.

Big Ed met our respective parents, on his insistence, and they were alright with us doing these things with him on occasion. However, Ed never gave us condoms, girly magazines, or asked us details about our respective sex lives, or the lack thereof back then. Yes, we occasionally discussed sexual issues, but it was not the primary topics of our drive-arounds with him.

As far as I know, over the years, nothing of an overt sexual nature ever occurred between Ed and any of my buddies. As time went on, and we all reached adulthood (Big Ed, of course, was already way ahead of us), we stayed close friends with him.

(Much more on Big Ed and his role in my early life is found in JCM Book I.)

So, with my sort of similar and somewhat odd guy from my own past in Big Ed, I wasn't quite sure what was going on here with these young kids in Bensalem. I didn't see it as a crisis situation or something that I had to jump on right away because, well, the evidence so far just didn't support me arresting Scheck nor was it indicative of a sexual crime necessarily being imminent. Certainly, none of the parents seemed to feel that way. He was definitely strange and arguably suspicious, but not arrest-worthy, at least not yet. I should talk to him and see what he says about his relationship with these kids. If nothing else, maybe I can scare the committeeman/auditor from doing anything illegal with them. Sometimes in these type situations it's the most an investigator can do.

As it turns out, that opportunity never presented itself. Well, not that exact opportunity, anyway. But, as I came to learn in life, where one door closes, another door opens.

* * * * *

As the days of November grew colder and darker, and after I had a few days off and Lt. Eckert had a few other days off (and/or he was diligently working at the White House on the Viola Mini-Task Force), I never had the chance to advise him either verbally or via our usual written memo means of what I had found out regarding the politician and his teenage boy entourage. So, I kept the interview notes in a folder in my CID desk and awaited the chance to interview Scheck. I would do it first thing next week and fill in the lieutenant accordingly.

However, within just a day or two of these initial interviews of the teenagers, on Friday, November 16th, right before lunch, lo and behold, I got the memo. Yes, THE memo. It was from the Deputy Chief himself. I suppose my name should have been typed in all caps to reflect his recent penchant for yelling my name, but it wasn't. In mostly lower-case lettering, and in less than thirty words or so, I was advised of my new assignment. In three nights, on November 19th, I was to report to Patrol Division, specifically a certain patrol squad starting its 9P-7A shift, and then and there I was to assume the position of patrol sergeant.

So, after almost eleven full months under the nose of Zajac and Eckert in CID, it was off to patrol I was going.

This is actually good news to me. But I couldn't help but ask myself…What took them so long? And why now?

Hmmm…let me think about this….

My sudden transfer wouldn't have anything to do with the investigation of Joe Scheck, would it? Am I getting too close to something, someone, here? Did Zajac or Eckert get a phone call? Is that why I'm being shuffled off to patrol all of a sudden? But if so, why would my lieutenant have assigned me that case in the first place if he didn't want me to learn about this committeeman/auditor and his teenage boy sex-life (so far) shenanigans?

Well, I didn't know the answers to these questions, not then, anyway. All I knew was that I was happy to be out of CID. I know it would mean I was off the 8-4 shift and I'd be working weekends again, but that's okay. I could take an hour or two of comp time on the evenings of my grad classes and still manage fine. It was all very doable and this transfer was actually a very welcome change in my professional life.

Upon checking the roster of the squad I was to supervise, I knew I was friendly with most of the officers. That fact should help make it an easier transition for me. It would be my very first time working as a patrol sergeant, but I knew I could do it. I had been away from patrol and wearing a uniform for over a year and a half, but it'll all come back to me once I…

Wait! "…wearing a uniform…?"

Uh-oh! There's a problem here, a potentially big problem. I CAN'T go to patrol anytime real soon and for a very logical and pragmatic reason. I better tell Zajac of this right away. Fingers, start typing that memo.

My "problem" was two-fold, as in the folds found in one's shirts and pants. It just struck me that I owned no uniform shirts and pants. My leather gear, holster, nightstick, etc., were still in my locker, but not the actual clothing itself which comprised the new uniform of my police department.

Going back in time a bit...within a few months of Chief Viola arriving at the BPD, and after commenting that he thought our then-uniforms made us look like "bus drivers," he ordered every patrol officer and supervisor to get new ones. The new uniform shirts would be a different shade of gray, and the new pants would have a light blue stripe down the outside of each leg. They did look nicer than the old uniforms, I must admit.

Unfortunately, somewhere in that process starting over two years ago, as a CID suit-and-tie wearing acting detective then full sergeant, I never got around to ordering the new uniform shirts and pants. I turned in the old ones, but I never got the new ones. I knew from my tenure as the admin officer it would take several weeks to get these items, even if I ordered them today.

Back to the present...What do I do now? What does the Deputy Chief do now?

Well, that's why Zajac gets paid the big bucks. That's why HE is the Deputy Chief once again! He'll come up with the solution. Guaranteed!

I sent the DC a memo regarding my uniform situation within an hour of receiving my transfer notice. Within a few hours I had his response back. In so many words, it read: "You will order your new uniform shirts and pants immediately. In the meantime, you will report to your new assignment. You will temporarily wear civilian clothes while sergeant of your patrol squad."

So...I'm to be a uniformed patrol sergeant, supervising uniformed patrol officers, driving a marked patrol car, but wearing, at least initially, civilian clothing. Okay, that's a first. I've never seen or heard of anything such as this situation before in my agency or elsewhere. But we are in Bensalem, after all, the PD where virtually anything goes, at least under this current regime.

Well, I've now got my orders, uniform or no uniform, and I will of course obey them. I wasn't sure exactly yet what I would wear on my first few tours of duty, but as I'm working a 9P-7A shift for those first four days, I won't be seeing any bosses around the place, and more importantly, they won't be seeing me. In that case, I'll wear whatever I want to wear. All Zajac's memo said was "civilian clothes" were in order.

Let me see now...What do I have hanging in my closet that would be even a little bit fashionable, comfortable, durable, warm, not too dark, would cover my .357 Magnum in my old Tac Squad shoulder holster, yet should it be needed give me quick access to it? Geez, this isn't as easy as I thought it would be.

That last Friday afternoon in CID was uneventful. Lt. Eckert was in the White House that day, and the one or two detectives on-duty then said "good luck," etc., as I walked out the back door for the last time. It was a quiet departure for me, just as I preferred.

Once again, however, it would prove to be the quiet before the storm in my BPD-related life.

Over that weekend, I went through my closet and even the attic and decided on what to wear on my next few shifts as a patrol sergeant, sans an official uniform. My wife couldn't believe that the powers-that-are would have me doing everything that a uniformed patrolman/supervisor would be doing, but wearing regular street clothes while doing it. I reassured her that it would only be temporary and I'd make sure to be careful out there. She was right, though. It was hard to believe.

Regarding my temporary "uniform," I knew I wasn't going to be wearing anything of value while on these shifts. I didn't want to get in a wrestling match with a drunk or two and have any of my good clothes soiled or ripped. So, I gathered up a few older, plain long-sleeved shirts, two pairs of not-so-new khaki pants, and I managed to find and dig out my late father's old winter coat. This zippered, cold-weather overcoat wasn't anything fancy, but it was warm, it had deep pockets, it was light brown in color (so I could be seen at least a little bit at night if on the highway), and even a hood if it happened to be raining or snowing. I'm not even sure why I had saved the coat in the five-plus years since his death, but I figured if anyone could keep me safe (and warm) out there it would be Wally, looking down from above. This would be especially true as he wouldn't want anything bad happening to his favorite coat.

Okay, so temporary wardrobe crisis was over. For now, anyway.

I headed into work for my first ever shift as a patrol sergeant on 8:30 that Monday evening, November 19th. The 5P-3A squad was already on the streets, and now it was my new squad coming in to get ready for the late-night shift, all the way until 7:00AM the next morning. As by design, these two shifts overlapped each other for six hours, so there were extra officers on patrol during the busiest times of the night.

I've stood at enough roll calls to know how to handle this one, my first ever on the OTHER side of the line. It went well as I read to my ten new subordinates what cars were recently stolen, who was wanted for one felony crime or another, which officer had which sector, and the like. I didn't bother to check their guns, their other equipment, or their uniforms that first night. It would have been pretty strange considering the "uniform" I was wearing. So, they had their assignments, gathered their freshly charged flashlights and portable radios, and off into the night they went. I certainly didn't feel like hanging around HQ as I had seen enough of this place over the last year, so I told them I'd be out there with them before long.

As it turned out, my joining them would be delayed a few hours on this particular night. But it would be for good reason.

Before heading out on the streets, I walked up front to the dispatcher's office, said hello to them, and asked if there was anything else I should know. The two of them told me that so far it has been a quiet evening and there wasn't much else going on out there. We agreed that we were all hoping it would stay that way, especially on this, my first night ever as a patrol sergeant. They assured me they would do their best to keep it that way. We all chuckled and went about our business. Out of habit from my time in CID, I went through some of the calls from the last few days. After noting that most of them were very routine, one of them eventually caught my attention.

I didn't have a whole lot to go on, as I was only reading through the dispatcher's log sheet and listening to what one of them then told me about the initial phone call he received, but it seems that on Friday evening the BPD was contacted by a woman who wanted to report an adult "flasher" of some sort involving a male friend of her fourteen-year-old son. It had occurred in the Cornwells area of Bensalem. That was really all I had at the time. The call was subsequently handled that evening by an officer on the 5-3 shift. As it so happened, that officer was on the last night of that shift right now.

So…could this have anything to do with my case from last week? It's a long shot, but as it happened in the Cornwells area, and it involved a young male teen, I should probably check it out. So, I dug out the officer's incident report and read it. It had some basic information on it but little in the way of specifics. I needed more.

Once I left HQ and got to my patrol car (remembering to check under the back seat for weapons, evidence, etc., just as I always did in the past), I picked up the mike and requested the officer who took the aforementioned report on Friday to meet me. I didn't want what I was about to ask him going all over the Bucks County police airwaves. So instead, a one-on-one meeting between us it would be.

In just a few minutes, the officer and I met at the darkened gas station at the intersection of Street Rd. and Hulmeville Rd. I started asking him some questions about his report. He briefly described to me what the kid told him regarding what allegedly happened to his friend in the last week or two, where it happened, the circumstances, etc.

From his driver's seat to my driver's seat, through two open car windows, the officer continued by relating to me, "The kid said he was told by the victim that it was some local guy that all the neighborhood teenagers knew, but he didn't know his name...or wouldn't give it up to me, anyway."

I then asked the officer, "When did the incident occur?"

"The kid said his friend told him it was a week or so ago, but he doesn't know the exact date."

"So...seven to fourteen days ago," I uttered aloud.

"Yeah, that sounds about right," the officer responded, not really knowing what I already knew or now suspected.

If this time frame is accurate, this incident may have occurred before I was even assigned this case by Lt. Eckert. That makes things even more interesting IF, in fact, it's connected to my earlier investigation.

I wrote down what I needed of the victim kid's info, thanked the officer, and we drove off our separate ways. Without even driving back to police HQ, without even getting my file which should have still been in the CID sergeant desk's lower drawer, I drove immediately to the address of the young victim. I let dispatch know I would be "10-6," that is, busy for a while, and I gave the address where I'd be. With portable police radio at low volume in hand, I then knocked on the door of the house.

As I was awaiting someone to open the door, I found myself wondering...Am I a CID sergeant right now or a patrol sergeant? I'm wearing civilian clothes but I am driving a patrol car. I suppose outer appearances of either car or person didn't matter at this place and time. Nonetheless, I decided regardless of whatever specific position I held or did not hold right now I was still a police officer and an investigator, first and foremost. Let me put both those skillsets together in an attempt to figure out just what I have here in this case involving the young teen. Maybe it's nothing, maybe it's something...but I was determined to know one way or the other before this night was over.

Fortunately, the police radio was relatively quiet and it stayed that way for the next hour-plus. As such, it gave me some flexibility here to channel a bit of my former position of CID sergeant and fulltime investigator. There'd be plenty of time for my new position, I was sure, with or without an official uniform. But first this....

Even though it was about 10:15 at night, a school night no less, a woman finally came to the door after I pushed the small, lighted button adjacent to it several times. Luckily, it seemed I hadn't awakened her. I identified myself by flipping open my wallet which contained my badge and picture ID. After she turned on the porch light she looked me up and down a few times somewhat hesitatingly. But upon seeing the marked police car in her driveway she relented and invited me inside her house. She didn't seem to focus on the issue of me in civvies yet driving a marked car. That was good. When asked, she acknowledged to being the mother of a certain fourteen-year-old boy and that he was, in fact, at home. That was good, too.

I next apologized to her for my late and unannounced visit, but I assured her this was very important. The mom was okay with it and invited me into her living room. She had no apparent idea as to the reason I was there.

I first assured the woman that her son was not in any trouble but that I had to talk to him. He may have been a witness to a crime, I advised her, and I needed to get a firsthand description of what happened. She was surprised to hear all of this, but agreed nonetheless to call her son downstairs to meet with me. Upon doing so, the skinny, somewhat short for his age, young teenager then joined us. Billy (fictitious name, of course), walked over and stood alongside his mom. I reached out my hand to shake his, he offered his in kind, and I introduced myself. It was now just the three of us in the living room about to have a chat which, quite frankly, none of us knew at that point exactly where it would lead.

Naturally, I started the conversation. Without telling either of them what I already knew about this case and the other local boys, a weird Bensalem politician, or anything of the sort, I simply asked Billy to tell me what he recently told his friend about a certain incident that took place when he was riding his bike. I assured the boy and his mother that it was important for me to hear what he himself had to say regarding whatever it was that happened to him a week or two ago. I continued that I couldn't simply proceed with this matter based solely on what someone else who heard about it had informed me. In effect, I had to learn of it directly from the source. That would be Billy. He seemed to understand this notion.

It didn't take long for Billy to figure out that it was his neighborhood friend who must have told his own mom, with her then calling the BPD. I didn't deny this scenario as it now made sense to my interviewee as to how the police came to learn about this incident. But as I really didn't yet know specifically what happened to him on that day, or exactly who else was involved, I told him to forget the how or the why of me being at his house tonight but simply that I now wanted to hear his version of the story. So, after looking at his mom for twenty seconds or so, then down to the floor, sort of clenching his teeth and slowly rubbing his hands together at the same time Billy sat up straight, looked at me, and began to talk.

It seems one day after school sometime during the last two weeks, the boy really couldn't remember exactly when, he was riding his bicycle through the nearby Ramblers Field. This was an area on Hulmeville Rd., south of Street Rd., and not too far from the boy's house in the Cornwells neighborhood of Bensalem. It had a few fenced-in baseball playing areas on it, and a large field where cars would park when games were underway. He couldn't remember the precise time he was there, but knows it was not quite dark yet as the sun hadn't completely set. We agreed that it was perhaps around 3:30 to 5:00 that day.

Billy continued by telling us that while by himself there riding his bike, with few if any other kids or adults in the general area (as November is not baseball season), he happened to notice a lone, dirty, dark-colored car pull off of Hulmeville Rd. onto the open field. After a very short time, the car drove in his direction and even seemed to be following him at a distance. He thought he recognized the car and the driver, but wasn't completely sure at first as it was mostly behind him up until this time. Upon doing a few more laps riding up and down the dirt and grass field/parking lots between Hulmeville Rd. and the baseball diamonds, he noticed the car still driving slowly and maintaining the same approximate distance to the rear of him.

However, Billy stated in a strikingly more animated manner, this was about to change. In a matter of just seconds, the car sped up, drove around him and in front of him and all of a sudden it came to a complete stop about fifty feet ahead of him. The teenager advised his mom and me, almost apologetically, that he really had no choice but to continue riding his bike towards the rear of this car as there were puddles or other obstructions on either side of him and he couldn't readily veer to his left or right in an attempt to avoid a close encounter with the car.

447

In continuing his same bike riding pace, and as he approached the area of the rear bumper on the driver's side of the now-stationary car, he noticed the front door quickly fly open. What he saw next, he readily admitted, really shocked him.

Now about ten minutes into this interview of Billy, with his mom sitting next to him on their living room couch, I observed her to be as much compelled by this story as I was. The boy was very matter-of-fact in his relating of it and didn't hesitate or seem to forget any of the pertinent details up to this point. Neither of the two adults in the room knew exactly where this was all going or who else may be involved in it. However, I was pretty sure we were just about to find out.

Billy continued, "So, I ride my bike right next to where the car had stopped and, and, almost like he planned it this way...the guy opens the door and swings his legs out towards me. And, uh, I could see his pants, uh, his pants were down around his ankles, his underwear too, and he was...uh...uh..., well, you know, touching himself."

I always hated doing this to crime victims, especially younger victims of sex crimes, but I had to ask them more specific questions of what they had experienced at the time of whatever incident it may be that they're reporting. The case and the possible prosecution depended on it. This matter was no exception.

"Billy, can you be more detailed as to what, if anything, the man was doing at that time?"

After a sideward glance toward his mom, Billy looked back at me, cleared his throat, and said, "Uh, yeah, well, he was, you know, going up and down on his...you know, uh, penis, real fast with his hand and looking at me the whole time and sort of smiling. I guess...uh...he was, you know, uh, jerking off. He even said 'Huh,' or something like that to me when I was the closest to him. I think I slowed down 'cause I was so surprised at what I was seeing, at what he was doing and all that, but then I sped off, crossed Hulmeville Rd., and came right home. I don't think he followed me."

Billy then looked directly at his mom and said, unsolicited, "No, I never told you about it. I don't know why, I just didn't. Sorry."

Mom touched Billy's hand and told him it was okay and that telling it now to the police officer was the right thing to do. She glanced in my direction, our eyes met, and she nodded her head approvingly at me. That was reassuring, especially after my experience with a few of the other moms from last week.

I was forced to ask the teen a few more questions, unfortunately some of the more graphic variety, and he answered them the best he could. Then, it came to the most important question of the night to him.

"Do you know this man? Do you know his name?"

Billy responded without hesitation, "Yeah, sure, I do. I thought you already knew it. It's Joe Scheck. All the kids around here know him. I've known of him for a couple of years. He drives around here all the time."

So, it WAS Joe Scheck. I knew this man was trouble from the very first kid's description of his very strange proclivities. I knew he wasn't just TALKING about sex with these kids. He was most likely acting out on his little fantasies too. He certainly did with this kid, Billy.

My next very important question to Billy was whether Scheck had ever tried anything like this before with him. He told me "No," this was the one and only time. Although he heard Scheck liked to talk about sex to his friends (none of the boys I had already interviewed), he never heard of him doing anything quite like this before.

Okay, well one time is certainly once too many in this type of crime, with this type of guy, with this type of victim...meaning a child. An arrest is forthcoming, no doubt. I'd still need some more details and a commitment of sorts from Billy. Go slow though, Jim, go slow....

Needless to say, Billy, my young teenage victim, was very confident in relating to me who it was he saw that day, even following-up by describing Scheck as well as his car in great detail to me. Actually, his entire rendition of what he just told me reeked of confidence; embarrassment perhaps at times, but with full assuredness nonetheless as to the vivid details. He'll make a good witness, I thought to myself, if it ever comes to that.

Now, if we could only narrow down the date that this incident occurred. It wasn't absolutely critical to making the arrest, to making the case, but it would help.

After a short break in which we talked about school, sports, and similar young teenage interests, I inquired further of Billy, "Can you possibly think of anything that could help you figure out the exact day this happened?"

I asked the mom at the same time if she had a desk or wall calendar we could borrow. She said she did and provided me with it. I pointed to it and we went over his school schedule, possible doctor appointments, sports practices or games, TV shows, anything at all which could maybe help us figure out when this incident happened.

As of now, we knew the *where*, we knew the *what*, and most importantly, we knew the *who* involving this incident. But knowing specifically the *when* of it would really help further this case and any future prosecution of Scheck.

Billy and I went back and forth with the date issue, mom too, looking at the calendar and agreeing that it was probably during the second week of November. Other than that, however, he just couldn't recall which specific day it could have been.

"Okay, how about this? Do you recall the weather that day?"

He didn't except he knew it wasn't raining.

"By chance, was there any sort of car accident or police activity along Hulmeville Rd. that I can check in the PD records and maybe establish the date?"

No, nothing.

"Hmmm…any fire trucks speed by that day?"

"No, not that I remember…but wait," Billy, now standing up in his living room said, "Now that you've asked that…I remember hearing the sirens going off. Yeah, that's right, just about the time I saw Joe, you know, doing what he was doing…the fire alarms were blasting. My friend's dad is a volunteer fireman and I pay attention to those things. I'm not sure if that helps, but it's all I can remember right now about it."

I thanked him for that sudden memory jolt. I wasn't sure exactly what I could do with this info, but it's better than nothing.

I was about to leave the house but before I did so I had to ask both mom and son one more very important question. That was, would they be willing to follow-through on this matter and, in fact, be willing to press charges against Scheck? Could they offer me a commitment here tonight to do so?

The mother didn't answer the question immediately. Instead, she told me that through Billy she had heard of Joe Scheck before and knew that he had befriended some local boys over the last few years. From the little she knew, she thought him a bit strange, but as he had no previous direct contact with her son, she hadn't really been too concerned about the guy in the past. She was sure her son never had any significant contact with him, and Billy reassured his mom and me once again that he hadn't. It was only this one time a week or so ago at the field.

The mom was now slowly becoming angry at this man and how he DARED to do this to her son. After fuming just a bit, she provided me with a resounding "YES," that she wanted to press charges. Billy, standing right next to her, aware now of her anger and upon hearing the emphasis with which his mom was framing her words, shrugged his shoulders and said he would too. I really would need a strong level of commitment from both of them here, so it was a relief to hear mom and son in total agreement. I explained to both that Billy may have to testify in court one or more times, etc. He and his mom said they were fine with doing whatever it would take to resolve this matter. They knew this guy broke the law, was "sick and perverted," and they wanted him to pay for it.

That was all I needed to hear. As it was now after 11:00, and Billy had school the next day, I told them I was going to depart. I asked them to keep this interview and this incident a secret for now (besides the one friend he already told) as I didn't want Joe Scheck or anyone else finding out about the BPD involvement before I could get the warrant for his arrest. They agreed to do so. I told them I would be in touch with them over the next few nights and would advise them about the arrest once it occurred so they wouldn't be surprised by reading about it in the newspaper. They thanked me and said goodbye.

So, off I went, now with only seven and one-half hours left of my patrol shift. Once inside the patrol car, however, I didn't radio "10-8," back in service, to the dispatcher. Not yet, anyway. I first wanted to drive by Joe Scheck's house and check out his car. As the boy provided me a detailed description of the vehicle, I wanted to see if the actual car matched what he told me.

Billy never did copy down or memorize the car's tag number, but as far as the make, model, color, approximate year, and even a dent of some sort on it, the kid had it right on the money. (He knew his automobiles.) I could see this when I slowly drove by Scheck's home and there was the car, clearly illuminated under a street light.

"22-7 (me) is now 10-8!"

I was now back in service with my new squad. It was around 11:30PM. My uniformed charges did fine without me so far. I knew they would. But I also knew besides handling these officers and any patrol-related situations which may arise tonight, I had to handle this case too. I probably could have turned the whole thing over to CID, connected the dots for them, but something told me not to. Something told me that if I did that, this matter would not be resolved anytime soon, if at all. So, I decided right then and there, as I was driving directly across from the Rambler's Field area where the incident occurred, this was my case, it was assigned to me, and I was going to be the one to take it to its logical conclusion and arrest this guy. I didn't know exactly when, but it would be this week before 7:00AM on Friday morning. I had to get him off the streets even if it meant him spending Thanksgiving in jail. It would be too bad if he was to miss the Scheck family turkey dinner that day.

But first, I had to figure out when this incident with Billy on his bike actually occurred. Let me see here…what did he say about fire sirens going off on that day?

I knew I was just about there with this case. I could probably call the Bucks DA's office tomorrow and get the approval to swear out an arrest warrant for Scheck. But I had to do more to figure out when exactly this incident with the boy on the bike and the man in the car occurred. Again, it wasn't absolutely crucial for the case to have this date confirmed, but it would make it more sellable to the DA's office, and eventually perhaps, to a judge and jury.

So, I kept working on it that night….

In 1984, there were at least five volunteer fire departments in Bensalem. Three of them, the Nottingham, Eddington, and Cornwells departments, would each have been within potential earshot of the Ramblers Field on whatever day the incident occurred. Eddington and Cornwells were the closest to the area, perhaps within one-half mile as the crow flies to their respective locations. The Nottingham station location was a mile or so away in a straight line, but it couldn't be ruled out as there were no natural or manmade impediments between the locations which would necessarily dampen the siren sound from firehouse to field. It is at the station houses of those three fire departments that I would begin my search to determine if any of them responded to a fire (or at least sounded an alarm) on a Monday through Friday sometime during the last two weeks, sometime between 3:30 and 5:00 in the afternoon.

I didn't want to waste any time on this matter. As such, I knew that the stations were generally closed overnight (if there wasn't a nighttime fire somewhere), but some of the members came in as early as 4:00AM to open up their respective facilities for the day. So, starting around 4:00AM that morning, on still my first shift as a patrol sergeant, I drove to each of the three fire companies in an attempt to determine which of them, if any, sounded their alarm in the late afternoon in the not-too-distant past. Fortunately, these individual departments were not all that busy on a daily basis so it shouldn't be too difficult to figure out when, or if, one of them may have done so.

I believe it was the Eddington firehouse I went to first, as it was the closest to Ramblers Field. Without providing any details as to why I was asking this question, the volunteer firefighter in the office portion of the firehouse nonetheless gladly checked his records and told me that there were no alarms anytime during the last two weeks between 3:30PM and 5:00PM. He even showed me the master black book where they recorded all of their fire-related activities. I thanked him and went on my way. My next stop, to the Cornwells firehouse, provided the same results, that is, no alarms matching up to those times. I was down to one more firehouse, and interestingly, of the three aforementioned station houses, it was the one farthest away from the scene of the crime.

Around 5:30AM, I drove to the Nottingham firehouse on Street Rd., near Richlieu Rd., and found one old-timer inside the place. When I knocked and walked in and identified myself, he looked at me, saw my marked car outside yet my rather bland non-official clothing and playfully inquired, "Where's your uniform, Sarge?"

I told him an abridged version of my recent transfer story, leaving the politics out of it, and advised him why I was there. He said he'd be glad to help me but added, "I don't understand why you're out here with no uniform or equipment. I wouldn't send any of my firefighters to do their job without their proper uniforms or equipment, that's for sure." I politely agreed with him, but was really in no mood to discuss uniform versus non-uniform matters with him. He was right, of course, but I'd save this banter for some other time and place.

"Yeah, I hear ya, but about that alarm being triggered, 3:30 to 5:00, on a weekday...."

The in-house firefighter walked over to another part of the building, found a book which was virtually identical to the books at the other two firehouses, opened it and started flipping through the pages. Finding the most recent page he used his index finger and moving down the page he came to a stop on a specific line.

"Let's see," the crusty older volunteer mumbled, "it looks like at 4:15PM on November 8th we hit the alarm. There was a shed fire at...."

That's all I needed to hear. I actually saw it too, as I peeked over the man's suspender-bearing shoulders (holding up HIS uniform pants) as he was scrolling down the book page. I could clearly see the notation itself indicating the date and time of the alarm being sounded.

I requested a photocopy of the page and he made one for me. I gave the man a solid handshake and thanked him for his time. As I was leaving I told him I'd stop back sometime in uniform, just to show him I actually owned one. He laughed and said, "Anytime, Sarge. Hey, by the way... what's this all about?"

I just kept walking to my car, waving to him on the way out.

Now I knew, it was on Thursday, the eighth of November, that this offense occurred. Billy said he heard the alarm just about the same time as Joe Scheck opened his car door. That pinpoints the time of the incident down to practically the minute. This victim was going to be a great witness. And this was going to be a great case, certainly in terms of prosecuting it. Now, I just have to get the warrant approved by an ADA, get it signed by a magistrate, and then go arrest the Bensalem Township Auditor. No problem....

When I returned to HQ that morning at 6:15AM, and knowing no detectives would be in yet, I went back to CID and got the file out of my former desk drawer. The file was just where I left it. After going over the paperwork of my officers from overnight, which fortunately was a quiet shift for everyone, I took the file, my various notes from the last ten hours, and went home. My goal was to get a good day's sleep and call the DA's office in Doylestown by mid-afternoon. And that's exactly what I did.

When I awoke at around 2:00PM, I ate "breakfast," pulled out the file, went over my notes from the night before, called the DA's office in Doylestown, and asked for the "on-call ADA." This was protocol for making a planned arrest with a warrant, as opposed to an officer making an "on view" arrest at the scene at the exact time of a crime. Once the ADA got on the line, I ran the whole case by him. After listening intently, taking his own notes, and asking a few follow-up questions, he eventually posited that I had probable cause to attain an arrest warrant for Joseph Scheck. We agreed that the listed charges would be Indecent Exposure, Open Lewdness, and Corruption of Minors. I thanked him and said goodbye.

For no reason other than extreme caution, and maybe just a little bit of paranoia, at no time during the call did I tell the ADA of Scheck's political affiliation within Bensalem Township politics. As far as he knew, he was just a regular person who committed this crime and whom I was now going to arrest. I didn't know this ADA's connections within the political substructure at either the County level or at the Bensalem level, but as Scheck's office and position were in and of themselves not germane to this incident or this crime, it went unmentioned during our phone call. I simply didn't want to risk any politician, or for that matter politically connected law enforcement officer, getting to Scheck before I did. I wanted this as a complete surprise to him at the time of his arrest, whenever that would be.

On that Tuesday night's shift, I went in to HQ again at 8:30, awaiting my squad to show up. Much like the night before, I went through roll call and got them out in short time and on patrol. I would be joining them, I told them, but I first had some admin matters to take care of here at HQ.

One of those matters included first finding out who was the on-call district magistrate for the night. I found out and called their office and told the staff person that I'd be there around midnight to get an arrest warrant signed. She said the magistrate would be there.

The next matter was to prepare the probable cause affidavit and the arrest warrant itself. I had done both before on numerous occasions as a detective and knew it wouldn't take me all that long to complete them. As such, I began pecking away at the typewriter in the secretaries' area. I didn't want to use the typewriters in CID as there were detectives back there, specifically one or two that I didn't necessarily trust. It would have looked odd for a patrol sergeant to be typing an arrest warrant around those guys. I knew they would have peered over my shoulders to see just who it was I would be arresting and I wanted to avoid that possibility. So, I did it behind the closed doors of the where the secretaries sit during the daytime, adjacent to the dispatcher's room.

Perhaps I should have pulled out the typewriter ribbon when I was done with the warrant and affidavit, like the detective on Zajac's first night back in office, but I didn't. I didn't deem it necessary, and it wasn't.

By midnight, I drove to one of the adjoining towns to the on-call district magistrate's office. I presented to him my completed probable cause affidavit and arrest warrant. A few minutes later in his courtroom I raised my hand and swore on a Bible that all I attested in the two documents was true and accurate to the best of my knowledge. In front of the magistrate I signed the documents, he signed the documents, he put his seal on them, he kept his copies, and gave the remaining copies to me. I thanked him and left his office.

I was now holding in my hand an arrest warrant for Bensalem citizen Joseph Scheck. That's really the only way I saw him as during the course of this investigation, nothing more, nothing less. However, I knew others, from the media to his fellow politicos, not to mention some police department higher-ups and their elected/appointed wives, would focus on Joseph Scheck the Bensalem Auditor, a GOP Committeeman, a Boy Scout leader, and a member of the Knights of Columbus. Oh, and no doubt me, the non-uniform wearing patrol sergeant, who arrested him.

In view of all this, I knew my investigation was sound. What Billy told me was truthful, this pending arrest was legal, and Scheck did what he did (although, of course, he's innocent until proven guilty). But it would still come down to this current regime that it was me who was the arresting officer of one of THEIR politicians representing THEIR present regime.

I didn't care. This guy, in his own way, was a menace to society, certainly the young, teenage boy society, and he had to be dealt with accordingly. I was assigned this case and I was going to close out this case. And I'll do it tomorrow night, as soon as I start my shift.

Signed arrest warrant, you're residing in my locker for now. See you first thing tomorrow night.

On Wednesday, November 21st, the night before Thanksgiving, I once again got the troops out and on their way by just a little after 9:00. One of the newer guys even said to me, "Geez, Sarge, we don't see much of you out here at night."

I responded, "Yeah, I know. You'll be seeing more of me though by tomorrow night once I clear up some stuff from my CID days. I'm sure it'll be a nice quiet shift with everyone taking it easy after their big Thanksgiving meal. I'll connect with you then. I promise."

Regarding this particular officer, just barely past his rookie year, I would in fact meet up with him the following night. We'd have a nice talk. I'd even give him some sound professional advice after he requested it. But, interestingly, he wouldn't follow it. It would turn out to be anything but a "nice quiet shift" that next night.

Before all that though…there was an arrest to be made.

I found Officer Tim Carroll walking around HQ. He was a patrolman on the 5P-3A shift. He was a friend and a guy I trusted implicitly within the department. He definitely was not aligned with the Dark Side. I asked him if he was particularly busy right now. He said "not really." I asked him where he was assigned. He told me Sector

4, the Cornwells area. I advised him to meet me at Rambler's Field at 9:45. He did.

On the field area, very near to where Joe Scheck exposed himself to Billy, I explained to Tim about Scheck and what I was doing. He was all ears and very enthusiastically said, "Let's go and arrest this guy!"

I enthusiastically concurred with Tim and off we went to Joe Scheck's home. His car was out front. That was good to see. Tim and I parked our patrol cars to the front and rear of his, tight to his car's bumpers so he couldn't readily drive away if he somehow got past us. We walked up and knocked on the door. A guy answered the front door who very much fit Billy's description of Scheck. I asked him his name. He said, "Joe Scheck." He then added, "Is there a problem officers?"

As Tim and I made our way inside the front door into his living room, I responded, "I HOPE there are no problems here tonight Mr. Scheck. You're under arrest. Please put your hands up and turn around so I can search you. If you come along peacefully, I assure you that any problems will be kept to a minimum."

Scheck looked like he had been hit in the back of the head with a two-by-four. He was in total shock. After a few seconds, with hands straight up in the air, he managed to ask me with some incredulity, "Uh…what is this for? What did I do?"

While patting him down for possible weapons, "Mr. Scheck, you're being charged with Indecent Exposure, Open Lewdness, and Corruption of a Minor. The incident occurred on the afternoon of November 8th at Rambler's Field. Here's a copy of the warrant and affidavit. You can look at it for a minute, but then I'm putting the cuffs on you. Oh, and you have the right to remain silent…," and so on. No weapons were found on him.

The walloped-in-the-head look slowly morphed into one of forlorn, fright, and fear. For thirty seconds or so I allowed Scheck to read over the arrest warrant. With Tim and I securely on each side of him as he scanned the documents, his body language indicated to me that he was all but giving up as his shoulders collapsed, his knees buckled ever so slightly, and he put his hands out in front of him to be shackled. I told him to put his hands behind his back, then I would handcuff him. He put down the papers and did so. Once he was cuffed, we got his coat, draped it over his slouched shoulders, and walked him out his door, locking it behind us. Into the back seat of my patrol car he went.

One Bensalem citizen, Joe Scheck, now under arrest. Let's see how long that mere description of him lasts.

Upon arriving at BPD HQ, I immediately secured my prisoner onto the temporary holding bench. Before I would do anything else, I wanted to call Billy and his mom. I did, and I informed them of the arrest of Joe Scheck. They were relieved to hear it. The mom even thanked me. That was refreshing, again, as compared to the earlier reactions I received from some of her other neighborhood mothers. As things would develop in this case, she would be one of the last people to thank me for doing what I did. The other remarks I would start to hear would not be so, shall we say, encouraging.

But first...the booking and processing of Joe Scheck was routine. He was polite and did what he was told to do in terms of being finger-printed, photographed, providing his basic pedigree information, etc. However, when I brought him back into the CID interview room (yes, back to my old haunts, and I didn't care who saw me), and after being fully read his Miranda warnings, and being advised that I'd like to talk to him regarding this incident, my arrestee respectfully told me that he preferred not to be interviewed right now. He should probably speak with his lawyer first, he mumbled in barely audible manner. It was at this time Joe requested to make a phone call. I allowed him to do so. It wasn't to his lawyer though. It was to his mother.

So, without any further options, as Scheck had now invoked his right to not be interviewed by the police, I returned him to the holding cell. Within an hour or two I would drive him to the on-call district magistrate in an adjacent township for his preliminary arraignment. There, after being formally read his charges by the judge, he was held in lieu of $50,000 bail. He was committed to Bucks County Prison, escorted there around 1:00AM by two constables.

I would go "10-8," back in service, upon re-crossing the Neshaminy Creek and returning to Bensalem Township around 2:00AM that night. I spent the rest of the shift, pretty much for the first time, being a patrol sergeant. I met with each officer, signed his log sheet, backed them up on some routine calls, and generally made my presence on the street known to them. For the first time I told them what I had been working on over the last few nights. They understood and were supportive of it. On the whole, they were a good bunch of guys, and could handle most calls on their own, without a supervisor needing to become directly involved every inch of the way.

But there was this one officer...only about two years out of the police academy. He was overall a good cop, but he would test me the following Thanksgiving night, well, actually on Friday morning around 4:00, after an adrenalin pumping thirty minutes. What I earlier advised him, what happened next, and where he wound up during and afterwards, would be emblematic of the professional "issues" I'd be dealing with in him.

And…there would be more to the Joe Scheck case in the next two days, in the next two weeks, and over the next few months. But first, let's finish out this holiday week. There's more still to come.

Chapter Forty-Three

I did my best to sleep at least six hours on Thanksgiving Day, 1984. We were hosting my wife's large family for a 5:00 dinner and I wanted to be up for it, literally and figuratively. It turned into an enjoyable seven hours between my awaking at 1:30PM and the time before going back to work for my final shift of this first tour-of-duty ever in my new role as patrol sergeant. I spent that afternoon and early evening at the house chatting with my in-laws, watching football games, and assisting with meal prep.

However, sometime during the dinner itself, along with the friendly back-and-forth family banter and the time-honored masticating of turkey, stuffing, cranberry sauce, maize (corn), and other traditional culinary delights, something from my other life hit me. It hit me hard and left me quiet and deeply contemplative for a longer time that it should have during this otherwise festive gathering around the Fitzgerald dining room table.

While others in my immediate and extended family were discussing school, work, sports, and issues normally talked about during a friendly holiday eating event, I became silent for a while. For some reason, I found myself becoming uneasy and concerned about the Scheck case and my arrest of him from the evening before.

These concerns involved self-imposed questions such as:

What if Billy changes his mind?

What if his mom decides this whole matter would be too traumatic for her and her son?

What if Billy and/or his mom decide after they read the forthcoming newspaper account of Scheck's arrest that they don't want to follow through on their "commitment" to this case?

What if someone gets to him, his mom, offers money, something else of importance, or even threatens one or both of them, for him/them to drop the charges?

What if, God forbid, something happens to Billy and he is physically incapacitated somehow, or worse, and can't follow through on his testimony?

How do I further the prosecution if any of these should happen?

Additionally, how do I protect myself in the event that even ONE of these factors comes to fruition?

As of now, I'm the only non-family or non-friend to have Billy's "word" that this incident happened several weeks ago as it did with Scheck. And I arrested the man based on it. Yes, I double- and triple-checked the facts, Scheck's story, Billy's story, knew what his teenage friend told the other officer, and the background of the entire situation. But was that enough? Not just for the upcoming preliminary hearing or even the possible trial, but my professional reputation too.

Throw in the eventual political ramifications of Auditor/Committeeman Scheck's arrest, where I stand among the politicians and appointed officials running Bensalem right now, including the ones married to the top brass of the PD itself, and it could become very problematical...for ME, depending how it all turns out.

So, I better find a way to further document and even "prove" that I acted in good faith and with due diligence throughout this week-long investigation. I better do it soon, too.

Okay...I think I figured out what to do. I will do it right after I go to work tonight. It would be after their Thanksgiving dinner that I would ask Billy and his mom to put up with me one more time. Yes, this will work. It should work, anyway.

"Jim, you're quiet there at the head of the table. Are you okay? And could you please pass the potatoes?"

That request from my mother-in-law sort of snapped me out of my mid-meal twilight zone moment. I indeed passed the potatoes and resumed participation in the real world as it was taking place around me. All was good about it too...the conversation, the food, and now my plan for later on this Thanksgiving eve.

With the meal over and the in-laws eventually gone, I dressed in my non-uniform and took off for work. Once at the police station that night, and for the fourth night in a row, I got the troops off on their patrol assignments with no delay or issues. For also the fourth night in a row, I told the guys I would be a bit delayed in joining them. They were fine with it. At least now they knew what their sergeant was doing during his "10-6" times. We agreed before we dispersed that it should be a quiet night. Holiday nights usually were in Bensalem. Usually...

I really just wanted a not-too-busy first hour or so while I go visit Billy and his mom one last time.

Oh, and that reminds me. I should call Billy's mom beforehand and tell her I'm stopping by. It's the least I can do.

That first hour was, in fact, uneventful. I was glad for it as I undertook my little follow-up meeting with Billy and his mother. The next six hours were quiet too. By about 4:00AM though, all hell would break loose. Well, at least for me. It should have also been for at least one young officer on my squad, but he didn't listen to me and he was nowhere to be found as Hades erupted. This is after the same officer specifically asked me for advice in the exact topic area of where he felt he was lacking in performing his job, and even in the exact geographic area of our town where the whole thing started.

I'll get back to this officer in a bit. First, let's talk to Billy....

Besides grabbing my flashlight and portable radio that night before entering my patrol vehicle, I brought with me one more item. It was a staple of my CID days, but not so much now in my newly assigned role. Tonight, however, I would borrow one from the backroom for a very specific purpose.

That item was a portable tape recorder. Oh, and a blank cassette tape too.

What I wanted to do at Billy's house was simple. I wanted to get him on tape telling me that which he told me the other night about the incident at Rambler's Field between him and Joe Scheck. Yes, I know, I probably should have done this while at his house the first (and only other) time so far, but quite frankly, that night and that part of the investigation developed so quickly that I really didn't know all that I was going to be learning before arriving there. However, it wasn't too late and I could now obtain a recorded version of Billy's encounter with Scheck on this night after their big meal. I was just hoping they weren't late eaters. Fortunately, they weren't.

I spent less than forty-five minutes at Billy's house. He and his mom were very accommodating regarding my request. While not giving them details regarding why I was doing this, I nonetheless told them it was "standard protocol" to get a taped statement from a witness or victim of a crime and that's why I was here tonight. I wasn't being untruthful here, as I had done it before with other victims and witnesses. It's just that in some cases it proves to be more critical than in others to undertake this extra step. This was one case which I

463

deemed to be more critical in that regard, for all the potential reasons articulated earlier.

So, I asked Billy and his mom if they'd be okay with me going through his "statement" once more, and this time tape recording it. They agreed right away. We then sat down in their living room again and with the recording device on the coffee table I asked many of the same questions as Monday night. And Billy answered them exactly the same way. It was good to hear that he was consistent with his story, even three nights later. No changes at all to it.

Once I got what I needed to hear, as well as what I needed to record, I thanked both mother and son and went on my way with tape recorder, and more importantly, tape in hand. I would keep the cassette at my house, under lock and key, just in case I may need it sometime in the future. Just in case….

I now had peace of mind regarding the Scheck case and could once again rejoin my troops as their patrol sergeant. I was looking forward to it. I just wanted to get to 7:00AM in one piece, sleep for a few hours, and begin what should be a great extended four-day holiday weekend.

It wouldn't quite work out that way, unfortunately. Not in the next few hours or even that Friday afternoon when I was called at home and ordered into the BPD for reasons initially unknown.

It would all make sense soon…or would it?

* * * * *

There was this officer, with now maybe three full years on the BPD, who was on my new squad. He was a strapping young man, in his early twenties, in good overall shape, and full of as we used to say, "piss and vinegar." In other words, he was a hard worker, always on the go, and wanted more than anything, I would later learn, to be perceived as a very good all-around cop. A few years earlier, as a new detective sergeant, I was responsible for his background check prior to him being hired. Through interviews of people who knew him, I could find nothing in his long-term or immediate past which would have precluded him from becoming a Bensalem police officer. As a result, he was eventually hired. I'll refer to him here as Officer Dan.

Dan could possibly have succeeded in attaining that desired level of very good all-around cop status in those early years, but somehow enroute to that goal he became professionally distracted. Somewhere in his training, street experience, or maybe even rooted in his personality, in his first year or two on the job he seemed to become fixated, perhaps even obsessed, with one type of crime and one type of crime only. Violators of same soon became his "public enemy(s) number one."

This "magnificent obsession" of Officer Dan's involved drunk drivers. As such, it would lead to a very high level of achievement for Dan, but only in one narrow slice of what it took to be that all-around cop he so wanted to be. At some point, even Dan himself felt he was short-changing his career with this professional myopia of his own creation.

Allow me to elaborate....

By Officer Dan's second year, with a number of these drunk-driving arrests under his leather belt, and after he made his formal request through the chain-of-command to then-Chief Viola, he was approved to go to the Pennsylvania State Police Breathalyzer Examiner Training Program. It surprised no one that he graduated the week-long school with top honors. Afterwards, back on the streets of Bensalem, he could not only make the on-view arrests of the intoxicated drivers on the highway, but he could then bring them to HQ and do his own testing of them. Dan saw himself as a complete officer at this point. Well, in regards to Driving Under the Influence (DUI) arrests, anyway.

After completing the Breathalyzer training course, Dan took it upon himself to become a virtual one man drunk-driving detector. He was unstoppable, well, except when he was actually stopping cars for various traffic violations. It's hard to believe, but he'd sometimes make three separate DUI arrests over the course of one ten-hour long night-time shift. Two such arrests per shift would be his average. He had hundreds of these arrests over his first few years on the BPD. He became so prolific and proficient at these arrests, all of which were standing up in court too, that the then-governor of Pennsylvania awarded this officer with the state's annual police drunk driving enforcement award several times over the next few years. The media picked up on Dan's arrest record, his annual awards, and articles were written about him and his seemingly one-track purposeful life while on patrol.

It may be apocryphal as I didn't actually witness it, but as the story goes, on one occasion Officer Dan was asked by a colleague at a pre-shift roll call, "Hey, Dan, if you pulled over a car and it was your own mother and she had been drinking, would you arrest her?"

After most of his squad mates were done laughing, Dan answered, with little hesitation and with a straight face, "Yes I would. Of course, it would depend on what she blew on the Breathalyzer."

Now THAT is a patrolman with an agenda, a patrolman on a mission, and yes, one could say a patrolman obsessed with a singular type of criminal offense, virtually to the exclusion of all other criminal offenses. He was SO agenda-/mission-oriented, he continued winning those statewide awards for it, year after year.

Which brings me to the conversation I had with Officer Dan that morning, around 3:00AM, barely ten hours after most of the rest of us had finished our Thanksgiving dinners. Interestingly, he is the one who came to me and started the conversation regarding his "problem."

I was sitting stationary in my patrol car at the time in the Hilton Hotel parking lot on Rt. 1 at Old Lincoln Hwy. My engine was off and I was just listening to and observing my immediate environs on all sides of me. As I learned back in my earliest weeks on the job from my training officer, "Trapper" Dave Huetger, by simply doing this sometimes it would be surprising what could be heard or seen. In effect, he would say, let the crime and/or the criminals come to you. As a patrolman and later a plainclothes officer I learned Trapper was correct, on numerous times too.

I recall early that Friday morning observing the Krispy Kreme doughnut shop located diagonally from my parked location on the northeast corner. It was open around-the-clock and was known to be robbed on occasion, so I thought I'd keep an eye on that place and look for any suspicious cars or people which may come onto the property. All I recall seeing then was a few customers sitting at the counter and two or three Philadelphia PD patrol cars pulling up to replenish their coffee and doughnut supplies. Funny how they'd leave THEIR jurisdiction (by about one-quarter of a mile over the Poquessing Creek) to get food and drink in MY jurisdiction. But I didn't care. They helped keep the robbers away too so we BPDers, as well as the doughnut shop employees and customers, appreciated their patronage too.

Directly across Old Lincoln Highway from me, on the northwest corner, was a large Pontiac automobile dealership. I was keeping an eye on that place too as in the past a car had been stolen out of the lot at nighttime. The facility was alarmed and it employed a watchman there every night, but he could only see so much of the expansive (and expensive) collection of new cars as they were displayed both inside and outside the several buildings. There was a chain link fence around the exterior of the well-illuminated lots and between that, the alarm system, and the guard, it was relatively rare for a car to be stolen overnight. But it did happen. So, I casually kept my eyes open in that direction too for any suspicious goings-on.

Of course, crime happened in the Hilton parking lot too, but it seemed pretty quiet on this coldish night. If there was any illegality taking place on these grounds, it was inside the hotel rooms and not really my concern right now. The lot itself was free of any activity at all, at least from my vantage point. That brought no complaints from this new patrol sergeant with less than four hours to go until my long weekend off.

It was around this time that Officer Dan reached out for me via the police radio. He wanted to meet with me. I advised him of my exact location and asked him to come there. He said "10-4" and that he'd be there shortly. Within ten minutes he was parked directly alongside of me, my car facing one way, his car facing the other.

With my window now rolled completely down, I asked, "What's up, Dan?"

"Not much, Sarge, I just wanted to touch bases with you while it's quiet out here and before we're off for four days. I know you've been busy with that investigation and arrest over the last few shifts."

"Yeah, I was, but that's all taken care of for now." I added, "I saw you were busy with a few arrests of your own this week, right? A DUI each night?"

He retorted, somewhat whimsically, "Just one per night this week. I'm slowing down I guess."

I half-laughed without instilling any editorializing into it, or at least I don't think I did. On the whole, I saw Dan as a good cop, a dedicated cop, who just happened to be laser-fixed on drunk drivers. I had no overt problem with it so far, but then I was still new to this whole patrol supervisory thing. He seemed to back up his fellow officers on their calls, well, when he wasn't tied up on one of his arrests. He was also responsive to the dispatchers' calls, had no significant civilian complaints filed against him (perhaps because they were too intoxicated to remember anything he MAY have done wrong to them), and generally did his job well.

But that morning it was Dan who shortly thereafter changed the topic from the generic to the specific. The fact that the issue he wanted to discuss was coming from Dan himself is what took me most by surprise during our conversation. I already knew from in-house departmental scuttlebutt what he would shortly be telling me was seen as a "problem" regarding him by some in upper-management. But I wasn't sure, certainly not yet, Dan saw it as a problem too. However, I was about to learn just what Officer Dan perceived as his own shortcomings.

467

He wasn't necessarily wrong here in his self-assessment, and I later commended him for his apparent awareness of it. Ironically, this very issue, in its own bizarre way, would manifest on varying levels in our respective lives before the next ninety minutes were up, and all beginning less than ninety yards from where we were sitting right now.

Time, space, me, Officer Dan, and his "problem," each finding themselves at the nexus of Rt. 1 and Old Lincoln Hwy. in Bensalem Township. What are the odds...?

After a few more work related incidentals as part of our chat, Dan became a bit more circumspect in his demeanor and confided to me what he saw as his problem. He proceeded to tell me that he didn't think he was a "complete cop." He knew he was doing great work in the area of arresting and convicting DUI drivers (he had the Governor's awards to back him up), but he wanted more out of his career. He wanted to make felony arrests, good felony arrests, which stood up in court and resulted in convictions. He told me he was aware of my track record as a young officer, both in uniform and in plainclothes. He was a rookie officer when I was a detective sergeant and he was knowledgeable of some of the investigations and arrests I had undertaken during that timeframe. Although it hadn't quite yet hit the newspapers, he knew about my very recent arrest of Joe Scheck and advised me he was impressed with how that whole case came together for me.

I interrupted Dan and thanked him for his seemingly genuine platitudes. Enough about my career, I thought. I wanted to know where he was going with all this. What did he want from me, from the BPD, and most important, from himself? I figured getting him to answer the last question would shine the light on him, his concerns, and how to best "fix" them.

"Sarge, I want to make other types of arrests. I want to catch the shooters, the rapists, the robbers, the burglars. I want to do something other than just stop these drunks driving their cars down the road. I want to make some felony arrests, quality ones, but I just can't seem to do it. I always seem to be at the wrong place at the wrong time, showing up late to the scene, whatever."

Hmmm...do I detect a mid-career crisis on the part of Officer Dan? He only has three years on the job though. He's at most, twenty-four years old. A bit early in his professional life to be feeling this way, I thought.

So, how do I handle this? Dan's a hard worker and takes his role as a BPD officer very seriously. He's on time, doesn't abuse his sick leave, and is respectful to authority. He presents an overall positive image, well, except for the seemingly ever-present toothpick hanging out of his mouth. (I told him earlier that night he can chew on it/them in his car to his heart's content, but when he's dealing with the public in any situation, to remove it. He agreed to do so.)

Toothpick placement aside, and switching back to career counseling mode, I suggested to him, "Dan, we've only worked together for four nights now, and I know I was busy doing my own case-related thing for much of it, but I want you to know that I think you're a good cop. You've certainly developed an interest, a proficiency, even an expertise in finding and arresting drunks. That's nothing to scoff at. It's important to get them off the streets when they shouldn't be driving. No argument there...."

He was nodding his head in agreement but then all of a sudden interrupted me. "But, Sarge, that's NOT all I want to do while on-duty every night. I mean, I come across the drunks and I can detect what they're doing pretty easily. I mean, I have that down to a science. It's like I have drunk driver radar. But, it's the REALLY bad guys I want to start catching in the act, or at least right after they commit their crimes. Do you know what I mean? Like you used to do!"

I wanted to be careful here. I didn't want to say something to Dan that would turn him off from doing ANY work while on the job. There were enough of them on the BPD already and we didn't need another one. I certainly didn't want to tell him to stop arresting DUIs. That would be wrong too. So, what do I tell him here?

After thinking for a minute while listening to a routine call from dispatch to another officer, I slowly figured where to go with Dan. I simply reinforced to him something that maybe no one has told him in a while, or maybe even never told him. That is, the basics of what I believed it took to be a successful street cop. So, over the next few minutes, that's what I did. I simply told Dan to know his assigned sector inside and out, check his occupied and unoccupied buildings, stop any suspicious cars and/or pedestrians if he has probable cause, respond to calls from dispatch quickly, and use his common sense while on patrol.

Repeating to Dan what Trapper told me years ago that sometimes, just sometimes, there's nothing wrong with just sitting in one place and taking in the sights and sounds around you. Sometimes, as I had been told and which I knew actually worked, you'll hear that barking dog, that glass smashing, the tires squealing, the person screaming, and it will tell you something is afoot. It MAY be innocent, or accidental, but it also may be the real thing, as in a real crime taking place. If you work on that overall philosophy, I told Dan, you'll make those arrests. You can't force them to happen, but they'll be there if you stay diligent, patient, and most importantly, observant.

"Sarge, you make it sound so easy. Is that what worked for you all these years?"

"Dan, first of all, I'm not THAT old. I've only been on eight years, you know. But yes, absolutely this philosophy, this mentality, has worked for me. You don't have to always be on the move, putting miles on the patrol car, driving around your sector like a pinball in the middle of a high-scoring game. Let the crime and the bad guys come to you sometimes. Trust me, it works."

Dan sat back in his seat, rubbed his eyes a bit, shifted his toothpick, and said, "I hear ya. Maybe I am trying too hard sometimes. Maybe I gotta slow down a bit. From what you say, that's how good things happen on the job. I mean, felony arrest-wise, right? I suppose luck is involved sometimes too, eh?"

I replied, "Dan, I think that luck actually has very little to do with matters such as this. It may be some measure of 'luck' that has you in a certain area at a certain time when something is going down, but it's skill and experience that allows you to then recognize and handle the situation as it unfolds in front of you."

"You know, Sarge, no one has really laid it out to me quite like you did tonight. I want you to know I appreciate your advice, your time, and your concern here."

In all earnestness, I told him, "No problem. You're welcome, Dan. I gotta tell you...you're a good cop. I see that in you already. Keep making those DUI arrests. But at some point, don't necessarily go looking for them. Look for other sorts of behavior and activity and crime that will take you to the next level of arrest making. You can do it. I know you can. Just remember, let it come to *you* sometimes."

I continued, "Even here in Sector One, this is a good place to park. You're only a short distance away from almost anywhere you'd be sent to, and you've got the Rt. 1 strip right in front of you. That's why I cruise around here and just park here sometimes. It's worked for me...."

For now, I didn't want to overburden Dan with advice or become too heavy-handed or detailed with what I was telling him. I wanted to keep it basic and simple, for both of our sakes. I figured we could talk again next week and see where we are with this situation.

I eventually told Officer Dan that I wanted to check on one of the other officers who was on a call in another sector. He thanked me again and said he learned a lot in the last fifteen minutes or so. I told him I was glad to help and that he'd get to where he wanted to go. I meant it, too.

I said goodbye to Dan and drove from the scene. As I zig-zagged out of the Hilton parking lot and out onto northbound Rt. 1 to head to the other officer's location, I watched as Dan took off behind me right away, southbound on Rt. 1, toward the Philadelphia border.

Oh well, Dan just couldn't sit still it seems.

It's a shame too as that all-hell-breaking-loose scenario was just about to...well, break loose. It would be starting right across the street from where Dan and I had been sitting.

Perhaps the concept of "luck" did play a role in Dan vacating the scene when he did. Not for him though, but for two other guys about to pull off a very dangerous caper.

Chapter Forty-Four

At around 3:45AM on the Friday morning after Thanksgiving, after my hopefully meaningful advice to Dan, and after backing up an officer at his call on Street Rd., I requested yet another one of my guys to meet me at the Bensalem High School as I wanted to sign his log sheet. (Sergeants are supposed to do that every shift, if possible. It shows they're "checking up" on their officers.) We met there and we sat for a while and discussed multiple and sundry issues. However, I never did get to sign his sheet though. Something sort of came up....

This officer was the first person to show me the short blurb in the "Police Blog" section of that morning's hot-off-the-press *Bucks County Courier Times* regarding the arrest of Joe Scheck the night before. It didn't include too much in the way of details (nothing about his political connections), but the matter was clearly public information now. I certainly hadn't called anyone in the media, but I know the paper's reporters and editors routinely check with the various Bucks County police departments as well as the on-call district magistrates in their attempts to obtain any newsworthy crime related information for their daily publications. Apparently, that's what happened here and the arrest of Scheck was now out there for all to read. (A longer article about Scheck's arrest with many additional details, positioned on the front page of the BCCT, would be published over the weekend.)

In the empty high school parking lot, the officer and I talked about Scheck, the investigation, and the newspaper article, with our discussion eventually drifting off onto other PD related matters and even some personal topics. Included in our conversation was the fact that it was getting pretty cold outside, with some recently iced-up street sections, as well noticing that a light fog was slowly enveloping us. At one point, weather commentary aside, we simultaneously stated that we now had only about three hours left on our shift. After a long midnight shift, we agreed we'd be at our respective homes and hopefully asleep before long.

I forget after all these years what exactly we were talking about after discussing the surrounding meteorological conditions and what time we may be going to bed later this morning, but whatever the issue may have been came to a sudden and demonstrative halt as a result of what we were about to hear over the police radio. It was one of those relatively rare but at the same time stop-whatever-you're-doing-and-listen-up moments for a cop.

"BEEP! BEEP! BEEP!"

Upon hearing this electronically produced emergency signal, initiated by one of the BPD dispatchers, both of us seasoned officers knew right away what to do. Without even saying goodbye to each other (and me never getting around to signing his log sheet), the two of us immediately put our respective gear selectors into "Drive" and headed toward the parking lot exit out onto Hulmeville Rd. We didn't even know yet where we were going or what had happened, but we knew it wasn't here on the otherwise dark and serene Bensalem High School grounds. Within seconds though, we heard the rest of the message from dispatch.

"22-cars, the theft of two new dark-colored Pontiac Trans-Ams just occurred at _____ Pontiac dealership at Rt.1 and Old Lincoln Hwy! The guard reports that he saw two white male drivers proceed past him and drive through the chain-link fence at high speed, one after another, and then head northbound on Rt. 1! More info forthcoming!"

Okay, this doesn't happen every night. Not just one vehicle theft, but two, and not just any cars, but brand-spankin' new Trans Ams.

Oh well, Jim, time to get to work here. That's what you're paid to do in these situations. You're a patrol sergeant now, in a patrol car… whether wearing a patrol uniform or not.

I first contacted the Sector 1 car and made sure he was enroute to the dealership. I wanted him to make sure the guard was alright and, assuming he was, to get further "flash" information from him regarding the brazen thefts.

I next had the BPD dispatchers make sure that the Penndel Borough, Middletown Township, and Falls Township PDs were each notified of these cars possibly heading in their directions. They were to the immediate north of Bensalem up Rt. 1 and not on our radio band, so I wanted to make sure they were advised to be on the lookout for them. The Pennsylvania State Police and Philadelphia PD were notified too, just in case they happened upon the two cars.

After that, I wanted to know the whereabouts of my individual officers. As I was driving, I went through an informal checklist with each of them. As was practiced protocol, they were individually broadcasting that they were in the process of positioning themselves at various major Bensalem intersections in an attempt to locate and possibly stop either of these vehicles. (These intersections were designated by pre-established codes just in case a fleeing felon had access to a police scanner.) Upon listening to each of my guys sound off, it occurred to me that the only squad member not broadcasting his whereabouts was Officer Dan.

After hearing from everyone else on my squad, I decided to try and raise Dan on the radio. "22-7 (me) to 22-12 (Dan), what's your 10-20 (location)?"

No response.

Okay, that's weird, nothing from Dan...especially as we had been talking right across the street from the Pontiac dealership barely thirty minutes ago. Geez, if he had stayed there with lights out and engine off (as we HAD been) he would have possibly witnessed the whole thing as the cars apparently drove through the fence on the Old Lincoln Hwy. side of the business. He would have seen AND heard it, plus possibly even smelled it too as the cars were apparently laying lots of rubber during their high-speed, fence-crashing getaway. That could have been the very type of arrest that Dan and I had been talking about for him.

"22-7 to 22-12, what's your 10-20 please?"

Nothing.

While the other officers were setting up at various township intersections, the officer I had just been talking to at the high school pulled out of the lot ahead of me and decided to turn left, southbound on Hulmeville Rd. Alright, so he's heading toward the center of town. Well, I might as well go right, northbound on Hulmeville, and spread things out a bit. Why not, especially as the whole Street Rd. corridor from the Pennsylvania Turnpike overpass to State Rd. seemed to be pretty well covered by my squad members. So, I'll go a bit off the beaten path a bit. You never know....

But, where the hell was Officer Dan?

"Dispatch, keep calling 22-12! Get a status on him!"

"10-4!"

"696 (BPD dispatch) to 22-12, what's your 10-20? 22-12?"

Silence.

It was my turn again. "22-7 to 22-cars, has anyone seen 22-12 recently? I was with him at the Hilton parking lot barely a half-hour ago."

Silence or negative responses.

Geez, I'm trying to locate these two stolen Trans-Ams, but I'm also trying to locate one of my officers. I certainly hope there's no connection here. Could Dan have come upon them somewhere and something bad have happened to him? I certainly hope not.

With Dan very much on my mind, I was still driving north on Hulmeville Rd., attempting at the same time to possibly intercept these cars. Of course, it's unlikely they're still both together. If so, they would stick out like…well, two brand new, stolen Trans Ams. No, they've probably separated and are almost to their chop-shop location by now, wherever that may be. Not to be "chopped," of course, as they were brand new cars, literally fresh off the lot. They'd be sold whole, to someone, somewhere, if they did manage to reach their intermediary destination. Although, come to think of it, the two thieves DID bust through a chain-link fence in the process of stealing these cars. There would be some paint damage, at a minimum, to the cars as a result. Stolen car middlemen don't like damaged cars, especially if stolen right off the lot with the stickers still on the rear side windows.

Hmmm…just why were these cars stolen?

So, I have two recently stolen high-performance cars on the loose and an out-of-pocket patrolman? Could it get any more tenuous than this? Well, I think it just did thanks to Mother Nature.

The fog was getting a bit thicker in the direction in which I was heading and there were some icy patches developing on the roadways too. I could still see safely in front of me, but not as far off into the distance as I would like. The rear of the car was ever-so-slightly sliding a bit at certain sections of the road. What a smart night to steal a car, make that two cars, I recall thinking at the time. Fortunately, there were virtually no other cars on the roads. At least none that I could see through the fog, anyway.

For no conscious reasons that I can recall, my instincts had me turn off of Hulmeville Rd., at the gas station, onto westbound Bristol Rd. I then proceeded past the small shopping center onto westbound Neshaminy Blvd., into the heart of a residential area of Bensalem known as Neshaminy Valley.

(What has since been renamed Pasqualone Blvd. in Bensalem was called Neshaminy Blvd. in 1984. For consistency purposes, I will continue here to refer to this roadway by its name at the time this event occurred.)

I wish I could say here that I had an actual plan in motion, but I didn't. My experience and street-sense only told me that if I wasn't the closest to the scene of the crime (which I wasn't when this one occurred) and responding directly there, I should instead go in a round-about way in the direction to where the criminal may have fled, allowing for the requisite time and distance calculations, of course. My hope in those instances was always to find the getaway car or the criminal himself as he's fleeing the scene. So, that's what I did on this night.

But I was really only partially focused on these two stolen cars. My primary focus was still with Officer Dan. Where was he? I was becoming more and more concerned about him as I was driving more and more into increasingly foggy conditions.

One more time, "22-7 to 22-12?"

After a few seconds, a response, finally. "22-12 to 22-7, proceed."

Dan's on the air. Okay, that's great to hear.

"22-12, what's your 10-20, what's your status?"

After a bit of radio silence an almost too calm, perhaps even a somewhat dejected sounding Officer Dan, advised for all on the police radio band to hear, "Yeah, I'm 10-4. I'm at Salem Harbor Apartments. I'm, uh, 10-6 right now."

Dan's out of service? At Salem Harbor Apartments? I didn't hear him take a call there or pull a car stop there. That's about as far away from the scene of the car thefts as one could be and still be geographically inside Bensalem Township. This apartment complex was located in the far southeastern corner of Bensalem, between the Delaware River and State Rd., just before crossing over the Philadelphia line. What's he doing down there? Well, whatever it is, and for whatever reason he's busy ("10-6"), at least he sounds okay.

I was about to ask Dan what he had going on in the apartment complex, especially as all the rest of the squad was involved in looking for these two hot cars. However, I became sidetracked by what was now ever so slowly coming into my line of vision in front of me.

As I approached in a westerly direction on Neshaminy Blvd. its intersection with Declaration Drive, I slowed down as I came to the four-way stop sign. While Neshaminy Blvd. was wide enough for two cars in each directional lane, it was generally used by drivers as a single lane road each way. The wideness, however, was appreciated by drivers at intersections such as where I was now as cars could turn left and right and not necessarily impede the flow of other traffic in doing so.

As such, I came to a complete stop on my side of the intersection, with the lane all to myself. What I then observed on the other side of the intersection in BOTH lanes coming in the eastbound direction towards me, and which was now clearer to me through the fogginess, gave me what is clearly known in official police parlance as one of those "HOLY SHIT!" moments.

Sitting across from me and presently at a complete stop at their intersectional line, just as I was at my opposing intersectional line, was not one, but two vehicles. Upon immediate closer inspection, I could plainly see they weren't just any two vehicles. They were both dark-colored Pontiac Firebird Trans-Ams. Even in the foggy conditions, I could make out the color scheme of the cars and the iconic spread-winged eagle on the two side-by-side hoods as each was partially illuminated by a nearby overhead streetlamp. Even if my vision had been further impaired because of the enveloping fog, the sounds of their V-8, 190 horsepower engines would have otherwise given them away. One such Trans Am presented its own very distinctive and powerful engine sound; two, much more so.

At this point, without a doubt in my mind, I realized I had just come upon the two very recently stolen cars. The three of our cars were presently stopped at the same off-the-beaten-path and now otherwise empty intersection at the same time, me facing one way, those two facing the other, towards me. As the nanoseconds were ticking away in my brain at this time and place, the conundrum of the moment began to register, especially as the drivers of the two stolen cars seemed in no immediate rush to go anywhere. There may be a reason for their hesitation.

So Jim's brain, what are the known facts here? To them? To me?

Let's break it down...

A. The two drivers KNOW they are in stolen cars.

B. I KNOW these are two stolen cars.

C. Yet...the two drivers don't NECESSARILY know that I know they are stolen cars.

So...for the next few nanoseconds, while I buy some precious time here, what's behind Door C may just work to my advantage.

But first things first here. I gotta get on the radio.

In a relatively calm voice, while holding the mike at mid-chest level so the car thieves wouldn't see what I was doing, I stated, "22-7 to 696, be advised I have BOTH stolen cars at the intersection of Neshaminy Blvd. and Declaration Drive! They're occupied but sitting still right now, both facing eastbound! They see me, too. Backup requested!"

"10-4, 22-7!"

"Other 22-cars in the area? 22-7 has both stolen cars located and they're occupied! Proceed to vicinity of Neshaminy Blvd. and Declaration Drive!"

My colleagues began radioing that they were on their way.

This was one of those times and places as a cop when you knew that things were about to get hairy...very hairy. My adrenalin had already been pumping through my system at a moderate rate of speed, but now it was quickly approaching maximum velocity. In addition, the hairs on the back of my neck were at full attention and my hands were starting to sweat. These, of course, are all signs that the body and mind know something out of the ordinary, make that extraordinary, was happening and about to get even...hairier.

I became immediately cognizant that this present scenario was NOT going to end in a routine and low-keyed manner. I was absolutely positive of that. Not with these two guys who not only jointly coordinated the successful thefts of their respective muscle cars, but then drove them through a friggin' fence at a well-protected automobile dealership in the process of doing so.

These two drivers weren't exactly your sophisticated and debonair master jewel thieves or sweet-talking and erudite international con men looking to quietly and discreetly ply their criminal skills against unsuspecting victims to purloin items of value from them. No, these were obviously two risk-taking adrenalin junkies who more likely than not stole these cars for the fun in it more so than for the profit in it. And now, I was next in line to play a role in their late night, fog enshrouded, nerve-racking fun, with high-speeds about to be added to the equation just to make it more adrenalin-producing for them.

Okay, now how do I handle this? I'm here with not just one, but two stolen cars. They're both ready to take off on a moment's notice too. They're not just regular cars either. These are two high-performance cars. I could see AND hear the engine size from my proximity to them. And me, all by myself in a car that is not exactly a four-cylinder family mini-van, but certainly no match on the open road against these two built-for-speed cars. In terms of any help, the next closest police car was at least five minutes away from me.

What do I do here? What do I draw on to minimize the danger yet maximize their arrest possibilities?

IF this was to turn into a car chase, it wouldn't be my first. I've engaged in a few already during my prior years in patrol. Fortunately, none went much farther than a mile or two before they ended, with no injuries to anyone either directly involved or to bystanders. Sometimes, when a pursuit finally would come to an end, it would then turn into a foot chase as the driver would in these cases bail out of the car and begin running away. Of course, sometimes there were passengers in the car too and they would also start running once the car came to a stop or crashed. I learned a long time ago not to waste any time chasing the passengers out of a stolen and/or just-chased car. I learned later it's hard to convict them of anything in the courts. So, when there was a multiple-person foot chase in a stolen car situation, I always went after the driver. He's the most legally complicit in the criminal act so he's the one most worth pursuing.

As anyone who's ever been in a car chase can attest (whether as the chaser OR the "chasee"), the adrenalin does begin pumping at a fast and furious rate very early on. It starts when the gas pedal is first pushed to the floor and lasts until at least twenty minutes after it's all over. There's no getting around that physiological response to the high speeds involved, I can assure you.

From the outset of a chase, some less experienced officers can't seem to help themselves in one particular area. It involves their communication skills, or more precisely, their lack thereof. That is, they lose almost all physical control and management of their vocalization process. In other words, they insist on screaming at full volume over the radio for most of if not the entire duration of the pursuit. It is almost impossible to understand them many times as they're calling out directions and mileposts to their police colleagues who are trying to catch up to their rapidly moving locations. These officers can become completely incomprehensible due to their loudly yelling of what they're trying to articulate on the radio. More than once in my police career I got on the air and interrupted the officer and actually ordered him to speak in a calmer, more understandable tone on the radio. It never worked.

This uber-adrenalin experience during car chases also explains why many officers are observed and/or caught on video beating or otherwise physically manhandling a just-extracted driver from his car at the end of a pursuit. It's almost impossible after driving at breakneck speeds on highways or along urban streets to NOT overreact to some degree once the perp/driver is out and on the ground. I'm not justifying this potentially abusive behavior at all, but merely pointing out that there are physiological as well as psychological elements behind it. Believe me, I know. It almost cost me my life.

Probably the closest I ever came to being killed or seriously injured by "friendly-fire," that is, being shot by another police officer, occurred not during a several mile-long car chase itself, but in its immediate aftermath. It was sometime in 1980, during my second stint in patrol at the BPD. I recall it being a late-afternoon weekday pursuit initiated by another officer. He and a few police cars were chasing a guy in a stolen car in and out of traffic, into oncoming lanes, through a strip mall parking lot, and the like. Finally, with me in my patrol car and not even engaged in the actual chase itself, I managed to intercept the vehicle and cut it off in the middle of the busy intersection of Street Rd. and Old Lincoln Hwy., effectively blocking him in with nowhere else to go. Approximately four police cars caught up with the suspect vehicle at the same time. That would be me and the three other officers who had been chasing the stolen car.

The driver of the hot car immediately jumped out and started running. I bolted out of my car and ran after him. I managed to tackle him and take him to the ground. He was still struggling a bit with me, mostly by squirming on the ground and resisting me putting my handcuffs on him. That's when out of the corner of my eye I could see Officer Tony Rihl, running over to my location in the middle of the street with his shotgun in hand. (Yes, the same Officer Rihl who was seriously injured just months later in the robbery arrest scenario in which Officer Bob Yezzi was killed.)

As the suspected car thief was still resisting arrest on the ground, with me more or less on my knees straddling him in an attempt to hold him down by his chest, head, and at least one shoulder, I could peripherally see Tony running up to us. Once alongside of us, I watched as he hauled back and in full pile-driver mode brought the butt of the shotgun directly onto the car thief's left shoulder. I had no initial problem with Tony doing this in an attempt to assist me gain the physical advantage necessary to arrest and handcuff this guy, but there was one little problem that occurred as the butt of the shotgun made contact with the guy's shoulder blade. That one little problem was that there had been a shotgun shell previously racked into the chamber of the weapon, the safety was off, and somehow, someway, the shotgun discharged. The barrel was directly next to and just slightly above my head as it did.

WTF?! I felt like my right-side eardrum had just been blown out.

No surprise, I had trouble hearing from that ear for my rest of the time at the scene that day. But the direct hit to the shoulder and/or the errant discharge did manage to accomplish its purpose as it startled both me and, even more so, the car thief. It no doubt hurt his shoulder too, besides one or both of his ears. As a combined result, the guy finally stopped fighting me and put his hands out and meekly surrendered.

In retrospect, I would have rather kept fighting the suspect on the ground and managing to get him into the cuffs by some other means than having a twelve-gauge shotgun discharge its double-ought buckshot within six inches of my head. Luckily Tony had good aim, I guess, and the pellets went straight up into the air after the butt-to-shoulder maneuver on his part.

Needless to say, back at the station Tony and I had some words after this incident, including some up-close and personal dialogue. He did ultimately apologize though (into my left ear), saying he did not know there was a live shell in the chamber. I accepted his apology, but told him firmly that I did not want him bringing a shotgun to any scene with me in the future. He reluctantly agreed.

Tony Rihl was then and remained an excellent police officer up until his eventual retirement from the BPD. This particular incident was, well, a rare mistake on his part, and he admitted it. No one got hurt from it and as far as I know nothing like it ever happened again involving Tony and a mistimed shotgun blast alongside another officer's head. That's a good thing.

Now, back to those two stolen Pontiac Trans-Ams facing me from across Declaration Drive....

Interestingly, the driver in the vehicle on the inside lane did something which at first surprised me. It was something I did not expect from a car thief. That is, he decided to put on his turn signal. In doing so, he was at least suggesting to me that he was about to make a left turn onto northbound Declaration Dr. How courteous that even while behind the wheel of a stolen car the driver not only comes to a complete halt at a stop sign but also uses his turn indicator to signal his intentions.

Despite the car's now blinking intentions, no car made a turn. No car made a move. Not yet, anyway. That included me, too.

As I was listening to my colleagues over the radio racing to my location, well everyone except Officer Dan, I figured I'd be a courteous police officer back at the driver. I'd allow the turning car to make its left in front of me. So, I did what any courteous driver would do when allowing another car to turn in front of it. I exhibited the international symbol of, "Yes, you may turn in front of me." I did a quick on and off of the high-beam lights at him.

I realized at this point, still on my own here, there was no way I could or would chase both cars. Unless they followed each other and drove in a straight line to their destination, which was unlikely, I would have to ultimately choose one of the cars, follow it, and radio the direction of the other car as it was leaving the scene for one of the newly arriving officers to locate. But in conjunction with this just-developed strategy, I would also have wanted to continue to buy as much time as I could here. One way I would do that is by NOT putting on my red lights and siren just yet. Of course I knew these were the two stolen cars (see earlier Option B) but they didn't know, yet, I knew they were two stolen cars (see earlier Option C). They may have suspected I knew something was amiss, but no one was showing their hand (or foot) yet.

So, I sat at the intersection awaiting the stolen car with its signal on to make the left turn. But he was apparently a courteous driver too. Shortly after I flashed my high-beams at him, guess what he did? He flashed his high-beams a quick on and off back at me. He was now allowing ME to proceed straight ahead and he would then make his turn after me. Again, how nice of him.

Well, one good "turn" deserves another, whether based on niceness, courteousness, or something else. So, I flashed my beams once again at him. (If you've lost count, we're up to three high-beam flashings so far; two by me, one by him.) I decided then and there I wasn't entering this intersection until one of these cars moved. We've been here now sitting stationary for close to forty-five seconds. It seemed like an eternity to me and I'm sure it did to the car thieves too. But I was in no rush. Apparently they weren't either.

Approaching the full minute mark of this fog-encased, exhaust fume emitting, engines purring, headlights flashing, two-versus-one Mexican Standoff at this innocuous intersection in the middle of a usually quiet residential area, things finally took a turn; literally, in this case. The inside Trans did, in fact, slowly make its left turn onto Declaration Dr. I slowly made my own right turn to follow it. Again, in an attempt to buy as much time as possible while awaiting the cavalry, I deemed this would be less suspicious than me making a U-turn to follow the other car. I wasn't sure how long it would be before this particular Trans-Am I was now following would decide to hit the gas and speed off, but I knew I was staying on him until that time came.

Of course, I immediately got on the radio and advised dispatch (and the other cars) the direction I was now following Trans-Am #1.

I also advised that I last saw Trans-Am #2 proceeding eastbound on Neshaminy Blvd. I even instructed the nearest approaching police vehicle to go after that car for now and I would stick with #1. Or, at least I'd try....

At this point, everyone either on location or listening over the airwaves knew it was just a matter of time until this scenario would blow up. It didn't take much more time…just seconds actually. After slowly trailing Trans-Am #1 several hundred feet on Declaration Dr., he apparently knew the gig was up. And he let me know that he knew the gig was up with his right foot. All of a sudden and without warning (yet not a surprise to me) the car I was behind by maybe fifty feet floored it and within six seconds was at an easy 75 MPH and pulling away fast from me. It took me a bit more than six seconds, but before long I was at 75 MPH too, not far off his tail, in full pursuit with red lights and siren now on to make it official.

It was me and the driver of Trans Am #1, mano a mano, with nothing between my front bumper and his rear bumper, engaged in a high-speed car chase through residential Neshaminy Valley at a time when very fortunately there was no other traffic or pedestrians. (If there HAD been traffic and/or pedestrians, I never would have initiated the pursuit.)

As mentioned earlier, I knew enough from hearing other cops in car chases that I had to control my vocalizations whilst so engaged in my own chase. So, I consciously kept my vocal cords under control and in check. I subconsciously may have wanted to scream my instructions/directions at the top of my lungs, but I consciously worked to NOT do that. I was understandable to my dispatchers and my fellow officers, of that I was assured then and later. My only real disadvantage when compared to the other driver was that I could only steer with one hand as I needed the other hand to hold the microphone. I've done it before and that was the least of my problems right now.

This other driver also had two distinct advantages over me. Firstly, he had a faster car. Secondly, he knew where he was going as he approached each intersection, even if only a few seconds before I would find out. But those few seconds could make a difference in him and/or me making a turn at these rates of speed. Luckily, I knew the streets and roads ahead of me. I wasn't sure if he did or not.

Now fully engaged in this chase, the next largest cross-street coming at us was Constitution Drive. The Trans Am driver veered right onto it and I followed him, all eight tires squealing as we did so. The road was wide enough and empty enough that the driver was now pushing his car at 85 MPH. I followed suit. After negotiating a few subtle turns in the roadway, Speed-Racer was now approaching Bensalem Blvd. He had to jam on his brakes to safely make the turn onto it, but once he did, he floored it again, now going southbound.

This whole time, of course, I'm transmitting to my colleagues where I'm heading, the streets I'm passing, and what the other driver is doing. Officers know to keep off the radio during these tense situations as it's always just one police car, or in my case the only police car, which should be transmitting. My troops heard me advise when we had just flown (almost literally) over Neshaminy Blvd., still southbound on Bensalem Blvd. through more residential areas. At this point, if looking on a street map, we've done a rough horseshoe design from where I first saw the cars to where we were now.

I recall thinking then and there that it was only a matter of time. Between the ice and the fog and the speed, something had to give with one of our cars, and not in a good way. And it did shortly thereafter. It was along this stretch of roadway that the Trans Am hit a small patch of ice. In doing so, his car did a 180-degree spin in front of me and banged up hard against a curb. It momentarily brought the driver to a complete stop. As such, I had the opportunity to pull up right next to the car. I purposely drove tight to his driver's side door so he couldn't readily jump out and run. Amazingly, I wound up next to him almost like I was meeting with one of my officers to sign his daily log. Our heads were about four linear feet from each other's and I got a very good glimpse of him through the closed windows. He got one of me too. Right before he hit the gas again, he reminded me that he was the driver of Trans Am #1. Yes, he put up his middle finger at me to let me know that he was, in fact, NOT driving Trans Am #2. Well, that was at least one of the interpretations of his little hand gesture.

After letting out one or more profanities within the interior of my car directed towards "driver number 1" and this increasingly intense and rapidly moving situation, the Trans Am somehow managed to steer free of my location. After partially hopping the curb and driving along with two wheels on the sidewalk, it got back fully onto the macadam itself and was now speeding northbound on Bensalem Blvd. That means I did my own 180-degree turn and began heading in that direction too. However, for some reason this guy seemingly wanted to proceed in his original direction because once he came again to Neshaminy Blvd. he did a wheel-squealing U-turn and managed to get back southbound on Bensalem Blvd. again. As he passed me in the opposite direction, I went to the intersection, did the same thing, broadcasting it all accordingly. I was NOT going to lose this guy I told myself. No way, no how!

As Trans Am #1 (now so-numbered for TWO reasons) continued on Bensalem Blvd. towards Bristol Rd., the driver this time safely made it past the patch of ice where he had spun out just thirty seconds or so before. I avoided it too. Once clear of that area, the driver really hit the gas and was now approaching 85 MPH again. However, what he didn't count on was yet another patch of roadway ice ahead of him. And as muscular and high-performance as his stolen sports car may have been, it was no match for the laws of nature, specifically, those involving flat sheets of frozen water. Thus, his car and all four tires hit the rather large patch of ice and this time did a full 360-degree turn before its rear tires slammed into a curb once again, except this time the force and speed of the spin dictated that the car was to go airborne. It did, spinning the whole time while going up at least fifteen feet in the air. It then came down hard, nose first, ultimately crashing down onto its roof.

Okay, add this as yet another "HOLY SHIT" moment to that night. Watching the brand new Trans Am, with its youthful driver inside, go completely airborne, spin around, come down on its front bumper, then square on its roof, could not bode well for car and metal, not to mention person and flesh. I was observing this singular car wreck taking place at first in front of me, then alongside of me, and then behind me, as I was going fast enough that I actually had to pass the still-spinning upside down car to slow down enough to make a quick U-turn, and then backtrack to the scene. While doing so I got on the radio, gave my specific location of Bensalem Blvd. just north of Bristol Rd., advised of what just happened, and that I would need a rescue squad and a flatbed tow truck to proceed here right away. I KNEW the car was severely damaged and would need a flatbed to right it and tow it away, but what I was also concerned about was the driver. If he did survive this crash, he would no doubt be seriously injured. That was certainly my preliminary diagnosis of him and his probable condition at this point in time.

I parked my car and exited with flashlight under my arm and portable radio in my right hand. I wanted my left hand free to go for my gun…just in case this guy was still alive, had a weapon of some sort, and even crazier than I may have already thought he was. I slowly walked toward the upside-down car which had just finally stopped spinning. The roof was at least partially collapsed onto the body of the car itself. At the same time, I noticed red fluid slowly running out from the driver's area. Not a good indicator, I said to myself.

Finally, off in the distance I first heard, and then saw, a police car coming my way. It was good to have another car in the area that was neither stolen nor being chased. It pulled up, the officer got out, and quickly surveyed the scene next to me. He first asked me how I was doing. I told him I was fine. Hard to believe, as I related to him, that I didn't crash or hit anything during the entirety of the chase. However, we were sure that the driver was not all that fine based on where the roof was now meeting the body of the upside-down car. My colleague agreed that the guy was probably wedged into the floor of the car's interior which was now up where the car's roof would normally be found. We also agreed that the red liquid slowly making its way down the street may have been blood.

Geez…I didn't want this thing ending this way. I hope the driver is okay. It may take us a while though to find out.

Other officers eventually arrived and the rescue squad got onto the scene at what must have been around 4:30. Despite all of our concerns and searching in and around the vehicle, including calling to the person to answer us, none of us could see any visible evidence of a person, a body, or parts thereof. One of the medics opined that the red fluid draining away from the car did not appear to be blood, but perhaps brake fluid. Okay, that was a good sign…I guess.

The heavy-duty tow truck finally showed up at 5:00AM and the driver/operator started doing his job. With various cables, winches, and jacks, he managed to turn the car over onto its four wheels. He backed off, as did the rescue squad personnel, and several of us officers walked cautiously over to the now upright car. We were looking inside for a person in any condition, be it injured, trapped, or dead. We searched the front seats, the front floor, the back seat, the back floor, even under the hood and in the trunk area.

But, believe it or not, the driver was nowhere to be found. Not in the car, not in the immediate area, not on that night.

As the newly arriving officers and I pieced together the scene and the timing of it all, somehow, someway, once the car smashed down to the ground, and I had to drive past the spinning upside-down car and make a U-turn to come back to its location, that must have been the precise moment when the driver managed to crawl out from it and run off into the nearby apartment complex or an adjacent field. That was the only explanation which made any sense to us. We even looked for a blood trail to follow as this guy must have been hurt somehow. But there was no blood to be found. None at all. That was good for him, of course, but not for those of us who were looking for some sign of his whereabouts.

With the stolen car now on the flatbed, and no driver located, the other officers started to clear the scene and take off to finish the remaining hour or so of their shift. Fortunately, just a little while later, Trans Am #2 was found abandoned by one of my officers in the rear of a nearby shopping center. Besides a punched out ignition switch, it was in very good condition (as opposed to #1), but there was no driver with that car either.

It'll be up to the detectives to follow-up on these car thefts now. They'll take fingerprints off of the cars' exteriors and interiors and do their best to figure out the identity of the thieves through informants, witnesses, etc. I'll provide my detailed description of the thief to the assigned detective and that'll give him a place to start. I'm sure at some point he will show me a photo-array and hopefully I'll be able to pick out the #1 driver and he can then be arrested based on my eyewitness identification of him and other available evidence. That would be the plan, anyway.

Interestingly, as the tow truck driver was cleaning up the remaining debris on the street, and with me still on the scene of the crash, Officer Dan reached out for me via police radio. He never did make it to my location. He asked me to switch to the admin channel. I did. Our conversation went something like this:

"Sarge, is duty tow still at your scene?"

"Yes he is. He's just getting ready to leave though. Why?"

"Uh, before he leaves, could you ask the driver that once he drops off the stolen car to come and get me at Salem Harbor Apartments? I, uh, need a tow back to HQ."

"10-4. I can do that. What's the problem there? Did you breakdown? Have an accident?"

"No, negative. I'll talk to you at HQ. I'm...I'm okay though. The car's okay too."

"10-4. I'll tell him to proceed to you once he puts this car in the impound yard. What's your exact 10-20?"

Officer Dan provided me with his specific location within the apartment complex and I advised the tow truck driver of his next pick up.

Dan was a bit late getting into HQ that morning. It was after 7:00 and all of my other officers had already turned in their paperwork and had gone home. But I knew he wasn't going to be much longer so I waited for him. I wanted to know what his issue was that he never made it out of the far-off apartment complex during the car theft/car chase scenario from just a few hours earlier.

Around 7:15 the tow truck dropped off Dan and his patrol car right at the fuel pump behind the BPD. I saw out the window as he was putting gas in it.

No, it can't be. Don't tell me.

Yes, he did eventually tell me.

Once Officer Dan parked his car and gathered his equipment he came into the sergeant's office. It was just the two of us. He was upset. I could see it. Dan advised me that I shouldn't have waited for him as he knows it was a busy night and a busy week for me. I agreed it was but told him I wanted to see him anyway before we went off-duty for four days. Before I could even end that last sentence he blurted out something like, "Go ahead, yell at me if you want! I deserve it! I'm a really stupid ass!"

I replied, somewhat surprised, and in non-yelling mode, "Why, Dan, for what reason?"

"Because I ran out of f**kin' gas down at Salem Harbor Apartments, that's why! How stupid could I be? Then as soon as the car putters to a stop, I hear that you spotted the two stolen cars. Jesus, do you know how f**kin' dumb that made me feel? Especially after the talk we just had at the Hilton parking lot?"

I asked, "Uh, by chance, is there a problem with the car's fuel gauge?"

"Nope, it's fine! This is on me! It's one hundred percent on me! Tell me off, put me in my place, write me up…whatever you gotta do Sarge, do it! I deserve it!"

I never did yell at Dan that morning. That's not my style, certainly not in this sort of situation. He knew that, but he said what he said to me out of frustration as to how his shift eventually turned out that morning.

I wasn't going to write up Dan, either. I simply told him that he should go home, get a good day's sleep, enjoy his time off, and we'll talk again next week when we come in for the 5P-3A shift. I reassured him regarding what just happened that no officers had been hurt, we recovered the two stolen cars, and we will eventually get the two thieves. It's really not that big of a deal.

Dan handed me his paperwork, thanked me for not chastising him, and agreed that we should have a follow-up conversation next week. We said goodbye and both started for home.

As I was finally walking out of the BPD door that morning, I must admit I couldn't help but think…so much for my talk to Officer Dan a little more than four hours ago about just sitting sometimes and letting criminal activity come to you. Not only did he NOT sit and watch this ballsy double-car theft occur across the street from where we had been talking but instead he drove to one of the far corners of Bensalem Township, all the while NOT keeping an eye on his gas gauge. Then, he runs out of fuel.

Damn…did he hear anything I said to him during our chat?

Apparently not.

Should I also have reminded him to fill up his gas tank when it approaches the one-quarter mark? I didn't think I would have to do that for him, not at this stage of his career.

Yes, we will talk next week.

Anyway, after all of this stuff, it'll be nice to finally be free of this place for a while. I could use a few hours of sleep and several days away to clear my mind.

But unfortunately, that wouldn't be the case. Remember, it's the Bensalem Police Department, circa 1984. Remember who's in charge.

Chapter Forty-Five

As was my custom on the final day of a midnight shift, I awoke around noon on that Friday. I was a bit groggy at first, but after a shower and a caffeine laden soft drink or two, I felt better. I could make it until 9:00 or so that evening, go to bed, and then get back on a regular nocturnal sleep schedule for the rest of the month.

As it was Black Friday, the big shopping day after Thanksgiving, with all the traffic problems that entails, I had no intention of ever leaving the house that day. I had enough driving overnight, to include the high-speed variety, to last me for a while. My two sons were home from their pre-schools and I thought I'd engage in some father-son time with them that afternoon. We'd have fun doing something. That was the plan, anyway. But there would be an interruption to my playtime with them later that afternoon. The interrupting would come from the Big Boss Man himself. He apparently had to see me and it couldn't wait until the following week.

The call to my home actually came from one of the BPD secretaries at around 2:00. I was essentially being ordered in to HQ by Deputy Chief Zajac. He had to talk to me about a matter at exactly 4:00. I asked her "what matter?" She wouldn't or couldn't tell me. I told her I'd be there anyway.

The good news was that I was about to earn at least two hours of overtime. That's the rule per our Police Benevolent Association (PBA) collective bargaining agreement if/when an officer gets called in for court or some other reason off of his regular schedule. That was fine but I was still curious as to just what was the reason he wanted to see me? I guess it's something pretty darn important.

Wait, I know! He wants to congratulate me on the two stolen cars I recovered last night. And he wants to make sure I'm physically okay. Yeah, that's it.

NOT!

I wasn't stupid. I guessed what it was about, but I'd go in like I didn't know. Sometimes ignorance can be bliss, especially if it's of the feigned variety.

So, I told the kids and my wife I'd be back shortly to continue doing whatever it was we were doing. I put on some casual clothing and went to HQ at the appointed time. I arrived there just before 4:00. I walked back to the DC's office and the door was closed. Nothing new there, it usually was closed nowadays. The same secretary who earlier called me, saw me, picked up the phone, pushed two buttons, and said simply, "He's here."

The woman then told me to have a seat and they will be with me soon.

"They," I wondered to myself. Who else does Zajac have in there with him?

I'd find out soon enough.

Before long, without the cheap construction-grade door even opening, I could hear at least two familiar words emanating deep from Zajac's seemingly overworked diaphragm.

"FITZGERALD!" Then he added, "GET IN HERE! NOW!"

I simply looked at the secretary, smiled, and said, "I think he means me. See ya…."

She smiled back and resumed her typing.

As I opened the door and walked into the office I immediately learned who the other person was. It was my former CID supervisor. Lt. Eckert was sitting in front of the desk with Zajac in his usual chair behind his desk. They both appeared very somber and serious. Their eyes and heads followed me as I sat down in one of the chairs with my back to the wall.

The ensuing conversation started almost immediately. It went more or less like this…

Me (just sitting down): "Hello, gentlemen, you wanted to see me?"

Zajac: "You know why you're here. It's about the arrest."

Okay, it was now confirmed to me why I was here, but I thought I'd maintain that faux ignorance thing for as long as I could. Just to see how they would react to it. Sometimes, just sometimes, it was fun to play with these guys when I knew I held the upper hand.

Me: "Actually, sir, there was no arrest."

Zajac: "What do you mean there was no arrest? I read the Incident Report."

Me: "You must have read the wrong one. I saw the guy, but no arrest was made. Not yet, anyway. I can't believe he got away from me after all that. The other one too."

Eckert: "Got away from you? The other one? What are you talking about? We know there was an arrest and YOU made it. Why else would we have called you in here today?"

Me: "I don't know…to maybe congratulate me? To make sure I was okay? I mean, it was pretty hectic out there as this whole thing unfolded last night."

Zajac (after looking frustratingly at Eckert and then back at me, with voice raised): "This isn't about LAST night, Fitzgerald! I could care less about that. This is about Wednesday night. When you arrested the township accountant, bookkeeper, or whatever the hell he is! What's his name, John Speck or something like that?"

Me: "Oh, THAT arrest. Actually, it's Joe Scheck, sir." (As if Zajac didn't know his name OR appointed political position.)

Zajac: "Yeah, whatever!"

Me: "Okay, I thought at first you meant the car chase from last night where I recovered the two stolen Trans-Ams in Neshaminy Valley. You know, we were going pretty fast when…."

Zajac (interrupting): "Do you know I received calls all day on Thanksgiving about this arrest! From the press, elected officials, you name it! And I knew nothing about it!"

Me: Silence, but looking concerned.

Eckert: "Well, answer the question."

Me: "What question? He never asked me one."

Zajac (with telltale veins now pulsing on his forehead): "Why didn't I know about your arrest of this appointed township something-or-other guy? Why wasn't I or Lt. Eckert told about his arrest in advance?"

Me: "Wait, I'm missing something here. Do I now have to tell you personally about every arrest I'm making? In advance?"

Zajac: "When it's a high-profile guy like this one, yes you do! I don't want to sound dumb when I get these phone calls and I don't know anything about what happened in my police department."

I considered myriad options involving his use of the word "dumb," but I resisted each of them.

Me: "Oh, okay. I understand now. In the future I'll do so. No problem."

Zajac: "By the way, how did you even get involved in this case? You're in Patrol now. Weren't you just working vandalisms when you were still in CID?"

I couldn't believe the Deputy Chief just asked me this question. Didn't he know that his Man Friday, Lt. Eckert, personally assigned it to me? I certainly wasn't about to pass up on this opportunity.

Me (looking at and pointing directly at Eckert): "He's the one who assigned me the case, sir. But, he wasn't anywhere to be found afterwards once I identified Scheck as the subject. Then, you (looking back at and now pointing at Zajac) assigned me to Patrol Division. So, I just stayed with the case. It was just a regular investigation as far as I was concerned. I didn't care one way or the other whether this guy was some kind of a politician or not. Should that have made a difference to me?"

Zajac gave a long, hard look at Eckert. A few other veins on his forehead were now becoming prominent. Eckert shuffled in his seat and conspicuously pulled at the front of his buttoned shirt collar.

Geez…did my then-lieutenant somehow forget he assigned me this investigation barely two weeks ago? Did he NOT tell Zajac that he gave me this case? Me, the guy who was just supposed to answer phones and work vandalism investigations during my waning days in CID? Did Eckert not know who the pervert/politician/perp was from the very beginning?

I suppose if the lieutenant wasn't off on his Viola-Mini Task Force witch-hunt at the White House most of the time, he would have known these things. Or, he did know all these things but for some reason didn't tell the Deputy Chief? Now why would that be…?

Zajac (now looking back in my direction and meeting my eyes): "SERGEANT Fitzgerald, I'll repeat myself so I'm real clear here! The next time you're going to arrest a high-profile person in Bensalem Township, I want to know in advance! That's an order! Can I make it any more simple than that?

Me: "No sir, I get it. You're very simple. You know, if I may add here…."

Zajac (once again interrupting me): "No you may not! I'm done! Get out of my office!"

Me: "Yes, sir. You two have a nice rest of your day."

Them: No response, eyes following me contemptuously out of the office.

I walked out and closed the door behind me.

I didn't walk far though. I stopped by the secretary's desk right outside Zajac's office and made small talk. I really wasn't listening to her though. I was listening instead through the door in an attempt to hear what was being said between the DC and the DL. I could readily hear that the Deputy Chief was not very happy. He seemingly was not very happy with his trusty Detective Lieutenant either. I couldn't make out the exact words, but there were the f-words (both "Fitzgerald" and the other single-syllable one ending in "k") being thrown about quite liberally, actually by both of them. I couldn't now see Zajac's protruding veins, but I was imagining that by this time they had come loose at their ends and were squirming around his head like the snakes of Medusa. What a picture....

Okay, back to reality here.

After submitting my overtime slip for two hours, I went home and Sean and Dan and I picked up horsing around where we had left off. After a delicious dinner of leftover turkey, I went to bed circa 9:00 and slept very well through the night. Following that I had a great four days off from work.

I think, make that I know, I deserved it.

* * * * *

Back to the Joe Scheck case....

I knew somewhere down the line, somehow, someone would try to get to Billy and convince him or scare him into not testifying in the case against Joseph Scheck. I just knew it. And it did happen. I learned of it on December 3rd. One of Billy's friend's moms tracked me down at the PD and advised me of what had recently happened. I then got to work...again on this case, even as a newly minted patrol sergeant.

I saved a copy of the BPD report I wrote regarding the matter, and I'll relay portions of it below. It is two pages long and I submitted the original to the investigative file on December 8th of that year.

It reads, in part, as follows:

> "On 3 Dec 84, this officer had occasion to speak with one 'Billy_____.' Billy stated at this time that during the week of 26 Nov 84, while at _____ School..., he was confronted by one of his teachers' aides about the court case in which he is involved. The teachers' aide, Betty _____ (not her real first name) said to him during a conversation after one of his classes that he should not testify in this case because when the subject gets out he may try to get him and hurt him. Billy states that this conversation occurred after what is known as a 'round

table' discussion. During these discussions, students sit in a circle in a classroom and discuss various problems or concerns which may be affecting their lives at the present time. For a short time, the case involving Billy was the topic of the conversation and Betty was, in fact, the moderator of said discussion. It was after this class that Betty called Billy to the side and made the above statement.

"On 7 Dec 84...this officer interviewed Betty. She stated that yes, she does know Billy_____ and that he is, in fact, a student of hers during the morning classes. She stated that she did have a conversation with him regarding this court case but she did not tell him that he should not testify. She merely states she advised him after he brought the incident up during the round table discussion that perhaps he should keep the matter to himself. She reiterated that she did not say to him at any time that he should not testify in court or that the man might hurt him.

"Betty advised this officer that she is, in fact, a neighbor of Joseph Scheck and a friend of his, however, she reemphasized that she did not say anything of this sort to Billy, nor would she, because she knows of the seriousness of the charges. It was shortly after this that Betty began crying and sobbing uncontrollably and saying that she wanted to quit her job at the school.

"She stated that she wants absolutely nothing to do with Billy from this point on and that she was very upset.

"...She just wished to end this matter and forget about the whole thing. This officer advised her that the situation would continue to be monitored but hopefully would not turn up or develop again."

(End of report.)

In what could have been a potential criminal case of Obstruction of Justice and/or Tampering with/Intimidation of a Witness, "Betty" was not arrested. After we talked things out a bit, I decided not to pursue it any further. I did happen to believe Billy and what he told me that Betty said to him after class that day (and I did NOT believe her), but I didn't want to make the poor kid into a fulltime court witness, testifying against yet another adult at yet another criminal proceeding. I figured I'd save him for the upcoming preliminary hearing involving Scheck and leave it at that. If more of this tampering or intimidation-like evidence surfaced, I'd handle it accordingly.

No other similar incidents occurred, as far as I ever knew. Billy was fine. His teacher Betty didn't further attempt to intimidate him. Next for me, and more importantly my witness/victim, was a courtroom date with Joseph Scheck. Let's see how he does there.

* * * * *

On December 11, 1984, the preliminary hearing was held for Joseph Scheck on the charges of Indecent Exposure, Open Lewdness, and Corrupting the Morals of a Minor. It was held at the district magistrate's office in Bensalem, but the regular magistrate, Chris Ritter, was not the presiding judge. As he knew Scheck and his family, he found it best to recuse himself from these legal proceedings to avoid even the perception of a conflict of interest. As such, another Bucks County district magistrate sat in his place on the bench that day.

Previous to the hearing, I had requested one of the Assistant District Attorneys (ADAs) from Doylestown to attend this preliminary hearing and represent the Commonwealth in presenting the prima facie case. This made sense as it was an important matter and I didn't want to take any chances on something going amiss, legally speaking, in the courtroom. I had acted as an ADA in other cases at the preliminary hearing level in the past, and successfully so, but I decided not to do so on this occasion.

Billy was the only person to testify that day. He did a great job answering the questions from the ADA. He stuck to the facts and told the judge and those assembled in the courtroom exactly what he had told me on two different occasions. At one point, he was asked by the ADA to point to the person in the room who had exposed himself to him at Rambler's Field on the day in question. Billy pointed directly at Joe Scheck and said, "That's him, right there," indicating the defendant. There wasn't much of a cross-examination of Billy by Scheck's attorney, if there was one at all.

At the end of the hearing the visiting district magistrate ordered Scheck to stand trial in county court. He then released Scheck on his own recognizance. (I learned that day Scheck had made bail a few days after his arrest.)

In an article published in the *Bucks County Courier Times* on December 12, written by Joseph Grace, near the end, it reads:

"Several township Republican Party members were present at the district court in Bensalem Tuesday before and after the hearing. Scheck is a GOP committeeman and an appointed township auditor.

"Township Supervisor Mary Komada said after the hearing the Republicans attended because Scheck 'is a Republican committeeman and we're concerned.'"

(End of article.)

As the article relates, Supervisor Mary Komada, one of Stephen Kelly's fellow Board members and one of his acolytes, was present for Scheck's hearing. As the story relates, she wasn't the only politician or politically-connected person there in the courtroom that day. One of the other "politicians" present there was Lt. Robert Eckert's wife, Theresa Eckert, an unabashed acolyte of Komada's. Following the township political chain of command, that also made her an acolyte of Stephen Kelly, as she was appointed Tax Collector for Bensalem Township by the Chairman himself earlier this year. I already knew who she was and I observed her in the back of the courtroom during the hearing. I did not engage her in any conversation, nor did I personally hear anything she may have said before, during, or after the proceeding.

However, a day or two later I was contacted by another BPD officer I trusted and respected and who happened to be in the courtroom for other purposes on the 11th. He told me then and there he overheard Mrs. Eckert make a statement and he thinks I should be made aware of it. He continued that she apparently told one or more persons around her, and loudly enough for other nearby people to hear, in so many words, "Sergeant Fitzgerald better know what he's doing with this Joe Scheck arrest because this may just cost him his job." If these weren't the exact words, they were darn close to it.

I thanked my fellow officer for passing along this information. I told him I wasn't all that concerned about anything politician Theresa Eckert might have to say...much the same way I felt about anything her all but-politician husband might have to say.

I kiddingly advised the other officer that I better make sure my taxes are all paid and up-to-date though. She does hold SOME power in the township, I guess. We half-laughed, shook our heads in collective benign resignation, and went our separate ways.

* * * * *

Sometime in mid-1985, Joe Scheck and his attorney reached a plea agreement with the Bucks County DA's office. He would plead guilty to one or two of the charges, be put on two years' probation, and receive some mandatory psychological counseling. He would do no jail time.

I was asked by the ADA in advance about this plea arrangement. After some thought and consideration and discussion with Billy and his mom, we all reluctantly agreed to it. I concurred to it mostly to preclude Billy from having to go through a potentially lengthy trial and all that would entail to a fourteen-year-old boy. It was the right thing to do at the time...at least I thought it to be.

As far as I know, Joe Scheck was never arrested again. I believe he stepped down from his various positions within Bensalem Township politics in early 1985. However, he seemingly remained active in the Boy Scouts and the Catholic Church for many years to come...for better or worse.

Joseph Scheck died of cancer in 2006. He was single.

* * * * *

Back to the double-stolen car case and chase....

Now-Detective Steve Moran, (fellow one-time rookie, for a while fellow Tac Squad member, future Chief), was assigned the case of the two stolen Trans-Ams. After a week or so of some excellent investigating on his part, he came up with a suspect. He put that guy's picture in a six-person photo array, showed it to me, and I immediately picked out one of them as the driver of Trans-Am #1. I couldn't forget his face or his finger for a while back then, so it was a relatively easy ID for me. He was a Bensalem resident and a known car thief. Within a few days, he was arrested. The thief ultimately confessed to the stolen car caper, and also gave up Trans-Am #2 driver.

Driver #1 told Det. Moran that it was on a lark that night that they went out to steal the cars from the dealership on Rt. 1. They were bored with nothing else to do and decided to give it a go. A friend dropped them off in the area, they scaled a fence, and with their various car theft tools, they got to work. He told Steve he couldn't believe that in the middle of Neshaminy Valley, at four in the morning and in the fog, a police car happened upon him/them. Otherwise, he said, they could have joy-driven their stolen muscle cars the whole next day. But it was not meant to be.

The thief added that he also couldn't believe he survived the high-speed crash with virtually no injuries. At the scene, after immediately coming to his senses, even while upside-down, he managed to crawl out of the still-spinning car and run into the nearby apartment complex. He had a friend who lived there, knocked on his door, and laid low for the rest of the night. He was hurting a bit afterwards, he said, but nothing major was wrong with him. Lucky guy....

Steve suggested to the admitted thief that he could have died that night. He didn't seem to care. He simply said back to Steve, "But I didn't, did I? And what a bad-ass car I had! Hey, by the way, can they fix it?" Steve never answered that last question.

I lost track of this guy, as well as his wing-man in the other stolen Trans Am. Something told me back then that they wouldn't go too far in life without either getting arrested again, hurt, or killed pulling similar stunts as on that Black Friday morning.

* * * * *

Lastly, Officer Dan....

DUI Dan and I talked the next week, and on numerous occasions after that while I was still his sergeant. It seems that at least once per tour of duty we would have an informal "counseling" session, although neither of us referred to it as such. He eventually made some pretty good felony arrests over the course of the next year or two. He never stopped arresting the drunk drivers, however, and won a few more awards for it, as that skillset was apparently in his blood.

Interestingly, in one of my Villanova management courses in '85, as a semester-long project, I had to identify a "problem employee" and come up with weekly solutions in how to best deal with him. I chose Officer Dan. (Of course, as here, I didn't use his real name.) The professor even commented after reading my first several papers in which I reference him that he was a most unusual candidate as a problem employee. We agreed he was very motivated to do his everyday job, but mostly in just one area of it, and it was clearly limiting his full potential. Dan was not the type of problem employee that most of the professor's students wrote about in his class, he later told me.

By the end of the semester, and after numerous advisory sessions from car-to-car, I feel Dan had definitely matured and developed a more comprehensive view of the police profession and his role as a patrolman. He was good already, but he was now turning into an even better all-around police officer. I included his "progress" in my final paper for the course.

I received an "A" for my grade that semester. More importantly, what I included in the various course papers, and what I incorporated in real life with Officer Dan at the same time, seemed to actually work. Just lending an ear, and providing common sense approaches to doing one's job more effectively and efficiently, can be very helpful to a struggling employee in most cases.

Officer Dan eventually went on to a successful career in the BPD, retiring after doing his full twenty-five years. Oh, and I happen to know he never ran out of gas in his patrol car again…to many drunk drivers' dismay, no doubt.

Chapter Forty-Six

My uniform shirts and pants finally came in sometime over the Christmas holidays, 1984. Now I was the complete patrol supervisor. I retired my dad's overcoat once and for all when the new apparel finally arrived. I felt much better going to work now in the uniform I should have been wearing all along rather than the makeshift plainclothes-in-a-patrol-car look that had been mandated of me for a month-plus. I now not only felt the part of a uniformed sergeant, but I looked the part too.

Along with Officer Dan, my first patrol squad after coming out of CID was an interesting mix of pro-Zajac, pro-Viola, and a few who were generally neutral. I really didn't care where they fell on that continuum. I simply told them at the various roll calls that I wanted them to do the job they're paid to do, stay safe, and to back up our fellow officers. If they could make some good arrests, write some quality traffic tickets, and generally not do anything stupid on top of all that, it was even better. As it turned out, these men were not difficult at all to manage on an everyday basis. There were no prima donnas among them, unlike a few of the detectives that I left behind in CID.

In fact, I wasn't really even keeping count, but when the monthly stats for December came out for each of the five patrol squads, my squad happened to be at the top of the list. That was a very nice feeling, and totally unexpected. I wish I could claim I possessed some special management skills or unique leadership abilities which resulted in my squad coming out number one for that month, but I really can't put a finger on any one supervisory talent of mine at the time which may have led to it. From an overall management-style perspective, I simply told my officers early on, much like I did with the detectives in CID when I was first appointed their supervisor, that I wasn't here to babysit them or micro-manage their every day (or every night) activities. This general philosophy seemed to work for me and for them. My squad's numbers during the first two weeks of 1985 were very good too.

But alas, all good things must come to an end. This scenario wasn't meant to last. I think my squad's numbers were actually too high, and the present management would have none of that, not with me at the helm, anyway. It simply didn't fit their narrative as it pertained to Sergeant James Fitzgerald.

Around mid-January, a memo was put in the admin book that the squads were about to be realigned. I'm not saying the patrol lineups were changed ONLY because my squad had done so well during my first month and a half as its sergeant, but this change did come as a surprise to almost everyone in the patrol division, especially as no explanation was ever provided for the sudden realignment of officers and sergeants. And from the relatively easy-to-manage squad to which I was assigned fresh out of CID, I was about to be put in charge of the antithesis of such a squad. So much so, as a matter of fact, that before we even worked an actual shift together my new squad earned itself a nickname. That would be, "F Troop."

F Troop was a mid-1960s television situation comedy. In the show, a squad of misfits and malcontents were assigned to the U. S. Cavalry's fictional Fort Courage in the 1860s Wild West. As can be surmised, there wasn't much the men in this unit could or would do by the rules, whether intentionally, through laziness, or as a result of their sheer stupidity.

At the non-fictional "Fort Bensalem" in early 1985, if there was a patrol officer who was a trouble-maker, a big-mouth, prone to indolence, disrespected authority, otherwise flaunted standard police department protocols and conventions and/or was a misfit or malcontent, he was now working for me as a member of our own modern-day, not-for-television version of F Troop. It wasn't an accident that these guys wound up on my troop, I mean, squad. I was sure of it, especially as management's rationale previously was to split up these officers with just a few on each squad and spread the wealth, or more accurately, the dearth.

If it was by happenstance on my last squad that the stats for December and even early January were at the top, it was most definitely NOT by happenstance that my numbers with this squad would most assuredly be at or near the bottom. That's why, I'm sure, this rogue's gallery of Bensalem patrol cops now comprised my new command. Individually, each of them to a man was one of the lowest producers on his previous squads. Making it even more challenging for anyone attempting to supervise them, most seemed to be proud of it.

"F Troop" was a fitting nickname for my new squad. The "F" possibly standing for "Fitzgerald," but just as likely standing for a certain crass four-letter word, perhaps followed by "Up."

On the night of F Troop's first ever roll call, right at the start as they lined up in front of me, I said to them, "Well, to a man, they've assembled the best of the best here, right guys?" They laughed. It was a good ice-breaker, and my obvious forage into sarcasm was appreciated. However, getting serious after the normal recounting of recently stolen cars, runaway teens, burglar alarm problems, and the like, I additionally told the nine officers that night I expected them to play by the rules every single shift and do exactly what's expected of them. I ended that first roll call by telling them that I knew that I was being watched very closely by the "higher authorities" and because of that I wasn't going to be taken down by any member of this new squad. Out of necessity and self-preservation, I told them, "I will write you up and recommend discipline if you give me cause to do so. I know if I don't, it'll be ME getting written up. Understand?" They did.

Even though most of these guys were on the Dark Side (and thus rarely, if ever, disciplined by the Zajac regime), and knew I was NOT a player on their team, they seemed to comprehend where I was coming from. Or, at least they pretended so.

I was none of my new squad mates' friend or on their same side politically within the BPD. Notwithstanding, I assured them I would back them up on their calls, car stops, etc., and I would otherwise support them when they honestly screwed up if they at least TRIED to handle a matter properly. I would NOT, however, support them if it involved dishonesty, overt laziness, or otherwise as a result of them simply not doing their job. Regarding that last part, I was very clear to my new squad during this first-ever roll call. And, yes, this initial roll call went a bit longer than most. I had a lot to say to them. They had a lot to hear from me.

By the second night's roll call, I advised my new band of officers that if a notice was placed in the admin book that ordered them to follow some new protocol, check a certain building, write up so many pedestrian stops, wear their hat when out of their car, etc., I would also type up my own individual memos to them. These memos would clearly mirror the same "order" as in the admin book and during each shift I would meet with my officers, sign their daily logs, and then have them sign the separate "Sergeant Fitzgerald memo" stating that they read the original memo in the book and they understood and they would follow/obey the new rule.

After all, if Captain Hughes (he was promoted sometime over the last year) saw one of my officers driving an unwashed patrol car, or had parked his personal car in an unauthorized spot in the back lot (both top level priorities to Hughes), or an officer's numbers were down in some category for the month, and the Captain wanted to go after the individual patrolman administratively, the supervisor (as in, me) could also be held responsible via the ever-present "Failure to Supervise" rule violation. This would be true even if the same supervisor (again, as in me) was nowhere near the scene of the alleged infraction. If such a scenario was to play out and I was to be written up because of this purported lack of supervision on my part, I wanted to present as exculpatory evidence signed memos that each officer was made personally aware of whatever the particular rule du jour may have been. It wouldn't necessarily mean that there'd be no disciplinary problems for me at that time, but at least I'd have some level of a defense if it ever came down to it.

As hard as this may be to believe regarding F Troop, after only a few weeks I actually found myself working quite well with these guys - most of them, anyway. A few of the officers actually raised their traffic ticket writing output although, of course, there was never a "quota" on any squad of mine. My guys' overall misdemeanor and felony arrest stats were up too.

Was this a coincidence…or something else?

Looking back at the early interpersonal dynamics of this newly-formed patrol squad, I happen to think what may have broken the ice between their self-actualized sergeant and their own tendencies toward professional lethargy occurred during, of all things, a bar fight late one night. I was there in the middle of my squad duking it out as a handful of drunken males were in the process of destroying the interior of a Bensalem nightclub. Those of us present got a bit banged up, but we definitely gave more than we received to the intoxicated pugilists, all of whom were pretty banged up themselves by night's end, as well as under arrest.

Fighting alongside someone and covering his or her back can accomplish much in terms of a bonding mechanism developing between people to include, naturally, police officers or military members. In these relationships, rightly or wrongly, it's generally an "us-against-them" mentality under which the uniform-wearing entities are patrolling, protecting, and/or on assignment. One may still not like a certain guy or gal squad mate on a personal level, but once that fellow officer comes to the defense of the other in a life-threatening situation, from flying fists to flying bullets and everything in between, that primal bond and mutual professional respect is then established, sometimes forever.

To some degree, I believe this is what happened between me and my F Troop subordinates. That, and the fact that the officers also came to know me as a no-nonsense, by-the-book supervisor who was not about to be taken down by the Dark Side because of THEIR actions or inactions, all contributed to their eventual if somewhat reluctant respect for me. Well, most of them anyway.

Surprisingly, despite many of my BPD friends' and associates' predictions that my new squad would totally "tank" on me, leading to subsequent disciplinary problems for me, what actually occurred was just the opposite. When the latter half of January's stats were posted, and then February's stats too, it seems that F Troop was right in the middle of the five squads. Not at the top, but by holding the third place spot, definitely not at the bottom either. If the regime was going to come after me for "Lack of Supervision" or "Neglect of Duty" or similar charges regarding my officers' activity level or lack thereof, they'd have to also go after the two patrol sergeants whose squad numbers were a good bit lower than mine. Knowing that one of the sergeants was a card-carrying Dark Sider, I was positive I was safe…for now, anyway.

What did happen though, to the surprise of many in the BPD once again, including me, was yet another switch of my schedule. It also involved a switch of my squad. Apparently, instead of waiting for the individual F Troop members to mess up and take me down with him/them, management decided on another strategy. That being, if the Zajac goon squad of non-conformists and anti-workers were actually getting along with and even producing for Sergeant Fitzgerald, the administration would have to move in the complete opposite direction. At least that's what they thought would work for them here.

So, the memo came to me advising that I was to be switched out with one of the other sergeants and put in charge of yet another patrol squad. Some individual officers were transferred too. Interestingly, my new squad was now comprised of guys with whom I was known to be friendly. It was common knowledge that some of our wives were even friendly with each other, too. Most of the nine of them were pro-Viola, with maybe one or two being, at best, neutral.

I suppose Zajac's rationale shifted from putting me in charge of officers I didn't know or like very much who were also trouble-makers and non-producers, to putting me in charge of a squad of hard-working guys with whom I was known to socialize and consider as my friends. And, almost to the man, they were known to NOT be supporters of the present Deputy Chief.

In effect, the regime was putting all of its "rotten eggs" into one basket. They were "Grade A" eggs in this case, certainly from a productivity and work ethic perspective. I was to be their new leader. Perhaps this would be an easier way for the Dark Side to bring down the now highest ranking member of the former Viola team still coming to work every day (me), along with some other known Viola supporters on the squad at the same time.

They could only hope.

* * * * *

It was either late February or very early March of '85, when I took over this new squad. It was a blessing working with guys who really needed very little supervision or watching over. I did away with the "Sergeant Fitzgerald memo" notion as I knew these officers would follow the rules and not set themselves (or their supervisor) up for an easy hit by Zajac and Company. Knowing this made going to my job much easier every day. IF the regime was going to ever take me down, or one or more of my men, they'd have to really dig hard to do so. I was sure of this fact.

As it turned out, the Dark Side would, in fact, dig hard for their desired results. The regime thought they found early on what they so desired in regards to disciplining me. However, the dirt they were digging up actually wound up burying them instead. They were just small shovels full at first, but it would prove to be the beginning of the end for them and their maddening managerial *modus operandi*.

Interestingly, exactly three years earlier during the spring of 1982, as a brand new detective sergeant, I experienced a very rewarding, exciting, and challenging few months working various investigations and making arrests involving a pedophile priest, two fake baby abandoners, and an international hitman/fugitive. Now, in the spring of 1985, life again would prove to be, well, at the very least challenging for me, yet for completely different reasons while under a completely different BPD management.

Like in '82, this challenging timeframe started in mid-March and went through mid-June of that year. During this current springtime, all kinds of allegations and accusations would be forthcoming from the regime towards me and, in turn, from me back at the regime. Being fifteen months now under the collective thumbs of Zajac, Eckert, Hughes and the other departmental troglodytes, I decided to stop merely playing defense with them and for the first time go on the offense when the opportunity permitted me to do so. It did and I did.

On Saturday, March 16, after barely two full shifts with my new squad, we were working the first day of a 7A-5P. We were short-handed from the outset, but nonetheless tried to muddle through for the first few hours. It became very busy by mid-morning with officers all over the township on various calls and time-consuming initial investigations. With the officers' lunch times approaching, I made an executive decision around 10:00 that morning. I had the dispatcher call the home of one of our squad members who was on his scheduled "group day" to come in and work the rest of the shift. He agreed to do so and within an hour or so the extra officer had joined us. There is no question that his added presence contributed to the safety of his fellow officers and Bensalem citizens alike that day. At shift's end, as I expected of him, he handed me an overtime slip for those six hours. As he expected of me, I signed it.

Everything seems pretty simple, right? Well, it wasn't.

Remember who I was. Remember who was in charge.

It took the Dark Side some time, but on April 5th I received a short memo from the "Lieutenant's Office." There was strangely no actual person's name on it, not even a set of initials. The essentially anonymous memo instructed me to answer, in writing, why I called the officer in to work on March 16 and also why I didn't first attain the duty-lieutenant's permission.

My April 9th response to the ghost written memo read, in part, as follows:

> "On that date, my squad had four officers on days off.
> Three were off for school and one was on his group day.
> At approximately 0730 hours that date, Officer _____
> was dispatched to the area of Rt. 13 and Buttonwood
> Ave. to handle a commercial burglary. Shortly thereafter,

he discovered a second burglary in the vicinity. He was subsequently unavailable for two-and-one-half hours that morning on those calls alone.

"Based on the knowledge that I was going to be short an officer for several hours (due to aforementioned burglary) and the fact that it was a seasonably warm holiday weekend (St. Patrick's Day), I took it upon myself to call another officer into work. It must be pointed out that no Neshaminy Mall Officer was in on that date. If, in fact, a Mall Officer was due in that day his presence would have sufficed in supplementing the squad and no call-in would have been necessary.

"My experience in patrol is that the first warm weekend of the Winter/Spring months is generally very busy with all types of calls. I was correct in that matter as that day was very busy with calls including burglaries, car accidents, retail theft arrests, and even an 'assist officer' call. (A Bucks County Sheriff had problems with approximately fifty youths drinking and causing a disturbance at the Delaware River access area.) Couple that activity with the officers taking their lunches between 1100 hours and 1400 hours, the possibility existed that only one or two officers might be available for emergency calls during those hours.

"Since assuming Sergeant duties approximately 3 years ago, I have never needed the approval of a Lieutenant to have an officer work on his day off, or after his tour of duty ended. I felt this situation was no exception and I was not about to disturb an off-duty lieutenant regarding what I thought was a relatively minor decision."

(End of memo.)

There was no immediate response from the "Lieutenant's Office" as a result of my memo to it/him/them. I believe I explained my position rather well in that the safety of officers and civilians alike would have been jeopardized without at least one extra patrolman on duty that day. I made a "relatively minor" decision then and all turned out fine for my squad. I was now awaiting the lieutenants', or more accurately the Deputy Chief's, next move. I was sure his best people were on it.

Yes...to have been a fly on the DC's office wall back then. I can hear him now.

"Let's see...how can we punish Sergeant Fitzgerald for what he did? How DARE he call in one extra officer to make the streets safer on that day? Who does he think he is?"

But still nothing, no response at all. Well, until....

If the overtime-officer scenario wasn't quite enough to get me at first, I suppose what I did exactly one month to the day afterwards put the final nail in my administrative coffin. If you thought the action I undertook on March 16th was reprehensible and beyond the pale, wait until you learn about what happened four weeks later.

On April 16, while on a night shift, at 12:05AM, along State Rd., I observed some taillights in the field of an abandoned factory complex. The area was still referred to as Publicker's even though the former distillery had closed down years before. Cars shouldn't be in there for any reason now, certainly at midnight, so I decided to investigate.

When I first pulled into the otherwise empty field, I did some damage to the undercarriage of the police car by running over a hard-to-see cutoff fence post sticking out of the ground. I knew I hit something right away, but my vehicle was still drivable, so I continued to check out the suspicious car. Within seconds I determined it was two local teenagers making out in the back seat. I attained their ID, everything matched up, and I chased them out of the lot. It was all very routine. But the damage was done to the undercarriage of my car. So, I limped back to the police station, wrote up the problem, and then took another patrol car for the rest of my shift.

One day later, on April 17th, I received a memo which ordered me to write a memo to explain how I came to damage the police car. It didn't take them long this time, did it?

Below, instead of my April 17th response to Capt. Hughes, I'll include his memo of two days later (April 19th) to Deputy Chief Zajac, also provided to me, which summarizes what I had wrote in my initial memo and clearly Hughes's fact-devoid thought processes at the time.

"On 16 April 1985 Sergeant James Fitzgerald was operating patrol car 22-10 when he entered the grounds of the old Publicker Company. He drove over an obstruction damaging the vehicle's frame and other under-carriage parts.

511

"Sergeant Fitzgerald submitted a report on 17 April 1985 explaining circumstances leading to the damage of the vehicle, explanations which I find unsatisfactory.

"1. He stated that he went into the lot to check out a suspicious car which turned out to be teenage lovers. There was no entry on his daily Patrol Log regarding the suspicious vehicle or its occupants. There was also no radio transmission of this incident. It is my opinion that you cannot see a vehicle in that lot from State Road at that time of the evening unless it has its lights on. If, in fact, Sergeant Fitzgerald went back into the lot to check for stolen or suspicious cars as he mentioned in his report, then I am sure he was previously aware of the obstruction to the entrance to the grounds.

"2. Sergeant Fitzgerald stated he may have been traveling at five or ten miles an hour when he hit the obstruction. Lieutenant Walsh and I drove to the scene the next day and when turning off of State Road into the drive to the lot there is a drop of several inches and the obstruction is also right in front of this. I feel that the only safe speed going through the gates into the entrance would be a crawling speed of five miles per hour or less.

"It is my opinion, therefore, that Sergeant Fitzgerald used poor judgment and that the damage occurred because of his negligence. I feel that he is in violation of 4.16 of the Rules and Regulations, under Conduct Becoming an Officer: 'Damage to Police Department Property Resulting from Negligent Action.'

"The penalty under this section is a reprimand to ten days' suspension for a first offense. After much deliberation, I recommend that Sergeant Fitzgerald be suspended for one day, without pay, namely 9 May 1985."

(End of memo.)

I don't believe ANY of Capt. Hughes's workplace "deliberation" ever went much beyond whether to do the daily newspaper's crossword puzzle first or read the comics first. Nonetheless, after this alleged "deliberation" on his part, I was now on the receiving end of a suspension day.

Will there be more to come for me? After all, there's still that pending matter regarding my preposterous call-in of the extra officer. Yet…it's been a while though. Maybe they forgot about it.

As it so happens, there was a Police Benevolent Association (PBA) meeting on Monday evening, April 22. I was a bit distressed about my three squad/schedule changes over the last four months, not to mention my recent disciplinary issues and the recommendation that I be suspended for at least one day so far, and I took this opportunity to raise my hand and speak out among my peers. (No one above the rank of sergeant was allowed in the PBA.) I initially waited my turn. I listened to some of my colleagues also complaining about their harassment issues involving upper-management. Then, I spoke my piece.

The gist of what I had to say took most by surprise. I don't believe it had ever been brought up before at a PBA meeting. Quite simply, I suggested that we, the rank and file of the BPD, should move beyond merely having the relatively benign and toothless PBA as our representative entity. We should perhaps consider forming a relationship with a national law enforcement association to speak and act on our behalf. Yes, I suggested that evening that we should look into contacting the nationwide Fraternal Order of Police (FOP) and requesting that they come in and represent the BPD's officers for future salary/benefits negotiations, as well as provide legal resources to us when so needed. I made the motion, someone seconded it, and it was agreed that I would contact my good friend, Rob McCarthy, now a sergeant in the Philadelphia PD and also an elected officer of that department's FOP, for guidance in creating such a BPD liaison. The PBA meeting essentially ended with my motion.

Interestingly, I noticed a few of the officers, all Zajac boys, walking hastily out of the meeting room at the same time. When I finally walked out into the parking lot of the facility where our meeting had been held, I saw one of these officers at a public payphone, surrounded by a few of the other guys. Their animated conversation with whoever was on the other end of the line suddenly went into whisper-mode once my group walked by them.

Hmmm…what could have been so important that these guys had to make a phone call from this parking lot, immediately after our PBA meeting? And to whom? I had some suspicions, as did several of my fellow officers, but I let it rest for the night. I was tired and it was time to go home. I had to be in work early the next morning.

On the morning of April 23rd, the very next day after the PBA meeting and my proposal to bring in the FOP as our "union," I was personally handed yet another memo by Capt. Hughes. It was from the Deputy Chief. It stated that I was to be suspended one day for the vehicle damage and for two days for calling in the extra officer on March 16. That's three days' suspension total if you're keeping count.

It was remarkably as simple as 1-2-3 for them; one memo, two incidents, three days off. It was a victory at last for the Dark Side. I guess they'd teach me not to add one extra officer to the streets, cause relatively minor damage to a police car or, God forbid, call for the FOP as our bargaining representative. It was now my firm opinion that it was Deputy Chief Zajac who had been called from the payphone the night before with the "radical" news regarding me wanting to unionize the place. That was my initial hunch and as far as I was concerned, it was now confirmed.

In actuality, this was really not a surprise to me. I was expecting additional suspension days all along. (Not that it was deserved, just that I was anticipating it.) It was simply a matter of when and for how long. As such, I had a game plan in mind for the last month-plus. Now, it was time to put it into motion.

As every Bensalem township employee knew at the time, as per Pennsylvania municipal code as well as the police department's collective bargaining agreement, when served with a disciplinary action of any kind, the officer/employee had ten days to appeal the findings. When I was suspended for two days back in 1980, the night the Phillies won the World Series, I ultimately decided to not appeal it. I regretted that decision ever since as it was a bogus charge.

This time would be different though. As such, I didn't waste any time in initiating two very specific actions. Within forty-eight hours I made a telephone call and then contacted certain people. A third action, which I did not initiate but participated in nonetheless, unfolded about ten days later. Each of these actions would intertwine as they played themselves out.

Firstly, on April 26th, I notified the PBA Grievance Committee by memo that I wished for a full review of my recent double-suspension. As per their protocol, and upon a preliminary review of the paperwork associated with my case, they agreed to hold a "hearing" and look into the recent disciplinary actions against me. That was good news for me.

Secondly, on April 26th, I called Peter Hileman. He had been the ADA/prosecutor of the home invasion gang I had arrested in 1981. I was aware that he had just recently resigned from the Bucks County District Attorney's office and was now in private practice in Doylestown, Pennsylvania. As such, I retained his services.

Per my specific instructions on that very day, acting as my newly retained attorney, Pete wrote and mailed a certified letter to the Bensalem Township solicitor. I helped Pete with some of the wording in it. The letter informed the Township that "Sgt. James Fitzgerald is appealing his recent three-day suspension." As was my right, I would be demanding a public hearing, open to whomever wanted to attend, including the local media (hopefully), to dispute my suspension in front of the five Board of Supervisor members.

I could have asked for a private hearing, as that would have been my legal prerogative too, but I wanted this issue out there front and center for all to hear and/or read. Also, Pete and I later decided to send a follow-up letter to the township which would demand that Mrs. Patricia Zajac recuse herself from my appeal hearing as it was her husband, the Deputy Chief, who was bringing the charges against me. That would mean one less politician who could rule against me at my appeal. (I suppose this nepotism thing can have its occasional downside too.)

Interestingly, Peter's office never received a response to the letter. I did though, well, in a way.

Within just days of the Township receiving the official letter from my attorney requesting the public hearing to appeal the charges against me, I found the below memo, dated May 2nd, in my mail slot. It was supposedly from Deputy Chief Zajac, yet with no initials or signature of any kind on it. It reads:

> "I have reviewed the reports submitted to me concerning the two incidents where disciplinary actions were recommended against you. I have also had several discussions with my staff and with P.B.A. President Jerry Judge. As a result of those discussions I am reducing the punishment in both incidents to a letter of reprimand."
> (End of memo.)

Again, I would love to have been a fly on the wall in whatever office the "discussions" took place regarding the disciplinary actions against me. I guess they realized that a public hearing would not be in the regime's overall best interests. In a way, I was disappointed. I really wanted a public hearing. I had already been working with Pete Hileman on his cross-examinations of both Capt. Hughes and Deputy Chief Zajac. Pete would have no doubt torn them new…well, usually hidden body parts. Of that I was convinced.

I learned here how people such as Zajac, Hughes, and their ilk will back down once lawyers are involved and advocating on the side of the person being harassed and bullied in a workplace situation. In view of that, I decided to keep this tactic in mind for future reference. It was a good decision on my part, if I do say so myself, especially as any backing down on their parts was only temporary. These people apparently had very short organizational memories.

At some point during all of this I also talked to Jerry Judge after he, as the newly elected PBA President, insisted on meeting with the Deputy Chief regarding my disciplinary matter. Jerry later told me Zajac seemed reluctant to reduce my original "punishment," but he did so anyway, telling Jerry that he could be a "fair guy" too.

Zajac never did volunteer to Jerry that he was also in receipt of the certified letters from my attorney. Despite not acknowledging their existence to the PBA President or my lawyer, the letters apparently performed their designed function very well as I was no longer facing multiple suspensions.

The dropping of my "punishment" to JUST a letter of reprimand wasn't good enough for me though. I violated no rules or regulations in the overtime matter. I did nothing that a dozen other BPD officers hadn't done to their police cars involving accidents and minor car damage over the last year with NONE of them having been disciplined in any manner. So, on May 2nd I made a follow-up request to the Grievance Committee to still review my case even though it was now only a matter of a letter of reprimand, and not an actual suspension. Once again, they agreed to review my matter.

As it turned out, May 6th was a busy day for me. There was a surprise or two on tap for me that evening…the good kind of surprise, in fact, for a change.

* * * * *

On May 6th, at 4:30PM, the PBA Grievance Committee, composed of seven volunteer rank and file police officers and detectives, after

516

reading and reviewing all of the documents related to the two separate incidents, met and interviewed me. Five of the committee members showed up at the "hearing" and each engaged me in substantive discourse. They asked me probing and relevant questions and I answered them honestly and to the best of my ability. I presented evidence in my case too, including a copy of a memo out of the admin book from just several months earlier which actually instructed patrol officers to check the vacant Publicker's lot for stolen cars. One of the committee members took copious notes the whole time. Within two days, the committee would submit their two-page opinion to the Deputy Chief.

After meeting with the Grievance Committee at the police department that afternoon, I went home. It was a scheduled day off for me. At around 6:30 that evening I received a phone call. The caller and the call itself caught me totally by surprise. It was from Township Manager Marge Strange. She "ordered" me to call Supervisor George Ciotti, one of the five elected members on the Bensalem Board of Supervisors. She gave me his phone number and I called him.

Ciotti, as of late, was the consistent lone dissenting vote on the Board. Of all the votes over the last year-plus involving the police department, from the firing of Viola to the re-hiring of Zajac, and all the political nonsense since then, he was always the sensible "1" vote to the nonsensible "4" vote when it was "4-1."

Supervisor George Ciotti was a successful local business person and an honest and by-the-book elected official. Someone, either inside or outside of the BPD, must have called him, explained my disciplinary situation, requested his intervention, and he saw this as an opportunity to do something right to help a little guy (me) who was caught up in this ongoing political and departmental malfeasance. I had never actually met the man before, but I was about to get to know him just a little bit over the course of the next few hours.

During our two-minute or so phone conversation George asked me if I would meet him in front of the township building at 8:30. He wanted me to attend an official Executive Session with the Board of Supervisors at that time. I hesitatingly said I would, but I'd need to know what was going to happen at the meeting. He said, "Trust me, we'll get to the bottom of this issue with you and Zajac and Hughes."

Before I even responded to George's request I told him that I very much respected him from afar for trying his best to right the crooked ship that is the current BPD and the Township on the whole. I added,

"…and if you think this is the right thing to do, and it will help my cause and the cause of the other officers in the department being harassed and intimidated, I'll be there."

"Okay," Supervisor Ciotti said, "Meet me there at 8:30 sharp. Oh, and wear a suit and tie. It'll make a difference."

"Sure, whatever you say, sir," and we ended the call.

(As can be seen here, Ciotti and I never did talk about my specific disciplinary situation before the meeting. That would be important to know for yet another memo I would be compelled to write about one month later.)

After getting dressed, at the last minute I retrieved my former CID leather-bound note pad from the desk in my house. I'm glad I did as the copious notes I would be taking over the next few hours would prove very important to me, in the short-term as well as the long-term.

I showed up right on time and there was Supervisor George Ciotti waiting for me at the bottom of the steps of the township building. (As a reminder, the police department occupied the whole first floor, with the township offices on the second floor.) As we walked up the concrete stairs to the top floor George merely said to me that once inside the meeting room he was going to ask me some questions and I should answer them honestly. I told him, "No problem, I can do that," as we walked into the conference room.

In the room I took a seat next to George. I wasn't initially introduced nor referenced by him or anyone else. For the next ten minutes or so, the various politicians talked among themselves regarding some relatively mundane and innocuous zoning issues, corporate tax levies, and requests to put up new stop signs at various township intersections. I paid little attention as none of this concerned me.

Then, as if on cue, someone knocked on the closed door. The person was granted permission to enter and of all people to walk into the room, it was Capt. Bob Hughes. I had no idea he was supposed to be here tonight. And once his eyes met mine, I was sure by his reaction that he didn't expect to see me in that room either. He took the empty chair to the right of Mrs. Zajac. I recalled thinking then and there that I suppose Hughes is the right-hand man to both husband AND wife. How cozy.

Within a few minutes after the routine matters had been fully addressed, George Ciotti shifted gears and advised his fellow supervisors that he wanted to discuss the matter of the various disciplinary actions being leveled against Sgt. James Fitzgerald. He then gestured toward me, in effect, introducing me to the group. I nodded my head politely toward everyone.

Immediately, one of the other elected supervisors, Mary Komada, spoke up and said, "Oh, you're one of our police officers? I thought you were a lawyer here on some other matter."

I'm not sure why Supervisor Komada stated what she did. I hadn't said a word yet at the meeting, but I guess I was attired and carried myself in what she perceived to be a "lawyerly manner." Or, maybe it was my official looking leather-bound note pad. Either way, I took it as a compliment. However, that would be the extent of any complimentary language afforded me that evening. In fact, thanks to the mumbling and fact-deprived Capt. Hughes, it would pretty much go all downhill from that point on.

Fortunately, like any well-dressed lawyer (or well-dressed cop), I took some good notes that evening. Some while still in the meeting room, and then filling in the rest immediately upon returning to my home.

My two pages of handwritten notes are replicated below. They are transcribed here exactly as I wrote them at the meeting and immediately thereafter at the desk in my house. (Occasional parenthetical inclusions are added for clarification purposes.)

> "Executive Session w. Bensalem Twp. Board of Supervisors
> - May 6, 1985
> - 8:45PM
> - Bensalem Twp. Bldg.
> - Present: (Supervisors) Patricia Zajac, Mary Komada, Peter Reed, Geo. Ciotti, (Township Manager) Marge Strange, Capt. R. Hughes, Sgt. J. Fitzgerald
>
> Remarks
> - Ciotti asked Hughes to describe why I was suspended/reprimanded.
> - Hughes stated:
> • (Fitzgerald) was grossly negligent, careless, with a disregard for police property.
> • He (Hughes) knows I didn't do it intentionally.
> • (Hughes) doesn't know what I would be doing at Publicker's field in the first place, probably meeting with my men.
> • He (Hughes) only took over patrol several weeks ago and is trying to 'come down hard' on guys like me.

- When asked of my record and reputation, (Hughes) stated I write him 'wise guy' like memos, questioning his memos.
- (Hughes) stated he had nothing to do with disciplinary action involving overtime issues. Only this one.
- (Hughes) 'Sergeant Fitzgerald is a liar. He's making these things up to cover something up. He couldn't have seen that car, I checked it out in daylight. He couldn't see the car and turn right in to check it out. It was poor police work all the way around. He never even made a written report out on it.'
- (After being asked by Ciotti if other officers with car accidents/damage were similarly disciplined... Hughes) is going to check out all of the accident reports for the last year, and if a reprimand or suspension is needed, the officer will get it.
- Ciotti: 'You're (Hughes) punishing an officer for being aggressive. You want all the men (officers) to be wimps?'
  Hughes: 'Well, no. But Sgt. Fitzgerald was clearly wrong here.'
- Upon meeting ending...
- Sgt. Fitzgerald to Capt. Hughes w. board members still present.
  'I demand you retract what you said about me. You called me a liar in front of these people. If you have proof of that, or of a conspiracy or a cover-up, then charge me with it. Otherwise, my reputation and credibility has been offended here...'
  Hughes (interrupting): 'I never called you a liar. I stated that...that (some hesitation) in my opinion, you were lying.'
- Board members agreed to end meeting and have Deputy Chief review Grievance Committee recommendation and see if change is warranted.
- I thanked board members for their time.
- End of meeting approximately 9:10PM."
  (End of notes.)

Immediately outside of the meeting room, Supervisor Ciotti shook my hand and thanked me for acquitting myself so professionally during the relatively short meeting. He made that statement just as Capt. Hughes was walking by us. I know Hughes heard it and I'm glad he did. I was also sure that he was on the phone with the Deputy Chief within minutes of the end of the meeting. Or, perhaps he simply instructed Mrs. Zajac to tell her husband what had occurred later that night before going to bed. Again, what a cozy relationship.

I left the township building and had no further direct or even indirect interactions with George Ciotti. It was one-and-done with him or any similar such maneuver on his or anyone else's part regarding my departmental well-being. To this day, I'm not sure how he ever found out about my then-problematic situation. But he did, he took action, and I was appreciative of it then as I am now.

What happened at this surprise meeting on this May 6th evening would come into play over the next month and again about six months later. I wasn't about to let the officious Capt. Hughes get away with what he said about me in that forum. He could have disagreed with me all he wanted about what he believed happened to the car on that night. But to call me a "liar" in one form or another in front of people who may someday be the deciders as to whether I get a departmental promotion could not and would not stand as far as I was concerned. I would see to it.

Yes, I was on offense now, and it was my turn to take some swings.

* * * * *

On May 8th, the summary opinion of the Grievance Committee regarding my disciplinary actions was provided to the Deputy Chief. It reads, in part, as follows:

"After looking at the facts, the Grievance Committee sustained with Sgt. Fitzgerald's grievances against both his charges.

"Regarding calling in the officer on his day off when the squad was shorthanded, the committee included the following:

A. "It has been both Sgt. Fitzgerald's and the Committee's experience that an unexpected warm weekend tends to produce a large amount of complaints. After the Committee reviewed each officer's daily report (patrol log) on Squad Four it appeared to the Committee that Sgt. Fitzgerald made a proper and sound judgment;

B. "Sgt. Fitzgerald was not provided with a complete Operation Procedures for Sergeants as per schedule and manpower strengths;

C. "On a memorandum written by Capt. Traenkle in 1982, it states 'It is recognized that at times the possibility exists that we will have a bare minimum of personnel on the street. If this does occur, it will be the Sergeant's responsibility to cancel scheduled time off if the need should arise.' Nowhere here does it state that a Sergeant should contact a Lieutenant or any other high ranking official before making this decision."

Regarding the damage to the vehicle charge, the Grievance Committee wrote the following as part of their findings:

A. "In the report from Captain Hughes to Deputy Chief Zajac, Sgt. Fitzgerald's motive for entering the Publicker's lot was questioned. A police officer has the right and responsibility to check every area in his sector... Furthermore, reflecting back to memorandum #1726 (found in admin book in roll call room) which informed the patrol division to patrol the Publicker's lot due to the fact that stolen vehicles were being dropped in that area...this clearly shows that Sgt. Fitzgerald's motive was with good intention;

B. "...Total cost to repair vehicle 22-10 came to $336.63. The committee feels that if Sgt. Fitzgerald was traveling any faster than the estimated speed the extent of damage to vehicle 22-10 would have been far worse and the cost of repair would have been greater;

C. "After reviewing Capt. Hughes report to Deputy Chief Zajac, the Committee found that Capt. Hughes only expressed opinions and no facts were presented. Also, Capt. Hughes's investigation of the location was done in daylight which makes it easier to observe any obstruction or abnormality in or on the pavement. Capt. Hughes was not aware of the exact location of where the suspected vehicle was parked. Taking this into consideration, the Committee feels that Capt. Hughes cannot determine whether a vehicle can or cannot be seen from State Rd."

"The Grievance Committee's investigation was meant to be unbiased and was attempting to reach an honest decision based on police reports presented by both Sgt. Fitzgerald and Capt. Hughes. We hope that you can come to a decision which will be both fair to Sgt. Fitzgerald and the Patrol Division."

(End of report.)

With knowledge of this report, and after what happened the night before, I didn't waste any time. On May 9th, the day after my impromptu appearance at the Executive Session of the Board of Supervisors, and being called a "liar" in front of them by the Patrol Captain, I got to writing. I sent a memo to Deputy Chief Zajac respectfully requesting him to investigate how and why one of his upper-management members would refer to me in such a way, with no offered proof, only opinion, in front of the various elected officials at the meeting on that evening.

I received no response to this memo.

As I had not heard back from Zajac regarding my May 9th memo, I resubmitted virtually the same correspondence, simply re-dating it June 12.

Zajac's belated response back to me on June 14th reads exactly as follows:

"I have reviewed your memo dated 09 May 1985, concerning allegations against Captain Robert Hughes.

"Captain Hughes has informed me that he was asked, by Supervisor George Ciotti, during a supervisors' executive session on 06 May 1985, to explain charges that had been placed against you.

"Executive sessions of the Board of Supervisors are held in private to allow those taking part in discussion to express themselves freely. It appears to me Captain Hughes did just that, as did you when you spoke to the Board.

"The Board of Supervisors had the opportunity to listen to both of you and judge for themselves who's telling the truth and who's lying.

"Since I expect my staff, when questioned by the Township Board of Supervisors, to be frank and express themselves openly, I cannot find fault with Captain Hughes' actions during the May 6, 1985 meeting.

"Therefore, no disciplinary action will be taken against Captain Hughes.

"This investigation has also raised some additional questions in my mind as to how this matter came to be in front of the Board of Supervisors without the normal sequence of events taking place.

"Please answer the following questions by return memo. Your reply is to be made no later than 17 June 1985, 1600 hours.

"1. Did you discuss your disciplinary problems with any Board member prior to the executive session on 06 May 1985? If so, what was discussed and with who did you discuss it?

"2. Did you ask Supervisor George Ciotti to intervene for you and help out with your disciplinary problem?

"3. When did you first learn that you were to attend the supervisors meeting concerning your disciplinary action? Who did you learn it from?

"4. Did you advise your immediate supervisor that you were attending the supervisors meeting on 06 May 1985?"

(End of memo.)

In turn, my June 17th response to the Deputy Chief was quick, easy, and, of course, entirely truthful. After the "To" and "From" part of the memo, my remaining response consisted of three words, a date, a time, and one name.

"1. No.
"2. No.
"3. 06 May 1985, 6:30PM, Supervisor George Ciotti.
"4. No."
(End of memo.)

It took Capt. Hughes almost five years and three different BPD administrations to do it, but he can now finally claim "mission accomplished." After refusing to "fix" his niece's speeding ticket, his August 5, 1980 admonition that he will "make life very difficult...around here" for me, had now come to pass. The suspension and calling me a "liar" in front of various politicos was his eventual payback to me. It didn't take much "deliberation" on my part to realize that at least in this one rarified instance, Hughes was indeed a man of his word.

Bottom line, it didn't surprise me that Zajac would try to flip this whole incident around on me. (It also wouldn't be the last time this page of their playbook would be used against me, either.) I never did expect any disciplinary action to be taken against Captain Hughes. At the same time, I knew the regime was very curious as to how I ever wound up in front of four members of the Board on that early May evening. So, I asked, they responded; they asked, I responded.

* * * * *

This particular on-and-off series of allegations, accusations, and incriminations ended right here. As far as I knew, the letter of reprimand was still in my personnel file. That was okay though as its presence may actually benefit me and my case down the line.

I decided once this springtime of '85 course of events came to a halt that it was time to begin the process of building a new strategy, one harassing memo at a time. My official lawyer of record now, Peter Hileman, was continuing to advise me too. While he wasn't pushing any specific legal recourse on me, he was very clear in that he believed I was being genuinely harassed at my workplace. I didn't necessarily need him to tell me that but I came to agree with him anyway. He also advised there were remedies for these types of situations. I listened to him. Before we ended discussing this episode of organized and multi-pronged harassment against me, my lawyer simply suggested that I keep good notes and retain every piece of written correspondence with my name on it. I told him I was way ahead of him, but thanks anyway for the reaffirmation. Before hanging up Pete reminded me that he was only a phone call and a lawsuit away. I thanked him.

Hmmm...maybe Pete was on to something here. It's not my style and it's unprecedented so far in my life, but a civil suit against these reprobates is certainly worth thinking about. I could probably knock down their ill-stacked house of cards with what they've done to me already. Maybe....

It's possible though, after all of this, the Dark Side will simply leave me alone. After all, lots of time and energy was spent on these memos going back and forth. In the long run, to what avail? Surely even THEY must get tired of this form of management-by-harassment. I know I was. But, as I was to learn, they weren't tired of it at all. Instead, it was becoming the new-normal for them and it was seemingly empowering them along the way.

So, with my lawyer just a phone call away, a civil suit may just be something to keep as a very viable option. A potentially powerful option, but one with risks attached to it at the same time. And the timing of it all would have to be just right....

Fortunately, I suppose, the evidence would keep falling onto my lap over the next several months. Each harassing memo, it seemed, being more bizarre in content than the one preceding it. These guys liked to put everything in writing. I learned to save every last scrap of the paper they wrote it on.

Good for me. Bad for them.

Oh, but there were still these damn headaches. They were not going away. In fact, over the last few months, they were as frequent and as painful as ever. What the hell could be causing them?

I better seriously look into these head-splitting migraines, or whatever they are. A good neurologist may be needed. Or, a good lawyer.

Maybe both....

* * * * *

Lest we forget about who USED to be in charge of my police department....

Former BPD Chief Rich Viola was apparently keeping busy during the last few months with his attorneys, as well as with at least one other person too. This busy time culminated with a perfunctory hearing in front of the Bensalem Board of Supervisors on the evening of April 8th, 1985. Then and there, to the surprise of many and to the chagrin of some, Viola arrived at this oft-postponed hearing at the township building with a guest witness for his defense. And not just any guest witness was he. It was none other than former Philadelphia Police Commissioner and later mayor, Frank L. Rizzo. Talk about bringing out the big guns. In the Philadelphia metropolitan area during the '60s through the early '90s, there weren't any guns bigger than those of

Frank Rizzo. And it didn't take him long that night before he started firing away.

On April 9th, the *Bucks County Courier Times* included a front page article in their morning edition. It was written by Joseph Grace. It read, in part, as follows:

> "Declaring he was 'fed up with politicians who try to run police departments,' Frank L. Rizzo testified Monday night in Bensalem on behalf of suspended township Police Chief Richard Viola.
>
> "Flanked by a small entourage of aides and illuminated by TV news cameras, Rizzo entered the township municipal building to testify at disciplinary proceedings for Viola, a former (Philadelphia PD) police sergeant before he became Bensalem chief.
>
> "Rizzo called misconduct charges filed against Viola 'utterly ridiculous,' but said he doubted Viola would be vindicated by the supervisors' board, which is sitting in judgment on the case.
>
> "'There's been an injustice,' Rizzo said. 'But he (Viola) is not going to win here.' The former mayor said he 'absolutely' believed Viola's suspension was motivated by politics.
>
> "'They send messages to police chiefs,' Rizzo said, referring to politicians. 'You do what we want you to do, or you're finished. And you know who suffers most? Not the police. Not the politicians. The people.'
>
> "After testifying for about an hour behind closed doors, Rizzo emerged from the auditorium, declared the proceedings an 'outrage,' and left with his driver and aides."
>
> (End of article.)

There was to be no decision or vote regarding Viola after this hearing, regardless of whether Frank Rizzo appeared as the star witness or not. The Board of Supervisors would take their time with this matter. After all, Viola was suspended (well, actually injured-on-duty AND suspended), and out of the regime's hair at the present time. Lt. Eckert, still squatting at the so-called White House behind the police department building, marched on with his case against Viola, alleging (as per the same aforementioned newspaper article) "…a wide range of offenses, including stealing money during a police raid, abusing criminal suspects and making politically motivated arrests."

So, the beat went on and on regarding this Bensalem taxpayer-funded machine in its (and its operators) ongoing attempt to bring former Chief Richard Viola down once and for all. There would be a whole lot more of the taxpayers' money to be wasted on this politically and ego-motivated venture before it was all over.

Like Rizzo said, and was eventually proven correct, what was happening here to Viola and the BPD was truly an "outrage."

(+Bonus Chapter 46a, 46b, 46c, 46d)

April 8, 1985, Disciplinary Proceedings
Left to right: Frank L. Rizzo, Supervisor Tom Walls, Richard Viola
(Photo courtesy of *Bucks County Courier Times,* Ron Brown)

Chapter Forty-Seven

"Crimson flames tied through my ears,
rollin' high and mighty traps
pounced with fire on flaming roads using
ideas as my maps..."
(Bob Dylan, *My Back Pages*)

The intermittent brush fires ("crimson flames") in my everyday BPD life, some of which I had just recently managed to stomp out, nonetheless continued to grow in intensity and volume for me. They were spreading and burning ever hotter as the summer of '85 progressed towards the fall. There was little relief in sight and no fire engines or firefighters I could see coming to rescue me (on "flaming roads"). I knew I'd have to put them out mostly on my own, each one of them, before I got burnt beyond recognition. But I gotta somehow figure out a way to do it (using "ideas as my maps").

Let's see...there's water, there's oxygen depletion, there's even chemicals. I suppose they could work, but isn't there at least one additional method - one arguably outside the box and a bit unusual.

I'm aware that in some varieties of forest fires, and even in some uncontrolled semi-rural conflagrations, firefighters are known to start their own fires to prevent the spread of the original one. It seems counter-intuitive at first, but it actually does make sense.

So, would that be an option here for me? Essentially "fighting fire with fire?"

As life moves on for me at the BPD during these incendiary times, I'm getting figuratively tinged on my extremities on an almost daily basis. I DO NOT want to sit and wait for my pending immolation by these ego-driven arsonists.

I may just have to start my own symbolic fire, or fires, in this place (and set my own "high and mighty traps"). It's perhaps the only way

I can adequately safeguard myself and at the same time extinguish these police/politician pyromaniacs and their increasingly destructive blazes once and for all.

So, let me take stock here...I've got the kindling wood, I've got the matches, I just need additional fuel sources. I have some stored away already, but I'll need more of it, much more of it. Now where could that come from...?

Take a wild guess as to who will be providing me with that additional necessary accelerant, and lots of it. If you figured it would be Zajac himself and his assorted band of fire-setting cronies, you're right on the mark.

* * * * *

Going back in time about a year, but while still on the subject of fires, firefighters, and the like, as it so happened, one of Bensalem's most popular volunteer firemen, Nick Pasqualone, 54 years of age, died suddenly of a medical condition unrelated to his position as Chief of the Cornwells Fire Company. Incidentally, starting in 1981 until his death three years later, he had also been one of the five elected members of the Bensalem Board of Supervisors.

From what I knew of Nick and his overall reputation, he seemed like a decent guy, a good family man, and a steadfast proponent of the volunteer firefighters in Bensalem Township. As they say, however, politics makes for strange bedfellows.

For whatever reason during Nick's abbreviated three years as an elected Supervisor, he chose to cast many of his votes with Stephen Kelly and/or Kelly's like-minded elected counterparts. It was four of them, including Mary Komada and Patricia Zajac, as well as the just acquitted Stephen Kelly, who in January of '84 ushered in and then continued to back the quagmire of an administration under which we were presently toiling in the BPD. (Again, Supervisor George Ciotti was the one dissenting vote of the five.)

When Nick Pasqualone died in mid-1984, a partisan seat-warmer by the name of Peter Reed was appointed to temporarily fill his Board position. Naturally, since Kelly and his two political cohorts appointed him, Reed voted in lockstep with them. But since Reed was only appointed to his position temporarily, he would have to run for election in November of '85 to hold on to that seat. That's when things started getting very intriguing in Bensalem, politically-speaking, anyway.

Stephen Kelly had already announced he was not going to run again for elected office in Bensalem. His twelve years in office was apparently enough for him. Many, many people agreed. He wasn't showing up for most meetings anyway during his last year in office, only doing so when his vote was absolutely needed. His days were effectively numbered in Bensalem as he must have had other avenues he wanted to explore, or re-explore, in his life. His further damage would be limited to whatever he and his three voting co-minions could do through early January of 1986.

That damage, it would turn out, would be substantial.

Bottom line...Kelly and company had held a 4-1 majority since he retook his post-acquittal throne in January of '84. As Kelly had decided not to run for another term, with Pete Reed having to run in the upcoming November '85 election to keep his appointed seat, and with George Ciotti deciding he had enough as a Supervisor, that meant there was an ever so slight possibility that there could be a shift in the majority of the five-person Board of Supervisors; emphasis, of course, on "ever so slight." For this to happen, Reed would have to lose, as well as the three untested rookie Republican party candidates would have to win against their three Democrat party opponents. IF the trio of longshot Republicans won, it would mean beginning in January of '86 this threesome would represent the majority on the Board of Supervisors. Mary Komada and Patricia Zajac would represent the minority. As far as many of us in the BPD were concerned, a 3-2 majority worked just as well as a 4-1. We would gladly take those numbers, as long as it was the right three representing the right majority.

Remarkably, before Pasqualone's untimely death, it seemed as if this Board was destined to hold the majority for years to come. But Nick's demise in '84 certainly changed the political landscape in Bensalem. There was hope that if in the unlikely chance all three of these Republican/GOP candidates could get elected into office this coming November, things would change. From the perspective of many people, both inside and outside the BPD, it would be for the better. Needless to say, I was one of those people. Even though I was pretty much a political neophyte prior to this upcoming election, certainly on the local and county level, maybe it was time I became just a bit more involved.

And...I did. Actually, I became very involved. I'm neither proud nor ashamed of this decision and the overt acts I undertook in doing so. My self-preservation and, as far as I was concerned, the sanctity and security of the BPD and Bensalem Township itself were on the line.

What were my choices?

* * * * *

There was a Police Benevolent Association (PBA) meeting in June of '85. I attended it, just as I tried to attend most of them. Toward the end of it I spoke up once again about the possibility of the BPD rank and file joining the Fraternal Order of Police. A substantial number of my colleagues in attendance agreed aloud that it may be a good idea, it should be further researched, and I was still the one to do it. I said I would do it. The meeting ended.

Amazingly, within twenty hours, I would learn again what the Dark Side thought of this notion.

When I came into work the very next day after the PBA meeting, there was a memo in my mail slot; nothing new there, of course. It was from the Deputy Chief; nothing new there, either. It was not good news for me; so nothing new all the way around.

The memo advised me I was being "temporarily" transferred out of my present squad assignment as patrol sergeant. As it read in the short paragraph, my one and only new duty was to be the now-fulltime BPD Property Clerk, aka Evidence Custodian, for an amount of time deemed necessary by management. My one and only supervisor was to be Captain Hughes.

Lucky, lucky me!

This came as a complete surprise to me as I had no forewarning regarding any potential assignment change. I don't know for sure, but maybe, just maybe, the Dark Side really didn't want anything to do with the FOP coming into the Bensalem PD. (Gee, do you think?) Not here, not now, and certainly in no way with me as the catalyst in bringing this national organization to represent the BPD officers. So, the message was sent loud and clear by yet another written memo to me with yet another schedule and assignment change.

I was to finish my current patrol shift with my squad and report the following Monday morning to the man who just about a month ago formally and officially called me a "liar" in front of the people who run the township.

Yeah, this should be a fun new assignment.

This was now my fourth involuntary squad change in the last seven months. It wasn't any easier this time either, trying to re-calculate my work schedule as well as my personal schedule for the remainder of the calendar year.

For most people in their jobs, being laterally transferred to another department, division, unit, or whatever it may be called in their particular company or institution, where they mostly work Mondays through Fridays and 9:00 to 5:00, would be a move which at most may be a minor inconvenience. For a member of law enforcement, other first responders, the security industry, the health services field, and/or any employment where staffing is required around the clock and on weekends, it can throw off plans for an entire year for the just-transferred (or re-transferred) person. If expected and planned for, the issues may be minimal. After four such transfers in less than seven months' time, it was anything but minimal for me.

If I had plans to attend someone's upcoming wedding, graduation, a reunion, go on vacation, a get-away weekend, undergo medical tests, take or teach Villanova or other classes, an FBI exam, or any similar event which may require advanced travel bookings, financial, days off, and/or personal commitments, it could become very problematic and disconcerting to have a forced and surprise schedule change as had just happened to me, yet again. It affects both the short-term and the long-term aspects of a person's life, not to mention their family's life, too. One would have to hope after such a surprise transfer, if he or she was scheduled to work on certain future dates which HAD been regular days off before, that he/she could now use vacation or comp time to take the necessary time off. That could never be a guarantee though, as someone with more seniority at the new assignment may already have that particular time off officially approved. Or, if the administration is screwing with that person already anyway (as was clearly happening to me), they could simply refuse to grant the now-needed requested time off.

The BPD management clearly didn't care at all about this issue with me. Transfer away, they must have thought, at least when it came to Sgt. Fitzgerald. We'll show him what it means to exercise his free speech rights.

The FOP in the BPD? No, we don't think so! Suspension the first time after the subject was broached, transfer the second time, and this one to a position that while I knew how to do it, I didn't want to do it.

In fact, I determined shortly after this transfer that I was now the only officer in the entire department in a position that he or she did

NOT put in for, want, or desire. Literally, everyone in Patrol, CID, Admin, of any officer position or supervisory rank, was where they wanted to be at the present time - except now me. I was later advised by some senior officers with long institutional memories, no one except me had ever been transferred around from squad to squad, position to position, with such little notice, as many times, for obviously punitive purposes, in the known history of the department.

Arsonists, brush fires, out-of-control blazes, fueling up, my own planned fire-starting, a deceased firefighter/politician, an upcoming election, new/old/temporary candidates and politicians, forced transfers, even more harassment…yes, these are all starting to converge on a grand scale at the same time and place for me. Their ultimate convergence and the resultant effects of same will shape the history of Bensalem Township and its police department for decades to come.

It will further shape me, too, big-time.

Now, where are my friggin' matches?

* * * * *

To add some further context to Bensalem politics in 1985, and to make sure the reader is aware that it was not just me alone taking on the Dark Side, nor the only one being victimized by the forces within, I want to include several newspaper articles from those dark days, as well as an editorial. They summarize, over just a ten-day period, not just the malicious micro-managing and harassment by the present administration towards many of its employees, but its self-serving macro-managing of the entire PD, if not the entire Township, at the same time.

The first article was in the *Bucks County Courier Times* (BCCT), on the front page directly below the masthead, and written by reporter Joseph Grace. It's dated August 20, 1985.

The headline reads, "**Bensalem PBA criticizes department administrators.**"

The article reads, in part, as follows:

> "An organization of Bensalem police officers has sent three letters to the township supervisors, one of them addressing the suspended status of Police Chief Richard Viola, and two others criticizing department administrators.

"The Bensalem (PBA), which represents the department rank-and-file in contract negotiations and personnel matters, hand-delivered the strongly worded letters to the supervisors before their public meeting Monday night.

"The letter regarding Viola states that should the supervisors vote to fire him, the PBA believes the chief's post should be left vacant until Viola's anticipated legal appeals are resolved.

"If Viola is fired and loses his appeals, the PBA letter then advocates an 'open, competitive examination' to fill the chief's post, according to a copy of the letter obtained by the (BCCT).

"The second letter alleges the development of a trend by department administrators of 'selectively harassing' police officers who file complaints with the PBA over personnel matters.

"The harassment has taken the form of transferring the complaining officers to different squads, which disrupts the officers' vacation time and the entire squad's schedule, the letter alleges.

"The third letter claims that police administrators appointed three patrolmen as acting sergeants by passing over a list of eligible officers who ranked higher than the appointees on the last promotion test conducted by the department.

"PBA President Jerry Judge, who signed each of the letters, said the police group was 'not trying to dictate policy' by sending them.

"'We just want to be treated fairly,' Judge said in a phone interview Monday night. 'We're not children. We're adults. And we don't think we should be harassed for stating our opinions. We had no recourse but to do what we did.'

"Deputy Police Chief Theodore Zajac, Jr., the department's commanding officer and rumored replacement as chief if Viola is fired, is not mentioned in the letters specifically. However, taken as a whole the three letters are critical of his administration.

"Zajac declined to be interviewed about the letters. Asked Monday night at the board's meeting if he had seen them, he said 'No,' and walked away.

"However, a police source close to Zajac disputed the impression that the letters represented the view of the entire PBA, which comprises more than 50 officers.

"The source, who declined to be identified, said the officers who submitted the letters represented less than 50 percent of the PBA. Then the source said, 'In fact, they represent less than 5 percent' of the police group.

"...Judge said he sent the other two letters himself as a 'responsible' PBA president. 'They're not vindictive letters,' he said, 'they're more like, Wake up.'

"Judge, a nine year Bensalem police veteran, said uncertainty over the Viola case and bad feelings between groups of officers – some of whom support Viola, some of whom back Zajac – has contributed to a deteriorating state of morale.

"'This is the worst I've ever seen it,' Judge said.

"...Official reaction from the township to the letters Monday night was mixed.

"One official termed them 'position papers from a labor organization.' Supervisor George Ciotti supported the letters and said he would request an outside study of the department's management.

"Supervisor Chairwoman Mary Komada said, 'They came from Jerry Judge. Everyone knows where he stands. If you didn't get your PAL, you'd be mad too.'

"Komada's comment was an apparent reference to a Police Athletic League program proposed by Judge. The program was never begun for a number of reasons, Judge's wife said late Monday night."

(End of article.)

On August 21, 1985, on page B18 of the BCCT, an article also written by Joseph Grace has the headline, "**Bensalem orders Zajac to respond to letters.**"

The piece was framed by a photo of Zajac on the left side and Jerry Judge on the right side. The article re-summarizes the three PBA letters and the revelation of an apparent late-night ordering of the Deputy Chief by the Board to submit in writing his rebut to them.

Interestingly, also on August 21, near the end of Section A of the BCCT, the top editorial on the left hand side of the Editorial Page included the simple headline of "**Bensalem needs help**." In it, the unnamed editor posited, in part:

> "It should come as no surprise that there's dissent among the ranks of Bensalem police. What is surprising is the vehemence of that dissent and the threat it poses to the fragile authority being exercised by the current administration.
>
> "...All three letters were hardly ringing endorsements of the Zajac administration.
>
> "...Supervisor George Ciotti has a good idea. He thinks the township ought to commission an outside study to look at how the department is being managed.
>
> "...We urge the supervisors to give Ciotti's recommendation some serious consideration. They made the mess. They owe it to taxpayers to clean it up."
>
> (End of editorial.)

Lastly during that torrid second half of August, 1985, this headline was found on page 3B of the *Philadelphia Inquirer*, attached to an article written by Amy S. Rosenberg.

"Bensalem fires police chief for alleged misconduct."

The headline referring to the now-officially fired Chief Viola says it all. In a 4-1 vote, Supervisors Kelly, Komada, Reed, and Zajac voted to officially fire Viola, twenty months after his suspension. No surprise there for even the casual follower of Bensalem politics and police in the late summer of '85.

As such, the Bensalem mid-'80s passion play continued to drag on. Act Four, its fiery final act, was just about to begin.

Things were definitely beginning to get hot in this place. The fires were all around me. However, as if somehow reborn or resurrected, seeing the burning light as never before, I proclaimed to myself...

> "... 'We'll meet on edges soon,' said I, proud
> 'neath heated brow,
> Ah, but I was so much older then, I'm
> younger than that now."
>
> (Bob Dylan, *My Back Pages*)

Chapter Forty-Eight

The evidence closet, located in a five foot by eight-foot room at the rear of CID, was a mess until Chief Viola came into office in late 1981. By the time I was promoted to detective sergeant in April of '82, it was in much better shape. The four detective sergeants back then, under the tutelage of (and including) Jack Robinson, were each considered evidence custodians. We carried out this important function along with the rest of our CID related duties.

Before Viola, there was one old-time detective whose desk was adjacent to the evidence closet door, and the whole system back then was based on index cards and this guy's (hopefully) good memory. He was known to leave evidence on top of, alongside of, in, or under his desk for days if not weeks at a time, and there was very little in the way of a verifiable chain-of-custody system. (That is, a documentable means to indicate where a piece of evidence had been secured at all times.)

Pre-Viola, if a court date was pending, and an officer needed that knife or gun he confiscated off an arrestee, it was always smart to walk back to the aging detective's desk a whole day or two in advance to make sure he could find the needed item, or at least the index card he kept in his drawer which may tell him where the evidence was possibly stashed. More than a few criminal cases were summarily dismissed back in the day when needed evidence couldn't be readily located. It usually showed up within a few days or weeks, but by that time it was too late.

When Viola took over, upgrading the evidence closet and the entire evidence collection system was one of the first items on his agenda. He brought with him copies of the Philadelphia PD's four-part carbon-copy evidence submission forms. In a month's time, with nearly identical forms for the BPD, a new system was put into effect. For the first time, a master evidence control book was also maintained. In it, the submitting custodian would log in date order each and every evidence entry by consecutive numbers, then the officer's name, case number, where it was stored, and at some point its final disposition. It was retained when not in use inside the always locked evidence closet.

Viola initially referred to the old-school detective/property clerk's work area as "Pop's Candy Store," as there were always various items of evidence strewn on his desk and all around it. Needless to say, "Pop" was relieved of his evidence custodian responsibility by month number two of Viola's regime. That's when the detective sergeants were assigned the duties. With a much more streamlined system, and four "custodians" (with Robinson as a backup) to enter, maintain, and retrieve evidence, it made for a much more efficient and effective system.

Along with the other criminal cases and supervisory responsibilities during my time in CID as a detective sergeant, then-Lt. Robinson entrusted me with helping him redo the entire evidence room and system. This included putting in new shelving, creating alpha-numeric designators for specific shelf areas, a separate locked drawer for smaller valuables, multiple temporary evidence storage lockers in the rollcall room for overnight evidence submissions, attaining an old truck trailer and positioning it at the rear of the BPD parking lot where bicycles and other larger items could be stored, and securing a safe deposit box at a local bank for maintaining cash which may have been confiscated during the course of an arrest and/or search. None of this had ever been in place before. Now it was.

By the time I was transferred out of CID in late '84, the evidence system was running very smoothly. "Pops" had retired some time before and his haphazard methods went along with him. Officers and prosecutors alike were very satisfied with the new evidence control procedures now employed at the BPD.

Since the modernized evidence system wasn't the idea of Deputy Chief Zajac or Lt. Eckert, and with other issues more pressing on their respective desks (e.g., firing Viola, multiple transfers of me, lowering departmental morale), they had very little interest in how evidence was maintained and controlled during their now-eighteen months in office. As a result, when the closet in CID and the other storage facilities were found to be bulging at their seams, and some recently submitted evidence couldn't be located in time for court, they decided they needed someone right away who knew what he was doing to come in and remedy the problem. Even though there were other detective sergeants who had been performing evidence custodian duties for the last year or so, they were apparently deemed too "important" for this relatively mundane tasking.

So, without good ol' Pops to provide the fix, Zajac reached out and asked me for help. Well, actually, he didn't ask. I was ordered to "temporarily" undertake evidence custodian duties "fulltime," if that makes any sense. It didn't take me long to assure myself that the FOP remark from the previous evening had everything to do with this new assignment of mine. Even if Pops had still been around and available, I'm damn sure it would have still been me doing this re-overhaul once again of the BPD evidence system.

So...I showed up as ordered on that first Monday morning to Hughes' office. As I walked through the long, dark paneled hallway from the rollcall room, I once again heard that all too familiar refrain from that (unfortunately) all too familiar voice and person.

"JIM FITZGERALD, HOW ARE YOU ON THIS FINE MORNING?!"

It had been awhile since I'd experienced Deputy Chief Zajac's non-melodious, totally unnecessary pronouncement of my name at near-full volume. With a rhetorical tag question too, added for good measure as he sometimes did. I had no doubt he was reveling in his recent order/assignment change and to where I was now banished. I suppose on this "fine morning" (at least for him) the DC just had to address me as such before I walked into the belly of the beast, aka, Captain Hughes' office.

My headache for that day had its genesis at right about the same time I hearkened the first syllable that Zajac shrieked in my direction. It would get much worse by day's end.

I did manage to take a deep breath and respond to the DC. I replied, "Never better! Straight day-work with weekends off. I love it. How about you?"

Without answering, Zajac merely turned with coffee in hand and walked into his office.

I was lying to him, but a little misinformation never hurts in these type situations. He'll at least think about what I said for a while. It may lead to yet another schedule change for me. I can only hope.

After my brief hallway encounter with The Loud One it was into Hughes' office, just a few feet away. This morning would be the first time I was forced to talk directly to him since he publicly called me a "liar." I figured I'd start with a bang, even if completely contradicting myself from what I just said to Zajac.

After knocking on Hughes' closed door and him authorizing my entry, I approached his newspaper covered desk and I told him point-blank that I did not want this new detail. I made it clear to him that I wanted to stay with my squad in patrol. I even offered to train anyone he or the DC would choose instead of me. Within a week, I guaranteed him, this other person could be doing this job and doing it well. I readily shared with Hughes that I had talked with two senior officers in Patrol Division over the last few days who would LOVE to be taken off the streets and given a Monday through Friday, 8-4 job. Let's give it to someone who actually wants it, I strongly advised the Captain, as I provided him with their names.

Without acknowledging my statement or suggestion in any manner, Hughes closed his newspaper, stood up, and simply told me to follow him. We walked right around the corner from his office and he pointed to my new work area. It was the sergeants' office in the roll call room. I was to sit at the desk in the cramped, windowless quarters during hours when the patrol sergeants didn't use it, and "straighten out this whole evidence mess."

"Okay, whatever…but let me ask you…?"

For not the first time nor the last, Hughes did not allow me to finish my statement or question to him. Instead, he mumbled on, "You won't be spending much time in this office over the next few months," Hughes almost gleefully advised me. I was about to find out why.

"To begin with," Hughes barked at me in his usual rapid, vapid, and sometimes incomprehensible marbles-in-the-mouth speech style, "the trailer out back is overloaded with bikes, canoes, car parts, and other large and unwieldy items. We need a complete and detailed inventory of everything that's in it. If it can be legally gotten rid of, we want to do it. Understand, Fitzgerald?"

I guess the Captain simply assumed I understood. Without waiting for even a nod of the head from me, he handed me a set of keys to each of the various evidence facilities. He then did an about-face and walked out of my new space and back into his own office, slamming the door behind him for apparent effect. Yes, I understood. His comics and crosswords were there and they were calling his name.

Within the time of our ever-so-brief interaction, I had a pretty strong feeling that Hughes didn't want to be supervising me any more than I wanted him to be supervising me. But as per our Fearless Leader's orders, we were stuck with each other for now. And, as expected, our relationship wouldn't exactly be growing any closer in the near future.

I'd be a "liar" if I told you otherwise, or at least Captain Hughes would so label me. For once though, he'd actually be right.

I remember in my early youth on certain timely occasions my father referring to an old radio program called *Fibber McGee and Molly.* It aired years before I was even born but the main character, Fibber, apparently lived a relatively normal life in a relatively normal house with his relatively normal wife. However, there was this hallway closet which was somehow anything but normal. It seems that whenever the husband would open its door all kinds of miscellaneous items would fall on top of him. According to my dad, the weekly visit to "Fibber McGee's closet," even if regularly anticipated by the show's millions of listeners, provided them with the belly laughs they were looking for while sitting in front of their large living room radio speakers.

Why mention this long-forgotten radio broadcast? Well…you're about to hear of a similar closet of mine, in a manner of speaking. Except, what happened to me wasn't expected by anyone, including me, and it certainly wasn't funny.

As so instructed that first morning at my new job, my mission was to sort out the mess inside the trailer at the rear of the BPD parking lot. Being the ever-obedient public servant that I was, within a few minutes I departed my new sergeants' office space with clipboard and keys in hand. I walked out the metallic blue roll call room door and crossed the parking lot to a place where I figured I'd be spending lots of time over the next few weeks.

Upon arrival after the very short stroll, I climbed the four wooden steps leading up to the trailer's rear doors. I bent over and put the key marked "trailer" into the industrial-strength padlock. The locking mechanism opened effortlessly and I removed it from the door clasp where it had been hanging. I then pulled the standard trailer door handle up, out, and over as I proceeded to swing the right side door open. Everything was routine so far. However, within a second or two, and without any warning whatsoever, with the door open only several inches and still grasped in my right hand, it all of a sudden flew out of my grip and rapidly proceeded to swing on its hinges into full open position. At virtually the same time as the door continued its outward motion to meet up with the side of the trailer, I noticed a large blackish blur pass directly alongside of me. By the time I could turn my head to see what it was, I came to realize it was a mid-sized truck tire which had just rolled out the door directly by me and down the steps across the parking lot. A second or two later, a brown-colored Dodge car fender slowly plopped down onto the steps alongside of me, narrowly missing my quickly retracted right arm. It then proceeded to slide downwards until it came to a metal-on-asphalt screeching halt as the front of it hit the parking lot surface.

For some reason at this exact time and place, my dear departed dad's descriptive summary of that old radio show came to mind. That closet, which for some reason the guy opened every week, only to have hat boxes, tennis rackets, ironing boards, bowling balls, and various other household items knock him down onto the floor, was no longer just a vague anecdotal memory. This trailer was now MY Fibber McGee's closet, except with no discernible laugh track in the background. Certainly none that I heard, anyway.

Fortunately, I managed to dodge (pun intended) both rolling and/ or falling car parts and I wasn't hurt on this first half-hour of my first day of my new assignment. A lesser man (or maybe a smarter man) could have claimed an injury to his arm or leg and been placed on disability (IOD), for a while. But not me. That wasn't my style.

The trailer, rendered somewhat safer to enter by me later that day, was to be my work home for the next eight weeks. Hughes wasn't lying this time. It would be my place of business for easily seven hours each work day, with only my lunchtime and precious other little time inside HQ being anywhere even close to climate controlled. And there would be no assistance from anyone, including the Deputy Chief, Capt. Hughes, other officers, Fibber McGee OR Molly.

Once I could focus my eyes to safely look inside the trailer, with a flashlight in hand of course, I could see there was complete inaccessibility to the front section of it, some eighty feet away. This was as the result of piles and piles of potentially dangerously packed and stacked (if not tossed) bikes and other items too large and too bulky to put into the interior CID evidence closet. At some point, I'd have to slowly remove each item to the rear of the trailer, out the swinging doors, and down the steps in any attempt to inventory the items at the very front of the trailer. It would not be very easy, to say the least, especially when considering the stifling heat index inside the long, windowless, metallic box on its semi-flattened rear tires.

I can clearly attest here that neither Jack Robinson nor I had left this trailer in this condition when we were still managing the evidence system at the BPD. It had been fully walkable on one side all the way to the front and everything had been dutifully categorized, tagged, and carefully stacked and secured. Others who had taken over in our relatively brief absence obviously let the trailer (and I would soon find out the CID evidence closet) in disarray. Now, it was my job to straighten out the mess left behind after multiple months of mismanagement and/or just not giving a damn about it.

Interestingly, while working in the intense summer heat in this large oblong-shaped sweatbox, my mind would sometimes wander. Maybe these wanderings were the result of the excessive temperatures, dehydration, boredom, or something else. I don't know. However, whatever brought them about, it was during these times that I came to see this trailer mess as a metaphor for the present condition of the BPD. It was mismanaged, not taken care of, ignored, and all behind closed doors. Now, after all of this, they want it fixed.

Actually, the more I thought about it, as bad as this trailer was, it may be much easier to fix it than the mismanaged, not taken care of, and ignored police department behind the closed doors of the building just across the lot from me.

Good luck to whoever gets THAT tasking. I know it ain't gonna be me doing it.

By my second day on the new job, right before lunch, with my shirt's underarms already soaked from sweat, I asked Captain Hughes if I could come back "dressed down" for the rest of the day and possibly for the immediate future while undertaking my trailer evidence duties. I emphasized to him that the temperatures were expected to be in the high-80s to 90s for the rest of the week. I even pointed to the open newspaper still on his desk and advised him to check the weather forecast. I was hoping to convince him that by wearing short pants and a plain white short sleeved tee-shirt while inside the trailer, and immediately outside of it in the hot sun while positioning the various items of evidence alongside of it to attain serial numbers, makes, models, etc., it would make my job much more easy. More importantly, I added, I could probably then even work faster and complete this trailer evidence assignment even sooner.

Hughes didn't think twice regarding what he next had to say. (This was an ongoing trait of his. Sometimes, it seems, he didn't even think once.) He said "No," and that I will continue to wear my full uniform each day on the job with no exceptions. He then added one more item to our discussion as I was walking out of his office to go on my lunch break. He now wanted me to fill out a daily log sheet for each workday.

He told me he noticed that I was gone almost 45 minutes yesterday for lunch when I'm only allowed 30 minutes. I responded to him that it's about a five minute ride to and from my house. Hughes responded, "Well, where were you for the other five minutes?" He was dead-serious, too.

I thought about his question a bit and remembered where and how I spent those five minutes. I then proceeded to tell the Captain that I backed up one of the uniformed officers on a car stop on Hulmeville Rd. on the way back to HQ.

"You don't have a problem with that, do you?"

Hughes said, "I do. That's not your job. You're assigned here now as fulltime property clerk...until told otherwise. Make sure your daily log reflects everything you do each day and I expect you here for seven hours and twenty minutes each shift, doing the job you're tasked with doing."

"Yes, sir, I'll start filling out a log sheet completely every day, just as you ordered. In full uniform, too. Gotchya."

Kill 'em with politeness, right?

"Yeah, that's right," Hughes dismissively retorted. "Now get back out to your trailer. You're far from done there."

I first went to lunch. I carefully watched my time too. I didn't want to overstep my bounds or, God forbid, back up a fellow officer on a car stop on my way there or back. After all, I had bikes and other miscellaneous items to count and that was the clear departmental priority over officer safety, at least when it came to me.

I did, in fact, follow Captain Hughes' advice; to the letter, actually. I fully obeyed my time restrictions, getting in exactly at 8:00AM, leaving exactly at 4:00PM with just thirty minutes at my home for lunch, signing in and signing out at the exact half-hour mark. And, as also ordered, I started filling out the daily log sheets.

Interestingly, in the recent history of the BPD, these forms were only for uniformed patrol officers and their sergeants. Never was I aware of any officer working an inside job, in a non-patrol position, having to fill out one of these logs. I was apparently the one and only. But as I knew I was "special" to this administration, there were special rules just for me. Being that "special" person, I wanted to make sure I did exactly what I was supposed to do as per my orders from the good Captain. However, even THAT got me into trouble within a few days.

Please allow me to elaborate....

In the upper right hand corner of the BPD daily log, across a straight line after "Officer," "Badge #," "Day," and "Date," there was this one last block that simply read "Weather." So, just as when I was in patrol, I continued filling in the weather for each day at my new position. Usually, back in those halcyon patrol days, I would simply write "Clear," or "Rain," or "Snow" in that block. But I wanted to make sure now I filled out the whole log completely, as per the very clear and concise orders from Captain Courageous himself.

In doing so, it took Hughes a bit longer than I thought it would, but by the end of week two of my new assignment I was met by him just as I was about to leave for the day. At that precise moment, holding half-a-dozen daily logs in his hand, he held them out and pointed to them and directly ordered me to no longer complete the "Weather" block on them. I was caught off guard and asked him in return why and for what reason. A few of my uniformed colleagues who happened to be in the room looked at me, at him, and at each other, their shoulders simultaneously shrugging as if to say, "Wait! Sgt. Fitzgerald is in trouble for something to do with the weather? How the hell did he do that?"

Hughes then made it clearer for me and all within earshot, "You know why, Fitzgerald! You always have to be the wise guy, don't you? Now I'm ordering you, NO MORE WEATHER COMMENTS! LEAVE THAT BLOCK ON THE LOG BLANK. THAT'S AN ORDER! GOT IT?!"

"But, Captain, you wanted the log filled out completely. You told me that just over a week ago, right in your office."

"Fill it out like I told you, but leave out the smart-ass weather comments. Don't f**k with me! I'm telling you, Fitzgerald, don't f**k with me!" Hughes walked away, both hands clenched in fists of rage, partially crumbling the log sheets in one of them.

"Okay, so...everything but the weather comments. I got it. As you wish...," I responded to his back as he returned to his office area.

One of the uniformed officers, waiting until the Captain left the room observed, "So, Fitz, raining on Hughes' parade again, eh?"

I nodded, smiled, and winked my eye at my colleague's attempt at climate humor. I got it. He got what I was doing too.

So, here's the rest of the story. For the last two weeks, I had been putting in the high temperature of each day on the log. I had a mini-thermometer I brought with me from home and recorded the temps outside, as well as inside the trailer. Upon filling out my log at day's end, I would include in the "Weather" block the high temperatures as so recorded on my little mercury-filled weather device. For this whole time so far, certainly by mid-afternoon each day, the numbers were almost always in the very high 80s or well into the 90s, and usually with matching humidity levels. After a few of these days (and possibly suffering from early heat stroke symptoms), I got the idea to add a few TV weather-related terms such as "Oppressive," "Dangerously Hot and Humid," and/or "Very Uncomfortable" next to the temps. These words were apparently what raised Hughes' own "temperature" and he chased me down to tell me about it.

Anyway, I dutifully followed Hughes' revised order. There would be no more temperature and heat-index references on my daily log. I would continue to keep my own "log" though of both inside and outside temps. I may just need them at some point in the future; the near future even, when it begins getting really "hot" around this place.

After just a few days on my new mission, I started to bring a large red picnic-style jug of ice water with me to my elongated metallic "office." I wanted to make sure I stayed hydrated while working in full uniform in the hot sun and in the windowless, vent-less, truck trailer. I also brought in a portable AM-FM radio to keep me company as well as monitor the weather. If a thunderstorm was heading my way, I was not about to stay in my eighty-foot long lightening rod of a workspace. Lastly, for extra safety sake, I dug out an old construction hardhat I had at my house. I wore it every time I entered the trailer. I actually didn't put it on as a joke or to make a statement, but for safety purposes. Really!

On occasion, a few fellow officers with whom I was friendly would stop by with a Slurpee from the nearby 7-11. They'd even stay and talk for a while. On at least one such occasion, Capt. Hughes stepped out of the front glass doors of the PD and stood there across the parking lot watching me talk to the "visiting" officer. He had his arms folded across his chest the whole time but would look at his watch on occasion too as if timing my interaction and whether it was "work" related or not. After a few minutes of catching up with my former squad mate, and showing the officer a piece of broken bike and pointing to my clipboard for the visual effect, he drove off in his patrol car. Hughes then walked back inside of HQ, apparently satisfied for now that he had done his job.

I told you, I was really "special" at this time.

As all good things must come to an end, the long hot summer of 1985 finally did too. It took me just about that whole time, costing me blood, sweat, (no tears), and a few major league headaches, but by early

September I finally managed to get the evidence trailer into manageable working condition. It was now even safe to walk through it again. Yes, Fibber McGee's old "closet" was now fixed. No more items of evidence falling on my head, or almost taking out my arm and legs.

Along the way, I reconfigured the trailer's interior for the first time with clearly identifiable alpha-numeric sections, installed a few hanging racks for the larger items, and even put in some battery operated overhead lights near the front section. Every item which had to be maintained for court or other purposes was properly tagged and now logged into the master evidence book. Other items, after checking with the submitting officers (IF their names were known), were either returned to their owners, set to be destroyed, or forwarded to the county to be "escheated." (That's an official, court-ordered manner to legally dispose of items of certain categories of evidence.) There would eventually be a Bensalem Township sponsored "Bike Auction" and many of the previously unclaimed bicycles would be removed from our inventory in that way too.

While I would still visit the trailer over the next few months when needed as part of my everyday property clerk duties, my main work was now within the four walls of the BPD, where it was the actual evidence closet itself in CID which needed to be reconfigured, restructured, and essentially reclaimed from a year or so of neglect. (Yes, that earlier trailer-as-PD metaphor would apply here too.)

While the meteorological conditions were much more tolerable inside of HQ (I could finally leave the jug of ice water at home), the people I was now forced to work with or under made for some similarly difficult scenarios. It may not have been as hot and humid in there, but it could definitely still be as dangerous.

Maybe I should continue to wear that hardhat.

The upcoming month of September, 1985, would not be an easy one for me. There would be numerous interpersonal interactions between me and various BPD management members, as well as with one starry-eyed detective, none of which was provoked by me or invited in any sense. Lots of paper was pushed in my direction too, some of it quite asinine in topic and content. I responded, of course, sometimes in kind.

It took me a while, and phone calls and visits to a former criminal justice associate of mine, but I eventually realized by the end of this calendar month that the Dark Side had provided me the additional fuel supply I had been counting on; you know, for that fire I'd have to set around this place to save it...and me. Ironically, Zajac and his cronies were essentially delivering the necessary accelerant right to my little office doorstep. Their timing couldn't have been better. Well, for me. Not so much for them.

Here at the beginning of September, we were at eight weeks and counting....

Chapter Forty-Nine

1943 - In the German POW camp Commandant's office, upon their initial meeting…

(British) Group Captain Ramsey: "Colonel Von Luger, it is the sworn duty of all officers to escape. If they can't, it is their duty to cause the enemy to use an inordinate number of troops to guard them and their sworn duties to harass the enemy to the best of their ability."

Later that same day, in the same POW camp prisoners' barracks, upon a long-awaited reunion…

Group Captain Ramsey: "Roger, did the Gestapo give you a hard time?"

(British) Squadron Leader Roger Bartlett: "Not nearly as rough as I now intend to give them."

Ramsey: "Roger, personal revenge must be kept out of what we have to do here. Too many lives are at stake."

Bartlett: "What my personal feelings are is of no importance. You appointed me Big X, and it's my duty to harass, confound and confuse the enemy to the best of my ability…That's what I intend to do. I'm gonna cause such a terrible stink in this Third Reich of theirs that thousands of troops will be tied up here looking after us."

Ramsey: "Have you thought of what it might cost?"

Bartlett: "I've thought of the humiliation if we just tamely submit, knuckle under and crawl."

The above two separate dialogue snippets are from the 1963 movie, *The Great Escape*. The credited screenwriters are James Clavell and W. R. Burnett. I saw it in the theater with my parents when it was first released. To this day, it remains one of my favorite films. It's based on a true story, first told in a book of the same title by Paul Brickhill.

As the World War II-themed movie's plotline advances, the viewer learns of the various Allied officers who are anguishing under extreme conditions while being held in a German prisoner-of-war camp, and ultimately the means by which they choose to deal with their captivity. To a man, they refuse to give in, to acquiesce, or to meekly accept the indignity of being confined to a place where they are harassed and dehumanized on an almost daily basis by their captors.

In response, the men dig; three separate tunnels in all. In doing so, they eventually orchestrate one of the largest mass escapes in modern history.

As the British officer Ramsey (actor: James Donald) boldly states to the German Commandant (actor: Hannes Messemer) upon his arrival at the new prison camp, and later that same day engages in an earnest discussion with fellow POW officer Bartlett (actor: Richard Attenborough), it's clear that these two British officers, whether speaking directly to the enemy or to each other, know what is at stake in their present situation, not to mention the world outside of their barb-wired stalag. As intimated in their rhetoric, these men are fully aware that they cannot presently confront the enemy one-on-one, certainly not as POWs in a well-guarded prison. So, they have to think outside the box, if not outside the camp. As a result, they decide to go about challenging the enemy by other means…breaking out of the place en masse.

The two British officers eventually agree that even if their elaborate plans to escape never come to full fruition and/or do not meet all of their lofty expectations, their pending actions will nonetheless cause the enemy to devote so many soldiers to guard them, police them, and ultimately hunt them down (the ones who do manage to escape), that it would weaken the German army's collective effectiveness and possibly even contribute to their eventual defeat at the hands of the Allies.

The POWs know very well that they can't presently drop bombs on the enemy, overtake them with tanks, or engage them by more direct means on a battlefield. Instead, they choose to "…harass the enemy to the best of their ability" in other ways. Throw in some aggravated attempts to "confound and confuse" and both agree, even if somewhat reluctantly, they could really do some damage to the Third Reich. These men did just that…in the book, the movie, and most importantly, in real life.

Mostly on a whim and because it had been a while, I rented *The Great Escape* at my local Bensalem video store during the summer of '85. After watching it for the first time in many years, I was reminded once again of the inner strength, determination, innovativeness, and cunning of the composite characters representing the actual men who plotted this real-life escape. At no time in their captivity did they fall victim to the old adage, "If you can't beat 'em, join 'em." To the contrary, it was the notion of fighting one's enemy by whatever means available to them which became their everyday goal, all in an attempt to muck up the works (for the Germans) as best they could.

This movie and its characters served as an inspiration for me when I needed it most and as I was dealing with my professional situation at the BPD, to include its Commandant, "Colonel Von" Zajac. I just had to start digging those tunnels.

To be very clear here, I would never compare my then-life at the BPD to those of POWs during the Second World War, or any other war for that matter. Those military veterans were/are true heroes and their lives were no doubt hellish every single day of their forced captivity. In my own little piece of BPD hell, I was definitely not a literal prisoner as I went home every night to my family. That made a BIG difference, of course. But, I must say, along with many others in my department, I was put in situations at times of being humiliated, dehumanized, and clearly f**ked with in numerous ways, by numerous people, with the fear of being demoted or even fired seemingly omnipresent.

In view of this, it became very obvious to me it was time for me to launch multiple offenses, on multiple fronts, to dig those tunnels, to start those fires within the BPD. It wouldn't necessarily be about me escaping this place (although I was trying), but instead for now to neutralize the enemy in any way I legally could do so.

Yes, I clearly knew who my enemy was. It was they who had declared war on me. They weren't just MY enemy, however; the whole stalag, make that the whole BPD, needed to be liberated from their "stink." This upcoming month of September, and going into a bit of October, convinced me of it once and for all.

At month's end, when I finally met with that former criminal justice associate to discuss this plan of mine, he asked me if the BPD bosses had been giving me a difficult time in the recent past.

I responded to him with all forthrightness, determination, and sincerity, "Not nearly as rough as I now intend to give them!"

* * * * *

The memos started flowing...from all directions, from numerous people, regarding different topics, sometimes on the same day. It seemed to be raining the damn things.

So, there was this one lieutenant. I've never mentioned him here before because he played virtually no role in my career up until this point. Other officers, especially some of the senior guys, hated him with a passion and spoke negatively about him at every turn. When still a young officer, he had apparently married the daughter of Chief Rempe, who had been the head of the BPD before Larry Michaels. Afterwards, his career took off, all the way to the position of lieutenant. (I guess this guy started the whole BPD nepotism trend.) With his father-in-law as his boss, he seemingly got away with being very strict and officious towards his various BPD underlings, whoever they may have been. Then, dad-in-law eventually retired, and the lieutenant remained stuck for years right in the middle of the BPD management pyramid. Few above him or below him seemed to like him or have any time for the man.

Me? I was neutral about this lieutenant. With no interactions at all of which to speak, I had neither reasons to like or dislike him. Not yet, anyway.

His name was Thomas Walsh.

To reiterate, Lt. Walsh never bothered me or harassed me one time in my employment at the BPD so far. I don't recall ever having even a single discussion with him about anything at any stage of my thus-far nine-year-long career. He was simply a non-entity to me, as I suppose I was to him. He seemed to get along with Rempe (of course), Michaels, Zajac, Viola, Zajac again, and just did what he was told to do under those chiefs. He was an administrative lieutenant most of the time I worked at the place and our paths rarely crossed professionally or personally, even during my year as the administrative sergeant. However, for reasons long lost to the past, he carried a legacy of being a very intolerant supervisor to many of the officers who had been around longer than me.

I should add, the lieutenant was a bit overweight; actually, very much overweight. As such, these older officers had all sorts of nicknames for him. One of them was "Fat Ankles." However, their favorite nickname contained three words, the first two beginning with the letter "F," and followed by "Walshey." The first "F"-word related to his build, and the second "F"-word was, well, the F-word itself, with "-ing" added at the end of it.

I had made it to almost mid-September with no new issues. I was in my little sergeant/evidence office about a third of each day, inside the CID evidence closet for another third, and either at lunch or (mostly) in the outside trailer for the other third. I was making progress too, evidence disposition-wise. For those first several weeks of the month I mostly kept to myself in the BPD and that was just fine with me. But that was all about to change...really quick and on multiple fronts.

Apparently at some point I strayed from my appointed mission, my relegated lot in life, was "observed" doing so, and had to be officially reminded of it and remanded for it. More precisely, I received a memo about it.

Said memo read exactly as follows:

> "TO: Sergeant Fitzgerald
> FROM: Lieutenant Walsh
> DATE: 13 September 1985
> SUBJECT: Information
>
> On several occasions, recently, you have been observed taking part in idle conversation, not related to your duties, with various members of the department and clerical staff.
>
> This practice is to stop immediately. In addition, you are to only utilize clerk typists Liz _____ and Carol _____ for all typing and secretarial duties. If for some reason they are unable to do your work, see me."
>
> (End of memo.)

Interestingly, and oddly, there was no signature or initials next to the lieutenant's name. Did he forget? Did he want an excuse to later say he didn't write it? Did he NOT write it? Maybe I should ask him.

I did.

Shortly after retrieving the memo in my mail slot, and reading and rereading it to make sure I wasn't somehow misconstruing it, I located Lt. Walsh sitting at his desk in his office. He was by himself. This was not unusual as few people seemed to ever talk to him. Now I was compelled to talk to him for what I believe was the first time in my career. It was ironic in many ways that I was forced into a "conversation" with him because of these alleged "idle conversation(s)" on my part.

Hmmm...maybe this will be the start of something more for Lt. Walsh and me. Maybe he really WANTS to talk to me, engage in conversation of the idle or non-idle variety, but he never knew how to approach me before. Perhaps he's just a lonely soul and this was his way of reaching out.

Oh God, please, don't let it be that!

It wasn't!

I knocked on Lt. Walsh's already open door. Without passing beyond the threshold, I succinctly asked him if he had just left this memo (holding it up) in my mail slot. I told him it was unsigned so I wanted to make sure it was actually from him.

The lieutenant looked up at me, grabbed at his neck with his index finger where his collar and clip-on tie met and twisted his whole head to the side once. (Picture comedian Rodney Dangerfield as he's stating to the audience, "I'll tell ya...I get no respect.") Walsh next swallowed hard, and subsequently nodded his head up and down.

Not exactly sure of what I observed in the midst of his various gestures, I further inquired, "Okay, just so I'm clear here...this memo ordering me not to engage in 'idle conversation' is from you, right?"

He kind of nodded his head up and down again. There was no neck/shirt/tie readjustment this time, but no eye contact either. He added maybe one extra nod. He was getting cocky.

For reasons I'm still not sure of, I then politely asked him, "Uh...do you want to sign it now? You must have forgotten to do so."

Hesitating at first, he eventually responded, as if thinking about his answer, "Eh....no...no, that's alright." He then nervously picked up the phone and proceeded to call someone, clearly an indication he was done talking to me.

So, there it was. After all these years, I had my first ever dialogue with Lt. Walsh. How...underwhelming it was. However, I did manage to determine that the unsigned memo was, in fact, legit. It came straight from the horse's mouth (no pun intended), or by way of his not-so-small nodding head.

Damn! Just who the hell does that Fat F***ing Walshey think he is?!

I walked the short distance back to my evidence/sergeant's office, closed the door, and started to think. Then it struck me. As a result of this just received memo, I'll bet unlike every other BPD employee who would stop and ask about a fellow worker's kids, their dog, the ball game the night before, a recent or upcoming vacation, last Sunday's church services, or whatever, I was the one all of a sudden chosen from all these people, and by written (albeit unsigned) correspondence no less, to NOT engage in "idle conversation." Me, and I was pretty darn sure to the exclusion of everyone else in the department! (I'll confirm this a bit later.)

And what's with the secretary restriction part of the memo? I guess Zajac and company wanted to know in advance what I was typing and to whom, so it was these two trusted secretaries for me and no one else. The women were no doubt instructed to then tell Zajac, Hughes, Eckert, or now "F.F." Walsh, what I was up to right after they had typed something for me. Again, no other employee had such a mandate given to them; just Sgt. Fitzgerald.

What the hell...?

It had been such a quiet (and more temperate) last few weeks, too. Did I say something again about the FOP? Geez, was I merely thinking about the FOP and someone found out? Can they do that here? This is crazy...!

To further confirm what I could that afternoon, over the course of the next few hours, as surreptitiously as I could manage, I quietly asked about five other people in their various offices, ones I could trust of course, if they too had received such a memo. I actually affixed it to my always-with-me clipboard, under a few evidence submission sheets, and showed it to various officers and staff members alike. No one had received a similar memo or had even heard about me getting MY memo until now. Nor were they aware of anyone being verbally warned to restrict their everyday conversational habits. Several of the people laughed out loud and thought I actually typed it myself. I assured them that I did not and that this was no laughing matter. But then I told them quietly I had to get back to work. After all, I didn't want to get caught engaging in "idle conversation" about my "idle conversation" memo.

Or wait...would this have been, in fact, non-idle, work-related conversation? I may need a clarification on that.

Naturally, I made a copy of the memo for my own file at home. That file was slowly growing thicker. I gotta come up with a better filing system. Let me think about that....

I thought about my potential strategies at home over the next two days. I came up with a few interesting ideas, but was vacillating on whether they were the right moves or not. It was a combined strategy that would be a bit over-the-top for me, but perhaps necessary if I wanted to attain further proof of the provenance of this memo. That being, was it simply Lt. Walsh sending it to an officer (me) he didn't really know at all and without cause as some sort of a throwback to his officious days of yesteryear? Or, was it more than that? Did it actually originate at the top, with this rotund puppet in a lieutenant's costume serving as the conduit for delivery? If so, was it done just to "routinely" harass me, to keep me "in check" and spread the wealth among management while doing so?

I'd have to ponder my options if I truly wanted to find out more about this quasi-mystery memo. I'll keep this recently contemplated strategy on the back burner for now. Let's see what unfolds when I'm back at work. That next scheduled shift of mine was the following Monday, three days later.

That Monday would turn into a pretty busy day for me and the Dark Side before it was over. The "stink" would become virtually unbearable.

* * * * *

Amazingly, before a strategy of any sort on my part was set into motion on that subsequent Monday, a whole additional unsolicited scenario unfolded between me and Lt. Eckert in CID. What he did to me and why he did it made no sense at all. But that was becoming the new normal around here. Eckert was right up there with the others in the BPD's Axis of Evil when it came to engaging in activities which defied the conventional precepts of those notions commonly referred to as logic and common sense. Well, at least as it applied to Sgt. James Fitzgerald.

To best describe what happened that day between the two of us, with Capt. Hughes finding himself eventually mixed up in it too, I'm going to provide for the reader a document I handwrote in my office that day at 1:00PM. I did it then so later I wouldn't forget the details of what happened. It is self-explanatory. It reads exactly as follows:

"On 16 Sep. 85, at approx. 1015 hrs., while working in the evidence locker (located in the C.I.D. room), I closed and locked all evidence doors up so I could go to the bathroom, & finish some paperwork in the temp. evidence storage room. Upon leaving C.I.D. room I left evidence log book on Det. Moran's desk. Det. Moran is on vacation this week.

"Approx. ½ hr. later, at 1045 hrs., I returned to Det. Moran's desk to retrieve evidence log book only to find it was gone. I knew I had left it on Det. Moran's desk which is located directly adjacent to evidence closet door, but it was gone. Being positive that I had left said book there, I didn't know what to make of the missing book. Just in case, I began searching all of the evidence facilities for the missing book. I also searched and asked around for book in the front dispatcher area, roll room, bathroom, etc. Finally, at approx. 1105 hrs., I saw Capt. Hughes and I asked him if he knew where the book was. He replied that Lt. Eckert gave it to him. It was unknown to me at this time why Lt. Eckert would take the book off of the desk where I left it and give it to someone else. I then retrieved book and went about my work.

"Approx. 1200 hrs., when I next saw Lt. Eckert in his office, I went to his office and the following dialogue took place:

Fitzgerald: 'Why did you hide the evidence book on me, Lt. Eckert?'

Eckert: 'I didn't hide it, I gave it to Capt. Hughes.'

Fitzgerald: 'Why didn't you just give it to me instead of Capt. Hughes?'

Eckert: 'I don't have to answer to you Sgt. Fitzgerald. Did you leave the book there?'

Fitzgerald: 'Yes, I've been working there all day and I'll be there the rest of the day working.'

Eckert: 'The book shouldn't be left out.'

Fitzgerald: 'Well, you should have still given it to me instead of Capt. Hughes. It took me 20 minutes to find it. That's a waste of 20 minutes of taxpayers' money!'

Eckert: 'The book shouldn't have been there and neither should you have. You're not allowed back here anymore. C.I.D. is for detectives only so you stay out of here!'

Fitzgerald: 'Ok, whatever you say. Thank you!'

Conversation ended approx. 1202 hrs.

I am presently in a quandary as to how I can complete my evidence duties if I can no longer go into C.I.D. The evidence locker is located in C.I.D."

(End of my handwritten notes.)

There was absolutely NO precedence in the BPD for the evidence book NOT being temporarily left out on the detective sergeant's desk (when they were still the evidence custodians) or on one of the two desks nearest the door to the evidence closet. (Steve Moran's desk was closest to the door.) The book in and of itself was not evidence. It was merely a line-by-line register of where the evidence items were recorded. The evidence submission cover sheets, safely stored at all times inside of the evidence closet in CID, contained all the same information.

There was no reason for this action on Eckert's part. He simply took it upon himself to do this to make my day difficult, or at least a portion of it. He must have been bored as his "frame Viola" investigation at the White House was mostly behind him now. And, yes, what he did was a clear waste of taxpayers' money for those twenty minutes. Of course, it was a drop in the bucket of wasted taxpayer money when compared to the last eighteen-plus months of this administration and their questionable undertakings. Plus, as Eckert's wife was the official Bensalem Tax Collector, maybe that comment hit home for him. Literally….

As was well known then and written of here earlier, Eckert's former mentor and friend, the now retired detective not-so-affectionately called "Pops" by Viola, used to leave actual items of evidence themselves out on or under the same desk, for days at a time, frequently misplacing them for additional days at a time. He was never confronted about it except finally by Chief Viola. Now, the lieutenant is upset at ME for leaving a simple book out in a secure area while I go to the bathroom? Who was going to steal it, another detective? Well, no, in this instance it was actually a Detective Lieutenant named Eckert who "stole" it.

This is when I decided to employ my weekend-devised strategy, or at least one component of it. To this day, I'm not sure I would have actually followed-through on it if Eckert hadn't played his little game with me with the hidden book earlier in the morning. But he started the game with me, it was time for me to play back with him and the other Dark Siders who I knew would react in kind.

As per that plan, right after I "found" the secreted-away book that morning, I took the half-page "idle conversation" memo and made a full-page copy of it. Then, in red marker type pen, beneath the profound typewritten words of Lt. Walsh (or his ghostwriter), I added my own words to the memo.

In large, red, upper-case lettering, I wrote, "DO NOT TALK TO ME!" Beneath those five words, still in red, I wrote in slightly smaller font, "Only work related business discussed here!" I then taped the memo onto the front corner of my desk in the sergeant's office. It was readily visible for anyone to see who came into my office or who walked by it.

Hey, I wanted to make sure I obeyed Lt. Walsh's edict. I wanted to give fair warning to all that I was NOT to be engaged in conversation, well, at least of the "idle" kind. In this office, with this sergeant (me), it was business only from now on. No exceptions. I made that very clear in my red-inked modified memo to anyone who would dare to try to break this new rule.

For the rest of that Monday, fellow officers and staff would pass by my office, see the bright red lettering under the memo, walk in, read the original advisory by the lieutenant, and comment in various forms and versions, "What the hell is this?" Or, "This is ridiculous!" Or, "You mean that Fat F**kin' Walshey gave this to you?" I would only shrug my shoulders in silence and purse my lips as if to say, "Sorry, but I can't talk to you about it."

The officers and I would then quietly discuss whether talking about this memo was "idle conversation" in and of itself. I'd ask them if they had been given such notice, either in writing or orally, or if they were aware of anyone else receiving a similar notification. None had. No surprise there.

After literally everyone who visited me expressed their disbelief over such a command, in writing too, I made sure to turn the conversation toward the topic of evidence. As almost every officer had some item in the closet or the trailer that had to be adjudicated, this wasn't hard to do. I made it abundantly clear to everyone who stopped by that I do not want to hear about their family, their pets, their night classes, their medical problems, or anything that doesn't somehow entail the concept of "evidence." They agreed to do so, or more accurately not do so, for my sake. (Both parties may have winked and/or smirked at the other at the same time while formalizing this for-all-to-hear "don't talk to me" agreement.)

My self-notated version of the memo actually remained on my desk the entirety of that afternoon. However, upon coming in on Tuesday, the 17th, I saw that it had been removed. The tape was left behind, but the combined typewritten Walsh/handwritten Fitzgerald memo was now missing. Oh well, it served its purpose for the half-day it was affixed to my desk.

However, I wasn't done with this issue yet. As it turned out, neither were they.

Besides my "no talk zone" memo within a memo, I was determined to also collect some exculpatory evidence on my behalf. After all, I was the evidence custodian, so I might as well gather some for a possible big case of my own coming up sometime in the future. In doing so, I wanted to determine just who else was engaging in such non-essential chatter around the BPD. It didn't take long to find it as virtually everywhere I went I heard it. By Tuesday of that week, I thusly began compiling a list of those so engaged. It was silly, I grant you, but it was necessary for me on a few different levels. I was still doing my assigned evidence job for eight hours every day, but I was now also paying attention to others around me, and more intently than ever before.

Over several days that week, and without even trying, I came up with at least nine "idle conversation" incidents within the offices which comprised the BPD. I documented each event to include the date, time, where, participants, and topic. I just happened to walk by and hear non-BPD related dialogue involving Zajac, Hughes, Eckert, Walsh (of all people), detectives, secretaries, and the like. I made sure to not engage them as I was the only one among all of them who had a written order restricting me from doing so.

On September 18th, at 1:30PM, I hit pay dirt in my hunt for "idle conversation." It so happens, as part of my evidence duties, I was in one of the front administrative offices and bent over behind a row of filing cabinets. I was routinely attempting to locate an incident report regarding an old case to determine how I could best dispose of the evidence associated with it. Adjacent to me, two secretaries were merrily discussing matters definitely NOT related to their jobs or to police work at all. They knew I was there but they didn't care. Why should they? Either way, I noted their chatting dutifully on my clipboard (again on a document hidden under evidence submission sheets) and made a point of not joining them in their "idle" discourse. However, what happened next, and what was said and by whom, only further solidified for me the folly of the recent memo to me and how I was being truly set up, singled out, and harassed.

Clearly without knowing I was there, Captain Hughes sauntered his way into the secretaries' office. I was still on my knees going through a drawer at the bottom of a filing cabinet and out of his direct line of vision, but I could still manage to see him at an angle. When Hughes overheard the women innocently talking away he calmly muttered aloud with a shit-eating grin on his face, "This isn't an idle conversation is it?"

When the now two suddenly scared women didn't initially know how to respond, Hughes reassured them by laughingly telling them, "Well, that's alright."

This was too good to be true and I couldn't resist. Upon hearing the Captain's wiseass question and comment, I immediately stood up from behind the filing cabinets. He saw me looking at him as I was scribbling something on my clipboard at the same time. His face turned white and it looked as if he swallowed the shit which just covered that earlier grin. He stumbled and fumbled in an attempt to verbalize something to the secretaries, but upon pivoting to leave the room he could only advise them to "carry on." He seemed to forget why he came to their office in the first place.

The two secretaries smiled at me as I left their office. I smiled back, but didn't say a word.

Unbelievable, bizarre, very strange…, but most importantly, duly noted.

* * * * *

Going back again to that same Monday, after the hide-and-go-seek book incident with Eckert, and posting my redlined memo for all to see, I undertook two additional separate but related actions that afternoon. The first involved my daily log. You may recall that when first "temporarily" appointed to this evidence position in the early summer, I was told that I had to fill out an "Officer's Daily Activity Report," aka daily log, each and every day. I was the only BPD inside-guy ever required to submit one on an everyday basis. So, of course, I did one on this day. In the weather block, I wrote "Clear, 70s." That wasn't the problem with THIS particular log. No, on this one the problem was a few lines further down and had nothing to do with meteorological conditions. To be exact, it was what came after the standard first two lines of "0800 - Report on Duty," and "0810 - H.Q., Evidence work." On the next line on this day I wrote something different, yet completely accurate.

It read, "1045–1105, Search for evidence book, Lt. Eckert gave it to Capt. Hughes.?" (I included the question mark on the log for emphasis.)

As per that earlier order, I obediently turned in my log sheet to Capt. Hughes at the end of my shift on Monday, the 16th. And, just as with the log containing my weather block reportage of a month or so ago, by the next morning I was ordered to do this one over again too. This time Capt. Hughes didn't like what I wrote on that third line. I'm sure Eckert was shown it and he didn't like it either. So, I rewrote my daily log, once again, this time to the ordered specifications of deleting the "search for evidence book…" notation. Of course, I kept the original one which Hughes had returned to me. I had a feeling it may come in handy again before too long. It did.

565

The second issue on the afternoon of Monday, September 16th, involved Hughes verbally advising me that I was not leaving my position as evidence custodian anytime soon. In fact, I should consider the position now "permanent" as I was "uniquely qualified" to do it. When he told me this, and what else he wanted me to do, I immediately sat down and wrote out a memo to the Deputy Chief.

That afternoon, after being told by Hughes of my revised orders, I gave the below memo to Zajac's secretary and asked her to please give it to him. It read, in part, as follows:

"I was recently advised by Captain Hughes that I am to continue in the position of property clerk/evidence custodian until further notice, even after my present 'temporary' assignment is completed. The longevity of my stay was evidently further extended when I was told by Captain Hughes that you and he agreed that my name should be recorded on the records of the new safe deposit box at Provident Bank. I, along with Captain Robinson, are then to have keys to said box and together will be responsible for maintaining it and its contents.

"I do not want this new responsibility, nor do I want my responsibility as evidence custodian to extend past the eventual completion date of my present assignment. Although it is most flattering for me to know that you feel I am 'uniquely qualified' for this position, I don't believe my qualifications are limited to just this one area.

"This assignment should be completed by late October or early November, barring any further hardships. At that time I would hope to see my name resubmitted to the patrol schedule and…returned to one of the squads which I formerly supervised. Upon that reassignment I would be glad to spend any time necessary in training whoever it is that is to take my place as evidence custodian.

"Any questions you may have concerning this matter please feel free to re-memo me, and hopefully, via return memo, I can answer them. Thank you."

(End of memo.)

Neither Zajac nor Hughes ever responded in writing to this memo. Hughes simply told me a day or two later that this was my job for the foreseeable future, whether I like it or not. In so many words he said, "Get used to it here. You're not going anywhere."

Jack Robinson was scheduled to return to work the following week after his long IOD status. His almost year-long back problem was now somewhat resolved. Upon his return, he would be my direct supervisor in the evidence custodian capacity. Now there would be two of us doing this job fulltime, a captain and a sergeant. In most PDs, at least of the size of Bensalem at the time, it was one rank and file officer performing these duties. Not here though. After all, I was "uniquely qualified" to do this job. I guess Jack was too.

Capt. Robinson and I talked on the phone the same evening that Hughes told me of my now official long-term assignment and also being one of two custodians officially responsible for the new safe deposit box. Neither Jack nor I was the paranoid type. (Well, I didn't think so... more on this issue in the next chapter.) However, we agreed this would be the perfect setup to somehow frame us for alleged missing money down the line. We put nothing past this regime, especially involving large sums of money and their desire to get rid of the two of us uninvited guests to their ongoing party.

Jack and I would have to be careful, very careful, keep duplicate records, and have objective witnesses for everything we do, especially regarding the large sums of cash at the bank. That, we agreed, was a no-brainer.

Oh, and it apparently took Zajac a few days to catch up on everything, but at 8:10AM on September 19th, I was handed an envelope by one of the two secretaries now assigned as my personal typists. The memo inside read as follows:

"TO: Sergeant James Fitzgerald
FROM: Deputy Chief Theodore R. Zajac
DATE: 18 September 1985
RE: Judgment

On 13 September 1985 you were given a memo by Lieutenant Walsh concerning your taking part in idle conversation not related to your duties.

As a result of that memo you hung up a sign in your office advising people not to talk to you.

Such action on your part shows extreme lack of judgment and immaturity. By hanging up such a sign you showed little regard for your rank, and open disrespect for a superior officer. Such action on your part will not be tolerated.

I suggest in the future you exercise more self-control, and a better degree of judgment."

(End of memo.)

Bingo! The DC took the bait; hook, line, and sinker. It may not prove that Zajac authorized the original memo, but it certainly demonstrated after-the-fact that he condoned it. If nothing else, he was a now a co-conspirator in the ongoing harassment against me. (Duh!) That was what I needed to determine in this matter... and I just did.

This evidence custodian was collecting his own evidence for his own case, slowly but surely.

Oh, and if you think Zajac's criticism actually bothered me...well, you haven't figured me out quite yet. I knew he was wrong, others I greatly respected knew he was wrong, and that's all that mattered to me. Considering the source, I actually took it as a badge of honor that this man would think of me in such terms. I knew what I did with that altered memo and for what reason. Let him think what he wants in the meantime of my "judgment." I may just be surprising him before too long in that regard.

As an interesting aside, this most recent memo was also unsigned. There were no initials, nothing next to Zajac's name. Just like the original Walsh memo. I should point out here that virtually every other memo I've received (or wrote myself) at the BPD was signed or initialed by its sender. It was very odd that neither of these two recent ones were so marked. Was it a tepid attempt at plausible deniability on the Dark Side's part in case some time in the future this action should ever come back at them? Did Zajac realize, much like Walsh before him, how ludicrous of an "order" this was to give me, or anyone for that matter?

I really didn't care about the answers to those questions. All that concerned me was that my strategy worked.

I suppose their strategy worked too. Over the next few weeks, I rarely talked to anyone about anything at work unless it involved the words "Destroyed," "Escheated," "Returned," or "Retained."

However, my silence at work was made up for by lots of talking after workhours at home. Most of it was by phone. Lots could be covered, I learned, from 4:15 to 5:00 on a telephone line. A visit to the man to whom I was talking, this former criminal justice associate of mine, was also imminent. It would only make sense. We agreed telephonically that I had the fuel already for that large fire to be set. Little did we know, however, that before long a tanker truck full of the stuff would be delivered to me.

Ironically at the time, I wasn't even working on a specific long-term strategy. I didn't have to. In a sense, the Dark Side's own strategy became my strategy. Theirs was short-term, mine morphed into just the opposite. That was their mistake, and not their only one.

I was to experience at least one more incident during this ninth month of 1985. Again, it was unsolicited on my part and totally uncalled for on someone else's part. If I had been somewhat wavering before undertaking a certain major strategic move, this upcoming event and its follow-up made the eventual decision so very easy for me. It also served to strengthen and enhance what I was going to do. And I'll always have a certain detective to thank for it. So will the Dark Siders too for that matter.

Chapter Fifty

First, a bit of cultural history from the 1980s....
Trust me, it'll all make sense.

There was this very popular network television program in the U.
S. from the mid- to late-1980s. It was called *Miami Vice*. It was about two
Miami-Dade narcotics detectives and their adventures and experiences
in attempting to curb the then-notorious drug trade in South Florida.
It was flashy, fast-moving, topical, and very entertaining. It was one
of the top shows on TV for five years, and remained very popular in
reruns for a decade-plus afterwards.

The two main characters were Detective James "Sonny" Crockett,
played by Don Johnson, and Ricardo "Rico" Tubbs, played by Philip
Michael Thomas. Both were handsome, quick-witted, full of bravado,
and stylishly dressed to the hilt. Every week, every episode, the show's
two protagonists would battle international drug lords, narco-terror-
ists, domestic cocaine distributors, gun-runners, corrupt businessmen,
dirty politicians, and the like, and they'd always win. They were two
bad-asses with both their guns and their fists and were really cool,
dressed in the latest Miami-influenced clothing designs. Of course, by
each episode's end, they always got their man, and/or woman, as the
case may be.

So, why is this popular television series relevant to the BPD during
this same mid-'80s time frame? Well, because we were lucky enough to
have our own Sonny Crockett, or at least a detective who did his best to
model himself after this character, right in our own department. Yep,
Hollywood came to my town and my PD thanks to this officer. We'll
call this "Bensalem Vice" wannabe, Detective John Donson.

It started way back in March of '84 when Deputy Chief Zajac
appointed two detectives to a new "Narcotics Squad" within CID.
They were like the two investigators in *Miami Vice* except for one very

notable difference. That is, they rarely made any arrests. They were narcs, just minus the successful investigations, the apprehensions and, well, the narcotics. Otherwise, and much more importantly to the Dark Side, at least one of them, BPD's own Det. Donson, dressed and acted the part of his favorite character on what was without a doubt his favorite weekly TV show. If they made lunch boxes back then with the show's characters on them, Donson would have very likely carried one to work every day.

Sometime during or shortly after the first season of *Miami Vice*, it seems as if overnight John Donson transformed himself from a plain old traditional dark suit wearing detective into something much more, dare I say, flamboyant. His butterfly-like metamorphosis would have made Franz Kafka proud. It included Donson now coming to work wearing flashy neon-colored coats/jackets, coordinated slacks, open-collared shirts, necklaces, bracelets, no socks, off-white loafers, etc. They were probably purchased at the Men's Department of the Bensalem K-Mart store, but that didn't matter to him.

To top off his look, the Bensalem Vice narc (again, minus the actual narcotics) seemed now to have a perpetual two or three days' growth of whiskers and seemed to be letting his hair grow longer too. He was as cool as Sonny Crockett except, well, when he wasn't. That was, quite frankly, all the time. Donson's thinning and receding hair, uneven beard growth, and the slight paunch over his beltline took away from the look he was trying so desperately to create, or recreate, in a classic example of life imitating art.

Maybe this whole cool, South Florida persona could have worked for him in Bensalem, at least on some scale, if he and his partner had only made some arrests. But, as already mentioned, that occurred very infrequently. When there happened to be an actual arrest on their parts, it was either by accident, happenstance, or it fell in their laps as a result of some good work by uniformed officers in the Patrol Division. Even then, in most every case the amounts were small and there would be no attempt by our wannabe narcs to go up the criminal food-chain to arrest those actually distributing the contraband.

But, I gotta reiterate here, Det. Donson did look cool while making these non-arrests, undertaking these non-investigations, non-prosecutions, and gaining the subsequent non-convictions. His coolness was especially evident to him I'm sure, every time he passed a mirror or a plate glass window.

I was in CID when this faux Narcotics Squad was first created but I had little, if any, direct involvement with it or the two detectives. As

I was one of the part-time (then) evidence custodians for the department, I rarely received any evidence from them to lock away, send to the lab, or pull out for court because, again, there was virtually none ever submitted by the two of them.

As can probably be surmised, Det. Donson had been made a detective pre-Chief Viola through the former promotional testing protocol under DC Zajac. (Remember, he gave the written test to the "candidate," in private, and graded it himself.) Then, Donson was eventually appointed to this special squad by, who else, the top man himself. When he and one (and then another) partner were appointed to this Narcotics Squad, it was known to virtually everyone in the BPD that in actuality it was Zajac's "goon squad." Instead of chasing down druggies and those who would sell the stuff, the BPD's version of "Sonny" and "Rico" were suspected of following around our fellow officers (me included) and otherwise run interference for all that Zajac and his ilk were doing, or undoing, within the township.

I'm recounting the brief history of this rather insignificant squad and at least one rather insignificant detective on it because of what happened between me and this same officer in September of '85. It, along with the other notable incidents I've already referenced, each recorded dutifully on both sides by written memoranda, was the straw that broke this camel's back in these latter years of my time at the BPD. What occurred between me and this narco-minimalist (at least arrest-wise), and the follow-up actions by his/my superiors, convinced me once and for all to take that long contemplated proactive action and be the catalyst for change within the BPD.

I knew Officer (later Detective) John Donson since my earliest days on the BPD, well before his pretend-to-be Sonny Crockett days. I would never have called him a friend, but I initially got along with him to some degree as a sometimes squad mate. He had a few years on me in seniority, and a few years in age, too.

I learned early on that John was an unwavering devotee of then-Lt. Zajac. I didn't care at all back then one way or the other as Zajac had not fully spread his wings yet within the department and I really didn't know much about the man. As I wrote many chapters ago, in those days I just wanted to do the job, learn the job, and be the best cop I could possibly be.

During those early years in uniform, I remember one day when Donson and I met up at a call of a suspicious vehicle somewhere in the Neshaminy Valley area of Bensalem. Either I backed him up or he backed me up, I forget after all of these years who took the actual call. Anyway, upon our arrival, we didn't find the vehicle as it apparently had left the scene before we got there. For some reason, after talking to a witness or two, there was speculation by Donson that the car MAY be part of a federal law enforcement surveillance team, possibly belonging to the FBI or the DEA. He somehow came to the conclusion that they were conducting an investigation of some sort in this particular Bensalem neighborhood.

John was very adamant as we were clearing the scene that he was going to find a payphone and call Lt. Zajac at HQ right away. Perhaps naïvely, I asked him why. He responded without skipping a beat that Zajac always insisted upon knowing when the feds were working in Bensalem, even if it was just a suspicion. The lieutenant apparently expressed this sentiment to John as well as some of his other trusted officers in the department. In doing so, Officer Donson strongly suggested to me that I do the same when similar suspicions or facts present themselves regarding the feds working in Bensalem.

"Uh, okay, sure. I'll tell him…I guess. Should I just include it in the written incident report?"

"No, never in writing; the lieutenant prefers you to tell him in person or over the phone. He's that kind of guy. You know what I mean?"

I really didn't know what Donson meant, but I shook my head up and down as if I did.

As a further example of my then-naïveté, and without really knowing Zajac at all in those early days, I actually thought to myself afterwards, "Gee, this lieutenant is such a dedicated cop, such an excellent investigator, that he wants to know right away every time another law enforcement agency is working in his town. That way, he can call them up and assist in their investigation, surveillance, or whatever, in any way he can. What a guy, what a professional!"

Yeah…something like that.

This was most likely the logic when I was ordered back in 1981 by one of Zajac's people to investigate that alleged suspicious Cadillac in the Doral Apartment complex. If you recall, it was driven by then-Sgt. Viola of the Philadelphia PD, destined just a few months later to become the new Bensalem chief. Of course, he almost didn't make it to that position as I was compelled to point my gun at his head after our brief interaction. Luckily, it worked out okay that day for the both of us.

Anyway, this is the very short history of me with this now unabashed pro-Zajac detective acting like a TV character in our own PD. It's pretty clear to see where he was coming from, what he was, and who he was pretending to be. The only thing he couldn't pull off was being an actual narc. There would be no Emmys for him in that role.

So, here's how it all went down between me and Det. Crockett-lite, with the usual cast of Axis members soon finding their way into the middle of it.

Over the summer when I was first force-assigned my new evidence custodian duties, I had devised a simple "Evidence Disposition" form. It was designed in template format, easy to understand, with me just filling in the blanks as to certain questioned pieces of evidence, to include the original submitting officer's name, the property receipt number, case number, date it was submitted, name associated with the case (e.g., arrestee, victim, etc.), and description. I would put copies of these in individual officers' mail slots (former time card slots) and hopefully within a few days, he or she would get back to me with how I could dispose of the evidence. Again, their choices were to Destroy, Retain, Return to Owner, or Escheat. It was very simple.

Thanks to this streamlined form, and the hundred-plus copies I had distributed to officers of all ranks within the BPD, by late September of that year each returned them within days advising me how to handle the so-designated item of evidence. Some chose to tell me verbally in my office or did so by writing on the form itself and leaving it in a small box on the desk in the sergeant's office. Either method was acceptable. I had absolutely no problems with any officer previous to the incident which I'm about to relate. None at all! It was a good system and so far, it had worked flawlessly.

However, Det. John Donson must have been feeling his oats on this one certain day. Perhaps there was a big arrest he and Rico did NOT just make and he was cocky and sure of himself. In any event, his written responses on two evidence disposition forms were most unwelcome by me, not to mention highly unprofessional on his part.

Without boring the reader with the details of the evidence disposition protocol at the time, suffice it to say I would go through the evidence closet and find various items, determine the name of the officer who had submitted it, and fill out one of the aforementioned forms. Instead of hitting the officers with a different form every day listing just one item, I would begin to write them out and wait until I listed three or four items on each, perhaps from the same case or perhaps from different cases, and then put the form in their time slot. They may be dated from that first day in the closet, but then sometimes not put in their mail slots until a few days afterwards. No big deal, right?

Well, in the matter at hand with Det. Donson, it became a big deal.

I must have started a form on September 20th but apparently didn't put it in Donson's mail slot until the 23rd. I then found additional evidence and I sent another form to him on the 24th. After writing upon each one, Donson walked them back into my office, slammed them down in the middle of my desk with obvious disdain and defiance to me while I was sitting there, and left the room without saying a word.

Okay, that was weird. Whatever...he's weird, especially in the mauve leisure suit he was wearing that day. For some reason at first, I assumed it was only one form he left behind, but in reality it was two. Either way, I'll read it/them later.

The first returned evidence disposition memo I read (not knowing yet there was a second one), dated the 24th, simply had, in red ink, "I got this from you Fitz (and his initials)." The one listed item had "hold" written next to it.

That was kind of snarky, to say the least. What does he mean, he got it from me? That written line makes no sense. Plus, he's been a wise-guy to me recently when I would pass him in the hallway and at other times overhear him talking trash specifically about me in "idle conversation" mode with others.

So, how do I handle this? What do I do? I am a sergeant, after all. I do hold rank over this detective. How would Hughes or Eckert handle it if I walked into their offices exhibiting the same behavior with a form similarly written?

More importantly to me at the time, how would British Squadron Leader Roger Bartlett have handled it? Maybe it's time to borrow from the Big X model of dealing with my "enemy."

After thinking about it overnight, I decided to test the waters. Let's just see what happens here. As such, I sent Donson an official memo, dated September 25th. This memo to him required no response. I simply advised him that what he wrote to me was "most irregular" in that "I know very well that I am the one sending you...the (evidence disposition form)," and lastly on further correspondence, "...you will address me as Sergeant Fitzgerald, not 'Fitz'..."

Then, after putting that memo in Donson's mail slot and him apparently removing it, I found the second evidence disposition form he had slam dunked on my desk the previous day. On this one, dated the 20th, in red ink, Donson scribbled out that date and wrote next to it, "Wrong date – memo in time slot 9-23-85. Please be accurate!! Thank you (His signed name and initials.)" The listed items had either "hold" or "escheat" next to them.

Again, this response was unlike any others I had received over the last few months from all the other officers. What was written on this one and the way Donson came into my office and roughly deposited them onto my desk while I was sitting there was quite, well, rude and unprofessional, to put it mildly.

So, I sent him a second memo. This one required a written response from him back to me. I inquired of him, in writing, as to why he was questioning my accuracy because of "…one working day difference in the listed date…and the date you found it in your time slot." And "what effect did the one-day date differential have on your ability to determine the dispositions of the listed submissions?"

Simple questions, I thought. Perhaps he had simple answers. In any event, Donson was ordered to respond by written memorandum to me no later than the 26th, at 8:00AM.

I wasn't sure exactly what to expect Donson's response to be, but his actions actually surprised me. It probably shouldn't have considering the source and his upper-management role models, but it still did to some degree. I should have known that this "scene" was part of the script for this particular episode. After all, he was Sonny Donson, or at least he thought he was.

So, what did Donson do? Quite simply, within five minutes of receiving the second memo from me, he came into my sergeant's office. He asked me if there was a trashcan in the room. Before I could answer, and while walking towards the trash can, he ripped up the two memos I had just written to him and stuffed them into the can. He then walked out of my office.

I was surprised initially. But almost immediately thereafter I became elated that this incident unfolded as it just did. I couldn't wait to get home that afternoon and call the former criminal justice associate and tell him what had just occurred. When I made that call he asked me right away if I saved the ripped up documents. I told him, "Of course, I have them right here. They're being maintained in my own little evidence closet."

He said, "Good. We're gonna need them."

Based on my further phone conversation with the former associate, we agreed that I should refrain from personally confronting the officer and proceed instead to write him up for disciplinary charges. So, the next day, I did just that. On September 26th, I addressed a memo to Lt. Eckert, the head of CID and Donson's supervisor, with the subject line reading, "Detective Donson/Conduct Unbecoming an Officer." In it I detailed exactly what happened the day before, including Donson's "…obvious blatant act of disrespect for me and my rank" and that he was in violation of at least three departmental regulations.

Now, the ball was in Eckert's court. I didn't expect anything to actually happen to Donson, but I really wanted to see Eckert/Zajac's response to it. So did my former "associate."

Well, it took just about a calendar month, and another reminder memo from me to Lt. Eckert, but I finally got the response for which I was waiting. Just in time too, as the reader will eventually learn.

Lt. Eckert's two-page response memo to me was dated October 25th. The subject line was "Conduct Unbecoming." The first line read, "Please answer the following questions regarding the incident with Det. (Donson)." That was followed by nineteen questions back at me. Each of the numbered questions instructed me to describe in very specific detail, telling me to "justify in writing" each and every component of the detective's actions that day, as well as my own actions. The questions were well beyond the scope of the issue at hand. It was clearly an attempt to back me down and, of course, cover the backside of Donson.

I didn't bother to answer the nineteen interrogatories. Instead, I chose on October 29th to respond with another memo to Lt. Eckert. It read as follows:

"I am in receipt of your memo dated 25 Oct. 1985. The correspondence requests me to answer nineteen questions regarding the incident…with Det. Donson. Instead of answering each question individually as directed, I elect to answer them and address the whole matter in the following three paragraphs.

"The BPD Rules and Regulations which were violated by Det. Donson…are for one reason and one reason only. Det. Donson failed to respond to my memo of the previous day as he was ordered. He was asked several specific questions on that memo and given a specific time to respond to them. Up to and including this date, I have yet to receive a response from him. The charges preferred against him in my 26 Sept. memo to you are for failure to obey an order, et al, by virtue of his failure to respond and carry out said order. I believe that was made clear in my 26 Sept. memo to you, and again in my 24 Oct. follow-up/reminder memo to you.

"The mention in my initial memo to you of Det. Donson's actions while in the temporary evidence storage room was only to illustrate his obvious disrespect of my authority and my position professionally. I wanted to make sure that it was clear to you that I didn't believe that Det. Donson simply forgot to respond to my memo, but instead, that he had in fact deliberately failed to obey a direct written order given by me to him. His behavior on that day in question was indicative of his pre-determination to violate my order, and I felt it was important to convey same to you.

"The only request that I make of you, Det. Donson's immediate supervisor, is that the proper and just discipline be administered to him for his direct violation of a written order given by a superior officer. Ripping the memo up in front of me is not the issue here. If a veteran detective, or for that matter any officer, is allowed to continue aforesaid activities as such, so be it; that is then a reflection on him and the environment of which he is a part of and no direct concern of mine. However, for a subordinate to be allowed to violate any legal order, be it verbal or written, whether he agrees with it or not, which is given by a superior officer, would be a sad commentary and set a bad precedent for every officer of supervisory rank in the department.

"I will be awaiting your reply to this matter. Thank you."

(End of memo.)

It took Eckert until the morning of October 30th to respond, but it was a classic. It came in the form of a brief memo handed to me again by the same secretary who handed me Eckert's nineteen interrogatories memo. She's apparently not only the designated secretary for doing MY typing, but also the designated person to hand me THEIR memos. The present "leaders" of the BPD seemingly don't like getting up close and personal themselves with me, at least in regards to physically handing me their ongoing harassing (or cover-up) communications. Interestingly, and yet again, it was a memo which was unsigned and un-initialed. Perhaps there was, in fact, a method to their madness.

The memo read, in its entirety, as follows:

> "Your 29 October 85 memo was most helpful in narrowing the issues involved in this matter concerning Detective Donson.
>
> "I have reviewed all the reports in this matter and find that disciplinary action is unwarranted.
>
> "Detective Donson was advised by Captain Hughes on 25 September 85, just after receiving your two memorandums, that the matter would be taken care of by him.
>
> "Detective Donson was therefore relieved of his obligation to respond to you by a superior officer.
>
> "In the future, complaints against CID members should be referred to me prior to memos being sent by you to the CID person involved."
>
> (End of memo.)

What wasn't "helpful" in my first memo to Eckert? It laid out Donson's violations very clearly to him. All of a sudden, chain of command is important around this place? How does that explain Lt. Walsh's memo to me? He wasn't my boss...ever! What about Donson allegedly going to Hughes? They're not in the same chain of command.

None of this truly mattered to me on a professional level, not even on a personal level. This eventual outcome was very predictable, certainly as far as Bensalem Vice's Sonny Donson not being charged or disciplined in any way. It also didn't surprise me that Hughes would have somehow slithered his way into this matter, although I had real doubts as to his involvement being anything like it was written of in Eckert's memo. If that was the case, why didn't the Captain provide this cover story when I first submitted my memo to Eckert on September 26th? That would have made more sense, or at least been a more believable lie. I suppose delayed lies coming from this regime are as valid as ones told right away. Why would they care?

To reiterate, this was all superfluous to me. There was a higher agenda and mission in the works here by me at this same time. There would be another document coming in their direction from me within a day or so of Eckert's last memo. Their responses to that one wouldn't be quite as easy to cover-up, although no doubt they would try. Oh, and did I mention yet that this newer document would change the course of Bensalem politics and the police department forever. I almost forgot to include that little detail here. It would also result in the cancellation of "Bensalem Vice" for Sonny Donson. That's too bad....

But first, we have the month of October ahead of us. I made up my mind it was time to even further "...harass, confound, and confuse the enemy to the best of our ability." So, I did.

Four weeks and counting....

(+ Bonus Chapter 50a)

Chapter Fifty-One

"The darkest places in hell are reserved for those
who maintain their neutrality in times of moral crisis."
(Dante Alighieri, *The Divine Comedy*)

The reader may have picked up by now that I'm a multi-tasker. I am to this day and I was pretty good at it back in 1985 too. In view of that, besides the various memorable and "memo-able" incidents related in the prior chapter, I was involved in some other activity during that same timeframe. They included conversations and meetings with that "former criminal justice associate" of mine.

You've probably guessed by now this former associate of mine was Pete Hileman. I knew him and worked with him when he was a Bucks County Assistant District Attorney. You may recall it was me and Pete who travelled to the upstate Pennsylvania prison together to interview the convicted home invader. He was the lawyer who later in private practice represented me through several official letters when Zajac had suspended me for those three days earlier in the year. Of course, it was those letters to the Township which helped my original "punishment" get reduced to JUST a letter of reprimand.

Well, a few days after the "idle conversation" memo and series of events I knew I needed some help of the legal variety once again. And no, it wasn't for a lawyer to merely write an official letter regarding that stupid memo from Lt. Walsh. That would have been small-picture. I was now thinking big-picture, as big as I could frame it. So, I called the former Bucks County prosecutor and after a few phone conversations I made an appointment to meet him at his Doylestown law office. I wasn't sure what I was going to do yet, but I needed some good objective lawyerly advice. I knew he was the man to get it from.

I took a few hours of comp time one weekday afternoon and drove to Doylestown. I hadn't actually seen Pete in person for a few years, and it was nice to spend some time with him on this late summer afternoon, even if regarding such a problematic subject matter.

Pete Hileman was a tall, thin, dark haired, good-looking guy, in his mid-30s. He was a graduate of Villanova Law School. He had been an excellent prosecutor and I knew him to be a fair and honest man. He was married with a few kids and a religious person firm in his Christian belief system. I was familiar enough with this guy that I knew he wasn't trying to push anything on me, rip me off, or sell me a bill of goods just so he could rack up the billable hours. That wasn't his style or his reputation. I felt in good hands with this lawyer and he would tell me as it is, not just what I wanted to hear.

We hadn't talked very long on the day of that initial office meeting when Pete firmly provided me with some of that good objective advice I was seeking. In less than ten minutes of him hearing about my latest victimization at the BPD, as well as visually assessing copies of the most recent memos in my possession, Pete informed me of what I wanted to hear but in a strange way did NOT want to hear at the same time. He advised me that from all of which he was aware so far there was no doubt in his mind that there were numerous identifiable civil rights violations in regards to the treatment I had been receiving at the police department over the last twenty or so months. He went on to list some potential charges which could be brought against the Township, to include individual politicians and police supervisors alike.

After listening to him cite the various violations and civil remedies, I then asked Pete, "Okay, but do we have a winning case here? I'm about to put a lot on the line and I need an idea of the possible outcome."

Pete responded, "Jim, no legal case is ever a sure winner, and I'd be remiss if I told you otherwise. But I feel that your situation and your case definitely has merit and is certainly worth exploring further."

I appreciated Pete letting me know that there were no guarantees here. I was aware of that already, but I liked how he explained it nonetheless. I also felt compelled to advise him at the same time that this case was NOT about money. IF I would go this route, I wanted him to know I was not undertaking it for financial gain. It was about protecting myself and making the BPD a better place to work for everyone. He told me that he liked my approach and he'd do his best to help me in this attempt to right the wrongs which were being committed there on seemingly a daily basis, especially against me. IF there was an award or judgment of any kind, well, that would be a bonus for us (as in one-third for him, two-thirds for me). But we both adamantly agreed that I would not have that as my singular goal. "Change," yes, but not cash. We concurred that this philosophy made the most sense at this time.

As we were wrapping up our meeting that afternoon, Pete asked me if I had taken any time off due to sickness or emotional stress or the like since this harassment campaign started. I told him I was never one to abuse my sick time and had taken very little of it for that reason; vacation and comp time, yes, but not sick time. Despite not missing much work due to illness, he asked me anyway if there were any ailments or physical issues bothering me during the recent past.

"Well, Pete, since you asked…there are these headaches. They're actually pretty bad sometimes. I usually suffer through them at work but then once I get home I have to go right to bed in my attempt to get rid of them. Sometimes it works, sometimes it doesn't. Aspirin or meds don't seem to help at all either."

Pete, who was taking copious notes the whole time, then asked me, "When did they first start?"

I answered, "Uh…about a year and a half ago."

"Okay," my lawyer responded, "probably not a coincidence either."

I nodded my head in agreement.

Before I walked out his door that day, Pete strongly suggested that I do two things during the next week. First, I should make an appointment with a neurologist and undergo a full examination for my chronic headaches. Second, I should go see a psychologist and get assessed for any mental health related issues.

"Whoa, Pete, what's going on at the PD is really bothersome and maybe, just maybe, the cause of these headaches, but I don't have any psychological problems. I mean, it's not like they're driving me nuts or anything like that."

"No one is suggesting that, Jim," my lawyer calmly explained, "but we need to explore every possible option here. IF we file this lawsuit, I want all our ducks in a row. And IF these headaches can be attributable to your daily workplace experience, it will only strengthen your case. And really, a psych eval is not out of the ordinary in a matter such as this. There may be something that shows up that can prove helpful to us in our case. So, you'll at least consider it, right?"

I agreed with Pete that I would "consider" his requests, even if somewhat reluctantly regarding the part about seeing the shrink. But he was now representing me, I was about to start paying him, so I guess

I should listen to the man. And I think it was the first time either of us used the word "lawsuit" with each other. We had sort of hinted around about it using terms like "taking civil action" and "beginning the legal process," but now the actual "L" word was out in the open. It was all of a sudden a bit overwhelming, and a bit scary.

Literally while shaking Pete's hand and saying goodbye that afternoon, I told him that I still wasn't sure I wanted to actually do this but I was glad we at least talked today. He was fine with my attitude as he said it was a healthy way to approach a very serious potential course of action. I told him I'd make the doctor appointments and I'd let him know the diagnoses as we said goodbye.

Of course, that evening I discussed all of this with my wife, Eileen. I wanted her on board too with whatever it is I, and we, would be doing here. She was supportive of this potential action, process, or even lawsuit as we started referring to it. She saw me with the headaches and knew there was something definitely wrong as I never had experienced anything like them before in my life. Quite frankly, she had already recommended that I see a doctor regarding this ongoing problem, but I kept putting her and it off. Now, I agreed, the time was right.

I happened to know of a certain psychologist in Philly. He did a lot of work with the Philadelphia PD and even (at least) one Bensalem cop who had confided in me that he had gone to him. He had an excellent reputation. So, I gave him a call and within a few days we met at his office.

During my first meeting, or I suppose "session," with the police psychologist, we simply talked. It seemed to go relatively well and he made me feel better about myself, all things considered as of late. He was concerned about my chronic headaches and was hoping between him and the neurologist we could find a way to minimize them, if not get rid of them completely.

I also remember very clearly what the shrink told me after our two hours together. He said, "Jim, from what I preliminarily see here, I can tell you that you're a normal person in a very abnormal situation. Not many people would have handled all you've been through as well as you have so far."

I replied, "Thanks…I guess."

The psychologist next wanted me to come back to his office and undergo some formal testing. I agreed to do so.

Regarding the neurologist, it took the better part of six weeks and numerous medical examinations such as MRIs, CAT scans, X-rays, or whatever the various type tests were called back then, all focused on my head. When the results came in, they were all negative. There was no physiological explanation for my headaches. That was the good news, but then what the hell was causing them? Well, I was about to find out.

With no apparent medical reason for my headaches, the neurologist then interviewed me for twenty minutes one morning. He got around to asking me, "Mr. Fitzgerald, are there any external factors in your personal life, work life, or other issues which could possibly be causing these headaches. You know, stress and related factors are known to cause headaches such as you've described to me."

"Well, Doc, have you ever heard of the Bensalem PD...?"

I went on to explain in a generic sense what my life was presently like for eight hours per day, forty hours per week, for the last twenty months.

The medical doctor's final diagnosis that day was, "Mr. Fitzgerald, I would suggest to you that since all your test results have produced absolutely no indication of brain damage, tumors, lesions, fractures, or anything of the sort, it is most likely your present workplace situation which is contributing to your headaches. If you can remedy that scenario somehow..."

"Thanks, Doc, I hear you loud and clear. I'm working on it. I appreciate your time."

It wasn't any real surprise to me, but I needed to hear it from a medical expert. I had little doubt that he was right on the money with what he told me.

Now it's confirmed...the f**kin' BPD and its leadership was causing me these ongoing headaches, taking valuable time away from me that I should otherwise have been spending with my family, friends, and living like a "normal" human being. This changes the entire paradigm. If I was hesitating before, now I MUST do something about it.

The last Saturday in September I travelled again to the psychologist's office in Northeast Philadelphia. He gave me two formal, written tests. They were the Minnesota Multiphasic Personality Inventory (MMPI) and the Clinical Analysis Questionnaire (CAQ). The shrink told me afterwards, even before he assessed the written tests, that I should immediately begin extended sick leave. He provided me a note for it.

As such, I started calling out sick every day starting the week of September 30th.

On October 4th, with my permission, the psychologist mailed a letter to both me and Pete Hileman. The shrink wrote a summary of my reasons for coming to his office, a brief history of what I've been experiencing at the BPD, and the results of my interview with him and of the two formalized tests.

The letter/report read, in part:

> "It is my opinion that Mr. Fitzgerald is a sincere and dedicated police officer who is telling the truth about what is happening to him."
>
> The document continued, "The results of the MMPI indicated that he is in a Paranoid state, which I believe is a direct result of his experiences in the police department. The results of the CAQ indicated that he is depressed, withdrawn, and feels persecuted. I recommend that he see a physician for possible (non-addictive) medication for the depression and to begin psychotherapy once or twice a week for the next few weeks. I do not believe that he should return to work for at least thirty days."
>
> (End of letter.)

I talked to Eileen, my wife, and Pete, my lawyer, after receiving this correspondence from the psychologist. I agreed to just one of his recommendations. I would take the time off. It would be three weeks of total sick leave.

I believe I met with the shrink one more time at his office. However, I never went the drug route. An occasional beer on occasional nights worked just fine for me in that regard. Especially during the three weeks that I was off. It was amazing how the headaches seemed to disappear during that timeframe…not one of them, as a matter of fact.

Regarding my time off, I called in sick every morning for those three weeks. I eventually turned in the generic note from the psychologist explaining nothing more than my ongoing headaches as the reason for my absence from the evidence custodian position for which I was "uniquely qualified." For obvious reasons, for present and future possible employment, I didn't want anything in writing at the BPD regarding "stress" or "depression" or even "paranoia" on my part.

The issue of "paranoia" was no doubt based on me telling the shrink that I KNEW I was being followed or monitored at various times by one or more of Zajac's goons on the BPD. I KNEW for fact they would cruise slowly past my house on my one block-long residential street in both marked and unmarked cars at times. I saw them or my wife saw them on my street on more than one occasion during the second half of 1985.

Other BPD officers, of the same non-Dark Side persuasion as me, also experienced these "drive-bys" at their respective homes. I suppose it was an attempt to determine who was visiting who in our alleged "conspiracy" to counter the Zajac regime, but these were also clear attempts to intimidate us at the same time.

It didn't work, not with me or my fellow officers who also happened to be on the goon squad tour guide. In fact, it only emboldened us. I enjoyed waving to the officers as they drove by my house a few times. I suppose telling a psychologist about these exact issues and incidents could possibly make one appear to be paranoid, even if they were actually happening in real life. Nonetheless, he dutifully noted it in his report.

As Joseph Heller wrote in his 1961 novel *Catch-22*, "Just because you're paranoid doesn't mean they aren't after you."

That would be me in 1985...well, sort of. Not clinically "paranoid" I would suggest, but very aware that there were people out to get me virtually every day of the week at every turn of the bend. I clearly have the memos and the drive-by sightings to prove it.

* * * * *

Several of my trusted fellow BPD colleagues and I were, in fact, taking turns meeting at our various homes to discuss political strategies during September and October of '85. The word of one or two of these rendezvous must have somehow leaked out within the department. It then became imperative for the Dark Side to determine just who was a part of this clandestine movement. They knew the leaders (me, Jerry Judge, John Knowles, other PBA officers) but they wanted to know of our more recent recruits. No doubt, Sonny and Rico from the Narco Squad were sent on these critical missions. Hey, they weren't making any arrests, so why not investigate their fellow officers during these off-duty house gatherings?

During these meetings we would joke among ourselves that we felt like members of the French Underground movement during World War II. Except it was Bensalem, not Paris. We weren't cutting phone lines or blowing up bridges and train tracks. We were instead putting together a master plan to get the present Vichy-like government out of power once and for all.

While there were numerous BPD officers very tired of this present regime, there were about fifteen of us "true believers" committed to actively overthrowing it. That's really all we needed. We approximately fifteen truth-believing officers, after several of these secret meetings at our various homes, came up with a master plan.

In *The Great Escape*, the officers in charge named their three separate tunnel projects as "Tom," "Dick," and "Harry." The fifteen or so of us co-conspirators casually referred to that movie and those three tunnels during our varied meetings. As such, we decided to undertake a three-prong approach to "confound and confuse" the Zajac government once and for all.

This tri-level strategy included the so-named "Operation Media," "Operation Get-Out-The-Vote," and the top-secret "Operation X," aka, Tom, Dick, and Harry. I told my fellow underground saboteurs that I will be with them in a supportive role for both "Op M" and "Op GotV" and provide any and all assistance I could. They knew that. But I also told them in no uncertain terms that they'd have to trust me with "Op X." It was so top-secret that I couldn't share the mission with anyone, not even these fifteen, the brain-trust of our newly formed cabal. They understood.

I learned from not getting chosen for a private sector job I had inter-viewed for a few months ago how loose lips do, in fact, sink ships. I wasn't risking this last phase of the three-part strategy to a leak of information.

Of course, Operation X was my pending lawsuit against the Township. I knew before too long exactly when I would be filing it. As much as I liked, respected, and trusted these other BPD officers, I couldn't risk that information getting out before the suit was officially signed, sealed, and delivered in Doylestown and served on the defend-ants themselves.

So, along with Jerry Judge, we delegated one team and one team-leader to be in charge of Op M and one team and one team-leader in charge of Op GotV. I would be solely in charge of Op X. They trusted me and believed me. "I appreciate that," I told them. "Now, let's get on Tom and Dick as they're critical to our success too. I'll take care of Harry."

Our underground group kicked around lots of ideas, but the one we settled on initially was what came to be called the "List of Complaints."

We talked among ourselves during several of these clandestine meetings and elicited further information from fellow officers between them. As a result, in late September and through official PBA channels, a documented litany of issues that had dogged the BPD since the inception of this new regime was released for all to read. Some were Chief Viola related, some were individual officer related, and some were general departmental morale related.

The PBA authored a first draft version of this document and placed several copies in the Patrol Division roll call room. A copy was also surreptitiously provided to one of the elected township Supervisors, George Ciotti. Oh, and one copy managed to find its way to the *Bucks County Courier Times* (BCCT), too. It was amazing how that seemed to happen sometimes....

An October 2nd, 1985 article in the BCCT concerning this early version of the "list of complaints," written by Staff Writer Joseph Grace read, in part, as follows:

> "A list of complaints by Bensalem police officers about the department's management has sparked a dispute between three township supervisors who have not seen the list and one who has.
>
> "The list, developed by officers who head the department's PBA, prompted Supervisor George Ciotti last week to propose that the township seek a management review of the force by the state Department of Community Affairs.
>
> "Ciotti's motion requesting the review died for lack of a second at last week's supervisors meeting. Other supervisors present were Chairwoman Mary Komada, Patricia Zajac and Peter Reed.
>
> "Komada said Tuesday she allowed Ciotti's motion to die because neither he nor police association leaders have provided her or her colleagues with a copy of the complaints.
>
> "'It's pretty hard to address something that nobody wants you to see,' Komada said.
>
> "Officer Jerry Judge, president of the PBA, said Tuesday the organization has decided to give the supervisors a copy of the complaints after the names of certain officers are deleted.

"Judge said those officers 'fear reprisal' from the department administrators if their names are left on the list submitted to the supervisors. He said the list would probably be provided by the end of the week.

"The complaints number about 35 and center on assertions that department officials use harassment and favoritism to manage the force, according to Judge and other police officers.

"However, other officers disagree the department is poorly managed under the administration of ...Zajac.

"'It's a handful of guys complaining,' Officer Charles Maddocks said after a recent PBA meeting to discuss the complaints and morale problems. 'We've got it good here.'

"Judge and others counter that their views are supported by a majority of the department. Judge said he expected the 55 to 60 members of the PBA to vote within the next few weeks on whether they support a DCA study.

"Zajac has declined to comment on the situation.

"...(Jerry) Judge criticized Komada for comments she made at the meeting with the PBA regarding the future of the department and its police officers.

"'She said,' 'If you don't like it here, quit,' Judge said. He said Komada also threatened to disband the department and have the township patrolled by the Pennsylvania State Police.

"Komada acknowledged she made the comments, but not in the context claimed by Judge."

(End of article.)

A revised and updated list, which was expanded to forty-five separate "complaints," was eventually provided to all five Township Supervisors. Multiple copies were also made available for our fellow police officers.

(See +Bonus Chapter 51a for the full "Complaints" document.)

There were a few iterations of this document, but the referenced version is the official one finally presented to our fellow officers, the Board of Supervisors, and yes, the media. Many of the specific "complaints" involve me. Quite frankly, that is because much of the top-down harassment of the last twenty months did, in fact, involve me. Specifically, complaints 15, 19, 20, 21, 22, 23, 24, 31, 32, and 33 related directly to my then-everyday existence at the BPD. (Most were written of here in earlier chapters.) Others, of course, related indirectly to me while some were specific to fellow officers and/or the department as a whole.

Interestingly, and actually humorous in some ways, when our team of operatives finally decided upon the forty-five official complaints, for various reasons we decided to "black out" four of them. It was for no truly strategical reason other than one was more or less repetitive to an earlier one, another involved an officer who decided at the last minute he didn't want his incident mentioned, one was a matter possibly going to civil court, and the last one contained a few simple typos. So, in a time before ready access to personal computers, word processors, and printers (the list was typed at someone's home on their electric typewriter), instead of a simple "delete" of the items to be removed, we merely used low-tech black electrical tape to cover the four unwanted entries. We then made multiple photocopies off that original.

The funny aspect of it all was when the final list was ultimately made public for all to read, the Dark Side members, while upset at the whole notion of the list itself, became even more openly distraught when considering the four deleted points. It was those blacked out items which several of them somehow felt could be even MORE damaging to their cause and they were adamantly concerned about those four entries eventually being un-deleted, or more accurately, un-taped.

I suppose each of these officers, including Zajac himself, wondered what lay beneath each piece of photocopied black electrical tape and if it involved something they did or said and would it/they be "outed" at some later time. It's amazing how the unknown can truly frighten some people, especially people with multiple skeletons already in their departmental closets.

* * * * *

With the "List of Complaints" as part of Operation Media, our secret group wanted to next launch Operation Get out the Vote. We did so in various ways. One was an agreement by at least twenty of us, from the fifteen true believers along with others we recruited, to begin engaging in active politicking for the three Republican (aka GOP) candidates running for Supervisor. As such, we commenced to contact literally every Bensalem registered voter we personally knew and asked, if not strongly suggested of them, to vote for the Republican candidates. Naturally, we explained why, too.

I made a lot of phone calls during the month of October just for this reason. Many of our respective spouses did too. Eileen called multiple friends and present and former work colleagues who lived in Bensalem and asked them to vote Republican on November 5th.

In terms of my own contacts, I had coached or served as an assistant coach on my son Sean's T-Ball and Little League Bensalem-based baseball teams for the last three years. I happened to save the roster of each team. On each roster were the parents' names and home phone numbers.

Well, guess who I called? If you guessed each and every one of them, you'd be correct. I did it off-duty, of course, mostly during the three weeks I was on sick leave. By the end of these multiple brief conversations, after asking each mom or dad how their child was doing, is he/she still playing ball, etc., I attained a verbal "Okay" from each parent that they would vote for the three candidates I suggested. As there were probably fifteen different kids on each team, each with a mom and a dad, that was ninety potential votes right there for the three candidates. I also asked them to advise their Bensalem-residing family members, friends, neighbors, and whoever else could legally vote to also consider pulling the lever for this trio of candidates. They liked me as a coach, knew I was the "friendly cop," and each assured me telephonically they would do so.

During this same period of time, I also attended various church and school functions (all after work hours or on weekends). While there, and engaged in casual conversation with the other parents, I unabashedly suggested to them before our little chats were over to please consider voting for the three Republican guys. No separation of church and state (or school) for me in these desperate times. My youngest, Dan, then three years old, was in a local daycare program. Yes, I petitioned all of those people too as I would see them before and after his afternoon class. I made sure not to go overboard or come across as a zealot, but as I got to know some of these people over the last year or two, the requests came to me quite naturally.

I know, I know...this is NOT what a police officer should be doing, off-duty or not. I had never undertaken such politically-oriented actions before and I can assure you, never afterwards. But the way I looked at it, if you're a Bensalem cop and you somehow got your spouse elected or appointed to an important political position (not to mention your daddy before that), then all was fair in love, war, and an election year for the rest of us.

One of my fellow officers in the Patrol Division semi-kiddingly told me in those weeks prior to the election that when he would conduct car stops, and it turned out the driver was a Bensalem resident, he would not issue him/her a traffic ticket if the person agreed right then and there to vote for the three Republicans running for office on November 5th. Naturally, the driver and sometimes even the passengers agreed; anything to avoid getting a ticket, right? I politely warned the officer that this sort of activity MAY be pushing it a bit, and perhaps he should stick to phone calls and other solicitations for votes when he's not actually working and in uniform. He laughed and said he'd "think about it." To this day, I'm not sure if what he told me was true or not. But if he didn't care, neither did I. Just get the vote out...and for the right three candidates.

There was a PBA meeting scheduled for late October, just a few weeks before the big election. As the List of Complaints was now out for all to read, there was a good deal of media coverage regarding it and other PD related issues (Operation Media), so the meeting was sure to generate a large turnout. As such, I came up with yet another idea for Op Get out the Vote. I got together with Jerry Judge a week or so before the planned meeting and strongly advised he consider it.

I suggested to the PBA President that we break precedent and invite some "outsiders" to our next meeting. That is, we ask each of the three Republican candidates and each of the three Democratic candidates to come to our meeting and agree to a question-and-answer session with us, the officers of the BPD. Jerry liked the idea and he went about to formally invite each candidate.

Interestingly, the three GOP candidates immediately welcomed the invite and jumped on the opportunity by agreeing to show up for our meeting. However, to a person, the three Democratic candidates refused to appear.

Hmmm...what does this decision in and of itself tell us about the Dem candidates? Who the hell are their political advisors?

The PBA meeting took place and it was a crowded event. It was relatively civil and the three Republican candidates answered each question put to them. There were some posturing and agenda-driven (if not pre-scripted) questions and comments on the part of the more vocal Zajac supporters, but they were put in their place by either the candidates themselves or fellow PBAers. Not everyone heard exactly what they wanted to hear that evening, but the three men running for elected office presented themselves as honest and firm in their beliefs, acknowledged that the PD had its problems, and fixes of some sort were necessary. At the end, Jerry Judge as well as most of the rest of us thanked them for taking the time and conveying their interest in the BPD and its issues. The same certainly couldn't be said for or to the three Dems who didn't even bother to show up that night.

I attended but was purposefully quiet at this PBA meeting. I was in touch with Pete Hileman on an almost daily basis at this time, and when I advised him of this meeting he encouraged me to go but also encouraged me to remain circumspect while there. We both knew that anything I would say publicly, and possibly in anger or frustration, could come back to potentially haunt me once my lawsuit was filed. So, I bit my tongue a few times that evening when certain Zajac supporters made certain statements or asked certain loaded questions. It was intelligent advice my lawyer gave me. What I had to say was indeed about to be yelled from a figurative mountaintop within days so it was prudent not to jeopardize any part of it at this meeting. I simply watched and listened…and took good notes.

It wasn't long before Joe Grace, the BCCT reporter, found out about the meeting. In fact, it was covered very prominently in the next day's newspaper. Someone had called him right after the meeting was over. (Apparently it was by someone who had taken good notes while there.) The story he wrote, while objective in topic and content, was very accurate. It certainly didn't make the Democratic candidates look very viable in their blanket refusal to even attend the meeting. That decision alone made the three of them appear to be uncaring and unresponsive to the important issues which concerned the BPD. Their no-show would not go unnoticed.

With examples each of Operation M and Operation GotV illustrated above (there were others, too), it was soon time for Operation X to be launched. I was somewhat anxious about it, but I knew it was the right thing to do. Well, I was hoping it was the right thing to do. If nothing else, I was absolutely positive the timing of it was right.

Hours and counting….

Chapter Fifty-Two

Calling out sick during the first three weeks of October proved to be a very smart decision on my part. It was an excellent recommendation by my short-term psychologist and slightly longer-term lawyer. And, as an extra added result, I had no headaches during this extended sick leave. It was the first time in well over a year that I went longer than three to four days without one of these debilitating head-throbbing events.

Now, to get rid of them for good....

During this time, I was still in contact with my fellow faction members as they would stop by the house or I would talk to them on the phone quite often. Me being absent WITH official leave didn't impede any of our concurrent operations either as I could do as much if not more in that regard while being away from the BPD for those twenty-one days or so. Yes, the freedom from both work and headaches at the same time allowed me to accomplish much in my ongoing personal, professional, and legal life.

Needless to say, it was great to spend extra time with my young sons, as well as take care of some interior home chores that I had been putting off for a while. I believe I painted two whole rooms of the house during those three weeks. I also wrote a paper for my current Villanova course, which I still managed to attend on its regular class nights once a week.

When calling out sick at the BPD, the policy was that the officer or employee was not supposed to leave his/her house for any reason during their scheduled shift except for, of course, medical appointments. So, between the hours of 8:00AM and 4:00PM, Monday through Friday, I stayed within the four corners of my property. After hours and during the weekends, I had no restrictions at all and did what I had to do in the outside world.

All things considered, my prolonged medical leave provided me with valuable time to spend with my family, friends, do house and school work...and oh yeah, plot, plan, and conspire the overthrow of a certain political party and its puppet police administration. You know, regular, everyday stuff that we just don't take the time often enough to do in our busy lives.

And...with my headaches non-existent during this timeframe, that's what I did. From after school Whiffle-ball games in the backyard with my two young sons, to parsing the final wording of a lengthy civil action with my attorney on the phone immediately afterwards, it made for a wonderful time for my kids and their future plaintiff-dad alike.

When finally back at work after this three-week reprieve, my batteries would be fully recharged and I'd be ready to face the enemy once again. I was actually looking forward to it because I knew what was coming right around the bend. They didn't, but I did. I had the advantage for once in this regard. It was a good feeling too, especially with no recent headaches to deal with.

Perhaps the Dark Side members would be feeling some head pain before too long. That was at least one of the motivations behind Harry, aka Operation X. Let's hope it works.

* * * * *

During one of the nights I was home on sick leave, I received a call from Jerry Judge. It was around 10:00PM. He seemed a bit disconcerted and off-kilter when he first got on the phone with me. That was unusual for the Jerry I knew. Remember, he's the guy who spent multiple rounds in the boxing ring toe-to-toe against both Larry Holmes and George Foreman, as well as other prizefighters. He was even stabbed in a bar fight yet kept punching away. I knew it took a lot to rattle his cage.

After first inquiring how I was feeling, Jerry asked if he could stop by my house so we could talk about something. He didn't want to discuss any of it on the phone. I told him, "Sure, come on over."

Jerry arrived at my place in his patrol car around 10:30. He initially stayed in the driver's seat until I came out to the curb to talk to him. Stepping outside the car on this mild and starry-skied fall evening, with his police radio crackling away in the background (although his sector was quiet), he began to relate to me the strange series of events which unfolded just a few hours before, and with two very unlikely people. I was all ears.

It seems Jerry was on his regularly scheduled 5P-3A shift this evening. After only an hour into it, around 6:00, he received a radio message to return to HQ. Once there, he was directed to go to Deputy Chief Zajac's office. As instructed, he walked back to CID where the office was located and knocked on the closed door. Upon being granted permission to enter he could see it was the Deputy Chief himself and the Bensalem Township Solicitor, that is, the lawyer for our town and, by extension, the Dark Side. His name was Emil Toften. He was one of several Bensalem lawyers. This administration seemed to require numerous legal practitioners for all they were attempting to undertake, overtake, do, and undo.

Without even being invited to sit down on one of Zajac's office chairs, Jerry was matter-of-factly told that the three of them were going for a ride together. He was made to feel that he essentially had no choice but to proceed with these two men on this particular evening to an as-of-yet unknown location. Jerry reluctantly agreed to do so.

Shortly afterwards, the trio got into the Deputy Chief's unmarked police car and drove. In doing so, as the car crossed the western boundary lines into Lower Southampton Township, exiting Jerry's normal patrol sector at the same time, he told me a feeling of dread came about him. He honestly believed there was a set-up of some sort in the works and that bad could only come of it. His instincts were not that far off.

"Just where are they taking me and for what reason?" Jerry later told me he was pondering along the way. He had his .357 Magnum and two potentially lethal fists at his immediate disposal, but he wasn't sure even these weapons would be of help to him tonight.

The three of them eventually arrived at an inconspicuous office building located outside of the township. It was the Solicitor's private business office. For some reason, Zajac and the lawyer felt that this meeting and their eventual conversation would be better suited for them if removed from within the jurisdictional lines of Bensalem. So, this was the place. As it so happened, the two others would do most of the talking as this meeting would progress. Jerry would do most of the listening.

After some basic pleasantries upon first walking into the law office, the conversation casually turned to Jerry's actions over the last few months as the PBA President. Once this topic was broached, according to Jerry, the conversation never went back to being pleasant again.

Before long Jerry was being told in no uncertain terms, mostly by Toften the lawyer but with Zajac the Deputy adding his own two cents when appropriate, of the potential problems Jerry was causing for himself and his family. Before fifteen minutes passed he had been strongly advised that his ongoing letter writing campaign and public statements to the media regarding what was happening within the BPD could, in fact, lead to serious career and legal ramifications for him. As in being sued, disciplined, fired and even (gulp) arrested.

"Oh, yeah?" Jerry later told me he said to them, "I want you to explain to me just what you mean by that. But first, where's your restroom?"

Jerry confided in me that night in front of my house that he was, in fact, getting a bit stressed during this triangulated approach from the two township politicians, well, with one of them supposedly a Deputy Chief of Police. However, he wasn't about to show it. He was being threatened by a potentially dangerous left-right combination, but he refused to let either of them land any punches. He'd parry their blows. He'd duck and weave. He'd lie on the ropes. That's what prizefighters do. That's why Jerry casually tried to change the subject and buy some time with a quick restroom visit. His counter-punching would come later.

End of round one.

Upon Jerry's return, the borderline polite but otherwise very stern and officious rhetoric on the part of the lawyer and the Deputy Chief continued through the next phase of the discussion. In so many words, Jerry was told to cease and desist his letter writing and BCCT reporter chats which were critical of Zajac's administration...or else! They even presented Jerry with a multi-page document of some sort for him to sign. It was written in lawyerly language in which he would agree to stop such allegedly subversive behavior toward the regime. Naturally, Jerry refused to sign it.

End of round two.

Emil Toften then cited some Pennsylvania civil statutes as well as the rules and regulations of the BPD disciplinary code in an attempt to explain where Jerry was going wrong. Jerry casually cited back the First Amendment of the U. S. Constitution, as in his right of free speech, etc., to explain to them where they were going wrong.

End of round three.

The attorney and his client were at a stalemate, a loggerhead, and going nowhere fast. A split decision in this bout just wouldn't work for them.

Jerry then described the end of the conversation as going something like...

"Officer Judge, you're missing the point here," Toften reminded the PBA President. "We don't want to actually sue, suspend, terminate, or arrest you. Really, we don't. Right, Ted?"

Zajac, seemingly caught off-guard, added, "No, Emil, of course not."

"But," the lawyer continued, "you've got to stop writing these letters and talking to the reporters. If not, you will face the gravest of consequences. Understand? That's why you should sign this document...to protect yourself."

Jerry simply retorted, "I hear ya. But I'm not signing your document. I'll find some other ways to protect myself."

End of round four.

"Well, Jerry, I then have one more question for you. Is it you writing the letters, or is it someone else? Now, if it's not you, and you tell us who's really writing them, well, that could be very helpful here in your case."

Lawyers are the very curious kind, aren't they?

Very demonstratively placing his large hands on the lawyer's desk and while looking directly at him, Jerry replied, "You know, as a reminder, Emil, a majority of the Bensalem officers elected me as their PBA President. I have a responsibility to them. So, I really can't make any promises to you of any kind at this point in time. I'll continue in the meantime to do as my fellow elected officers and I deem fit. And as my name is on the bottom of each of those letters, you can assume I am the one who authorized them. Is that helpful for YOUR case?"

"So," the lawyer quickly retorted, "when you say you 'authorized' them, does that mean you're their author? Or, do you mean it like you approved of them? This is important."

Jerry smiled at the both of them and simply responded, "Yes!"

DC Teddy Z. and Solicitor Emil T. looked at each other quizzically, whispered something when they thought Jerry wasn't paying attention, and then immediately suggested that they leave the premises.

End of round five.

In the car ride on the way back to BPD HQ, there was a chilling silence. Upon parking Zajac's police car and before Jerry exited the rear seat, the Deputy Chief turned around and asked him once again, "Jerry, who's writing the letters? I really want to know."

"I told you, I authorized them, each and every one of them. Understand? Goodnight, gentlemen. I have a sector to patrol for about five more hours. Thanks for the enlightening conversation."

End of round six.

Winner by TKO, Jerry Judge.

Within thirty minutes, the PBA President was at my house telling me the above story.

"Damn, Jerry, they really tried to intimidate and scare you, didn't they? Are you okay with all of this?"

"I'm fine. And yeah, they tried Fitz, but they didn't succeed, not at all. They have me really pissed-off though."

I empathized with Jerry, "I understand. Look, if you want to take a break from all of this…"

The PBA President interrupted me, "No, just the opposite… How about writing us a new letter. We're overdue. What, it's been about a week? And let's hit 'em hard, really hard! Make sure the Courier gets a copy too."

"I'm on it, Jerry. We'll figure out a topic or two. It's easy with these guys…."

Clearly, it took a much harder punch than either of these guys could deliver to beat "Irish" Jerry Judge. And he, make that we, were about to deliver a hell of a one-two punch ourselves in the next bout.

So, if it hasn't been surmised by now…I was, in fact, the ghost writer for the vast majority of Jerry's letters as PBA President. Not all of them, but most of them, especially during the months leading up to the election. He was very appreciative of it, too.

Jerry was (and remains) a smart guy as well as a good writer. (I know as I read many of his incident reports as his sergeant.) But he felt I had certain flair in making salient points, in painting vivid pictures, and doing it all in two pages or less on official PBA stationery. He would thus read what I wrote, officially "authorize" it, and sign it. Off to our fellow officers, the politicians, or the newspaper they would go…most times to all three entities.

We had quite a partnership going on at this time with Jerry as President and me, I suppose, as his chief speech writer. Actually, he did very well giving "speeches" on his own to the media and as PBA President. He didn't need any help in that arena. I was the guy putting his other words to paper, the written ones, each done in conjunction with my own words and my own set of papers which would appear shortly in the form of a lawsuit.

Yes, that would be Operation X.

* * * * *

In an October 28, 1985 edition of the BCCT, reporter Joseph Grace wrote the following article. It appeared in the paper's "Voter's Guide."

The headline read, "**Police interference flayed in Bensalem.**" In part, it read:

"Bensalem Supervisor Stephen Kelly is rarely seen in township political circles these days. He lives in Florida and flies north infrequently to attend township meetings. His term expires this year and he is not running for reelection.

"But the outspoken, blond-haired Kelly, a board veteran of 12 years, remains a focal point this fall in a pivotal election campaign for three supervisors' seats.

"'He is the single biggest issue I hear when I knock on voters' doors,' said Jack Maher, 48, an Andalusia businessman running as a Republican candidate for the board.

"Republican campaign leaflets claim the Democratic candidates, if elected, will hire Kelly as township manager, a position he applied for earlier this year.

"The three Democratic candidates opened an interview by raising the Kelly issue and heatedly denying they would hire him.

"'The Republicans are trying to push their dirty linen into the Democratic camp,' said James Pallante, 44, a department store executive sales manager and Democratic candidate.

"None of the six candidates for three board seats said they would consider Kelly for the manager's position.

"Running with Maher on the Republican ballot are Joseph Francano Jr., 44, a tire store manager who is chairman of the township water and sewer authority, and Paul Rauer, 31, an attorney.

"Pallante's Democratic running mates are Jane Pasqualone, 47, a Bensalem school bus driver and widow of Supervisor Nicholas Pasqualone, and John Wolaniuk, 40, who manages a family-owned concrete company.

"...Other issues raised in the campaign include the management of the township police department...

"Allegations by some police officers that department administrators use harassment and favoritism to control the 67-member force have led those officers to request a management study by the state Department of Community Affairs.

"While the department's rank-and-file officers and the supervisors debate the need for a DCA study, the situation has become a campaign issue. All six candidates said they would request the study, but cited varying reasons.

"...In addition, the question of who should run the department – Deputy Chief Zajac or ex-Chief Viola – remains an issue despite five years of divisive debate.

"...Pallante and Wolaniuk supported the firing, but Pasqualone said she lacked information to take a position, noting the hearings that led to the dismissal (of Viola) were private. The three said they preferred a court ruling to decide the case.

"Francano and Rauer took a more conciliatory stance, saying they would discuss a settlement of the case with Viola's attorneys if elected. They declined to state if they wanted Viola to return as chief.

"Maher said he, too, preferred a judicial ruling to decide the issue. If Viola won on appeal, he said he would welcome him back as chief. If he lost, Maher said the post should be opened to all interested parties, including Zajac."

(End of BPD-related portion of article.)

So goes the fundamental issues in Bensalem as per the BCCT voter's guide, just one week prior to the election. It's only a few days before yet additional articles, and a highly damning editorial, would be found in the same newspaper. My name would be prominently mentioned in each of these. It would be for reasons soon to be obvious.

Chapter Fifty-Three

After three headache-free weeks on sick leave, I came back to work on the morning of Monday, October 21st. I wrote in my notes from that day that no supervisor of any rank asked me how I was feeling, how I was doing, or the like. There was not even the elevated in volume, screechy, almost desperate voice of the Deputy Chief asking "JIM FITZGERALD, HOW THE HELL ARE YOU?" from twenty feet or so away. For whatever reason, I didn't see Zajac that week. I'm sure if he had been around, I would have heard him, and all too loudly.

Management's overall lack of sympathy was really no surprise to me, but you'd think even a smidgen of humanity would have been found within just one of these so-called leaders and they would have said something remotely kind to me. But, believe me, my feelings weren't hurt. In fact, it only served to reinforce for me the type of environment in which I was presently working and the personal and professional demeanors of people presently running the show.

By that Wednesday, I received a memo from Capt. Hughes instructing me that starting the following Monday I would be on a 3:00PM to 11:00PM shift through that Friday, November 1st. As Jack Robinson was now back at work and assigned those hours, it was so ordered that I would work the same shift as him for one week. Yet another schedule change for me. I remained the only employee in all of Bensalem Township, police or otherwise, whose schedule was changing as frequently and without notice.

I'm not sure of the precise reason why I was put on these evening hours for five days. Maybe it was so the Dark Side operatives could watch me and Jack easier, especially as the big election was the very next week. They would be too late though. I'd be taking a half-day off during this first week back to conduct official business with someone. My wife would be accompanying me too.

That official business involved Eileen and I travelling to Pete Hileman's Doylestown law office to review the final version of the nineteen-page complaint attached to my lawsuit. Upon both of us reading it and approving of every word in it, we signed it. Pete then asked me one more time if I was positive that this is what I wanted to do. Eileen and I looked at each other and agreed simultaneously, "Yes, we're doing it!"

(Pete had explained in an earlier phone call to both me and Eileen that including the two of us as plaintiffs made perfect legal sense. After all, both of us were directly affected by the actions of the BPD management and the various politicians. As such, each of us would be suing the parties involved and thusly both had to sign the complaint's "Verification" page. So, we did.)

Pete then advised us, "Okay, it'll be filed first thing tomorrow. It may take a day or two to make its way through the various courthouse channels, but the eleven named defendants will receive their certified letters by week's end. At that time, the media will be aware of it too."

I then officially advised Pete that I wanted him to call reporter Joe Grace of the BCCT and provide him with a formal press release regarding my legal action. I authorized him to do so immediately upon the official filing. He said he would call the journalist within an hour of it being duly filed in the courthouse. He'd fax him a copy of the lawsuit, too.

That was it. Decision made. There was no going back.

Interestingly, there were no qualms or second-guessing at all on my part or Eileen's part. I actually felt a relief of sorts as the tedious work involved in preparing this lawsuit was now over. It was now in the hands of the court and the lawyers and out of mine. Knowing this, I still didn't have a clue as to where it would take me. I hadn't the foggiest notion of its end results. I didn't even know if it would make things better or worse for me at the BPD. But I did know absolutely, positively, it was the right thing to do and this was the right time to do it.

Someone had to take a stand, and a legal stand at that, against this mob mentality which currently ran the BPD and the Township. The Dark Side and their political cronies pushed me to this. Now it was time to push back, and do so in a way which would inflict the most damage upon them possible. That was certainly my goal, anyway.

Operation X was now officially launched. It would further enhance and facilitate Operations Media and Get-out-the-Vote. That was one of its purposes. The timing of it wasn't by chance.

Borrowing again from *The Great Escape*, the figurative tunnels Tom, Dick, and Harry, couldn't have opened up at a better time. The days where many of us in the BPD were forced to "...tamely submit, knuckle under and crawl..." were over. It was time to cause our own "stink" in this "Reich" of theirs.

* * * * *

It didn't take long. On the morning of Wednesday, October 30, in the *Bucks County Courier Times*, front page above the fold, the following article appeared. It was written by reporter Joseph Grace.

"Sergeant files lawsuit against Bensalem police."

"A Bensalem police sergeant has filed a lawsuit against his department and the township supervisors, alleging his superiors have harassed him and hindered his career because of his perceived allegiance to former Police Chief Richard Viola.

"Sgt. James Fitzgerald, a nine-year department veteran, filed the lawsuit Friday in Bucks County Court against the supervisors, the department, and five police administrators, including Deputy Chief Theodore Zajac, Jr.

"The complaint alleges that under Viola, Fitzgerald was promoted to sergeant after placing first in competitive testing, and eventually became supervisor of the department's criminal investigations division.

"Viola was suspended by the supervisors in January 1984 for alleged misconduct. Zajac then assumed command of the force and 'singled out' Fitzgerald for reprisals because of his perceived allegiance to Viola, the lawsuit claims.

"Fitzgerald was removed from the investigations unit and transferred to patrol duty. He was suspended without pay for three days this spring on 'unsubstantiated' charges, the complaint says. The suspension was later reduced to a written reprimand by Zajac.

"Fitzgerald's attorney, Peter Hileman, a former prosecutor in the Bucks County district attorney's office, said his client's career was 'on the rise based on merit and accomplishment,' but that his fortunes reversed 'dramatically' after Zajac assumed command.

607

"The lawsuit, which seeks more than $20,000 in damages on each of (nine) counts, also says the supervisors were aware of the alleged harassment of Fitzgerald and did nothing to counter it.

"Zajac declined to comment on the lawsuit, saying he had not yet received a copy. Township Solicitor Emil Toften said he also had not seen the complaint, but termed it 'laughable.'

"'It's a political lawsuit,' Toften said. 'I believe it to be a spurious-type suit entered without reflection.'"

(End of article.)

Interesting that the well-paid Township Solicitor, Emil Toften, "had not seen the complaint," yet could still find it "laughable" and somehow know it is "political," a "spurious-type," and "...without reflection."

I always wondered about the "reflection" a guy like Toften would see when looking at himself in the mirror every day. Perhaps that was "laughable" too, but he just never realized it.

As by design, the lawsuit specifically referenced the BPD, the Bensalem Board of Supervisors, as well as individually naming DC Zajac, Capt. Hughes, Lt. Eckert, Lt. Dechant, Lt. Walsh, and elected Supervisors Komada, Zajac, Reed, and Kelly. These actions were brought against the latter persons "individually" as well as in his/her official "capacity" as a member of Bensalem police management or as an elected official.

After the "Parties" were named and described, and the "Facts" were listed, the following "Causes of Action" were then enumerated:

"Count I – Intentional Infliction of Emotional Distress; Count II – Interference with Employment Relations; Count III – Intentional; Count IV – Defamation; Count V – Injurious Falsehood; Count VI – Civil Rights Action; Count VII – Conspiracy; Count VIII – Breach of Contract; Count IX – Loss of Consortium."

Virtually all of the "Causes" as referenced above have been enumerated upon in the preceding chapters of this book to one degree or another. From Hughes "ordering" me to fix a ticket, to him calling me a liar in front of the various Board of Supervisor members, to each of Zajac's, Eckert's, Walsh's, and Dechant's separate or coordinated harassment events, they were all included.

I was on a 3:00PM – 11:00PM shift the day my lawsuit hit the newspaper. Before work that day, I received repeated phone calls at home from my friends and colleagues on the BPD. They were calls of congratulation, gratification, and appreciation for finally someone taking the bulls by their respective horns and trying to rid the place of all the accumulated...well, bullshit.

A few insiders to the cause asked me that day, "So THIS was Operation X/Harry, right?"

I told them it was. They now understood the secrecy up until this time.

I thanked each caller before he or she hung up but individually reminded them that our job was not yet done. Operation X now had to fully meld into the existing Operations Media and Get-out-the-Vote. They concurred and all agreed that we would keep making phone calls and suggesting to Bensalem voters what lever to pull next Tuesday. Again, this was NONE of our previous styles as police officers, but it was necessary, make that absolutely critical, to the future of this township and its citizens, not to mention the overwhelming majority of its cops.

When I came into work at 3:00PM on the day the lawsuit went public, I was met right away by Capt. Jack Robinson. He was all smiles, shook my hand, patted me on the back, and had nothing but positive things to say to me. He consciously wanted to undertake a public and demonstrative acknowledgment of what I had just done. It showed to anyone who witnessed it in HQ that day he was in solidarity with me regarding the filing. That was a great feeling too.

As I had even kept my pending lawsuit a secret from Jack, he was as surprised as anyone this morning to read of it in the newspaper. He asked me if Viola had known about it in advance. I responded, half-smiling, "No, not a person was told of it. This was a top-secret mission all the way."

Jack reaffirmed to me that keeping quiet was the right way to go about it. I concurred as we began working on the various and mundane evidence closet issues.

That afternoon and evening, a few other officers and detectives came up to me and shook my hand, telling me "good job," and the like. Some of them would look around first, just to make sure there were no bosses nearby before they said anything to me. (After all, the "idle conversation" memo had never been officially rescinded.) I didn't blame them but I certainly didn't care who heard me say what. Interestingly, none of the named defendants was seen by me that afternoon or evening. Not a one. Geez, if I knew I could have gotten rid of them this easily, I would have filed the suit eighteen months earlier.

Regardless of who was or wasn't there that day it was nice to be teamed up with Jack again. His sore back was mostly healed and he was ready and able to be here doing what he was paid to do. That is, digging through filing cabinets, a messy closet, and a truck-trailer counting and itemizing pieces of evidence. Oh, and with a sergeant at his side too.

Clearly, this was not the most effective utilization of higher-paid BPD management members, but then this administration never pretended to be effective; or efficient, for that matter. Why would they start now?

On Friday, November 1st, the *coup de grace* for the Dark Side, the existing Board members, and the three Democrats running for office, reared its beautiful head (in my opinion) in the form of the lead editorial in the *Bucks County Courier Times*. It read:

> **"With eyes wide open"**
> "The writing was on the wall. But since the Bensalem supervisors simply closed their eyes to the problems brewing inside their politically ravaged police department, they now have what ought to be an eye-opening lawsuit to contend with.
>
> "The suit was filed by Sgt. James Fitzgerald, a nine-year veteran of the police department. According to the suit, Fitzgerald has been 'singled out' for reprisals because of his perceived allegiance to former Chief Richard Viola.
>
> "Fitzgerald's accusations should come as no surprise to the supervisors; other officers have lodged similar complaints. Though they didn't do so by name – something the supervisors spitefully used to discredit the grievances – they did make their fears known through the Police Benevolent Association. Clearly, that should have been enough for the supervisors to do something.
>
> "The PBA's request that they launch a management study of the department seemed to make sense. It would

have indicated some attempt by the supervisors to clear up the problems – if indeed any exist. And it might have precluded the filing of a lawsuit by an officer who feels he has nowhere to turn.

"Instead, the request was all but ignored by the supervisors with the exception of George Ciotti. The reason clearly had more to do with politics and less to do with good government.

"The election-minded supervisors responsible for Viola's firing and his current replacement can ill-afford the political cost of a study that might seriously question their judgment and criticize their actions. The candidates they hope will join them in maintaining control of township would be dirtied by this process.

"So doing the best thing for taxpayers – not to mention a police department alleged to have serious morale problems – took a back seat to what would best serve the political objectives of Bensalem's power-hungry supervisors. This, no matter what it might cost taxpayers in the way of court settlements, legal fees and police protection.

"That's why Bensalem taxpayers need to take a closer look at the candidates seeking their votes on Tuesday. Electing more of the same will only doom the township – and the people who pay the bills – to more divisiveness and the inevitable lawsuits and legal fees that kind of mentality brings.

"For starters, voters ought to be wondering why the Democratic candidates refused to attend a question-and-answer session sponsored by the PBA earlier this week. Their official response – that the police department shouldn't be involved in politics – doesn't wash.

"As employees of the township – and in some cases, residents – cops have a right to know where their would-be bosses stand, especially on their request for a management study. Spurning the invitation was far from an indication that the candidates are interested in good relations with the largest department in township government.

"This gives us cause for concern, as it should voters. The message here is succinct: Don't go to the polls without a clear understanding of what's at stake."

(End of editorial.)

Wow! I couldn't have said it, or written it, any better. The objective, anonymous editor hit the nail, actually multiple nails, right on their respective heads. While he or she was certainly supportive of me and my lawsuit, the best part of the whole editorial in my humble estimation was that it ran just five days before this very meaningful election. And it specifically advised "taxpayers...to take a closer look at the candidates seeking their votes Tuesday. Electing more of the same will only doom the township...."

Well said, well written, well timed.

The expressed editorial opinions were the precise points I was hoping to make with Operation X, and precisely to be so enumerated just days before the big election. Once again, not a coincidence, I can assure you.

Timing is everything, they say. Those who say that are one hundred percent correct.

Now, it was just waiting some time for the election results to come in on Tuesday night. That night couldn't come soon enough.

Chapter Fifty-Four

November of 1985 would be one crazy month in Bensalem Township, Pennsylvania; much of it involving the police department. And you probably thought the craziness quotient there had already peaked. Well, it hadn't. Not by a long shot.

This craziness began on election day, the first Tuesday of the month....

I voted right after work on November 5th. (I was back on 8AM – 4PM shift by then. Yes, another schedule alteration for me, but an expected one this time.) My polling location was at Bensalem High School, which was a relatively short distance from my home. After getting changed into my civvies, I brought my dog Mickey with me for the walk there. I tied him up outside while I went in and performed my civic duty.

While at the voting location, taking my time walking there, hanging around a bit, and taking my time walking home, I saw a number of people with whom I was familiar. They were neighbors, fellow St. Ephrem School and Church members, parents of former little leaguers, and other individuals I knew from my eight-plus years living in Bensalem. If they were observed heading towards the voting area and I knew them, I casually suggested to them once again for whom they should consider voting. If I saw them heading out of the area, I casually asked them if they remembered to vote for the candidates I had mentioned to them in the weeks before.

Every single person responded to me in a friendly manner and in the affirmative that afternoon. That was good enough for me. Having my cute little dog with me didn't hurt either. And yes, if Mickey had been eligible to vote that day, he would have pulled the lever for the three GOPers. His dog-sense would have told him as much.

Just to make it perfectly clear here, and despite how it may seem, I wasn't working at the polls that day. I wasn't officially working for any one party or any one candidate during this particular election cycle. Police officers by law are not permitted to do so in the U. S. (Or at least they shouldn't be doing so in the U. S.) However, merely on my walk there and my walk back, if I saw someone I knew, I would talk to them and off-handedly mention their voting options to them. Most of them I had spoken to on the phone well prior to election day. I trusted them to do the right thing on this, the actual election day.

It seems the people I talked to that day did the right thing, at least as far as I was concerned from my informal entrance/exit polling. Or, they were pretty good liars. Time would tell, of course. Specifically, in about six hours from when Mickey and I left the high school/voting area to walk home. It would seem like six dog years for me as that afternoon into evening into night dragged on like molasses going uphill. I'm sure Mickey felt the same way too.

I'd like to make one more political related point very clear here. It is important for me to convey at this juncture. When I write of the three Republican and the three Democratic candidates in the 1985 Bensalem Township elections, I must add that these six people and their respective parties had little, if anything, to do with the policies, philosophies, ideologies, or platforms which many voters back then associated with either the GOP or the Dems. As in many local elections in the U. S., certainly in 1985 Bensalem, they are/were parties of opportunity and expediency for each candidate. Perhaps one or more of the candidates would happen to subscribe to some or all of the political viewpoints of the national party or even the state party, but that was certainly not a requirement or even expected of them at the local level in Bensalem. These six ran in the two parties which recruited them, which happened to be the one to which they were previously registered. They then sought the votes from their electorates accordingly, with local issues as the primary (if not only) factors in their respective campaigns, certainly more so than anything on the national parties' platforms.

In closing here, no matter what one's political affiliations may be then or now, i.e., Democrat, Republican, liberal, conservative, libertarian, or something else altogether, I want to emphasize that the two party choices back in the mid-1980s in Bensalem had little to do with the ideologies of either party as they existed then, or for that matter, today. In other words, it was politics as usual in 1985 Bensalem, that being very local politics, with issues of national relevance rarely, if ever, even mentioned.

Besides word of mouth, as in knowing someone in a particular candidate's office or higher up at the party level (of which I didn't know either), the only way I or many others in Bensalem could monitor the election results in almost real-time on that Tuesday evening was via AM radio. This would be done by tuning into a particular small-wattage local station with the call letters WBCB. It was located at 1490 near the far end of the dial. I had found in the past that reception for this station could be dicey on even the clearest of nights and knew it was best to have an external antenna of some variety to better pick up the sometimes static-filled transmissions. I managed to jury-rig one that evening consisting of a clothes hanger, bell wire, and aluminum foil. It worked…well, mostly.

I recall very well on this election evening putting my two sons to bed, turning off the television, and then moving around to different windows within various rooms of my house with my boom-box style AM-FM radio/cassette player with modified antenna in hand in an attempt to obtain the best reception possible. Naturally, I was tuned into WBCB in my attempt to learn of the election results relating to Bensalem Township. The station covered news, sports, and politics throughout most of Lower Bucks County, but I was only interested in what was happening election-wise in Bensalem on this night. So were my BPD colleagues I knew who were either working their shifts or listening at their homes to the same reporters over the same radio airwaves as me.

It took until about 11:00 that night, three hours after the polls closed, but the news finally found its way through the twin speakers of my portable radio. What I heard then and there was difficult to understand or distinguish at first. I wanted what I was hearing to be repeated several times as the station tended to fade out for crucial descriptive soundbites as the wind, solar flare-ups, or some other invisible meteorological condition briefly interfered with the radio waves at just those crucial times. I can still recall at least twice that night certain mid-sentence key words being wholly indecipherable by me. In fact, they were absolutely critical key words that I just couldn't quite make out, yet on which everything depended.

I can almost still hear the on-air WBCB reporters broadcasting something like, "…And in Bensalem tonight, the...(static)…-idates have swept the ticket with all three being elected to office…" Okay, it was a sweep! That's good to know! But WHICH party's "-idates" swept? Damn! This is tortuous!

Ultimately, with my make-shift antenna stuck outside a partially open upstairs bedroom window, I was pretty sure I finally understood and comprehended the on-air reporters and what they were conveying. But I still made a phone call to confirm it. I had to know for sure.

I recalled over prior years seeing the iconic black and white photograph from 1948 of Harry Truman holding up the front page of a newspaper with its headline reading "Dewey Defeats Truman." Of course, the incumbent Truman won that U. S. presidential election against Thomas E. Dewey. The *Chicago Daily Tribune* had called it wrong. Needless to say, I did NOT want the media equivalent happening here in Bensalem in 1985 if WBCB somehow also called it wrong. I needed proof. I needed confirmation. I needed it from a reliable source, or people with connections to a reliable source. So, I made those calls to people who knew people in Bensalem politics. One of those calls sealed the deal.

That news was, that proof was, that confirmation was…the radio reporters had called it right. It was, in fact, a sweep. It was a Republican sweep. The three GOP candidates, Jack Maher, Joe Francano, and Paul Rauer won, and won big. Actually, how big they won didn't even matter. Even if it was by one vote each, it made no difference at all. But, as it so happens, they beat out their Democratic Party rivals by relatively large margins. That was all I needed to hear. That was all my underground BPD colleagues needed to hear. That's all the concerned citizens of Bensalem needed to hear, or read, in the next day's newspaper.

THEY WON!

WE WON!

The good guys, certainly in my estimation, were about to regain the upper hand in Bensalem and at the BPD. The other guys, well, they tried and they failed…miserably. They had the reins for almost two years now, twenty-two long months to be exact, but their end was nigh. Their style of management by non-objective objectives just didn't pan out for them. And interestingly enough, we wound up beating them at their own game; that being, Politics. (Yes, with an upper-case "P.")

The voters got it right this time. All of our team's pre-election hard work paid off. Operation Media, Operation Get-out-the-Vote, and my own Operation X (aka Tom, Dick, and Harry) delivered in just the ways we hoped they would. The strategies employed by our little faction, really only about a dozen police officers with some late-arriving reinforcements, working off-duty and behind the lines, managed to alter the politics of Bensalem Township and its police department… well, possibly forever. Not a small accomplishment considering the well-entrenched political juggernaut we were going up against in the Kelly/Zajac machine.

But it was official…Bensalem's poor man's Napoleon had met his political Waterloo. Zajac, and his fellow abusive minions, along with their collaborative do-nothings and know-nothings, were about to be neutralized, removed, put out to pasture, exiled, or…well, pick your metaphor. It couldn't have happened to a more deserving bunch of guys.

With the excitement of it all, a late evening champagne toast with Eileen, patrolmen and detectives stopping by my house to do high-fives, phone calls going until almost 1:00 AM, and my overall internal adrenalin rush, I didn't get much sleep that night. It didn't matter. I was up at 7:00AM, bright eyed and bushy tailed once again for the first time in a long time.

Coming into work that next day at 8:00 was truly a memorable experience for me. It's like I had been reinvented, rejuvenated, even reborn, certainly from a professional standpoint. Others around me in HQ felt the same way. Well, not all of them, of course. A few of their tails weren't bushy at all, and solidly between their legs. You can surmise by now who they may be.

I saw Deputy Chief Zajac later that morning. To his credit, he made it into work, albeit not until around noon. Funny, when we eventually crossed paths there was no impersonal, snarky, across-the-room, way-too-loud greeting from him. Not even a mumbled barely-there acknowledgment of me. He also looked like he hadn't slept very well overnight; perhaps for different reasons than me though.

Well, for his sake, at least Zajac's wife still held her elected office as her supervisor's seat hadn't been in contention. However, she will shortly be part of a two-person Board minority. That will be different for her, and her husband. What the heck; maybe our illustrious leader will find a way to get his father back into politics, or an aunt, uncle, sibling, or some other family member, and attempt once again to reverse his mostly self-inflicted misfortunes.

Or…maybe the DC won't have to wait that long. Maybe there was something in the works already among these political lame ducks and their co-conspirators at the top of the BPD rotten food chain. I know these people. I know them, unfortunately, all too well. Something tells me that they won't be going down without one last fight. Even if it

617

makes absolutely, positively, no sense at all, in any way, shape or form, fiscally, legally, or politically. If it benefits them personally, professionally, financially, and/or egotistically, they'll do it despite the short-term or long-term costs to everyone else.

Just remember who we're dealing with here, having recently met their "Waterloo" or not. Nothing should be a surprise by now. And within weeks we'll all know just what their next move would be. It would shock even the more jaded among my colleagues.

No, their strain of "stink" in the BPD wasn't completely gone yet. Not if the Dark Side/Reich could help it in the dying throes of the Kelly/Zajac administration.

Be prepared to hold your figurative nostrils even tighter for a while.

* * * * *

Speaking of a "stink," the next few days in the BPD reminded me of being in a morgue. The Dark Siders were either out sick, not in the office, or behind multiple closed doors. It was not a good time for them. Not at all....

Just for kicks, I brought in a *Bucks County Courier Times* the day after the big election and left it on top of my evidence office desk in the sergeant's office. It merely sat there, bold headlines up, positioned in such a way that anyone walking in the roll call room by the office could clearly see the article about who won and who lost the election. I placed the paper at the same corner of my desk as the "idle conversation/don't talk to me" sign from circa six weeks before. I was hoping the irony would be obvious to all, to include, "Yes, you can talk to me once again."

Later that same afternoon, when I was out of my office for a short bit of time, someone came in and removed the newspaper. It was "Deja vu all over again" (thanks, Yogi Berra), with no doubt a newly and severely depressed Dark Side member secretly taking it upon himself to remove what he saw as an offensive piece of paper from my desktop. Hmmm...did Det. Donson come in and rip it up and stuff it in my trash can? No, all the wind was now out of his sail; it probably was not him. I also wondered if I'd be getting another memo from the Deputy Chief telling me how I exercise bad judgment in putting these type documents on my desk.

Actually, forty-eight hours later I did receive a memo from ol' Teddy boy himself. What a difference a day or two makes, not to mention a lawsuit, and an election which didn't exactly go his way.

618

The aforementioned memo was to me, from Zajac, still unsigned/ un-initialed, and read,

> "You will work with Captain Ronald Traenkle to produce a new performance evaluation form to be utilized by the department. Please meet with me on Thursday, 14 November, at 1500 hours with your preliminary ideas and paperwork."
> (End of memo.)

What?!?!? Me? Traenkle? Both of us actually assigned to do something by this regime NOT demeaning, NOT beneath our pay grade, NOT involving most of my workday in sauna-like conditions in a dilapidated truck-trailer? This was too good to be true. Or, was it?

Traenkle and I talked about our alleged new "assignment" a bit before our meeting with the Deputy Chief. I told him in one of my recent grad courses at Villanova we had spent several classes on the topic of performance evaluations in the corporate world, government agencies, and the like. He knew I even wrote a paper on the topic and we agreed that I should bring it in and give Zajac a copy during the scheduled meeting.

("A" and "Excellent work, Jim" were written on the front page by the professor when he returned it to me. I left these remarks on the copy for the Deputy Chief to see. I'm sure he would have graded it differently, of course. That is, if he would even bother to read it.)

Traenkle and I had the meeting in Zajac's office on the 14th of November. It was very routine, perfunctory, and polite. It lasted no more than ten minutes with both Traenkle and me officially assigned to come up with a workable evaluation form to replace the all but useless one we had for years around the department. (Viola had talked to me when he was still in charge about devising a new one, but when he was summarily canned so was that project idea.)

During the brief meeting that day, I knew it was killing Zajac to exhibit such self-control in his very office in the company of the very people who he knew wanted to rid him from his very position. It was even tougher in that he knew we were both very obviously elated about the election results of barely eleven days ago. We maintained our professionalism, of course, but our elation was clearly simmering under the surface, and he saw it. Nonetheless, the lame duck DC playacted his role very well; in fact, almost too well. It's as if he actually cared about this issue of performance evaluations and, for that matter, the police department itself.

Both Traenkle and I agreed upon leaving his office that he was up to something. He was being TOO nice, TOO approachable, TOO, well, unZajac-like. Of course, he knew anything he said to me or wrote to me in a memo could potentially be additional evidence against him in civil court down the line. I'm sure the township solicitor (the one who finds things he does not read "laughable") told him to handle me with kid gloves and treat me fairly; again, even if it was ripping him apart inside.

My lawsuit never came up during our brief meeting that day. It's as if it was never filed and Zajac was never one of my defendants. But it was filed, the local newspaper wrote a scathing editorial about it right afterwards, and the election results followed. The three issues weren't unrelated. Zajac knew this, I knew this, and inside it was tearing him apart, especially during those ten minutes I sat across from him in his office discussing the mundane subject of officer performance evaluations. I believe for the first time, the Deputy Chief evaluated MY performance around the BPD in a different light, and he didn't like this version any better than the past ones.

* * * * *

Things began to make sense about one week later on a Monday evening. That's when the boom came down; that being the political boom on an already ravaged police department. Like many of us suspected at the time, Zajac and company were doing some plotting and planning of their own. They were not going down without a fight. The combined forces of the Dark Side had worked too hard by means of various political machinations to attain positions they otherwise couldn't earn or didn't deserve. They couldn't simply quit now because of some "stupid" election results. They had barely six weeks left of their Board of Supervisors majority. They weren't about to let that month and a half go to waste without gettin' what's due to them.

So came the Board meeting of November 18, 1985.

On November 19, the front page BCCT headline, with story by Joseph Grace, read as follows:

> **"Bensalem makes Zajac chief, promotes 6 other policemen."**

"In a sweeping series of moves in its police department, the Bensalem supervisors Monday night elevated Deputy Chief Theodore Zajac, Jr. to chief and promoted six other officers.

"The promotions, approved for the most part by four board members, two of whom leave office in January, drew criticism from three supervisors-elect who will take seats on the board next year.

"'I'm disappointed,' said Jack Maher, elected earlier in November to a six-year term. 'This has to cause dissension within the department. Guys were passed over who were more qualified.'

"The supervisors who approved the promotions disagreed. 'I think we promoted the people who were most qualified for the positions and who have acted in the positions for more than a year,' said Supervisor Stephen Kelly, a 12-year board veteran whose term ends in January.

"An ally of Zajac, Kelly flew back from Florida, where he works as an urban planner, to attend the meeting and vote for the appointments. Board Chairwoman Mary Komada and Supervisor Peter Reed joined Kelly in voting for Zajac.

"Supervisor Patricia Zajac, the chief's wife, abstained from voting for her husband's appointment, but joined with Kelly, Komada and Reed in approving these other promotions.

* Lts. Robert Eckert, Thomas Walsh and Robert Dechant were promoted to captain. The promotions leave the 67-member department with six captains and no lieutenants.

* Acting Sgt. William Thompson and Detective Joseph Dunner were promoted to sergeant.

* Officer David Clee was promoted to detective.

"Supervisor George Ciotti, who along with Kelly and Reed will leave office in January, voted against all the promotions, calling them a 'prearranged charade.'

"For Zajac, 42, a 20-year department veteran, the appointment was the culmination of five years of struggle with township politicians.

"... 'After what my family went through, I'm not elated, but I'm glad it's over with,' Zajac said after his appointment. 'I can't put into words what my family went through while I was the target of politicians.'

"Zajac acknowledged that he met with the three Republican supervisors-elect two weeks ago to discuss what would happen if the lame-duck board appointed him as chief.

"'I told them if the board offered me the position, I'd take it,' he said. 'They told me they're interested in what's best for the community. If they let me do my job, I'll get this department back to being number one in Bucks County.'

"Zajac's primary task would appear to be mending a rift between factions of the department, one loyal to him, one supportive of (Richard) Viola. The ex-chief is appealing his firing in Bucks County Court, and suing the supervisors in federal court.

"A number of officers supportive of Viola expressed outrage over the promotions, particularly those involving the rank of sergeant and detective.

"The officers asserted these promotions violated the township's contract with the officers, which reportedly stipulates that promotions should be based on competitive testing results.

"The question of whether a test was given for sergeant and detective was disputed Monday. Some officers claimed the test was invalid because it was given three years ago. Komada said the supervisors knew a test had been given, but that she had not seen the results.

"Officer Jerry Judge, president of the PBA...said the officers would take some unspecified action.

"'There will definitely be a response,' Judge said. 'Unfortunately, the township won't like it, and the people of Bensalem won't like it.'

"Komada, a dissident Republican who has split from the mainstream township GOP organization, defended the promotions as necessary to address the dissension in the department.

"Komada said the board received letters last week from several of the officers they promoted. The officers stated in the letters they might sue the township if they were not promoted to the positions they were holding, she said.

"Asked for reaction to the objections of the supervisors-elect, Komada said, 'What gives them the right to tell us what to do?'"

(End of article.)

Near the end of the aforementioned Board meeting, the supervisors also agreed (unanimously, believe it or not) to formally invite the Pennsylvania Department of Community Affairs (DCA) to "review the management practices, promotion policies and other matters of all (Bensalem) township departments." Not JUST the police department, but ALL the various departments.

Outgoing Supervisor George Ciotti had been requesting such a DCA study for months. But on this night, during this meeting, and AFTER the supervisors already voted to promote Zajac and his six cohorts-in-kind, THEN they decided to bring in this state agency for a review. I suppose they knew that the DCA would never approve of the above promotions once they actually saw what was going on in the BPD under Zajac, so they better make them beforehand. And they did.

Many, many BPD officers were upset about the results of Monday night's Board meeting, where promotions were given away like cheap door prizes. Independently, another well-known entity saw through the malevolence at the same time. He/she chose to write of it accordingly, even if anonymously.

As such, one only had to go to page six of the November 20th BCCT to read just what one of its editors thought of the move by the outgoing majority of the Board of Supervisors. The editorial's headline and narrative follows.

"The Bensalem follies."

"When the curtain went up on Bensalem's theater of the absurd Monday, there was something for everyone: drama, suspense, comedy, catcalls – even a surprise ending. A special treat came in the form of a cameo appearance by a travelling magician known in sorcery circles as Stephen (now-you-see-him-now-you-don't) Kelly.

"The disappearing supervisor flew in from Florida for Monday's entertainingly scripted show – ah, meeting – one of the few he's attended lately, to cast the deciding vote on a proposal to promote Deputy Police Chief Theodore Zajac to chief.

"Zajac's wife, Patricia, a supervisor, was forced to abstain. And with Supervisor George Ciotti firmly opposed to the promotion, Supervisors Mary Komada and Peter Reed needed to pull another vote out of their hats.

"The trick worked. Too bad taxpayers don't know the magic words; they might have made Kelly disappear long before he started costing them money.

"Which is what Monday's decision to promote Zajac and six of his underlings could do. It's not that Zajac shouldn't be chief or the other officers don't deserve promotions. They might. But that's not the point.

"The point is, part of the purpose of the Department of Community Affairs study the supervisors requested in a surprise encore performance is to determine whether promotion policies are fair.

"Among the complaints of disgruntled police officers is that promotions are being handed out on the basis of favoritism – in other words, to those who supported Zajac and opposed his predecessor, former Chief Richard Viola.

"What's worse, the promotions approved by the supervisors may have violated contract guidelines, a matter those who claim they were passed over are hinting they'll take to court. Similarly, Viola's firing could be overturned by the courts, which would leave the township with too many chiefs and not enough deputy chiefs – not to mention chiefs' salaries.

"Clearly it would have made more sense – both financially and legally – to wait for the results of the study, to use it as a guide for promotions and as a way to gauge Zajac's administrative abilities.

"Zajac has been under fire since he was handpicked by Kelly to replace Viola. Whether the criticism has been unfair is hard to say with any degree of certainty. One thing can be said with certainty: Zajac has not been a healing force. Police officers continue to line up on both sides of a department split by politics and forged into angry camps by alleged favoritism and reprisals.

"Still, the study should help the new board of supervisors understand what's needed to bring peace to their warring police department. Unfortunately, the incoming majority may find it legally difficult and no doubt costly to undo Kelly's spell and implement study recommendations of its choosing or court orders it might not have any choice but to enforce.

"Indeed, Monday's performance was entertaining. But the best trick of all – or the worst from a taxpayer's point of view – is that residents could be footing the bill for their supervisors' black magic for a long time to come."

(End of editorial.)

So, that was November. I'm sure the recently promoted Dark Siders celebrated a very happy Thanksgiving that year. The seven of them had much for which to be thankful, no matter the level of political malfeasance and impropriety by which some of them were rewarded.

The PBA wasn't laying down on this though. There wasn't much we could do about the just promoted chief or three captains, as their ranks did not fall under the BPD bargaining agreement. But the two men promoted to sergeant, and the one to detective...these would not stand. We'd do our damnedest to fight these outright violations of our contract.

However, believe it or not, the Dark Side wasn't done yet. One last boom was set to fall. It became a not-so-nice Christmas present for the entire BPD, especially ten of its members.

Chapter Fifty-Five

In late November, I decided to pull out the September 16th memo from my home file, copy it, and resend it to now-Chief Zajac. It was the memo in which I requested to be relieved of my evidence custodian duties and reassigned as a patrol sergeant. If you recall, it was never answered in writing, only with a smug response from the usually smug Capt. Hughes. This time, with a brief new cover memo attached, updating my earlier request, I forwarded it to his office. I figured now was a good time to re-remind our vaunted leader of my vocational interests.

Strangely, it worked.

It was hard to believe when I first read it, but lo and behold, on December 2nd, a notice appeared in the roll call room info book which stated that effective December 9th I was to be the new patrol sergeant for Squad II. It was from *Chief* Theodore R. Zajac. I guess that notice made it official.

Geez, what a difference a couple of months makes. It apparently took him making Chief to come to realize that I was, in fact, "uniquely qualified" to do something other than being the department's evidence guy. I'm sure being a defendant in my lawsuit didn't hurt either.

Also on December 2nd, now-Chief Zajac put out a notice for any/all interested officers to respond to him regarding which sort of training they would like to receive. There was an accompanying list of approximately ten different training schools. Officers, if so inclined, were instructed to respond with their top three choices.

Again, what's up with this? Training opportunities for the rank and file? Under Zajac? It must be the new and improved Ted Zajac. He must really, really like us now.

Or, once again, something is up with our Chiefy. Time will tell, I was convinced once again. And with his Board's time running out, I knew it couldn't be too far into the future.

Anyway…since the Chief asked, I returned a memo to him on the same day advising I was interested in the following schools: 1) Hostage Situation/Stress Shooting Course, 2) Unarmed Self-Defense/Mechanics of Arrest, and 3) Survival Techniques.

It should not come as a surprise here, but no one in the BPD ever heard anything about these courses again. I suppose some things are just too good to be true, including the benevolence of ol' Ted Zajac.

Plus, with this otherwise quiet before the storm, it seemed more and more that the new administration…no wait, the new, lame duck administration…both upstairs with the politicians and downstairs with the politicians, er, I mean police managers, had other agenda on their mind.

Now what could that be?

As for me, starting on December 9th, it was nice to be in full uniform again as I took over Squad II. I forget what shift I started on and even who was on my squad. Whatever it was, whoever they were, I found just being out on the streets of Bensalem, minus a clipboard full of evidence sheets and crawling through a truck-trailer or a closet, was a very welcome change.

As the days and the few weeks progressed into December, my colleagues knew things were going to be different once the three new Supervisors were sworn in that first week of January. It would just be a matter of waiting out the next few weeks, enjoying the Christmas holidays, and in my case being appreciative of working again as a real supervisor of other cops.

None of us knew what the immediate or long-term future held for us in the BPD. Would Zajac remain in charge? Would Viola be brought back? Would someone else be brought in? Would there be one chief, two chiefs, three chiefs? In any of those scenarios, at least Stephen Kelly and his majority of misfits would no longer be in charge of the township. It and the BPD would have proper stewardship once again.

For now though, as the holiday season of 1985 was approaching, many of us were grateful for where we were and hoping for the best in the New Year, the very early New Year. In view of that, it was agreed in early December that the underground faction members who conspired to mastermind the political defeat of the Dark Side forces owed it to themselves to have a nice night out to celebrate the victory and pending changes in the administration.

After comparing everyone's work schedules, and with a few people willing to burn some vacation or comp time or switch schedules for the night with other officers, approximately twelve of us, along with our respective spouses, met at a certain high-end restaurant outside of Bensalem Township. Jerry Judge had been there before and personally recommended it.

After a heartfelt and moving toast by the PBA President ("Tom," "Dick," and "Harry" somehow made it into his words) and a great dinner, he made sure after the meal was over that we each ordered the restaurant's famous apple pie a la mode. The dessert made for a great ending to an evening of celebration for the twenty-four of us. It also made for a well-deserved and memorable exclamation point to a hard-fought battle against forces admittedly much more powerful than us, but who were nonetheless beaten fair and square at their own game. We collectively concurred our victory was the result of the fearlessness, diligence, intelligence, as well as street smarts of the people sitting at the long table that evening.

David can beat Goliath, as we came to learn. You just need big enough stones.

* * * * *

While the twelve-plus of us were celebrating, others were conspiring. Goliath was seriously wounded, but not quite dead yet.

Within the highest ranks of the BPD, as well as their soon to be unemployed political counterparts, they were plotting and planning their scorched earth exit. They couldn't leave well-enough alone, or more accurately bad-enough alone. So, they brought down yet another boom on the worker bees within the BPD. This one was less than a month after the most recent boom came crashing down upon an already morale-deficient department. But the Dark Side did get their seven promotions out of that one, didn't they? Now, they must have decided, let's go in the complete opposite direction. Yes, instead of promoting officers....

Late on the Monday evening of the 16th of December, at the last Bensalem Township Supervisors meeting of the calendar year, and the last time this particular majority would ever vote together, it happened. Behind closed doors it must have been said, "F**k with us, we'll show you what we can do!"

Yep, these lame ducks came out of those closed doors and f**ked us good!

That is, the majority coalition of the Supervisors, including Mrs. Patricia Zajac herself, voted to layoff twenty-three township employees, including ten police officers. The lone vote against the layoff was the one constant level-headed member of that Board, George Ciotti. But, of course, his vote alone wasn't enough to cauterize the wound, make that multiple wounds, caused yet again by this Board and their newly crowned king, make that Chief, Ted Zajac, Jr.

I forget if I was working the night when the layoffs occurred and called Jerry Judge at home, or if he was working and he called me at home. Either way, we were both very upset that this decision was made, especially after earlier voting to make Zajac the chief and questionably promote six other officers at the same time.

So, we commiserated together...the Township can afford those seven new upper-management salary expenditures, but not the money required to pay the salaries of ten hardworking patrol officers? (All of those laid-off were in the Patrol Division as the policy was "last hired, first fired.")

Jerry wanted me to pen a letter to the *Bucks County Courier Times* right away. He'd sign anything he said, "just put it to paper and call these people any names you want." I was with him all the way and we started taking individual notes on the direction and tone of the letter. No holds barred on this one, I told him. He agreed. We decided, after we calmed down a bit, to meet with the rest of our faction and do whatever it was that we could to get these laid-off officers back on the job and supporting their families.

Besides just the officers' families and their situation, the citizens of Bensalem were now that much less safe with two fewer policemen per shift on the streets to protect them. What were these politicians thinking? Actually, the better question is, of whom were these politicians thinking?

That was an easy one to answer. It was themselves, of course. Oh, and Ted Zajac, too, who's both politician and police chief. What a pair!

The BCCT gave its normal and very accurate coverage to the police layoffs, even interviewing some of the officers recently victimized by the Kelly/Zajac Board. Jerry gave a few excellent sound bites too, as he always did. However, we agreed to hold off on sending the letter itself to the newspaper. We wanted it to gain maximum coverage possible. It wouldn't have that level of coverage this close to Christmas Day. So, it was decided we'd send it in right before the new Supervisors took office. It also gave me some extra time to get it right. I put everything I had into this one too. Something told me it may be my last PBA letter writing assignment, so I wanted to go out with a bang - make that an explosion.

I wrote it, showed it to Jerry, and he loved it. After he signed it, I then personally drove it to the BCCT offices in Falls Township, Pennsylvania, and dropped it off. They waited a few days and then made it the top letter to the editor on their January 5th, 1986 editorial page.

The headline and the full body of the letter read as follows:

> **"Bensalem police official outlines case against chief and supervisors."**
>
> "Editor, Courier Times:
>
> "As president of the Bensalem Township PBA, I am compelled to write this letter to protest the most recent act of political malfeasance committed by the outgoing majority members of the township Board of Supervisors. Their 11th hour laying off of 10 police officers culminates what can only be perceived as a 2-year-long endeavor to humiliate, demoralize and ultimately suck the lifeblood from the majority of the Bensalem Township police officers.
>
> "All of this while continuing to reward present Chief of Police Ted Zajac and his assorted band of police department cronies. The rest of us, the rank and file, the working street cops, had to endure the ongoing harassment, disciplinary actions, contract violations, etc., which were forced on us so the supervisors and Chief Zajac's patronage system could thrive.
>
> "It certainly came as a slap in the collective face of police and taxpayers alike to watch the layoff of the officers for 'budget deficit' reasons when during the last 24 months:
>
> - An overall total of approximately $200,000 was spent to fire Chief Richard Viola, only to have a Bucks County judge decide recently that the firing was politically motivated.
> - Seven officers promoted recently, including Zajac from deputy chief to chief, when both he and the supervisors knew the Viola appeal was pending.

The overall costs of these highly questionable promotions require an extra $25,000 per year in the police budget. Chief Zajac, of course, said he knew nothing of this.

- A two-man narcotics squad which has yet to make a substantial drug arrest in the last two years, yet its members continue to average between 20 and 35 hours overtime per man, per month.
- A full chief's uniform and all its accessories ordered by then Deputy Chief Zajac for himself a full five months before Chief Viola was even fired. Chief Zajac, of course, said he knew nothing of this.
- A brand new unmarked police car for Chief Zajac.
- Paying the Township Solicitor his substantial hourly fee for researching, preparing and subsequently forwarding an official legal notice to me, advising that if I did not stop questioning and commenting on the management tactics of Chief Zajac, I and the PBA would be sued by the Township.
- An officer being "suspended" for nine days because he did not qualify at first on the pistol range, instead of giving him an inside desk job until he could qualify. When the officer contested the suspension through his attorney, the Township was forced to pay the officer for those 90 hours, even though he did not work any of them.

"The list could go on. Suffice to say that with a qualified, professional police chief in charge, and a board of supervisors not so hell-bent on wastefully

spending taxpayers' money to achieve personal goals, these layoffs never would have happened. Chief Zajac knew these layoffs were coming, but sticking true to form, he of course stated he knew nothing of this either. His one rather subdued comment to the board of supervisors regarding the layoffs came only after a half dozen officers stormed into his office on the night of the last township meeting and practically forced him to say something publicly.

"It's strange that in most of the recent major developments in the police department, Chief Zajac knew nothing about them. Hmm. Just who is running this department anyway? It doesn't seem like Ted Zajac is. I wonder if Mary Komada ordered a chief's uniform, too.

"I welcome the three new supervisors, Jack Maher, Paul Rauer and Joe Francano, who take office on Jan. 6. They are sorely needed and long overdue. Hopefully, the changes this police department is in dire need of, especially at the top, are very near. If ever there was a time to reorganize a police department, to raise its rock bottom morale, it is now.

"I have just returned from police headquarters where I and some 32 other officers were there to meet with Chief Zajac for a scheduled grievance hearing regarding the recent promotions which he sanctioned and which we PBA members feel is a blatant violation of our contract. Coincidently, Chief Zajac called in sick today.

Jerry Judge
President, (Bensalem Police) PBA"
(End of letter.)

Jerry was very proud to put his name to this letter. He knew every word was the truth. I was very proud to have written it. I knew every word was the truth too. This administration made it very easy for me. Hyperbole was never needed when writing about this crew.

The above letter was published in the January 5th Sunday edition of the *Bucks County Courier Times* (BCCT). Certainly, back then, the Sunday edition of any newspaper was always the most read and had the highest weekly circulation. It was excellent timing, once again, that the PBA's cause received this kind of coverage. And, interestingly enough, as the letter had been delivered to the BCCT a few days before, it apparently had time to circulate throughout the editorial board room. As a result, that anonymous editorial author surfaced once again to write another beauty.

Almost directly alongside Jerry's letter, also in the same Sunday edition, the following headline and editorial was found.

"Political quackery"
"Members of the outgoing board of supervisors in Bensalem Township are giving new meaning to the

phrase lame duck. Or maybe they've been daffy all along. Whatever their states of mind, taxpayers should be relieved that saner folks take over the reins of government on Monday.

"Already Supervisor-elect Jack Maher said the incoming majority on the board will reinstate 10 police officers who were laid off by the outgoing majority in a mindless attempt to avoid the stigma of a tax increase. Most of the other 13 full- and part-time employees, who became sacrificial lambs at least week's Monday night massacre as well, 'probably' will get their jobs back too, Mahr said.

"That the new board will be pressed into crisis management the first day on the job is indicative of the state of affairs in Bensalem. The outgoing board – first under the leadership of Chairman Stephen Kelly and later under the thumb of underling Mary Komada – carved out a record of unmatched political buffoonery.

"Taxpayers long will pay for their foolishness.

"Sharp increases in insurance and the cost of municipal pension fund notwithstanding, the legal bills run up by the supervisors may have played a role in the need for a tax increase as well. And taxpayers soon could be footing the bill for two police chiefs and yet another legal battle over who should be chief, if former Chief Richard Viola is vindicated in Bucks County Court.

"Appointing a replacement for Viola before all legal channels had been exhausted was a clear attempt by the outgoing majority to wrap its political tentacles around the most powerful department of municipal government. So far that squeeze play merely has served to polarize further the already divided rank and file members of the department.

"Open warfare going on between cops, the supervisors and the man who replaced Viola – Supervisor Patricia Zajac's husband, Theodore – was never more evident than during Monday's hostile meeting. Angry over the surprise layoffs, officers engaged the supervisors in heated debate and pressed their new boss for an explanation as to the role he played, according to sources.

"None, he reportedly told them, claiming he didn't know what his wife and her playmates on the board were up to. Right.

"Is it any wonder Zajac hasn't attracted the support – or the respect – of men who increasingly are being forced to pick sides against their instincts and their will?

"And so the new supervisors take their seats amid chaos and crisis. The challenge ahead of them is clear; the solutions are not.

"Taxpayers can only hope that good sense will replace political nonsense; that what you know, not who you know, will become the board's new barometer; that professional leadership will be the keynote for a community so long dominated by amateur political hacks."

(End of editorial.)

Thank you anonymous BCCT Editor for seeing it, and more importantly, telling it like it is. You are (and still remain) on the right side of history.

However, it wasn't only on the Sunday of this first weekend in January that some of us BPDers attempted to convey our position to the people of Bensalem. As it so happens, on the day before, our little faction had some other tricks up our collective sleeves.

For one of these tricks a number of us chipped in some hard-earned cash to accomplish it. Lots of people would then know about it as that was by design.

The other trick, I undertook on my own. It didn't cost me a cent and it involved only one other person. But I had to time it ever so precisely.

These two events would result in a well-planned simultaneous air-and-ground attack...in a manner of speaking. No animals or humans were hurt though, I can assure you.

Some of the latter were pretty pissed-off about it, but that wasn't my concern. In fact, it was a very pleasant by-product.

Chapter Fifty-Six

The "air attack" idea had its origins during the course of a late night shift sometime around the Christmas holidays of 1985. At that point I was three weeks or so into patrol sergeant mode and I was thoroughly enjoying it. I had a great squad and we worked together very well. But, we all agreed, there was still a strange and uncomfortable uncertainty surrounding us and what the immediate and long-term future may hold, especially with ten of our colleagues still laid-off.

Yet again, it was a bit disconcerting being a Bensalem cop at this time; probably less so for me and my friends as opposed to the various Dark Siders. I empathized with them to some degree as they were going through what many of us went through exactly two years ago once the Stephen Kelly acquittal became a reality and we knew all hell was about to break loose.

Rest assured though, my actual level of empathy for Zajac and his motley crew was to a very, very low degree. They'd have to find a way to manage the change in administration just as I had done twenty-four months before. As it played itself out, some did and some didn't.

During a particular quiet stretch of night on one of these late December 9P-7A shifts, probably around 5:00AM, a few of us met in an empty parking lot off of Street Rd. to share some coffees, hot chocolate, and conversation. While sipping said beverages and trying to keep warm by standing near the running car engines, among other issues the three of us were discussing was what more could we possibly be doing to hasten the re-appointment of Chief Viola now that things were about to change within the political structure of our town.

This current mindset had been brought about as the result of a recent hearing in Bucks County Court involving Viola's wrongful termination lawsuit against Bensalem Township. It had filtered down to us that the judge overseeing his suit opined in open court that the former chief had been fired for clearly political reasons. That was very good to hear coming from the judge's lips, although no surprise to any of us. With that, many of us were even more confident the lawsuit was heading in the direction of a victory for Viola with him having his termination ruled unlawful and ultimately overturned.

It was only a matter of time, we were told...only a matter of time.

As we continued conversing that night, we wondered aloud - was there a way, even in some whimsical manner, maybe by doing something we haven't done or even thought of before, of moving the hands of the Bensalem clock forward, specifically as it related to Viola and the three newly elected supervisors. Something we could do which would remind them, encourage them, to perhaps do the right thing sooner rather than later.

Hmmm...what would be some of our options here?

We knew as police officers we were limited in what we could publicly say or do in this type of situation. Of course, Jerry Judge, as PBA President, could say and do many things because of the elected position he held. (And I was glad to help him express many of those words, certainly of the written variety.) However, as the three of us continued discussing various options during that cold early morning, we collectively admitted to being impatient with the much-too-slow legal process which we had been living and working with for almost two years now. We felt there was still something else we could do to hasten matters along. It would have to be innovative, outside-the-box, and along with all of that maybe even laugh-worthy. It would also have to be informative and very adamantly make our point as well as possibly serving to expedite what we all hoped would be inevitable – the rehiring of Chief Viola. Yes, we knew Jerry's (and my) PBA letter would be at the newspaper any day now. But was there something else we could do, perhaps before that, to really drive home what we were trying to impress upon people here?

At the same time the three of us were weighing our various choices, from off-duty officers holding "We Support Viola" placards in front of HQ, to highway billboard signs, to newspaper ads, to TV commercials, a small to mid-sized airplane just happened to fly over our heads. I first heard it and then silently watched its outline of blinking lights pass above us. It wasn't all that far above us as it was most likely on its approach to nearby Northeast Philadelphia Airport.

The happenstance flyover of the soon-to-land aircraft became the impetus for me of a certain event which eventually came to pass within a week or so. In the meantime, that's when with hardly a conscious thought, while looking up at the red and white lights heading southward and out of sight on its approach to the unseen landing strip, the synapses of my brain made their lightning fast electrical connections. With little, if any, hesitation, I all but involuntarily stated it aloud.

"Wouldn't it be cool to hire one of those banner planes? You know, the kind you see flying down the shore during the summertime. It could fly over Bensalem with a banner behind it saying something like 'Bring Viola Back Now.'"

My colleagues each chuckled and agreed with me that it was a really "cool" idea. However, as quickly as we all came to the same semi-humorous opinion as to its unarguable coolness factor, the notion all but faded away as we also agreed that it would most likely not be doable. We commiserated that there is probably no such plane company in the area, or if there was, it would probably be very expensive to undertake, and even if not all that costly, it most likely wouldn't be able to make our agreed upon arbitrary deadline of the weekend before the first Township meeting of the new Board majority. With all of those downers attached to my initial ever-so-cool idea, we figuratively shrugged our shoulders and moved on to other topics.

Perhaps by happenstance once again, it seems that just a few minutes later another one of my officers showed up at our semi-secretive, pre-arranged rendezvous location. After quickly grabbing his coffee, which had been kept warm by its placement on one of the car hoods, he joined us in mid-conversation. When one of the other guys just happened to mention my banner plane idea in passing, he looked up after a long sip of his hot beverage and nonchalantly said, "Yeah, I know someone who does that."

Wait! What? You do? Who?

Please, tell us more.

The relatively newer officer (he just missed being one of those laid-off) volunteered that someone he knew, be it his neighbor's former high school classmate, brother-in-law's cousin, friend of a friend, or someone like that, worked at the nearby Middletown Township (Pennsylvania) airport, Buehl Field. He added that he believes this person is somehow connected to a company which has single-engine airplanes which tow short ads behind them and fly them wherever the customer wants them flown.

While looking at my two colleagues, I then stated to the newly arrived officer, "Uh, this may sound crazy, but could you somehow get in contact with this person, whoever it is and whoever he knows, and find out what it would cost to do this for, I don't know, an hour, half an hour, or something like that, over Bensalem one day in the next week?"

639

He replied, "Yeah, sure. I'll call him later today when I wake up."

I then asked all three of my subordinates if the cost to set up such a flight was within reason, would they be willing to chip in and lay out the cash to get it done. Without thinking about it, each of them immediately said they would. We quickly added that "the more the merrier" would be ideal though. Mostly for cost related reasons, of course.

I told them I would contact Jerry Judge, make sure he was on board with it, and start moving this idea forward. But we needed to know what it would cost and when it could be done. Both would be critical to this operation ever getting off the ground. (Yes, pun intended.) After all, we're cops on cops' salaries. We couldn't or wouldn't want to spend TOO much on this endeavor, as cool as it may be. Plus, we'd want it done before the first meeting of the new Board of Supervisors scheduled for January 6th.

The so-assigned officer said no matter how many calls it took him he'd have all the required info for us by tonight at 9:00, our last night on this shift. We agreed this would become the fourth official "Operation" in our mission to get Chief Viola back to his rightful and deserved position. We quickly named it "Operation Flyover." We were confident it would be as successful as the other three, and kinda fun at the same time.

As there was about an hour and a half left to our shift at this point, the sergeant in me took over our early morning coffee break. I advised the three officers it was time for us to get back to work. I instructed them to check their shopping centers and industrial parks for any signs of overnight burglaries, vandalisms, or similar such criminal activity. They promptly did so, found no indications of any such crimes, and back at HQ we bid adieu for the day at 7:00. It was time to get some sleep.

Upon my awakening later that afternoon, I called Jerry and he was onboard with Operation Flyover. In fact, he loved the idea. He reminded me that Capt. Jack Robinson had a friend at Buehl Field too. He was right, so we got Jack involved in Operation F too. We agreed after a few phone calls to tell our various friends and colleagues about this crazy notion. We each knew some regular everyday Bensalem citizens who would be very glad to play a role in this mission and possibly help with the operational expenses. Let's bring 'em on board, I strongly suggested to Jerry and later that day, Jack.

Even before roll call at the beginning of that last night's shift, between what Jack Robinson and the officer told me we had attained the information we needed regarding the guy at the banner plane company. We learned that Saturday, January 4th, was an available date to do the flyover; weather permitting, of course.

I forget exactly how it all came together from that point on, how many people actually chipped in, who handled the money, what was the exact cost, etc. However, I don't think any of us paid more than $20 each for the flight. We agreed, for various reasons (mostly money-related), that thirty minutes circling over the center of Bensalem Township would suffice for our purposes here. The banner would read very close to what I stated that first morning. It would say, "Bring Chief Viola Back Now." We added "Chief" to the signage to make sure everyone who saw it knew exactly to whom it referred, that we saw him as the legitimate boss of the BPD, the heir again to his once-throne, and we wanted to put it in writing...even if just on a plane-towed banner for now.

Interestingly, unlike our earlier three Operations, with this one we told everyone involved to absolutely talk it up. Yes, please pass the word that something important would be "in the air" around 1:00 on Saturday afternoon. We didn't care if the Dark Siders found out about this one. In fact, we wanted them to know all about it, to include even that other Chief, Ted Zajac.

I figured former (and hopefully not "former" for long) Chief Viola would want to know about this aerial act too. So, once it was confirmed I called him the day before and suggested he take a walk outside on Saturday afternoon at 1:00 and look up in the sky. He said he'd make sure to do so. Before we hung up, he thanked me for the solidarity and support, and not just on this day, but for the entirety of the last two years. I responded, "No problem. Just bring some solidarity back to the PD once you return." He guaranteed me he would.

After much careful planning, Saturday, January 4, 1986, at exactly 1:00, Operation Flyover was launched...literally. On that clear and sunny day, I happened to be working a 7A-5P shift. I brought my 35mm camera with me that day. If possible, I wanted to capture the moment on film for posterity.

Because of my other lone-wolf plan (the aforementioned "ground assault"), I was parked at a shopping center in the Neshaminy Valley area of Bensalem. Then and there, right on schedule at 1:00, I heard the low but steady whirring of a plane's engine from a distance to the north of me. Within twenty seconds or so, as the whirring increased incrementally in volume, I observed in the sky a fixed-wing aircraft approaching my general location. Upon closer inspection I could see it was towing a banner. Once it crossed the approximate location of the Neshaminy Creek, which served as the northern border of Bensalem, I could clearly see it was OUR plane towing OUR banner.

Unbelievable! This is SO friggin' cool!

Seeing this plane do its first half-circle over the township, my township, filled me with an overwhelming set of mixed feelings, personally and professionally. It was just five simple words, twenty-two letters in total, "Bring Chief Viola Back Now." Yet, with my eyes and head initially following this plane from north to south, I realized that the flying message represented so much to me...so much good, so much bad, so much aggravation, so much harassment, so much hard work, and now finally, so much to look forward to.

I'm not sure of the plane's exact altitude for the duration of its thirty-minute circular flight, but it was low enough to make the banner very easy for anyone to read. I took photos with my camera's regular lens and then I switched to a telephoto lens. I wanted to make sure I captured the airborne moment then and there for all time.

Shoppers and pedestrians alike walking not far from me and my patrol car saw what I was doing and also looked up into the sky. At least two separate people pointed to the plane, pointed to me, and clapped their hands together as if to say, "I'm with you, Officer!" At least one other in a passing car beeped his horn and waved at me. All of this was refreshing to see and hear. I proudly tipped my cap to each of these supportive folks in response.

The police radio was fun to listen to during that half hour too. My squad members had good senses of humor and were full of chatter about it being a sign from the heavens, flying words of wisdom, and the like. I recall one of them saying over the radio, borrowing from the old *Superman* radio and television series, "Look, up in the sky, it's a bird, it's a plane, no, it's...a banner plane supporting Chief Viola!" Another officer was heard to say, "Ze plane, Boss, ze plane," as a reference to the diminutive Tattoo character from the late '70s to early '80s television series *Fantasy Island*.

The anticipation building towards it, the actual half-hour airshow itself, and its eventual aftermath all made for a great workday. We still answered our calls, made an arrest or two, but the plane and the sign defined the shift as unique from all others, certainly of any I've ever worked as a law enforcement officer.

This whole banner plane stunt, and that's really what it was, a stunt, served a few useful purposes that day. It further bonded the officers of our faction, it was a visible and high-flying manifestation of our hard-fought victory, and it reminded everyone who took the time to look up in the air (or even heard about it later) what and who it was we believed to be the most salient solution for the myriad problems of the police department. That is, to bring Chief Viola back now!

The plane with its five-word sign was silly in some ways, I grant you. But sometimes it takes silly things, planned or unplanned, to accomplish in certain situations what can't be done at the time through other more serious channels. If nothing else, it can add some humor when needed. It did on this day, and it was much deserved and much welcomed. And remember, our situation wasn't over yet. Viola was still the ex-Chief of Bensalem, Zajac was still the Chief, and ten of our fellow officers were still laid-off. All three of these matters had to be rectified, somehow. Maybe this was the start.

So, this was interesting, fun, timely, and all that, but I also needed to make a stop and talk to someone. He was someone important, newly important, certainly within Bensalem Township. His home was near my present location. That wasn't by accident.

Now, if I can time this just right…the ground assault would be next.

Of the three newly elected township supervisors, I felt I potentially had the most in common with Paul Rauer. He was around my age, grew up in Northeast Philadelphia, and was directly involved in the criminal justice system as a lawyer. I had spoken with him briefly the evening the three Republican candidates came to the PBA meeting back in October. He told me after the formal session that if elected, he would like to talk to me more about the PD and the direction it should be heading in '86 and beyond. I told him I'd be glad to discuss any of these matters with him when the time was right.

I figured the day the Viola banner plane was flying overhead would be the right time for this talk. The plane would also make for a nice visual over my shoulder, consciously or sub-consciously, for Paul to see. So, timing was important here too. With that in mind, I drove the police car the few blocks, parked it, and with the plane still buzzing above me, I knocked on his door. Fortunately, he was home.

Paul recognized me right away. It didn't hurt that I had a name plate on my uniform coat which would remind him of just who I was. But he didn't need it. He greeted me with, "Hi Jim, how are you? Is everything okay?"

I assured Paul all was fine, and as he had mentioned those two months ago that he would like to talk one day, I told him I was hoping that this could be that day. He agreed and invited me to come inside. However, I politely asked him instead to grab his coat and step outside. He looked at me rather quizzically at first, but then said, "Sure, no problem."

Paul and I talked that afternoon for about ten minutes. That's really all I wanted with him at this point as I didn't want to press my luck, especially on this unannounced visit. Being outside now, I was hoping he would see the plane pass by at least once. He did. He smiled and read aloud the banner's words slowly for both of our sakes. He commented, "I like the message - short and sweet. Someone, some group, is pretty serious about bringing Viola back as chief, eh?"

As we both watched the plane slowly break from its circular flight path and head back toward the airfield in Middletown Township, I responded, "Yes, Paul, we are. And there are lots of us."

"I hear you, Jim, and I can read too," the Supervisor-elect half-laughingly retorted as he watched the plane fade into oblivion north-bound above the Neshaminy Creek area.

On the small front porch of his house, I advised the soon to be sworn-in Supervisor that pointing out the banner plane wasn't the reason I was here today. That part, I told him, was coincidental as I just happened to be in the area, things were quiet, etc. (Well, that was more or less true.) However, I acknowledged, it did serve as a timely backdrop for our discussion today. He agreed.

I then continued with Paul with what he already knew, but I felt was important to repeat. That is, the police department as it had been managed over the last two years was in shambles and morale was at an all-time low. The place absolutely had to be fixed and at the very top was where to start. I ended my initial statement by also reminding him, "We also must get the ten officers who were laid-off back on the job. Can you really try to do that? And very soon?"

Paul responded, "Yes, that's number one on our agenda. We're gonna do our best to rehire them Monday night. All of them."

I thanked him for that but before I could say anything else, Paul outright asked me, "Jim, is bringing Viola back as Chief the answer to all these problems?"

I responded bluntly, "Yes, it is. For now, it's the only answer. Probably down the line, in a few years, a brand new chief from the outside will be warranted. But for now, for legal purposes as well as departmental morale and productivity purposes, we need Viola back, and immediately, if not sooner, if I may say so."

Paul nodded his head as if he was highly appreciative of my comments to him. He maintained a poker face and didn't give me an answer one way or the other regarding Viola, but he affirmed that he would be meeting with the other two Supervisors-elect on Sunday afternoon and they would be putting together the game plan for their first ever official public meeting on the following Monday night.

I thanked Paul for his time and told him I'd be there in the township auditorium for his swearing in and their first Board meeting. He thanked me, shook my hand, and said he may want to talk to me again at some point about various other departmental issues. I told him that would be fine and gave him one of my business cards after writing my home phone number on the back. He took it from me and placed it inside his wallet.

And that...was that.

During one half-hour starting at 1:00 on that Saturday afternoon, I participated in what I earlier euphemistically referred to as an "air and ground assault." The "air" part was pre-planned and all I did that day was watch it unfold and take some photos. The "ground" part was a little more complex that same day and time as I wasn't exactly sure how Paul Rauer would greet me at his home, especially unannounced. But in life, one has to take chances sometimes, especially when the stakes are high. They were high on that January weekend before the first ever meeting of the newly elected Board majority. With that in mind, I decided to leave nothing to chance. It paid off.

* * * * *

I worked the next several day shifts to include Monday, January 6th. As I was off that evening, I found myself in the township auditorium for the much anticipated meeting. Along with many other officers and concerned citizens, Joe Grace from the *Bucks County Courier Times* was there too. His article, dated January 8, 1986, and the accompanying headline are as follows. (Staff writer George Mattar also contributed to this story.)

"In surprise vote, Bensalem rehires Viola as its chief"
"Bensalem Police Chief Richard J. Viola, fired five months ago for alleged misconduct, was rehired as

chief Monday in a surprise move by three supervisors moments after they took office.

"The rehiring, which took place in a township auditorium filled with more than 150 people, reversed a two-year chain of events that began with Viola's suspension and culminated in his dismissal in August.

"Viola's return as chief of the 69-member department, which officials said was effective immediately, cast in doubt the status of current Chief Theodore Zajac, Jr.

"A decision on Zajac has not been made and will occur after consultation between Viola and the three new supervisors, Supervisor Jack Maher said.

"However, Maher said Zajac told him recently that he would resign from the department if Viola were to return as chief.

"Zajac said in a telephone interview later Monday night that he was uncertain how Viola's rehiring would affect his position.

"'I don't know,' Zajac said. 'I'm not sure what they're going to do with me yet.'

"Zajac said Viola is not certified as a police officer under state law, an issue raised at the time of his original suspension.

"The supervisors who rehired Viola addressed that by stipulating his return was contingent on him obtaining the certification.

"Viola, surrounded in the township building lobby by supporters after his rehiring, was reserved in his public comments.

"'I am gratified, extremely gratified, that the board gave me my job back,' Viola said.

"The three supervisors who voted to rehire Viola were Maher, Joseph Francano, and Paul Rauer. The three were sworn into office on Monday night as political control swung to them. Maher was selected as board chairman.

"Supervisors Mary Komada and Patricia Zajac, the chief's wife, both of whom voted in August to fire Viola, abstained from the vote to rehire him. They made no public comment.

"The two other board members who had voted to fire Viola, Stephen Kelly and Peter Reed, left office Monday as their terms expired. They did not attend the meeting.

"The township police department had been split by a five-year struggle for control between Zajac and Viola, and between the politicians who support each official.

"The officers who support Viola reacted with unrestrained jubilance Monday night.

"'I hope this ends the polarization of the police department,' said Capt. Ronald Traenkle. 'Will it? Only time will tell.'

"Other officers were more cautious. 'I'm apprehensive because it's not over,' said Capt. Robert Dechant. 'I'm not looking forward to the weeks ahead. I just hope it's the beginning of some kind of end, so that we can get back to the business of serving the people.'

"The rehiring was accomplished in an atmosphere already highly charged with emotion following the reinstatement of nine officers who were laid off last week for budgetary reasons.

"A lame-duck board of supervisors said the layoffs of the police officers and other municipal workers were necessary to avoid a 21 percent tax increase.

"On Monday the new board reinstated the police officers, but stopped short of bringing back the other workers. They said they would amend the budget before Feb. 15, leaving open the probability of a tax increase.

"The reinstated police officers, their families and friends roared their approval at the supervisors' actions. Several of the officers slapped hands above their heads.

"'Schwabbie's back!' one yelled, a reference to reinstated Officer Donald Schwab.

"A 10th officer who was laid off, Patrolman Juan Diaz, submitted his resignation and was not reinstated. 'We lost Officer Diaz, a big loss,' Francano said.

"Moments later, Rauer read a prepared statement in which the township stated it was dropping all charges lodged against Viola in exchange for his ending his dismissal appeal in Bucks County Court.

"'This has been the most controversial issue in Bensalem in recent years,' Rauer stated. 'We came to the conclusion that there was no merit to the case against Richard Viola.'

"As Rauer read, Viola appeared suddenly from within the overflow crowd and moved to a position in front of the supervisors' wooden podium.

"After Viola agreed to drop his appeal in county court, the supervisors rehired him, and the crowd once more roared its approval.

"Rauer declined to speculate how much the board would be willing to settle the case for."

(End of article.)

Well, if it's in the BCCT, it must be official. And it was. Chief Richard J. Viola was back and in charge once again of the BPD.

The two-year long nightmare of mismanagement, poor management, and/or no management, with the plummeting departmental morale and productivity rate to match, was all but over. The Dark Side was no more. At least they were no longer in charge of the place. There were remnants of it and them still floating throughout the BPD afterwards, but nothing or no one of any great concern to the everyday running of the department.

Now, what the hell do we do with two chiefs? And a few other members of upper-management?

I have some ideas.

Part 6 -
The Return of the Chief

Chapter Fifty-Seven

My last shift on day-work that week was Tuesday. As it so happens, that was newly re-appointed Chief Viola's first full day back at work. I made sure to be inside HQ at 8:00AM when he strolled in the door. When he did, he was met by a hearty round of applause by many. But of course, not everyone.

Despite the mostly warm welcome, it was agreed by many that Viola's task now that he was back in charge would not be an easy one. To begin with, what would he do with Zajac and now-Capt. Eckert? They were the ones who along with Stephen Kelly railroaded him out of the department two years before. They were also defendants in his ongoing federal lawsuit, just as they were in my lawsuit. They'd now be under Chief Viola's thumb, managerially speaking. He'd have to handle them carefully, but handle them nonetheless.

This situation was truly hard to fathom. That is, the BPD now officially had two chiefs, six captains, no lieutenants, and at least ten sergeants. Talk about being a top-heavy management pyramid, not to mention top-heavy with mostly empty suits or uniforms. All of this being Zajac's doing, too. Welcome back, Chief Viola!

In the meantime, I had my sights on someone else in management, another one of MY defendants. I knew his Achilles heel too. I was going after it. And that was no "lie."

It was inexplicably gratifying, once again, being in the chief's office and actually seeing Rich Viola sitting behind the desk. There were boxes already lined up and Zajac's stuff was being taken off the wall and from shelves and moved to the office directly next door. It was the same adjacent office where the former Deputy Chief was assigned the last time he was working under Viola. But now he would also be a Chief. But, wait, Viola was Chief...

This was getting confusing. Well, actually, it wasn't.

Within a few hours that day the other chief, Ted Zajac, now ordered to wear his full uniform to work, would be put back in charge of the BPD auto fleet. It seems to have been a position for which he was "uniquely qualified."

Later that same morning, Captains Eckert, Walsh, and Dechant would be permanently assigned to the radio room, in charge of the dispatchers, and dispatchers only. The three of them were also ordered to wear full police uniforms when on duty. Walsh and Dechant were assigned to a split late night shift, but Viola wanted Eckert on straight day-work. He wanted to make sure Eckert saw him a few times each day now that he was back and in charge again. That alone, Viola figured, would be torture enough for Eckert.

On the other side of the coin, Capt. Jack Robinson would be back as head of CID. Capt. Ron Traenkle was put in charge of the Patrol Division once again.

That left just one upper-management person unassigned on Viola's first day back. That would be Capt. Bob Hughes. That's where I came in.

When I joined the small gathering in Viola's office that morning, it was nice to see so many smiling faces once again. They were the smiling faces of officers who were hard workers, with self-motivated dispositions, high personal and professional ethics, who happened to have excellent investigative, arrest, and prosecution records, and/or were excellent supervisors. This, of course, was the antithesis of the immediate prior regime where it was who you knew (Zajac) and practically what you did NOT do, that got you ahead. Not a very good way to run any organization, much less a law enforcement agency.

As the people in the Chief's office were slowly leaving and getting back to work on this first day of the second Viola administration, the man himself called me aside. When it was just the two of us in the uncrowded and bare walled office, he took the time again to thank me for maintaining my loyalty to him and to the spirit of what the BPD should be.

I told Viola, "You're welcome." However, I continued in all seriousness, "I gotta tell ya, Chief…it wasn't so much my loyalty to you during these last two years but more my total disrespect for the management style of the guy who used to sit in this room. He and his people made it very difficult for me, and many others in this department, to ever develop any sort of loyalty to them or respect for them."

"Actually, Chief," as I was ending this part of our conversation, "and I mean this with all due respect…it was less about you and more about them that determined my attitude here and how I ultimately handled myself. To any stand-up guy who had to look in the mirror each day, Zajac and company made it rather easy in how to comport oneself under such circumstances."

Viola readily acknowledged he understood completely and would have expected nothing less of me and the others who were here every day (or at least some of those days) and suffered the consequences for not being a Zajac ring-kisser. I appreciated his gratitude.

The new and once-again Chief then asked me if there was any particular assignment I would like.

"Chief," I responded, "believe it or not, I'm perfectly happy as a patrol sergeant right now. I have a good squad and if it's okay with you, I'd like to stay there. I was cooped up inside HQ for most of your forced absence dealing with the usual half-dozen CID shit-for-brains and then later crawling around the evidence closet and trailer. So, for the immediate future anyway, the freedom of being out on the road in my present role works just fine for me."

"You got it," Viola responded. "In Patrol you'll stay for now. We'll talk again in the next few weeks and see where things are then."

"Great, Chief, thanks. By the way, have you reassigned everyone in upper management yet? I'm curious as to who is going where."

"Not everyone, Hughesy is the last one I have to find a spot for. Any suggestions?"

Well, if the Chief is gonna ask me...

"Yeah, how about a permanent midnight shift for him, working the dispatch room like the other captains? I think that would be a perfect fit. Know what I mean?"

"Excellent idea, Jimmy. Let me get one of the secretaries to type the memo and..."

"Please," I interrupted the Chief, "let me type it. Unlike the others I was forced to write to Hughes over the last nine months, this one will be my pleasure to do, believe me. You can sign off on it and I'll personally hand it to him right afterwards. Okay?"

"Sure, go for it. Write whatever you want. I'll sign it."

Within minutes I was sitting at a typewriter outside of the chief's office typing away at the memo. It would be from the chief, to Capt. Hughes, and it would instruct him that until further notice he would be assigned to the 11P-7A shift, Monday through Friday, in uniform, supervising the dispatchers; no one else, just them. Like the other captains, he would even relieve them on the radio when they were on lunch or bathroom breaks. I happily included that part of his new job description in the memo too.

Once done, I took the memo to Chief Viola, he quickly read it, signed it, and "ordered" me to personally hand it to Hughes. I followed his order with great urgency and expediency.

You may have figured out by now that the person with the Achilles heel I referenced a bit ago was, in fact, Capt. Hughes. I knew from various sources in the past that above all else on this job there was one aspect of it he truly loathed. And while Hughes was the furthest thing from the noble warrior of Greek mythology, he nonetheless possessed a job-related weakness of his own…and I happened to know of it.

You see, he didn't do midnight shifts very well. When working such hours in his distant BPD past they allegedly caused Hughes all sorts of sleeping problems. These shifts would also interfere with his well-known nighttime socializing schedule. So, as there was still an opening on the overnight shift for a radio room supervisor, who would be better qualified, if not "uniquely" so, than Capt. Hughes?

Well, that's how I saw it anyway. Chief Viola agreed, too.

With signed memo in hand, and after a bit of searching around HQ, I finally found the captain sitting in, of all places, the radio room. How ironic, I recall thinking at the time, that Hughes just happened to be sitting in the very room where he would shortly be assigned fulltime, although on very different hours than those to which he was accustomed. Actually, I was told a short while later, Capt. Hughes whispered to someone that he was staying in the radio room this morning for a while because he wanted to be as far away as possible from the celebratory activity in and around the new chief's office. He knew since the November election that his days as the primary enforcer and hitman for Team Zajac were over. Today, I'm sure Hughes knew, was the first day of the rest of his life in the BPD. He better enjoy working today. As per the memo I just typed and was about to give him, it would be the last DAY he would be working for the foreseeable future.

I walked into the general area of the radio room where Hughes was sitting and heard him in mid-conversation with one of the dispatchers. It was an "idle conversation" I couldn't help but notice right away, but I didn't really care. It seemed most of the workplace conversations in which I ever heard him engage would fall into that category, so today was nothing new.

As I wanted to savor this moment for as long as I could, I proceeded directly next to the captain and in turn engaged in an also idle conversation with the other dispatcher at her console. Hughes didn't get up and move away at first, but as he saw me holding an envelope in my hand with his name clearly on the front of it, he knew something was up. Over the next minute or two, as he was clearly becoming uncomfortable about the mystery document in my clutches, he slowly began stirring in his seat. And, with me using the envelope as a strategic prop in my hand while talking, with his name clearly visible on it in all upper-case font moving up and down only a few feet from his face, he finally said to his fellow conversant at his dispatch post, "Well, okay, see ya later."

Not so fast! I then immediately switched from one conversation to begin another.

"Oh, Bob, while I have you here...don't leave just yet."

Bob (yes, I referred to him that way intentionally) stopped in his tracks, turned around, and our eyes met for the first time that morning. I then slowly held up the envelope and handed it to him. I told him as he grasped it, "This is from Chief Viola. He wants you to open it right away." I didn't want to give Hughes the opportunity to put it aside for later. I wanted him to open it in front of me. He did, and I watched intently as he read it.

It seems the captain read it twice, just to make sure he understood it. All Hughes said, in clearly a less-sure and less-cocky voice than usual was, "Yeah, sure, no big deal. I've always liked these hours," as he walked away.

Now who was lying?

It was very gratifying to be the one who not only typed this memo to Hughes but to be the one to actually hand it to him and watch him read it and react to it in real-time. I know he knew from whom it originated (me), even if it had Viola's name on it. That was good enough for me at this time and place.

This was nothing more than a minor moral victory for me, no more, no less. However, it was well worth it knowing that this man, Bob Hughes, who had done his best to cause me aggravation and frustration, not to mention those friggin' almost daily headaches, for the next few months wouldn't be sleeping very well. I hope every time he laid his head down on a pillow to go to sleep at 8:00AM, he thought of me handing him this envelope. Make that, when he TRIED to go to sleep at 8:00AM....

Within a few months, Captains Un-Courageous, aka Hughes, Walsh, Eckert, and Dechant, were put on a rotating shift schedule minding the store in the radio room/dispatch office. After they teamed up and complained to Chief Viola, each of them eventually got off of their initially-assigned steady shifts and was placed on an around-the-clock schedule, including weekends. For the foreseeable future, however, their duties remained pretty much the same.

I have a feeling when these four received their captain bars, three of them at the recent mid-November Board meeting, with Hughes a few years before, they never envisioned their immediate futures being assigned to the radio console and running registration and wanted checks on vehicles called in by the "lowly" patrol officers. But that's where they were now once the Zajac dealt house of cards came tumbling down upon them. In each of their own cases, they were their own worst enemies. Now they had to live with it, and themselves.

* * * * *

In closing this chapter, it's time to close on these aforementioned people. If you're not sick and tired of reading about them, I gotta tell you, I'm sick and tired of writing about them, even thirty-plus years after my dealings with them. As none of these men played any role at all in the rest of my tenure at the BPD, or for that matter in the rest of my personal or professional life, it's time to say goodbye to them once and for all.

In case you happen to be curious as to how some of these people spent their final days in the BPD or its political environs, here's how it played out. They're listed in alphabetical order.

Capt. Robert Dechant retired with his full pension in 2000. He died in 2009.

Barry Denker, Esq., later Witness Protection Program protectee, died in 1996 in Albuquerque, New Mexico, of heart related problems. (If you didn't pick up on it then, the "article" snippets in Chapter 37 are actually from his obituary.)

Capt. Robert Eckert left the BPD for parts unknown sometime in '86 or '87. He quit, he didn't retire, so there was no full pension for him. Oh, and his wife was no longer the Bensalem Tax Collector as of January of '86. It seems that neither of their jobs worked out for them in the long run.

Capt. Robert Hughes actually managed to find his way to the rank of Major in the next BPD administration. He retired with full pension in 1996.

Capt. Thomas Walsh retired with his full pension in July of 1986. He died in the 1990s.

In January or February of '86, barely a month or two after Viola took over, Chief Theodore Zajac happened to be riding as a passenger in a patrol car. The vehicle was rear-ended by another car while sitting at a Bensalem intersection. The Back-Up Chief sustained alleged back injuries and he immediately went out on IOD status. This turned out to be his last day ever as a working Bensalem police officer, Bensalem politician, or both. Zajac was eventually allowed to fully retire on an injury related pension with an additional "buyout" from the Township of approximately $65,000. A bargain at any price, I would suggest. Patricia Zajac, his wife, finished out her six-year term as Supervisor and did not run for office again.

Time to move on....

(+Bonus Chapter 57a)

Chapter Fifty-Eight

Going back in time a bit first...you may recall on the night in January 1984 of Stephen Kelly's triumphant post-acquittal return as Chairman of the Board of Supervisors that his first two official acts were to suspend/fire Viola and then reappoint Ted Zajac, Jr., as his Chief. Later that same evening there was a well-attended police bacchanal in the CID area where, among other matters ongoing, the song *Innocent Man* by Billy Joel was played at full volume several times by one of the very jubilant detectives. It was meant to signify, of course, that Kelly, Zajac, et al., were those innocent men who were now fully vindicated and back where they belong. Its playing then and there served as the musical highlight (or lowlight) of a disturbingly celebratory evening in the CID room.

I mentioned back in that earlier chapter that this song would reappear once again before this whole saga played itself out. Well, it did, one more time. In doing so this next time, it added forever to the musical soundtrack of the brand new BPD administration during the first days of Viola's triumphant return. It was well received at the time of its second playing, although by an entirely different audience. Funny how that works.

The *Innocent Man* encore event happened very quickly and without any of the obvious preplanning which marked the first time the song was played on the tape deck in CID. This time, it was different. You see, one morning I just happened to be in the area of CID to see Capt. Robinson regarding one matter or another. While there, *Innocent Man* just happened to be playing on one of the secretaries' desktop FM radios. Looking up and around, I happened to notice the CID area was chock-full of detectives of varying political persuasions, to include the *Innocent Man* DJ from that party night just about two years prior.

What are the odds?

With this uncanny confluence of coincidental events, I simply couldn't resist the temptation.

Yes, before the song was even a few bars long, and with a wide grin and a few winks to certain nearby people, I carefully moved the secretary's radio to one convenient corner of her desk and directed the speakers toward the back of the CID room. I then turned up the volume and made sure everyone in the room could hear the song, whether they wanted to or not. I left it at the high volume setting for the duration of the tune. Its melody and lyrics were reverberating all around the desk filled room, from Chief Viola's office on one side to the back corners of CID on the other.

When the DJ/detective responsible for the two-year-ago prearranged song rendition happened to hear it once again on this day, on a regular FM radio station this time, it must have hit a musical note…or nerve. Probably the latter, because before Billy Joel's second chorus was complete, without looking at anyone, the detective stood up from his desk, threw down a pen, grabbed his coat, walked by me and directly in front of Viola's occupied office, exiting CID and the building itself to parts unknown.

From this detective's perspective, this was HIS song, HIS anthem, HIS ballad, about HIS people, the last time we all heard it together. What a difference two years and a new Chief makes, eh? Especially if it's the former Chief and the one who was TRULY innocent.

"…Because I am an innocent man…"

Yes, you were; yes, you are, Chief Viola. Thanks one more time, Billy Joel.

* * * * *

As there was good news in regards to who was leaving the BPD, one as a result of alleged physical injuries sustained in a fender-bender and at least one other for alleged personal reasons, there was also good news in terms of someone who came back into the fold. That would be former detective Ken Hopkins. You may recall he quit the police department during the first year of the Dark Side re-regime and went to work as an investigator in one of the Atlantic City casinos. Shortly after the new Board took over, and once Viola was officially back in charge, Ken contacted the Township and it was agreed he could return at his previous full rank and time served. He was a great investigator, a class guy, and thusly welcomed back to CID by Chief Viola and Capt. Robinson as well as the majority of his fellow officers. That included me too.

Viola didn't give Ken much time to get re-acclimated to his previous position in CID. Within a week or two, along with some new cases he had been assigned, he delegated to Det. Hopkins the task of forming a drug squad within the BPD. He wanted a REAL one too, not like the pretend television version that was recently cancelled due to very poor ratings.

Ken was assigned the mission of building this new squad, and in doing so he went about looking for the right two officers to staff it. They had to be hard-working, street-smart, have a familiarity with the drug trade and the people engaged in it, know the inherent dangers involved, and be willing to work long and usually late night hours. He found those two officers in Tim Carroll (he assisted me with the '84 arrest of teenage-boy flasher Joe Scheck) and T.J. Campellone, a hard working officer with about four years' experience under his belt. They were both still in the patrol division but with their successful arrest records as well as their overall work accomplishments, they were definitely the right officers for the task. To no one's surprise, they started making quality drug arrests right away.

Within a few months, T.J. voluntarily left the unit (for unrelated personal reasons) and Tim was then joined by John Knowles. I mentioned John earlier as he was the officer who in early January of '84 told me what he heard of my supposed pending demotion and showed me the departmental hit-list of checked names of Viola supporters that he happened to find in the roll room.

John was a former BPD radio dispatcher who took the police entrance exam a year or two after I took mine and eventually made his way onto the department as a patrolman. He was a Bensalem native and came from a family of twelve kids. His father was a well-liked and well-respected physician who ran a small but successful family practice in Bensalem for decades.

Interestingly, John Knowles became a card-carrying, life-long "enemy of the people" when during one of the very rare Dark Side sponsored award ceremonies for officers not directly affiliated with their team, he did something to really piss them off...and they never forgave him.

It seems John was at a weekly Monday evening township meeting sometime in early 1984 to receive a well-earned commendation for one of his many exceptional arrests. As per tradition, after receiving the framed award he and several other so-commended officers would walk down a short line of police bosses and elected officials to shake their hands. As per that tradition, John proceeded down that line and shook the hands of the first several people. However, when he came to Stephen Kelly, positioned somewhere in the middle of the pack, he pulled his hand back and walked directly in front of him. He didn't even make eye contact with him. Once John passed Kelly, he then continued shaking the hands of the remaining several people on the dais. The officers then left the township auditorium and the general meeting resumed.

The word got back to us that after the meeting Kelly was beside himself about John's public snubbing of him. He let his then-Deputy Chief know about it too. How dare one of HIS police officers embarrass him thusly in public?

The word never got back to us how Zajac answered his boss.

John told me later that he simply couldn't shake the hand of this particular elected township supervisor, even if the man had managed to be acquitted of his federal meth distribution charges. In good conscious, John said, he just couldn't do it. Debbie Knowles, his very nice wife, in the audience that night, couldn't believe what she just observed her husband do. Or not do. In the long run, like a good spouse and a good friend, she supported him wholeheartedly. So did many others in the BPD, including me.

Needless to say, departmental award ceremonies for non-Dark Siders were few and far between afterwards. Actually, they were virtually non-existent. That'll teach 'em not to shake Stephen Kelly's hand.

I can almost hear Kelly say back then, "Damn it, as an elected Bensalem Township Supervisor, when I put my hand out, I expect something in it."

Well, you came up empty-handed that Monday night, didn't you, Stephen? In my opinion, John Knowles should have received another commendation for that act alone.

Tim Carroll, the other new BPD narc, was Philadelphia born and bred like me. He attended Archbishop Ryan High School, a rival Catholic school to mine, having graduated a year after me. He was hired by the BPD in 1977. Tim had a B.S. degree too, getting his at Delaware Valley College, near Doylestown, Pennsylvania.

Coincidently, Tim and I both had friends who were officers on the Philadelphia PD. Some of them happened to even know one another. Occasionally, with some pre-planning, Tim and I would meet with these friends/officers on the Philly-Bensalem border late at night when our shifts happened to correspond and the police radios were otherwise quiet on both sides of the jurisdictional line. This didn't happen too often, but it was nice when we could sometimes work it out and the four or more of us could compare agencies, bosses, bad guys, and other relevant and some not so relevant issues over hot beverages as we watched the sun come up over our respective jurisdictions.

When the new BPD drug squad was first proposed by Chief Viola, Ken wanted my input in the selection process as I was the only one who actually worked with most of the applicants on the streets as a patrolman and later as a sergeant. I fully advocated for T.J. and Tim to Detective Hopkins, Chief Viola, and Captain Robinson. We eventually agreed unanimously in choosing them for this squad, then welcoming John Knowles onboard later when T.J. went back to patrol.

As when I was appointed to the Tactical Squad, this wasn't a promotion per se for these officers. That is, there was no elevation in rank or salary. It was a lateral transfer. But it was considered by many to be a highly desired position. A number of officers put in for it and those of us with say in the selection process agreed that out of all of them these three were ultimately the cream of the crop.

As it turned out, no one was disappointed with these officers' appointments except, I would suppose, the local drug dealers. As 1986 progressed into 1987, the team of Tim Carroll and John Knowles, supervised by Ken Hopkins, made more drug arrests than any other police department in Bucks County, including the Bucks County Detectives themselves. They also worked very closely with Ken Anthony, a Pennsylvania State Police (PSP) trooper assigned to his agency's narcotics division which covered Bucks County.

Tim and John, sometimes with the assistance of the PSP and/or other agencies, would bust lower-level drug guys and then convince them to name their mid-level suppliers. On a number of occasions, they even convinced the mid-level suppliers to name their high-level drug suppliers, to include those selling not just marijuana, but also cocaine, P2P, meth, as well as other Schedule I drugs. Arrests would be forthcoming.

It would usually all start with what were known as "buy-busts." That is, Tim and John would convince an already arrested guy that they could get him a "deal" of some sort and he could reduce his charges and ultimate prison sentence if he would help them get the next person up the drug distribution ladder. When one of these buy-busts was set up, Tim and John would confirm that the cooperating witness's pockets were empty of any drugs, they'd watch him as they sent him into a known drug house, apartment, hotel, or motel room with marked bills, and the purchase would be made. The cooperator would come out, show the two narcs the just bought drugs and they'd do a quick chemical field test to make sure it was the real stuff. When it was confirmed to be an actual illegal drug they'd then have the uniform cops already on standby come around the corner, bust down the door, and the arrest(s) and search would follow.

Shortly thereafter, when the new arrestee was confronted with his immediate and long-term future in the criminal justice system, invariably Tim and John would convince him to do the same thing against the guy up the ladder from whom HE bought his drugs. If it was in Bensalem, they could run this next phase on their own. If it was elsewhere in Bucks County or Pennsylvania, they would bring in Trooper Anthony and/or the Bucks County Detectives and take down the next drug house...and so on.

Tim Carroll and John Knowles were very successful in their first several years as they plied their trade as narcs in the BPD. Their arrests made headlines several times per month during this period and it resulted with everyone in our department looking great. The Bucks County Detectives, the PSP, the DEA, and even the FBI on more than one occasion let Chief Viola know that they truly appreciated the work of the BPD drug squad. This was especially appreciated as these agencies had virtually no contact with the previous BPD drug squad. As a side benefit, many other criminal cases would be made and duly prosecuted, even those not directly associated with the drug trade, as a result of some of the arrests made and subsequent interviews of the druggies by these two very effective narcotics officers on the new squad.

The juxtaposition of the immediate past drug squad and the new drug squad was as different as Chief Zajac was to Chief Viola, and Det. Donson and partners were to Officers Carroll and Knowles. It was hard to believe there actually WAS a drug squad at the BPD which pre-dated the work of the current one. It didn't matter anymore. Tim Carroll and John Knowles, as supervised by Ken Hopkins, were doing the job now, and doing it very well.

Drug dealers in Bensalem be aware! And this time we really mean it!

* * * * *

It wasn't only the drug squad who was making quality arrests during this time frame. A certain patrol sergeant, unleashed on the streets of Bensalem for the first time after being cooped up for the better part of two years performing menial tasks at HQ (e.g., in charge of vandalism investigations, evidence closet, truck trailer, etc.) made a pretty good arrest himself before too long. And, as a patrol sergeant, making arrests wasn't even necessarily his primary function. No, it was supervising his officers and facilitating THEIR abilities to make arrests, serve the public, etc., which was his priority. But, as mentioned once or twice before here, old habits die hard, especially when they come to catching bad guys.

This so-referenced patrol sergeant was, of course, me. And, while I was a pretty good patrol supervisor, I also could make a pretty good arrest myself every once in a while. Interestingly enough, one particular arrest would initiate the opening of several doors for me which, once stepped through, would usher me onto the next stage of my profession.

As I've stated here numerous times, but it's worth repeating... timing can be everything in life. And this forthcoming series of events would certainly reinforce that notion.

But first, the crime and the arrest....

On February 13, 1986, with me barely nine weeks back in patrol sergeant status, an attempted robbery occurred at the Beneficial Savings Bank located at Street and Hulmeville Rds. It occurred at 2:20 in the afternoon. I was working the 7A–5P shift and wasn't far from the scene when the bank alarm call was broadcast over the police radio. Once the dispatcher telephonically contacted the bank and found out it was, in fact, an actual attempted robbery, and the proper secret code was received that the gunman had departed the scene, it was duly transmitted. Hearing that information, I parked my car out front and cautiously proceeded inside.

(Many of us in the BPD remembered the years ago bank robbery alarm situation involving Sgt. Gene Ashton - referenced at the very beginning of this book - and what happened to him when he did NOT wait for the secret code. If you recall, he walked in on an active robbery in progress. He was held hostage for a while and was very fortunate to escape with his life.)

I took this attempted robbery rather personally because it happened to occur at my personal bank branch. Upon entering the crime scene, I soon came to realize that my favorite teller was the intended victim. It was her second time as such, too. Yes, ironically, the same bank and the very same teller had been robbed by the same gunman only three months earlier. He got over $5800 that last time.

The victim teller on this day was physically alright but quite emotionally distraught when I first walked over to her. However, between her sobs, deep breaths, and comforting words and gestures from her co-workers, all of which I encouraged as a way for her to calm herself, within a minute or two she managed to provide me with the info I was ever so anxiously requesting.

The woman described the attempted robbery suspect to me as a white male, about six feet tall, in his 50s, with grayish hair, and wearing a yellow baseball-type cap. Another employee sitting at one of the bank's front desks managed to obtain an excellent description of the almost-robber's vehicle as he fled the scene. He told me it was a mid-'70s white Firebird Trans Am. With this info in hand, I walked toward the glass windows at the front of the bank and via my portable radio I relayed the suspect and car flash information over the airwaves for all my squad members to hear. They would know what to do with it.

As I ascertained just a minute or two later, once the aforementioned teller heard the robber say to her, "Give me all your money," she immediately recognized his voice, his appearance, and the gun itself from the previous stick-up. With the weapon pointed directly at her, she decided right then and there to simply run from her window to the end of the counter and crouch down on the floor. The gunman, flummoxed and seemingly not knowing what to do next, proceeded to exit the bank. He still had his gun in his hand but with no other tellers at their windows he left with no cash in his free hand.

Interestingly, as with almost every at-gunpoint robbery victim I've ever interviewed on scene shortly after its occurrence, the description of the handgun by this teller was remarkably consistent. It was either "big" or "large" or some such similar word. That's how she and most of the others I've interviewed over the years tended to recall firearm dimensions immediately after an armed robbery. I fully understood and respected their possible distortional descriptions relating to weapon size. It's only natural when one is held that close to a person's face that the actual size is never fully comprehended. Gun size, I came to realize, is clearly in the eyes of the beholder, especially when the barrel is pointed within just inches of those eyes.

For this case, I knew it would be the description of the man, what he was wearing, and the car which would prove to be the most valuable evidence. So, I put that info out there hoping one of my squad mates or other officers in surrounding jurisdictions would pick up on it and locate the car, the man, or hopefully both.

However, despite the relatively detailed descriptive information broadcast and rebroadcast over police radios throughout the whole of lower Bucks County, to include over the PSP and the Philadelphia PD radio systems, there were no identifications or stops of the car or its driver during the next half hour. He seemed to have made a clean getaway.

Damn...!

Once the BPD detectives arrived on the scene at the bank they took over the interviewing of the tellers and the other witnesses, as well as beginning the forensic processing of the bank for fingerprints and other evidence. As was customary, since bank robbery (even an attempted one) is a federal offense, the FBI would be notified. Sometimes they would come to the scene right away; sometimes it would be later in the day or even the next day, depending on their availability at the time. However, since the BPD was once again under the leadership of Chief Viola, he had now reestablished a positive working relationship with the various federal authorities in the area. As such, they would entrust the immediate follow-up of the bank robbery to the Bensalem investigators. The FBI would take the case over at some point in the near future when appropriate.

By around 2:40 that afternoon I departed the crime scene in my patrol car. My job there was done. I immediately got on the radio and instructed my officers to start checking out other banks in the area as this suspect may be hard-up for money. Since he struck out at the Beneficial Bank, he may try to rob another one. Bank robbers have been known to attempt another robbery shortly after a failed one, depending many times on their level of financial desperation.

(Some bank robbers are actually very predictable in their timing. Usually, if they are junkies, desperate for their next drug fix, and depending on the amount of the "take" at their last successful bank robbery, it can be predicted to almost the day when they will strike again.)

While driving westbound on Street Rd., I also started assigning my guys to check the various apartment complex parking lots in an attempt to find the white Trans Am. It would be a longshot as I didn't necessarily think this guy would be a "local," but as the same bank was robbed twice in less than three months, it's possible he was a resident of Bensalem, or at least a long-term visitor. After assigning different complexes to different officers, I drove the half-mile or so to Knights

Rd., turned left to proceed southbound, and upon reaching Dunks Ferry Rd., I drove into the sprawling Doral Apartments parking lot. I figured it would be like looking for a needle in a haystack in this place, but it would be as good of a place as any for me to check right about now.

I proceeded to zig and zag throughout the serpentine roadways of the expansive garden complex which was the Doral Apartments. After about ten minutes of scanning the lot for an older American made white sports car I found myself in one of the southwest corner parking areas. There, I came upon a row of parked vehicles. One of them was backed into its spot. It happened to be an unoccupied, mid-'70s, white Trans Am.

(As Pennsylvania was then and remains now one of the very few U.S. states with registration tag placement ONLY on the rear of cars, to me it was always a clue something may be amiss when any car was parked in its slot rear-end first. When I would routinely notice such a vehicle parked that way, it was usually worth checking the car's tag and vehicle identification number, aka VIN, to make sure all was copasetic about it. Sometimes it was, other times it was not.)

I got out to check the registration plate on this Trans Am. On the way to the rear of the car, I did three other things. First, via my portable radio, I advised dispatch of my specific location and that I was checking out a white Trans Am. Secondly, I felt the hood area. It was hot. That means the engine had been running recently which suggests the car had just been parked here a very short while ago. Thirdly, I looked inside the car's windows to view its interior. Upon doing so something caught my attention right away. It was a yellow baseball cap sitting on the back floor. It very closely matched the teller's description of the cap worn by the robber during this and the previous robbery.

When I finally made it to the rear of the Trans Am I called in to the dispatcher the tag number. I also requested backup to my locale as this was becoming more and more interesting.

I was pretty certain I had found the getaway vehicle and stated as much over the airwaves. At that point, the crime scene essentially shifted from the bank to my location at the Doral Apartments. I stayed with the car, blocking it in so it couldn't be driven away if by chance the suspected gunman appeared on the scene. And, with that possibility in mind, I was also ever vigilant in monitoring the area around me, both at ground level and up in the surrounding buildings. This suspect was armed, and I didn't want him taking a surprise shot at me from either up close or from an open second floor apartment window or balcony.

So, I watched...I stayed alert...I waited....

The dispatcher provided me with the plate registration information over the air. It was not stolen and came back to that make, model, and year of car, but to an address not associated with Doral Apartments or anywhere in Bensalem or even nearby. Hmmm....

Within a few more minutes the reinforcements arrived. They included several of my squad mates as well as Capt. Jack Robinson and a few detectives who had just departed the bank. We more or less surrounded the car, the small section of the parking lot, and the buildings in the immediate area. What we didn't know at first was whether this guy, if he was in fact the bank robber, could see or hear the growing police presence down in the parking lot below or adjacent to him. We just weren't sure yet on what side of the building his unit was located and how much of our activity he could readily observe. In other words, we may or may not hold the element of surprise in our favor. We'd prefer to have it, but there was presently no means of knowing one way or the other.

Coincidently, a person walked out of one of the buildings just as we were establishing our inner and outer perimeters at this location. He didn't match the description of our bank robber so I felt free to ask him if he happened to know who owned the white Trans Am. Fortuitously, he did. He pointed up to the exact unit where the owner lived. When further asked, he described him as a 50-something, gray haired, white male. He lived there with a woman but he didn't know his name.

Okay, thank you, sir. Now please get back inside your residence and don't come out until we tell you it is okay.

He obeyed. He didn't have much choice.

In the next minute or so, Capt. Robinson brought out a bullhorn from his trunk and pointed it up in the direction of the apartment in which the car's driver supposedly lived. After the usual bullhorn squelching sounds dissipated, Jack's booming and now very clear voice could be heard. It was heard specifically ordering the man in apartment 40-57 (fictitious unit) to come outside with his hands visible.

It took a few minutes, and a few more loud squelches, but after the order was repeated several times by Capt. Jack a man eventually walked out of the front door of the building with his hands up. He exactly met the description of the bank robber as provided to me by the teller. While still focusing on the suspect, a few of us stole side-glances at each other and nodded as if to say, "Yeah, we got 'em." I approached him with my gun drawn and once he was thoroughly searched for weapons, I handcuffed him.

The detectives took over and brought the suspected bank robber into HQ. I assigned two officers to guard the outside of his empty apartment as a search warrant for it was being prepared. I also called for a tow truck to come and bring the car into our impoundment yard for it to be searched. I then left the apartment complex. As my shift was over at 5:00 I went home without knowing too much more about this suspect and this case.

Ken Hopkins called me at my house later that night and told me we hit the jackpot with this guy. Through a fingerprint check, Ken told me it was determined that his name was James Joseph Murphy. He was wanted by the U. S. Marshals and the FBI. It seems he escaped from a federal penitentiary in Chicago in 1982 and subsequently he committed bank robberies in Illinois, Minnesota, Florida, and now Pennsylvania. He stole over $70,000 during the course of this three-plus year crime spree.

Murphy eventually confessed to the attempted robbery on this day at the Beneficial Savings Bank and also at the same branch on November 22nd of last year. The search of his apartment turned up the gun. It was a toy gun, but one which looked very authentic, certainly to the bank teller I interviewed that afternoon. It not being a real gun took nothing away from the charges against this guy. Other incriminating evidence was found in Murphy's residence and in his car too.

In the end, it wasn't just "case closed" with this attempted robbery arrest today, which in and of itself would have been great. But it was "case closed" on multiple actual bank robberies in at least three other states as well as a prison escape. Not a bad closure rate for the BPD, and all in one day too.

I'm glad I happened upon the white Trans Am in the Doral Apartments parking lot that afternoon shortly after the robbery. So was the FBI when a few months later the Philadelphia Division Special Agent in Charge (SAC), Wayne G. Davis, sent Chief Viola and the BPD an official letter offering "sincere appreciation and congratulations" to me and the others that day in effecting Murphy's arrest. We were also informed by the FBI that he pleaded guilty to his various crimes and was sentenced to fifteen years in federal prison.

I know the Beneficial Bank teller was glad to hear of Murphy's sentencing too. I told her about it one day as I was cashing my paycheck. While counting out some twenty dollar bills for me I noticed her grinning from ear to ear with the satisfaction of learning she would never see him OR his gun again, be it real or a very authentic looking replica.

I grinned back at her and let her know I agreed.

The teller quit her job within a few months. Two robberies at gunpoint (real or fake) in less than half a year was too much. I can't say I blamed her.

Chapter Fifty-Nine

By chance, a week or so after the bank robbery I happened to be in HQ. I recall I wasn't on a day-work shift but I believe I may have been there for the now-monthly patrol sergeants' meeting. For whatever reason I was at HQ, afterwards I walked into the CID area as it was friendly confines for me once again. I wanted to see what was new with the Chief, the Captain, and maybe even a few detective colleagues in CID.

I don't think Viola was in that day but upon walking toward Robinson's office door I could see he was in there with a visitor I didn't recognize. It was a professional looking man who was approximately my age. As I assumed it was a private meeting I turned around to walk away. However, when Jack saw it was me, he immediately called me into his office.

When I was barely through the doorway Capt. Robinson articulated very matter of fact-like to both me and his guest, "Sgt. Jim Fitzgerald, I'd like you to meet Special Agent Frank Brown (fictitious name) of the FBI. The Bureau is taking over the Beneficial Bank robbery cases and he's here to retrieve the evidence, our reports, and whatever else he needs. C'mon in Jim, have a seat!"

I walked in, extended my hand to shake Frank's, and sat down in one of the chairs in Jack's office. I told the noticeably fit and trim FBI agent in the well-cut suit and brightly polished shoes that it was a pleasure to meet him.

In his also matter of fact-like response the FBI agent stated, "Same here, Sgt. Fitzgerald. I read the initial reports in this case and I've been talking to Capt. Robinson and I want to congratulate you on making this arrest last week. I believe you now know Murphy was wanted for prison escape as well as numerous BRs, er, bank robberies, from here to Illinois. Your arrest closed lots of cases in various FBI divisions east of the Mississippi, including here in the Philadelphia Division."

"Well, thanks. I appreciate you saying that. It was really a team effort though. Capt. Robinson is the one who convinced the suspect to come out of his apartment and…"

Jack butted in, "Yeah, but Jim here was the one who first found his car. We'd all be still looking for the perp otherwise."

After some related small talk, the Captain added, "Anyway, Jim, I'm going to give Frank the evidence in a few minutes here. But I'm glad you stopped by today and you two had the occasion to meet."

Both Frank and I concurred as we shook hands. I bid him farewell after our brief three-way conversation and left the office. He went with Jack to retrieve the toy gun, yellow cap, and other materials from the bank robbery. I made one or two other stops around HQ.

Having just met that agent though, the rest of the time there I was thinking, and wondering….

Coincidently, the FBI agent and I just happened to cross paths one more time outside in the parking lot as he was putting a Xerox box full of evidence into the trunk of his car. Interesting timing this would turn out to be regarding me and this man, now twice in one afternoon, and especially as I had been just thinking, and wondering….

Without much conscious aforethought, I walked over to the agent. A question had popped into my head. It's one which I've been pondering for some time now. Agent Brown would be the ideal person to direct my inquiry and since he's here, and it's the second time I'm running into him….

I again told Frank it was nice meeting him inside and reminded him that if there's anything he or the FBI may need from me regarding this case, to please not hesitate to ask. He thanked me again for facilitating the Murphy arrest and my just-now offer to continue to assist in any way I could. We then got to talking about the Bureau, his background, and a few related matters.

When it came to me, among other issues I mentioned to the agent was that I had recently read something in the news that President Reagan and/or Congress were debating the lifting of the hiring freeze within the federal government. I told him that I had been curious to ask someone associated with the feds as to when hiring may be starting up again. And since he was right here, I asked Brown if he happened to have heard whether the government would be hiring again; specifically, in his agency.

Seemingly having talked to similarly interested cops prior to this in their own backyards or elsewhere, Frank waited until one of my fellow uniformed officers strode by us and then replied in a somewhat lower volume.

"Jim, I recently learned through our Applicant Coordinator that we're going to be resuming special agent testing in the next month or two. May I ask...are you interested in joining the FBI?"

Standing by the trunk of his dark-colored Bureau car, I looked away from the FBI agent for just a moment, glancing at the BPD building to my right side and turning my head to glance at the evidence trailer to my left side. In the no more than two seconds that I took in these separate visualizations, the last two years of my career flashed before my eyes. It wasn't a welcome flashback either. The faces, the assignments, the memos, the headaches, all seemed to be swirling around inside my brain like a slow moving tornado at this exact juncture in time. Then, as quickly as it all began, the tornadic swirl of bad memories came to a sudden halt.

That's when I came back to the present and responded to the agent, "Well...you know, Frank... I think I'd like to at least explore my options."

"Sure, I understand. Jim, if I may ask...how old are you?"

"I'm 32."

"Okay, you're fine there. I assume you know that 35 is the maximum age for the FBI to hire special agents. Also, do you have a college degree?"

"I'm aware of the age factor and, yes, I do have a BS degree. In fact, I'm finishing up my Master's at Villanova as we speak."

"That's good to hear, Jim. No doubt you'll be a very competitive candidate. Listen, I'm going to give you my business card. On the back I'm going to write the name and direct phone number of the Philadelphia Division's Applicant Coordinator. Call her and mention you spoke to me. She can send you all the necessary paperwork and you can get started on the process. I think you'd be a great asset to the FBI...if you would decide to come on board, that is."

We shook hands one last time and Frank left in his vehicle. I put the business card in my shirt pocket and drove home.

When I got to my house I figured...what the heck? So I called the FBI, asked for the person on the back of the card, and was actually put through to her. Her name was Jerri Williams and she was very helpful that day. She, in fact, confirmed what Frank had told me regarding the hiring process. I requested her to send me some additional information. She did.

Within a week, for the second time, I received a several-paged special agent application in the mail from the FBI. I filled it out exactly as I had the last time, except on this application I had to check off one extra box. That was the box which indicated that I had previously taken the test. Underneath that little box, in small print, it reminded the potential applicant that he/she only had two opportunities to take the FBI entrance exam. If the candidate falls below the cutoff score the second time, he/she would not have another chance to take the test again.

That meant for me if I wanted to pursue this professional opportunity with the FBI, this would be the last time I could do so. Essentially, it was one and done for me at this point.

It hit me then and there. I gotta get it right this time because there will be no next time for me, not with the FBI anyway. That was an indisputable fact I had to deal with accordingly. Perhaps this time I'd have to do something out of the ordinary.

I decided on the very day I took my completed application to the post office and mailed it off to the Philadelphia FBI office that IF I'm going to take this exam one more time I will have to approach this one differently. That is, I will have to properly prepare for it. Unlike when I took the PACE (federal government multi-agency job test) back in the mid-'70s, and then the prior FBI test just about two years ago, I'd better actually study for this one, in some way or in some manner. At a minimum, I'd need to buy one or more of those red and blue professional study guides I would see in the various bookstores at the mall. Or, perhaps even hire a tutor with some expertise in these types of tests.

Summing up my situation here...I knew I was a relatively intelligent guy, and I could do very well in undergrad and now grad courses. I was well read with very good common sense and street sense. I came to realize, however, that there was an art to taking these standardized tests. I needed to learn to be a bit more, well, artful when taking such a test, especially in the math portions, which I was sure was always my weakness. So, bottom line here, I was determined to not go cold into this event with little or no preparation such as I did in my two prior federal test-taking events over the last ten years. This one would be different for me because there would be no second chances, certainly not with this agency.

As my new test-taking strategy was forming, I thought of a relatively new company in the Andalusia area of Bensalem which could possibly be of help to me. I had been there once before in the last year and met the manager regarding a minor outdoor vandalism problem of some sort. He was a nice guy. I wondered if he still worked there.

The company's name was the Sylvan Learning Center (SLC).

While on a day-work shift a week or two after mailing my application, I stopped in the SLC storefront facility. The same manager happened to be there. He recognized me and advised that the vandalism was only that one-time incident and thanked me for however it was I handled it back then. I said, "You're welcome. Anytime."

Slowly switching gears, I advised the manager of my very specific needs on this day. I confided in him that I was about to take the FBI exam and wanted to know if there was anyone in his employ who perhaps specializes in prepping someone for such tests. I told him I'd like to focus on the math portions, but I'd be open to go over any test-taking hints (i.e., the "art" thereof) which could be shared with me. Upon his non-verbal direction, I followed the manager into his office. Once there, he spun through his desktop Rolodex and eventually stopped and pulled out a business card. Holding it up to me the manager strongly suggested that this is the person I wanted. I was assured that this particular tutor knew his stuff regarding state and federal test-taking as he's successfully provided similar training sessions in the past. And it so happens he's also a math teacher at a Philadelphia high school.

Good enough for me, I told the SLC manager. Now, how do I go about hiring him?

The manager and I worked out the financial details in the office that day. This teacher/tutor didn't come cheap, but I was convinced that it would be money well spent on my part. With that in mind, later that evening I called the referred gentleman and we arranged to meet four separate times over the course of the next four weeks. For purposes of having a quiet workspace, we agreed to hold our hourly sessions at my house when Eileen and the kids were not there. The final two-hour session, a review, was set for the week before the exam.

When we finally met, the tutor was a guy a few years older than me who wore round gold-rimmed glasses and had his long hair in a ponytail. He reminded me of a hippie from the late '60s. That didn't bother me one way or the other as he was seemingly a very bright guy, especially in the multiple types of problems we knew I'd be tasked with solving in this upcoming FBI special agent exam. Once started, we focused on math, to include basic algebra, geometry, fractions, decimals, percentages, and the like. We went over all the different types of questions I could expect in the test. He provided me with an excellent study guide too.

As we progressed over the next several weeks, I was reminded of some of the math formulae from my years ago high school classes. With this excellent one-on-one tutoring (which, unfortunately, I had never taken advantage of in my student days) this stuff actually started making sense to me. I could figure out the written problems the tutor was presenting to me better and even faster with each passing week. I was practicing on my own too, of course.

I knew I was never going to become a math genius at this stage in life, but that wasn't my goal here. I just wanted to get through this test with a passing grade. That was my only objective for now, certainly from a written test perspective. The rest of the hiring process I could handle when the time presented itself. I was sure of that. I just had to get my foot in that fed door, specifically the FBI door, which meant I had to pass this test.

Upon receiving the official response in the mail from the FBI, I now had a confirmed test date. It was set for early April. When it was only a week away, and during my last multi-hour overview session with the tutor, I felt very comfortable. I knew for the first time in my life I had truly prepared for one of these standardized federal government examinations and I was ready to go. The date was marked on my calendar. It happened to be on a scheduled day off and I was very much looking forward to the challenge.

Then, something came up. It was something not completely unexpected, yet caught me off-guard at the same time. And it also involved the FBI. It was very strange timing, to say the least. It again got me thinking, and wondering....

So it came to pass...literally three or four days before the FBI special agent examination I was beckoned to Jack Robinson's office late one afternoon. I believe I may have just started a 5P-3A shift and he was still at HQ. He later told me he purposely stayed late that day and waited until I was done roll call and got my troops out on the street. That's when he told me to follow him back to his office. So, I did.

Once inside, the Captain closed his office door and we both sat down. I was really curious what he had to tell me or ask me. This wasn't his usual style. Not an hour after his usual quitting time anyway.

Jack then inquired, "What are your plans for this coming fall?"

"Eh...the fall, what do you mean? What part of this coming fall?"

"Say...between late September and early December?"

"Well, Jack, I don't know. That's like six months from now. I'll be here as far as I know. Do you know something different?"

During this very brief discourse, my mind was wandering all over the place. I knew I wasn't in trouble for anything, but I also knew that I was taking an FBI test in just a few days. Did Jack somehow find out about it? Did Jack think I had already taken the test and passed it and was on my way out of the BPD? Did the hippie tutor talk?

O Captain! My Captain! (Thank you, Walt Whitman.)

What do you know or what do you think you know?

My captain, Jack Robinson, from his seated position behind his desk ever so-demonstrably held up an already opened envelope and slowly pulled a letter out of it. Once he unfolded it I could see the FBI seal on the top of it. It seemed to be official about something - I just didn't know what yet.

That's when the head of CID ended the guessing game. While clearly smiling he said, "Well, Jim, I told you it may take them a few years, and it did. But it looks like you're just about next in line in the Philly area to attend the FBI National Academy (FBI-NA) in Quantico. It would be in September. According to this letter, it would be the 147th Session. Do you think you could find the time to go?"

"Holy Shit! That's what this is all about? You mean two and a half years after you nominated me to the NA, this is finally coming to pass?"

"That's what this letter says. Here, read it."

I read it. It was just one page, very basic, and also signed by SAC Wayne Davis. (He signed the earlier letter congratulating/thanking me for the bank robbery arrest.) It made it clear that the BPD was at the top of the list of the approximately one hundred police departments in the Philadelphia Division to send one of its nominated officers to the NA. As I was the only one presently nominated from my department, it was my name and my name alone which was included as eligible. In the last paragraph it requested the Chief to contact the local FBI-NA Coordinator in Philadelphia. Once he did so and officially sanctioned my attendance there, the wheels would start turning.

"Jack, if you want to know if I'm still interested in attending the NA, you gotta know that I am. Yes, have Viola call or write to whomever and let's light this candle. Absolutely! I'm in! This is such great news!"

Jack told me he had already spoken to Viola and the Chief assured him that my attendance was a done deal. Viola merely wanted Jack to talk to me and make sure I was still interested. Once that was established, he'd contact the Philly FBI office, talk to his people there, and move the process along.

Any law enforcement officer would be crazy to NOT want to attend the NA, especially as it was usually a multi-year wait just to be considered. And no, I wasn't crazy. I told the Captain, however, that I should probably run this whole scenario by my wife and make sure she's okay with it. This shouldn't be a problem with her, I assured him, as it wouldn't be a complete surprise. Eileen knew from several years ago that I had been nominated to the NA by Viola and Robinson. Naturally, though, I wanted to make sure she would be okay with handling the household and our two kids for the eleven weeks I was away. I told him I'd call tomorrow.

Upon running it all by Eileen later that evening she was, in fact, okay with this professional advancement opportunity, despite the fact that I'd be in Quantico, Virginia, for almost three months. I let her know, very truthfully, that I would definitely miss her and the two boys while away. However, we both knew it was offered to such a select few U. S. law enforcement officers that it would be preposterous to pass on it. So, we agreed. I/we wouldn't pass on it. Plus, I promised Eileen that as I'd have a BPD unmarked car to drive back and forth from Bensalem to the NA, I'd do my best to be home most weekends. She liked hearing that part. So did seven-year-old Sean and four-year-old Dan.

I called Jack the next day and told him to advise the FBI that I was ready, willing, and able to attend the 147th Session of their National Academy. Whatever they need, I'll give them. Whatever they want done, I'll do it. Just let me know. Jack said he'd have the Chief call later that day and start moving the process along.

I thanked Capt. Robinson yet again for nominating me in the first place over two years ago, and then following through now with this next stage. He said he was glad to do so as I deserved it. While still on the phone, I then couldn't help but ask him how he felt this would have been handled if the letter just happened to have arrived during the Dark Side's regime. Without any hesitation he was adamant in his telling me that my attendance at the NA would have never been approved by them, for one bogus reason or another. But would they have also tried to remove my name off the list all together? Could they have done so?

By coincidence (maybe, maybe not) the NA invitational letter regarding me wasn't sent out until about three months into the new Viola regime. If it had been anytime in '84 or '85, Jack and I agreed that the letter would have never even been shown to me and that regime would have done everything in its power to get me OFF the list itself.

Before hanging up that day Jack and I concurred that it didn't matter anymore. That was then, this is now, and those days and those people are slowly fading off into everyone's collective institutional memories. This fall I was heading to the FBI-NA, the most prestigious law enforcement academy in the world. Right now, that's all that concerned me.

The timing of it all was perfect. It was the ideal scenario.

Right?

Well, perhaps not so fast here....

When I hung up the phone with Capt. Robinson I looked at the kitchen wall calendar and was reminded of something. According to the date circled in red, the FBI special agent exam was now only three days away. With the phone call barely ended I started thinking a bit more clearly about these very recent events and that's when it became a dilemma for me. Not too bad of a dilemma I suppose, but one of some measurable proportions nonetheless.

The dilemma involved the fact that the two highest ranking BPD supervisors were now strongly advocating for me and fully endorsing me to attend this much-desired and hard-to-get-into FBI training academy class. It has been in the works for me for two and a half years now. Their/our department would then arguably become a better organization with at least one more supervisor (me) as a graduate of the National Academy.

At the same time, unbeknownst to them, I was about to take an entrance exam to possibly become a special agent in the same agency which also runs this separate and distinct police officer training academy I've been nominated to attend. If I'm successful in taking this test, I would possibly quit the BPD to work for that agency...as a special agent.

I was being pulled in two directions here. Interestingly, both involved the FBI. One was at a very early stage at this point. I mean, I'd still have to pass the damn written exam in a few days and then there would be numerous other steps to take. The alternate one, by all measures, was essentially a done deal. I just had to take care of some routine administrative issues and I'd be spending eleven weeks in Quantico in the fall.

So...how do I handle this? What are my choices, what are my obligations? Are there ethical and/or moral issues at hand here?

Do I tell Viola and Robinson of my possible long-term intentions with the FBI? Do I ask them to put my NA processing on hold until I know one way or the other whether I pass the entrance exam and may be leaving the BPD? However, even if I pass the written test, it is by no means a guarantee I'll be hired by the FBI.

This is perplexing. It's the proverbial fork in the road which I'm facing here. There are no guarantees of results in either direction, even if both forks happen to lead to the FBI Academy. One is short-term but with many advantages to my future police career in the BPD or perhaps at another department. The other is a whole change of venue for me, literally, but with no guarantees that there will even be a venue change.

What DO I do?

I eventually did the smart thing and I believe the right thing. It took talking to my wife and some deep soul-searching to figure it out, but it made perfect sense to me afterwards.

As no department or agency was promising me anything here, I must again take matters one step at a time and address each separate opportunity as they present themselves and in the order in which they are presented. I reminded myself that I already told Capt. Robinson to follow through on the NA appointment paperwork for the fall session.

So...that's done!

The special agent exam is in three days. I reminded myself that I've already filled out the application and signed up for it, not to mention spent time and money prepping for it. I'm going to take it.

So...that's done!

Plus, for perhaps one of the first times in my life I was coming to grips with something about myself. It wasn't necessarily easy to reckon with, but I had to, and starting right now too. That is, I was not a kid anymore. I was rapidly approaching the ripe old age of 33. With the maximum hiring age for FBI special agents at 35, my window of opportunity with that agency was slowly closing down. Again, it was one and done with this next test, and now with only slightly over two years to possibly get it done.

In the end, I simply decided to follow through on both of these options as they presented themselves and see where each one leads. I will take the exam in a few days and I will not say anything to the BPD management regarding it. There's simply no need for them to know anything right now and I'll leave it that way. Furthermore, I will allow BPD management to continue my application to the NA and we'll let that run its natural course.

As was my philosophy when I began seriously job hunting near the end of my college days...whoever offers me a viable position first, they will be the one I go with. If another opportunity comes along after that, well, I'll cross that bridge then and there.

That made the most sense and is fair to all involved, to include me, the BPD, and the FBI.

My last working shift two nights before I took the special agent exam was a 5P-3A. I don't recall the specifics of a certain call that night but it somehow involved one or more disorderly persons in an upscale local restaurant. I subsequently went there to assist my officers who were already on the scene. The details of this incident aren't all that important but it seems once I arrived there as the supervisor-in-charge we collectively managed to bring the heretofore escalating situation under control. Upon arriving I took over and advised my officers to handle the matter in a certain way, the management of the establishment to do something or other, and the trouble-makers to quiet down, pay their bill, and eventually go on their way. Before long, all three disparate entities thanked me for showing up and making the difference at the scene of the disturbance before it became even more problematic, where it had seemed to be heading. There were no arrests necessary and everyone was glad of it. All parties left in one piece; no foul, no harm.

The manager of the establishment later telephoned the captain (it was Capt. Walsh) who was on that overnight shift with me and complimented me for a job well done. The captain actually told me about it and said he would pass it along to Chief Viola via memo. That was nice of him, especially considering it was only the second memo he had ever written to me or about me, not to mention he was still a defendant in my lawsuit.

Also, as my squad and I were about to leave HQ to go home at 3:00AM, the two officers who were on the earlier scene went out of their way to thank me for showing up when I did on their call. In their macho way in front of the others in the roll room they extended kudos to me for addressing the initially escalating situation as I did and thusly calming things down so everyone could get home in a timely fashion on this night. I told them I appreciated their nice words. Now, let's go home and have a few well deserved days off.

Why relate the above relatively innocuous anecdote of how I handled a very routine police matter? Well, quite honestly, because of how it made me feel at this time-critical professional junction in my life. I had some upcoming decisions to make, and in its own little way this late night incident confused things for me just a bit.

The whole of the next day after this restaurant call I was overcome with a feeling of great satisfaction regarding my role as a patrol sergeant on the BPD. It had been a while since I felt this way. Throw in the relatively recent bank robbery arrest and I knew that I was doing a pretty good job out there, now that I was finally allowed out there once again. It was reassuring knowing that not only members of the public were complimentary about my presence on the scene that night (the manager and the customers), but my own men seemingly appreciated me and my supervision too.

I thusly found myself at a stage in which I was thoroughly enjoying my squad, my squad mates, my overall work life, and my everyday life. Things were all looking up for me.

It got me yet one more time thinking, and wondering....

* * * * *

Just as it was supposed to, the clock-radio alarm went off on that mid-week morning at 6:30. I had set it the night before at 10:30 shortly before my head hit the pillow. I wanted a good night's sleep. And I got one. I slept like a baby. I was getting up bright and early on one of my days off because I had an exam to take. And it wasn't just any exam. No, this one could possibly lead the way to me becoming a special agent of the FBI.

So, with all the pre-planning and prepping for this exam, not to mention the excitement of the challenge associated with it, what did I do when the alarm went off?

I hit the snooze button.

However, I don't believe I actually fell back to sleep during my ten minutes of bonus dozing time. I was in that nether-world where you're sort of awake but still sort of asleep. You're not really dreaming but your mind goes in and out of consciousness and all kinds of thoughts and ideas enter and leave in those six hundred or so seconds between the initial few notes of the preliminary wake-up song which happens to be playing on the radio station and the subsequent you-better-really-wake-up-now song. You kinda know the next song is coming, so your brain allows you just enough latitude to formulate the relevant elements of your semi-dream state, all while subconsciously ticking down the minutes and seconds of remaining snooze time.

I recall in my horizontal half-asleep, half-awake state half-asking myself, then half-answering myself...

"Jim, this test today...Do you really want to take it? Do you really NEED to take it? Do you really want to/need to leave the BPD? Things are pretty good there now. The bosses like you and respect you. Your men feel the same way. Even the public calls and compliments you. I mean, dang, you're going to the FBI-NA in the fall, isn't that good enough? Isn't that good enough...isn't that good enough...?"

Then, all of a sudden and out of nowhere, a very familiar momentary apparition came into my head. It was similar to the one from just a month or so before while in the parking lot with Agent Brown. But this time it was even more disturbing, and seemed to continue much longer. It was those same Dark Side regime faces but they were now contorted in Picasso-like non-symmetrical and multi-colored fashion. There were also multiple memos falling about me from above like giant sized snowflakes. I found myself running among the oversized pieces of white paper towards what appeared to be the Gates of Hell. Once inside I could see I had just walked through the entrance to a certain evidence truck-trailer, but then I couldn't get out. Lastly, there were barely recognizable men in uniforms with jackhammers pounding away at my head. All of these images were in my brain once again in a slowly swirling tornado fashion in various forms, colors, sizes, and at various intensities.

This dream/nightmare was mind-numbing, it had me tossing, turning, and...it eventually startled me out of my half-sleep. As such, I sat straight up, shook my head back and forth a few times, rubbed my eyes with my hands, and asked myself, "What the hell am I still doing in bed?"

Just then, the alarm went off. Of all songs, it was The Animals 1965 classic, *We Gotta Get Out of This Place*.

Geez, was this a message from God? From the FBI Director? From Eric Burden, the Animals lead singer? Whatever or whoever, it's time to get up and get outta this bed!

The alarm/song woke up my wife too who was next to me. She knew I was startled and must have been having a bad dream.

"Jim, are you okay? You're getting up for the FBI test, right?"

"I'm...I'm okay. Yes, I am taking the test. No doubt about it, especially with the dream I just had and this song playing on the radio."

"What dream? What song?"

"I'll tell you later. I gotta get outta this place...and to the FBI office."

It was most definitely time to get up, put on my test-taking suit, eat a quick breakfast, and drive downtown to take a certain exam. I may or may not pass it, or even get a high enough score to otherwise be competitive, but damn if I'm staying in bed today. I do NOT want that dream again. Plus, in terms of reality, I've put up with too much over the last two years to not at least make an attempt at this opportunity. The headaches may be gone, the ones who caused them may be gone or neutralized, but those damn bad images still pop up every once in a while. I gotta do something to get rid of them. Maybe going to the FBI-NA will be enough. Maybe… but I really should hedge my bets. I must try to go to the next level in my professional life.

I will take this test today! And I will pass it!

Then I'll figure out what the hell I'm doing.

I took the special agent exam on April 10th, 1986, in a large classroom in the Philadelphia Division with at least fifty other professionally dressed people between the ages of 24 and 34 – each man and woman my competition. When it was all over I wasn't sure exactly how I fared on it, but for some reason the math portion seemed easier than the last time I took it. I even finished that section before the allotted time ran out. That was a first. Thanks, hippie tutor man. The other parts didn't seem all that difficult either. My ongoing review of the study guide over the last four weeks seemed to make these questions and queries much easier to answer too.

Not a bad day, all in all, especially as I was home by 2:30 or so. At just about the same time, Sean and Dan were also getting home from school. It turned into a fun afternoon for us and another great bonding experience for father and sons. Sean and Dan seemed to enjoy hangin' out with their dad too on this sunny and warmish day. After a long, cold winter, this was one of the first times we had a chance to play a little baseball game together in the backyard. We may not have done so since my headache-related three weeks of sick leave the previous October.

Man, how things have changed for me and the BPD since then.

Things would be changing too for the agency to which I was applying. Actually, this change began less than twenty-four hours after I walked out the door of the Philadelphia Division. It would be as the result of one of the darkest days in FBI history.

* * * * *

On the morning of Friday, April 11, 1986, in the outskirts of Miami, Florida, two FBI agents were killed in a shootout with a pair of serial bank robbers. Both heavily armed robbers were killed too. As my wife and I were watching the network news that evening regarding the murders of Special Agents Jerry Dove and Ben Grogan, and the serious injuries to other agents on the scene, she turned to me afterwards and asked, "Gee, Jim, are you sure you want to be an FBI agent?"

I responded in all sincerity, "Eileen, I'm not sure yet if I do or not. But this very unfortunate Miami incident will not influence my decision one way or the other. I think you know that about me by now." She agreed that she did.

Little did I know starting nineteen months later, at a location south of Bensalem and north of Miami, I'd be in the daily company of one of the surviving agents of this tragic day, this tragic shootout. His name was Ed Mireles.

Ed hated the word, but he was truly the "hero" of that day in Miami. (More on Ed and my relationship with him in JCM Book III.)

* * * * *

Sometime in late May or early June of that year, I received an envelope in the mail at my house. It was from the FBI. I knew my test results were contained therein. I was nervous. I had opened at least two similar federal government envelopes over the last ten years and they had contained not-so-good news. What would this one tell me? I suppose I better open it to find out.

Let's see…reading down, first sentence, second sentence, next paragraph, all routine stuff so far. Hey, here it is, in the second paragraph as clear as day.

Yes, I did it! I passed the test! Finally!

Yippee yi yo ky ay!

The letter didn't say too much more other than that my score was passing and I was in further consideration for the special agent position. It ended with it stating that I would be receiving the next part of the application package in the mail before long. That was good enough…for now.

There wasn't much celebration though. It was only one small step forward in this long process. Eileen was happy for me, but as she was literally the only other person outside of the FBI who knew about this, we kept any celebrating very close to home and very low-keyed.

Within a few weeks, a package came in the mail from the FBI. It was a thick manila style envelope. It contained the multi-paged, detailed, totally comprehensive special agent application. It asked many, many questions, to include every address I've ever lived and the name of every person with whom I ever cohabited. Besides parents, sisters, and now a wife and kids, this would include former college roommates too. It also asked all kinds of questions regarding extended family history, academic history, work history, criminal history, drug usage history, and whether I was a Communist or sought to overthrow the U. S. government. At least these last few series of questions were easy for me to answer.

Easy or not, each and every question had to be answered completely and honestly. If not the former, the application was kicked back to the candidate and the hiring process delayed. If not the latter, the hiring process was ended. No lies permitted on an FBI application. No relevant omissions permitted either.

It took me the better part of a week, doing some research and making some phone calls to find out where various college roommates may now be living and how they could be contacted (I was eleven years out of college at this point), but I was pretty sure I had filled out everything the application requested. I was required to include my signature on the very last page indicating that all of the information was complete and truthful. I was sure that it was, so I signed it, sealed it in a new manila envelope, and sent it back certified mail to the FBI office in Philadelphia.

I knew my fifteen-page application was truthful. I was positive as to the "letter-of-the-law," it was complete too. But…it wasn't. I failed to mention one brief little chapter of my distant past life. (This coincides with a certain chapter in JCM Book I.) Having read and reread the application though, it didn't seem as if it was necessarily relevant. But I came to learn it was, or at least the FBI thought it was. I would be asked about it somewhat later in the hiring process.

However, for now, the application was in the mail. Within a day or so I even had confirmation that the FBI received it. Now, it's just waiting for them to get back to me. I've waited this long, I can wait a bit more.

During this time, I had a pretty good feeling that I'd be residing at the FBI Academy in Quantico for at least one extended stay within the next few months as an FBI-National Academy attendee. The question I was asking myself more and more though was would it be just that one stay or perhaps another much longer stay in the not too distant future, leading to a possible whole new career.

Time will tell, but first I'd have a few more questions to answer for the FBI regarding that "whole new career" opportunity…and the answers to those questions would go back almost fifteen years.

Chapter Sixty

In the meantime...

You may remember Sgt. Whacky, my former plainclothes tactical squad supervisor. He was known for always carrying multiple guns, wearing cheap Indian jewelry, and otherwise mismatched clothing. You may also recall he told me on my first day on the Tac Squad that I didn't belong there and a year or so later told my six fellow squad members setting up for a bank robbery stakeout that he expected at least three of us to be killed that day. He was my personal nominee for boss of the year back then. (Not!)

Well, in early 1986 he was in uniform as a (gulp!) patrol sergeant. As such, we would occasionally be working the hours between 9:00PM and 3:00AM when our ten-hour shifts overlapped. It was during one of these six-hour overlaps which resulted in me for the first and only time in my entire law enforcement career initiating charges against a fellow law enforcement officer, not to mention fellow sergeant, for "Dereliction of Duty" and "Failure to Respond to a Required Police Action," or similarly worded offenses, both resulting from what I saw to be an act of overt cowardice.

It started like this...

Sometime around 11:30 on a late winter or early spring Saturday night there was a robbery-with-a-knife call in the parking lot of an apartment complex on Rt. 1. Several patrol cars showed up with me and Sgt. Whacky being among them. I forget exactly after all these years how it initially went down, but I do recall there was a pretty specific description of a male with a knife given by the robbery victim and then broadcast over the air by the first officer on the scene. Shortly thereafter in one of the adjacent complex parking areas I saw a person who matched that description, I called it out on my radio, I exited my vehicle and I approached the man. He then began running away from me at full speed through the parking lot. I immediately gave chase on foot. In doing so, I happened to run directly alongside Sgt. Whacky's car. He had his window down as I ran by and I could see the smoke from his cigarette swirling upwards out from it. At no time did my fellow uniformed sergeant attempt to exit his car, drive his car alongside me or behind me while I was running after the suspect, or even call in on the radio "officer in foot pursuit" in an attempt to further assist me and/or arrest the robbery suspect. Nothing even close! He just sat there casually puffing on his cigarette as I ran directly by him.

The potentially violent felon made it around the corner of one of the buildings, behind a dumpster, and over a six-foot high wooden fence before I could get even within forty feet of him. Using my portable radio, I broadcast that he was now in the adjoining neighborhood of Nottingham and I instructed other units to head over there to search for him. I then turned around and started walking back to my car, catching my breath and readjusting my uniform shirt which had pulled out during my sprint. On the way, I couldn't help but notice Sgt. Whacky still sitting in his car at the same location where I had just passed him, still smoking his cigarette, listening to some country music on his radio which I could now hear as I got closer to him.

With clear agitation in my voice, and now alongside the driver's side door I said to my fellow sergeant, "Thanks for the back-up here! Did you see me run by you in foot pursuit less than a minute ago?"

"Oh, was that you? I...I...didn't notice."

"What the f**k do you mean you 'didn't notice?'" Yes, I was very agitated at this point!

Whacky doubled-down. "I mean, I saw people running, but I wasn't sure what was going on. You know how it is sometimes in the dark...."

I retorted, louder than before, "That's bullshit! You respond to this call and you couldn't do ANYTHING? You know the guy I was chasing matched the description of the suspected robber with the knife, right? You couldn't have driven alongside of me to cut this guy off with your car? I could've tackled him from behind and made the arrest then. For that matter, could you have even put 'officer in foot pursuit' over the radio so other officers could come this way and assist me since you weren't willing or able to?"

As Sgt. Whacky threw his gearshift into Drive, he mumbled something like, "Well, maybe next time. I'm outta here!"

I mumbled something loud enough back at Whacky as he was pulling away. It rhymed with "truckin' grass troll." He heard it too.

And this guy holds the same rank as me?! For that matter, he's even a police officer to begin with?!

I went off duty at 3:00 that night. I didn't sleep well once I got to bed. I then took a good bit of my Sunday afternoon to contemplate my next move regarding what happened the night before. My contemplation eventually led me to sitting down at one of the typewriters on that Sunday evening when back at HQ. In doing so I composed a memo in which I laid out the exact scenario as to what happened twenty-four hours earlier. I next gave the two-page, single-spaced memo to the patrol captain on duty that weekend. It happened to be Capt. Tom Walsh. (Yes, he of the "idle conversation" memo from eighteen months or so earlier.) This was literally only my third direct interaction with him…ever. Well, besides naming him in my lawsuit. But this one was a bit different than these prior interactions with him. I wasn't keeping my mouth shut this time – not for him, not for anybody.

Upon reading my memo later that shift, the captain sometimes known as Walshey (among other nicknames) asked me if I was sure I wanted to follow-through on this charge. He reminded me that an accusation related to "cowardice" carries a lot of weight within a police department and could have many long-term implications. I told the captain I very much understood the seriousness of it and ALL its potential implications. But as it was my ass on the line the night before chasing the knife-yielding robbery suspect with Sgt. Whacky sitting idly by in his idling car doing nothing to assist me, well, yeah, I want to officially lodge these charges against him, and, yeah, I want the word "cowardice" referenced throughout. Let the "implications" fall where they may, I told him.

"Okay, I'll look into it," Walshey said to me, once again pulling on his tie and shirt collar a la Rodney Dangerfield. We then parted company with me further understanding why so few BPD officers respected him.

That was the last night of my 5P-3A shift. I was off for a few days and then came back to work by week's end. Upon my return, Capt. Walsh called me into his office and told me he had a conversation with Sgt. Whacky concerning my allegations. He told me that Whacky's version of the story was not all that different than mine, but he swore he didn't know it was me running by him chasing the robbery suspect. However, I was told, Sgt. Whacky assured Walsh that he would be more diligent the next time and react differently if confronted with the same situation.

In other words, Sgt. Whacky was sorry and it wouldn't happen again. He also emphasized to the captain that he was not a "coward."

I was glad to confirm that Sgt. Whacky was at least made aware of my use of that word in the context of what occurred that night.

Lastly, the sergeant decided he was going to get his eyes checked. Perhaps he did need new glasses after all. That's how the captain known as Walshey ended our chat regarding the sergeant known as Whacky.

I could have pushed this issue to the limit and insisted on formal charges being lodged against my former Tac Squad sergeant. I felt I had every legitimate right to do so, along with several patrol officers who witnessed the whole thing from afar. But I didn't. I had a feeling my days at the BPD were numbered and I really didn't want my last year here involved in disciplinary hearings, appeals, and whatever else may come of it. I also really didn't want Sgt. Whacky to get suspended over this matter either. I just wanted him adequately admonished in hopes he would react more professionally the next time such a situation would unfold before him.

That's where I left it with F. F. Walshey regarding this matter and for that matter with his career. He retired several months later.

I never spoke to Sgt. Whacky after that incident and after a year-plus I would never see him or interact with him again. No loss there on my part. The man remains to this day at the top of the list of people I chose to NOT emulate or imitate in any way during the rest of my law enforcement and/or supervisory career. He earned this distinction on multiple levels during his interactions with me as well as others. It's the least I could do for the various people I would come to supervise in the future.

* * * * *

Strangely, yet by design, the summer of '86 found me balancing two unrelated pending FBI opportunities. One was internal through my police department, that being my proposed attendance at the FBI's National Academy. The other was external to my police department, that being my proposed attempt to become one of the FBI's special agents.

My special agent application had been received at the Bureau. That I knew. However, they were seemingly taking their time in processing it (and me) as I had not heard anything from them since mailing it off to them a few months prior. I was okay with that as long as they finished what they had to do before I turned 35 years of age in June of '88. I wouldn't want them taking THAT much time.

On the other hand, my NA "application" was a different story. It was moving along quickly. As the 147ᵗʰ Session's starting date was getting closer, I had to partake in several specific and mandated activities for me to be officially sanctioned to attend.

One of the first such activities was getting a complete medical check-up to make sure I could handle the physical regimen while in Quantico. I did so and passed with flying colors. No surprise there.

Next on the list was a mandatory half-day introductory meeting at the FBI Philadelphia Division for soon-to-attend NA candidates. As instructed, I showed up there at the designated time and date and was met by the NA Coordinator. I wasn't alone either. Several other Philadelphia area law enforcement officers who were scheduled to attend the 147ᵗʰ Session this coming fall were there too. It was six of us at this meeting as the Philly Division had a half-dozen NA slots it was filling this upcoming session.

(Then as well as now, every one of the FBI's 56 divisions is allotted a certain number of individual slots each session for the NA; the bigger the division usually the more slots they're allocated. They're divided up accordingly as long as it adds up to 250 candidates per session, with four sessions per year.)

One of the officers at this meeting was a Philadelphia PD supervisor, another was a Pennsylvania State Police supervisor, yet another was a New Jersey State Police supervisor. The other three of us were police supervisors from smaller municipal departments. The other two were lieutenants at their respective departments, including James Swope from the nearby Bristol Township Police Department.

As a sergeant, I believe I was the lowest ranking supervisor at this meeting. Hopefully, when I get back from the NA, I'll have the opportunity to get promoted to lieutenant, to captain, and then who knows how high up the law enforcement ladder.

During this meeting at the Philadelphia FBI office, the six of us were told that we could dress "business casual" while at the Academy. That meant no tee-shirts, jeans, or sneakers during the day. Open collared shirts, khaki-style pants, and casual non-athletic type shoes were fine. However, we should also bring a jacket and tie with us for some events or for some classes in which we would be required to dress a bit more business-like. Of course, we were told to bring a nice suit for our December graduation day, although that seemed so far away for us on this warm summer afternoon.

Interestingly, this whole dress code thing at the FBI Academy would create quite a stir during the latter part of my stay there. I had nothing to do with it at all, but I was there and a witness to the specific incident. It seems a bunch of other visiting law enforcement officers pushed their luck, dress code-wise, and they wound up paying a heavy price for it. The group of them having been summarily "dressed-down" afterwards would be an understatement.

More to follow....

Back to the meeting in the local FBI office...at some point my five LEO brothers and I were each handed course packets. We learned that day that there were certain core courses which we had to take while there, and other courses we could choose as electives. Constitutional Law as well as Police Management courses were mandatory and every NA student had to take them. There were other elective courses offered that interested me, especially as I discovered the FBI Academy had a direct academic affiliation with the University of Virginia (UVA). As such, the FBI instructors were all designated adjunct professors at UVA. (Each instructor, I would learn, held the rank of supervisory special agent with at least a master's degree. The law course instructors were, of course, lawyers.) With such an academic cross-affiliation, I came to understand that I had a choice of various courses in which I could earn either three undergraduate credits or three graduate credits.

As I had all the undergrad credits I needed, those didn't concern me. But graduate credits? Geez, if I can enroll in at least two graduate-level courses while at the FBI Academy, each officially sanctioned by UVA, I could then transfer those credits to Villanova and be that much closer to finishing my master's degree. (Much as I did with the three graduate credits from the POSIT-POLEX course at Penn State in '84.) This was turning into a better deal than I ever imagined.

After another hour or two at the FBI office, and a few more blocks of instruction in terms of what to expect while living in Quantico for those eleven weeks, the six of us FBI-NA candidates said goodbye to one another. We each agreed we'd meet up again about 200 miles south of here in late September.

Unfortunately, as it turned out, one of the candidates I had just met wouldn't be there for the upcoming session. His absence would be the result of some decisions, or lack thereof, involving the U. S. Congress.

696

Without getting into the political morass here, suffice it to say that sometime in the late summer of '86 it was learned that President Reagan and Congress couldn't agree on various governmental budgetary issues. In the midst of all of this it seems that the FBI National Academy, along with a multitude of other federal programs, was not initially allocated funding for fiscal year 1987. As the U.S. government fiscal year begins October 1, which would be within the first actual week of the 147th NA, the entire session's funding was in jeopardy. In other words, if the federal funds were not so-allocated, it wasn't going to take place. At the time, it would be the first NA session ever cancelled for any reason except, I believe, during World War II.

Damn, just my luck! What a time for the President and Congress to not get along.

However, someone in the FBI came up with an idea. It was a good one too.

Literally with about a month to go, in late August of that year, each of the 250 upcoming NA candidates' departments received an official letter in the mail. In that letter, the budgetary issue was explained in full.

Essentially, the letter from the FBI Director succinctly related the aforementioned budgetary issues and the problems they were causing for the upcoming National Academy session. The letter thusly ended with a question. It read, in so many words, "If the federal budget isn't approved soon, and if the costs of sending your department's candidate to the NA isn't thusly covered, would your agency be willing to allocate the approximately $2,500 in costs for your candidate to still attend?"

Each chief of police/agency head was instructed to respond to the letter one way or the other to the local FBI office, in writing, by mid-September. Apparently, if enough agencies said "yes" and would agree to individually fund their candidates, the 147th session would go on as scheduled.

I was shown that letter a few days after it was received at the BPD. However, before I ever knew about it, Chief Viola and Captain Robinson first went to Township Manager Marge Strange to discuss the situation with her. Once on board with it, she then brought the issue to the attention of the five elected supervisors. A decision was eventually reached by them. Well, by the three majority Republican supervisors anyway. The other two Democratic supervisors abstained. Their joint decision apparently had something to do with the fact that they were still defendants in my lawsuit.

When all was said and done the BPD agreed, in fact, to pay the $2,500 to send me to the National Academy in the possible event the Congressional budgetary stalemate wasn't resolved by then and the federal government wouldn't cover the costs for me to attend. The letter was written, signed, and mailed back to the FBI by Chief Viola. By the time I learned of this it was already a done deal.

It was very nice to hear from my police bosses and their political bosses (well, the three newer ones, anyway) what had been done for me. I thanked them yet again for this opportunity, especially now that it may cost Bensalem Township $2,500 just to send me to the NA, when attendance before that had always been tuition-free.

However, as I already knew, nothing is ever actually "free" in life. There is always a hidden cost somewhere.

* * * * *

My lawsuit against Bensalem Township and multiple present police supervisors and politicians, as well as a few already departed or almost so, was still pending. Pete Hileman and the new township solicitor had been going back and forth on it doing their lawyerly thing since the beginning of the year. Pete kept me in the loop regarding the various offers and counter-offers. None up to this point was satisfactory.

In mid-September, Jack Robinson called me in his office one day. Our talk went something like this...

Jack: "Jim, I was in a meeting today with the Township Manager and the new Solicitor. We were discussing a number of budgetary matters and one of them was your lawsuit. I know the Solicitor has been talking to your lawyer and I'm sure he's keeping you abreast of things, but they're really hoping to resolve some of these financial matters sooner rather than later, your suit included. And, you know, with the Township recently agreeing to pay the whole freight with you going to the National Academy, well, I think they're kind of hoping that in turn you'd perhaps consider dropping the lawsuit."

Me: "Oh, okay. I see, sort of a quid pro quo here, eh?

Jack: "Well, yeah, I guess that's one way of looking at it."

Me: "Hmmm... Well, Jack, I told you and anyone who would listen from day one - this lawsuit was never about the money. It was about protecting myself and possibly, just possibly, turning this doomed ship of a police department around. It was a definite last resort on my part as I'm not the litigious type. I think you know that."

Jack: "I do. I hear everything you're saying. Look, I'm just the messenger here. I'm not trying to talk you into anything. You and your lawyer have a right to resolve this issue in any way you two deem appropriate. I know the hell you went through for the two years those assholes were in charge around here. Believe me, I felt it too. I'm simply telling you that I've been asked to discuss this matter with you. And, just so you know, I've agreed to drop my lawsuit for my unlawful demotion in early '84. I'm settling it for the back pay owed me and attorney's fees."

Me: "Okay, I hear ya Jack. Let me talk to my lawyer and my wife and see what we can come up with. I'll get back to you in the next week."

That night I spoke to Eileen. The next day I talked to Pete. My lawyer and I discussed all of our options. We weighed the pros and cons of each and every one. By the end of that phone call I told Pete of my decision. It wasn't an easy one, but I knew for me it was the best one.

I wanted to drop the lawsuit. My only demand at this point was that all of my attorney's fees and costs are reimbursed to me. As a good lawyer should, he asked me at least twice before we hung up if I was sure about this decision. I told him, "Yes." He then told me he'd contact the Bensalem solicitor and advise him accordingly.

A day or so after that I stopped in CID and told Capt. Robinson of my decision. He asked me in all sincerity if I was sure it was the right thing to do. He reemphasized that he didn't want me to think that he was trying to talk me into anything against my will. I told him he wasn't and I again reminded him my lawsuit was never about financial gain on my part. He nodded in understanding with both of us at the same time agreeing our PD was a different place now, a better place now. I restated to him that I was very appreciative of not only attending the upcoming FBI-NA, but that the township would be willing to pay my way there if necessary. In view of all of this, the least I could do would be to drop the litigation against my employer. So, rightly or wrongly, smartly or dumbly, that's what I did.

What neither Capt. Robinson nor Chief Viola knew at the time was that I was also attempting to gain actual employment with the FBI. The more I thought about my lawsuit back then, to include the time involved in potential future depositions, hearings, trials, etc., and as my hiring process was slowly moving along, I decided I simply wanted this litigation to be over and done with. I knew the FBI would not or could not refuse to hire me because of a pending lawsuit against my PD. That would have been wholly illegal on their part. However, I now viewed this legal action as a relic of my past and as something whose time and purpose had come and gone. While very necessary at the time, this entire matter now was simply something I wanted off my plate and in my personal and professional rearview mirror.

So, yes, my current job quest figured into my decision-making too when it came to dropping my lawsuit...again, rightly or wrongly, smartly or dumbly. Bottom line, as I came to realize more than ever, I got out of the lawsuit what I wanted.

Several days before leaving for Quantico, Eileen and I (remember, she was a co-plaintiff) signed a slew of documents at my lawyer's behest. In doing so, the formerly referred to "Operation X" came to an official end. Within several weeks a check for $1963.86 came in the mail from Bensalem Township to my house representing the full amount owed to me for my legal expenses. Operation X was, without question, a resounding success. In the grand scheme of things, it was money well spent - especially as I was later reimbursed for every cent of it.

It was now time to move on. Well, at least for eleven weeks.

Chapter Sixty-One

With a babysitter for the two kids, Eileen and I had a very nice dinner at an upscale Doylestown, Pennsylvania, restaurant on the Friday evening before my National Academy departure. It was my little way of thanking her in advance for what would be a challenging next eleven weeks for her taking care of most, if not all, of the family responsibilities while I was away at Quantico.

As newlyweds, Eileen and I had been apart when I attended the Pennsylvania State Police Academy in Hershey for my first multi-month law enforcement training stint. That was for twelve weeks in the fall of 1976. The NA would be one week less. Ten years later, however, there were two little kids in the household. That certainly changed the familial paradigm. Nonetheless, all parties agreed to give it a go. I was very appreciative of them for agreeing to do so.

Speaking of Sean and Dan, several weeks before I was scheduled to leave on my excellent professional adventure, I told them if they promised to be good for their mom in my absence, I would give them a special treat of their choosing before I leave. All they had to do was come up with a reasonable request and I assured them I would deliver. They did, although I'm not sure how truly reasonable it was on their part.

At seven and four years old, like many other boys of their ages at the time, my sons enjoyed watching professional wrestling on TV. While doing so over the last few weeks, they saw the commercials for a big title match coming up at the Philadelphia Spectrum on September 20th. Once I put my "promised to be good" deal on the table the boys all but begged me to take them to it. If so, they assured me and their mom, they'd be "good" for the entirety of the time I was away. I discussed this with Eileen and she had little, if any, desire to go to a Worldwide Wrestling Federation event. However, I eventually convinced her it would be a fun, if not ethnographically interesting, experience.

It was that, and so much more.

Upon arriving at the Spectrum that Saturday night in South Philadelphia, the one saving grace for Eileen was that the Monkees were performing a concert across the street at the open-air Veterans Stadium. We couldn't see them but we could clearly hear their music as we waited in line the thirty minutes or so to get into the sold-out arena. She would have much preferred to have been at the Vet to see the '60s rock and roll band perform. Instead, she acquiesced to watching a bunch of sweaty men in tights bash each other with flying dropkicks and head slams, not to mention folding chairs and stepladders.

Once inside the arena for the next several hours we anxiously awaited the main event. That's when Hulk Hogan lost to Paul Orndorff by disqualification. (Something about the Hulkster using brass knuckles and/or shoving the ref.) It was...interesting, to say the least.

Sean and Dan enjoyed themselves that evening at the Spectrum, so we did too. That's what Eileen and I convinced each other anyway. The boys, perhaps as a result, were relatively well-behaved during my prolonged absence. They even managed to refrain from bashing each other with folding chairs and brass knuckles while I was away.

Bless their little hearts....

* * * * *

On a warm and sunny Sunday afternoon, the 28th of September to be exact, after numerous hugs and kisses with my wife and boys in front of the house, with the official letter of invitation from the FBI-NA, I departed Bensalem to begin a remarkable eleven-week stay at their Academy in Quantico, Virginia. I'd certainly miss Eileen, Sean, and Dan over the next almost three months, but at least I would be home practically every weekend. I promised her and the kids that much and I did keep my word.

As I would come to realize, Bensalem to Quantico being only about three and a half hours apart by car (circa 215 miles) would prove to be a big advantage for me. The vast majority of police officers around the U. S. and internationally who would be attending the 147th NA Session were saying goodbye to their loved ones too this very weekend. However, most of them would not see their family members again until they returned home on or around December 12th. I was fortunate in that regard as I could come home every Friday night. Sometimes geography happens to work in your favor.

After driving the entire 215 miles southbound on I-95 that Sunday afternoon, getting off the interstate at the "Quantico Marine Corps Base" exit, and snaking along a tree-lined winding two-lane road an additional few miles westbound through the military base, I arrived on the FBI Academy grounds right around 3:30. I was in awe of the sprawling facility at first sight.

The Academy complex officially opened its doors in 1972, just a few months after the death of J. Edgar Hoover. It was only fourteen years old when I showed up there for the first time. It was in excellent overall condition and I could see why it was referred to as the premier law enforcement academy in the world. And, I would later learn, it wasn't merely the brick-and-mortar design of the place. Its international reputation was earned as a result of the personnel inside of it too.

Unlike present time, there was little security at the FBI Academy in 1986. Students, staff, and for that matter anyone else could drive right onto the actual grounds of the complex during those halcyon days. The exterior doors themselves were locked at all times but everyone either temporarily or permanently assigned there had keycards to gain interior access.

Most assuredly, the security measures at the FBI Academy are different today.

(The remainder of my description of the FBI Academy and its environs is from what existed and what I experienced in 1986. Needless to say, additional buildings and other infrastructure have been added, expanded, and/or modernized since then.)

The FBI Academy is laid out much like a mid-sized rural college campus. It has a three floor classroom building, two high-rise dorm buildings, one very large auditorium, one mid-sized auditorium, a three floor library, a good-sized cafeteria, an extra-sized gymnasium, an almost 25-meter swimming pool, a non-denominational chapel, helicopter landing pads, and other useful and practical facilities-within-a-facility. It also has a fake little town immediately adjacent to it. Hogan's Alley is its name.

The campus is spread out over 547 wooded acres which the U. S. Marines kindly lease to the FBI on a yearly basis for the sum of one dollar. I suppose the only real differences between the FBI Academy and a regular college campus are the outdoor shooting ranges and the inside barroom. Oh, and that fake town too.

There are several firearms ranges on the east side of the Academy grounds. How else can future and present law enforcement agents/ officers learn and further hone their shooting skills? There's almost always the sound of gunfire during the daytime at the Academy, sometimes in the early evening too. As exploded gunpowder has its own distinctive smell, that seemed to be pervasive in the air too when anywhere near the ranges.

Regarding the barroom…the Academy is about thirty minutes from the closest towns of Quantico and Stafford. It takes that long because you have to drive really slow on the USMC base roads. If caught speeding, even a few miles above the posted speed limit, the young Marine police officers assigned there will pull you over in a heartbeat and write you a ticket no matter what kind of badge you may flash at them. If caught driving drunk, they'll lock you up without blinking an eye. So, it makes sense to have a full-service bar right on the Academy campus. That way, after a long day in the classroom or on the range, or at both venues, the adults assigned there do not have to drive anywhere to enjoy a few alcoholic beverages. More importantly, they don't have to drive back. It is only opened from 7:00 until 10:00 each weekday evening, and until 11:00 on Friday and Saturday nights. It's called The Boardroom.

I don't believe too many U. S. schools of higher education have firearms ranges and a bar right on campus, certainly none I've ever attended or visited. Of course, the strictest rule of all at the FBI Academy is that you can shoot first and drink at the bar later, but never, ever, the other way around. No one has ever argued with that rule.

Hogan's Alley included a carefully laid out façade of various businesses, stores, and even a pretend movie theater over several urban-like blocks, all fake. The so-named Biograph Theater in Hogan's Alley always had the same movie, *Manhattan Melodrama*, displayed on its overhead marquis. This wasn't by coincidence. It was outside the REAL Chicago Biograph Theater in 1934, after watching *Manhattan Melodrama,* that notorious bank robber and murderer John Dillinger was cornered and gunned down by FBI agents. It serves as a little bit of criminal justice history to remind those who may pass by this part of town.

However, unless an NA student decides to take a stroll through the Academy grounds and purposefully walks up the hill to this pretend town, he or she won't otherwise spend any real time in this otherwise unreal place. It was designed and is maintained to give young agents-in-training various learning experiences in a city-like environment as they conduct their assigned faux investigations. Since the NA attendees are all senior law enforcement officers/supervisors, already with years of city/town law enforcement experience under their belts at this stage of their careers, they don't need this specific type of training at the FBI Academy. So, the make-believe city of Hogan's Alley, Virginia, is saved for the younger special agents-to-be who may not have such experiences yet.

(More on Hogan's Alley in JCM Book III.)

When I initially walked inside the Academy main building my very first day there, I was directed to a long table where I gave my name to a staff person. There were numerous people sitting at numerous tables with file-type boxes in front of them. Once the woman I was talking to saw my official letter and found my file and confirmed I was who I said I was, she gave me my clip-on badge and a folder with numerous handouts in it. She advised I had time to proceed to my dorm room and unpack my belongings. Then, at 5:00 everyone was to meet in the large auditorium for the official National Academy welcoming ceremony.

Okay, I can do that. But how do I find my dorm room from here, and then get to the auditorium? I mean, this place is so large.

That would be easy as a tour guide was provided to us. How convenient....

Several of us NA attendees who showed up at the same time were introduced to a young man who was wearing a different color badge than us. As we found out, he was one of the many FBI New Agent Trainees (NATs) at the Academy for their almost four months of training. He and his fellow FBI agents-in-the-making on this day were assigned to provide tours of the Academy to those of us who were just arriving on the first day of our NA session. So, off we went, with us older guys following the younger tour guide hither and yon through the even-larger-than-I-first-imagined Academy complex.

The tour took us about twenty minutes. As we walked a bit, we talked a bit. It turns out that the NAT actually wasn't all that much younger than me, but there was no reason to bring that up at the moment. He was definitely much younger than the other four or five guys with us on the walking tour. I would find out later so was I, and by a good bit.

Amazingly, as we continued our perhaps half-mile interior stroll, we found that the separate buildings were attached to each other by about one hundred foot-long, glass-enclosed bridges. There were at least eight of them at the time. If you can picture numerous hamster cages connected by clear plastic tubes, well, that was the layout of the FBI Academy. If so desired, a person assigned here could spend their entire time inside the buildings (and hamster tubes) of the Academy as he/she could get to class, the gym, the pool, a small indoor firing range, the cafeteria, and for that matter a barber shop, a bank, a PX, a dry cleaner, a U. S. Post Office, and the all-important Boardroom, without ever stepping outside into the fresh air. Again, amazing....

Our NAT/tour guide eventually allowed us to get our suitcases and garment bags from our cars in the parking lot and he walked us to our respective dorm rooms. While we began to unpack, he told us he would wait downstairs in the elevator lobby until 4:50 when he would escort us to the large auditorium for the welcoming ceremony. That gave us about thirty minutes. It would be a quick unpacking.

Each of the then-two dorm buildings was seven stories tall. Other than the first floors which contained miscellaneous offices and a TV/lounge area each, the top six floors of both structures consisted entirely of dorm rooms. Between them they could hold a multitude of invited guests. I found my room in the Washington Dorm (the other building was the Madison Dorm) and walked inside for the first time. Each dorm room was the same for both NATs and NA attendees, although the two groups tended to be assigned to different floors from the other.

Every dorm room in the Washington and Madison buildings consisted of two single beds, two nightstands, two desks, two bureaus, and two closets, with a large window overlooking the Academy grounds. They measured roughly twelve by twenty feet. There were no locks on any of the dorm room doors. That's because there was never a reported theft at the FBI Academy.

I would certainly hope not!

Each dorm room was connected by a common bathroom to another identically laid-out room. The bathroom, designed to be shared by four people, had two sinks, two toilets, and two showers. So, my roommate and I shared the bathroom with two additional NA police officer attendees from the room on the other side. The four of us would get to know each other pretty well over the next eleven weeks, that's for sure. Sharing one bathroom tends to do that to people, for better or for worse.

By 5:00 on that first Sunday afternoon at Quantico, we newly arrived police officers managed to find our way to the larger of the two auditoriums. It was located in one of the far corners of the Academy grounds. The cavernous room with an elevated stage in the front was designed to hold at least 1,000 people. On this day, however, there were only 125 of us in the front few aisles of the room. We came to learn that day because of the ongoing political issues in Washington, D. C., and the fact that the 1987 fiscal budget had not yet been passed, our NA session was only half the size of a normal one. The missing 125 who had been nominated and who had planned to come here obviously did not have an agency behind them which was willing to foot the $2,500 tuition bill in the event the funding never came through. Thus, this was a smaller session size, by half. At least one of the no-shows was the lieutenant from the smaller Philadelphia area department I had met at the FBI orientation back in the summertime. He wasn't as fortunate as me in that regard.

Thank you, BPD. Not for a whole lot lately, but for at least offering to pay my freight here if the worst case budgetary scenario presents itself.

The attendees that afternoon were welcomed by the new Assistant Director (AD) of Training at the FBI Academy, James Greenleaf. He seemed like a decent and friendly guy. He appeared to take very seriously his new position in charge of all training at the Academy, to include new agent training, in-service training, and the National Academy training. He advised us that there were at least 750 people at any given time going through some level of instruction at the Academy. The number was slightly lower (by 125 people) during this 147th NA Session because of the ongoing budget stalemate, but it was still at near-full house conditions nonetheless.

AD Greenleaf assured us that he and his staff would attempt to make our eleven-week stay at the FBI Academy as enjoyable and rewarding as possible. One brand new initiative that he was working on is what he referred to as "Enrichment Night." It was going to officially commence every Wednesday night starting sometime in early November. For starters, the cafeteria would offer specially cooked meals on those nights. They would be served on upgraded, candlelit tablecloths. There would even be mood music playing in the background. These upcoming Wednesday nights would usually reflect a theme of some sort tied into the meal. Then, afterwards, in the same auditorium where we were now sitting, an invited speaker with an expertise relevant in some way to the criminal justice system would give a presentation to the various attendees. Once initiated, the AD mentioned as an aside, the only condition regarding this evening was that for this one meal and/ or speaking engagement per week, the guests, students, et al., would have to meet a minimum dress code. That would mean wearing a sport coat, button-down shirt, and a tie.

Okay, no big deal to me, I remember thinking at the time. It seems like a nice effort on the FBI Academy's part. It could perhaps even be actually "enriching" too, depending on the speaker. As it's pretty casual around here apparel-wise most of the time, I can certainly "dress-up" at least one night per week when so requested. The first Enrichment Night is still a month-plus away and I'm sure we'll be notified of it well beforehand and reminded of what we're supposed to do then and there.

Before he left the stage that late afternoon, the AD went on to advise us that starting a year ago the U. S. Drug Enforcement Agency (DEA) was also presently training their personnel here at the FBI Academy. In essence, the FBI Academy was also the DEA Academy, whether the latter agency preferred it that way or not. (They did not.) This would include their New Agent Trainee classes, in-service training for their present agents, as well as the DEA's own version of the National Academy. This was called something like the "DEA Drug Investigators Academy." This course consisted of approximately fifty police officers from various U. S. departments here at the FBI Academy for eight weeks receiving specialized training in drug investigations.

On a certain upcoming Wednesday evening, it would be a large group of these DEA-invited police officers, all FBI Academy guests, who did not take very well to being "enriched." And…the aftermath wouldn't be pretty.

Back to our first night welcoming ceremony in the auditorium… when the AD was done his remarks he turned the proceedings over to another FBI Academy administrator. His name was Tom Colombell. Supervisory Special Agent (SSA) Colombell further introduced himself and then began discussing basic issues related to class scheduling, cafeteria hours, office and ancillary business hours, phone usage, laundry room rules, upcoming legal holidays, the eventual graduation ceremony, dealing with the U. S. Marine military police in the area, and the like. It was valuable information which we all needed to hear. Tom presented it all in a light-hearted yet edifying manner. That was his trademark as he was the well-liked and well-respected FBI agent supervising the everyday running of the National Academy. I later learned that he had held this position for a few years already and was very much appreciated by the NA students and his fellow FBI agents and instructors alike.

Before graduating from the NA in December, I would share some private news with Tom. He was helpful to me once he learned that news and for a time thereafter. I would also share with Tom my idea regarding the NA officers and their relationships with the New Agent Trainees going through the Academy at the same time. It can safely be said that before the next calendar year was over both Tom and I mutually benefited from what we did for the other.

Back yet again to that initial Sunday night...as his last closing pronouncement that evening, SSA Colombell advised the 125 of us that we were to be divided into three separate sections. We were to meet with our respective NA Counselor and each one of these men would take over from there. Once segregated alphabetically by our last names, the forty-two members of my section met off to one side of the auditorium. The counselor instructed us that we were going to follow him to the cafeteria and then after "chow" we'd be off to one of the classrooms. There we'd get to know him and each other a little bit better.

Once again with a tour guide, this time our own NA counselor, the three dozen-plus of us walked through at least four hamster tubes and eventually found our way to the cafeteria. The few other men with whom I had been speaking so far agreed that we were all hungry and looking forward to a nice meal. We were hoping our first dinner here would be a good one. It did not disappoint.

From that all-important daily eating perspective...upon walking through the cafeteria's receiving line where the food was served by various kitchen staff, there were always at least two entrees with multiple side dishes from which to choose. Upon entering the dining hall itself, it was seen to measure approximately 150 feet by 150 feet. To make any U. S. visitor feel just a little more at home, the interior of the dining area had the fifty U. S. state flags, as well as flags of Puerto Rico and the District of Colombia, framed and behind glass above the windows surrounding the eating area. A well-stocked salad bar was found in the center of the dining hall. (At breakfast time, it contained different brands of cereal.) In addition, there were also soda, juice, and milk machines off to the sides of the room. Last but not least, there were two separate machines which dispensed cold and delicious vanilla and chocolate custard as a daily dessert treat. Waffle cones were available too.

All in all, for an institutional-style cafeteria co-located at a large law enforcement academy, it wasn't bad food three times a day. In fact, I'd say it was pretty darn good food. While I've never been considered a "foodie" by people who know me, and readily acknowledging that some meals there were definitely not as good as others, I can still say

I was never disappointed culinary-wise even once while dining at the FBI Academy cafeteria. But then again, I'm not a foodie.

Our subsequent hour-plus meeting in one of the classrooms after dinner provided even more valuable information for me and my new section-mates. As I came to learn, our NA counselor was a special agent assigned to the Los Angeles Division. To give its agents in the field an occasional break from their everyday duties, the FBI allows them to request once or twice during their career a stint as a counselor at the FBI Academy. Depending on the personality of the agent, as well as other related factors, they may choose to put in for a counselor slot in the National Academy or in New Agent Training. The former is definitely a bit more laid back of a position as all of the counselor's charges are older, experienced law enforcement supervisors. No babysitting required for these guys. The latter, however, calls for the counselor to be more of a mentor, a hand-holder, and yes, sometimes even a babysitter as the NATs are relatively young and many are for the first time in a training academy environment of any kind.

Our counselor was definitely suited for us, a bunch of senior police officers, now all living and working together for the next eleven weeks. He was definitely NOT our babysitter, nor was he ever required to be one for us.

Still in the classroom that first evening, there were further introductions and brief self-bios of my other forty-one section-mates. I could see and hear, being barely ten years into my law enforcement career, that I was the youngest person in my section. As my stay at the Academy continued over the next several weeks, I became aware that I not only had the least law enforcement service time out of my 124 fellow session-mates, but at 33 years of age I was also the youngest in the entire 147th Session. I think by at least five years too. Some of the older guys referred to me occasionally as "Kid." That never bothered me.

I didn't necessarily realize it then but this would be just about the last time in my life where I would be called "Kid" in any similar sort of professional venue. Those days would soon be behind me - and forever, I'm sad to say.

There were five international students in the 147th. They were from the U. K., Canada, The Netherlands, South Korea, and Thailand. My classmates and I couldn't help but notice the South Korean NAer had some trouble with the English language at first. However, with his dictionary in hand and almost constantly in use, he eventually managed his NA experience just fine. Interestingly, as I had relatively new Korean-American neighbors in Bensalem, for the first month at Quantico I felt that perhaps I should invite him home for a weekend so he could visit with some fellow country-people. I must say though, with there being language issues between me and this particular NA colleague, as well as also between me and my neighbors, I simply found it too difficult to arrange. Perhaps I should have tried harder to be the liaison in this international situation. In the long run, I can assure you, my South Korean classmate did very well during his eleven weeks at Quantico.

* * * * *

Of course, I was at the FBI-NA to learn. And learn I did.

I enrolled in the law and police management courses as they were both mandatory. My primary elective courses were Police/Media Relations, Advanced Concepts of Criminology, and Future of Policing. The last two were the graduate courses I chose. Each of the courses required some serious studying, written papers, one or more in-class presentations, and entailed a mid-term and final exam. These were actual college courses and thusly taught that way. I loved it, especially as I was taking two grad courses on "company time" and having the "tuition" fully covered. What a deal!

There was another one credit course each student needed to choose as an elective. Jack Robinson advised me back in the summer when I showed him my course packet to take one of the excellent firearms courses offered to the NA students. It did seem like a cool course upon reading its description, but then I saw another one which really caught my eye.

This other one credit course was titled "Introduction to Computers." As something told me computers would play more of a role in my future career than firearms, at least on an everyday basis, I ultimately decided on that course. I'm glad I did. I spent several hours a week in the FBI Academy computer classroom and learned all the basics of computer usage, to include word processing. I typed (keyboarded?) my first ever term papers using word processor software at the FBI Academy. I got "As" in them too. What a pronounced difference from using a typewriter. In fact, this one credit course so influenced me that within a few weeks of my NA graduation I bought my first CPU, monitor, and printer at a local Bensalem computer store. Thanks to the FBI-NA, I personally had now finally entered the computer age.

Speaking of computers, the future, and related such issues... one of my two NA graduate courses, "The Future of Policing," was taught by Supervisory Special Agent (SSA) Timothy Walters (fictitious name). As its description sounded interesting, about twenty students initially signed up for his course and we were all in his classroom on the first full day. However, when Walters told the class of the number of required readings, written paper requirements, and presentations due throughout the course, all but four dropped out. (Like in a regular college, a student at the NA could drop/add an elective course during the first week.) I was one of the four who stayed. It wasn't so much my keenness for this course, or my keenness for this instructor, but it was the only other grad course which would fit into my already tight academic schedule. Since hard work never scared me, I figured I'd stick it out.

The Futuristics course, as we came to call it, turned out to be somewhat interesting and thought-provoking, despite or perhaps because of the extra work we had to undertake to successfully complete it. The highlight of the course was when SSA Walters invited the noted futurist and author Alvin Toffler to Quantico for a series of talks. He was known then for writing *Future Shock* (1970) and *The Third Wave* (1980), among other books and articles relating to the future of humankind. That particular Wednesday made for a very interesting Enrichment Night when Toffler was at the Academy, on numerous levels as it would turn out.

Over the next nine years or so I maintained a loose, long-distance association with SSA Tim Walters. I was even one of the charter members of "The Society of Police Futurists," which he founded. However, our relationship unfortunately went decidedly south during the time of a certain major FBI investigation which was centered in San Francisco in the mid-1990s. Too bad.

(More on this in JCM Book III.)

My undergrad police management course carried the title of "Managing Marginal and Unsatisfactory Performance." It was taught by SSA Arthur Meister. I admired Art right away for his laid-back yet very informative style of teaching. He would not only share various recognized theories of management and supervision with me and my classmates, but he would also incorporate various real-world examples to make his points. The tall and lanky instructor had been an actual police supervisor in the past, and now he was teaching it. That was a great combination in my view.

SSA Meister, like me at the time, had been a police officer for ten years prior to joining the FBI. He had been a trooper in the Connecticut State Police with six years in patrol and the last four years in Major Crimes. Although originally from different sized law enforcement agencies a few states apart, I found from a career perspective I could relate to Art in numerous ways. We hit it off personally too as he would occasionally stop by the Boardroom before going home and drink a beer or two with me and some of his other NA students.

As part of Meister's course, we had to identify a past or present police officer under our individual supervision who was not performing up to par. I once again chose Officer Dan (keeping him anonymous, of course), the BPD patrolman who made the many, many DUI arrests every year but who was admittedly not achieving much else during his regular tours of duty. In this course though (as opposed to my Villanova course several semesters before), I could paint the complete picture of Dan and how with a little encouragement and guidance from his supervisor (me), he finally turned things around and became a much more complete police officer. SSA/Instructor Meister complimented me on my problem scenario and how I eventually came to address and remedy it.

Neither Art Meister nor I knew it at the time, but just about a decade later our paths would cross again. It would be for several years then, not just several months. It wouldn't be in a teacher/student relationship, but something somewhat similar.

(More on this in JCM Book III.)

Lastly, all NA students were required to take a physical fitness course. As such, the forty-plus of us in our section met two to three times per week in the gym and were encouraged to use this almost three-month time period to get ourselves back into a good fitness regimen. The classes themselves would include organized jogging, calisthenics, volleyball, basketball, and the like. We even played the other two NA sections in various sports as part of a late afternoon intramural program.

By the second or third day of the NA, when in our gym clothes for the first time, we were each individually weighed by a gym staffer on a calibrated scale. With a cloth tape, our waists were measured too. Then, during the last week of the NA, we would all be weighed and measured again. Our class, like the ones before us and after us, would then have listed on a large chart in the gym how many pounds and how many inches were collectively lost over our eleven weeks in Quantico. Every class seemed to lose upwards of 750 pounds and twenty feet or so off of their waistlines. Our class's total loss was smaller, of course, because we had only half the people as the other NA sessions. However, from what I remember, our numbers were still pretty significant at around 400 pounds of weight loss and ten feet off our waists. Not bad....

There was also a swimming program at the FBI Academy for whoever wanted to join it. It was simply called "Swim the Potomac." No, the participants would not actually swim in the nearby river, but instead in the Academy pool. If within eleven weeks said swimmer would swim a total of thirty-four miles, the equivalent distance from Quantico, Virginia, to Washington, D. C., he or she would then be awarded with the official tee-shirt, a small plaque, and their name so-noted at poolside.

During the previous summer I had gotten into distance swimming at a pool club in the Bensalem area to which my family and I belonged. As a former lifeguard, it didn't take me too long to get back into it. By Labor Day weekend, I was already swimming one-half mile in that particular pool. Could I possibly reach my goal of swimming thirty-four miles in the FBI Academy pool over an eleven-week timeframe? Well, I decided I was going to give it a try.

It took sixty-four lengths of the Academy pool to equate one mile. I started slow but by the third week I was swimming a mile every other day. I doubled up sometimes and swam two days in a row. Also, during the two weekends I stayed at Quantico near the end of my tenure there, I actually swam 128 lengths, two whole miles, on those Saturday afternoons. I'd record my mile(s) after each swim on a whiteboard chart on the wall near the main entrance to the pool. The miles eventually started adding up.

I did, in fact, complete my watery goal. It was in my eleventh week at the Academy, just in the nick of time. At the dinner-dance the night before our formal graduation, with Capt. Jack Robinson as well as my wife, Eileen, in attendance, I was publicly awarded the official green tee-shirt and the plaque. I still have the tee-shirt, although I may have misplaced the plaque after all these years. I was the only one in the 147th Session to attempt the "Swim the Potomac," or at least complete it. I remain proud of that accomplishment to this day.

My time in the pool helped my class's final numbers too as I had lost five pounds and took an inch off my waist. No doubt it was mostly due to my strict swimming regimen. I was by no means overweight when I went to Quantico, but a few pounds and an inch off certainly didn't hurt me.

* * * * *

Everyone in the 147th received the good news at the same time during our third or fourth week at Quantico. We were all requested to attend an important meeting in the auditorium one October afternoon immediately after our classes ended. Many of the instructors even showed up, yet no one knew what it was we were going to hear. Upon practically all of us 125 students taking our seats, along with various staff, faculty, and our five counselors, AD Greenleaf came out onto the stage. That's when he told us just a short while ago he had received a phone call from FBI HQ. The news he wanted to share with us was that Congress had finally passed a budget for fiscal year 1987. President Reagan was expected to sign it. In this budget, the NA had been fully funded for the entire fiscal year. It included our present session too.

Upon learning of this information the NA attendees burst into applause. Granted, we were already there, and granted, our respective PDs had already agreed to pay our way, but it was still great to hear the future of the National Academy was secured for at least this year and hopefully beyond. Almost everyone in attendance knew an officer in some neighboring department who was on the list to attend the 147th but because their PD couldn't/wouldn't commit to paying for it, they weren't able to come. While still sympathetic toward them, we were at the same time glad that this valuable law enforcement tradition would continue to be funded for some time into the future. Those other officers who didn't make it to the 147th would most likely be reinvited sometime during the next year.

It was good news for everyone involved, from me representing the Bensalem PD to present and future National Academy attendees from other departments; thank you Congress and President Reagan.

* * * * *

I got to know my roommate the best of all during my time at the NA. His name was Alfonso Graham. He was a great guy. He was probably fifteen years older than me and a captain at the Milwaukee Police Department. He also happened to be African-American, one of several in our session. Along with anecdotes from his present personal and professional life, it was also very interesting when Al later told me of his exploits being one of the first African-Americans on his police force some twenty years earlier. He lamented they weren't always easy times for him and his fellow black officers back then, from dealings with the public as well as with some of his white officer colleagues. After time, however, Al said his PD's culture vastly improved. I never heard my roommate even once complain of any current racial issues in his agency. His PD wasn't perfect in that regard, he told me during some of our late evening dorm room chats, but a clearly much better place than when he came on board as a rookie.

From race to gender...there were no women National Academy attendees in my session. There had been female NA attendees before me, but up to and including my time there they had been relatively few and far between. As women had only entered the realm of sworn law enforcement officers in the U. S. in the early 1970s, barely fifteen years prior, I suppose not many had yet climbed the management ladders in their respective agencies to be eligible for attendance at the NA. However, that wasn't the case with the NATs. From what could clearly be observed there were a significant number of women among those fledgling FBI agents at the Academy. Eventually, in later years, the NA would catch up in that regard too.

(For clarification purposes here, the FBI did not/does not recruit National Academy attendees. As in my case, each potential candidate has to first be nominated by their own police department/law enforcement agency. Then, when space, time, and FBI background checks permit, that officer will be selected to attend.)

From race, to gender, to dysfunctional police departments...over time I shared with my roommate, as well as with other NA attendees, the trials and tribulations I experienced at the BPD during '84 and '85. Eventually, a number of the attendees shared similar stories about their own departments throughout our eleven-week session. In the Boardroom one evening near the end of our NA time, with confirmation coming from neighboring Bristol Township PD's Lt. Jim Swope (he apparently read the *Bucks County Courier Times* too), I was crowned the winner of an informal contest we created among ourselves. Yes, I was voted the NAer who came from "the most f**ked up department in the 147th Session." It was an ignominious "win" on my part, but I accepted the figurative crown nonetheless.

I did make sure to remind everyone at the NA that the BPD was a much better place now. That didn't matter though. Despite some pretty bizarre stories regarding some other officers' home departments, my two years of tales involving the Dark Side regime outdid them all.

Lucky, lucky me. At least I drank for free the rest of the night.

Chapter Sixty-Two

The first of AD Greenleaf's so-called Enrichment Nights was planned for a Wednesday in early November. I believe it was the same night futurist/author Alvin Toffler was at the Academy. I don't think anyone, including the prescient Dr. Toffler, would have been able to predict what would happen in the cafeteria that evening and then over the next two days. None of us actually residing there at the time could have done so either.

This incident would eventually become a part of FBI folklore, told in various forms, with various reported outcomes. But I was there that evening and I was there the next two days. I saw what happened. I lived what happened.

Here's what happened….

Since the upcoming Wednesday was to be the first-ever Enrichment Night at the FBI Academy, the word went out the week before that there would be a special meal, special drinks, and even special dinner-time music played over the cafeteria PA system. Then, there would be a presentation by a special guest (Dr. Toffler) in the auditorium after-wards for all to enjoy. It seemed like a special night was on tap to be had by one and all.

Not a bad idea, AD Greenleaf. I know I was kinda looking forward to it.

Oh, but there was just one little "catch" for all to know in antici-pation of this evening. It was relatively minor yet seemingly impor-tant to those in charge at the Academy. That was, "Proper attire, including jacket and tie, are to be worn at this and every Wednesday Enrichment Night in the cafeteria." These words were found on the numerous multi-colored flyers posted on the walls and in the halls of the Academy, as well as heard from every instructor and NA counselor in the days leading up to this particular night.

Okay, again, a relatively minor request of the guests at the FBI Academy. We can do this. I can do this. I mean, wearing casual clothes is usually preferred at mealtime for most people here, but what the heck. One night of getting a little dressed-up is not going to kill anyone.

Well, it never did kill anyone at the FBI Academy. However, it may have practically killed some law enforcement officers' careers. As I mentioned before, it wasn't going to be pretty.

I forget if I swam that afternoon or came right from a class, but either way I made sure to first stop in my dorm room to put on a button-down shirt, a tie, and a sport coat over a pair of dress pants and decent shoes before walking into the cafeteria. Again, it was no big deal to me. It was now required this one night of the week so that's how I dressed, or more precisely, redressed. I'd go to the guest's talk afterwards and then change back to my more comfortable attire for the rest of the evening at the Academy. It was a small price to pay for what seemed like a well-planned and well-coordinated evening meal and speaker presentation.

I recall walking through the cafeteria serving line that evening and the workers ladling a delicious looking meal onto the dish on top of my green plastic tray. It was lasagna or a similar such Italian dish. I made sure to grab some slices of freshly sliced garlic bread near the end of the line too. Upon walking into the dining hall itself I was surprised to see that there were actually red and white checkered tablecloths on the individual tables. That was a different look for this place. There were lit candles and carafes of red wine on each table along with clear plastic cups to serve as our little wine glasses. That was definitely a different look too. Classic Italian music was playing in the background, which further enhanced the overall ambience of this initial Enrichment Night at the FBI Academy. The theme was, I believe, "An Evening in Florence."

After lining up at the salad bar and pouring a little olive oil (of course) over my just constructed antipasto dish, I found a table where I joined a few of my NA classmates. Before the breaking of bread, digging into my salad, and thoroughly enjoying the generous portions of the well-presented pasta meal, my six NA colleagues and I agreed to a toast. Holding up our half-filled plastic cups of Chianti, one of us said something like, "If you gotta be away from home and loved ones, this ain't a bad place to be - to our further enrichment! Cheers!"

We touched our glasses (actually plastic cups), drank, and then we ate. The lasagna may not have been the best I've ever eaten, but I gotta say it was still pretty darn good. The ambience, as artificial as it may have been in a law enforcement training academy on a military base, was appreciated nonetheless. Well, by most of us in attendance anyway.

It was near our dinner's halfway point when those at my table looked up, around, and at each other as we each first heard a somewhat far-away rumbling. Over the next minute or so we came to realize it was getting closer, whatever it was. What had been a somewhat off-in-the-distance rumbling was now approaching us and had transitioned to a more human-like banter mixed in with some indecipherable blathering. Then, as the odd bantering morphed into an even odder blathering, a sort of cocky laughter took over. It was the kind of laughter you hear when someone doesn't really seem to be sure why they're doing whatever it is they're doing, so they forcibly laugh out loud as a sort of defense mechanism. Multiply that by approximately fifty people and it becomes even odder, if not genuinely ominous.

Before long, the fifty or so people were upon us, entering the dining hall one at a time. As the well-known old Italian love song *O sole mio* happened to be the background music playing at the exact moment, the first few of these uncomfortably laughing, blathering murmurers were heard to be singing to the tune. As others in their same group would enter the dining hall behind the initial entrants they too would slowly join in the chorus. None of these "singers" seemed to know the lyrics to the rest of the Italian language song, but as they filtered in one-by-one, each carrying his own tray of pasta and salad, those three Italian words, "O sole mio," were repeatedly "sung" over and over again, even well into the next musical offering.

Geez, and these guys haven't even had any wine yet. Or at least I didn't think so.

I should add here that it was apparent each of the fifty newly arrived and lyrically-challenged dinner guests must have previously read or heard of the Enrichment Night's dress code as, from a very technical perspective, they were in accord with it. Well, one specific part of it anyway. You see, each one of them was wearing a tie. Yes, they did so to a man, and their ties were as plain as day for all to see on each of them. However, upon even a furtive glance, it was glaringly noticeable that something was amiss.

It seems that each of these men had forgotten the button-down shirt and jacket part of the well-publicized dress code. Instead, each and every one of them had on a tee-shirt, an undershirt, or a three-button collared sport shirt, over casual pants, with the tie loosely affixed around their necks, but with no jacket. Some had their ties draped down in front of them (where they're normally found), others had the ties on backwards where it would drape down their backs (where they're not normally found).

Suffice it to say by the time the fifty of these men sat down at their tables, with tee-shirts/undershirts/sport shirts, front and back ties and all, they had already made quite a demonstrative entrance. Even if no one else thought so, they certainly thought they were funny. They couldn't seem to stop laughing at or with themselves. Then, they started drinking the Chianti at their tables. Needless to say, the Italian lyrics they were attempting to mimic after that point were even more difficult to understand. Actually, so was their English as the evening wore on.

If you haven't surmised by now, these fifty men were all investigators enrolled in the DEA-run and sponsored police officer academy. They were in their seventh week and ready to graduate in nine days. They had been at the FBI Academy for almost two months already and it seems they collectively felt that this whole Enrichment Night thing, and its mandated dress code, just wasn't for them.

So, instead of these officers simply jumping into their cars and driving the half-hour to Stafford or Quantico and eating in a restaurant of their own choosing, dressed of their own choosing, they took it upon themselves to make the first time Enrichment Night at the FBI Academy into their own personal mini-rebellion. How DARE someone tell them that they have to wear a tie (with the standard button-down shirt and jacket) to a themed dinner event at the Academy's cafeteria?

Yeah, we'll show the FBI! We'll wear our friggin' ties, but over tee-shirts and three-button sport shirts and some even down our backs! That'll teach 'em!

I had always heard it wasn't a good idea to mess with the FBI. I learned after that night that this also applied to the inside of their training Academy cafeteria, and especially on their inaugural Enrichment Night.

By the next morning at the Academy, this story had already spread like wildfire. The NA attendees who were not in the cafeteria at the exact time when the DEA police officer students marched in wanted to hear all about it. Those of us who were there and dressed accordingly (which everyone else was...NA, NAT, staff, faculty alike) gladly retold the story. In the classroom that Thursday, our NA counselor was very circumspect about what happened the night before. He was usually a funny guy, telling jokes and the like. But there was something about what took place on this first-ever Enrichment Night that he didn't want to talk about, or certainly not discuss in any humorous manner. We all had a feeling that a nerve had been struck, a very sensitive FBI nerve, and that something dynamic was in the works in terms of a response. We just didn't know what or when.

Late that Thursday afternoon, the Academy lobby area was bristling with activity. People I sort of recognized from my time there were milling about with suitcases, garment bags, book bags, and the like, and talking loudly among themselves. Much of the talk was of the unfriendly and angered variety. There was a definite pall cast over the Academy environs which was difficult to describe, yet was evident to all of us. No one with any official status said anything to us, nor was anyone privy to any rumors which may explain the unusual movement in and about the Academy grounds. It seemed numerous people were leaving the campus, and by what they were carrying with them, it didn't appear to be for just an extended weekend. We who had been there for a while now knew it was not usual Thursday afternoon or evening activity. That was for sure.

By Friday morning, less than thirty-six hours after the dining hall incident, our counselor gave us the news in the classroom. The other two sections' counselors advised their charges of the same information at the same time. No doubt, the NATs as well as the rest of the faculty and staff were learning of and/or imparting the identical news around the same time too. That was, the DEA police officer academy had been officially disbanded by AD Greenleaf. Each and every one of the fifty attendees had been sent packing...literally. Their planned graduation ceremony in eight days was cancelled. There would not even be the all-important certificate of completion for them because, well, they didn't complete the course. Lastly, each of their agency's heads would be notified by the FBI in an official letter of what occurred on that fateful Wednesday night which then resulted in the seventh week termination of their eight-week course.

So, I guess you don't, in fact, mess with the FBI. That would include with a new Assistant Director of Training at their Academy where you are an invited guest there.

And really guys, all you had to do was dress up a little bit for one dinner. Geez....

This DEA drug investigators academy was well-known at the time as an important and sought-after training program among police officers and detectives who worked in narcotics. Like the FBI National Academy for law enforcement managers, graduation from this course further enhanced the careers of the attendees who were fortunate enough to be nominated for it and then complete it. However, to have attended this particular course in the fall of 1986 and then be ordered to leave it just about a week before graduation was not a good thing. In fact, it was a very bad thing. It was without a doubt a significant blow to each of the officers' careers and a black mark on their respective professional resumes. There was no getting around it.

However, even the FBI can be compassionate at times. Really, it can. As it played out, and as I later learned, over the next year, after some political pushback and what I heard to be even some overt begging on the part of the sent-home officers, their agencies, and the DEA, AD Greenleaf relented. Well, he relented a little bit. No, the officers weren't invited back for a graduation ceremony. That was never part of any negotiations. But Greenleaf agreed (apparently still reluctantly) that the officers could receive their certificates of completion from the DEA indicating that they had finished the course...even though they really hadn't. They were embarrassingly forced to leave the FBI Academy a whole week early and they never did have their graduation ceremony, so I suppose it was ultimately agreed upon by all parties that would be punishment enough.

The DEA shared FBI Academy space for the better part of the next thirteen years or so. I happen to know they (the DEA) were never thrilled about it. They wanted a training facility they could call their own for their personnel and their police officer academies. I don't blame them. When the federal budget saw fit to allocate the funding, the DEA finally opened its own training facility in Quantico in 1999. It was about a half-mile down the road from the FBI's facility. The DEA was and no doubt still is very grateful for it.

In the grand scheme of things, I suppose what occurred that November evening in 1986 at the FBI Academy was a relatively minor matter. No one was hurt and no laws were broken. But as I have written here before and have provided other examples…timing is everything in life. With a brand new Assistant Director in charge of the place, the fifty DEA sponsored police officers choosing that night to "protest" was wrong on numerous levels. Most of all, however, it was bad timing. Mix in their proven bad judgment and it was a recipe for disaster, certainly from a professional perspective.

I've never witnessed or heard of a similar multi-person incident such as the now infamous Enrichment Night dress-down at either of the FBI or DEA academies, whether when conjoined or separate, or for that matter at any other law enforcement training establishment in the U. S. I can only wish for their sakes the fifty of these men learned a lesson that night and next day, even if the hard way. Hopefully it was learned vicariously by others in similar surroundings too as time went on, even if only by the years later folklore version of the tale.

* * * * *

In my tenth week in Quantico, in the Classroom Building, one mid-afternoon I happened to walk by the second floor NA office message board and noticed on it a pink piece of notepad paper with my name on it. It was a message to call Eileen at her workplace. It clearly said "No Emergency." If it had been a crisis call of any sort, the staff would search out the NA student and allow him to make a call right away. That wasn't the case here.

Hmmm…a message of this sort from home was a first for me here at the Academy. I wonder what it could be. I know, I'll call my wife and find out.

I found an available payphone a few minutes later and called Eileen at work. She told me she went home at lunch time and among other things while there she checked the mail. In it was a letter from the FBI. She told me she didn't open it because in the upper-left hand corner of the envelope there was language to the effect that stated it was a federal offense to open this letter by anyone other than the addressee. As such, she didn't want to take any chances, especially since it was clearly from the FBI. I knew she was half-kidding, but also half-serious. I responded in the same hybrid-tone to her that I didn't think it necessarily applied in this case, especially as we're husband and wife. But, either way, as she had brought the intact envelope back to work with her she told me she could open it right now and read it to me over the phone if I gave her "the okay." I gave her "the okay" and requested her to open it and read to me what it says. She proceeded to do so.

It was a one-page letter from the FBI's Philadelphia Division. As Eileen read it to me, it initially reiterated that I had taken and passed the written special agent exam earlier in the year. It next stated that I had "passed" my preliminary background investigation. It then advised that the oral interview would be the next step in the exam process. The letter ended with a short paragraph requesting me in the next two weeks to contact the Philadelphia FBI Office, specifically SA Jerri Williams, and let her know one way or the other of my continuing interest in this regard.

Holy Shit! This was for real! The FBI was moving ahead with my application and my processing. I made it through the initial background check and my interview was next.

But hold on. I gotta make sure of something here.

"Eileen, could you please read the whole letter to me again and slower this time. Before you do, it is MY name on the envelope and at the top of the page, right?"

My wife reread the entire letter and advised it was me to whom they were writing. Okay, well at least we confirmed that issue. I thanked her and told her to hold on to the letter and we'd further discuss it when I returned home next week.

After saying goodbye to my wife, I placed the phone receiver back into its cradle. But before opening the bi-fold, half-glass door of the booth I said aloud once again, this time to myself and at a slightly higher volume, "Holy Shit!"

It was the blessed invective of the positive variety, if you haven't already so gathered.

At first, I didn't tell a soul about this letter. Not in the Commonwealth of Pennsylvania, not in the Commonwealth of Virginia, nor anyone else in the remaining two commonwealths and forty-six states. And as I had at least thirteen more days to decide, I didn't call SA Williams back yet either.

As my plan was to stay at the Academy over the forthcoming weekend, the last weekend before our graduation, I told Eileen that when I returned home on the following Tuesday, we would discuss this special agent opportunity that evening. If we decided the oral interview was the next logical step for me, for us, I'd call the Applicant Coordinator on the following Wednesday. That would be forty-eight hours before my National Academy graduation.

Geez, how strange is this scenario? I'm at the FBI Academy as an NA student and I just received a letter in the mail at my home from the same agency as they're further processing me to join their ranks as a special agent, or to at least take the next step in that direction.

It was, in fact, strange. And I was bursting at the seams to tell someone, anyone, about this somewhat strange scenario, or at least the strange timing of it all. But who would that be?

I know. There's someone I've been meaning to talk to here anyway as I have this idea. The timing may now be just right....

The next day, during one of my non-class periods, I stopped by the NA office and asked to talk to SSA Tom Colombell. He was there and invited me into his office. I asked him if it would be alright to shut his door as there were two issues I wanted to discuss with him and one was on the personal side...well, sort of. He agreed and as I sat down he closed his office door.

Tom was around forty years old in 1986. He had been in the FBI since 1973. I recall him telling a group of us that in his early special agent days he had successfully worked undercover as a trucker investigating stolen and hijacked trailers and merchandise. I could easily envision him in a yellow "Cat" hat, dirty overcoat, and cowboy boots in the cab of a big-ass eighteen-wheeler truck, not to mention hangin' out with his fellow good ol' boy truckers at the service areas and depots.

Tom was a big guy with broad shoulders. He could have been a football fullback in his youth. I know he was a good athlete as when he'd play in the NA officers versus FBI faculty/staff softball games, he could hit the ball over the fence almost every at-bat. On top of that, Tom was a gregarious guy who could swap funny and interesting stories with the best of them. He was good at remembering names too. That's always a valuable trait in business AND law enforcement for that matter. Lastly, Tom took his role as the FBI agent who was responsible for the smooth sailing of the NA ship very seriously. This was very obvious, and the NA students and later NA grads (of which there were many thousands) always appreciated him for it. Tom's dedication to them and to the tradition and institution of the National Academy was without peer at the time.

So, once in Tom's office, with the door closed, our conversation went something like this...

Me: "Tom, I want to discuss two things with you here. I won't take long, I promise."

Tom: "No problem, Jim, take your time."

Me: "Okay, firstly, I have an idea regarding a way to maybe further bridge the gap between the NA students at the Academy and the New Agent Trainees. As you know, we pass them in the hallways all the time, share elevators and even tables sometimes in the cafeteria, watch TV in the lounge rooms at night, yet I notice that neither group ever seems to really communicate with the other. Quite frankly, my fellow NA students think some of the NATs are arrogant and maybe even a bit stuck-up. It doesn't help the FBI's long-term relationship with local and state police once we're all out there ostensibly working together to catch bad guys. Do you know what I mean?"

Tom: "I hear ya, Jim. The FBI is always trying to find ways to better, as you say, bridge that gap between us and the rest of the law enforcement community. J. Edgar Hoover came up with the whole National Academy notion back in the 1930s as one way to do so. But, just so you know...here at the Academy, while the NA guys no doubt work hard at their courses and physical training and all that, don't forget, no matter what happens in that regard you guys still have a job to go home to. New agents at the Academy have no guarantees – actually none at all. If they fail their academics, firearms, defensive tactics, or screw up in some other way, they're out of a job. Period. That's why they seem pretty intense around here all the time. Hey, I went through here too as an NAT some fifteen years ago. I can relate to them. It can be pretty overwhelming for them at times, especially in their first month here. It's that intensity, worriedness, and quite frankly insecurity on their parts, at least with some of them, that perhaps some of us here see as arrogance."

Me: "Okay, I understand Tom, I really do. I can't offer much regarding the anxiety of the NATs' first month or so here, but I think I have something for later in their tenure at the Academy. To me, it makes perfect sense as everyone then benefits."

Tom: "I'm listening..."

Me: "So, here's my idea to maybe start to bridge that gap right here at the Academy. How about once the NATs are assigned to their respective divisions, I believe it's in their sixth week here, that some sort of a quasi-social event is set up by your office and the NAT office, maybe in the back section of the Boardroom some evening, where they get to meet police officers here at the NA from their soon-to-be assigned geographic regions? That way, these relationships can be forged early on for the NATs. At the same time the NA guys can talk to them in an unstructured and informal setting over a few beers regarding their home towns, their regions, and all parties can see that the other side is actually human and more than willing to work together. The NA officers can give their business cards to the NATs and right away, even on the brand new special agents' first day in their new office, they have a police department contact if they should need one. I don't think there's a downside to this idea. What do you think?"

Tom: "Jim, I think it's a great idea. I really do like it. Let me see if I can get something like that officially initiated around here with the NAT training staff. I do appreciate you bringing it to me. Now, you said there were two issues you wanted to run by me?"

Me: "Yeah, one more thing here…uh, believe it or not…I MAY be one of those NATs in the not too distant future attending one of these Boardroom meetings I just proposed to you. You see, after first applying for the special agent position in early '84, well let's just say after the hiring freeze, I finally took the test earlier this year, passed it, and literally just a day ago I received a letter in the mail at home that my oral interview is next on the horizon. You are one of the very few people that I'm telling so far that I MAY be back here again sometime before too long."

Tom: "Whoa! Jim, that's great news! Congratulations! I really mean that! Geez, you mean you were processing in the Philly Division for both the NA and special agent position at the same time?

Me: "That's right. Bizarre, eh?"

Tom: "Does your chief know? How about…it's Jack Robinson, right? He went through the 138th Session, right?"

Me: "No, neither of them is aware of this. I gotta tell you though, Bensalem PD is, or at least was, a really screwed up place, they both know it, and I don't think either of them would really care if I got out, despite them sending me here to the NA. I'm sure my chief would actually encourage me to leave as I don't think he'll be there much longer either. Jack, I'm not so sure about. Anyway, what I was going to ask you, Tom, is if it would be okay if I use you as a reference in any future proceedings with the FBI?"

Tom: "Absolutely. Just so you know though, as per Bureau rules, I can't officially endorse you or advocate for you, but if and when I get this program up and running that you just mentioned here, perhaps I can send you a personal letter on FBI letterhead thanking you for the suggestion and wishing you the best of luck, or something like that, in your special agent processing. It would go to you, not the Bensalem PD. Would that work for you?"

Me: "Yes it would. That would be great. Thanks so much for your offer to do so. When I get back here, if it's meant to be, I'll buy you a beer in the Boardroom. Fair enough?"

Tom: "Fair enough. I'll take you up on it. Have a great rest of your day and your stay here. You'll love the graduation ceremony, by the way. It's the best. Just remember though, IF you do come back as an NAT, and when you complete your training here, you'll see their graduation ceremony pales in comparison to the NA graduation. Just be forewarned. Enjoy this one next week."

I shook hands with Tom and left his office.

Tom Colombell didn't waste much time with my NA/NAT meet-and-greet in the Boardroom suggestion. He almost immediately wrote it up, formally proposed it to the Academy management, they liked it, and they went forward with it. It became a staple of every NA session and NAT class for the foreseeable future. All parties seemed to enjoy it and benefit from it at the same time. Tom even received a several hundred dollar cash incentive award sometime afterwards. He thanked me for it and eventually bought ME a beer in the Boardroom down the line.

Well before the beer in the Boardroom though, Tom sent me a very nicely worded letter about seven weeks after my NA graduation. It was a seemingly genuine "thank you" for the concept I presented him. At the end of the letter, he used wording that was about as close to an endorsement or recommendation as I believe he could possibly get away with. In the February 6 letter to me, SSA Colombell wrote, "I would like to offer my sincere best wishes concerning your potential employment as a Special Agent in the FBI. It is my hope that your interview...will be a successful one and that we will have an opportunity to meet here at Quantico again."

That works for me. Thanks, Tom.

Both SSA Colombell and I benefited from my short time at Quantico in the NA. He went on to a long and successful career running the FBI-National Academy. As a result, he has many friends and fans all over the world. I'm certainly one of them.

* * * * *

Every session leaves something of significance behind upon graduating from the FBI-NA. The buildings and grounds of the Academy contain numerous portraits, paintings, statues, plaques, memorials, and even some practical usage items donated by each session before it graduates. The 147th would be no exception.

Along with seven of my fellow classmates, I volunteered to be part of the Legacy Committee to collect funds and determine the best "gift" to leave behind for future students of any rank and/or agency who would be spending quality time at the Academy. As such, my colleagues and I eventually collected a total of $525 from our fellow NAers. We then took a vote and decided as a group to purchase something of a very practical nature for the Academy. It was therapeutic equipment for the trainer's room, located immediately adjacent to the gymnasium. We additionally commissioned a small plaque to be hung in the room.

On behalf of the 147th Session of the FBI National Academy, the plaque commemorated the strenuous physical exercise programs undertaken by many who come this way. Our donation of this rehabilitative-related equipment would serve to help those future attendees who may have pushed their bodies just a bit too hard in attempting to achieve their lofty workout objectives.

I happen to know for fact in the very near future this therapeutic equipment donated by my session, my committee, would come into everyday use by more than several attendees at the FBI Academy. Thanks to the conspicuousness of the wall plaque, the 147th was thanked out loud more than once during this timeframe for their wisdom in donating such well-needed apparatuses. It was definitely $525 well spent. To that I can later attest.

* * * * *

It was hard to believe, but December was a week old and it was just about graduation time for the 147th Session of the FBI National Academy. The other 124 attendees were making arrangements with their wives and loved ones over the handful of payphones around the complex for their big trip to Quantico to partake in the elaborate ceremony. I was no different, although I could do most of my planning over a prior weekend while at home. I was in contact with Chief Viola and Capt. Robinson and they both wanted to attend the ceremony too. That was great to hear.

As mentioned earlier, I stayed at the Academy the weekend before graduation. I had a few papers and a swimming assignment to complete. However, I drove back to Bensalem on the Tuesday of graduation week, and by Thursday morning, December 11, I was driving back to Quantico. With me was Eileen, my two sons, and my mother, Alma. I wanted all of them to be a part of the ceremonies these two days and share with me all that I was going to experience. They were the four most important people in my life at the time, so it only made sense.

There was a farewell dinner-dance in the FBI Academy cafeteria on the Thursday night before the next morning's graduation. It was for the NA students, their significant others, and selected guests. I was planning to attend for the whole evening but Chief Viola insisted on treating me, my wife, and Jack to dinner at the Quantico Marine Corps Base Officers' Club, located on the base on the east side of Interstate 95. (Remember, Viola was a Lt. Colonel in the Marine Reserves. As such, he had full officer privileges in Quantico.) So, with my mom babysitting the two boys at a local hotel, our first stop that evening was the Officers' Club. It was an exquisite and classy place with an historical ambience to it. The place also served great food. It was an overall excellent culinary experience for Eileen and me with these two very influential older men in my young professional life.

As Viola only drove there that afternoon for dinner on the Quantico base, he headed back to Bensalem right afterwards. He had some chief-related commitments the next day. Jack had driven separately and as he was an NA graduate he was authorized to come to the evening dinner-dance. The three of us then headed over there to the Academy for just the "dance" portion of the evening. Upon arriving there, albeit a bit later than most, it was great to finally meet the wives and girlfriends of the guys I had become friendly with over the last almost eleven weeks and introduce them to my spouse at the same time. Jack also enjoyed himself talking to some of the instructors he had from his stint there several years before me.

I wound up saying farewell to a bunch of guys that night as I knew it would be tough to see everyone tomorrow during or after the graduation ceremony. Jack, Eileen, and I then left and went back to our two separate hotel rooms to get a good night's sleep for the big day to come.

Friday, December 12th, 1986, was the actual graduation day of the 147th Session. To this day, it holds my own personal record of being the most ornate, elaborate, lavish, and impressive ceremony I have ever attended. I was so glad Eileen, my mother, Sean, and Dan were there to share it with me too.

The Marine Corps band and their flag bearers were present and they put on a great show. There were local, state, and federal politicians, chiefs of police, and family members from all over the U. S. and the world to celebrate the individual accomplishments of each of us graduating on this day from this prestigious and virtually one-of-a-kind law enforcement training academy. Eventually, after the pomp and circumstance as well as a few moving speeches, all 125 of our names were called (yes, every one of us who started the 147th also finished it), and we walked onto the stage to shake hands with FBI Director William H. Webster as he handed each of us our diplomas. It was a great day and a great celebration after a great eleven weeks.

Over the next hour or so as the clock approached 1:00, and after milling around a bit outside of the auditorium and later in other parts of the Academy, I said goodbye to the many friends I made over the time I spent here at the NA. They included both students and faculty members. It was sad to know that I would never see most of my NA classmates again, but we all realized that was the reality of a training environment such as this one. We also knew it was time to go back to our real worlds, the good and the bad of it, as we bade adieu to this home-away-from-home which had been ours for these very special seventy days.

As I finally drove away from the Academy with my immediate family in the car, adults as well as young children equally impressed with all they had experienced on this day, I recall looking in the rearview mirror and wondering to myself if I'd ever see this place again.

I wasn't sure, but to keep that option open I should probably make a certain phone call.

Top: December 1986, FBI Academy Pool, Jim Fitzgerald
upon completing last lap of 34-mile
"Swim the Potomac" exercise program
Bottom: December 1986, FBI NA Farewell Dinner, FBI Academy, Jim
Fitzgerald awarded "Swim the Potomac" tee-shirt
Left to right: Capt. Jack Robinson, Jim Fitzgerald

Top: December 11, 1986, FBI NA post-graduation, FBI Academy
Left to right: Alma Fitzgerald, Eileen Fitzgerald,
Jim Fitzgerald, Sean Fitzgerald, Dan Fitzgerald
Bottom: FBI NA graduation photo

Chapter Sixty-Three

I was back at work with my old patrol squad at the BPD by the following Monday. The officer I had appointed three months earlier as my acting sergeant brought me up to date on the various work-related happenings during my absence. Everything seemed fine with him, the squad, and for that matter the rest of the department. He did a good job in my stead.

It was nice seeing my subordinates again at my first roll call with them since late September. I was truly reinvigorated and ready to go that day. I was anxiously anticipating the application of all that I had learned over the last three months to their everyday supervision. This would include the designation of enhanced performance initiatives, the further distillation of their assigned workplace goals and objectives, as well as the ongoing facilitation of short-term and long-term professional growth opportunities within their present employment paradigms.

Yeah...or something like that.

Things hadn't seemed to change at the BPD all that much in my absence. The guys that I liked and respected were still there and the guys that I didn't like and didn't respect were still there. Well, most of them anyway. I'm sure both sets of people felt the same way about me, and neither entity seemed to really care. Everyone knew each other's number at this point and there was no reason to pretend otherwise. At least the good guys were still in charge of the place. There had been no coup in my absence. That was a relief.

Over the next week or two I was back at work I picked up from a few of my fellow officers of varying ranks an attitudinal shift of sorts. I would best describe it as a subtle jealousy or envy towards me, mostly of the professional variety. These were even from men whom I had considered quasi-friends, or at a minimum, trusted workmates in simpatico during our prior opposition to the Dark Side regime.

One of the BPD captains in particular couldn't seem to let go an obvious feeling of disappointment that I was the management member (of an even lower rank than him) who had been earlier nominated and then eventually chosen over him to attend the FBI-NA. I detected his negative vibes even before I shipped off to Quantico for my eleven weeks. However, through recent comments from him, some within earshot and some repeated later by others, I pretty much confirmed his apparent level of growing animus towards me. His negative commentary was usually in the form of an allegedly humorous aside or a semi-caustic quip of some sort, but I certainly got the message behind it.

It seemed without the Dark Side as the common enemy a few people with whom I had previously worked well and with whom I got along now wanted to shoot their figurative arrows and darts in my direction, usually from behind, too. I suppose they saw me as a threat of some sort. As a recent NA grad, they perhaps perceived me as the heir-apparent to Chief Viola's position when/if he would finally pull the plug and decide to leave this place.

Whatever...I knew who my friends were and they treated me the same respectful way, pre- and post-FBI National Academy. That certain captain, and the one or two other officers, didn't really concern me at all. I had neither the time nor the patience for them. For that matter, I wasn't even sure if I would be hanging around the BPD very much longer. In any event, my chief and his second-in-command, Capt. Jack Robinson, still liked me and respected me, of that I was assured.

Despite this noted divisiveness, I continued to perform my job as a patrol sergeant supervising a hard-working bunch of police officers to the best of my ability. As my squad almost always had the highest monthly stats, I must have been doing something right. So, I kept doing what I was doing, maybe even more proficiently now as an NA graduate. Or, at least those around me may have thought as much. I'd take it either way.

* * * * *

Taking care of my present everyday duties at the BPD was one thing. But I had a possible future in the FBI to plan for too. Again, time for some multi-tasking....

In terms of that potential future opportunity, I didn't let much time pass upon my return from the NA before I called the FBI office in Philadelphia. Upon doing so, I advised the Applicant Coordinator,

Special Agent Jerri Williams, that I was still interested in following through on my special agent application. I had two weeks or so to contact her after the receipt of the recent letter that my wife had read to me over the phone. Just about a day before the deadline, after speaking to Eileen and further evaluating my professional and personal life, I made the call.

Yes, SA Williams, please consider Jim Fitzgerald as still interested in joining the ranks of the FBI. In response she thanked me and advised me I would be hearing from her office before long to set up the next stage in the ongoing hiring process. That would consist of the panel interview.

After celebrating an excellent Christmas holiday season with my family, just a few weeks into January of '87, I received a call at home from the Applicant Coordinator. I was in the next group on the list to go through the interview process and she wanted to know what date would work best for me to come to the Philadelphia Division offices. We picked a day in mid-February. She told me that I'd receive a letter in the mail within a week confirming the date and what to expect while there.

As promised, the next letter from the FBI arrived several days later. It was simplistic in content and context. It stated that I would be interviewed on the agreed upon date by a three-member panel of special agents from the Philadelphia Division. Based on the interview results I would then be rated on a scale of one-to-five by each, with fifteen being the highest possible score. The letter didn't really provide any details as to what the interview would entail, what would be asked of me, or what I should otherwise expect. The only additional information was that the interview itself would take approximately forty-five minutes and the candidate should be prepared to answer various questions relating to his or her background as well as current events both domestically and internationally.

Okay…that narrows it down.

Well, as I've always been a news junkie and history buff I felt I was relatively well-versed at the time on most of what was happening in my area, my country, and my world. I got my news "fix" every day from at least two newspapers, a weekly subscription to *Time Magazine*, and I would usually watch the local and national network news each evening whenever I was at home. I didn't think I could do much more during this timeframe leading up to the interview as I didn't see any way to really "study" for this occasion. So, I didn't bother. I knew I didn't need a tutor for this particular stage of the FBI hiring process, so I saw no need to rehire the hippie school teacher. I was pretty sure there would be no math related questions asked of me by the three agents. I hoped not, anyway.

I decided I was simply going to be myself during this interview and let the panel members know I'm an experienced law enforcement officer/supervisor, almost done my master's degree, and oh yeah, a recent graduate of their own FBI National Academy. I will remind them too of the arrest of James J. Murphy from a year ago and all the bank robberies that were solved as a result.

I mean…why not? This would be my one and only chance to impress this panel and further make my case that I would be and could be an excellent FBI agent for them. I must put it all out there during my allotted three-quarters of an hour and give 'em everything I got. This would not be a time to be passive or humble. I couldn't come across as cocky, but I certainly could as confident. That was my game plan and I was sticking to it.

I debated whether or not to bring with me on the day of the interview a scrapbook of a dozen or so arrest-related newspaper clippings from my career as a Bensalem police officer. Eileen and I had been maintaining it since my first big arrest on my very first night as a rookie. It also contained a few departmental commendations I had received over the years. On the very last page of this plain black converted photo-album was the letter from the three interviewees' own boss, the Philadelphia FBI Special Agent-in-Charge, congratulating me and the BPD for the Murphy arrest. I'll make sure to show them that too. As SSA Tom Colombell had just recently sent me his official letter thanking me for the now-in-place NA/NAT Boardroom liaison evenings, with a definitively worded "best of luck in your FBI special agent position quest," I figured I'd bring that along to show them too.

I wasn't sure career-related "props" were necessary for this type of interview. But I'd have this scrapbook in my briefcase that day just in case I felt I needed the heavy artillery. One never knows….

The interview day was finally upon me. Unlike the day of the written test just about a year earlier, there was no hesitation or indecision on this morning when I awoke as to where I was going or what I was doing. On this cold, cloudy February morning, in my new suit, new shoes, and briefcase (with scrapbook inside) firmly in hand, it was off to 4th and Arch Streets in downtown Philadelphia to the Federal

Building, the FBI offices specifically, to undergo my scheduled interview with the three agents.

I was nervous on this interview day, but in an almost healthy way. They say even the most experienced of actors get stage-fright each time right before the curtain rises. Well, I had no plans on doing any acting today in front of these guys, but having some degree of "stage-fright" was probably okay for me. That's what I convinced myself anyway. I also kept repeating out loud during the entire drive there, "Be confident, be persuasive, but above all be yourself…if so, it'll be just fine." I was hoping that would work, anyway.

Once upstairs in the designated office in the FBI building I was met by a secretary who then introduced me to Special Agent Williams. The Applicant Coordinator with whom I had been previously communicating via mail and telephone calls was a tall, attractive, and nicely attired African-American woman, seemingly a few years younger than me. She made me feel comfortable right away while in her presence, despite the minor "stage-fright" otherwise permeating the whole of my insides. Jerri was very friendly and very professional the entire time. Not everyone can pull that off in the workplace, whether in the government or the private sector. However, she did both well.

After discussing a few administrative matters with SA Williams, we left her office area and she walked me down a non-descript corridor and into a non-descript room. Inside there were three male FBI agents sitting at a long table awaiting my arrival. She introduced me to them and as quickly as she entered the room, she left the room. I thanked the Coordinator as she walked out the door, nodded to the men at the table, and sat down in the one available chair in the room. It was already facing the three of them. Now, so was I, with about ten feet of air and floor between us.

It was just me and the three FBI interviewers in the room at this point. Oh, and my briefcase too. I made sure to bring it in here with me, just in case I may need those various props from my recent past.

Okay, I'm ready to go here. I'm pretty sure I am, anyway. What was I telling myself earlier in the car? Yes…just be yourself. I can do that. To help me in that regard, I took a deep breath, straightened my tie, pushed my hair back, looked at three men barely ten feet away and articulated a confident, "Good morning, gentlemen" in their direction. They responded in kind.

The interview went well. The forty-five minutes seemed to fly by pretty fast. Before too long into it, I felt that I had bonded with at least

two of my interviewers. One in definitely a positive way, the other…
well, let's just say we bonded in a crime-related way.

The lead interviewer on the panel identified himself as Special
Agent James McIntosh. Okay…why does that name ring a bell? Even
though he was seated the whole time, I could tell by the length of his
legs under the table and how he was sitting in his chair that he was
a tall guy. When I happened to mention in my personal introduction
that I was presently attending Villanova University and finishing up
my master's degree, McIntosh commented that he went there too,
having graduated back in the late 1960s. That's when I suddenly came
to the realization that I knew this man, or at least knew his name and
reputation.

McIntosh was a former basketball player, and a darn good one,
having grown up in Philadelphia and later playing the position of
center on Villanova teams that went to two National Invitational
Tournaments and one NCAA tourney. He was a very well-known local
high school and later college player in his day. Now, on this day, he
was interviewing me in my attempt to possibly become an FBI agent.

So…could I pass this tryout to make his present team?

I casually mentioned to SA McIntosh that I recalled his playing
days at Villanova, some of his fellow players, and even one of his
better games which I saw in person at the Palestra, the University of
Pennsylvania arena where many of the Philadelphia college teams
played at the time. He seemed to appreciate my recollection of his
playing days, not to mention the fact that I was presently attending his
alma mater. However, before long we moved on to other topics more
germane to a job interview. It was time.

After discussing some of these more relevant issues with the panel,
to include the ongoing drug problem in the U. S., the Mafia in the
Philadelphia area, the Soviet Union's ongoing aggressiveness, continued hostilities in the Middle East, the panelist to the immediate left
of SA McIntosh chimed in. Returning our discussion to a more local
flavor, he advised me he was very familiar with my police department
as he presently lives in Bensalem, in the Brookwood Apartments, as a
matter of fact. He also advised he was familiar with some recent crime
trends in my town.

Okay, I asked myself, where was this going? What does this other
panel member know about Bensalem crime trends and patterns? Are
there federal statutes being violated under my department's nose?

The BPD once again had an excellent relationship with the Feds,
including the FBI, ever since Chief Viola returned. If there was

something going on in my PD with a federal nexus, I'd like to think I would know about it - unless he's referring to something else entirely. The only thing I can think of is a recent string of residential burglaries in the area including, as it so happens, at his particular apartment complex. Maybe I should mention this....

"Well, SA Green (fictitious name), one of the more troubling trends of which I am aware concerns a burglary ring operating in Bensalem. We think they're out of Philly. I know a number of homes which have been hit recently, as well as some upscale apartments. I was just talking to one of our detectives last week about it. As a result, I'm making sure my officers are conducting their patrol checks through the various targeted neighborhoods and apartment complexes on a frequent basis."

That was all the truth, too.

I didn't know it beforehand, but it seems SA Green was aware of this recent crime trend from a very personal perspective. It was really, really personal as I was about to learn.

Somewhere between very humorous and very serious, SA Green replied, "Well, Jim, I hope you'll let me know if you identify the burglars who broke into MY apartment in early December. They took some cash, a camera, and some other items of value. I spoke with one of your investigators, I think it was Det. Lachman. He seemed helpful but so far no luck in arresting anyone or recovering the stolen items."

Geez, what are the odds of undergoing a panel interview in an attempt to join a certain prestigious federal investigative agency and having one of the interviewers be a felony crime victim in the town I'm presently charged with protecting?

At least I didn't put a gun to his head like I did with a particular Philadelphia PD sergeant before he was to become my boss. No, it wasn't quite that drastic here today. But still....

So, how do I handle this? Tell the agent I'm sorry? Tell him I'll talk again to the detective? Catch the actual burglars? Well, that last one WOULD be a nice gesture, but it's not gonna happen anytime today.

I was, in fact, aware of some possible suspects that CID had identified in just the last week. I didn't have much in the way of details but I told SA Green I'd have Det. Terry Lachman call him in the next day or two and hopefully provide him with some additional information regarding his case. He thanked me, seemed impressed that I was aware of the details of the problem, and we moved on with the rest of the interview. (Det. Lachman, at my request, did call the agent within the next few days. I knew I could count on Terry.)

The third special agent is the only interviewer with whom I seemingly had nothing in common, at least not basketball or burglary related. I was hoping and praying he never had his car stolen from the Neshaminy Mall or anywhere else in Bensalem. If he did, for better or worse, he never volunteered that information to me.

Near the end of the forty-five minutes, as the interview was clearly winding down, and even though I felt that it had gone extremely well so far, I nonetheless mentioned to the three agents that I had some material with me which may shed an even brighter light on my eleven-year career at the Bensalem Police Department. One or two of them responded, "Sure, let's see it."

I opened the briefcase which was beside me on the floor, removed the scrapbook, stood up, and placed it in front of SA McIntosh at the center of the three of them. I slowly started flipping through the pages. I emphasized that there was no need to read the individual newspaper articles themselves but by just scanning the headlines (and some photographs) they could see that I had made numerous quality arrests as an officer, detective, and sergeant over the last decade. On the last two pages were the bank robbery arrest atta-boy letter from their SAC and also the letter from Tom Colombell via the FBI Academy. The three of them added that they were impressed with my accomplishments to date so far. They seemed to mean it. I thanked them while closing the book and putting it back in my briefcase. I shook each of their hands and told them I hoped to see them again sometime.

Whether he was supposed to say it or not, SA McIntosh responded to my last comment with, "I have a feeling you will, Jim. Have a great rest of your day and stay safe out there. See you soon."

The interview was over. One of the agents walked me back to SA Jerri Williams' office and I said goodbye to him. I spoke with Jerri for just a few additional minutes. It ended with her telling me that my just-completed interview score, somewhere between zero and fifteen, will be added to my written exam score and I will be further ranked accordingly. At some point in the next month or two her office will contact me again to advise me of the next stage. I thanked her and left the building.

Whew! It was sooooo nice to be completely done with the competitive portion of my application process. Now, I just had to wait for the FBI to contact me again and see where this whole matter takes me next.

The FBI's formal letter writing stage seemed to be a thing of the past. Over the next several months it was almost all phone calls between me and the Bureau. Each of the calls originated from SA Williams' office.

I was fine with that. She was very easy to talk to and at the same time very informative.

Sometime in early April, Williams called my house and left me a message. I called her back the next day and she told me some very welcome news. That is, I had done exceptionally well in the panel interview with the three special agents. I scored a fifteen. She told me it was essentially a "perfect score" which was relatively rare in her experience. She added that I "must have really impressed these agents." I was at a momentary loss for words and simply retorted something like, "Thank you... this is great to hear."

Duh! A perfect fifteen! Of course it's great to hear.

Okay, though...what's next?

Jerri told me what was next. She wanted to conduct a "spousal interview" with my wife in the very near future. It's something the local offices began doing several years ago to make sure that the wives and husbands of candidates are aware of the various implications of becoming an FBI agent. The interview would involve both of us, not just Eileen. I told Jerri I was pretty sure my wife would be glad to talk to her.

After discussing this matter with Eileen, we picked a date and within two weeks she took a few hours off from her job on one of my scheduled days off and we drove downtown to the Philadelphia FBI Offices. Once there we met with SA Williams.

The whole meeting with Jerri, me, and Eileen took less than an hour. The Applicant Coordinator did most of the talking, but we had the occasional question to ask of her too. Most of what Jerri was trying to impress upon both of us was that there were some hardships attached to being an FBI agent, and she wanted both parties in the relationship to be cognizant of them before the hiring process progressed any farther. These hardships included me being away at the FBI Academy for about four months of training, an initial transfer to another U. S. city, long working hours, assignments which may keep me away from home for days, weeks, or even months at a time, and the possible subsequent transfer to yet another FBI division within a few years of arriving at my first office. Jerri added that relocating BACK to the Philadelphia FBI office, while certainly not impossible, could take me as long as ten to fifteen years.

Jerri slowed down her rhetoric at this point for a moment or two. It wasn't just to collect her thoughts, but also to allow the two of us to collect ours. We did, more or less.

I couldn't help but notice Eileen becoming somewhat uncomfortable and listless during the latter stage of our three-way conversation. I knew she felt she could manage me working late hours and even being away for extended periods of time. But moving from the only place she's ever called home? That, I could see, would not be easy to overcome here. Of course, we both knew in advance that my employment with the FBI would require me initially working at a division other than the one in Philadelphia. However, this was the first time we ever heard about it up close and personal and perhaps the first time it really sunk in for either of us.

I must add, this wasn't just Eileen's issue either. After all, the Philly area is the only place I had ever lived up until this juncture in time too. I was settled in, owned a house, my two sons were in good schools, and I had numerous family members and friends in the immediate area. I wasn't exactly thrilled about the possibility of leaving my hometown, but geez, this was the FBI. They offer so many professional opportunities, so many short-term and long-term advantages, so many chances to become an even better investigator, the ability to work major domestic and international cases, not to mention a better salary than the BPD, excellent benefits, a great pension plan....

Then, as both Eileen and I were separately contemplating all of these factors, including the moving-away-from-home scenario, SA Williams reinitiated the conversation. In doing so, she offered the one additional bit of information which would change everything, certainly from my wife's perspective. As almost an afterthought, she stated, "You know Jim and Eileen, within the last six months the Bureau has started a pilot program which allows new agents while still in training at the Academy to request New York City as their first office assignment. This is being done because the New York Division is such a difficult office to staff. As I'm sure you know, it's a high cost of living area, it's a difficult daily commute, and some agents just don't like working in a city as large as New York. Some have even quit the FBI after being assigned there. So, Jim, if you would be interested in specifically requesting the New York Office while at the Academy, there's a good chance you would get it as your first office. Then you could commute every day from Bensalem to there. I happen to know of a few agents who are making the daily roundtrip from there and other parts of Bucks County. You could probably jump in a carpool with them. Lastly, as you know, you'll be starting in the FBI at a GS-10 pay grade, plus the built in overtime pay. In every other Bureau division in the U. S. it takes seven years to reach GS-13. In New York, it's only three years until you're making Grade 13 salary. Anyway, I just wanted you to be aware of this particular recent development."

Through all of this, Eileen slowly started sitting up in her chair. Jerri had her attention once again. Before I could say anything my wife voluntarily offered to anyone who may be listening, "Yes, that's most likely what we would do if Jim decides to join the FBI."

I looked at Eileen from my chair to her chair somewhat quizzically and thought to myself, "Wait! We? What did WE just decide?" I didn't actually say anything though; not yet.

The interview ended shortly thereafter on a positive note. Jerri Williams shook both of our hands and advised us over the next week or two to discuss all of the issues which she presented us today. After that time, she would appreciate a phone call from me letting her know one way or the other whether I wanted to continue processing for the special agent position. I told her we would talk and I would make that call shortly. We thanked her for her time and left the office.

In the elevator down to the lobby, with both of us silently staring at the steadily descending floor numbers atop the door, Eileen made a simple yet emphatic statement to me. She said very matter-of-factly and without hesitation, "If you really want this FBI job-thing, you're driving to New York every day. I'm not moving anywhere. Understand!"

I understood. On the way home in the car that afternoon, my wife further laid out her reasons why she/we were not moving, with both familial and financial reasons comprising her strongest arguments. I counter-argued to a degree, but as we were still at only the mid-stages of this whole "FBI job-thing" hiring process, with no guarantees of anything yet, I suggested we delay this discussion until another time and place. Eileen agreed to do so, but then added that she would not be changing her mind.

I simply replied at that point, "Yes, Dear."

After several relatively intense husband and wife conversations (not arguments) over the next week, Eileen and I agreed that New York City, about seventy-five miles northeast of Bensalem, would be my new workplace if I decide to join the FBI and, of course, if they decide to actually hire me. In view of this "compromise," I called Jerri one morning and advised her that I was still interested in becoming an FBI agent and that both Eileen and I understood all of which the position entailed, from the positive to the negative. She told me she was glad to hear this and my processing would now continue. Before long she told me the Bureau would be digging further into my background.

This would include our financial records and interviewing neighbors and others who have known me over the years. Agents would also be contacting the BPD, but that wouldn't be for a few more months and before it begins she will notify me so I can notify them in advance. I thanked her yet one more time as we ended the phone call.

I supposed at this time my future was slowly being shaped for me... by my wife, Jerri, and the rest of the FBI. IF I was to be accepted into New Agent Training and IF I was to successfully complete said training, it was off to New York City I would go. That would certainly be a change from my medium-sized community and police department of Bensalem Township – a very substantial change, actually.

Interestingly, up until this stage of my life, even at 33 years of age, I could count on one hand the trips I had made to New York City. I always figured if I wanted to see a very large city I would simply drive or take public transportation to the nearest one, which happened to be the city of my birth, Philadelphia. Now, if this gig works out, I'll be in the Big Apple five days a week, at a minimum. That'll be about four hours per day in a car driving there from Bensalem and back.

What's my commute to the BPD now? Let's see, it's four minutes by car, a whole six minutes by bike.

So...what are those positives to joining the FBI again?

Actually, there are plenty of them. A longer commute, even a much longer commute, will NOT be one of the reasons for which I will decline this job offer. That much I know for sure.

Of course, the job still has to be offered to me first. I'll figure the rest out afterwards. There were still a few complications with which I would have to first deal.

You didn't think it would be THAT easy, did you?

Chapter Sixty-Four

Several miscellaneous matters to convey here, each related to my professional past, present, and/or future...

With my six University of Virginia graduate credits from my two NA courses successfully transferred to Villanova University, it turns out the Spring '87 semester in which I was presently enrolled and taking a course was to be my very last. Yes, five-plus years after starting in the Human Organizational Science program at 'Nova, with taking about a year off in the middle of it all, I was about to complete my final course requirement there in May. What a great feeling. All I had to do now was take the written "Comps," (a three-hour comprehensive exam with multi-part questions to be answered in bluebooks), pass them, then the Orals (a formal, in-person Q & A interview session with at least three professors in the program), pass that, and I would be awarded my M.S.

I managed to pass the Comps in the early fall of '87. However, the very final stage of my Villanova academic career would have to wait until the following spring, 1988. Suffice it to say, once I finally arranged to take the Orals at that time, I passed. I received my M.S. degree in the mail a month later. Academic mission accomplished.

Like I said to myself after attaining my B.S. degree from Penn State in '75, I was now officially done with my formal academic pursuits. Adding this additional M.S. from Villanova University to my resume was just about all I would ever need from a future career perspective. Right?

Wrong!

Believe it or not, I had one more degree in me. It would be another M.S. earned over fifteen years later. And of all places, it was from the same school that Villanova beat in the 1985 NCAA basketball championship game.

Looking back, it's fair to say if my first two academic degrees opened a number of professional doors for me, this next one, from Georgetown University, would knock others completely down... linguistically speaking, of course.

(More on this in JCM Book III.)

* * * * *

In early April of '87, Chief Viola asked me if I would consider coming out of patrol and reassume my role as the Admin Sergeant for a few months. It was a "temporary position," he assured me. The BPD was in the process of hiring ten new officers and he wanted my help in taking care of all that was necessary in facilitating their final testing stage, selection, uniform and equipment acquisition, police academy training, and the like. Captain Traenkle had been doing this job temporarily but once again he was being transferred elsewhere.

I knew when Viola "asked" something of one of his subordinates he was more or less strongly requesting it, if not ordering it. But since I liked the way he "asked," and I suppose I could use a few months of straight day-work with weekends off, I said "sure." So, even though I knew I MAY be a short timer at this place, I figured once again, "why not?" I did the job before and I knew what I was doing so the transition time would be minimal.

After being back in the Admin sergeant position for a few weeks, I remember meeting in my office one day with the final ten candidates who came out on top of the most recent police officer testing. It was shortly after they were officially sworn in upstairs. Six of them already had their Act 120 certifications so they could start on the streets right away (with a training partner, of course). However, four of the newly hired officers were required to attend the Philadelphia Police Academy to attain their accreditation. (The BPD was once again using the PPD Academy for their training. The PSP Academy was unavailable, too expensive, or not simply feasible for some reason at this time.)

One of the cadets was a young man named Fred Harran. He was originally from Brooklyn, New York, but after college found himself here in the Bensalem area and was about to become one of our "finest." I recall that day he was sworn in, and every other Thursday when he and his three colleagues would come in to my office for their paychecks, he would always seem to be the cadet to ask more than one intelligent question about either Bensalem Township itself, the management structure of the PD, the Bucks County court system, an issue or two which were discussed in class that week, or some other relevant matter pertaining to the criminal justice system in general. Upon taking in his usual well-thought out questions, I'd do my best to provide Fred with well thought-out answers.

In getting to know Cadet/Officer Harran a bit back in his very early days on the BPD, I couldn't help but see a bit of myself in him from ten-plus years ago in my early professional life. Like me back then, he was hard-working, very inquisitive, and wanted to learn. But, at the same time, Fred was a bit naïve and unsure of exactly what he was getting himself into here at the BPD. Just like me back in '76, I fondly (or not, at times) recall.

When I would eventually return to patrol sergeant status after the summer was over, and Fred had graduated from the PPD Academy, I'd cross paths with Fred on occasion when our shifts would overlap at night. I remember backing him up on several calls and car stops during that timeframe and noticing that he was handling himself and the situation at hand very well. I grew to like and respect the "Kid" and was sure he would go places in this PD.

I was later proven correct.

* * * * *

My last noteworthy BPD arrest occurred on April 20, 1987. I may have assisted in others before the year ended, but this was the last one I made on my own. The next day it was referenced in the *Bucks County Courier Times*. I suppose that would make it noteworthy.

It seems around 1:00 on a Monday afternoon a man came back to his house after being away from it for an hour or so and noticed a strange green Chevy in his driveway. He also noticed the front door of his residence kicked in. Needless to say, these two issues combined are almost never a good thing. This man apparently knew that. Very smartly, instead of walking inside and confronting a possible burglary in progress, the man went to a neighbor's house and called the police. Shortly thereafter an unknown subject walked quickly out of the house, jumped into the Chevy, and drove off with what was later determined to be the homeowner's rare coin collection. The description of the car and the suspect was put out over the radio. This would in turn hopefully locate the burglar, and maybe even the stolen coins.

Of course, I was looking for it too, although at the time I was assigned as the Admin Sergeant. I believe I just happened to be coming from my lunch break and I wanted to see if I could assist in any way.

So, it being a quiet day inside HQ I figured I'd head over towards that direction. Even Admin Sergeants gotta have fun sometimes.

For some reason, as the victim's house was not too far from the Neshaminy State Park, which borders the Delaware River in the northeast section of Bensalem on State Rd., I drove my unmarked car onto the grounds. The lot on this early spring afternoon was all but empty except for a lone green Chevy in one of the far parking areas. I could see from a distance that the one visible occupant in the parked car was intently looking down as if he was highly preoccupied with something he was doing. Fortunately, this preoccupation kept him from observing me as I made a wide sweep around the rear of his vehicle. I then pulled up tight behind it, in effect boxing him in his parking spot, called in the car's plate number, the car description, my 10-20 (location), and walked up to the driver's side window. Then and there, my sudden presence took the single occupant completely by surprise.

In my full uniform and with my left hand judiciously hovering directly above my holstered firearm, I requested identification from the driver. Upon him handing it to me I also asked him what was on his lap. He told me they were coins.

"Yeah, I can see they are coins. Are they yours?"

He responded, "No, I...uh...I just found them."

"Really? Where?"

The suspect knew from the intonation of those two words to him, along with incredulity expressed on my face, that I in no way believed what he just told me. After that, he didn't even try to answer any of my additional questions except with repeated "Uh, I don't know(s)."

By this time one of the regular squad officers came onto the scene and we ordered the suspect out of his car. We handcuffed him behind his back, told him he was being detained for suspicion of burglary and receiving stolen property and put him into the rear of the other officer's patrol car. I then ordered the officer to drive over to the location of the burglarized house. As less than thirty minutes had transpired between the time of the burglary and me finding this suspect, his car, and the coins, we could do a "show-up" with the victim. Upon the victim seeing the man through the back window of the police car, he positively identified him as the guy he saw exiting out his front door. The victim also described his coin case and it perfectly matched what was found in the green Chevy at the state park.

Later, when one of the BPD detectives began formally interviewing the suspect, he confessed. Not only did he admit to this burglary, but eventually to others in Bensalem and Lower Bucks County too, to include having knowledge of the break-in at the apartment of the FBI agent on my panel interview. We never recovered the items stolen from the agent's residence, but he was VERY happy our CID eventually identified and arrested the perp, thanks in part to me arresting this coin thief when I did. I made sure to call him with the news on the day of the arrest.

Not a bad pinch on a few levels. And at least the most recent victim got all of his stolen items back.

These are the best kinds of arrests…no one hurt, property recovered, multiple crimes solved, multiple felons off to jail upon conviction, and oh yeah, arresting the thief responsible for the burglary of the residence of one of the people who had a say in your future employment. I hit all five in this case. (Although, this agent had already given me a perfect score after my oral interview.)

As it turned out, this was the last occurrence of my name ever appearing in the *Bucks County Courier Times* for anything arrest related. I was fine with that. My Bensalem PD scrapbook was just about full. Maybe it's time to start a new one….

* * * * *

I was forced to deal with yet another dose of hardcore reality in my life. An acquaintance of mine, a Philadelphia Police officer, was killed in the line of duty. His name was William D. McCarthy. He was a first cousin of my good friend and also PPD officer, Rob McCarthy.

Officer Bill McCarthy was 31 years old with ten years on the job. His death occurred on September 22, 1987, alongside the Spectrum arena in South Philadelphia. Bill was a mounted officer when he and the horse he was riding, while engaged in crowd control at a Grateful Dead concert, were hit by a speeding pick-up truck. McCarthy died almost instantly of head injuries. His horse, Skipper, had to be put down on the scene.

Ironically, the driver of the aforementioned truck was an off-duty Philadelphia police officer. He was subsequently charged with and later pleaded guilty to DUI and Vehicular Homicide. He was eventually sentenced to three-to-six years in prison.

I wasn't necessarily the best of friends with Bill McCarthy, but I knew him somewhat from various McCarthy family social events over the years. He was a great guy. When his very untimely death occurred he was living on N. Third St. in the Olney section of Philadelphia, just a few blocks from where I grew up. Bill left a wife and four young children. As expected, his funeral a few days later was quite the well-attended and ceremonious event.

Not that I was keeping a conscious count, but it occurred to me around this time that in just about seven years there have been four police officers I personally knew to one degree or another who died violent deaths while in the performance of their duties. They were Bob Yezzi of the Bensalem PD, Gary Farrell, Danny Faulkner, and now William McCarthy of the Philadelphia PD.

The four aforementioned police officers were much too young and their deaths so very much unnecessary in each and every one of their cases. And these were just the ones I knew....

RIP again to each of you.

(+Bonus Chapter 64a)

Chapter Sixty-Five

"Jim, it's Special Agent Williams. Please call me at the FBI office as soon as you get this voicemail. There's...a problem."

This was the brief message on my answering machine when I came home for lunch one late September day. Jerri's voice sounded a bit disconcerting at the time. It was different than her normal tone and pitch. She seemed very formal and serious too, more so than in our recent conversations. What's up with that?

Wait! It wouldn't be THAT issue, would it? I mean, could it? Please tell me it wasn't what I thought it may be.

It was, and I suppose I should have known.

Damn!

After a few attempts, I finally got ahold of Jerri later that afternoon. She was direct and to the point with me and remained very serious in her demeanor.

"Jim, I'm not sure what this all means but in the course of conducting the last aspect of your background check we came up with something which MAY prove problematic to your hiring."

"Uh...okay. What was it?" I was pretty sure I knew but I wanted to hear it from Jerri first.

She didn't hesitate in telling me.

"Well, upon checking our indices we found that you were under investigation by the FBI back in 1974. Yet, you didn't include it on your Bureau application. What can you tell me about this matter?"

Yes, this was the issue I was afraid it might be. It was back to haunt me again after thirteen whole years. It seemed like a lifetime ago to me. In many ways it was. But from an FBI record checking perspective it might as well have been yesterday.

They don't miss a trick, do they?

Geez, this was so long ago too. I was a long-haired college kid back then doing what college kids did. Well, some of them anyway. Now, in addition to being short-haired, I'm an accomplished mid-level law enforcement manager, relatively well-educated, married with two kids, who's even a graduate of this particular agency's own prestigious National Academy.

Damn! I couldn't believe this. Here we go once again. It's a trip down memory lane, a very specific lane, and I'm not looking forward to reliving even one aspect of this long ago and faraway part of my journey.

And no, it had absolutely nothing to do with drugs.

As recounted in detail in JCM Book I, in my late teens and very early twenties, it seems I had this little side avocation. It involved the making of fake ID cards. Specifically, they were U.S. Selective Service cards.

You see, sometime in the early '70s I managed to get my hands on a blank photocopy of a draft card. (Back then, every male U. S. citizen over 18 years of age had to register with the Selective Service System and acquire a draft card.) I then made several dozen additional photocopies from it, and over the next few years I typed fake names and fake dates of birth on them for one reason and one reason only. That was, for me and my not yet 21-year-old male friends (and some of their male friends) to get served in bars, beer distributors, and liquor stores. I gave away many of the cards for free but also charged between $5.00 and $7.00 for some of them.

What should have then been a very predictable eventuality to me did before long come to pass. That is, one of these card-carrying underage wannabe drinkers got caught trying to get into a bar in State College, Pennsylvania, (the home of Penn State University, where I was going to school at the time). He presented his plastic laminated-covered photocopy of one of these fake cards to the doorman. For whatever reason that night the card was confiscated by the doorman, the police were called by the bar owner, and the FBI was called by the police. The card-carrier (who is unknown to me to this day) apparently sang like a canary to one or more investigators, and within a week or two I was sitting in the State College Resident Agency explaining myself and my actions to a real, in-the-flesh, FBI special agent. That was probably the worst day of my life and it would become the overall worst several weeks of my life up until that point in time.

As it turns out, if I did anything right during this timeframe it was my candid admissions to the FBI agent as I fessed up to my equal measures of complicity and stupidity as it related to my little sideline. I reassured him numerous times the cards were being reproduced (and really, there weren't all that many of them) for one reason and one reason only. It was for me and my friends and acquaintances, while still underage, to be served alcoholic beverages in bars, to buy booze, etc. That was it. And despite the warnings written on the back of the actual Selective Service card that tampering with them or altering them was a felony and all that entails, I assured the special agent that my purpose in making them was not to unlawfully avoid the military draft or military duty, not to assist soldiers in going AWOL, not to muck up the records of the Selective Service System, and/or certainly not to commit acts of sedition against the U. S. Government. It was to simply make me and my friends age-appropriate for drinking purposes. That, of course, was the absolute truth.

I assure you, the then 21-year-old Jim Fitzgerald would not have been telling an FBI agent anything but the truth during this meeting. That would also be the case later when the now 34-year-old Jim Fitzgerald was retelling an FBI agent/applicant coordinator about this confounding time in my early adult life.

As I didn't know exactly what paperwork or old reports Jerri may have had in front of her at the time, I further related to her during this phone call in September of '87 that the agent in December of '74 told me he genuinely believed me and all that I had "confessed" to him in his office that day. I continued with Jerri that after being kept in limbo for about two weeks the State College FBI agent re-contacted me and officially advised there would be no further investigation or any prosecution of me for my small fake draft card sideline.

I advised SA Williams of all of this. In doing so I found myself for the second time in thirteen years formally acknowledging to an FBI agent that it was very stupid to do what I did, even if for relatively innocuous purposes. It seemed even stupider to me in '87 as an adult when forced to revisit those days and attempt to explain this component of the much younger Jim Fitzgerald to her. But I did, and I did so forthrightly. I was completely honest in '74 with that special agent and I was completely honest once again with this special agent. The first time, of course, it was a potential arrest by the FBI which was on the line. This time, it was a potential job with the FBI which was on the line.

As different as the issues may have been, each one and each outcome was equally important to me, even thirteen years apart. I was hoping this second time around the results would be once again favorable for me. I knew the statute of limitations had expired and I couldn't be arrested by the FBI for the draft card matter itself. But would I be hired by them? Is there a statute of limitations on youthful stupidity for candidates applying to the FBI?

If so, I was hoping to make it just under the wire.

As a seemingly important follow-up question from her during this phone call, SA Williams asked me why I hadn't included this specific information in my employment application to the Bureau. I advised her, once again with all sincerity, that I read and reread the application very carefully, line-by-line, and responded to every query with the exact information requested of me. After reviewing the entirety of the application numerous times, and answering each and every question completely, I told her I determined there was no one question which directly elicited information regarding the investigation from 1974.

I further advised Jerri that in one section of the application it asked of any and all adult arrests on my part, even if they subsequently resulted in acquittals. I responded accordingly (and in the negative). However, at no time on the 1987 special agent application did it ever directly inquire as to whether the candidate was ever actively investigated by the FBI or a "suspect" in one of their cases. As such, there was really no place to add that specific information. So, I didn't.

Lastly, I told SA Williams that I did, in fact, contemplate this situation in my application and tried to determine before I sent it off whether to include information regarding this matter back in '74. In thinking it through, I assumed it would most likely be in the FBI records somewhere and if it became an issue in my hiring, we would discuss it openly then. Well, that's exactly what was happening here, I politely reminded Jerri, and she appeared to accept it.

SA Williams seemed satisfied with my overall responses. She certainly knew I wasn't purposefully trying to hide anything from her or her cohorts at the FBI. Before we ended the call Jerri told me she'd get back to me regarding this matter after running it by her supervisors. I thanked her once again.

After the call, I must admit, I was a bit dejected and down in the dumps by this whole sordid affair coming back once again to bite me in the...lower posterior. But it was what it was, no more and no less, with no going back in time to change things. I didn't lie back then and I wasn't lying now.

I knew at the time I was going through the special agent processing that a candidate could have told the Bureau that he or she smoked pot and perhaps even ingested other harder drugs over the prior decade.

As long as these incidents weren't within the last few years, the candidate had essentially "cleaned up his/her act," and all of the other aspects of their background were in order, the FBI would still consider hiring the person. That philosophy, I hoped and prayed, would apply to me in this situation.

I tried to objectively think through this whole former draft card scenario and ask myself…was it really that big of a deal? Or if not even the actual situation itself a decade-plus ago, what about me not including it on my application, even though there was no one specific block or category which referred to such a matter?

No doubt, all of these questions will be answered for me soon. I knew it wouldn't take the FBI long to address them. And it didn't.

Within a few days, I had my answer from SA Williams. She told me over the phone that the FBI records were further checked and all was good. The very minor and relatively inconsequential '74 incident (her words) and its subsequent non-inclusion in my '87 application would not be a factor in my further processing and/or my potential hiring by the FBI.

Whew! That was good to hear. Make that very, very good to hear. The fake draft card saga of my early life was now finally behind me once and for all. Good riddance!

* * * * *

SA Williams advised me in our next phone conversation that the penultimate stage of my special agent candidate processing would begin shortly. That is, having an agent proceed to my place of employment and interview my supervisors and colleagues there regarding my overall work record, my character, my trustworthiness, and the like. She wanted to make sure this next necessary step would be okay with me from a timing perspective. We concurred that once this happened the proverbial cat would be out of the bag at my workplace in regards to me seeking a position with the FBI. I told her cat or no cat, it would be fine, but to give me a few days to tell a few of those supervisors first. She agreed.

The cat would have to remain in its bag for just a little bit longer.

With this next-to-last part of my special agent processing now imminent, I wasn't sure between Chief Viola and Capt. Robinson who to initially advise of this upcoming visit by an FBI agent which, of course, would signal to one and all the real possibility of me leaving the BPD to join that agency. But who do I tell first?

I mean, I've known Jack Robinson the longest and he was instrumental early on assisting in my career development and advancement. It was he who suggested to the relatively new Chief Viola that I be appointed to the acting detective position within a few weeks of him (Jack) being put in charge of CID. That certainly didn't hurt my future career track. Not to mention it was Robinson who nominated me for the National Academy. That was a really big deal, too.

However, Viola is, in fact, the chief (once again) at the BPD. Perhaps I should tell him before I tell Jack. Advising the very top guy in my organization this information first may be the most prudent. He's certainly been influential in my career too. Plus, the FBI would probably contact him initially anyway.

Let me think about this.

Work-wise, through a mutual agreement with my bosses it was decided that my second round as Admin Sergeant was soon to be over. I agreed that I would return to patrol in the next week or so. I was fine with that as I was actually looking forward to spending my last few months at the BPD on the streets, not as a desk jockey.

As it so happens, there was some sort of a luncheon for the secretaries one early October afternoon right before I was due to leave my administrative post. I travelled there in the car with Chief Viola. I'm not sure if Capt. Robinson attended or not, but if he did, he drove there on his own.

The ride to the restaurant with Viola and the luncheon itself were routine with nothing of any true relevance being discussed between us. However, on the ten-minute or so drive back to HQ, the Chief took me by surprise when out of the blue he inquired of me, in so many words, "Jimmy, what're your future plans for this place, your career? I'm asking you because I want you to know I'm not hangin' around here forever and there's no guarantee who will be put in charge once I'm gone. I think Zajac and his cronies are done for good, but with this town and these politicians anything is possible."

"Well, it's interesting that you...," but before I could finish my sentence, the Chief continued his verbal momentum.

"You know, the FBI is hiring. You should definitely look into that agency. They're the real deal. You're under 35, Jimmy, right?"

Geez, what are the odds? Just as I was about to tell Viola and Robinson what will be happening in a few days. Well, since he brought it up first, I guess he'll be the one I tell first.

"Ah, Chief...it's interesting you bring up this very topic. Yes, I'm still under 35. And...I was going to soon tell both you and Jack that I did take the FBI special agent exam early last year and passed it. I also did well at the panel interview earlier this year, and...uh...well, I suppose now is as good of a time as any to tell you...an FBI agent will be coming to you in the next week to complete the FBI's background check on me. He'll want to talk to you, probably Jack, and probably some others. So, uh, yeah, I am seriously thinking of joining the FBI, and probably sooner rather than later from what they're telling me."

"Jimmy, that is fantastic news! I am really, really happy for you! You are making an excellent move going with the Feds. This place is a f**kin' cesspool and it won't be getting better any time soon. I mean, the three new Republican majority members are good guys and doing the best they can, but it could all change again after the next election or the election after that. So, getting the hell out of here while you can and in one piece is a very wise decision on your part."

"Well, Chief, I appreciate you saying that. I know you've hinted before about being a short-timer here and I am certainly aware that this place is only one potential voting-cycle away from being turned back into the morass it was under the last regime. So, for these and other professional reasons I decided a few years ago to take a look at the FBI as the logical next step for me, career-wise. It took a while with the federal government hiring freeze and all that but it appears as if it may finally be coming to fruition."

"It'll be our loss here, Kid. No doubt you would have made a great lieutenant, captain, and who knows how much higher up the management ladder you would've gone. But seriously, I'm glad for your sake you're leaving this hellhole. If this place EVER gets straightened out, it'll be years from now. You don't want to wait around and go through all of that bullshit. I certainly don't plan on doing so either."

"Yeah, I hear ya Chief, loud and clear."

"Needless to say, Jimmy, I'll have nothing but good things to tell the agent who comes to see me. I'll probably know him anyway."

"Thanks, Chief, for that and for all the support over your two separate terms as chief here. Especially considering how we first met, right?"

We both chuckled at that one. I was just hoping afterwards my Chief didn't share with the FBI agent in a few days about that car stop incident from over six years ago. Of course, depending on exactly how Viola would describe the story of me holding my gun to his head back then, well, maybe it could actually work in my favor. If anyone could spin cop-on-cop gunplay positively, it would be good ol' Chief Viola.

It started to hit me right around this general timeframe that upon moving on to a new job at another agency or company...well, I would miss Chief Rich Viola. I realized then that wherever I may wind up in life, perhaps with the FBI or perhaps somewhere else, I won't be coming across another boss quite like him.

Viola was truly one of a kind, at least he had been in my life so far. As I described earlier, he's that rare Rolex-wearing, classic art-loving, international travelling, public servant who also happens to carry a badge and a gun, doing so with ten very nicely manicured and clear-painted fingernails.

Like I said...one of a kind, or damn close to being so. A Renaissance Man, no doubt - certainly in Bensalem, Pennsylvania, in the 1980s.

Okay, so it was now one boss down, one to go. I'll look for Jack Robinson later this afternoon and tell him the news. I don't want too much time to lapse between me advising these two supervisors of my big plans. That wouldn't be right.

Well, I did look for Jack but I couldn't find him. It wasn't until the next day when I saw him in his office and asked him if I could talk to him. He said I could and I closed the door. Before I could say another word to him or even sit down he blurted out, "So, I hear you're leaving us."

Apparently Viola told Robinson either later yesterday or this morning. I never did swear Viola to secrecy, so he didn't really violate my trust in that regard. However, I would have preferred to have broken the news to Jack myself about this issue. But that chance has now passed me by. Oh well....

As we talked a bit more, Jack seemed rather taciturn during our brief meeting. He told me even if somewhat reluctantly that he too was happy that I was moving on in my life and wished me "the best of luck and all that." Then, as with Viola, he also reminded me that the BPD still had many problems within it, to include many problem employees, most of them holdovers from the last regime, and they would be tough to deal with over the next few years. "So, yeah, your timing is excellent," Jack added as we were winding down our discussion.

Hmmm...Jack was definitely taking this news differently than Viola took it. He was saying the right things, congratulating me when and where he should, but it didn't seem from the heart. Or was it from the heart, but perhaps he was disappointed to some degree in learning that his semi-prodigy of all these years was leaving for bigger and brighter pastures.

Unlike after my recent talk with Viola, I was given the distinct feeling by Jack Robinson that he saw me as abandoning the BPD ship, or at least him, its primary Captain. He didn't put it in so many words, but I couldn't help but read behind the lines and observe his non-verbal clues in arriving at this opinion.

In any event, both of these two bosses were now told what was going on in my life and what to expect from the FBI around here sometime during the next week. They were both appreciative of me letting them know - well mostly - and I knew they wouldn't let me down during these upcoming interviews. They didn't, either.

Oh, and by the way, I'd miss Jack Robinson too once I left the BPD. He wasn't exactly a Renaissance Man like Viola, but nonetheless he was still very influential in my young career.

* * * * *

As per agreement well before the scheduled FBI in-house interviews came to pass, I was transferred back to the Patrol Division the second week of October. It was a welcome change for me. Or at least it seemed to be at the time.

Little did I know that my very first night back on the streets in over six months would take me to the scene of human carnage the likes of which I had never before experienced in my life, personally or professionally. It was one of those life-altering moments, at least for me.

Maybe it was, in fact, time for a career change.

Finishing up my Admin Sergeant duties mid-week, I took that Thursday and Friday off and came back to work on the 9P-7A shift on Saturday, October 11. It was the same squad I left earlier in the year and it was good to be "home" again, even if for just a few more months with these guys. I consciously chose to not advise the officers on my squad of my potential hiring by the FBI. Even though I told Viola and Robinson, I thought I'd wait until the agent actually showed up to do my workplace interviews before I told anyone else of my present career aspirations. A private sector almost-job scenario from two-plus years ago, and me stupidly telling someone about it before I ever should have done so, was still percolating inside my head. So, even though it was an entirely different situation I still decided to keep the FBI almost-job scenario with only my two bosses. If someone found out on their own through BPD scuttlebutt, I wouldn't necessarily deny it to them. For now, however, I was just keeping it under my hat, my once again out-of-its-box uniform hat, as I rejoined the Patrol Division.

I had taken a nap early on Saturday evening before coming to work so I felt pretty good as the clock struck midnight. I still felt fine even as it approached 3:00AM. The first two-thirds of my first shift on October 11th into the 12th was a relatively normal Saturday night/ Sunday morning for me and my squad. There were no unusual types of calls for us to handle, just those of the standard variety. The bars were now closed, the drunks were mostly home, and all was pretty quiet in Bensalem Township. Another four hours or so and I'd be home in my bed. I was looking forward to a good day of sleep.

The police radio calls throughout the Lower Bucks County bandwidth fell off to a trickle shortly after 2:00 that morning. The quiet was welcomed, certainly by me. As I would soon come to realize, however, it was the literal quiet before the storm. That's because around 3:20 all hell was set to break loose. As it so happened, I wasn't far from this part of hell at the time. I'd be one of the first police officers entering through the soon-to-open gates to that place too.

It's a place I don't want to ever see again.

The initial radio call that morning was a strange one and definitely not of the standard variety. A citizen had contacted dispatch around 3:20 advising that a vehicle was observed driving in the northbound lanes of I-95 in a southerly direction just south of Street Rd. That wasn't an easy accomplishment for a driver but I suppose he or she could have entered the I-95 northbound off-ramp to Street Rd. from the opposite direction for which it was designed, driven down the ramp from Street Rd., and onto the interstate itself. I recall saying to myself if this is an accurate call, the driver won't be getting very far at 3:20 on a Sunday morning. There would still be numerous vehicles on this busy section of highway and they'd all be heading in the prescribed northerly direction. Unfortunately, my solitary words to just myself would prove all too accurate.

Since I was already in the vicinity of the Woodhaven Mall, upon hearing the call I started heading the short distance towards the

Woodhaven Rd. on-ramp to I-95. This is an exit/entrance to the interstate approximately one mile south of Street Rd. If this car was heading southbound in the northbound lanes, and if by some motor vehicle miracle it made it this far, I may be able to see something as I approach the traffic cloverleaf. Or, perhaps see something in its wake.

I was almost correct here as I would very soon know something had definitely happened nearby…except it would not involve my sense of sight. Instead, it would be my sense of hearing.

As it was a dry and relatively warm October morning, I had the driver's side window down in my patrol car. When I slowed down on the Woodhaven Rd. on-ramp to northbound I-95, directly adjacent to the three lanes of interstate highway, I couldn't readily see anything of significance as it related to this call. However, within seconds I would hear it.

It was the unmistakable sound of metal meeting metal at high speed, with the unmistakable sound of screeching tires accompanying it. I deemed it to be to the north of my present location. Also, as I was quickly processing these audible indicators, I noted the rubber-meeting-asphalt sounds didn't come before the metallic crashing sound. Instead, they were immediately afterwards. That told me whatever car hit another car or other fixed object, it wasn't that driver, or those drivers, who were jamming on their brakes. It would be the cars coming up behind the scene reacting to whatever occurred in front of them. I instinctively said out loud to myself, "This is not good!"

I recall at this exact point in time longing wistfully for my Admin Sergeant position of the last half-year. It was a pretty good gig come to think of it, mostly dealing with vendors, budgetary matters, secretaries, enthusiastic new officers stopping by for visits, etc.

But that gig was over and done with now. I held a Patrol Sergeant's position again as of the beginning of this shift and it was my duty to respond to whatever it was that just happened, whether I truly want to or not.

I had no doubt at all the sounds I heard somehow involved the wrong-way driver call of just a minute earlier, but exactly what it entailed was still unknown to me. Whatever it may turn out to be, I knew it was onto northbound I-95 I must drive. My patrol car's lights and sirens were turned on but I was very cautious as I proceeded at reduced speed toward the incident my auditory sensors detected only seconds earlier.

Ears, eyes, and remaining senses...don't fail me now. I'm gonna need you.

Before driving much more than several hundred yards northbound on the interstate I began to see numerous pairs of red vehicle taillights ahead of me. However, they appeared to be stationary and at odd angles to the highway. Strangely though, as I continued forward, the vision field in front of me and in front of those cars worsened. It's as if a cloud from nowhere had descended over the angled red lights ahead of me.

As I mentioned earlier, it was a clear night. But there was this slowly cascading fog forming in front of me. In view of this, I greatly reduced my speed as I passed some stopped cars but continued driving around them and into this odd fog even as it totally enveloped my own vehicle.

By the way, I knew right away this wasn't a weather related fog. It's one which every police officer recognizes as soon as he or she first comes upon it on a highway. It's the fog of death.

The type of fog through which I was now driving is created by undercarriage and engine block dust and debris particles which "explode" out of a vehicle in multiple directions when one or more cars hit something or each other, especially at a high rate of speed. Add in the other vehicular collisions which occurred right after the first big one, they being cars mostly rear-ending each other, and I knew the fog would hover above this scene for some time yet.

With the temporary reduced visibility, I proceeded with even more caution as I crawled along the usual fast moving interstate. The spinning emergency lights on the top of my car cast an odd intermittent red and blue hue in the particle cloud through which I was now driving. (I turned the siren off at this point.) I knew I had to reach the front of this line of stopped and stalled cars, but I was slowed down as there were now people walking alongside of their vehicles seemingly in various stages of shock and dismay. Some were bloody, some were limping, some were yelling things out loud. However, I knew the very first car or cars in line would be where the worst of it all would be found. I had to get there, even if driving in and around stalled cars and seemingly shell-shocked and bloodied people.

Senses...I need all five of you on full alert right about now. Maybe even that sixth one which tends to appear at times like this for me.

Of course, in the midst of all this I had notified dispatch of what I heard and that I was proceeding to the scene in attempt to further determine what just happened. With the traffic on I-95 at a standstill in front of me as I zigged and zagged through the various stationary cars and clearly traumatized people, I requested back-up and the duty tow truck. I wasn't definitively sure yet if I'd need heavy-rescue and ambulances at the scene, but I called for them anyway. I'd rather be wrong in that regard than have the injured be forced to wait any longer for their medical treatment. As it would turn out, the ambulances could have taken their time. There would be very few needing serious medical treatment at this scene.

Along with the aforementioned requests to the dispatcher, I also advised her to contact the Philadelphia PD and/or the Pennsylvania State Police and request them to shut down I-95 northbound at Woodhaven Rd. As the BPD barely had ten officers on the streets right now (the 5P-3A shift had already gone home), I knew it would require some assistance from other agencies to control traffic as the rest of the morning unfolded.

The dispatcher made the telephonic request of the PPD and she told me several of their Highway Patrol units were enroute to assist in traffic control. She added at the close of her transmission, "...22-7, the Philly PD dispatcher advised me over the last fifteen minutes they had received numerous complaints of a vehicle driving northbound on I-95 at speeds well in excess of 100MPH. It had been described as a later model car with at least four or five people in it driving very fast and passing cars in a very dangerous manner. And it was heading towards Bensalem."

I responded with a simple "10-4" as I got even closer to the front of the line of stopped and stalled cars.

So, let me get this straight. Philly PD has its own reports of a car driving at triple digit speeds northbound on I-95 approaching Woodhaven Rd. The BPD gets a report of a vehicle driving southerly on the same northbound interstate approaching Woodhaven Rd. This could be even worse than I initially imagined.

I mean...what are the probabilities of two separate drivers of two separate cars each picking the same exact stretch of highway at the same exact time to be excessively speeding and/or excessively stupid-like driving the wrong way? I would say slim to none. But Jupiter aligned with Mars over Bensalem on the morning of October 12, 1987, at around 3:25. It was not in a good way, either. And I was destined to be the one of the first officers on the scene of this not-so-stellar alignment of death and destruction.

It would be hell on wheels, enveloped in the surrealistic fog of death....

As in my limited description of the autopsy of a homicide victim in an earlier chapter, for the same reasons I'll refrain from describing in detail the human carnage as I observed it at the scene of this accident. But, yes, despite the astronomical odds, the car which was still driving at upwards of 100MPH as it crossed into Bensalem and proceeded northbound on I-95 did, in fact, meet up with the vehicle which happened to choose this very night and very place to drive the wrong way on the same highway. Neither one of the drivers, it was subsequently determined, ever touched their respective brake pedals before their respective front bumpers met. It was somewhat akin to the classic paradox of the unstoppable force meeting the immovable object. It's a paradox which human beings should avoid involving themselves in at all costs, in virtually every situation. This one being no exception.

When I finally arrived at the front of the line, I could see two piles of mangled metal and steel seemingly at one with each other. By this time, drivers and passengers of some of the other cars on the scene had exited their own vehicles and began describing to me all at once and in frantic and desperate terms what they had just witnessed. I did my best in this first minute or so to ascertain that these people were physically okay. Amazingly, except for a few cuts and bruises among them, the ones to whom I was speaking were in overall pretty good condition. I instructed them to stand on the grassy shoulder of the roadway, out of harm's way. The dozen or so of them agreed to do so. With another officer who made it onto the scene, it was time to walk over to the two cars which originally impacted. I took a deep breath and prepared myself for the worst.

With the dust and debris particle cloud now all but gone, upon walking over to what used to be two fully functioning automobiles I could immediately see there was a solitary driver in one of the cars. I could also see there were at least five people in the other car. I could readily determine by their body positions, their observable trauma, and the fact none was moving nor breathing, that there were no living survivors to this initial cataclysmic collision. By the time heavy rescue and other back-up units arrived, it was officially determined it was a total of six dead. They were apparently killed instantly at the point and time of impact.

When all the eyewitness accounts were finally collected later that day it seems after dangerously bobbing and weaving past a number of vehicles all the way from downtown Philadelphia and into Bensalem along I-95, the northbound speeding car hit the southbound wrong-way car head-on. While there were no survivors within those two cars, fortunately (if that can be said here), despite the numerous rear-ended and side-swiped cars in the aftermath of the main collision no one else at the scene sustained any serious injuries.

The driver of the wrong-way car was a 23-year-old woman. It was never determined why or exactly how she came to be driving southbound in the northbound lanes of I-95.

The speeding northbound vehicle was a group of college-aged males, all attending Trenton State College (now The College of New Jersey). They were returning back to campus from a night of partying somewhere in Philadelphia.

It was eventually learned through blood-alcohol tests that both drivers had been heavily drinking that evening and were legally intoxicated. Booze doesn't figure very well into that whole immovable force/unstoppable object paradox scenario. Not at all, actually, especially with human beings involved.

I turned the scene over to one of my officers who specialized in accident investigations. I assured him that northbound traffic was being detoured onto Rt. 13 and Woodhaven Road and that he could take his time in attempting to figure out just what happened here. I assigned two other officers to assist him.

I-95 was eventually reopened by 7:00 that morning, after the bodies were removed and the numerous un-drivable cars were towed away. I helped out initially until the accident investigator officer had his bearings and could begin the tedious task of reconstructing the scene.

Strangely, even after all these years, my most memorable take-away of this incident resulted from me observing the two cars which initially struck each other being removed from the area. For the first time, in the dawn's early light, I could see clearly inside the interior of the woman's car. Among other things, I happened to notice a set of keys still dangling from the ignition. On the keychain was a shiny, long, thin plastic memento of sorts, the kind readily purchased off the rack in a novelty store. It was bright pink with white print on it. I couldn't decipher it at first so I walked over a bit closer and shined my flashlight directly onto it.

It contained six words, and six words only. Coincidently, the same number of fatalities as the result of this horrible accident.

It simply read, "Life's a bitch, then you die."

For this woman, and the other five young men, this may have been very true.

Chapter Sixty-Six

Back to that career change option I was exploring....

George Everly (fictitious name) was an FBI agent I got to know about a year and a half ago when he was doing the requisite background checks for my then-upcoming attendance at the National Academy. He had been working in the downtown Philadelphia office during that earlier time but in the last year he was transferred to the Lansdale Resident Agency, located in the northwestern suburbs of Philly. Now, he was about to finish up his second recent assignment involving me, to include my past and present employment status at the BPD.

By the time he wrapped up his assignment in mid-October, SA Everly told me that several of my bosses and some other co-workers he reached out for each gave me very positive reviews. I had no problems at all in this area he assured me. I was certainly glad to hear this news from him.

Everly later told me that the only odd part of his one-day visit to the BPD involved his interview with Capt. Ronald Traenkle. He added that he was not even scheduled to talk to Traenkle that day but as he was technically my boss again now that I was back in patrol, he walked up to George and all but insisted on being formally inter-viewed as it related to me and my potential employment with the FBI. George thusly agreed to interview him.

Once behind closed doors and before the interview officially started, Traenkle insisted to SA Everly that he did not want what he was going to tell him about me to ever be made available for me to read in the future. He wanted his information to be marked "Secret" or "Confidential" or something like that. Everly, not knowing what he was about to hear, simply told Traenkle, "Okay, sure."

As I was advised by George, as odd as his request was, Traenkle never actually said anything negative about me. Some of what the captain related to the agent was "at worst neutral" about me, but mostly what he said regarding my background, work ethic, etc., was favorable.

George told me he never experienced anything quite like this in all his years of doing police background checks for either officers nominated to the NA or who were in the special agent application process. That is, the police interviewee reporting nothing negative about a co-worker but then insisting for some reason on anonymity. "The whole interview was just so strange," Everly repeated more than once to me regarding his brief time with Capt. Traenkle.

I later told SA Everly that he didn't know the Bensalem PD and he didn't know Capt. Traenkle. If he did, it would have made sense…well, somewhat. I left it at that and so did he.

As I was now within several months, at the most, of never seeing Traenkle again, all of this had no effect on me whatsoever. It was time to move on from these people, certainly some of them.

Although I would have the opportunity in later years, I never did bother to check my personnel file to learn what Traenkle may have said about me during this pre-employment interview with SA Everly. I did not care one way or the other. I never asked George for the specifics either. I had, in fact, moved beyond these people, and this captain specifically.

* * * * *

By the last week of October, Jerri Williams called me and confirmed that my BPD interviews went over very well, apparently even the one involving Captain Confidential. It appeared to be smooth sailing from this point on and I was on my way to an official appointment to an upcoming FBI New Agent Training class. As we were approaching the end of October, she was looking at the possibility of me getting my official appointment letter within the next month or so advising me to show up at the FBI Academy in Quantico on a certain Sunday in January.

This news was great to hear. Jerri agreed with me. But, the Applicant Coordinator told me, there was just one last matter I had to take care of. It is the very last stage in my application process. That is, I need to undertake my pre-hire physical training evaluation.

Since the earliest days of my interest in becoming a special agent with the FBI, various people had been telling me, from SA Jerri Williams, SA George Everly, SSA Tom Colombell at the NA, and others, to make sure I was getting in top physical condition for my appointment to the FBI. Once at the Academy, they expected a candidate to be able to do a certain number of push-ups, sit-ups, pull-ups, and run the track at a certain pace. If these criteria could not be met by certain pre-set timeframes, the candidate was sent home. I'd also have to undertake a "trigger pull" test at some point too in the very near future. Hopefully these last few matters can all be scheduled at the same time, Jerri advised me.

I picked a date through SA Williams to meet one of the Philadelphia Division physical training (PT) coordinators at the U. S. Navy Yard in South Philly. I was instructed to wear sweat clothes and sneakers for my pre-Quantico PT evaluation. So attired, I showed up on the afternoon of Monday, November 2nd, and was met in the designated gymnasium by the PT instructor and five other candidates who, like me, were also scheduled for upcoming special agent classes at Quantico. We all sort of nodded our heads at each other and before long the PT guy had us individually doing our sit-ups, push-ups, and pull-ups. He had a clipboard and was counting and noting each exercise and how many of each we could successfully complete.

There was no "cheating" in this pre-test either. We had to touch our noses to the gym mat and then extend our arms fully vertical for the push-ups. It was the same with the pull-ups but in the opposite direction. We had to fully extend our arms downward and then proceed to pull ourselves up with our chin ultimately touching the horizontal bar each time. The run was one mile on a giant empty parking lot which could have doubled for a landing strip. We collectively ran halfway up the distance of the lot, turned around at a pre-set marker, and then came straight back at the instructor. He had a stopwatch, of course, and was timing us.

I wasn't the slowest or weakest one there that day, but I wasn't the fastest or strongest either. My ongoing bicycling and swimming cross-training regimen hadn't hurt me in terms of overall physical conditioning, but it didn't do a whole lot to greatly enhance these very specific forms of exercise. I guess I better start working on them even more so before long. I did.

Just when the five of us thought we were done at the Navy Yard that day, the PT instructor pulled out his .357 Magnum from the trunk of his car, made sure (and made sure again) the cylinder was empty of its six rounds, and with the weapon clearly pointed on an angle at a strip of grass he asked each of us separately to pull the trigger twenty-five times. He timed us doing this "exercise" too. I believe we had to complete this task in less than thirty seconds. From what I recall, each of us there pulled the trigger in the allotted amount of time that day.

This test, I later learned, was designed to make sure that special agent candidates had the hand and finger strength to pull a trigger enough times to prove he or she could do so in the event of an actual firefight. Apparently, some people, including some of the smaller female candidates, were having trouble passing this test. Without initially passing this trigger-pull exercise in the pre-PT test, the "failed" candidates were still authorized to go to Quantico and start in their New Agent class. However, if by the sixth week there they couldn't muster the index finger strength to pass this test, they would be told to leave.

I can tell you, rightly or wrongly, the FBI lost lots of otherwise qualified candidates to this exercise. For these and/or other reasons, the trigger-pull test was finally discontinued as a pre-requisite to graduate from New Agent class. Again, rightly or wrongly.

* * * * *

So...that was it.

I had now successfully completed every single step the FBI wanted me to undertake on my way to being assigned to a New Agent Trainee class. They seemingly had done everything on their end too as it related to my application processing and potential hiring. Now, it was just a matter of waiting. I have Thanksgiving coming up in a few weeks and the Christmas holidays not long after that. IF I get the official appointment letter anytime in the next month for me to show up at the Academy in January, the timing would be excellent.

In the meantime, Jim, enjoy the upcoming holidays with your family.

That's what I told myself. That's what SA Williams told me.

Perhaps, though, I, and she, were just a bit premature.

While I was still not completely ruling out some way, somehow, of vesting my pension at the twelve-year mark in September of '88, which would possibly mean me backing out of my FBI career aspirations and going with some other local, state, or federal agency in the near future, I gotta tell ya...it was quite exciting knowing I was on a very short list to be hired by the FBI. It's been a long time coming and it was still difficult to fathom that I may be just two months away from yet another

774

stint at the Academy in Quantico. This time though, it wouldn't be as a temporary NA attendee for eleven weeks. Instead it would be as a New Agent Trainee for four months, hopefully destined for a long career in the FBI afterwards.

As mentioned earlier, throughout the whole hiring process of the last year, to even include recent weeks, so as not to possibly jinx myself, besides my wife I had told virtually no one else in my life about my FBI application and the various and ongoing stages of processing I was undertaking. However, now on the brink of possibly being hired by the Bureau, and with my own workplace so notified, I figured I could cautiously begin to share this information with a few other folks. The first ones I told, of course, were my mother and three sisters. I let them know at a family function on the first day of November that although I was not one-hundred percent definite yet regarding exactly what was going to happen, I was nonetheless seriously considering becoming an FBI agent.

My family was very happy for me, especially my mom. As that September her 101-year-old mother, my grandmother, had died, it gave her some positive news to focus upon for a change. Of course, my family wanted to know if their son/brother would be moving away from the Philadelphia area IF I made this career choice. I told them there was a distinct possibility I could be transferred to another city but I was trying to work out a plan where I would be assigned to the New York Division with me then doing the long commute every day.

That was the tentative plan I shared with my various family members at the little get-together that day. My wife was nodding her head up-and-down at the same time on the couch nearby. In retrospect, I realized it was definitely more HER plan for me to drive back-and-forth to New York City every day from the Philly suburbs. But I told her I would do it and hopefully I could. I am, after all, a man of my word.

* * * * *

After the Navy Yard PT evaluation of my arms, legs, mid-section, and even index finger, each of which I "passed" just a few days before, I decided it was time to focus on work, the upcoming holiday season, and getting ready for what may come by the time January rolls around. Yes, that was the master plan all but set in stone for my immediate and short-term future.

However, the news I wanted to hear didn't wait for 1988. Hell, it didn't wait more than three days. Things were about to happen even more immediate and more short-term than I would have ever expected, and all by word of mouth too.

On Monday morning, November 9th, SA Jerri Williams called me at home and left a message to get back to her right away. I was on day-work shift through the next day and when I came home for lunch I immediately returned her call.

Geez, I wondered as the phone was ringing, what could it be this time? Not another problem, I hope.

After a few quick pleasantries, my conversation with the Applicant Coordinator went something like…

Jerri: "Jim, I know this is very short notice, but could you be in Quantico this Sunday, the 15th, to start your training?"

Me: "This coming Sunday?! You mean as in six days from now?!"

Jerri: "Yes, this Sunday."

Me: "Uh…Jerri…I thought you said it would be January."

Jerri: "Well, it was. But I just received a call from the Unit Chief of New Agent Training at the Academy and they had someone drop out of the next scheduled class and they called here as they happened to know I have a candidate ready to go. That's you, of course, Jim."

Me: "Right…yeah. Uh, geez, Jerri, you caught me kind of by surprise with this call. I mean, I was planning on spending the holidays here with my family, finishing up some projects around the house, giving two weeks' notice at work, and…."

Jerri: "Well, if you can't do it, I understand. I assume everything will still be in order for a January appointment."

Me, thinking: "Assume?" What exactly does she mean by that? Maybe I better take it down a notch.

Me, speaking: "Uh, I'll tell you what, Jeri. Let me get back to you on this. Let me think about it. I'll talk to my wife later today and see what she says about this change in plans. How about if I call you tomorrow?"

Jerri: "Sure, that would work. Could you make it before noon though? The Academy really likes to have the entire class set and ready to go a whole week before, so the earlier tomorrow the better. Could you do that, Jim?"

Me: "Yes, yes, I can call you by then. I'm not sure exactly what I'll have to tell you but I'll call you by noon. That I promise."

We then said our quick goodbyes.

Okay, so much for well-laid out plans.

Of course, this was not bad news. The FBI wanted me to start in just six days' time, not several months' time. This was definitely good news, right? Maybe? I better call my wife to find out though.

After several different calls to Eileen at her place of work, and several separate conversations later that evening, it was more or less agreed that if I was going to be away for four months anyway, it might as well start sooner rather than later. Plus, I'd make it home for Christmas Day as the Feds are always closed for business on that day. So it wouldn't be THAT bad.

Right, Dear?

Using the word "whatever" a few times as responses to questions and scenarios I posed to her, Eileen finally told me to simply call Jerri back the next day and tell her I could start the "FBI job-thing" this coming Sunday. She made sure to remind me to ask Jerri about the New York Division assignment "deal" she talked about when we were there for the spousal interview.

I told Eileen I would.

By noon on Tuesday, I called the Applicant Coordinator and told her after much discussion with my wife that I was good-to-go for Sunday, the 15th. Jerri was very happy to hear this from me. She very politely told me she wanted to quickly end this call so she could advise the Unit Chief at Quantico of this information right away. She told me we could talk more in the next day or so regarding further details about my now very rapidly approaching FBI appointment date at the Academy.

Okay, goodbye.

Whew! Decision made. I think....

The last of my four days of scheduled 7A-5P shift was Tuesday. As I left the building on Monday afternoon at the end of the shift (and after the first call that week with SA Williams) I recall thinking, "Geez, maybe just one more day of this." When I awoke on Tuesday morning and put on my uniform, I recall thinking, "This may be it...my very last day ever on the BPD."

As it came to be, Tuesday, November 10th, 1987, working a day-shift, and a rainy one at that, was the last time I ever wore a BPD uniform. These were the last ten hours I would ever be a police officer, a patrol sergeant, or hold any other similar type rank at my agency of eleven-plus years. It was a routine day, work-wise, but my mind was floating all over the place, from down south to Quantico all the way up north to New York City.

I wasn't thinking very clearly that day as I had made plans the night before to meet my sister Alma for lunch at one of the two Friendly's Restaurants in Bensalem Township. But I went to the wrong one and we never did meet up that day. It was my mistake as I should have proceeded to the one closer to the law office where she was working at the time. Duh! Again, I just wasn't operating mentally on all cylinders that shift with such a big change in my life now only days away.

As my workday ended that afternoon and I was signing off on the paperwork of my squad members, I said goodbye to each of them individually. I didn't go overboard or make a scene, but I knew this was my last shift ever as a patrol sergeant for the BPD. It was with definite mixed feelings that I walked out of the building that day.

Then, once again, I saw the evidence trailer of yore in the outside parking lot. A certain officious captain, with clipboard in hand, was monitoring the parking lot. I mumbled to myself, "F**k this place! I'm outta here!" And, so I was.

After work that day I went directly home. Once there, and before I took off my uniform, I had my wife take a picture of me in the living room with seven-year old Sean and almost five-year old Dan, each alongside of me. It was similar, in a way, to a picture Eileen took of me during my very first month as a police officer, way back in December of '76, with my parents on each side of me. I planned it that way. The photographs would serve as pictorial bookends to my Bensalem police career, with equally important people on both sides of me in each of them.

I called Jerri on Wednesday, a regularly scheduled day off. We had a nice chat that day and she confirmed that everything was now official. I would be sworn in as an FBI New Agent Trainee on Sunday evening at the Academy and start my training classes on the following Monday morning, five days from now. My graduation date would be February 19th.

I listened intently to everything Jerri had to tell me during our phone chat that day, taking copious notes as we spoke. Before we hung up I casually asked her when I could expect the official FBI letter to arrive regarding my hiring, my appointment, etc. She advised me, also casually, that she didn't have an answer for that question. My hiring and appointment were official as "it's in the computer," she assured me, but she could simply not guarantee a letter would be composed and provided to me before I would leave on Sunday.

Okay...that's interesting.

In so many words, all of them respectful and polite, I asked Jerri if she was serious. I mean…I'm supposed to quit my job, giving the BPD barely three business days' notice, and drive 215 miles to the FBI Academy this coming Sunday without a document of any sort advising me that I've been officially hired? Do we know as an absolute, positive fact they, someone, anyone, in charge at the FBI Academy, will be expecting me?

Don't get me wrong here. I trusted Jerri implicitly, and for that matter the FBI too. But I'm taking a REALLY big step in my life here, and now doing so in less than five days, which is about two months sooner than I originally thought I would be doing so. Is there any chance I could get a letter of some sort? Something in writing, even in handwriting, just to make it official?

Jerri still couldn't or wouldn't promise a letter, not even a faxed copy of a letter by week's end. With my moved-up appointment date it was unlikely the document could be prepared quickly enough by HQ in Washington, D.C. However, she reassured me several times over, I was officially hired, my name was in the computer on the master list for Class 88-2 (the year and month my class will graduate), and when I show up at Quantico they will, in fact, be expecting me, along with the other thirty-nine members of my New Agent Trainee class.

Hmmm…Well, I guess if you say so, Jerri. Who am I to doubt the FBI or one of its Applicant Coordinators?

I shrugged my shoulders and somewhat reluctantly advised Jerri I'd be at Quantico this coming Sunday afternoon. I knew my way there very well thanks to my stint at the National Academy last year, so I promised her I would not be late. SA Williams thanked me at the end of the call and left it that she'd contact me in the next day or two if there were any changes or new developments.

Jerri never did call as there were no changes or new developments. There was no letter either, as she told me there most likely wouldn't be. But based on her spoken word, yet not written word, I was pretty darn sure I was hired by the FBI and I was to be at Quantico by 5:00 on Sunday afternoon, November 15th.

So…I'll be there.

* * * * *

"…And so I quit the police department
And got myself a steady job…"
(John Lennon/Paul McCartney,
*She Came in Through the
Bathroom Window*)

Well…not quite, not yet.

It wasn't meant to be quite that easy for me.

I gotta tell you…I was really nervous about quitting my police department job without an actual letter of some sort affirming that I had another job. As I've mentioned on more than one occasion, this was an extremely difficult decision for me to make for various reasons, and now I was making it in a rush without any official documentation to back it up. Yes, I know neither Jerri Williams nor the FBI would lie to me or play games with me in this regard. But I'm old-fashioned. I like things in writing, especially involving life-altering changes to my (and my family's) every day existence.

Back in 1976, while still working as a store detective, I received a phone call while on the retail floor one day from a certain then-sergeant advising me I was hired by the BPD. Wisely, when I later called my dad to share with him the good news, he told me to not officially quit my department store job until I have it in writing from the BPD. I reluctantly agreed, but he was right. I did, in fact, receive that letter three days afterwards at home and it was then I officially put in my almost two weeks' notice at the store. That's how it should be, right?

But I didn't have that "proof" here, did I? Seemingly, I wouldn't until after I quit my police officer job and after I arrive at Quantico, where I was verbally assured I have the new job.

That's the FBI's story and they were sticking to it.

What do I do? How do I handle this?

I know, how about if I do nothing? Literally, nothing?

That may just work.

So, here was my plan. As I have months of unused sick time, I'm gonna call out sick for the upcoming weekend (I was due back to work on the 9P-7A shift on Friday night), drive to Quantico on Sunday, and officially report to my New Agent Trainee class. IF I have the job, then I'll take care of quitting the BPD during the next week. I can do that by phone and even mail a letter if I have to. But, first, I just gotta know that I AM actually an employee of the FBI.

Yeah, that should work. It'll have to. After all, Viola, Robinson, Traenkle, and other BPD bosses all used months and months of extended sick leave during the darkest days of the Dark Side regime. I barely used three weeks' worth of mine back then. I can use sick leave here for such an important reason. Or at least until I figure out just where I'm employed next week? I won't double-dip though. Once I figure everything out, I'll convert any used sick time to vacation time.

*****

With the short notice this time before going to Quantico (as opposed with the National Academy over a year ago), there was no time for elaborate farewell dinners with Eileen or All-Star championship wrestling matches with my sons. I know we went out for a planned family dinner somewhere in Bensalem on that Saturday night, my last night in town for a while, but it wasn't anything luxurious or fancy. It was special to me though as I wouldn't be seeing my wife and kids very much for the next four months, so I wanted to make the most of the limited time we still had together.

My boys were still pretty young then but I did my best to explain to them where I was going, what I was doing, and that I would no longer be a police officer. At their young ages, having a dad as a cop was still pretty cool. I know sometimes kids in their teens may resent having a parent as a police officer, but in this case "daddy policeman" (as Dan would sometimes refer to me) remained a positive thing. They weren't exactly sure yet what it meant for daddy to become an FBI agent, but they knew it had something to do with that place we visited just about one year ago with the really big and colorful graduation ceremony.

It came to me over dinner that last night in Bensalem as I was attempting to explain all of these new developments to my five-year-old and seven-year-old sons that I wasn't even a hundred percent sure myself of exactly what I was getting into here.

Geez, was I even fifty percent sure?

Let's see...I was driving 215 miles tomorrow to a place with nothing in writing indicating that I have a new job; I was starting the most prestigious law enforcement academy in the world (and arguably the most difficult) with no guarantee of graduating from it; IF I did manage to graduate, I didn't know what kind of actual work I'd be doing once officially designated a special agent; and lastly, I didn't even know for sure where I would be geographically assigned.

So, Sean and Dan, does this all make sense to you? Any of this?

I hope it does because I'm not sure it's all making sense to me.

But you know what, Kids? I'm going for it anyway.

It'll work out. I'll make it work out, one way or the other. I'm positive I will.

And...

Who knows where it will lead me?

Who knows what doors it will open for me?

Only time will tell, right?

Hint: In due time, specifically about eight and one-half years from this very point in my life, one of those aforementioned doors which opened to me was to a single-room cabin on a remote hillside in Lincoln, Montana. To say the least, its lone occupant was NOT very happy to see who was there. But then, as he would be later reminded, "You can't eat your cake and have it too."

It'll all make sense. I promise....

THE END...of JCM Book II

Epilogue

For those who may be interested, I never vested my PA/BPD pension. I couldn't. After many attempts to apply my unused sick leave, my accrued vacation leave, not to mention even trying to buy out the last year of my pension from the state, I just couldn't work it out. In the end, I was nine months short (of the twelve-year minimum) of vesting my pension when I eventually took my new job. It was a very tough decision, but I ultimately took the lump sum payout. For what it's worth, it was invested wisely. In fact, it's still growing in value.

The $500 or so potential annuity per month, before taxes, starting the month after my 50th birthday in 2003 and lasting the rest of my life, would have been nice. But to have chosen one of the several other available career options at the time, as in staying at the BPD or going with the Defense Contractors Investigative Service in September of '88 (see Bonus Chapter 66a) based on this one monetary issue alone would have been foolish on my part.

Sometimes in life it's not all about the money, to include potential future money. It's about the person, the situation, and what's best for him or her (and his or her family) in the long-run. Looking back, I know I made the right career decision.

Interestingly, and adding somewhat to my frustration even after the fact, by the early 1990s the FBI raised its minimum hiring age for special agents from 35 to 37. Coincidently, at around the same time, the Pennsylvania Municipal Police Pension Plan lowered the on-the-job time to vest one's pension from twelve years to ten years.

As I've been saying throughout here...it's all about the timing.

Sometimes it works for you, sometimes it doesn't.

Again, though, no regrets on my part.

* * * * *

In terms of the good guys I reference more than once in this book, each of whom I consider friends to this day (with a few sad exceptions), the following is a brief look at their careers since I left the BPD in 1987. In alphabetical order...

Sgt. Gene Ashton officially retired from the BPD in 1984 moving to his farm in Virginia. He died in June of 1993.

Officer Tim Carroll left the BPD in 1998 to join the Bucks County Detectives. As of late 2016, he remains there as a working detective.

Officer Dave "Trapper" Huetger left the BPD in 1980 after a thirteen-year career there. He moved out of Bensalem and it is believed he left the law enforcement profession too. He died in the early 2000s.

Detective Ken Hopkins retired in 1996. He died in the early 2000s.

Officer Jerry Judge fully retired in 1994.

Officer John Knowles left the BPD in 1997 to join the Bucks County Detectives. He fully retired in 2012.

Detective Terry Lachman left the BPD in 1991 to join the Bucks County Detectives. He fully retired in 2012.

Captain Jack Robinson fully retired from the BPD in 2004 with over forty years on the force. He tragically died as the result of a hunting accident in the Pennsylvania Poconos in 2013. He was 73 years old.

Not too long after Richard Viola was re-hired as Chief in 1986, his unlawful termination lawsuit was settled out-of-court with him receiving $150,000 from the Township. His lawyers received an identical amount. Viola subsequently left the BPD in 1988. This time, it was of his own volition. His "buyout package" upon leaving the BPD was $100,000. Rich (as I now refer to him) chose not to work in law enforcement from that point on in his life. He moved to the West Coast of the U. S. shortly after his time in Bensalem and remains (as of late 2016) living in that general area in full retirement. I happen to know - he's enjoying his post-law enforcement life immensely. He owns a newer-model Bentley motorcar. (Would you expect a Renaissance Man to drive anything else?)

* * * * *

In terms of the Bensalem Police Department itself, it did manage to straighten itself out before the 1980s were over. Chief Viola re-started the process. Upon his leaving, the Township decided to look once again outside of the department for its next police leader. In doing so, in 1989 another Philadelphia PD supervisor was hired. His name was Frank Friel. He had been a well-respected and experienced Captain on the PPD when he was hired by Bensalem. He enjoyed over eight successful years there as the newly titled Director of Public Safety. He resigned from the BPD in 1997.

After Friel left, Bensalem Township hired its next Director of Public Safety. This time, from within. It was one of my fellow rookies, Steve Moran, who rose through the ranks over the years and was eventually appointed to the top position in 1997. He successfully served in that capacity through 2007 when he officially retired.

And remember that bright and inquisitive young rookie who was hired shortly before I left the BPD in '87? The "Kid" who reminded me of myself in many ways and who I was pretty sure was someday "going places?" Well, he did.

Fred Harran was promoted to Director of Public Safety in 2006, upon Moran's retirement. (The one-year discrepancy is because Moran started burning unused leave time after stepping down from his position in '06. It was at that time when Fred officially took over the reins of the department.)

Director Harran remains in charge (as of late 2016) as the head of the now over one-hundred sworn officer Bensalem Police Department. Within its size-range, it is known as one of the most modern, innovative, diverse, and progressive law enforcement agencies in the state of Pennsylvania, if not the U. S. (The BPD HQ is also located in a new, state-of-the-art building.)

Kudos to Fred's stewardship and those who preceded him going all the way back to 1981, well, minus those two years in the mid-1980s.

Maybe, just maybe, I'd like to think I played a slight role, along with a few others, back in the day in starting this whole ball rolling in terms of taking the BPD from the Dark Ages/Dark Side/Chief Wars through its Age of Enlightenment and beyond. However, it was clearly under the later tutelage of leaders like Viola, Friel, Moran, and presently Harran, who eventually propelled the BPD into the 21st century and earned it the excellent reputation it enjoys today.

Keep up the tradition, Fred. The same goes to whoever follows you. I, and others, will still be watching.

* * * * *

In closing, I've been asked the same questions numerous times over the years, after telling and re-telling many of the Dark Side-related anecdotes contained in these pages. That is, do I consider my time at the BPD a mistake? Were they eleven wasted years? Would I or should

I have done anything different during those years other than what I wound up doing?

As some say, "hindsight is 20/20." They are generally correct in saying so. However, in a sober and clear-eyed retrospective all these years later, I would offer a resounding NO to each of those questions. Meaning, I regret nothing and I wouldn't trade those professionally formative years of mine for any other alternative life scenario. As tough as they were on multiple levels and on multiple fronts, those years, those people, and that place, essentially made me who I am today, and I'm a better person for it.

I learned much between the years of 1976 and 1987. My education was not just limited to the inner-workings of the criminal justice system. In addition to that field of endeavor, I also learned so much about human nature and the human condition itself, especially under some very harsh interpersonal circumstances. I learned about others, of course, but most importantly during this decade plus one year...I learned about *me*. Yes, I evolved from that fresh-faced, wet-behind-the-ears "Kid" as a rookie in 1976, to in many ways a battle-hardened veteran within my own profession by the time 1987 rolled around. Perhaps, as I look back, I became a bit too hardened, callous, and cynical at times, certainly when dealing on a daily basis with the Dark Side at its zenith (or, more accurately, nadir). It was necessary, however, for my professional survival, security, and sanity. I feel I really had no other choice at the time.

Bottom line here, dealing with the adversity I was forced to back then taught me in the long-run myriad additional life lessons. These would include: always sticking with my internal belief system, no matter how much it would be challenged; continuing to believe in my existing moral compass and ethical code, no matter who would question it; remembering my excellent parental upbringing when contemplating the difference between right and wrong, no matter what someone else may be doing; and most of all to NOT be afraid to be the person who is *Me*, James R. Fitzgerald, aka "Fitz."

I can very clearly see now much later in life that I learned who *I* was not during the "fat, dumb, and happy" halcyon days during the year-plus after first making sergeant in '82. No, it didn't occur during that timeframe. True strength, I came to realize, is rarely forged in uncontested, blissful, and peaceful times. It was instead during the subsequent bleakest days of the Dark Ages when I came to know the real person I was, or would gradually develop into. After those wounds ever so slowly healed, I'm glad to be that person now.

After one last look back at my eleven years at the BPD, it brings to mind one of my favorite historical quotes. It is by the German philosopher Friedrich Nietzsche.

It would be, "That which does not kill us, makes us stronger."

How right he was, how true that is.

* * * * *

My next professional adventure would not find me again mired in the trenches of partisan political nonsense. It wasn't that type of organization, certainly not at my level. For this I was greatly relieved.

However, it wouldn't stop me from learning still more about human nature and the human condition. To the contrary, this forthcoming two-decade stage of my life-journey would have me learning of an even Darker Side of humanity and, yes, inhumanity…that of the violent, criminal mastermind.

Stay tuned. My journey is far from over.

James R. Fitzgerald's story continues in
A Journey to the Center of the Mind
Book III:
The FBI Years
1987 - 2007

For free Book II bonus chapters and info regarding author events please go to:

www.jamesrfitzgerald.com

And one last time…

To those I have personally known during this book's timeframe who made the ultimate sacrifice in the performance of their law enforcement duties:

Officer Robert Yezzi, Bensalem PD,
End of Watch - August 12, 1980

Officer Gary Farrell, Philadelphia PD,
End of Watch – September 26, 1980

Officer Daniel Faulkner, Philadelphia PD,
End of Watch – December 9, 1981

Officer William D. McCarthy, Philadelphia PD,
End of Watch – September 22, 1987

…And to those law enforcement officers I will never personally know, your sacrifices will never, ever be forgotten!

RIP!

Made in the USA
Monee, IL
26 March 2022

93106686R00449